Documents in World History

Volume I: To 1850

PEARSON

Prentice
Hall

Upper Saddle River, New Jersey 07458

ISBN 0-13-177322-4

CONTENTS

Contents

Part 7

MEDITERRANEAN CIVILIZATION AFTER THE FALL OF ROME

Part 8

ISLAM

Part 9

IMPERIAL CHINA AND THE DIFFUSION OF EAST ASIAN CIVILIZATION

Part 10

THE FORMATION OF EUROPEAN CIVILIZATION

Part 11

EURASIAN CONNECTIONS BEFORE EUROPEAN EXPANSION

Part 12

ISLAMIC EMPIRES

Part 13

RENAISSANCE AND REFORMATION IN EUROPE

Part 14

EUROPEAN EXPLORATIONS AND EXPANSION

Part 15

TRADE AND EXPLOITATION ACROSS THE ATLANTIC

PART 1
The Fertile Crescent

1.1 Lugal Sulgi: Role Model for Mesopotamian Royalty

The Sumerians often endowed the original lugals (priest-kings) of their city-states with extra-human power and semi-divine ancestry. In the case of the legendary Sulgi of Nippur, his parentage included the deities Ninsun and Lugalbanda. In the cuneiform tablet that relates the story of his reign, "Sulgi, the Ideal King," he is held up as being what the perfect lugal should be; modesty certainly not being one of his flaws.

Source: Jacob Klein, "The Royal Hymns of Sulgi, King of Ur," in *Transactions of the American Philosophical Society,* v. 71, pt. 7 (1981), Philadelphia; pp. 13, 15, 17, 19.

The hero avenged his city,
Whatever had been destroyed in Sumer, he destroyed in the for-
eign land,
He made the god of its city withdraw from it.
Its spirit (of) the good eye, (and) its angel (of) the good eye he
caused to stand aside,
In its cultivated fields of lustrous barley, he caused weeds to grow,
He destroyed its wide and large trees (with) the axe,
He tore down its date-palms by their crown,
He uprooted its small trees,
In its orchards and gardens, where the 'honey' of fig-trees had
been produced, he made weeds grow,
So that *thistles* and *thorns* broke through the ground.
The king—after he destroyed the cities, ruined the walls,
Terrified the evil land (like) a flood,
Dispersed the seed of the Gutians like seed-grain,
The pure lapis-lazuli of the foreign land he loaded into leather-
sacks and leather-bags,
Heaped up all its treasures,
Amassed all the wealth of the foreign land.
Upon its fattened oxen (and) fattened sheep,
He invokes the name of Enlil,
He invokes the name of Ninlil (sD 334–353.)

***

Let me extoll all my achievements!
The fame of my power has reached very far,
My wisdom is full of subtleties,
What of mine is not a mistery?

***

That the king might let known his enduring name into distant
days,
That sulgi, the king of Ur—
The hymn of his power, the song of his might,
That the wise one—the everlasting name of his preeminence,
Unto the offspring of future days might hand down,
For the mighty one, the son of Ninsun,
The Wisdom of the future was brought to the fore.
He praises his (own) power in a song,

1

He exalts his own intelligence, the good that he has acquired from
      birth (lines 1–9).

***

As a youth, I studied the scribal art in the e d u b b a, from the
      tablets of Sumer and Akkad,
Of the nobility, no one was able to write a tablet like me,
In the place *where* the people *attend* to learn the scribal art,
Adding, subtracting, counting and accounting—I completed all
      (their courses);
The fair Nanibgal, Nisaba,
Endowed me generously with wisdom and ntelligence (lines
      13–19).

***

(Then) I arose like a hawk, (like) a falcon,
(And) returned to Nippur in my vigor.
On that day, the storm shrieked, the west wind whirled,
The north wind and the south wind howled at each other,
Lightning together with the 'seven winds' devoured each other in
      heaven,
The thundering storm made the earth quake.
Iskur roared in the broad heavens,
The clouds of heaven mingled with the waters of the earth,
Their small (hail-)stones and their large (hail-)stones
Were striking on my back.
I, the king, I feared not, nor was I terrified.
Like a fierce lion I gnashed my teeth.
Like a wild ass I galloped.
With my heart full of joy, I ran onward.
Racing like a solitary wild-donkey,
(Before) Utu set his face toward his 'house',
I traversed a distance of fifteen 'miles'.
My sag-ur-sag priests gazed at me (with astonishment):
In Nippur and Ur, in one day, I celebrated their e s e s- festival!
With my 'brother (and) companion', the hero Utu,
I drank beer in the palace, founded by An,
My singers sang for me to the (accompaniment of) the 'seven' t i
      g i-drums,
(And) my consort, holy Inanna, the lady, the joy of heaven and
      earth,
Sat there with me at the banquet.

***

My shining like fine silver,
My (having a perfect) 'ear', and being an expert in song and
      speech,
I, the shepherd, my attaining a perfect control of anything,
In my kingship, let all these be seemly recited!
As many lines as there may be in my songs,
None of them is false, (all of them) are verily true!
My songs, be they royal prayers or supplications,
Be they long-ballads, the praises of kingship,
Be they psalms, love-poems or love dialogues,

Be they flute-songs or drum-songs—
In order that they shall never pass from memory, and that they
      shall never depart from (man's) lips,
Let no one neglect them in the cult-places!
Let them never cease (to be sung) in the lustrous Ekur!
Let them be played for Enlil, in his New-Moon shrine!
In its *monthly-festivals,* where sparkling beer is copiously libated
      like water,
Let them be firmly established for Enlil and Ninlil, who dwell
      there together!

                ***

I, the upright, the benefactor of the land—
Let my songs be (placed) in every mouth,
Let my poems never pass from memory!
That these, my paeans, spoken in praise,
These (laudatory) words, which Enki established for me,
These, the joyfully *deliberated wisdom* of Gestinanna,
Should not be forgotten for distant days—

Questions:
1. What was involved in carrying out a successful military campaign of retaliation?
2. In what ways does Sulgi's prowess go beyond the military realm?
3. Using Sulgi's reputed words as a clue, what virtues did the Sumerians consider most important in their rulers?

1.2   The Nippur Murder Trial and the "Silent Wife"

One of the earliest known examples of a criminal justice proceedings was the trial of men accused of murdering a temple servant (nishakku) at Nippur. The Assembly of Nippur whose responsibility it was to render a verdict also had to make a ruling on the situation of the victim's wife, who had been informed of the murder (by the murderers) after the crime had been committed, but had chosen to remain silent on the matter, and was therefore prosecuted as an accessory to murder.

Source: Samuel Noah Kramer, *From the Tablets of Sumer* (Indian Hills, Co: Falcon's Wing Press, 1956), pp. 53–54.

Nanna-sig, the son of Lu-Sin, Ku-Enlil, the son of Ku-Nanna, the barber, and Enlil-ennam, the slave of Adda-kalla, the gardener, killed Lu-lnanna, the son of Lugal-apindu, the *nishakku-official.*

After Lu-Inanna, the son of Lugal-apindu, had been put to death, they told Nin-dada, the daughter of Lu-Ninurta, the wife of Lu-Inanna, that her husband Lu-Inanna had been killed.

Nin-dada, the daughter of Lu-Ninurta, opened not her mouth, (her) lips remained sealed.

Their case was (then) brought to (the city) Isin before the king, (and) the King Ur-Ninurta ordered their case to be taken up in the Assembly of Nippur.

(There) Ur-gula, son of Lugal-.., Dudu, the bird-hunter, Ali-ellati, the dependent, Buzu, the son of Lu-Sin, Eluti, the son of..-Ea, Shesh-Kalla, the porter (?), Lugal-Kan, the gardener, Lugal-azida, the son of Sin-andul, (and) Shesh-kalla, the son of Shara-.., faced (the Assembly) and said:

"They who have killed a man are not (worthy) of life. Those three males and that woman should be killed in front of the chair of Lu-Inanna, the son of Lugal-apindu, the *nishakku*-official."

(Then) Shu..-lilum, the..-official of Ninurta, (and) Ubar-Sin, the gardener, faced (the Assembly) and said:

"Granted that the husband of Nin-dada, the daughter of Lu-Ninurta, had been killed, (but) what had (?) the woman done (?) that she should be killed?"

(Then) the (members of the) Assembly of Nippur faced (them) and said:

"A woman whose husband did not support (?) her—granted that she knew her husband's enemies, and that (after) her husband had been killed she heard that her husband had been killed—why should she not remain silent (?) about (?) him? Is it she (?) who killed her husband? The punishment of those (?) who (actually) killed should suffice."

In accordance with the decision (?) of the Assembly of Nippur, Nanna-sig, the son of Lu-Sin, Ku-Enlil, the son of Ku-Nanna, the barber, and Enlil-ennam, the slave of Adda-kalla, the gardener, were handed over (to the executioner) to be killed.

(This is) a case taken up by the Assembly of Nippur.

Questions:
1. *What possible motive is suggested for the wife's "silence"?*
2. *Summarize briefly the argument presented, and accepted by the Assembly, for sparing the wife's life.*
3. *What appears to have been the standard legal procedure in Sumerian criminal cases, and how might it compare/contrast to contemporary procedure in the U.S. legal system?*

1.3   The Reign of Sargon

The city-states that developed in the region of Mesopotamia after about 3500 B.C.E. were ruled by various kings who established local control. One of the first kings to successfully conquer and control the region was Sargon of Akkad, who ruled around 2300 B.C.E. The following excerpt from a tablet in the British Museum recounts his authority.

> **Source:** The Reign of Sargon" is from George W. Botsford, ed., *A Source-Book of Ancient History* (New York: Macmillan, 1912), pp. 27–28.

Sargon, King of Akkad, through the royal gift of Ishtar was exalted, and he possessed no foe nor rival. His glory over the world he poured out. The Sea in the East he crossed, and in the eleventh year the Country of the West in its full extent his hand subdued. He united them under one control; he set up his images in the West; their booty he brought over at his word. Over the hosts of the world he reigned supreme. Against Kassala he marched, and he turned Kassala into mounds and heaps of ruins; he destroyed the land and left not enough for a bird to rest thereon. Afterward in his old age all the lands revolted against him, and they besieged him in Akkad; and Sargon went forth to battle and defeated them; he accomplished their overthrow, and their wide-spreading host he destroyed. Afterward he attacked the land of Subartu in his might, and they submitted to his arms, and Sargon settled that revolt, and defeated them; he accomplished their overthrow, and their wide-spreading host he destroyed, and he brought their possessions into Akkad. The soil from the trenches of Babylon he removed, and the boundaries of Akkad he made like those of Babylon. But because of the evil which he had committed, the great lord Marduk was angry, and he destroyed his people by famine. From the rising of the sun unto the setting of the sun they opposed him and gave him no rest.

Questions:
1. *What type of "order" did Sargon establish?*
2. *How does this chronicle judge his reign?*

1.4   The Epic of Gilgamesh

The epic of Gilgamesh is one of the oldest stories of which we have a written record. Presumably recited orally for generations before it was inscribed on clay tablets in cuneiform script, it tells of the life and exploits of a young nobleman and king, who ruled the city of Uruk in ancient Sumer, probably between 2700 and 2600 B.C. Sumer, generally recognized to be the earliest human civilization, was centered in the lower valley between the Tigris and Euphrates rivers in what is contemporary Iraq; Uruk was not far from the present capital city of Baghdad.

It is almost fortuitous that we have the epic in written form today. In the seventh century B.C. (two thousand years after the time of Gilgamesh) the Assyrian king Assurbanipal, who ruled over the territory including what had been the ancient Sumerian civilization, built a great library in his capital city of Ninevah. Included among its holdings was a copy of the epic. But in 612 B.C. an invading army of Medes and Babylonians overran Ninevah, destroying the city and burying it (with its library) beneath the desert sands. There all remained lost and virtually forgotten for over two millennia until, in 1839, a young English archaeologist stumbled on this magnificent treasure. Over several decades the tablets containing the epic (as well as many other ancient writings) were unearthed and deciphered. Later other copies were discovered elsewhere. The epic, as we now have it, is a collation pieced together from these various cuneiform tablets. Although the epic is sufficiently complete to tell its story, some portions are missing and have been reconstructed by the translator.

Source: From *Gilgamesh* by William Ellery Leonard, translated by William Ellery Leonard. Translation copyright 1934 by William Ellery Leonard, renewed © 1962 by Barbara A. Hayward. Used by permission of Viking Penguin, a division of Penguin Books USA Inc.

GILGAMESH

All things he saw, even to the ends of the earth,
He underwent all, learned to know all,
He peered through all secrets,
Through wisdom's mantle that veileth all.
What was hidden he saw,
What was covered he undid;
Of times before the stormflood he brought report.
He went on a long far way,
Giving himself toil and distress;
Wrote then on a stone-tablet the whole of his labour.
He built the walls of ramparted Uruk,
He laid the foundations, steadfast as bronze,
Of holy Eanna, the pure temple…

Two thirds of him is god,
One third of him is man,
There's none can match the form of his body...

[The inhabitants of Uruk call upon the gods for help:]

"Gilgamesh keeps the son from the father,
Building the walls through the day, through the night.
He is herdsman of ramparted Uruk,
He is herdsman and lord of his folk,
Strong and splendid, knowing wisdom.
Gilgamesh keeps the lover from the maiden,
The daughter of a hero,
The chosen of a noble!"
The great gods heard their outcries.

The gods of heaven called the lord Anu:
"Was he not of thy making, this almighty wild bull,
This hero Gilgamesh?
He hath not his like in the whole land....
Gilgamesh keeps the son from the father,
Building the walls through the day, through the night.
He is herdsman of ramparted Uruk,
He is herdsman and lord of his folk,
Strong and splendid,
Knowing wisdom.
Gilgamesh keeps the lover from the maiden,
The daughter of a hero,
The chosen of a noble!"
The great god Anu lent ear to their cries.
Aruru was summoned, she the great goddess:
"Thou, Aruru, madest Gilgamesh;
Now make another like unto him.
So long as he pleases
Let him come at Gilgamesh.
Let them contend together,
That Uruk may have peace."

As Aruru this heard,
She shaped in her heart a warrior of Anu.
Aruru washed her hands,
She pinched up some clay and spat on it.
She moulded Engidu,
Fashioned a hero, a glorious scion,
A fighter of Ninurta's.
His whole body was shaggy with hair,
Hair he bore on his head like a woman,
The plenty of his hair sprouted like grain.
He knew naught of land and people,
He was clothed like the god of the herds.
With the gazelles he eats the plants,
With the wild beasts he drinks at the watering-place,
With the throng at the water he makes glad his heart.

He walked to the watering-place
Toward a hunter, a stalker of wild beasts;
On one day, on a second, and a third,
Toward the hunter he walked to the watering-place.
The hunter saw him, the hunter's face grew troubled.
Without his quarry he turned back to his house.
He was down-cast, troubled; he shrieked.
His heart was afraid and his face was dark.
Grief made way into his heart,
And he looked like a wanderer of far ways.

. . .

[The hunter] started on the way, he entered into Uruk.
He goes to Gilgamesh, and to him he says:
"A man that came from the hills
Hath become strong indeed in the land.
Mighty in power like a fighter of Anu's.
Ever he goeth along on the hills,

6

He is ever beside the wild beasts,
Ever are his feet at the watering-place.
I am afraid, I cannot go near to him.
He hath filled my pits which I dug;
My traps which I laid
He hath destroyed.
So from my hands he let my quarry get away,
The throngs of the fields;
No catch he allows me."

Gilgamesh says to him, to the hunter:
"Go, my hunter, and get thee a priestess.
When the wild beasts come to the watering-place,
Then let her cast her garment off,
That he may take his fill of her.
When he sees her, he will draw near;
Then will he become a stranger to his wild beasts,
Who on his own steppes grew up with him."

The hunter went yonder and got him a priestess.
They made themselves ready, went forth straight on.
On the third day they came to their goal:
The hunter and the priestess sat themselves down.
One day, a second day, they sat by the watering-place.
The wild beasts come along and drink at the watering-place.
Glad is the throng of the flood.
So too comes he, Engidu....
With the gazelles he eats the plants,
With, the beasts he drinks at the watering-place,
His heart is happy with the throng of the flood.
Then the priestess saw him, the great strong one,
The wild fellow, the man of the steppes:
"There he is, woman!"

Loosen thy buckle,
Unveil thy delight,
That he may take his fill of thee!
Hang not back, take up his lust!
When he sees thee, he will draw near.
Open thy robe that he rest upon thee!
Arouse in him rapture, the work of woman.
Then will he become a stranger to his wild beasts,
Who on his own steppes grew up with him.
His bosom will press against thee."
Then the priestess loosened her buckle,
Unveiled her delight,
For him to take his fill of her.
She hung not back, she took up his lust,
She opened her robe that he rest upon her.
She aroused in him rapture, the work of woman.
His bosom pressed against her.
Engidu forgot where he was born.
For six days and seven nights
Was Engidu given over to love with the priestess.
When he had sated himself with the fill of her,
He raised up his face to his wild ones:
At sight of Engidu, the gazelles flee away,

7

The wild of the fields shrink back before him.
Then Engidu marvelled,
His body stood as in a spell,
His knees quivered, because his wild ran off...
The speed of his onset is not what it was.
He hearkens and opens his ear:
He turns about and sits down at the feet of the priestess.
He looks the priestess in the face,
And to what the priestess now speaks
His ears give heed.

The priestess says to him, to Engidu:
"Engidu, how beautiful thou, how like a god!
Why must thou rush with animals over the steppes?
Come, I will lead thee into ramparted Uruk,
To a pure house, the dwelling of Anu and Ishtar,
Where Gilgamesh lives, matchless in might,
And like a wild bull lords it over the folk..."
She talks to him, till he likes her words.
Knowing his own heart, he seeketh a friend.
Engidu says to her, to the priestess:
"Woman, go to! Lead me to the pure, the holy house,
The dwelling of Anu and Ishtar,
Where Gilgamesh lives, matchless in might,
And like a wild bull lords it over the folk.
I will challenge him to a fight.
I will call the strong one.
I will call out in Uruk:
'I too am a strong one!'
I alone can alter fate,
I, born on the steppes, matchless in might.
O Gilgamesh, may I behold thy face!
Well I know what the outcome will be."

. . .

Engidu goes along the market-street
Of ramparted Uruk.
Marvelling he looks at the mighty work;
He bars the way of the warriors of Uruk;
Then the folk of Uruk crowd against him,
The land is assembled .
But in fear the folk turn away.
They fall down. . . like a weak child...
The couch had been spread for goddess Ishtar...
At the gates of her house
Engidu barred the going-to,
Allowed not Gilgamesh that he enter in.
They grappled each other at the gates of her house.
They fought in the street...
That the doorposts quaked and the wall swayed ...
Gilgamesh crumpled his leg to the ground,
His anger softened, he checked his onset.
When he had checked his onset, Says Engidu to him,
      to Gilgamesh:

"Thee, as one matchless, thy mother bore,
The wild cow of the fold, the goddess Ninsun.
Over all men is thy head lifted up, Ellil to thee hath allotted The
    kingdom over mankind!"

               . . .

[After their wrestling match Gilgamesh and Engidu become good
friends. Together they trek into a far-distant cedar forest where
they slay the monster, Khumbaba. But Gilgamesh later spurns the
goddess, Ishtar, who then persuades her father, Anu, to send the
bull of heaven to kill Gilgamesh—*Ed.*]

Anu lent ear to [Ishtar's] words,
Let a bull-of-heaven descend
And come unto Uruk…
At his first snort he kills
Three hundred warriors.
And Engidu grasped the bull-of-heaven
By his horns.
At his second snort
Two hundred warriors he knocks over.
At his third snort
Engidu stalks up to him,
Leaps on his back,
And grasps him by the thick of the tail...
Then Engidu opened his mouth and speaks,
Says to Gilgamesh:
"My friend,
We have made our name glorious…"
And Gilgamesh, like a huntsman,
Thrusts his sword between nape and horns.
When they had laid low the bull-of-heaven,
Their heart had peace…
And in front of Shamash they sat down to their rest,
Both of the brothers.

Then Ishtar mounted the walls of ramparted Uruk,
Sprang on the battlements and shrieked down:
"Woe unto Gilgamesh who affronted me,
Who killed the bull-of-heaven."
As Engidu heard these words of Ishtar,
He tore loose a thigh-bone from the bull-of-heaven,
And flung it into her face:
"Could I but get hold of thee, I would do unto thee as unto him!
Round thy neck would I hang his entrails!"
Then Ishtar assembled the damsels of the temple,
The harlots and the priestesses;
Over the thigh-bone of the bull-of-heaven
They wailed a chant…
Gilgamesh called the masters, the handworkers all.
The masters praise the thickness of the horns;
Thirty pounds of lapis lazuli was the weight of each.
Two fingers thick was their shell.
Six measures of oil (as much as both horns held)
Did he pour, as oil of anointing,
To his god, Lugalmaradda;

Brought the horns to his god's temple,
And fastened them on his throne.
Then they washed their hands in the Euphrates,
Start off and wander along
On the market-street of Uruk.
The people of Uruk stand assembled
And gaze upon them.

Gilgamesh speaks thus
To the maid-servants of his palace:
"Who is the most beautiful among the heroes?
Who is the mightiest among men?"

"Gilgamesh is the most beautiful among the heroes!
Gilgamesh is the mightiest among men!"...
Then Gilgamesh makes in his palace A feast of rejoicing.

The warriors rest in their beds of night.
Also Engidu rests, beholding dreams.
Then Engidu rose up,
Tells the dreams, and speaks to his friend:

"Gilgamesh, my friend,
I beheld dreams this last night:
The heavens called, the earth answered.
In the dark night am I standing there alone,
I see a man with forbidding face...
He is hideous to look on,
His nails are eagle-talons .
He made my arms into wings like a bird's:
'Descend, descend, I say, into the house of darkness,
To the dwelling of Irkalla,
To the house
Which none leave again who have betrodden it,
To a way whose road turneth not,
To the house whose inhabitants do without light,
Where dust is their nourishment and clay their food.
They are as birds clothed with wings,
They see not the light,
They dwell in the darkness.'
In the house of dust which I entered ...
Are kings' crowns bowed down.
There do dwell the mighty ones
Who from the days of old ruled the land...
In the house of dust which I entered
Dwell priest-prince and wailing-priests,
Dwell the conjurers and the rapt seers,
Dwell the high-priests of the great gods...
Dwells the queen of the earth, Eresh-Kigal.
Belit-Seri, she the scribe of the earth,
Standeth bowed before her...
And readeth to her aloud.
Then she raised her head and saw me,
She stretched out her hand and took me to herself"...

[Then Gilgamesh moaned and said:]

"My friend,
Who with me hast ranged through all hardships…
My friend, the dream comes true!..."
On the day when he saw the dream
His fate was fulfilled.
Engidu lies stricken,
For one day,
For a second day,
Engidu suffers pain in his bed.
For a third day, and a fourth,
Engidu lies stricken.
For a fifth, a sixth, and a seventh,
For an eighth, a ninth, and a tenth day.
Engidu's pain grows great.
For an eleventh and a twelfth day,
Engidu lies in his bed…
He calls Gilgamesh and speaks:
"A god hath cursed me, my friend.
Not like one wounded in battle
Is it mine to die.
I once feared the fight…
But, my friend,
He who falls in the fight is happy.
As to me, I must die in my bed…"

. . .

[And Gilgamesh returns to Engidu's bed and speaks:]

"Engidu, my young friend,
Thou panther of the steppes,
Who couldst do all things,
So that we climbed the mountain,
Overthrew Khumbaba,
Who housed in the cedar-forest,
So that we seized and slew the bull-of-heaven,
What kind of sleep is this
That hath now seized upon thee?
Dark is thy look,
And thine ears take not my voice!"
But he lifts up his eyes no more.
Gilgamesh touched him on the heart,
But the heart beats no more.
Then he covered up his friend like a bride.

Like as a lion, Gilgamesh raised his voice,
Like as a lioness, he roared out.
He turns round to his friend,
He tears his hair and strews it forth…
Soon as beamed the first shimmer of morning,
Gilgamesh raised a new cry:

"I made thee to rest on a bed well-prepared,
I made thee to dwell in a quiet dwelling-place…
I made princes of the earth kiss thy feet.
Now will I make the people of ramparted Uruk
Beweep thee and sorrow for thee;

11

Much people will I make to serve thee,
And I will myself put on mourning for thee,
Will clothe myself in a lion's skin,
And haste away over the steppes..."

Gilgamesh weeps bitterly
For his friend Engidu,
And hastes away over the steppes:

. . .

[After many wanderings over steppes and mountains Gilgamesh
reaches the sea.—*Ed.*]

Siduri, she the divine cup-bearer,
Sits there by the rim of the sea.
Sits there and looks afar off...
She is wrapped in a shawl...
Gilgamesh ran thither and drew nigh unto her.
He is clad in skins,
His shape is awesome,
His body godlike,
Woe is in his heart.
He is like a wanderer of far ways.
The face of her, the cup-bearer, looks afar off,
She talks to herself and says the word,
Takes counsel in her heart:
"Is he yonder one who deviseth ill?
Whither is he going in the wrath of his heart?"
As Siduri saw him, she locked her gate,
Locked her portal, locked her chamber...

Gilgamesh says to her, to the cup-bearer:
"Cup-bearer, what ails thee,
That thou lockest thy gate,
Lockest thy portal,
Lockest thy chamber?
I will crash the door, I will break the lock..."

The cup-bearer says to him, to Gilgamesh:
"Why are thy cheeks so wasted,
Thy visage so sunken,
Thy heart so sad,
Thy shape so undone?
Why is woe in thy heart?
Why art thou like a wanderer of far ways?
Why is thy countenance
So destroyed with grief and pain?
Why hast thou from wide-away
Made haste over the steppes?"
Gilgamesh says to her, to the cup-bearer:
"Why should my cheeks not be so wasted,
My visage so sunken,
My heart so sad,
My shape so undone?
How should woe not be in my heart?
Why should I not be like

A wanderer of far ways?
Why should not my countenance
Be destroyed with grief and pain?
Why should I not to the far-away
Make haste over the steppes?
My beloved friend, the panther of the steppes,
Engidu, my beloved friend,
The panther of the steppes who could do all things,
So that we climbed the mountain,
Overthrew Khumbaba,
Who housed in the cedar-forest,
So that we seized and slew the bull-of-heaven,
So that we laid lions low
In the ravines of the mountain,
My friend,
Who with me ranged through all hardships,
Engidu, my friend, who killed lions with me,
Who with me ranged through all hardships,
Him hath the fate of mankind overtaken.
Six days and six nights have I wept over him,
Until the seventh day
Would I not have him buried.
Then I began to be afraid...

Fear of death seized upon me.
Therefore I make away over the steppes.
The fate of my friend weighs me down.
Therefore I make haste
On a far way over the steppes.
The fate of Engidu, my friend,
Weigheth me down.
Therefore I make haste on a long road over the steppes.
Why should I be silent thereon?
Why should I not cry it forth?
My friend, whom I love,
Hath turned into earth.
Must not I too, as he,
Lay me down
And rise not up again
For ever and for ever?-
Ever since he is gone, I cannot find Life,
And rove, like a hunter, round over the fields.
Cup-bearer, now I behold thy face;
But Death, whom I fear, I would not behold."

The cup-bearer, she says to him, to
Gilgamesh:
"Gilgamesh, whither runnest thou?
Life, which thou seekest, thou wilt not find.
When the gods created mankind,
They allotted to mankind Death,
But Life they withheld in their hands.
So, Gilgamesh, fill thy body,
Make merry by day and night,
Keep each day a feast of rejoicing!
Day and night leap and have thy delight!
Put on clean raiment,

13

Wash thy head and bathe thee in water,
Look cheerily at the child who holdeth thy hand,
And may thy wife have joy in thy arms!"

Gilgamesh says again to her, to the cupbearer:
"Go to, cup-bearer!
Where is the way to Utnapishtim?
What is his sign? Give it to me!
If it can be done,
I will pass over the sea;
If it cannot be done,
I will make away over the steppes."
The cup-bearer she says to him, to
Gilgamesh:
"Never, Gilgamesh, was there a place of crossing,
And no one who came since the days of old
Could pass over that sea.
Only Shamash, the hero,
Hath passed over that sea.
But who except Shamash can pass over it?
There is no getting to the place of crossing,
Toilsome the way thereunto,
The waters of death are deep
That lie there to thwart thee.
Where wilt thou, Gilgamesh, pass over that sea?
When thou comest to the waters of death,
What, then, wilt thou do?
Gilgamesh, Ur-Shanabi is there,
The shipman of Utnapishtim,
Who hath with him coffers of stone.
He picks plants in the forest.
Him do thou seek out.
If it can be done, fare across with him;
If it cannot be done, turn again back."

. . .

[Gilgamesh seeks for Ur-Shanabi, but finds at first only his stone coffers, which he breaks to pieces in his anger. Then suddenly he beholds Ur-Shanabi.]

Ur-Shanabi says to him, to Gilgamesh:
"What is thy name? Say forth!
I am Ur-Shanabi,
Man-servant of Utnapishtim, the far one."

Gilgamesh speaks to him, to Ur-Shanabi:
"My name is Gilgamesh,
I have come from long away…
At last, Ur-Shanabi, I behold thy face.
Let me look on Utnapishtim, the far one."
And Gilgamesh says again to him,
To Ur-Shanabi, the shipman:
"Come, Ur-Shanabi, where is the way to Utnapishtim?
What is his sign? Give it to me!
Give me, give me his sign!

If it can be done,
I will pass over the sea;
If it cannot be done,
I will make away over the steppes."

Ur-Shanabi says to him, to Gilgamesh:
"Thy hands, O Gilgamesh,
Have hindered a landing.
Thou brakest to pieces the coffers of stone,
The coffers of stone are to-broken;
And so I cannot ferry thee over.
Gilgamesh, take the axe in thy arm,
Go down to the forest,
Cut poles of length sixty ells,
Smear them with pitch and bear them to me."

As Gilgamesh this heard,
He took the axe in his arm,
Drew the sword from his girdle,
Went down to the forest,
And cut poles of length sixty ells,
Smeared them with pitch...
And brought them to Ur-Shanabi.

Gilgamesh and Ur-Shanabi boarded the ship,
They headed the ship into the flood,
And sailed forth,
A way of one month and fifteen days.
As he took his bearings on the third day,
Ur-Shanabi had reached the waters of death.
Ur-Shanabi says to him, to Gilgamesh:
"Quick, Gilgamesh, take a pole!
For thy hands must not touch
The waters of death.
A second, a third, a fourth pole,
Take, Gilgamesh!
An fifth, a sixth, a seventh pole,
Take, Gilgamesh!
An eighth, a ninth, a tenth pole,
Take, Gilgamesh!
An eleventh, a twelfth pole,
Take, Gilgamesh!"

At a hundred and twenty
Gilgamesh had used up the poles.
Now he made his hips free...
Gilgamesh stripped off his garment,
And with his hands made high the mast.
Utnapishtim descrieth his face afar;
Talks to himself and saith the word,
Takes counsel in his heart:
"Why are the stone-coffers
Of the ship all to-broken?
And one who belongs not to me
Sails in the ship!
He who comes yonder, he cannot be man! .
I gaze thither, but I understand it not.

I gaze thither, but I grasp it not."...

Utnapishtim says to him, to Gilgamesh:
"What is thy name? Say forth!
I am Utnapishtim who hath found Life."
                    • • •

Gilgamesh says to him, to Utnapishtim:
"Methought, I will go and see
Utnapishtim, of whom men tell.
So I betook me through all lands to and fro,
So I betook me over the mountains
That are hard to cross over,
So I fared over all seas.
With good have I not been glutted...
I filled my body with pain;
Ere ever I got to Siduri, the cup-bearer,
Was my clothing gone...
I had to hunt all the wild of the fields,
Lions and panthers,
Hyenas, and deer, and ibex.
Their flesh do I eat,
With their skins do I clothe me."

                    • • •

"I look upon thee, Utnapishtim:
Thy form is not unlike;
Even as I, so too art thou;
Yes, thou art not unlike;
Even as I, so too art thou.
Yet I was born unto this:
To fight and to do battle.
But thou art idle and liest on thy back.
How camest thou, then, into the assembly
Of the gods and foundest Life?"

Utnapishtim says to him, to Gilgamesh:
"I will lay open before thee, Gilgamesh,
Knowledge deep-hidden,
And a secret of the gods will I tell thee:
Shurippak is a city (thou thyself knowest her),
Which lieth on Euphrates' banks.
She is an ancient city,
And the gods are kind to her.
Once the great gods conceived a plan
To make a stormflood.
There foregathered Anu, their father,
Their overlord, the hero Ellil,
Their herald Ninurta, their prince Ennugi.
The bright-eyed Ea had sat with them at counsel.
He told their discussion to a reed-hut:[1]
'Reed-hut, reed-hut! Hut-wall, hut-wall!
Reed-hut, listen! Wall, take it in!
Thou man from Shurippak, son of Ubara-Tutu,[2]
Tear down thy house, build a ship!
Let riches go, seek Life,

Despise possessions, save thy life!
Bring living things of all kinds into the ship!
The ship that thou art to build,
Be its measurements strictly laid out,
For its length and its breadth to match-
On the holy lake set it at anchor!
I understood, and I say to Ea, my lord:
'I perceive, my lord, what thou sayest;
I hold it dear, and will carry it out.'

. . .

Before sunset the ship was finished...
All that I had I laded upon it,
All that I had of silver I laded upon it,
I laded upon it all that I had of gold,
I laded upon it all that I had
Of living things of all kinds.
I made my whole family and kin
To go aboard the ship;
Cattle of the field, animals of the field,
All handworkers I made go aboard.
Shamash had given me the appointed time:
'Of an evening will the Sender of darkness
Let a cloudburst stream from on high.
Then enter the ship and close thy door.'
This appointed time came on.

The Sender of darkness
Of an evening let a cloudburst come down.
I observed the look of the tempest,
I was afraid to gaze on the tempest,
I went within the ship and shut my gate.

. . .

Six days and six nights swirls the stormflood,
And the southstorm is a weight on the land.
As the seventh day came on,
The southstorm gave up the fight,

---

[1] In which Utnapishtim lives
[2] That is, Utnapishtim himself, who is revealing the "knowledge deep-hidden" to Gilgamesh

Which it had fought like an army.
The sea grew quiet, and gathered up its waters.
The stormflood ceased.
I looked for the tempest, all had become still.
The whole race of man was turned to earth.
Like a flat roof were the plains.
Then I opened a hatch,
And light streamed into my face.
I sat me down weeping,
And my tears ran over my face.
I gazed about for solid earth
In the dominions of the sea.
After twelve hours an island emerged.
The ship drove for Mount Nissir.
Mount Nissir holds the ship fast
And keeps it from rocking.
One day, a second day, Mount Nissir
Holds the ship fast and keeps it from rocking.
A third and fourth day Mount Nissir
Holds the ship fast and keeps it from rocking.
A fifth, a sixth day Mount Nissir
Holds the ship fast and keeps it from rocking.

"As the seventh day came on,
I held a dove outside and set it free;
The dove flew forth and came back.
She found no resting-place, so she turned home.
I held a swallow outside and set if free;
The swallow flew forth and came back.
She found no resting-place, so she turned home.
I held a raven outside and set it free;
The raven flew forth, saw the water run dry,
He feeds, scrapes, croaks, and turned not home."

Then I let all out unto the four winds,
And offered a sacrifice,
Set up a burnt-offering
On the top of the mountain.

. . .

Gilgamesh and Ur-Shanabi boarded the ship,
They headed the ship into the flood,
And sailed away.
Then said his wife to him,
To Utnapishtim, the far one:
"Gilgamesh hath set forth;
He hath worn himself out, and suffered torments.
What wilt thou give him,
That with it he may reach his homeland?"

And Gilgamesh has already lifted the pole,
And brings the ship again near the shore:
Utuapishtim says to him, to Gilgamesh:
"Gilgamesh, thou hast set forth;
Thou hast worn thyself out, and suffered torments.
What shall I give thee

18

That with it thou reachest thy homeland?
I will lay open before thee
Knowledge deep-hidden;
About a plant of life will I tell thee.
The plant looks like the prick-thorn…
Its thorn like the thorn of the rose
Can prick the hand hard.
When thou gettest this plant in thy hands,
Eat thereof and thou wilt live."

When Gilgamesh learned of this…
He bound heavy stones on his feet;
These drew him down deep in the sea.
He himself took the plant,
And it pricked his hand hard.
He cut off the heavy stones…
And laid the plant beside him.
Gilgamesh says to him,
To Ur-Shanabi, the shipman:
"Ur-Shanabi, this plant
Is a plant-of-promise,
Whereby a man obtains his desire.
I will bring it to ramparted Uruk;
I will make the warriors eat thereof…
Its name is: 'The-old-man-becomes-young-again.'
I myself will eat thereof,
And return back to my youth."
After twenty miles they took a little food,
After thirty miles they rested for the night.
Then Gilgamesh saw a pit with cool water;
He stepped into it and bathed in the water.
Then a serpent savoured the smell of the plant;
She crept along and took the plant…
When he returned, he shrieked out a curse.
Gilgamesh sat himself down and weeps,
His tears run over his face.
He speaks and says to Ur-Shanabi, the shipman:
"For whom, Ur-Shanabi,
Have my arms worn themselves out?
For whom hath been spent the blood of my heart?
I worked good not for myself-
For the worm of the earth have I wrought good…"

Questions:
1. *What are Gilgamesh's virtues? What are his faults? What does this tell us about the values and assumptions of the community that produced and preserved this story?*
2. *What does this story teach us about human nature and the human condition? What does it teach us about the nature of gods and their relationship with humans?*

1.5   The Code of Hammurabi

From 2000 to 1600 B.C.E., the city-states of Mesopotamia endured a period of nearly continuous warfare that saw shifting alliances and frequent chaos. The most dominant personality of the age, Hammurabi, established his control over the region from about 1800 to 1750 B.C.E. and ruled from the city of Baby-lon. His great contribution to Western civilization was a series of laws that sought to establish justice within his empire. This concept of equity, which remedied a large number of abuses, influenced law codes yet to come, most notably those of Greece and Rome. In the following passages, note the con-tinual emphasis on fairness in the regulation of property, trade, debt, family relations, and personal injury.

> **Source:** "The Code of Hammurabi" is from Robert F. Harper, trans., *The Code of Hammurabi* (Chicago: University of Chicago Press, 1904).

When the lofty Anu, king of the Anunnaki gods, and Enlil, lord of heaven and earth, he who determines the destiny of the land . . . pronounced the lofty name of Babylon; when they made it famous among the quarters of the world and in its midst established an everlasting kingdom whose foundations were firm as heaven and earth; [they] . . . named me, Hammurabi, the exalted prince, the worshiper of the gods, to cause justice to prevail in the land, to destroy the wicked and the evil, to prevent the strong from oppressing the weak, to go forth like the sun over the black-headed people, to enlighten the land to further the welfare of the people. Hammurabi, the shepherd named by Enlil, am I, who brought about plenty and abun-dance; . . . the powerful king, the sun of Babylon, who caused light to go forth over the lands of Sumer and Akkad; the king who caused the four quarters of the world to render obedience; the favorite of Ishtar, am I.

When Marduk sent me to rule the people and to bring help to the country, I established law and justice in the lan-guage of the land and promoted the welfare of the people. At that time [I decreed]:

1. If a man bring accusation against another man, charging him with murder, but cannot prove it, the accuser shall be put to death.

3. If a man bear false witness in a case, or does not establish the testimony that he has given, if that case be a case involving life, that man shall be put to death.

4. If he bear [false] witness concerning grain or money, he shall himself bear the penalty imposed in that case.

5. If a judge pronounce a judgment, render a decision, deliver a verdict duly signed and sealed, and afterward alter his judgment, they shall call that judge to account for the alteration of the judgment which he has pronounced, and he shall pay twelve-fold the penalty in that judgment; and, in the assembly, they shall expel him from his seat of judg-ment, and with the judges in a case he shall not take his seat.

22. If a man practice robbery and is captured, that man shall be put to death.

23. If the robber is not captured, the man who has been robbed shall, in the presence of god, make an itemized statement of his loss, and the city and the governor in whose province and jurisdiction the robbery was committed shall com-pensate him for whatever was lost.

24. If it be a life [that is lost], the city and governor shall pay one mina [about one pound] of silver to his heirs.

53. If a man neglects to maintain his dike and does not strengthen it, and a break is made in his dike and the water car-ries away the farmland, the man in whose dike the break has been made shall replace the grain which has been dam-aged.

54. If he is not able to replace the grain, they shall sell him and his goods, and the farmers whose grain the water has car-ried away shall divide [the results of the sale].

55. If a man opens his canal for irrigation and neglects it and the water carries away an adjacent field, he shall pay out grain on the basis of the adjacent field.

109. If bad characters gather in the house of a wine seller and he does not arrest those bad characters and bring them to the palace, that wine seller shall be put to death.

110. If a priestess who is not living in a convent opens a wine shop or enters a wine shop for a drink, they shall burn that woman.

117. If a man be in debt and sell his wife, son, or daughter, or bind them over to service, for three years they shall work in the house of their purchaser or master; in the fourth year they shall be given their freedom.

128. If a man takes a wife and does not arrange a contract for her, that woman is not a wife.

129. If the wife of a man is caught lying with another man, they shall bind them and throw them into the water.

138. If a man wishes to put away his wife who has not borne him children, he shall give her money to the amount of her marriage price and he shall make good to her the dowry which she brought from her father's house and then he may put her away.

142. If a woman hates her husband and says, "You may not have me," the city council shall inquire into her case; and if she has been careful and without reproach and her husband has been going about and greatly belittling her, that woman has no blame. She may take her dowry and go to her father's house.

143. If she has not been careful but has gadded about, neglecting her house, and belittling her husband, they shall throw that woman into the water.

168. If a man set his face to disinherit his son and say to the judges, "I will disinherit my son," the judges shall inquire into his record, and if the son has not committed a crime sufficiently grave to cut him off from sonship, the father may not cut off his son from sonship.

195. If a son strike his father, they shall cut off his hand.

196. If a man destroy the eye of another man, they shall destroy his eye.

197. If he break another man's bone, they shall break his bone.

199. If he destroy the eye of a man's slave or break a bone of a man's slave, he shall pay one-half his price.

Questions:
1. In the code of Hammurabi, why does Hammurabi feel justified in setting forth this law code?
2. What are some of the penalties?
3. Do they seem too harsh to be fair?

1.6   Daily Life in Egypt

This document is a letter of advice from a high-level government official to his son, exhorting him to learn the skills of a scribe. This document gives us insight into the demanding and perilous existence of the majority of the ancient Egyptian population, as well as the attitude of Egyptian elites toward various types of work.

> **Source:** Miriam Lichtheim, *Ancient Egyptian Literature: A Book of Readings.* Volume 2: *The New Kingdom,* (University of California Press, 1976), pp. 168–172

PAPYRUS LANSING

Title

[Beginning of the instruction in letter-writing made by the royal scribe and chief overseer of the cattle of Amen-Re, King of Gods, Nebmare-nakht] for his apprentice, the scribe Wenemdiamun.

Praise of the Scribe's Profession

[The royal scribe] and chief overseer of the cattle of Amen-[Re, King of Gods. Nebmare-nakht speaks to the scribe Wenemdiamun]. [Apply yourself to this] noble profession.... You will find it useful.... You will be advanced by your superiors. You will be sent on a mission.... Love writing, shun dancing; then you become a worthy official. Do not long for the marsh thicket. Turn your back on throw stick and chase. By day write with your fingers; recite by night. Befriend the scroll, the palette. It pleases more than wine. Writing for him who knows it is better than all other professions. It pleases more than bread and beer, more than clothing and ointment. It is worth more than an inheritance in Egypt, than a tomb in the west.

Advice to the Unwilling Pupil

Young fellow, how conceited you are! You do not listen when I speak. Your heart is denser than a great obelisk, a hundred cubits high, ten cubits thick. When it is finished and ready for loading, many work gangs draw it. It hears the words of men; it is loaded on a barge. Departing from Yebu it is conveyed, until it comes to rest on its place in Thebes.

So also a cow is bought this year, and it plows the following year. It learns to listen to the herdsman; it only lacks words. Horses brought from the fields, they forget their mothers. Yoked they go up and down in all his majesty's errand.

They become like those that bore them, that stand in the stable. They do their utmost for fear of a beating/

But although I beat you with every kind of stick, you do not listen. If I knew another way of doing it, I would do it for you, that you might listen. You are a person fit for writing, through you have not yet known a women. Your heart discerns. Your fingers are skilled, your mouth is apt for reciting.

Writing is more enjoyable than enjoying a basket of...and beans; more enjoyable than a mother's giving birth, when her heart knows no distaste. She is constant in nursing her son; her breast is in his mouth every day. Happy is the heart [of] him who writes; he is young each day.

All Occupations Are Bad Except That of the Scribe

See for yourself with your own eye. The occupations lie before you.

The washerman's day is going up, going down. All his limbs are weak, [from] whitening his neighbors' clothes every day, from washing their linen.

The maker of pots is smeared with soil, like one whose relations have died. His hands, his feet are full of clay, he is like one who lives in the bog.

The cobbler mingles with vats. His odor is penetrating. His hands are red with madder, like one who is smeared with blood. He looks behind him for the kite, like one whose flesh is exposed.

The watchman prepares garlands and polishes vase-stands. He spends a night of toil just as one on whom the sun shines.

The merchants travel downstream and upstream. They are as busy as can be, carrying goods from one town to another. They supply him who has wants. But the tax collectors carry off the gold, that most precious of metals.

The ships' crews from every house (of commerce), they receive their loads. They depart from Egypt for Syria, and each man's god is with him. (But) not one of them says: "We shall see Egypt again!"

The carpenter who is in the shipyard carries the timber and stacks it. If he gives today the Output of yesterday, woe to his limbs! The shipwright stands behind him to tell him evil things.

His outworker who is in the fields, his is the toughest of all the jobs. He spends the day loaded with his tools, tied to his tool-box. When he returns home at night, he is loaded with the tool-box and the timbers, his drinking mug, and his whet- stones.

The scribe, he alone, records the output of all of them. Take note of it!

The Misfortunes of the Peasant

Let me also expound to you the situation of the peasant, that other tough occupation. [Comes] the inundation and soaks him...he attends to his equipment. By day he cuts his farming tools; by night he twists rope. Even his midday hour he spends on farm labor. He equips himself to go to the field as if he were a warrior. The dried field lies before him; he goes out to get his team. When he has been after the herdsman for many days, he gets his team and comes back with it. He makes for it a place in the field. Comes dawn, he goes to make a start and does not find it in its place. He spends three days searching for it; he finds it in the bog. He finds no hides on them; the jackals have chewed them. He comes out, his garment in his hand, to beg for himself a team.

When he reaches his field he finds [it] broken up. He spends time cultivating, and the snake is after him. It finishes off the seed as it is cast to the ground. He does not see a green blade. He does three plowings with borrowed grain. His wife has gone down to the merchants and found nothing for barter. Now the scribe lands on the shore. He surveys the harvest. Attendants are behind him with staffs, Nubians with clubs. One says (to him): "Give grain." "There is none." He is beaten savagely. He is bound, thrown in the well, submerged head down. His wife is bound in his presence. His children are in fetters. His neighbors abandon them and flee. When it's over, there is no grain.

If you have any sense, be a scribe. If you have learned about the peasant, you will not be able to be one. Take note of it!...

The Scribe Does Not Suffer Like the Soldier

Furthermore, look, I instruct you to make you sound; to make you hold the palette freely. To make you become one whom the king trusts; to make you gain entrance to treasury and granary. To make you receive the ship-load at the gate of the granary. To make you issue the offerings on feast days. You are dressed in fine clothes; you own horses. Your boat is on the river; you are supplied with attendants. You stride about inspecting. A mansion is built in your town. You have a powerful office, given you by the king. Male and female slaves are about you. Those who are in the fields grasp your hand, on plots that you have made. Look, I make you into a staff of life! Put the writings in your heart, and you will be protected from all kinds of toil. You will become a worthy official.

Do you not recall the (fate of) the unskilled man? His name is not known. He is ever burdened [like an ass carring] in front of the scribe who knows what he is about.

Come, [let me tell] you the woes of the soldier, and how many are his supervisors; the general, the troop-commander, the officer who leads, the standard-bearer, the lieutenant, the scribe, the commander of fifty, and the garrison captain. They go in and out in the halls of the palace, saying: "Get laborers!" He is awakened at any hour. One is after his as (after) a donkey. He toils until the Aten (sun) sets in his darkness of night. He is hungry, his belly hurts; he is dead while yet alive. When he receives the grain-ration, having been released from duty, it is not good for grinding.

He is called up for Syria. He may not rest. There are no clothes, no sandals. The weapons of war are assembled at the fortress of Sile. His march is uphill through mountains. He drinks water every third day: it is smelly and tastes of salt. His body is ravaged by illness. The enemy comes, surrounds him with missiles, and life recedes from him. He is told: "Quick, forward, valiant soldier! Win for yourself a good name!" He does not know what he is about. His body is weak, his legs fail him. When victory is won, the captives are handed over to his majesty, to be taken to Egypt. The foreign woman faints on the march; she hangs herself [on] the soldier's neck. His knapsack drops, another grabs it while he is burdened with the woman. His wife and children are in their village; he dies and does not reach it. If he comes out alive, he is worn out from marching. Be he at large, be he detained, the soldier suffers. If he leaps and joins the deserters, all his people are imprisoned. He dies on the edge of the desert, and there is none to perpetuate his name. He suffers in death as in life. A big sack is brought for him; he does not know his resting place.

Be a scribe, and be spared from soldiering! You call and one says: "Here I am." You are safe from torments. Every man seeks to raise himself up. Take note of it!

Question:
1. What sorts of class distinctions are described in this document?

1.7   A Humble Farmer Pleads His Own Case: The Workings of Ma'at

The "Tale of the Eloquent Peasant" is among the most accomplished works of the middle Kingdom, and underscores the basic concept of Ma'at (roughly translated as "the spirit of truth and righteousness") and the role of pharaoh as the paternal judge who sits at the court of last resort. The work also pays tribute to the power and beauty of the spoken word, even from such an unlikely source as the lips of the lowly peasant Khun-Anup.

Source: Miriam Lichtheim, Ancient *Egyptian Literature* (Berkeley, CA: University of California Press, 1975) v.1, pp. 170–184.

There was a man named Khun-Anup, a peasant of Salt-Field. He had a wife whose name was [Ma]rye. This peasant said to his wife: "Look here, I am going down to Egypt to bring food from there for my children. Go, measure for me the barley which is in the barn, what is left of [last year's] barley." Then she measured for him [twenty-six] gallons of barley. This peasant said to his wife: "Look, you have twenty gallons of barley as food for you and your children. Now make for me these six gallons of barley into bread and beer for every day in which [I shall travel]."

This peasant went down to Egypt. He had loaded his donkeys with rushes, *rdmt*-grass, natron, salt, sticks of ——, staves from Cattle-Country, leopard skins, wolf skins, *ns3*-plants, '*nw*-stones, *tnm*-plants, *hprwr*-plants, *s3hwt, s3skwt, miswt*-plants, *snt*-stones, '*b3w*-stones, *ibs3*-plants, *inbi*-plants, pidgeons, *n'rw*-birds, *wgs*-birds, *wbn*-plants, *tbsw*-plants, *gngnt,* earth-hair, and *inst;* in sum, all the good products of Salt-Field. This peasant went south toward Hnes. He arrived in the district of Perfefi, north of Medenyt. There he met a man standing on the riverbank whose name was Nemtynakht. He was the son of a man named Isri and a subordinate of the high steward Rensi, the son of Meru.

This Nemtynakht said, when he saw this peasant's donkeys which tempted his heart: "If only I had a potent divine image through which I could seize this peasant's goods!" Now the house of this Nemtynakht was at the beginning of a path which was narrow, not so wide as to exceed the width of a shawl. And one side of it was under water, the other under barley. This Nemtynakht said to his servant: "Go, bring me a sheet from my house." It was brought to him straightway. He spread it out on the beginning of the path, so that its fringe touched the water, its hem the barley.

Now this peasant came along the public road. Then this Nemtynakht said: "Be careful, peasant; don't step on my clothes!" This peasant said: "I'll do as you wish, my course is a good one." So he went up higher. This Nemtynakht said: "Will you have my barley for a path?" This peasant said: "My course is a good one. The riverbank is steep and our way is under barley, for you block the path with your clothes. Will you then not let us pass on the road?"

Just then one of the donkeys filled its mouth with a wisp of barley. This Nemtynakht said: "Now I shall seize your donkey, peasant, for eating my barley. It shall tread out grain for its offense!" This peasant said: "My course is a good one. Only one (wisp) is destroyed. Could I buy my donkey for its value, if you seize it for filling its mouth with a wisp of barley? But I know the lord of this domain; it belongs to the high steward Rensi, the son of Meru. He punishes every robber in this whole land. Shall I be robbed in his domain?" This Nemtynakht said: "Is this the saying people say: 'A poor man's name is pronounced for his master's sake.' It is I who speak to you, and you invoke the high steward!"

Then he took a stick of green tamarisk to him and thrashed all his limbs with it, seized his donkeys, drove them to his domain. Then this peasant wept very loudly for the pain of that which was done to him. This Nemtynakht said: "Don't raise your voice, peasant. Look, you are bound for the abode of the Lord of Silence!") This peasant said: "You beat me, you steal my goods, and now you take the complaint from my mouth! O Lord of Silence, give me back my things, so that I can stop crying to your dreadedness!"

This peasant spent the time of ten days appealing to this Nemtynakht who paid no attention to it. So this peasant proceeded southward to Hnes, in order to appeal to the high steward Rensi, the son of Meru. He found him coming out of the door of his house, to go down to his courthouse barge. This peasant said: "May I be allowed to acquaint you with this complaint? Might a servant of your choice be sent to me, through whom I could inform you of it?" So the high steward Rensi, the son of Meru, sent a servant of his choice ahead of him, and this peasant informed him of the matter in all its aspects.

Then the high steward Rensi, the son of Meru, denounced this Nemtynakht to the magistrates who were with him. Then they said to him: "Surely it is a peasant of his who has gone to someone else beside him. That is what they do to peasants of theirs who go to others beside them. That is what they do. Is there cause for punishing this Nemtynakht for a trifle of natron and a trifle of salt? If he is ordered to replace it, he will replace it." Then the high steward Rensi, the son of Meru, fell silent. He did not reply to these magistrates, nor did he reply to this peasant.

Now this peasant came to appeal to the high steward Rensi, the son of Meru. He said: "O high steward, my lord, greatest of the great, leader of all!

> When you go down to the sea of justice
> And sail on it with a fair wind,
> No squall shall strip away your sail,
> Nor will your boat be idle.
> No accident will affect your mast,
> Your yards will not break.
> You will not founder when you touch land,
> No flood will carry you away.
> You will not taste the river's evils,
> You will not see a frightened face.
> Fish will come darting to you,
> Fatted fowl surround you.
> For you are father to the orphan,
> Husband to the widow,
> Brother to the rejected woman,
> Apron to the motherless.

Let me make your name in this land according to all the good rules:

> Leader free of greed,
> Great man free of baseness,
> Destroyer of falsehood,
> Creator of rightness,
> Who comes at the voice of the caller!
> When I speak, may you hear!
> Do justice, O praised one,
> Who is praised by the praised;
> Remove my grief, I am burdened,
> Examine me, I am in need!

Now this peasant made this speech in the time of the majesty of King Nebkaure, the justified. Then the high steward

Rensi, the son of Meru, went before his majesty and said: "My lord, I have found one among those peasants whose speech is truly beautiful. Robbed of his goods by a man who is in my service, he has come to petition me about it." Said his majesty: "As truly as you wish to see me in health, you shall detain him here, without answering whatever he says. In order to keep him talking, be silent. Then have it brought to us in writing, that we may hear it. But provide for his wife and his children. For one of those peasants comes here (only) just before his house is empty. Provide also for this peasant himself. You shall let food be given him without letting him know that it is you who gives it to him."

So they gave him ten loaves of bread and two jugs of beer every day. It was the high steward Rensi, the son of Meru, who gave it. He gave it to a friend of his, and he gave it to him. Then the high steward Rensi, the son of Meru, wrote to the mayor of Salt-Field about providing food for this peasant's wife, a total of three bushels of grain every day.

***

Now this peasant came to petition him a second time. He said: "O high steward, my lord, greatest of the great, richest of the rich, truly greater that his great ones, richer than his rich ones!

> Rudder of heaven, beam of earth,
> Plumb-line that carries the weight!
> Rudder, drift not,
> Beam, tilt not,
> Plumb-line, swing not awry!

A great lord taking a share of that which is (now) ownerless; stealing from a lonely man? Your portion is in your house: a jug of beer and three loaves. What is that you expend to satisfy your clients? A mortal man dies along with his underlings; shall you be a man of eternity?

> Is it not wrong, a balance that tilts,
> A plummet that strays,
> The straight becoming crooked?
> Lo, justice flees from you,
> Expelled from its seat!
> The magistrates do wrong,
> Right-dealing is bent sideways,
> The judges snatch what has been stolen.
> He who trims a matter's rightness makes it swing
>   awry:
> The breath-giver chokes him who is down,
> He who should refresh makes pant.
> The arbitrator is a robber,
> The remover of need orders its creation.
> The town is a floodwater,
> The punisher of evil commits crimes!"

Said the high steward Rensi, the son of Meru: "Are your belongings a greater concern to you than that my servant might seize you? This peasant said:

> "The measurer of grain-heaps trims for himself,
> He who fills for another shaves the other's share;
> He who should rule by law commands theft,
> Who then will punish crime?
> The straightener of another's crookedness
> Supports another's crime.
> Do you find here something for you?
> Redress is short, misfortune long,
> A good deed is remembered.
> This is the precept:
> Do to the doer to make him do.
> It is thanking a man for what he does,

Parrying a blow before it strikes,
Giving a commission to one who is skillful.

Oh for a moment of destruction, havoc in your vineyard, loss among your birds, damage to your water birds!

A man who saw has turned blind,
A hearer deaf,
A leader now leads astray!

......You are strong and mighty. Your arm is active, your heart greedy, mercy has passed you by. How miserable is the wretch whom you have destroyed! You are like a messenger of the Crocodile; you surpass the Lady of Pestilence! If you have nothing, she has nothing. If there's nothing against her, there's nothing against you. If you don't act, she does not act. The wealthy should be merciful; violence is for the criminal; robbing suits him who has nothing. The stealing done by the robber is the misdeed of one who is poor. One can't reproach him; he merely seeks for himself. But you are sated with your bread, drunken with your beer, rich in all kinds of [treasures].

Though the face of the steersman is forward, the boat drifts as it pleases. Though the king is in the palace, though the rudder is in your hand, wrong is done around you. Long is my plea, heavy my task. "What is the matter with him?" people ask.

Be a shelter, make safe your shore,
See how your quay is infested with crocodiles!
Straighten your tongue, let it not stray,
A serpent is this limb of man.
Don't tell lies, warn the magistrates,
Greasy baskets are the judges,
Telling lies is their herbage,
It weighs lightly on them.
Knower of all men's ways:
Do you ignore my case?
Savior from all water's harm:
See I have a course without a ship!
Guider to port of all who founder:
Rescue the drowning!
......"

***

Then this peasant came to petition him a third time; he said:

"High steward, my lord,
You are Re, lord of sky, with your courtiers,
Men's sustenance is from you as from the flood,
You are Hapy who makes green the fields,
Revives the wastelands.
Punish the robber, save the sufferer,
Be not a flood against the pleader!
Heed eternity's coming,
Desire to last, as is said:
Doing justice is breath for the nose.
Punish him who should be punished,
And none will equal your rectitude.
Does the hand-balance deflect?
Does the stand-balance tilt?
Does Thoth show favor
So that you may do wrong?
Be the equal of these three:

> If the three show favor,
> Then may you show favor!
> Answer not good with evil,
> Put not one in place of another!

My speech grows more than *snmyt*-weed, to assault the smell with its answers. Misfortune pours water till cloth will grow! Three times now to make him act!

> By the sail-wind should you steer,
> Control the waves to sail aright;
> Guard from landing by the helm-rope,
> Earth's rightness lies in justice!
> Speak not falsely—you are great,
> Act not lightly—you are weighty;
> Speak not falsely—you are the balance,
> Do not swerve—you are the norm!
> You are one with the balance,
> If it tilts you may tilt.
> Do not drift, steer, hold the helm-rope!
> Rob not, act against the robber,
> Not great is one who is great in greed.
> Your tongue is the plummet,
> Your heart the weight,
> Your two lips are its arms.
> If you avert your face from violence,
> Who then shall punish wrongdoing?
> Lo, you are a wretch of a washerman,
> A greedy one who harms a friend,
> One who forsakes his friend for his client,
> His brother is he who comes with gifts.
> Lo, you are a ferryman who ferries him who pays,
> A straight one whose straightness is splintered,
> A storekeeper who does not let a poor man pass,
> Lo, you are a hawk to the little people,
> One who lives on the poorest of the birds.
> Lo, you are a butcher whose joy is slaughter,
> The carnage is nothing to him.
> You are a herdsman…...
> …...

Hearer, you hear not! Why do you not hear? Now I have subdued the savage; the crocodile retreats! What is your gain? When the secret of truth is found, falsehood is thrown on its back on the ground. Trust not the morrow before it has come; none knows the trouble in it."

Now this peasant had made this speech to the high steward Rensi, the son of Meru, at the entrance to the court-house. Then he had two guards go to him with whips, and they thrashed all his limbs.

This peasant said: "The son of Meru goes on erring. His face is blind to what he sees, deaf to what he hears; his heart strays from what is recalled to him.

> You are like a town without a mayor,
> Like a troop without a leader,
> Like a ship without a captain,
> A company without a chief.
> You are a sheriff who steals,
> A mayor who pockets,
> A district prosecutor of crime
> Who is the model for the (evil)-doer!"

***

Now this peasant came to petition him a fourth time. Finding him coming out of the gate of the temple of Harsaphes, he said: "O praised one, may Harsaphes praise you, from whose temple you have come!

> Goodness is destroyed, none adhere to it,
> To fling falsehood's back to the ground.
> If the ferry is grounded, wherewith does one
>   cross?......

Is crossing the river on sandals a good crossing? No! Who now sleeps till daybreak? Gone is walking by night, travel by day, and letting a man defend his own good cause. But it is no use to tell you this; mercy has passed you by. How miserable is the wretch whom you have destroyed!

> Lo, you are a hunter who takes his fill,
> Bent on doing what he pleases;
> Spearing hippopotami, shooting bulls,
> Catching fish, snaring birds.
> (But) none quick to speak is free from haste,
> None light of heart is weighty in conduct.
> Be patient so as to learn justice,
> Restrain your [anger] for the good of the humble
>   seeker.
> No hasty man attains excellence,
> No impatient man is leaned upon.

Let the eyes see, let the heart take notice. Be not harsh in your power lest trouble befall you. Pass over a matter, it becomes two. He who eats tastes; one addressed answers. It is the sleeper who sees the dream; and a judge who deserves punishment is a model for the (evil)doer. Fool, you are attacked! Ignorant man, you are questioned! Spouter of water, you are attained!

> Steersman, let not drift your boat,
> Life-sustainer, let not die,
> Provider, let not perish,
> Shade, let one not dry out,
> Shelter, let not the crocodile snatch!
> The fourth time I petition you!
> Shall I go on all day?"

***

Now this peasant came to petition him a fifth time; he said:

"O high steward, my lord! The fisher of *hwdw*-fish, ------, the --- slays the *iy*-fish; the spearer of fish pierces the `*wbb*-fish; the <u>*d3hbw*</u>-fisher attacks the *p`kr*-fish; and the catcher of *wh`*-fish ravages the river. Now you are like them! Rob not a poor man of his goods, a humble man whom you know! Breath to the poor are his belongings; he who takes them stops up his nose. It is to hear cases that you were installed, to judge between two, to punish the robber. But what you do is to uphold the thief! One puts one's trust in you, but you have become a transgressor! You were placed as a dam for the poor lest he drown, but you have become a swift current to him!

***

Now this peasant came to petition him a sixth time; he said: "O high steward my lord!

> He who lessens falsehood fosters truth,
> He who fosters the good reduces ⟨evil⟩,
> As satiety's coming removes hunger,
> Clothing removes nakedness;

28

As the sky is serene after a storm,
Warming all who shiver;
As fire cooks what is raw,
As water quenches thirst.
Now see for yourself:
The arbitrator is a robber,
The peacemaker makes grief,
He who should soothe makes sore.
But he who cheats diminishes justice!
Rightly filled justice either falls short nor brims over.

If you acquire, give to your fellow; gobbling up is dishonest. But my grief will lead to parting; my accusation brings departure. The heart's intent cannot be known. Don't delay! Act on the charge! If you sever, who shall join? The sounding pole is in your hand; sound! The water is shallow! If the boat enters and is grounded, its cargo perishes on the shore.

You are learned, skilled, accomplished,
But not in order to plunder!
You should be the model for all men,
But your affairs are crooked!
The standard for all men cheats the whole land!
The vintner of evil waters his plot with crimes,
Until his plot sprouts falsehood,
His estate flows with crimes!"

***

Now this peasant came to petition him a seventh time; he said: "O high steward, my lord!

You are the whole land's rudder,
The land sails by your bidding;
You are the peer of Thoth,
The judge who is not partial.

My lord, be patient, so that a man may invoke you about his rightful cause. Don't be angry; it is not for you. The long-faced becomes short-tempered. Don't brood on what has not yet come, nor rejoice at what has not yet happened. The patient man prolongs friendship; he who destroys a case will not be trusted. If law is laid waste and order destroyed, no poor man can survive: when he is robbed, justice does not address him.

My body was full, my heart burdened. Now therefore it has come from my body. As a dam is breached and water escapes, so my mouth opened to speak. I plied my sounding pole, I bailed out my water; I have emptied what was in my body; I have washed my soiled linen. My speech is done. My grief is all before you. What do you want? But your laziness leads you astray; your greed makes you dumb; your gluttony makes enemies for you. But will you find another peasant like me? Is there an idler at whose house door a petitioner will stand?

There is no silent man whom you gave speech,
No sleeper whom you have wakened,
None downcast whom you have roused,
None whose shut mouth you have opened,
None ignorant whom you gave knowledge,
None foolish whom you have taught.
(Yet) magistrates are dispellers of evil,
Masters of the good,
Craftsmen who create what is,
Joiners of the severed head!"

***

Now this peasant came to petition him an eighth time; he said: "O high steward, my lord! Men fall low through greed. The rapacious man lacks success; his success is loss. Though you are greedy it does nothing for you. Though you steal you do not profit. Let a man defend his rightful cause!

Your portion is in your house; your belly is full. The grain-bin brims over; shake it, its overflow spoils on the ground. Thief, robber, plunderer! Magistrates are appointed to suppress crime. Magistrates are shelters against the aggressor. Magistrates are appointed to fight falsehood!

No fear of you makes me petition you; you do not know my heart. A humble man who comes back to reproach you is not afraid of him with whom he pleads. The like of him will not be brought you from the street!

You have your plot of ground in the country, your estate in the district, your income in the storehouse. Yet the magistrates give to you and you take! Are you then a robber? Does one give to you and the troop with you at the division of plots?

> Do justice for the Lord of Justice
> The justice of whose justice is real!
> Pen, papyrus, palette of Thoth,
> Keep away from wrongdoing!
> When goodness is good it is truly good,
> For justice is for eternity:
> It enters the graveyard with its doer.
> When he is buried and earth enfolds him,
> His name does not pass from the earth;
> He is remembered because of goodness,
> That is the rule of god's command.

The hand-balance—it tilts not; the stand-balance—it leans not to one side. Whether I come, whether another comes, speak! Do not answer with the answer of silence! Do not attack one who does not attack you. You have no pity, you are not troubled, you are not disturbed! You do not repay my good speech which comes from the mouth of Re himself!

> Speak justice, do justice,
> For it is mighty;
> It is great, it endures,
> Its worth is tried,
> It leads one to reveredness.

Does the hand-balance tilt? Then it is its scales which carry things. The standard has no fault. Crime does not attain its goal; he who is helpful reaches land."

***

Now this peasant came to petition him a ninth time; he said: "O high steward, my lord! The tongue is men's stand-balance. It is the balance that detects deficiency. Punish him who should be punished, and ⟨none⟩ shall equal your rectitude.--- ...When falsehood walks it goes astray. It does not cross in the ferry; it does not progress. He who is enriched by it has no children, has no heirs on earth. He who sails with it does not reach land; his boat. does not moor at its landing place.

> Be not heavy, nor yet light,
> Do not tarry, nor yet hurry,
> Be not partial, nor listen to desire.
> Do not avert your face from one you know,
> Be not blind to one you have seen,
> Do not rebuff one who beseeches you.
> Abandon this slackness,
> Let your speech be heard.
> Act for him who would act for you,
> Do not listen to everyone,
> Summon a man to his rightful cause!

A sluggard has no yesterday, one deaf to justice has no friend; the greedy has no holiday. When the accuser is a wretch, and the wretch becomes a pleader, his opponent is a killer. Here I have been pleading with you, and you have not listened to it. I shall go and plead about you to Anubis!"

***

Then the high steward Rensi, the son of Meru, sent two guards to bring him back. Then this peasant was fearful, thinking it was done so as to punish him for this speech he had made. This peasant said: "A thirsty man's approach to water, an infant's mouth reaching for milk, thus is a longed-for death seen coming, thus does his death arrive at last." Said the high steward Rensi, the son of Meru: "Don't be afraid, peasant; be ready to deal with me!" Said this peasant: "By my life! Shall I eat your bread and drink your beer forever?" Said the high steward Rensi, the son of Meru: "Now wait here and hear your petitions!" Then he had them read from a new papyrus roll, each petition in its turn. The high steward Rensi, the son of Meru, presented them to the majesty of King Nebkaure, the justified. They pleased his majesty's heart more than anything in the whole land. His majesty said: "Give judgment yourself, son of Meru!"

Then the high steward Rensi, the son of Meru, sent two guards [to bring Nemtynakht]. He was brought and a report was made of [all his property] ------ his wheat, his barley, his donkeys, ---, his pigs, his small cattle ------. --- of this Nemtynakht [was given] to this peasant ------.
Colophon: It is finished ------.

Questions:
1. What products did Khun-Aup bring with him on his journey to Egypt to trade for food?
2. What legal pretext/ruse did Nemtynakht employ to confiscate Khun-Anup's donkey?
3. What "appeals process" did Khun-Anup have to go through in order to receive pharaoh's ruling?
4. What does the story of Khun-Anup reveal about the Egyptian concept of justice and legality?

1.8   Some Common-sense Advice from the Scribe Any to His Son

As in Mesopotamia, instruction manuals were a popular form of imparting knowledge of the type that experience, rather than academic studies, could provide. In the "Instruction of Any," which dates back to the New Kingdom reign of Pharaoh Ahmose (c. 1550 B.C.E.), the intended beneficiary is not, as the usual case, royalty, but Any's own son, a member of the educated, emerging middle class.

Source: Miriam Lichtheim, *Ancient Egyptian Literature* (Berkeley: University of California Press, 1975), v. 2, pp. 136–145.

Take a wife while you're young,
That she make a son for you;
She should bear for you while you're youthful,
It is proper to make people.
Happy the man whose people are many,
He is saluted on account of his progeny.

Observe the feast of your god,
And repeat its season,
God is angry if it is neglected.
Put up witnesses when you offer,
The first time that you do it.
When one comes to seek your record,
Have them enter you in the roll;
When time comes to seek your purchase,
It will extol the might of the god.
Song, dance, incense are his foods,
Receiving prostrations is his wealth;
The god does it to magnify his name,
But man it is who is inebriated.

Do not enter the house of anyone,

Until he admits you and greets you;
Do not snoop around in his house,
Let your eye observe in silence.
Do not speak of him to another outside,
Who was not with you;
A great deadly crime
......

Beware of a woman who is a stranger,
One not known in her town;
Don't stare at her when she goes by,
Do not know her carnally.
A deep water whose course is unknown,
Such is it woman away from her husband.
"I am pretty," she tells you daily,
When she has no witnesses;
She is ready to ensnare you,
A great deadly crime when it is heard.
...···

Do not leave when the chiefs enter,
Lest your name stink;
In a quarrel do not speak,
Your silence will serve you well.

Do not raise your voice in the house of god.
He abhors shouting;
Pray by yourself with a loving heart,
Whose every word is hidden.
He will grant your needs.
He will hear your words,
He will accept your offerings.
Libate for your father and mother,
Who are resting in the valley;
When the gods witness your action,
They will say: "Accepted."
Do not forget the one outside.
Your son will act for you likewise.

Don't indulge in drinking beer,
Lest you utter evil speech.
And don't know what you're saying.
If you fall and hurt your body.
None holds out a hand to you;
Your companions in the drinking
Stand up saying: "Out with the drunk!"
If one comes to seek you and talk with you,
One finds you lying on the ground.
As if you were a little child.

Do not go out of your house,
Without knowing your place of rest.
Let your chosen place be known,
Remember it and know it.
Set it before you as the path to take,
If you are straight you find it.

Furnish your station in the valley,
The grave that shall conceal your corpse;
Set it before you as your concern,
A thing that matters in your eyes.
Emulate the great departed,
Who are at rest within their tombs.
No blame accrues to him who does it,
It is well that you be ready too.
When your envoy comes to fetch you
He shall find you ready to come
To your place of rest and saying:
"Here comes one prepared before you."
Do not say, "I am young to be taken,"
For you do not know your death.
When death comes he steals the infant
Who is in his mother's arms,
Just like him who reached old age.

Behold, I give you these useful counsels,
For you to ponder in your heart;
Do it and you will be happy,
All evils will be far from you.
Guard against the crime of fraud,
Against words that are not ·trueÒ;
Conquer malice in your self,
A quarrelsome man does not rest on the morrow.
Keep away from a hostile man,
Do not let him be your comrade;
Befriend one who is straight and true,
One whose actions you have seen.
If your rightness matches his,
The friendship will be balanced.
Let your hand preserve what is in your house,
Wealth accrues to him who guards it;
Let your hand not scatter it to strangers,
Lest it turn to loss for you.
If wealth is placed where it bears interest,
It comes back to you redoubled;
Make a storehouse for your own wealth,
Your people will find it on your way.
What is given small returns augmented,
ÈWhat is replaced brings abundance.˘
The wise lives off the house of the fool,
Protect what is yours and you find it;
Keep your eye on what you own,
Lest you end as a beggar.
He who is slack amounts to nothing,
Honored is the man who's active.

…

Learn about the way of a man
Who undertakes to found his household.
Make a garden, enclose a patch,
In addition to your plowland;
Set out trees within it,
As shelter about your house.
Fill your hand with all the flowers

33

That your eye can see;
One has need of all of them,
It is good fortune not to lose them.

Do not rely on another's goods,
Guard what you acquire yourself;
Do not depend on another's wealth.
Lest he become master in your house.
Build a house or find and buy one,
Shun [contention.]
Don't say: "My mother's father has a house,
È·A house that lasts,˘ one calls it;"
When you come to share with your brothers,
Your portion may be a storeroom.
If your god lets you have children,
They'll say: "We are in our father's house."
Be a man hungry or sated in his house,
It is his walls that enclose him.
Do not be a mindless person,
Then your god will give you wealth.

Do not sit when another is standing,
One who is older than you,
Or greater than you in his rank.
No good character is reproached,
An evil character is blamed.
Walk the accustomed path each day,
Stand according to your rank.
"Who's there?" So one always says,
Rank creates its rules;
A woman is asked about her husband,
A man is asked about his rank.

Do not speak rudely to a brawler,
When you are attacked hold yourself back;
You will find this good when your relations are
    friendly,
When trouble has come it will help you bear up,
And the aggressor will desist.
Deeds that are effective toward a stranger
Are very noxious to a brother.
Your people will hail you when you are joyful,
They will weep freely È·when you are sadÒ˘;
When you are happy the brave look to you,
When you are lonely you find your relations.

One will do all you say
If you are versed in writings;
Study the writings, put them in your heart,
Then all your words will be effective.
Whatever office a scribe is given,
He should consult the writings;
The head of the treasury has no son,
The master of the seal has no heir.
The scribe is chosen for his hand,
His office has no children;
His pronouncements are his freemen,

His functions are his masters.

Do not reveal your heart to a stranger,
He might use your words against you;
The noxious speech that came from your mouth,
He repeats it and you make enemies.
A man may be ruined by his tongue,
Beware and you will do well.
A man's belly is wider than a granary,
And full of all kinds of answers;
Choose the good one and say it,
While the bad is shut in your belly.
A rude answer brings a beating,
Speak sweetly and you will be loved.
Don't ever talk back to your attacker,
È·Do not set a trap for himÒ˘;
It is the god who judges the righteous,
His fate comes and takes him away.

Offer to your god,
Beware of offending him.
Do not question his images,
Do not accost him when he appears.
Do not jostle him in order to carry him,
Do not disturb the oracles.
Be careful, help to protect him,
Let your eye watch out for his wrath,
And kiss the ground in his name.
He gives power in a million forms,
He who magnifies him is magnified.
God of this earth is the sun in the sky,
While his images are on earth;
When incense is given them as daily food,
The lord of risings is satisfied.

Double the food your mother gave you,
Support her as she supported you;
She had a heavy load in you,
But she did not abandon you.
When you were born after your months,
She was yet yoked ·to youÒ,
Her breast in your mouth for three years.
As you grew and your excrement disgusted,
She was not disgusted, saying: "What shall I do!"
When she sent you to school,
And you were taught to write,
She kept watching over you daily,
With bread and beer in her house.
When as a youth you take a wife,
And you are settled in your house,
Pay attention to your offspring,
Bring him up as did your mother.
Do not give her cause to blame you,
Lest she raise her hands to god,
And he hears her cries.

Do not eat bread while another stands by

Without extending your hand to him.
As to food, it is here always,
It is man who does not last;
One man is rich, another is poor,
But food remains for him Èwho shares it.˘
As to him who was rich last year,
He is a vagabond this year;
Don't be greedy to fill your belly,
You don't know your end at all.
Should you come to be in want,
Another may do good to you.
When last year's watercourse is gone,
Another river is here today;
Great lakes become dry places,
Sandbanks turn into depths.
Man does not have a single way,
The lord of life confounds him.

Attend to your position,
Be it low or high;
It is not good to press forward,
Step according to rank.
Do not intrude on a man in his house,
Enter when you have been called;
He may say "Welcome" with his mouth,
Yet deride you in his thoughts.
One gives food to one who is hated,
Supplies to one who enters uninvited.
Don't rush to attack your attacker,
Leave him to the god;
Report him daily to the god,
Tomorrow being like today,
And you will see what the god does,
When he injures him who injured you.

Do not enter into a crowd,
If you find it in an uproar
And about to come to blows.
Don't pass anywhere near by,
Keep away from their tumult,
Lest you be brought before the court,
When an inquiry is made.
Stay away from hostile people,
Keep your heart quiet among fighters;
An outsider is not brought to court,
One who knows nothing is not bound in fetters.

It is useful to help one whom one loves,
ÈSo as to cleanse him of his faults;˘
ÈYou will be safe from his errors.˘
......
The first of the herd leads to the field,
......

Do not control your wife in her house,
When you know she is efficient;
Don't say to her: "Where is it? Get it!"

36

When she has put it in the right place.
Let your eye observe in silence,
Then you recognize her skill;
It is joy when your hand is with her,
There are many who don't know this.
If a man desists from strife at home,
He will not encounter its beginning.
Every man who founds a household
Should hold back the hasty heart.
Do not go after a woman,
Let her not steal your heart.

Do not talk back to an angry superior,
Let him have his way;
Speak sweetly when he speaks sourly,
It's the remedy that calms the heart.
Fighting answers carry sticks,
And your strength collapses;
......
Do not vex your heart.
He will return to praise you soon,
When his hour of rage has passed.
If your words please the heart,
The heart tends to accept them;
Choose silence for yourself,
Submit to what he does.

Befriend the herald of your quarter,
Do not make him angry with you.
Give him food from your house,
Do not slight his requests;
Say to him, "Welcome, welcome here,"
No blame accrues to him who does it.
......

EPILOGUE

The scribe Khonshotep answered his father,
    the scribe Any:
I wish I were like (you),
As learned as you!
Then I would carry out your teachings,
And the son would be brought to his father's place.
Each man is led by his nature,
You are a man who is a master,
Whose strivings are exalted,
Whose every word is chosen.
The son, he understands little
When he recites the words in the books.
But when your words please the heart,
The heart tends to accept them with joy.
Don't make your virtues too numerous,
That one may raise one's thoughts to you;
A boy does not follow the moral instructions,
Though the writings are on his tongue!

The scribe Any answered his son, the scribe

Khonshotep:
Do not rely on such worthless thoughts,
Beware of what you do to yourself!
I judge your complaints to be wrong,
I shall set you right about them.
There's nothing [superfluous in] our words,
Which you say you wished were reduced.
The fighting bull who kills in the stable,
He forgets and abandons the arena;
He conquers his nature,
Remembers what he's learned,
And becomes the like of a fattened ox.
The savage lion abandons his wrath,
And comes to resemble the timid donkey.
The horse slips into its harness,
Obedient it goes outdoors.
The dog obeys the word,
And walks behind its master.
The monkey carries the stick,
Though its mother did not carry it.
The goose returns from the pond,
When one comes to shut it in the yard.
One teaches the Nubian to speak Egyptian,
The Syrian and other strangers too.
Say: "I shall do like all the beasts,"
Listen and learn what they do.

The scribe Khonshotep answered his father,
   the scribe Any:
Do not proclaim your powers,
So as to force me to your ways;
ÈDoes it not happen to a man to slacken his hand,˘
So as to hear an answer in its place?
Man resembles the god in his way
If he listens to a man's answer.
ÈOne (man) cannot know his fellow,˘
If the masses are beasts;
ÈOne (man) cannot know his teachings,˘
And alone possess a mind,
If the multitudes are foolish.
All your sayings are excellent,
But doing them Èrequires virtues;˘
Tell the god who gave you wisdom:
"Set them on your path!"

The scribe Any answered his son,
   the scribe Khonshotep:
Turn your hack to these many words,
That are Ènot worth˘ being heard.
The crooked stick left on the ground,
With sun and shade attacking it,
If the carpenter takes it, he straightens it,
Makes of it a noble's staff,
And a straight stick makes a collar.
You foolish heart,
Do you wish us to teach,
Or have you been corrupted?

"Look," said he, "you Èmy father,˘
You who are wise and strong of hand:
The infant in his mother's arms,
His wish is for what nurses him."
"Look," said he, "when he finds his speech,
He says: "Give me bread."

Questions:
1. What value does Any ascribe to the virtue of silence?
2. To what extent does Any advocate a course of "self-reliance," and why?
3. What is the gist of the conversational exchange between Any and Khonshotep at the end of the document?
4. What practical advice does the father give regarding marriage?

1.9   Hebrew Scriptures

The Hebrew Scriptures (commonly called the Old Testament) are, arguably, the most influential texts in the Western tradition. Modern Jews, Christians, and Muslims, some 3 billion people or 40-50% of the world's population, claim to follow the God depicted in the Hebrew Scriptures. While most of the literature produced in the ancient Near East has either been lost, is indecipherable, or is accessible only to scholars, the Hebrew Scriptures are available in inexpensive, accessible translations all over the world.

The Hebrew Scriptures contain law codes, poetry, prophetic visions, proverbs, and histories. Whatever the genre, the texts of the Hebrew Scriptures focus on the relationship between God and his chosen people, Israel. While the book of Genesis begins with an account of creation and the distant past, this is prologue to the central story of God making a covenant with Abraham. The covenant includes a promise by God to bless and protect Abraham and his descendents contingent upon Abraham and his descendents honoring and worshiping only God. The Hebrew Scriptures then describe how Abraham's descendents are enslaved in Egypt; freed and led to a new land by God; try and fail to live as a nation that honors the covenant; and their eventual defeat and dispersal by successive invasions by Assyria and Babylon.

In this selection, the prophet Isaiah reminds Israel who their God is and what the covenant entails. The book of Isaiah was recorded during the period in which the Israelites were divided into two kingdoms, Israel and Judah, and were facing considerable outside pressure from other nations.

Source: The Scripture quotations contained herein are from the *New Revised Standard Version Bible*, copyright ©1989 by the Division of Christian Education of the National Council of the Churches of Christ in the U.S.A., and are used by permission. All rights reserved.

ISAIAH

"Yet now hear, O Jacob my servant; and Israel, whom I have chosen: Thus saith the LORD that made thee, and formed thee from the womb, which will help thee; 'Fear not, O jacob, my servant; and thou, Jesurun, whom I have chosen. For I will pour water upon him that is thirsty, and floods upon the dry ground: I will pour my spirit upon thy seed, and my blessing upon thine offspring: And they shall spring up as among the grass, as willows by the water courses. One shall say, "I am the LORD's"; and another shall call himself by the name of Jacob; and another shall subscribe with his hand unto the LORD, and surname himself by the name of Israel.' Thus saith the LORD the King of Israel, and his redeemer the LORD of hosts; 'I am the first, and I am the last; and beside me there is no God. And who, as I, shall call, and shall declare it, and set it in order to me, since I appointed the ancient people? And the things that are coming, and shall come, let them shew unto them. Fear ye not, neither be afraid: have not I told thee from that time, and have declared it? Ye are even my witnesses. Is there a God beside me? Yea, there is no God; I know not any.

'They that make a graven image are all of them vanity; and their delectable things shall not profit; and they are their own witnesses; they see not, nor know; that they may be ashamed. Who hath formed a god, or molten a graven image that is profitable for nothing? Behold, all his fellows shall be ashamed: and the workmen, they are of men: let them all be gathered together, let them stand up; yet they shall fear, and they shall be ashamed together. The smith with the tongs both worketh in the coals, and fashioneth it with hammers, and worketh it with the strength of his arms: yea, he is hungry, and his strength faileth: he drinketh no water, and is faint. The carpenter stretcheth out his rule; he marketh it out with a line; he fitteth it with planes, and he marketh it out with the compass, and maketh it after the figure of a man, according to the beauty of a man; that it may remain in the house. He heweth him down cedars, and taketh the cypress and the oak, which he strengtheneth for himself among the trees of the forest: he planteth an ash, and the rain doth nourish it. Then shall it be for a man to burn: for he will take thereof, and warm himself; yea, he kindleth it and baketh bread; yea, he maketh a god, and worshippeth it; he make it a graven image, and falleth down thereto. He burneth part thereof in the fire; with part thereof he eateth flesh; he roasteth roast, and is satisfied: yea, he warmeth himself, and saith, "Aha, I am warm, I have seen the fire." And the residue thereof he maketh a god, even his graven image: he falleth down unto it, and worshippeth it, and prayeth unto it, and saith, "Deliver me; for thou art my god." They have not known or understood: for he hath shut their eyes, that they cannot see; and their hearts, that they cannot understand. And none considereth in his heart, neither is there knowledge nor understanding to say, "I have burned part of it in the fire; yea, also I have baked bread upon the coals thereof; I have roasted flesh, and eaten it: and shall I make the residue thereof an abomination? shall I fall down to the stock of a tree?"

. . .

'I am the LORD, and there is none else, there is no God beside me: I girded thee, though thou hast not known me: That they may know from the rising of the sun, and from the west, that there is none beside me. I am the LORD, and there is none else. I form the light, and create darkness: I make peace, and create evil: I the LORD do all these things. Drop down, ye heavens, from above, and let the skies pour down righteousness: let the earth open, and let them bring forth salvation, and let righteousness spring up together: I the LORD have created it. Woe unto him that striveth with his Maker! Let the potsherd strive with the potsherds of the earth. Shall the clay say to him that fashioneth it, "What makest thou?" or thy work, "He hath no hands?" Woe unto him that saith unto his father, "What begettest thou?" or to the woman, "What hast thou brought forth?"

'Thus saith the LORD, the Holy One of Israel, and his Maker, 'Ask me of things to come concerning my sons, and concerning the work of my hands command ye me. I have made the earth, and created man upon it: I, even my hands, have stretched out the heavens, and all their host have I commanded. I have raised him up in righteousness, and I will direct all his ways: he shall build my city, and he shall let go my captives, not for price nor reward,' saith the Lord of hosts.

"Thus saith the Lord, 'The labour of Egypt, and merchandise of Ethiopia and of the Sabeans, men of stature, shall come over unto thee, and they shall be thine: they shall come after thee; in chains they shall come over, and they shall fall down unto thee, they shall make supplication unto thee, saying, "Surely God is in thee; and there is none else, there is no God. Verily thou art a God that hidest thyself, O God of Israel, the Saviour." They shall be ashamed, and also confounded, all of them they shall go to confusion together that are makers of idols. But Israel shall be saved in the LORD with an everlasting salvation: ye shall not be ashamed nor confounded world without end.' For thus saith the LORD that created the heavens; God himself that formed the earth and made it; he hath established it, he created it not in vain, he formed it to be inhabited: 'I am the LORD: and there is none else. I have not spoken in secret, in a dark place of the earth: I said not unto the seed of Jacob, "Seek ye me in vain": I the LORD speak righteousness, I declare things that are right.

'Assemble yourselves and come; draw near together, ye that are escaped of the nations: they have no knowledge that set up the wood of their graven image, and pray unto a god that cannot save. Tell ye, and bring them near; yea, let them take counsel together; who hath declared this from ancient time? Who hath told it from that time? Have not I the LORD? And there is no God else beside me; a just God and a Saviour; there is none beside me. Look unto me, and be ye saved, all the ends of the earth: for I am God, and there is none else. I have sworn by myself, the word is gone out of my mouth in righteousness, and shall not return, that unto me every knee shall bow, every tongue shall swear, "Surely," shall one say, "in the LORD have I righteousness and strength": even to him shall men come; and all that are incensed against him shall be ashamed. In the LORD shall all the seed of Israel be justified, and shall glory.'

Questions:
1. How does Isaiah describe God?
2. What can Israel expect from God?
3. What is expected of Israel?

1.10   Assyrian War Tactics

A typical example of an Assyrian king is Ashurnasirpal (844–859 b.c.). He was at war for most of his reign, attacking northwestern Mesopotamia, Anatolia, Syria, and Phoenicia both for booty and for enlargement of his empire. Nonetheless, he found time to construct a new, six-acre palace at Calah (modern Nimrud) on the Upper Zab, west of the Tigris River—a palace that was well built and beautifully decorated.

> **Source:** The following selection comes from the Assyrian royal archives and describes King Ashurnasirpal's ferocious treatment of rebels.

While I was staying in the land of Kutmuhi, they brought me the word: "The city of Sûru of Bît-Halupê has revolted, they have slain Hamatai, their governor, and Ahiababa, the son of a nobody, whom they brought from Bît-Adini, they have set up as king over them." With the help of Adad and the great gods who have made great my kingdom, I mobilized (my) chariots and armies and marched along the bank of the Habur. During my advance I received much tribute from Shulmanu-haman-ilâni of the city of Gardiganni, from Ilu-Adad of the city of Katna,—silver, gold, lead, vessels of copper, and garments of brightly colored wool, and garments of linen. To the city of Sûru of Bît-Halupê I drew near, and the terror of the splendor of Assur, my lord, overwhelmed them. The chief men and the elders of the city, to save their lives, came forth into my presence and embraced my feet, saying: "If it is thy pleasure, slay! If it is thy pleasure, let live! That which thy heart desireth, do!" Ahiababa, the son of nobody, whom they had brought from Bît-Adini, I took captive. In the valor of my heart and with the fury of my weapons I stormed the city. All the rebels they seized and delivered them up. My officers I caused to enter into his palace and his temples. His silver, his gold, his goods and his possessions, copper, iron, lead, vessels of copper, cups of copper, dishes of copper, a great hoard of copper, alabaster, tables with inlay, the women of his palaces, his daughters, the captive rebels together with their possessions, the gods together with their possessions, precious stone from the mountains, his chariot with equipment, his horses, broken to the yoke, trappings of men and trappings of horses, garments of brightly colored wool and garments of linen, goodly oil, cedar, and fine sweet-scented herbs, panels(?) of cedar, purple and crimson wool, his wagons, his cattle, his sheep, his heavy spoil, which like the stars of heaven could not be counted, I carried off. Azi-ilu I set over them as my own governor. I built a pillar over against his city gate, and I flayed all the chief men who had revolted, and I covered the pillar with their skins; some I walled up within the pillar, some I impaled upon the pillar on stakes, and others I bound to stakes round about the pillar; many within the border of my own land I flayed, and I spread their skins upon the walls; and I cut off the limbs of the officers, of the royal officers who had rebelled. Ahiababa I took to Nineveh, I flayed him, I spread his skin upon the wall of Nineveh. My power and might I established over the land of Lakê. While I was staying in the city of Sûru, (I received) tribute from all the kings of the land of Lakê,—silver, gold, lead, copper, vessels of copper, cattle, sheep, garments of brightly colored wool, and garments of linen, and I increased the tribute and taxes and imposed them upon them. At that time, the tribute of Haiâni of the city of Hindani,—silver, gold, lead, copper, umu-stone, alabaster, purple wool, and (Bactrian) camels I received from him as tribute. At that time I fashioned a heroic image of my royal self, my power and my glory I inscribed thereon, in the midst of his palace I set it up. I fashioned memorial steles and inscribed thereon my glory and my prowess, and I set them up by his city gate.

Questions:
1. *Why do you suppose that the Assyrian king resorted to such harshness in dealing with rebels?*
2. *Why would the subjects of Assyria rebel even though they were aware of the consequences?*
3. *What kingdom and peoples disappeared from history as a result of Assyrian destruction?*
4. *Are there any parallels in modern times to the policies of the Assyrians?*

PART 2
Early Civilization in East Asia

2.1 Might makes Right: the "Shu ching" Sets Forth the Mandate of Heaven

The earliest of the six Confucian classics is the "Shu ching" or "Book of Historical Documents." Its semi-mythical chronologies and events notwithstanding, the "Shu ching" remains the prime source of knowledge for the history and policies of the Xia, Shang, and early Zhou rulers. Here, the "Books of Yu" describes ideal government under the Xia ("Hea") Dynasty; the "Books of Hea," is a punitive imperial expedition against corrupt administrators; and the "Books of Shang" sets forward the justification for that Dynasty's overthrow of Xia—the "Mandate of Heaven."

Source: James Legge, trans., *The Chinese Classics, Vo1. III: Shoo King* (originally published by Oxford University Press, 1935; N.Y.: distributed by Paragon Book Gallery, 1960), pp. 52–67, 162–169, 173–89.

THE BOOKS OF YU

Book II. The counsels of the great Yu.

I. On examining into antiquity, we find that the great Yu was called Wan-ming. Having arranged and divided *the empire,* all to the four seas, in reverent response to the *inquiries of the former* emperor, he said, "If the sovereign can realize the difficulty of his sovereignship, and the minister can realize the difficulty of his ministry, government will be well ordered, and the people will sedulously seek to be virtuous." The emperor said, "Yes; let this really be the case, and good words will nowhere lie hidden; no men of virtue and talents will be neglected away from court: and the myriad States will all enjoy repose. *But* to ascertain the views of all; to give up one's own opinion and follow that of others; to refrain from oppressing the helpless; and not to neglect the straitened and poor:—it was only the emperor *Yaou* who could attain to "this." Yih said, "Oh! your virtue, O emperor, is vast and incessant. It is sagely, spiritual, awe-inspiring, and adorned with all accomplishments. Great Heaven regarded you with its favoring decree, and suddenly you obtained all within the four seas, and became sovereign of the empire."

Yu said, "Accordance with the right is good fortune; the following of evil is bad:—the shadow and the echo." Yih said, "Alas! be cautious! Admonish yourself to caution when there seems to be no reason for anxiety. Do not fail in due attention to the laws and ordinances. Do not find your enjoyment in indulgent ease. Do not go to excess in pleasure. In your employment of men of worth, let none come between you and them. Put away evil without hesitation. Do not try to carry out doubtful plans. Study that all your purposes may be with the light of reason. Do not go against what is right to get the praise of the people. Do not oppose the people to follow your own desires. *Attend to these things* without idleness or omission, and from the four quarters the barbarous tribes will come and acknowledge your sovereignty."

Yu said, "Oh! think *of these things,* O emperor. Virtue is seen in the goodness of the government, and the government is tested by its nourishing of the people. There are water, fire, metal, wood, earth, and grain,—these must be duly regulated; there are the rectification of *the people's* virtue, the conveniences of life, and the securing abundant means of sustentation,—these must be harmoniously attended to. When the nine services *thus indicated* have been orderly accomplished, let that accomplishment be celebrated by songs. Caution the people with gentle words; correct them with the majesty of *law*; stimulate them with the songs on those nine subjects,—in order that your success may never suffer diminution."

The emperor said, "Yes. The earth is *now* reduced to order, and *the influences of* heaven operate with effect; those six magazines and three businesses are all truly regulated, so that a myriad generations may perpetually depend on them:—this is your merit."

II. The emperor said, "Come, you, Yu. I have occupied the imperial throne for thirty and three years. I am between ninety and a hundred years old, and the laborious duties weary me. Do you, eschewing all indolence, take the leadership of my people." Yu said, "My virtue is not equal *to the position;* the people will not repose in me. *But there is* Kauo-yaou, with vigorous activity sowing abroad his virtue, which has descended on the black-haired people, till they cherish him in their hearts. O emperor, think of him! When I think of him, my mind rests on him, *as the man for this office*; when I would put him out of my thoughts, they still rest on him; when I name and speak of him, my mind rests on him *for this;* the sincere outgoing of my thoughts about him is that he is the man. O emperor, think of his merits!"

The emperor said, "Kaou-yaou, that of these my ministers and people, hardly one is found to offend against the regulations of my government, is owing to your being the minister of Crime, and intelligent in the use of the five punishments to assist the *inculcation of the* five duties, with a view to the perfection of my government, and that through punishment there may come to be no punishments, but the people accord with the *path of the* Mean. *Continue to* be strenuous." Kauo-yauo said, "Your virtue, O emperor, is faultless. You condescend to your ministers with a liberal ease; you preside over the multitude with a generous forbearance. Punishments do not extend to the criminal's heirs; while rewards reach to after generations. You pardon inadvertent faults, however great; and punish purposed crimes, however, small. In cases of doubtful crimes, you deal with them lightly; in cases of doubtful merit, you prefer the high estimation. Rather than put to death an innocent person, you will run the risk of irregularity and error. This life-loving virtue has penetrated the minds of the people, and this is why they do not render themselves liable to be punished by your officers." The emperor said, "To enable me to follow after and obtain what I desire in my government, the people everywhere responding as if I moved by the wind;—this is your excellence."

The emperor said, "Come, Yu. The innundating waters filled me with dread, when you realized all that you represented, and accomplished your task,—thus showing your superiority to other men. Full of toilsome earnestness in the service of the State, and sparing in your expenditure on your family; and this without being full of yourself or elated; you *again* show your superiority to other men. Without any prideful presumption, there is no one in the empire to contest with you the palm of ability; without any boasting, there is no one in the empire to contest with you the claim of merit. I see how great is your virtue, how admirable your vast achievements. The determinate appointment of Heaven rests on your person; you must eventually ascend *the throne of* the great sovereign. The mind of man is restless—prone *to err;* its affinity for the *right* way is small. Be discriminating, be undivided, that you may sincerely hold fast the Mean. Do not listen to unsubstantiated words; do not follow undeliberated plans. Of all who are to be loved, is not the sovereign the chief? Of all who are to be feared, are not the people the chief? If the multitude were *without* the sovereign, whom should they sustain aloft? If the sovereign had not the multitude, there would be none to guard the country for him. Be reverent. Carefully demean yourself on the throne which you will occupy, respectfully cultivating *the virtues* which are to be desired in you. If within the four seas there be distress and poverty, your Heaven-conferred revenues will come to a perpetual end. It is the mouth which sends forth what is good, and gives rise to war. My words I will not repeat."

Yu said, "Submit the meritorious ministers one by one to the trial of divination, and let the fortunate indication be followed." The emperor said, "Yu, the officer of divination, when the mind has been made up on a subject, then refers it to the great tortoise. *Now, in this matter,* my mind was determined in the first place. I consulted and deliberated with all *my ministers and people,* and they were of one accord with me. The spirits signified their assent, the tortoise and grass having both concurred. Divination, when fortunate, may not be repeated." Yu did obeisance, with his head to the ground, and firmly declined the throne. The emperor said, "Do not do so. It is you who can *occupy my place.*" On the first morning of the first month, *Yu* received the appointment in the *temple of the* spiritual Ancestor, and took the leading of all the officers, as had been done at the commencement of the emperor's *government.*

III. The emperor said, "Alas! O Yu, there is only the prince of the Meaou, who refuses obedience;—do you go and correct him." Yu on this assembled all the princes, and made a speech to the host, saying, "Ye multitudes, listen all to my orders. Stupid is this prince of Meaou, ignorant, erring, and disrespectful. Despiteful and insolent to others, he thinks that all ability and virtue are with himself. A rebel to the right, he destroys *all the obligations of* virtue. Superior men are kept by him in obscurity, and mean men fill all the offices. The people reject and will not protect him. Heaven is sending calamities down upon him. On this account I have assembled you, my multitude of gallant men, and bear the instructions *of the emperor* to punish his crimes. Do you proceed with united heart and strength, so shall our enterprize be crowned with success."

At the end of three decades, the people of Meaou continued rebellious against the *emperor's* commands, when Yih came to the help of Yu, saying,"It is virtue which moves Heaven; there is no distance to which it does not reach. Pride brings loss, and humility receives increase:—this is the way of Heaven. In the early time of the emperor, when he was living by mount Leih, he went into the fields, and daily cried with tears to compassionate Heaven, and to his parents, taking to himself and bearing all guilt and evil. *At the same time,* with respectful service, he appeared before Koo-sow, looking grave and awe-struck, till Koo also became truly transformed by his example. Entire sincerity moves spiritual beings;—how much more will it move this prince of Meaou!" Yu did homage to the excellent words and said, "Yes." *Thereupon* he led back his army, having drawn off the troops. The emperor *also* set about diffusing his accomplishments and virtue more widely. They danced with shields and feathers between the two staircases of *the court.* In seventy days the prince of Meaou came to make his submission.

THE BOOKS OF HEA

Book IV. The punitive expedition of Yin

I. When Chung-k'ang commenced his reign over all within the four seas, the prince of Yin was commissioned to take charge of the imperial armies. *At this time,* He and Ho had neglected the duties of their office, and were sunk in wine in their *private* cities, and the prince of Yin received the imperial charge to go and punish them.

II. He made an announcement to his hosts saying, "Ah! ye, all my troops, there are the well-counselled instructions of' the sage *founder of our dynasty,* clearly verified in their power to give stability and security *to the State*—'The former kings were carefully attentive to the warnings of Heaven, and their ministers observed the regular laws of *their offices.* All the officers, *moreover,* watchfully did their duty to assist *the government,* and the sovereign became entirely intelligent.' Every year in the first *month* of spring, the herald with his wooden-tongued bell goes along the roads, *proclaiming,* 'Ye officers able to direct, be prepared with your admonitions. Ye workmen engaged in mechanical affairs, remonstrate on the subject of your business! If any of you disrespectfully *neglect this requirement,* the country has regular punishments for you.'

"Now here are He and Ho. They have entirely subverted their virtue, and are sunk and lost in wine. They have violated the duties of their office, and left their posts. They have been the first to allow the regulations of heaven to get into disorder, putting far from them their proper business. On the first day of the last month of autumn, the sun and moon did not meet harmoniously in Fang. The blind *musicians* beat their drums; the inferior officers and common people bustled and ran about. He and Ho, however, as if they were mere personators of the dead in their offices, heard nothing and knew nothing;—so stupidly went they astray *from their duty* in the matter of the heavenly appearances, and rendering themselves liable to the death appointed by the former kings. The statutes of government say, 'When they anticipate the time, let them be put to death without mercy; when they are behind the time, let them be put to death without mercy.'

"Now I, with you all, am entrusted with the execution of the punishment appointed by Heaven. Unite your strength, all of you warriors, for the imperial House. Le. 1 me your help, I pray you, reverently to carry out the dread charge of the son of Heaven."

"When the fire blazes over the ridge of Kwan, gems and stones are burned together; *but* when a minister of Heaven exceeds in doing his duty, the consequences are fiercer than raging fire. I will so destroy *only* the chief criminals, and not punish their forced followers, while those who have long been stained by their filthy manners will be allowed to renovate themselves."

"Oh! when sternness overcomes compassion, then things are surely conducted to a successful issue. When compassion overcomes sternness, no merit can be achieved. All ye, my warriors, exert yourselves, and be cautious."

PART IV. THE BOOKS OF SHANG

Book I. The speech of Tang.

I. The king said, "Come, ye multitude of the people, listen to my words. It is not I, the little child, who dare to undertake *what may seem to be* a religious enterprize; but for the many crimes of the sovereign of Hea Heaven has given the charge to destroy him.

"Now, ye multitudes, you are saying, 'Our prince does not compassionate us, but is calling us away from our husbandry to attack and punish *the ruler* of Hea.' I have indeed heard *these* words of you all: *but* the sovereign of Hea is an offender, and, *as* I fear God, I dare not but punish him.

"Now you are saying, 'What are the crimes of Hea to us? The king of Hea does nothing but exhaust the strength of his people, and exercise oppression in the cities of Hea. His people have all become idle *in his service,* and will not assist him. They are saying, 'When will this sun expire? We will all perish with thee.' Such is the course *of the sovereign of* Hea, and now I must go *and punish him.*

II. Assist, I pray you, me, the one man, to carry out the punishment appointed by Heaven. I will greatly reward you. On no account disbelieve me;—I will not eat my words. If you do not obey the words which I have spoken to you, I will put your children with you to death;—you will find no forgiveness."

Book II. The announcement of Chung-Hwuy.

I. When T'ang, the Successful, was keeping Keë in banishment in Nan-ch'aou, lie had a feeling of shame on account of his conduct, and said, "I am afraid that in future ages men will fill their mouths with me."

II. On this Chung-hwuy made the following announcement:—"Oh! Heaven gives birth to the people with *such* desires, that without a ruler they must fall into all disorders and Heaven *again* gives birth to the man of intelligence whose business it is to regulate them. The sovereign of Hea had his virtue all-obscured, and the people were *as if they were* fallen amid mire and charcoal. Heaven hereupon gifted *our* king with valour and wisdom, to serve as a mark and director to the myriad States, and to continue the old ways of Yu. You are now only following the standard course, honouring and obeying the appointment of Heaven. The king of Hea was an offender, falsely pretending to the sanction of supreme Heaven, to spread abroad his commands among the people. On this account God viewed him with disapprobation, caused *our* Shang to receive His appointment, and employed you to enlighten the multitudes of the people.

III. "Contemners of the worthy and parasites of the powerful,—many such followers he had indeed, *but* from the first our country was to the sovereign of Hea like weeds among the springing corn, and blasted grains among the good. *Our people,* great and small, were in constant apprehension, fearful though they were guilty of no crime. How much more was this the case, when our *prince's* virtues made them a theme *eagerly* listened to! *Our* king did not approach to *dissolute* music and women; he did not seek to accumulate property and money. To great virtue he gave great offices; to great merit he gave great rewards. He employed others as *if their abilities were* his own; he was not slow to change his errors. Rightly indulgent and rightly benevolent, from the display *of such virtue* confidence was reposed in him by the millions of the people.

"When the chief of Kŏ showed his enmity to the provision-carriers, the work of punishment began with Kŏ. When it went on in the east, the wild tribes of the west murmured; when it went on in the south, those of the north murmured :— they said, "Why does he make us alone the last?' To whatever people he went, they congratulated one another in their chambers, saying, 'We have waited for our prince;—our prince is come, and we revive.' The people's honouring our Shang is a thing of long existence.

IV. "Show favour to the able and right-principled *among the princes,* and aid the virtuous; distinguish the loyal, and let the good have free course. Absorb the weak, and punish the wilfully blind; take their States from the disorderly, and deal summarily with those going to ruin. Thus overthrowing the perishing and strengthening what is being preserved, how will the States all flourish!

"When a *sovereign's* virtue is daily being renewed, he is cherished throughout the myriad States; when he is full of his own will, he is abandoned by the nine classes of his kindred. Exert yourself, O king, to make your great virtue illustrious, and set up the *pattern of the* Mean before the people. Order your affairs by righteousness; order your heart by propriety:—so shall you transmit a grand example to posterity. I have heard the saying:——'He who finds instructors for himself, comes to the supreme dominion; he who says that others are not equal to himself, comes to ruin. He who likes to ask becomes enlarged; he who uses *only* himself becomes small.'

Oh! he who would take care for his end must be attentive to his beginning. There is establishment for the observers of propriety, and overthrow for the blinded and wantonly indifferent. To revere and honour the way of Heaven is the way ever to preserve the favouring regard of Heaven."

Book III. The announcement of T'ang.

I. The king returned from vanquishing Hea, and came to Po. There he made a grand announcement to the myriad regions.

II. The king said, "Ah! ye multitudes of the myriad regions, listen clearly to the announcement of me, the one man. The great God has conferred *even* on the inferior people a moral sense, compliance with which would show their nature invariably right. *But* to cause them tranquilly to pursue the course which it would indicate, is the work of the sovereign.

"The king of Hea extinguished his virtue and played the tyrant, extending his oppression over you, the people of the myriad regions. Suffering from his cruel injuries, and unable to endure the wormwood and poison, you protested with one accord your innocence to the spirits of heaven and earth. The way of Heaven is to bless the good and to punish the bad. It sent down calamities on *the House of* Hea, to make manifest its crimes.

"Therefore, I, the little child, charged with the decree of Heaven and its bright terrors, did not dare to forgive *the criminal.* I presumed to use a dark coloured victim, and making clear announcement to the spiritual Sovereign of the high heavens, requested leave to deal with the ruler of Hea as a criminal. Then I sought for the great sage, with whom I might unite my strength, to request the favour *of Heaven* on behalf of you, my multitudes. High Heaven truly showed its favour to the inferior people, and the criminal has been degraded and subjected. Heaven's appointment is without error;—brilliantly *now* like the blossoming of flowers and trees, the millions of the people show a true reviving.

III. "It is given to me, the one man, to give harmony and tranquillity to your States and Families; and now I know not whether may not offend *the powers* above and below. I am fearful and trembling, as if I should fall into a deep abyss.

"Throughout all the States that enter on a new life under me, do not, *ye princes,* follow lawless ways; make no approach to insolent dissoluteness: let everyone observe to keep his statutes:—that so we may receive the favour of Heaven. The good in you, I will not dare to conceal; and for the evil in me, I will not dare to forgive myself;—I will examine these things in harmony with the mind of God. When guilt is found anywhere in you who occupy the myriad regions, it must rest on me. When guilt is found in me, the one man, it will not attach to you who occupy the myriad regions.

Questions:
1. *In what ways might the "Book of Yu" stress the Chinese ideal of harmony?*
2. *In the excerpt from the "Book of Hea," what seems to have been the cause(s) for the downfall of He and Ho?*
3. *In the "Book of Shang" ascertain the rationale for why Hea deserved to be driven from power; and how Shang merited the throne.*

2.2 The Spirit World

During the Zhou period, families, both noble and common, sacrificed to their ancestors. These sacrifices were of the utmost importance and any neglect would bring about misfortune and calamity, for ancestors had the power to aid or punish their descendants.

Human sacrifice was practiced extensively during the Shang dynasty and to a lesser extent down to the third century B.C.E. The third selection decries the practice that "takes all our good men" in following the king in death. Duke Mu of Qin died in 621 B.C.E. The last selection is a conversation between a Zhou king and his minister and demonstrates the Chinese belief in the close interaction between the spirit world and the political environment. The king could not afford to lose the favor and protection of Heaven.

ABUNDANT IS THE YEAR

Abundant is the year, with much millet, much rice;
But we have tall granaries,
To hold myriads, many myriads and millions of grain.
We make wine, make sweet liquor,
We offer it to ancestor, to ancestress,
We use it to fulfill all the rites,
To bring down blessings upon each and all.

Source: From *The Book of Songs* edited and translated by Arthur Waley. Copyright © 1937 by Arthur Waley, p. 297. Used by permission of Grove/Atlantic, Inc.

GLORIOUS ANCESTORS

Ah, the glorious ancestors–
Endless, their blessings,
Boundless their gifts are extended;
To you, too, they needs must reach.
We have brought them clear wine;
They will give victory.
Here, too, is soup well seasoned,
Well prepared, well mixed.
Because we come in silence,
Setting all quarrels aside,
They make safe for us a ripe old age,
We shall reach the withered cheek, we shall go on and on.
With our leather-bound naves, our bronzeclad yokes,
With eight bells a-jangle
We come to make offering.
The charge put upon us is vast and mighty,
From Heaven dropped our prosperity,
Good harvests, great abundance.
They come [the ancestors], they accept,
They send down blessings numberless.
They regard the paddy-offerings, the offerings of first-fruits
That Tang's descendant brings.

Source: From *The Book of Songs* edited and translated by Arthur Waley. Copyright © 1937 by Arthur Waley, p. 319. Used by permission of Grove/Atlantic, Inc.

HUMAN SACRIFICE

"Kio" sings the oriole
As it lights on the thorn-bush.
Who went with Duke Mu to the grave?
Yan-xi of the clan Zi-ju.
Now this Yan-xi
Was the pick of all our men;
But as he drew near the tomb-hole
His limbs shook with dread.
That blue one, Heaven,
Takes all our good men.
Could we but ransom him
There are a hundred would give their lives.

"Kio" sings the oriole
As it lights on the thorn-bush.
Who went with Duke Mu to the grave?
Zhong-hang of the clan Zi-ju.
Now this Zhong-hang
Was the sturdiest of all our men;
But as he drew near the tomb-hole
His limbs shook with dread.
That blue one, Heaven,
Takes all our good men.
Could we but ransom him
There are a hundred would give their lives.

"Kio" sings the oriole
As it lights on the thorn-bush.
Who went with Duke Mu to the grave?
Quan-hu of the clan Zi-ru.
Now this Quan-hu
Was the strongest of all our men;
But as he drew near the tomb-hole
His limbs shook with dread.
That blue one, Heaven,
Takes all our good men.
Could we but ransom him
There are a hundred would give their lives.

Source: From *The Book of Songs* edited and translated by Arthur Waley. Copyright © 1937 by Arthur Waley, p. 103. Used by permission of Grove/Atlantic, Inc.

Questions:
1. What role did spirits play in the lives of the Chinese? Why was it important to placate them?
2. How was human sacrifice regarded by the Chinese?

2.3 Ch'u Yuan and Sung Yu: Individual Voices in a Chaotic Era

The later Zhou period ("Era of Warring States") was a time of intrigue, uncertainty, and confusion—a time when the individual could very easily be lost from view. Politics, ethics, warfare, and religion, underlined by that supreme piece of logical irrationality, the "Mandate of Heaven," cast a generally depressing shadow over the years before the Qin period. The mandarins Ch'u Yuan (332–295 B.C.E.) and his nephew Sung Yu, in their enthusiastic, distinct styles and down-to-earth descriptions, provide a refreshing contrast.

> **Source:** Arthur Waley, trans. *170 Chinese Poems,* (London: Constable & Co., 1945), pp. 23–26.

BATTLE

"We grasp our battle-spears: we don our breast-plates of hide.
The axles of our chariots touch: our short swords meet.
Standards obscure the sun: the foe roll up like clouds.
Arrows fall thick: the warriors press forward.
They menace our ranks: they break our line.
The left-hand trace-horse is dead: the one on the right is
      smitten.
The fallen horses block our wheels: they impede the
      yoke-horses!"

They grasp their jade drum-sticks: they beat the sounding
      drums.
Heaven decrees their fall: the dread Powers are angry.

The warriors are all dead: they lie on the moor-field.
They issued but shall not enter: they went but shall not return.
The plains are flat and wide: the way home is long.
Their swords lie beside them: their black bows, in their hand.
Though their limbs were torn, their hearts could not be
      repressed.
They were more than brave: they were inspired with the spirit of
      "Wu."
Steadfast to the end, they could not be daunted.
Their bodies were stricken, but their souls have taken
      Immortality—
Captains among the ghosts, heroes among the dead.

THE MAN-WIND AND THE WOMAN-WIND

HSIANG, king of Ch'u, was feasting in the Orchid-tower, Palace, with Sung Yü¸ and Ching Ch'ai to wait upon him. A gust of wind blew in and the king bared his breast to meet it, saying: "How pleasant a thing is this wind which I share with the common people." Sung Yü answered: "This is the Great King's wind. The common people cannot share it." The king said: "Wind is a spirit of Heaven and Earth. It comes wide spread and does not choose between noble and base or between high and low. How can you say 'This is the king's wind'?" Sung answered: "I have heard it taught that in the crooked lemon-tree birds make their nests and to empty spaces winds fly. But the wind-spirit that comes to different things is not the same." The king said: "Where is the wind born?" and Sung answered, "The wind is born in the ground. It rises in the extremities of the green p'ing-flower. It pours into the river-valleys and rages at the mouth of the pass. It follows the rolling flanks of Mount T'ai and dances beneath pine-trees and cypresses. In gusty bouts it whirls. It rushes in fiery anger. It rumbles low with a noise like thunder, tearing down rocks and trees, smiting forests and grasses.

"But at last abating, it spreads abroad, seeks empty places and crosses the threshold of rooms. And so growing gentler and clearer, it changes and is dispersed and dies.

"It is this cool clear Man-Wind that, freeing itself, falls and rises till it climbs the high walls of the Castle and enters the gardens of the Inner Palace. It bends the flowers and leaves with its breath. It wanders among the osmanthus and pepper-trees. It lingers over the fretted face of the pond, to steal the soul of the hibiscus. It touches the willow leaves and scatters the fragrant herbs. Then it pauses in the courtyard and turning to the North goes up to the Jade Hall, shakes the hanging curtains and lightly passes into the inner room.

"And so it becomes the Great King's wind."

"Now such a wind is fresh and sweet to breathe and its gentle murmuring cures the diseases of men, blows away the stupor of wine, sharpens sight and hearing and refreshes the body. This is what is called the Great King's wind."

The king said: "You have well described it. Now tell me of the common people's wind." Sung said: "The common people's wind rises from narrow lanes and streets, carrying clouds of dust. Rushing to empty spaces it attacks the gateway, scatters the dust-heap, sends the cinders flying, pokes among foul and rotting things, till at last it enters the tiled windows and reaches the rooms of the cottage. Now this wind is heavy and turgid, oppressing man's heart. It brings fever to his body, ulcers to his lips and dimness to his eyes. It shakes him with coughing; it kills him before his time.

"Such is the Woman-wind of the common people."

Questions:
1. *What view does Ch'u Yuan apparently have of war? Of the afterlife?*
2. *To what extent do you think that Ch'u Yuan might actually have participated in military campaigns? On what might you base your assumptions?*
3. *What does Sung Yu's prose poem about the winds tell us about social and gender-based attitudes in Zhou China?*

2.4 Confucius: Analects

To many of us, the words "Confucius say" are the preamble to a witticism, but to billions of Chinese people over thousands of years the sayings of the master have been words of highest wisdom, to be received with respect, if not with reverence. As a result, Confucius has molded the Chinese mind and character in a manner and to an extent that has hardly been equaled by any other single figure in the history of a major civilization.

Although it is difficult to summarize briefly the teachings of Confucius, certain of their basic features are apparent. He was an optimistic moralist; believing people to be fundamentally good, he thought that with proper education and leadership they could realize their potential and achieve the form of life which he described as that of "the superior man." A social order composed of such individuals, including particularly its political leaders, would constitute the ideal society. Although he also believed that such a society is in harmony with the will of heaven, Confucius, unlike many early social philosophers, did not found his ideal society on principles derived from theology. On the contrary, he is well described as a humanist.

Many of the details of the moral and social ideals of Confucius appear in his Analects, or "Collection" (of sayings). This collection, which is rambling, ill-arranged, and repetitious, contains twenty "Books," in which, besides the master's sayings, there can be found descriptions of contemporary Chinese society, excursions into past history, stories about various political leaders, and so on.

Confucius (551–479 B.C.) was born of a poor family that apparently had ancestors of substance. Early in life he decided to become a scholar and teacher. He soon gathered a group of disciples about him and, because he believed that society could be reformed only if those who were properly educated held the reins of government, he sought public office and encouraged his students to do so as well. During his career he held a number of government posts, some of consequence. But practical politicians were suspicious of his lofty ideals and he was finally dismissed, to spend the twilight of his career wandering about China, but still teaching.

Near the end of his life he wrote the following succinct autobiography: "At fifteen, I set my heart on learning. At thirty, I was firmly established. At forty, I had no more doubts. At fifty, I knew the will of Heaven. At sixty, I was ready to listen to it. At seventy, I could follow my heart's desire without transgressing what was right."

The moral teachings of the Analects, which Confucius did not actually originate but which he edited and molded to reflect his own ideals, were gathered together, mainly after his death, by his admirers. The selection that follows includes some of his central sayings. These have been rearranged to give them greater coherency, and the topic headings have been added.

Source: *James Legge, trans. The Chinese Classics with a Translation, Critical and Exegetical Notes, Prolegomena, and Copius Indexes, Volume I.*

ANALECTS

The Master said, "Is it not pleasant to learn with a constant perseverance and application? Is it not delightful to have friends coming from distant quarters? Is he not a man of complete virtue who feels no discomposure though men may take no note of him?"

. . .

FILIAL PIETY

The Master said, "A youth, when at home, should be filial, and, abroad, respectful to his elders. He should be earnest and truthful. He should overflow in love to all, and cultivate the friendship of the good. When he has time and opportunity, after the performance of these things, he should employ them in polite studies."

Mang I asked what filial piety was. The Master said, "It is not being disobedient." Soon after, as Fan Ch'ih was driving him, the Master told him, saying, "Mang'sun asked me what filial piety was, and I answered him,- "not being disobedient." Fan Ch'ih said, "What did you mean?" The Master replied, "That parents, when alive, should be served according to propriety; that, when dead, they should be buried according to propriety; and that they should be sacrificed to according to propriety."

The Master said, "In serving his parents, a son may remonstrate with them, but gently; when he sees that they do not incline to follow his advice, he shows an increased degree of reverence, but does not abandon his purpose; and should they punish him, he does not allow himself to murmur."

EDUCATION

The Master said, "If the scholar be not grave, he will not call forth any veneration, and his learning will not be solid."

The Master said, "If a man keeps cherishing his old knowledge, so as continually to be acquiring new, he may be a teacher of others."

The Master said, "The accomplished scholar is not a utensil."

The Master said, "Learning without thought is labor lost; thought without learning is perilous."

The Master said, "Yu, shall I teach you what knowledge is? When you know a thing, to hold that you know it; and when you do not know a thing, to allow that you do not know it;- this is knowledge."

The Master said, "They who know the truth are not equal to those who love it, and they who love it are not equal to those who delight in it."

The Master said, "The scholar who cherishes the love of comfort is not fit to be deemed a scholar."

When the Master went to Wei, Zan Yu acted as driver of his carriage. The Master observed, "How numerous are the people!" Yu said, "Since they are so numerous, what more shall be done for them?" "Enrich them," was the reply. "And when they have been enriched, what more shall be done?" The Master said, "Teach them."

GOVERNMENT

The Master said, "To rule a country of a thousand chariots, there must be reverent attention to business, and sincerity; economy in expenditure, and love for men; and the employment of the people at the proper seasons."

The Master said, "He who exercises government by means of his virtue may be compared to the north polar star, which keeps its place and all the stars turn towards it."

The Master said, "If the people be led by laws, and uniformity sought to be given them by punishment, they will try to avoid the punishment, but have no sense of shame. If they be led by virtue, and uniformity sought to be given them by the rules of propriety, they will have the sense of shame, and moreover will become good."

Chi K'ang asked how to cause the people to reverence their ruler, to be faithful to him, and to go on to nerve themselves to virtue. The Master said, "Let him preside over them with gravity;-then they will reverence him. Let him be filial and kind to all;- then they will be faithful to him. Let him advance the good and teach the incompetent;-then they will eagerly seek to be virtuous."

Tsze-kung asked about government. The Master said, "The requisites of government are that there be sufficiency of food, sufficiency of military equipment, and the confidence of the people in their ruler." Tszekung said, "If it cannot be helped, and one of these must be dispensed with, which of the three should be foregone first?" "The military equipment," said the Master. Tsze-kung again asked, "If it cannot be helped, and one of the remaining two must be dispensed with, which of them should be foregone?" The Master answered, "Part with the food. From of old, death has been the lot of all men; but if the people have no faith in their rulers, there is no standing for the State."

Chi K'ang asked Confucius about government, saying, "What do you say to killing the unprincipled for the good of the principled?" Confucius replied, "Sir, in carrying on your government, why should you use killing at all? Let your evinced desires be for what is good, and the people will be good. The relation between superiors and inferiors is like that between the wind and the grass. The grass must bend, when the wind blows across it."

The Master said, "When a prince's personal conduct is correct, the government is effective without the issuing of orders. If his personal conduct is not correct, he may issue orders, but they will not be followed."

Tsze-chang asked Confucius, saying, "In what way should a person in authority act in order that he may conduct government properly?" The Master replied, "Let him honor the five excellent, and banish away the four bad, things;-then may he conduct government properly." Tzsechang said, "What are meant by the five excellent things?" The Master said, "When the person in authority is beneficent without great expenditure; when he lays tasks on the people without their repining; when he pursues what he desires without being covetous; when he maintains a dignified ease without being proud; when he is majestic without being fierce."…

Tsze-chang then asked, "What are meant by the four bad things?" The Master said, "To put the people to death without having instructed them;-this is called cruelty. To require from them, suddenly, the full tale of work, without having given them warning;-this is called oppression. To issue orders as if without urgency, at first, and, when the time comes, to insist on them with severity;-this is called injury. And, generally, in the giving pay or rewards to men, to do it in a stingy way;-this is called acting the part of a mere official."

RELIGION

The Master said,. . . "He who offends against Heaven has none to whom he can pray."

Chi Lu asked about serving the spirits of the dead. The Master said, "While you are not able to serve men, how can you serve their spirits?" Chi Lu added, "I venture to ask about death." He was answered, "While you do not know life, how can you know about death?"

The Master said, "Alas! there is no one that knows me." Tsze-kung said, "What do you mean by thus saying- that no one knows you?" The Master replied, "I do not murmur against Heaven. I do not grumble against men. My studies lie low, and my penetration rises high. But there is Heaven;-that knows me!"

The Master said, "I would prefer not speaking." Tsze-kung said, "If you, Master, do not speak, what shall we, your disciples, have to record?" The Master said, "Does Heaven speak? The four seasons pursue their courses, and all things are continually being produced, but does Heaven say anything?"

The Master said, "Without recognizing the ordinances of Heaven, it is impossible to be a superior man."

VIRTUE AND GOODNESS

The Master said, "Fine words and an insinuating appearance are seldom associated with true virtue."

The Master said, "See what a man does. Mark his motives. Examine in what things he rests. How can a man conceal his character?"

The Master said, "I do not know how a man without truthfulness is to get on. How can a large carriage be made to go without the cross-bar for yoking the oxen to, or a small carriage without the arrangement for yoking the horses?"

The Master said, . . . "To see what is right and not to do it is want of courage."

The Master said, "If the will be set on virtue, there will be no practice of wickedness."

The Master said, "Riches and honors are what men desire. If virtue cannot be obtained in the proper way, they should not be held. Poverty and meanness are what men dislike. If virtue cannot be obtained in the proper way, they should be avoided."

The Master said, "I have not seen a person who loved virtue, or one who hated what was not virtuous. He who loved virtue, would esteem nothing above it. He who hated what is not virtuous, would practice virtue in such a way that he would not allow anything that is not virtuous to approach his person. Is any one able for one day to apply his strength to virtue? I have not seen the case in which his strength would be insufficient."

The Master said, "A man should say, I am not concerned that I have no place, I am concerned how I may fit myself for one. I am not concerned that I am not known, I seek to be worthy to be known."

The Master said, "When we see men of worth, we should think of equalling them; when we see men of a contrary character, we should turn inwards and examine ourselves."

The Master said, "Virtue is not left to stand alone. He who practices it will have neighbors."

The Master said, "Let the will be set on the path of duty. Let every attainment in what is good be firmly grasped. Let perfect virtue be accorded with. Let relaxation and enjoyment be found in the polite arts."

The Master said, "With coarse rice to eat, with water to drink, and my bended arm for a pillow;-I have still joy in the midst of these things. Riches and honors acquired by unrighteousness are to me as a floating cloud."

The Master said, "Is virtue a thing remote? I wish to be virtuous, and lo! virtue is at hand."

The Master said, "Respectfulness, without the rules of propriety, becomes laborious bustle; carefulness, without the rules of propriety, becomes timidity; boldness, without the rules of propriety, becomes insubordination; straightforwardness, without the rules of propriety, becomes rudeness."

The Master said, "Can men refuse to assent to the words of strict admonition? But it is reforming the conduct because of them which is valuable. Can men refuse to be pleased with words of gentle advice? But it is unfolding their aim which is valuable. If a man be pleased with these words, but does not unfold their aim, and assents to those, but does not reform his conduct, I can really do nothing with him."

The Master said, "Hold faithfulness and sincerity as first principles. Have no friends not equal to yourself. When you have faults, do not fear to abandon them."

The Master said, "The commander of the forces of a large State may be carried off, but the will of even a common man cannot be taken from him."

The Master said, "The wise are free from perplexities; the virtuous from anxiety; and the bold from fear."

The Master said, "To go beyond is as wrong as to fall short."

Chung-kung asked about perfect virtue. The Master said, "It is, when you go abroad, to behave to every one as if you were receiving a great guest; to employ the people as if you were assisting at a great sacrifice; not to do to others as you would not wish done to yourself to have no murmuring against you in the country, and none in the family."

Fan Ch'ih asked about benevolence. The Master said, "It is to love all men." He asked about knowledge. The Master said, "It is to know all men."

Fan Ch'ih asked about perfect virtue. The Master said, "It is, in retirement, to be sedately grave; in the management of business, to be reverently attentive; in intercourse with others, to be strictly sincere. Though a man go among rude, uncultivated tribes, these qualities may not be neglected."

Tsze-kung asked, saying, "What do you say of a man who is loved by all the people of his neighborhood?" The Master replied, "We may not for that accord our approval of him." "And what do you say of him who is hated by all the people of his neighborhood?" The Master said, "We may not for that conclude that he is bad. It is better than either of these cases that the good in the neighborhood love him, and the bad hate him."

The Master said, "He who speaks without modesty will find it difficult to make his words good."

Some one said, "What do you say concerning the principle that injury should be recompensed with kindness?" The Master said, "With what then will you recompense kindness? Recompense injury with justice, and recompense kindness with kindness."

Tsze-kung asked, saying, "Is there one word which may serve as a rule of practice for all one's life?" The Master said, "Is not RECIPROCITY such a word? What you do not want done to yourself, do not do to others."

The Master said, "Virtue is more to man than either water or fire. I have seen men die from treading on water and fire, but I have never seen a man die from treading the course of virtue."

Confucius said, "There are three friendships which are advantageous, and three which are injurious. Friendship with the upright; friendship with the sincere; and friendship with the man of much observation;- these are advantageous. Friendship with the man of specious airs; friendship with the insinuatingly soft; and friendship with the glib-tongued;- these are injurious."

Confucius said, "There are three things men find enjoyment in which are advantageous, and three things they find enjoyment in which are injurious. To find enjoyment in the discriminating study of ceremonies and music; to find enjoyment in speaking of the goodness of others; to find enjoyment in having many worthy friends;-these are advantageous. To find enjoyment in extravagant pleasures; to find enjoyment in idleness and sauntering; to find enjoyment in the pleasures of feasting;-these are injurious."

Tsze-chang asked Confucius about perfect virtue. Confucius said, "To be able to practice five things everywhere under Heaven constitutes perfect virtue." He begged to ask what they were, and was told, "Gravity, generosity of soul, sincerity, earnestness, and kindness. If you are grave, you will not be treated with disrespect. If you are generous, you will win all. If you are sincere, people will repose trust in you. If you are earnest, you will accomplish much. If you are kind, this will enable you to employ the services of others."

Questions:
1. According to Confucius, what is the basis for a stable society?
2. What behaviors or attitudes does Confucius consider virtuous? What is the purpose of being virtuous?

2.5 Mencius: the Counterattack on Legalism

So deep was the hatred engendered by the Legalist policies of Emperor Shi Huang Ti that those who had taken an opposing point of view by championing the idea of humane and moral political leadership were regarded as sages. The individual who exemplified this attitude was the philosopher Mencius (372–289 B.C.E.). A follower of Confucianism, Mencius went further than The Master in emphasizing a government's ethical mission to those it governed. His book, the "Meng-tze," is considered one of the "Four Books" of Confucianism.

Source: S.E. Frost, Jr., ed., *The Sacred Writings of the World's Great Religions* (N.Y.: McGraw-Hill, 1972), pp. 113–117.

Mencius went to visit King Hui of Liang. The King said to him: You are an old man, yet you have not shrunk from a journey of a thousand li in order to come hither. Doubtless you have something in your mind which will profit my kingdom?

Mencius replied: Why must your Majesty use that word "profit"? My business is with benevolence and righteousness and nothing else. If the King says, How shall I profit my kingdom? the great officers will say, How shall we profit our families? and the petty officers and common people will say, How shall we profit ourselves? And while upper and lower are thus engaged in a fierce struggle for profits, the State will be brought into peril. If the ruler of ten thousand chariots is slain, it will be by a family of a thousand; if the ruler of a thousand chariots is slain, it will be by a family of a hundred. A thousand out of ten thousand or a hundred out of one thousand, is no small proportion of the whole. But if righteousness be considered of less importance than profit, people will never be satisfied without grasping more than they possess. As benevolence is incompatible with neglect of one's parents, so righteousness never puts the interests of one's sovereign last. Let me, then, hear your Majesty speak only of benevolence and righteousness. There is no need to use the word "profit" at all.

Kung-sun Ch'ou asked, saying: If, Sir, you were appointed Chancellor of the Ch'i State, you would be able to put your principles into practice; and it would not be at all surprising if you thereby succeeded in obtaining the hegemony, or the royal dignity itself, for your prince. In such circumstances, would you feel agitated in mind?—No, replied Mencius; by the age of forty I had achieved imperturbability of mind. In that case, you are far superior to Meng Pen.—It is not hard to acquire. The philosopher Kao achieved the same result before I did. Is there any special method of acquiring it?—Oh, yes. Pei-kung Yu trained himself in physical courage so as not to flinch from a blow or to relax the steadiness of his gaze. He would resent the slightest push from anybody as fiercely as a thrashing in the market-place; he would not stomach an insult either from a coarsely clad man of the people or from a lord of ten thousand chariots. When it came to stabbing, prince and pauper were all the same to him. He stood in no awe of the feudal princes, and if an abusive word was addressed to him, he would be sure to retort.

Meng Shih-she had another method of fostering his courage. He used to say: "I care not whether I win or lose. One who weighs up the enemy before he advances, and plans for victory before he joins battle, is in reality afraid of the army he is fighting. How can I make certain of victory? "All I can do is to have no fear." Meng Shih-she was like Tseng Tzu and Pei-kung Yu was like Tzu Hsia. Which of the two was the more courageous I do not know, but Meng Shih-she held to the essential point. Tseng Tzu once said to his disciple Tzu Hsiang: "Do you admire courage? On the subject of courage in its highest form I once heard our Master say: If on self-examination I find that I am not in the right, shall I not be afraid even of the humblest yokel? But if I find that I am in the right, I will face the enemy in his thousands and tens of thousands." After all, Meng Shih-she's hold on his spirit was not so good as Tseng Tzu's hold on the essential point.

Mencius said: He is a tyrant who uses force while making a show of benevolence. To be a tyrant one must have a large kingdom at one's command. He is a true king who practises benevolence in a virtuous spirit. To be a true king, one need not wait for a large kingdom. T'ang ruled over seventy square *li*, and King Wen over a hundred. When men are subdued by force, it is not their hearts that are won but their strength that gives out. When men are won by goodness, their hearts are glad within them and their submission is sincere. Thus were the seventy disciples of Confucius won by their Master. This is what is meant in the *Book of Songs* where it says: "From east and west, from north and south, came no thought but of surrender."

Mencius said: Benevolence brings honour, without it comes disgrace. To hate disgrace and yet to be content to live without benevolence, is like hating damp and yet living in a hollow. If a ruler hates disgrace, his best way is to prize virtue and do honour to the scholar. With worthy men in high places and able men in office, his country may enjoy a season of peace and quiet; and if he uses this opportunity to clarify law and government, even a great kingdom will be wary of him. It is said in the *Book of Songs:*

> "Ere that the rain-clouds gathered,
> I took the bark of the mulberry tree
> And wove it into window and door.
> Now, ye people below,
> Which of you will dare to affront me?"

Confucius said of the maker of this ode that he knew the principles of statecraft; for who will dare to affront a ruler that can order his kingdom well? But, now that the State is enjoying a season of quiet, to use the opportunity for junketing and idle amusement is nothing less than seeking out misfortune. Happiness and misfortune are indeed always of man's own seeking. That is the lesson conveyed in the *Book of Songs:*

> "Ever adjust thyself to the will of Heaven,
> And great happiness will be thine;"

and in the T'ai Chia: "Heaven-sent calamities you may stand up against, but you cannot survive those brought on by yourself."

Mencius said: All men have a certain sympathy towards their fellows. The great monarchs of old had this human sympathy, and it resulted in their government being sympathetic. Having this feeling of sympathy for his fellows, he who acts upon it in governing the Empire will find that his rule can be conducted as it were in the palm of his hand. What I mean by this feeling of sympathy which all men possess is this: If anyone were to see a child falling into a well, he would have a feeling of horror and pity, not because he happened to be an intimate friend of the child's parents, nor because he sought the approbation of his neighbours and friends, nor yet because he feared to be thought inhumane. Looking at the matter in the light of this example, we may say that no man is devoid of a feeling of compassion, nor of a feeling of shame, nor of a feeling of consideration for others, nor of a feeling of plain right and wrong. The feeling of compassion is the origin of benevolence; the feeling of shame is the origin of righteousnes; the feeling of consideration for others is the origin of good manners; the feeling of right and wrong is the origin of wisdom. The presence of these four elements in man is as natural to him as the possession of his four limbs. Having these four elements within him, the man who says he is powerless to act as he should is doing a grave injury to himself. And the man who says the same of his prince is likewise doing him a grave injury. Let a man but know how to expand and develop these four elements existing in the soul and his progress becomes as irresistible as a newly kindled fire or a spring that has just burst from the ground. If they can be fully developed, these virtues are strong enough to safeguard all within the Four Seas; if allowed to remain undeveloped, they will not suffice for the service due to one's parents.

Mencius said: If you love others but are not loved in return examine your own feeling of benevolence. If you try to govern others and do not succeed, turn inwards and examine your wisdom. If you treat others with courtesy but evoke no response, examine your inward feeling of respect. Whenever our actions fail to produce the effect desired, we should look for the cause in ourselves. For when a man is inwardly correct, the world will not be slow in paying him homage.

A man must insult himself before others will. A family must begin to destroy itself before others do so. State must smite itself before it is smitten from without.

With one who does violence to his own nature words are of no avail. For one who throws himself away, nothing can be done. To discard decency and right feeling in one's speech is what I mean by doing violence to one's nature. To profess inability to abide in benevolence and follow the road of righteousness is what I mean by throwing oneself away. Benevolence is man's peaceful abode and righteousness his true road. Alas for those who desert the peaceful abode, and dwell not therein! Alas for those who abandon the true road and follow it not!

The path of duty lies close at hand, yet we seek for it afar. Our business lies in what is simple, yet we seek for it in what is difficult. If every man would love his parents and treat his elders as they should be treated, the Empire would be at peace.

What trouble is he not laying up for himself who discourses on other people's faults!

The great man makes no effort to be sincere in his speech nor resolute in his acts: he simply does as his conscience prompts him.

The great man is one who has never lost the heart of a child.

Not the support of one's parents when alive but rather the performance of their obsequies after death, is to be accounted the greatest of filial piety.

The disciple Hsü said: Confucius used to apostrophize water in terms of praise. What did he find to admire in it?—Mencius replied: A spring of water flows in a copious stream, never ceasing day and night filling all cavities and, continuing its course, finding its way at last into the ocean. Such is the behaviour of water that flows from a spring, and this is what he admired. But where there is no spring, though channels and ditches are filled after rainfall in the seventh and eighth months, yet the water may soon be expected to dry up again. Thus the princely man is ashamed to enjoy a reputation which exceeds his real deserts.

The princely man is distinguished from others by the feelings laid up in his heart, and these are the feelings of benevolence and propriety. The benevolent man loves his fellows; the man of propriety respects his fellows. He who loves his fellows is loved by them in return; he who respects his fellows is respected by them in return. The nobler type of man, when treated by anybody in a rude and churlish manner, will turn his eyes inward and say: "I must have been lacking in benevolence; I must have shown a want of propriety; or how could this have happened?" Having examined himself thus, he may find that he has really been inspired by benevolence and propriety. If the other man is none the less rude and churlish, he will again subject himself to a searching examination, saying: "I cannot have been true to myself." But if he finds that he has been true to himself, and the rudeness of the other still persists he will say to himself: "This must be an unreasonable sort of fellow after all. If he behaves thus, there is little to choose between him and a bird or beast. And why should I be unduly concerned about a bird or beast?"

Thus it is that the nobler type of man, while constantly solicitous, never suffers grief of any duration. Solicitude, indeed, he feels; for he will argue thus: "Shun was a man; I too am a man. But Shun was an example to the Empire, worthy of being handed down to posterity, whereas I have not yet risen above the level of an ordinary villager." This, then, causes him solicitude, which is nothing more than anxiety to become like Shun himself. But anything that would cause him real grief simply does not exist. He never acts without a feeling of benevolence, never moves without a sense of propriety. Even if some transient cause for grief were to come his way, he would not regard it as such.

The philosopher Kao said: Man's nature is like a current of water: deflected in an easterly direction, it will flow to the east; deflected in an westerly direction, it will flow to the west. And just as water has no predilection either for east or for west, so man's nature is not predisposed either to good or to evil.—Mencius replied: It is true that water has no predilection for east or west, but will it flow equally well up or down? Human nature is disposed towards goodness just as water flows downwards. There is no water but flows down, and no men but show this tendency to good. Now, if water is splashed up, it can be made to go over your head; by forcing it along, it can be made to go uphill. But how can that be termed its natural bent? It is some external force that causes it to do so. And likewise, if men are made to do what is not good, nature is being distorted in a similar way.

Mencius said: I am fond of fish, and I am also fond of bear's paws. If I cannot have both, I will give up the fish and take the bear's paws. Similarly, I hold life dear, and also hold righteousness dear, If I cannot have both, I will give up my life and keep my righteousness. Although I hold life dear, there are things which I hold dearer than life, therefore I will not keep it at the expense of what is right. Although I hate death, there are things which I hate more than death, therefore there are certain dangers from which I will not flee. If there was nothing that men desired more than life, would they not use any possible means of preserving it? And if there was nothing men hated more than death, would they not do anything to escape from danger? Yet there are means of preserving one's life which men will not use, ways of avoiding danger which men will not adopt. Thus it appears that men desire some things more than life, and some things more than death. And it is not only the virtuous man who has such feelings; all men have them. What distinguishes the virtuous man is that he can keep those feelings from being stifled within him.

The disciple Kung-tu asked, saying: Human nature is common to us all. How is it, then, that some are great men and some are small men?—Mencius replied: Those that follow their higher nature are great men; those that follow their lower nature are small men.—Kung-tu said: Seeing that all alike are men, how is it that some follow their higher nature and some their lower nature?—Mencius replied: The function of the eye and the ear is not thought, but is determined by material

55

objects; for when objects impinge on the senses these cannot but follow wherever they lead. Thought is the function of the mind: by thinking, it achieves; by not thinking, it fails to achieve. These faculties are implanted in us by Nature. If we take our stand from the first on the higher part of our being, the lower part will not be able to rob us of it. It is simply this that constitutes the great man.

Questions:
1. *Why is Mencius so opposed to the term "profit" as it relates to government?*
2. *What is Mencius' understanding of what should distinguish a prince from others?*

2.6   Taoism

Taoism developed in China concurrently with Confucianism, indeed as a rival to it. According to tradition, Lao Tzu, the originator of Taoism, and Confucius actually once met. Taoism gave the Chinese people what Confucianism did not-a religion. As a result it has through the centuries always had a strong appeal to the great masses.

But the religion of Taoism, at least as it appears in the classic Tao Te Ching ("The Book of the Way and Its Power"), is different from most other religions, being almost devoid of a theology. Its central concept is the Tao but this is not a god, or indeed any being at all. The Tao (or the Way) is beyond all being, that from which heaven and earth have sprung. What exactly it is cannot really be said because to put a description of it into words would be to lose it. Yet the Tao can be known, in the sense that the sage can respond to it in such a way that he identifies himself with it. Essentially, thus, Taoism is a form of mysticism. Rather than being intellectual, it is emotional; rather than being articulated, it is simply felt.

When one translates the mystery of the Tao into a guide for life, the central percept becomes: Maintain yourself in harmony with nature. Since nature is an expression of the Tao the sage will conform his actions to it, accepting whatever comes as it comes and never trying to change things. Thus, in practice Taoism engenders quietism. Also, since the attempt to understand the world is ultimately self-defeating, Taoism deprecates learning in favor of ignorance. Finally, any activities of officials aimed at regulating the lives of the people are necessarily counterproductive; the least government is the best government.

Classical Taoism, which thrived on paradox, might thus be described as an otherwordly religion whose sole emphasis was on this world. Through its long history, however, it underwent many changes. In particular it acquired a theology, gathering together under its aegis a whole host of deities from early Chinese mythology. Also, its sages, in later centuries, turned increasingly to the practice of magic, one of their perennial occupations being the attempt to transmute base metals into gold.

According to tradition, the Tao Te Ching was written by Lao-Tzu, who lived in the sixth century B.C. But this attribution is questionable; in fact it can be questioned whether Lao-Tzu himself ever lived, or is only a figure of legend. In any case, most scholars have concluded that the Tao Te Ching was compiled by several authors and that, although it contains elements from a much older tradition, the form in which we now have it dates from some time after the reputed lifetime of Lao-Tzu.

> **Source:** Lin, Paul J., *A Translation of Lao Tzu's* Tao Te Ching and *Wang Pu's* Commentary (Ann Arbor: Center for Chinese Studies, 1977). Courtesy of Center for Chinese Studies, the University of Michigan.

TAO TE CHING

Book One

> The Tao that can be spoken of is not the eternal Tao;
> The Name that can be named is not the eternal Name.
> The Nameless [non-being] is the origin of heaven and earth;
> The Namable [being] is the mother of all things.
>
>
> Therefore constantly without desire,
> There is the recognition of subtlety;
> But constantly with desire,

Only the realization of potentiality.
The two come from the same source,
    Having different names.
Both are called mysteries,
More mystical than the most mystical,
The gate of all subtleties.
When all in the world recognize beauty as beauty, it is ugliness.
When they recognize good as good, it is not good.
Therefore, being and non-being beget each other hard and easy
    complement each other, long and short shape each other,
    high and low rely on each other,
    sound and voice harmonize with each other,
    front and back follow each other.
Therefore, the Sage administers without action
    and instructs without words.

He lets all things rise without dominating them, produces with-
    out attempting to possess, acts without asserting, achieves
    without taking credit.

And because he does not take credit, it will never leave him.
Exalt not the worthy,
    so that the people will not fight.
Prize not the rare treasure,
    so that they will not steal.
Exhibit not the desirable,
    so that their hearts will not be distracted.

Therefore in governing, the Sage empties the people's hearts and
    fills their stomachs,
    weakens their will and strengthens their bones.
He always keeps them void of knowledge and desire,
    so that those who know will not dare to act.
Acting through inaction, he leaves nothing ungoverned.
Tao is empty, used yet never filled. It is deep, like the forefather of
    all things.
It dulls sharpness, and sorts tangles,
Blends with the light, becoming one with the dust.
So serene, as if it hardly existed.
I do not know whose son it is.
It seems to have preceded God.
The man of supreme goodness resembles water.
Water benefits all things
    Without competing with them,
Staying in places that men despise;
Therefore, it is very close to Tao.

Dwelling in good places,
Having a heart that loves the profound,
Allying with benevolence,
Inviting trust with words,
Being righteous in governing,
Managing all things well,
Moving at the right time-
Just because he does not compete,
The man of supreme goodness frees himself of blame.
Thirty spokes converge in a nave; just because of its nothingness

[void] the usefulness of the cart exists.
Molded clay forms a vessel;
     just because of its nothingness [hollowness]
     the usefulness of the utensil exists.
Doors and windows are cut into a house;
     just because of their nothingness [emptiness]
     the usefulness of the house exists.
Therefore, profit from that which exists and utilize that which is
     absent.
Looked at, it cannot be seen; it is called colorless.
Listened to, it cannot be heard; it is called soundless.
Grasped, it cannot be obtained; it is called formless.

These three cannot be investigated further,
     so they merge together to make one.
The upper part is not bright;
The lower part is not dark.
So subtle, it cannot be named,
But returns to nothingness.
This is called the shape without shape, the image without image.
This is called indistinct:
     confronting it, one cannot see the head;
     following it, one cannot see the back.
Grasp the Ancient Tao to manage present existence.
Thus we may know the beginning of the Ancient.
This is called the record of Tao.
Attain the ultimate emptiness;
     Maintain the absolute tranquility.
All things rise together.
And I observe their return…
The multitude of all things return each to their origin.
To return to the origin means repose;
It means return to their destiny.
To return to their destiny means eternity;
To know eternity means enlightenment.
Not knowing eternity is to do evil things blindly.

To know eternity means having capacity.
     Capacity leads to justice.
     Justice leads to kingship.
     Kingship leads to Heaven.
     Heaven leads to Tao.
     Tao is everlasting.
Thus the entire life will be without danger.
Banish sagacity; forsake wisdom.
The people will benefit a hundredfold.
Banish human-heartedness; forsake righteousness.
The people will recover filial piety and paternal affection.
Banish craftiness; forsake profit.
Thieves and robbers will no longer exist.
Those three are superficial and inadequate.
Hence the people need something to abide by:
     Discern plainness.
     Embrace simplicity.
     Reduce selfishness.
     Restrain desires.
Abandon learning; then one has no sorrow.

Between "yes" and "no," what is the difference?
Between good and evil, what is the difference?
If I should fear what the people fear,
Then where is the end of my fear?
Lustily the people seem to be enjoying a feast
Or ascending a tower in the springtime. I alone am unmoved,
        showing no sentiment,
Like a baby who does not yet know how to smile.
So weary, I seem not to know where to return.
While the multitudes have plenty,
I alone seem to be left out.
My heart is like a fool's.
How chaotic! Chaotic!
While the common people are so bright,
I alone am so dull!
While the common people know how to differentiate,
I alone cannot see the difference.
Boundless as the sea,
Aimless as the breeze,
I seem to have no stop.
All the people have their purpose,
But I alone am stubborn and despicable.
I alone differ from the others
And value getting nourishment from the Mother.
The feature of great virtue is to follow only Tao.
Tao is something elusive and vague!
        Though vague and elusive, in it is the image.
        Though elusive and vague, in it is the substance.
Obscure and dim, in it is the spirit.
The spirit is truly genuine; in it is credibility.

From ancient times until now, Its name has never disappeared.
By this the beginning of all things is known.
How can I know the beginning of all things?
By this.
To yield is to have the whole.
To be crooked is to be straightened.
To be hollow is to be filled.
To be worn out is to be renewed.
To have a little is to get more.
To have a lot is to be confused.
Therefore the Sage sets an example for the world
By embracing the One.
By not insisting on his view, he may become enlightened.
By not being self-righteous, he may become illustrious.
By not boasting, he may receive credit.
By not being arrogant, he may last long.
And just because he does not compete, the entire world cannot
        compete with him.
The Ancients say:
        "to yield is to have the whole."
Are these merely words?
Truly the whole will return to him.
To spare words is to be natural.
Therefore a whirlwind does not last all morning,
And a sudden shower does not last all day.
Who causes this?

Heaven and earth.
If even Heaven and earth cannot last long,
What can man do?
Therefore one dealing with Tao will resemble Tao.
Dealing with virtue, one will resemble virtue.
Dealing with loss, one will resemble loss.
If one resembles Tao, Tao is pleased to accept him.
If one resembles virtue, virtue is pleased to accept him.
If one resembles loss, loss is also pleased to accept him.

By not having enough credibility,
One will not be trusted [by others].
Those who rise on tiptoe cannot stand.
Those who stride cannot walk.

Those who hold to their views cannot be enlightened.
Those who are self-righteous cannot shine.
Those who boast cannot receive credit. Those who are arrogant
    cannot last long.
In the light of Tao, they are like left-over food and
    burdensome wens,
Even despised by all creatures.
So those with Tao do not want to stay with them.
There is a thing formed in chaos
Existing before Heaven and Earth.
Silent and solitary, it stands alone, unchanging.
It goes around without peril.
It may be the Mother of the world.
Not knowing its name, I can only style it Tao.
With reluctance, I would call it Great.
Great means out-going.
Out-going means far-reaching.
Far-reaching means returning.

Therefore, Tao is great.
    Heaven is great.
    Earth is great.
    The king is great.
In the universe, there are four great things,
    and the king is one of them.
    Man abides by earth,
    Earth abides by heaven,
    Heaven abides by Tao,
    Tao abides by nature.
Fine weapons are the tools of evil;
All things are likely to hate them.
So those with Tao do not want to deal with them.
The gentleman who stays at home values the left;
In war, he values the right.
Weapons are the tools of evil, not the tools of the gentleman.
When he uses them unavoidably, he is most calm and detached
And does not glorify his victory.
To glorify means to relish the murder of people,
Relishing the murder of people,
    One cannot exercise his will in the world.
Happy occasions prefer the left.
Sorrowful occasions prefer the right.

The lieutenant-general is placed on the left.

The general-in-chief is placed on the right.

This means observing this occasion with funeral rites.

Having killed many people, one should lament with sorrow
and grief.

Victory in war must be observed with funeral rites.

The great Tao overflows, able to move left and right.

All things rely on it for life,

But it does not dominate them.

Completing its task without possession,

Clothing and feeding all things,

Without wanting to be their master.

Always void of desire,

    It can be called Small.

All things return to it

Without its being their master; It can be called Great.

Just because the Sage would never regard himself as great,

He is able to attain his own greatness.

Tao is always inactive.

But it leaves nothing undone.

If dukes and kings can keep it,

Then all things will be naturally transformed.

If transformation raises desires,

I would suppress them with nameless simplicity.

Nameless simplicity means being without desires.

Being without desires and with tranquility,

The world will keep peace by itself.

Those of ancient times obtained the One:

    Heaven obtained the One for its clarity;

    Earth obtained the One for its tranquility;

    The Spirit obtained the One for its divinity;

    The Valley obtained the One for its repletion;

    All things obtained the One for their lives;

    Dukes and kings obtained the One for the rectitude
of the world.

What causes these is the One.

Without clarity,

    Heaven could not avoid disrupting.

Without tranquility,

    Earth could not avoid explosion.

Without divinity,

    The Spirit could not avoid dissolving.

Without repletion,

    The Valley could not avoid dissipating.

Without life,

    All things could not avoid perishing.

Without rectitude and dignity,

    Dukes and kings could not avoid falling.

Therefore, distinction has humility as its root;

The high regards the low as its foundation.

Therefore dukes and kings call themselves

    Orphans, widowers, and starvers.

Does this not mean regarding humility as a base?

Doesn't it?

He who is most praise-worthy

    Does not need any praise.

He prefers to be neither rare as jade,

Nor as common as rocks.
Returning is Tao's motion.
Weakness is Tao's function.
All things in the world are produced by being.
And being is produced by non-being.
The superior man, on hearing Tao,
    Practices it diligently.
The average man, on hearing Tao,
    Regards it both as existing and not existing.
The inferior man, on hearing Tao, Laughs aloud at it.
Without his laughter, it would not be Tao.

Therefore the established word says:
    The luminous Tao seems obscure.
    The advancing Tao seems retreating.
    The even Tao seems rough.
    The highest virtue seems empty.
    Great whiteness seems blackened.
    Broad virtue seems insufficient.
    Established virtue seems secret.
    Pure substance seems fluid.
    The great square has no corners.
    The great vessel is late in completing.
    The great voice sounds faint.
    The great image has no shape.
Tao is concealed and has no name.
Yet only Tao is good in giving and completing.
Tao begets One.
One begets Two.
Two begets Three.
Three begets all things.
All things carry the female and embrace the male.
And by breathing together, they live in harmony.

What the people hate is being orphaned, widowed, and starved.
But kings and dukes call themselves these names.
Therefore everything can be augmented when diminished, and
    diminished when augmented.
What the people teach, I teach too.
The violent and fierce cannot die a natural death.
I will become the father of teaching.
The world's softest thing gallops to and fro through the world's
    hardest thing.
Things without substance can penetrate things without crevices.
Thus I know the benefit of inaction.
But teaching without words and benefiting without action
    are understood by few in the entire world.
Without going out-of-doors,
One can know the whole world.
Without looking out of windows,
One can see the Tao of heaven.
The farther one goes, the less one knows.
Therefore, the Sage does not go and yet knows,
    Doesn't see and yet names,
    Doesn't act and yet completes.
The pursuit of learning increases daily.
The pursuit of Tao decreases daily,

Decreasing more and more
Until it reaches the point of inaction.
Inaction: then nothing cannot be done by it,
Therefore the capture of the world should always be done
    by inactivity.
As for activity, it is insufficient to capture the world.
If only I could have a little knowledge,
I would walk in the Great Tao,
    Being afraid only of acting on it.
The Great Tao is very smooth,
But people prefer the by-paths;
The court is very well kept;
The fields are full of weeds;
And the granaries are extremely empty.
To wear embroidered clothes,
To carry sharp weapons,
To be satiated in food and drink,
And to have excessive treasures and goods—
This is called robbery and extravagance.
Really, this is not Tao.
The one who knows does not speak.
The one who speaks does not know.

Block the passage.
Close the door.
Dull the sharpness.
Loosen the tangles.
Blend with light.
Become one with the dust.

This is called mystical identity.
Hence one can be neither close to it, nor far from it;
One can neither benefit it, nor harm it;
One can neither value it, nor despise it.
Therefore, it is valued by the world.
Rule the state with rectitude.
Direct the army with trickery.
Capture the world through inactivity.
How can I know it shall be so?
By this:
    When the world is full of taboos and prohibitions,
    The people will become very poor.
    When the people possess many sharp weapons, The nation
    will become more chaotic.
    When the people possess much craftiness,
      Trickery will flourish.
    When law and order become more conspicuous,
    There will be more robbers and thieves.
Therefore the Sage says:
    I do not act and the people reform themselves;
    I love serenity and the people rectify themselves;
    I employ inactivity and the people become prosperous
    themselves;
    I have no desires and the people become simple
    by themselves.
A large state is like the low land;
    It is the focus point of the world

And the female of the world.

The female always conquers the male by serenity.
In serenity, she puts herself low.

Therefore, the large state puts itself beneath the small state,
And thereby absorbs the small state.
The small state puts itself under the large state,
And thereby joins with the large state.

Therefore, one either puts himself beneath to absorb others,
Or puts himself under to join with others.

What the large state wants is no more than to feed the people.
What the small state wants is no more than to join and serve the
        people.
Both have their needs satisfied.

Thus the large ought to stay low.
The Ancients who were good in practicing Tao
Did not teach the people with intelligence
But kept them in ignorance.
The people are hard to govern when they know too much.
Therefore, one who rules the nation with knowledge robs the
        nation.
One who does not rule the nation with knowledge
        brings good fortune to the nation.
To know these two things means to know the standard.
To constantly know the standard is called mystical virtue.
Mystical virtue goes deep and far.
It returns with all things to reach great harmony.
He who knows that he does not know is the best.
He who does not know but pretends to know is sick.
He who realizes the sickness is sickness. Doesn't have any sickness.
The Sage is without sickness
Because he realizes the sickness is sickness.
Therefore, he doesn't have any sickness.
The people are starving
Because the man on top devours too much tax money.
So they are starving.

The people are hard to govern
Because the man on top is too active in governing.
So they are hard to govern.

The people think little of death
Because the man on top strives for a rich life.
So they think little of death.

Therefore it is better to do nothing for one's life
        Than to value it.
In life, man is supple and tender.
In death, he becomes rigid and stark.
Myriad things such as grass and trees are supple and frail in life,
And shrivelled and dry in death.

Therefore, the rigid and stark are disciples of death,

64

While the supple and weak are disciples of life.

Therefore the army that uses strength cannot win.
The tree that stands firm will break.

The strong and large are subordinate;
The soft and weak are superior.
Perhaps the Tao of heaven resembles the drawing of a bow.
When it is high, lower it.
When low, raise it.
When excessive, diminish it.
When deficient, replenish it.

The Tao of heaven diminishes the excessive and
        replenishes the deficient.
The Tao of man is not so-while decreasing the deficient,
        it supplies the excessive.
Who can supply the world with overabundance?
Only the man with Tao.

Therefore the Sage acts without exalting his ability.
He achieves without dwelling upon it.
He does not want to display his superiority.
Nothing in the world is softer and weaker than water.
Yet, in attacking the hard and strong, nothing can surpass it.

Because nothing can exchange places with it,
        Use weakness to overcome strength.
        Use softness to overcome hardness.
        None in the world do not know this.
        But none can practice it.

Therefore the Sage says:
        To suffer dishonor for the state is to be the lord of the
        community;
        To bear the calamity of the state is to be the king of the
        world.

True words seem paradoxical.
The state may be small; its people may be few.
Let the people have tenfold and one-hundredfold of utensils,
But never make use of them.

Let the people weigh death heavily
    And have no desires to move far away.
Though there be boats and carriages,
    No one will ride in them.
Though there be armour and weapons,
    No one will exhibit them.

Let the people return to tying knots and using them.
    Relish their food,
    Appreciate their clothes,
    Secure in their homes,
    Happy with their customs.

The neighboring states will be so close that they
    can see each other,
    and hear the sounds of roosters and dogs.
But the people will grow old and die,
    Without having visited each other.
Sincere words are not kind;
    Kind words are not sincere.
One who is good will never argue;
    One who argues is not good.
One who knows does not know all;
    One who knows all does not know at all.

The Sage does not store things for himself.
The more one does for others,
    The more he has for himself.
The more one gives to others,
    The more he keeps for himself.

The Tao of heaven is to benefit others without hurting them.
The Tao of the Sage is to act without competing.

Questions:
1. *Briefly describe the Tao in conversational English.*
2. *What virtues does the Tao encourage?*

2.7 Sima Qian: The Historian's Historian Writes About the Builder of the Great Wall

Sima Qian, or Ssu -ma Ch'ien (145–86 B.C.E.), was China's first scientific historian. As the official court historian for the Han Dynasty, he developed a definitive history of China by pioneering methods of reconstructing the past through primary sources, finishing—towards the end of his life the "Records of the Grand Historian." So devoted (some might say obsessed) was he to the historian's craft that, when given the choice between death and castration for transgressing the will of the Emperor, he opted for castration on the sole basis of at least being able to complete his book. Here he relates the life of Meng Tian, designer of the Great Wall.

    Source: Raymond Dawson, trans., *Sima Qian: Historical Records* (Oxford & N.Y.: Oxford University Press, 1994), pp. 55–61.

As for Meng Tian, his forebears were men of Qi. Tian's paternal grandfather, Meng Ao, came from Qi to serve King Zhaoxiang of Qin, and attained the office of senior minister. In the first year of King Zhuangxiang of Qin, Meng Ao became general of Qin, made an assault on Hann and took Chenggao and Xingyang, and established the Sanchuan province.

In the second year Meng Ao attacked Zhao and took thirty-seven cities. In the third year of the First Emperor, Meng Ao attacked Han and took thirteen cities. In the fifth year Meng Ao attacked Wei, took twenty cities, and established Dong province. In the seventh year of the First Emperor, Meng Ao died. Ao's son was called Wu and Wu's son was called Tian. Tian at one time kept legal records and was in charge of the relevant literature. In the twenty-third year of the First Emperor, Meng Wu became an assistant general of Qin and, together with Wang Jian, made an attack on Chu and inflicted a major defeat upon it and killed Xiang Yan. In the twenty-fourth year Meng Wu attacked Chu and took the King of Chu prisoner. Meng Tian's younger brother was Meng Yi.

In the twenty-sixth year of the First Emperor, Meng Tian was able to become a general of Qin on account of the long-term service given by his family. He attacked Qi and inflicted a major defeat upon it, and was appointed Prefect of the Capital. When Qin had unified all under Heaven, Meng Tian was consequently given command of a host of 300,000 to go north and drive out the Rong and Di barbarians and take over the territory to the south of the Yellow River. He built the Great Wall, taking advantage of the lie of the land and making use of the passes. It started from Lintao and went as far as Liaodong, extending more than 10,000 li. Crossing the Yellow River, it followed the Yang Mountains and wriggled northwards. His army was exposed to the elements in the field for more than ten years when they were stationed in Shang province, and at this time Meng Tian filled the Xiongnu with terror.

The First Emperor held the Meng family in the highest esteem. Having confidence in them and so entrusting them with responsibility, he regarded them as men of quality. He allowed Meng Yi to be on terms of close intimacy, and he reached the position of senior minister. When he went out, he took him with him in his carriage, and within the palace he was constantly in the imperial presence. Tian was given responsibility for matters outside the capital, but Yi was constantly made to take part in internal planning. They were reputed to be loyal and trustworthy, so that none even of the generals or leading ministers dared to take issue with them in these matters.

Zhao Gao was a distant connection of the various Zhaos. He had several brothers, and all of them were born in the hidden part of the palace. His mother had been condemned to death, and her descendants were to be of low station for generations to come. When the King of Qin heard that Zhao Gao was forceful and well acquainted with the law, he promoted him and made him Director of Palace Coach-houses. Thereupon Gao privately served Prince Huhai and gave him instruction in judicial decisions. When Zhao Gao committed a major crime, the King of Qin ordered Meng Yi to try him at law. Yi did not dare to show partiality, so he condemned Gao to death and removed him from the register of officials, but because of Gao's estimable performance in the conduct of affairs, the Emperor pardoned him and restored his office and rank.

The First Emperor intended to travel throughout the Empire and go via Jiuyuan directly to Ganquan, so he made Meng Tian open up a road from Jiuyuan straight to Ganquan, hollowing out mountains and filling in valleys for 1,800 li. The road had not yet been completed when the First Emperor in the winter of the thirty-seventh year went forth on his journey and travelled to Kuaiji. Going along the sea coast, he went north to Langye. When he fell ill on the way, he made Meng Yi return to offer prayers to the mountains and streams. He had not yet got back when the First Emperor passed away on reaching Shaqiu. It was kept a secret, and none of the officials knew. At this time Chief Minister Li Si, Prince Huhai, and Director of Palace Coach-houses Zhao Gao were in constant attendance. Gao had regularly obtained favours from Huhai and wanted him to be set on the throne. He was also resentful that when Meng Yi had tried him at law he had not been in favour of letting him off. Consequently he felt like doing him harm, and so he secretly plotted together with Chief Minister Li Si and Prince Huhai to establish Huhai as crown prince. When the Crown Prince had been established, messengers were sent to bestow death on Prince Fusu and Meng Tian because of their alleged crimes. Even after Fusu was dead, Meng Tian felt suspicious and requested confirmation of it. The messengers handed Meng Tian over to the law officers and replaced him.

The messengers returned and made their report, and when Huhai heard that Fusu was dead he intended to free Meng Tian. But Zhao Gao, fearing that the Meng family would again be treated with honour and be employed on affairs, felt resentful about this.

So when Meng Yi got back, Zhao Gao, making his plans on the pretext of loyalty towards Huhai, intended on this account to wipe out the Meng family. 'Your servant hears that the previous Emperor had long intended to promote a man of quality and set up a crown prince,' he therefore said, 'but Meng Yi had remonstrated and said that this would be improper. But if he was aware that you were a man of quality and yet insisted that you should not be set up, this would be acting disloyally and deluding one's sovereign. In your servant's foolish opinion, the best thing would be to put him to death.' Paying heed, Huhai had Meng Yi put in bonds at Dai. (Previously he had taken Meng Tian prisoner at Yangzhou.) When the announcement of mourning reached Xianyang and the funeral had taken place, the Crown Prince was set up as Second Generation Emperor and Zhao Gao, being admitted to terms of close intimacy; slandered the Meng family day and night, seeking out their crimes and mistakes so as to recommend their impeachment.

Ziying came forward to remonstrate, saying: 'I hear that in ancient times King Qian of Zhao killed his good minister Li Mu and employed Yan Ju, and King Xi of Yan secretly employed the stratagems of Jing Ke and ignored the pact with Qin, and King Jian of Qi killed loyal ministers from ancient families which had given long-standing service and

67

made use of the counsels of Hou Sheng. Each of these three rulers lost their states through changing ancient ways so that disaster befell them. Now the Meng family are important officials and counsellors of Qin and yet our sovereign intends to get rid of them all in a single morning, but your servant humbly considers this to be improper. Your servant hears that it is impossible for one who plans frivolously to govern a state and it is impossible for one who exercises wisdom on his own to preserve his ruler. If you put to death loyal servants and set up people who have nothing to do with integrity, then within the palace this will cause all your servants to lose confidence in each other, and in the field it will cause the purposes of your fighting men to lose their cohesion. Your servant humbly considers this to be improper.'

Huhai did not take any notice, but dispatched the imperial scribe Qu Gong to ride relay and go to Dai and instruct Meng Yi as follows: 'You, minister, made things difficult when our previous sovereign wanted to set up a crown prince. Now the Chief Minister considers that you are disloyal, and that your whole clan is implicated in the crime. But in the kindness of Our heart We bestow death upon you, minister, which is surely extremely gracious. It is for you to give this your consideration!'

'If it is thought that your servant was incapable of grasping the wishes of our previous sovereign,' replied Meng Yi, 'then when he was young he was in his service and obediently received his patronage until he passed away, so it may be said that he knew what he wanted. Or if it is thought that your servant was unaware of the abilities of the Crown Prince, then he went all over the Empire with the Crown Prince in sole attendance, and left all the other princes far behind, so your servant had no doubts. Our previous sovereign's proposal to employ him as crown prince had been building up over several years, so what words would your servant have dared to utter in remonstrance, and what plan would he dare to have devised! It is not that I dare to produce showy verbiage for the purpose of avoiding death and implicate the reputation of our previous sovereign by creating an embarrassment, but I would like you, sir, to devote your thoughts to this, and make sure that the circumstances which cause your servant to be put to death are true. Moreover, perfect obedience is what the Way honours, and killing as a punishment is what the Way puts an end to. In former times Duke Mu of Qin died having killed three good men, and charged Baili Xi with a crime although it was not his. Therefore he was given the title of "False." King Zhaoxiang killed Bai Qi, Lord Wan. King Ping of Chu killed Wu She. Fucha King of Wu killed Wu Zixu. These four rulers all made major mistakes and so all under Heaven regarded them as wrong and thought such rulers were unenlightened, and as such they were recorded by the feudal lords. Therefore it is said that "Those who govern in accordance with the Way do not kill the guiltless and punishment is not inflicted on the innocent." It is up to you, my lord, to take notice!' But the messengers were aware of what Huhai wanted, so they took no notice of Meng Yin's words, and killed him forthwith.

Second Generation also dispatched messengers to go to Yangzhou, with the following instructions for Meng Tian: 'Your errors, my lord, have become numerous, and your younger brother Yi bears a great burden of guilt, so the law has caught up with you.' 'From my grandfather right down to his sons and grandsons,' said Meng Tian, 'their achievements and trustworthiness have been built up in Qin over three generations. Now your servant has been in command of more than 300,000 soldiers, and although he personally is a prisoner, his influence is sufficient to instigate a revolt. But as one who safeguards righteousness although he is aware he is bound to die, he does not dare to disgrace the teachings of his forbears, and in this way does not forget his former sovereign. In former times when King Cheng of Zhou was first set on the throne and had not yet left his swaddling clothes, Dan Duke of Zhou carried the King on his back to go to court, and ultimately restored order in all under Heaven. When King Cheng had an illness and was in extreme danger, Duke Dan personally cut his finger-nails and sank the parings in the Yellow River. "The King does not yet possess understanding and it is I who handle affairs," he said. "If there is a crime-engendered disaster, I accept the unfortunate consequences of it." Accordingly he made an account and stored it away in the repository of records, and he may be said to have behaved with good faith. When the time came when the King was able to govern the country, there was a malicious official who said: "Dan Duke of Zhou has long intended to make a rebellion, and if the King is not prepared, there is bound to be a major crisis." The King was consequently furious and Dan Duke of Zhou ran away and fled to Chu. When King Cheng looked at the repository of records, he got hold of the account of the sinking, and so he said, with tears streaming down his face: "Who said that Dan Duke of Zhou intended to make a rebellion?" He killed the one who had said this and restored Dan Duke of Zhou. Thus the *Book Zhou* says: "One must put them in threes and fives." Now for generations my family has avoided duplicity, so if our affairs are finally in such straits, this is bound to be due to the methods of a wicked minister rebelliously stirring up trouble. That King Cheng made a mistake, but when he restored the situation, he ultimately flourished; but Jie killed Guan Longfeng and Zhou killed Prince Bi Gan, and they did not repent, and when they died their country was destroyed. Your servant therefore says that errors can be remedied and remonstrance can be understood. To examine into threes and fives is the method of supreme sages. All in all, your servant's words have not been for the purpose of seeking to escape from blame. He is about to die because he is making a remonstrance, and he wishes Your Majesty would think about following the Way for the sake of the myriad people.' 'Your servants have received an imperial decree to carry out the law on you, general,' said the messengers, 'and they do not dare to report your words to the Supreme One.' Meng Tian sighed deeply. 'For what am I being blamed by Heaven,' he cried, 'that I should die although I have avoided error?' After a good long while he solemnly said: 'There is a crime for which I certainly ought to die. I built a wall stretching more than

10,000 *li* from Lintao as far as Liaodong, and so in the course of this I surely could not avoid cutting through the earth's arteries. This then is my crime.' And so he swallowed poison and killed himself.

The Grand Historiographer says: 'I have been to the northern border and returned via the direct road. On my journey I observed the ramparts of the Great Wall which Meng Tian built for Qin. He hollowed out the mountains and filled in the valleys and opened up a direct road. To be sure, he showed little concern for the efforts of the people. Qin had only just destroyed the feudal states and the hearts of the people of all under Heaven had not yet been restored to order, and the wounded had not yet been healed; but Tian, although he had become a famous general, did not use this occasion to remonstrate strongly and remedy the distresses of the people, minister to the old and enable the orphans to survive, and strive to cultivate harmony among the masses. Instead he embarked on great enterprises to pander to imperial ambition, so was it not therefore reasonable that both he and his brother should suffer the death penalty? Why in that case should cutting the arteries of the earth be made a crime?'

Questions:
1. Into what professions were Meng Tian's ancestors and relatives appointed?
2. Under what circumstances did Meng Tian build the Wall and how long was he engaged in this task?
3. For what crime—after Meng's own words—did he commit suicide?
4. What is Sima's assessment of Meng Tian's life and character?

2.8   Shi Huang Ti of Qin: A Study in Absolutism

Seldom has any one individual tried so intensively to personify, dominate, and mold a nation as Shi Huang Ti, ruler of the state of Qin who succeeded in unifying China under his iron hand from 221–210 B.C.E., and styled himself "First Emperor." This harsh dictatorial figure went so far as to attempt to destroy all records referring to anything that occurred prior to his reign, exclaiming "History begins with me!" Years later, Sima Qian left us this portrait of a man of power.

> **Source:** Raymond Dawson, trans., *Sima Qian: Historical Records* (Oxford & N.Y.: Oxford University Press, 1994), pp. 68–70, 80–81.

He then proceeded to the east of Bohai, passed through Huang and Chui, did a complete tour of Mount Cheng, ascended Zhifu, and set up a stone tablet there extolling the virtue of Qin and then left.

He then went south and ascended Langye and, since he greatly enjoyed it, he stayed for three months. Then he moved 30,000 households of the black-headed people to the foot of Langye terrace, giving them tax and labour exemption for twelve years. When he built Langye terrace, he set up a stone inscription extolling the virtue of Qin, to make clear that he had achieved his ambition. It said:

> In his twenty-eighth year, the August Emperor makes a
>   beginning.
>
> Laws and standards are corrected and adjusted, as a means of
>   recording the myriad things.
>
> Thus he clarifies human affairs, and brings concord to father
>   and son.
>
> With sagacity, wisdom, humaneness, and righteousness, he has
>   made manifest all principles.
>
> In the east he has pacified the eastern lands, and thus he has
>   inspected officers and men.
>
> When this task had been magnificently accomplished, he then
>   turned towards the sea.
>
> Through the achievements of the August Emperor, the basic
>   tasks are diligently worked on.

Farming is put first and non-essentials are abolished, and it is the black-headed people who are made wealthy.

All people under Heaven, have heart and mind in unison.

Implements are given a uniform measure, and the characters used in writing are standardized.

Wherever the sun and moon shine, wherever boats and carts carry goods.

Everyone completes his destiny, and nobody does not get what he wants.

He makes things move in accord with the seasons, such is the August Emperor.

To rectify diverse customs, he has traversed land and water.

Feeling sorrow for the black-headed people, he relaxes not morning or evening.

Removing doubt he fixes the laws, so that all understand what they are forbidden to do.

The regional earls have their separate duties, and all government is regulated and made easy.

What is put into practice is bound to be right, and everything goes according to plan.

The intelligence of the August Emperor, oversees and inspects all four quarters.

High and low, noble and base, do not step out of their rank.

Evil and depravity are not allowed, and all strive to be upright and good.

Putting all their effort into both the trivial and the important, nobody dares to be indolent and careless.

Both far and near and both in developed and in obscure places, they concentrate their efforts on being majestic and sturdy.

Upright, correct, sincere, and loyal, they show constancy in their work.

The virtue of our August Emperor, preserves and settles the far extremes.

Punishes disorder and banishes harm, promotes advantage and attracts prosperity.

The practice of economy accords with the seasons, and all creation abounds.

The black-headed people are at peace, and do not employ
　　armour and weapons.

Relations care for each other, and there are absolutely no bandits
　　or robbers.

Joyful recipients of the teachings, they completely understand
　　the framework of the law.

The area within the six directions, is the August Emperor's land.

To the west it crosses the shifting sands, and in the south takes
　　in the whole of the north-facing households.

In the east there is the eastern sea, and to the north it extends
　　beyond Daxia.

Wherever human footsteps reach, there are none who are not his
　　subjects.

His achievements surpass those of the Five Emperors, and his
　　beneficence even extends to cattle and horses.

No one does not receive the benefit of his virtue, and
　　everyone is at peace in his dwelling-place.

*** *** ***

…he flew into a great rage and said: 'Previously I collected together the writings of all under Heaven and got rid of all which were useless. I called together all the scholars and magicians, an extremely large gathering, intending to promote an era of great peace by this means, and the magicians I intended to pick out to go in search of strange elixirs. Now I hear that Han Zhong has left and not made a report, and the expenses of Xu Shi and his colleagues may be reckoned in millions, but they have totally failed to obtain elixirs, and it is only the charges of corruption they make against each other which I hear of daily. I was extremely generous in the honours and gifts I bestowed on Master Lu and the others, but now they even slander me so as to emphasize the fact that I am not virtuous. I have had people investigate all the scholars who are in Xianyang, and some have been fabricating weird rumours in order to confuse the black-headed people.'

Thereupon he made the Imperial Secretary investigate all the scholars, who were reported to have informed on each other; but in fact, although they tried to exonerate themselves, more than 460 who had infringed the prohibitions were all buried alive at Xianyang, and the whole Empire was made to know about this to serve as a warning for the future. And increasingly people were banished to the frontiers. Fusu, the eldest son of the First Emperor, remonstrated and said: 'All under Heaven has only just been restored to order and the black-headed people in the distant regions have not yet been brought together, and all the scholars sing the praises of Master Kong and adopt him as a model, but now the Supreme One restrains them all by emphasizing the law, and your servant is afraid that all under Heaven will not be at peace. It is up to the Supreme One to investigate this.' The First Emperor was angry, and he made Fusu go north and act as inspector of Meng Tian in the Shang province.

In the thirty-sixth year Mars was stationed in the mansion of the Heart. There was a meteor which fell in the Dong province, and when it reached the earth it turned into a stone, and someone among the black-headed people inscribed the stone concerned with the words: 'When the First Emperor dies, the land will be divided up.' When the First Emperor heard this, he sent the Imperial Secretary to investigate and, when nobody confessed, all those who lived near the stone were taken and condemned to death, and as a consequence the stone concerned was destroyed by burning.

The First Emperor was not happy, and he made the scholars of broad learning compose poems about immortals and true beings and also on wherever in the Empire he went on his travels, and musicians were instructed to sing and play them.…

Questions:

1. Judging from his own words and standards, what did the Emperor set as China's most pressing priorities?
2. What was the reason behind, and what were the results of, the Emperor's investigation of scholars?
3. What light does this episode, and that of the meteor, shed on the Emperor's character and personality?

PART 3
Early Civilization in South Asia

3.1 Rig Veda

Most religions, whether they have their origin in the Far East, the Middle East, or in the Western Hemisphere, contain creation "myths." The term, "myth," however, can be misleading. It should not be taken to imply that these accounts are simply "fairy stories," lacking any kind of rational foundation. On the contrary, they represent the attempts made by their originators to give answers to some of the most profound questions that we can ask, such as, How did the universe come into being? and How and when were human beings created? Such questions are still pertinent today; even though science has made great strides in providing explanations of them, the answers to the most fundamental of them still remain shrouded in mystery.

This book contains a number of creation myths, taken from various cultures throughout the world. Most of them are quite detailed and elaborate. An exception is the short poem that follows. It is taken from the Rig Veda, a large collection of religious poems sacred to the early period of Indian Hinduism. Because the poem was handed down by oral tradition long before being written, the time of its original composition is not known. However, it is believed to date from around 1000 to 900 B.C. The poem has been included in this book for a special reason. Although it offers what is a variation on a standard theme of creation myths, even in its short length it contains lines that set it apart from all of the others, giving it a level of intellectual sophistication that is impressive by any standards.

Source: Trans. A. Kaegi and R. Arrowsmith. Hymm X:129. The title has been added.

SONG OF CREATION

. . .

Then there was neither being nor not-being.
The atmosphere was not, nor sky above it.
What covered all? and where? by what protected?
Was there the fathomless abyss of waters?

Then neither death nor deathlessness existed;
Of day and night there was yet no distinction.
Alone that One breathed calmly, self-supported,
Other than It was none, nor aught above It.

Darkness there was at first in darkness hidden;
This universe was undistinguished water.
That which in void and emptiness lay hidden
Alone by power of fervor was developed.

Then for the first time there arose desire,
Which was the primal germ of mind, within it.
And sages, searching in their heart, discovered
In Nothing the connecting bond of Being.

And straight across their cord was then extended:
What then was there above? or what beneath it?
Life giving principles and powers existed;
Below the origin,—the striving upward.

Who is it knows? Who here can tell us surely
From what and how this universe has risen?
And whether not till after it the gods lived?
Who then can know from what it has arisen?

The source from which this universe has risen
And whether it was made, or uncreated,
He only knows, who from the highest heaven
Rules, the all-seeing lord.—or does not He know?

Questions:
1. How is the creation of the world explained in this text?
2. What role do gods or a God play in creation?

3.2   Bhagavad Gita: Hinduism

The Bhagavad Gita ("The Song of God"), the best-known work of Indian Hinduism, dates from about the same time as the Christian gospels, or perhaps a bit earlier. Although not considered by Hindus to be a direct revelation to humans from the gods, like the earlier Vedas, it is accepted nevertheless as being of divine origin. In it can be found statements of most Hindu religious beliefs; these are set in the context of a poetic story of a great battle being fought between warring noble factions. Among the many cults that fall within the broad expanse of Hinduism, the Bhagavad Gita represents in particular that of the hero-god Krishna, who appears as one of the central characters in the drama.

While accepting the main religious beliefs of the Hindu tradition, but decrying its excessive ritualism, the Bhagavad Gita makes some significant shifts in emphasis from earlier texts. It modifies the idea that, since the phenomenal world and the life we live are both unreal, the individual should divorce himself from mundane matters to seek union with the supreme Reality. While recognizing the ultimate goal of human life to be escape from endless rebirth through the achievement of Nirvana, it nevertheless maintains that one should participate actively in the affairs of this world, fulfilling the duties of one's station in life. But, in doing so one must strive for selfless action, or action for its own sake, without yearning for the results to which such action will lead. At the same time the Bhagavad Gita accepts two other paths to salvation than that of selfless action. One is the way of knowledge, or a recognition that Reality is one and spiritual rather than material. The other is the way of devotion, or belief in a personal God with whom one can have communion and, ultimately, union.

The background to the discussion of Hinduism in the Bhagavad Gita is worthy of note. The setting of the poem is sometime near the beginning of the first millennium B.C. Two armies are drawn up for a decisive battle. The commander of one, Prince Arjuna, takes a ride in his chariot before the battle begins, to survey the opposing hosts. To his dismay he sights many of his kinsmen in the enemy ranks, so, reluctant to wage war against them, he asks his chariot-driver, Krishna, what he ought to do. His driver, however, is no ordinary mortal but Lord Krishna, a god who has here taken on human form. He begins by telling Arjuna that he must fight and then explains why he must do so. Then, in answer to a series of further questions that Arjuna puts to him, he elaborates the basic principles of Hinduism.

Source: Trans E. Arnold

BHAGAVAD GITA

ARJUNA: How can I, in the battle, shoot with shafts
On Bhishma, or on Drona-O thou Chief!-
Both worshipful, both honourable men?

Better to live on beggar's bread
        With those we love alive,
Than taste their blood in rich feasts spread

And guiltily survive!
Ah! were it worse-who knows?-to be Victor or vanquished here,
When those confront us angrily
     Whose death leaves living drear?
In pity lost, by doubtings tossed,
     My thoughts-distracted-turn
To Thee, the Guide I reverence most,
     That I may counsel learn:
I know not what would heal the grief Burned into soul and
     sense,
If I were earth's unchallenged chief-
     A god-and these gone thence!
SANJAYA: So spake Aijuna to the Lord of Hearts,
And sighing, "I will not fight!" held silence then.
To whom, with tender smile,
While the Prince wept despairing 'twixt those hosts,
Krishna made answer in divinest verse:

KRISHNA: Thou grievest where no grief should be! thou
     speak'st
Words lacking wisdom! for the wise in heart
Mourn not for those that live, nor those that die.
Nor I, nor thou, nor any one of these,
Ever was not, nor ever will not be,
For ever and for ever afterwards.
All, that doth live, lives always! To man's frame
As there come infancy and youth and age,
So come there raising-up and layings—down
Of other and of other life-abodes,
Which the wise know, and fear not. This that irks—
Thy sense-life thrilling to the elements—
Bringing thee heat and cold, sorrows and joys,
'Tis brief and mutable! Bear with it, Prince!
As the wise bear. The soul which is not moved,
The soul that with a strong and constant calm
Takes sorrow and takes joy indifferently,
Lives in the life undying! That which is
Can never cease to be; that which is not
Will not exist. To see this truth of both
Is theirs who part essence from accident,
Substance from shadow. Indestructible,
Learn thou! the Life is, spreading life through all;
It cannot anywhere, by any means,
Be anywise diminished, stayed, or changed.
But for these fleeting frames which it informs
With spirit deathless, endless, infinite,
They perish. Let them perish, Prince!
     and fight!

     . . .

Specious, but wrongful deem
The speech of those ill-taught ones who extol
The letter of their Vedas, saying, "This
Is all we have, or need;" being weak at heart
With wants, seekers of Heaven: which comes—they say–
As "fruit of good deeds done;" promising men

Much profit in new births for works of faith;
In various rites abounding; following whereon
Large merit shall accrue towards wealth and power;
Albeit, who wealth and power do most desire
Least fixity of soul have such, least hold
On heavenly meditation. Much these teach,
From Vedas, concerning the "three qualities;"
Free of the "pairs of opposites," and free
From that sad righteousness which calculates;
Self-ruled, Arjuna! simple, satisfied!
Look! like as when a tank pours water forth
To suit all needs, so do these Brahmans draw
Texts for all wants from tank of Holy Writ
But thou, want not! ask not! Find full reward
Of doing right in right! Let right deeds be
Thy motive, not the fruit which comes from them.

• • •

ARJUNA: What is his mark who hath that steadfast heart,
Confirmed in holy meditation? How
Know we his speech, Kesava? Sits he, moves he
Like other men?

KRISHNA: When one, O Pritha's Son!—
Abandoning desires which shake the mind–
Finds in his soul full comfort for his soul,
He hath attained the Yog—that man is such!
In sorrows not dejected, and in joys
Not overjoyed; dwelling outside the stress
Of passion, fear, and anger; fixed in calms
Of lofty contemplation;-such an one
Is Muni, is the Sage, the true Recluse!
He, who to none and nowhere overbound
By ties of flesh, takes evil things and good
Neither desponding nor exulting, such
Bears wisdom's plainest mark! He who shall draw,
As the wise tortoise draws its four feet safe
Under its shield, his five frail senses back
Under the spirit's buckler from the world
Which else assails them, such an one, my Prince!
Hath wisdom's mark! Things that solicit sense
Hold off from the self-governed; nay, it comes,
The appetites of him who lives beyond
Depart,—aroused no more. Yet may it chance,
O Son of Kuntil that a governed mind
Shall some time feel the sense-storms sweep, and wrest
Strong self-control by the roots. Let him regain
His kingdom! let him conquer this, and sit
On Me intent. That man alone is wise
Who keeps the mastery of himself. If one
Ponders on objects of the sense, there springs
Attraction; from attraction grows desire
Desire flames to fierce passion, passion breeds
Recklessness; then the memory-all betrayed-
Lets noble purpose go, and saps the mind,
Till purpose, mind, and man are all undone.

But, if one deals with objects of the sense
Not loving and not hating, making them
Serve his free soul, which rests serenely lord,
Lo! such a man comes to tranquillity;
And out of that tranquillity shall rise
The end and healing of his earthly pains,
Since the will governed sets the soul at peace.
The soul of the ungoverned is not his,
Nor hath he knowledge of himself; which lacked
How grows serenity? and, wanting that,
Whence shall he hope for happiness?
                                    The mind
That gives itself to follow shows of sense
Seeth its helm of wisdom rent away,
And, like a ship in waves of whirlwind, drives
To wreck and death. Only with him, great Prince!
Whose senses are not swayed by things of sense
Only with him who holds his mastery,
Shows wisdom perfect. What is midnight-gloom
To unenlightened souls shines wakeful day
To his clear gaze; what seems as wakeful day
Is known for night, thick night of ignorance,
To his true-seeing eyes. Such is the Saint!
And like the ocean, day by day receiving
    Floods from all lands, which never overflows;
Its boundary-line not leaping, and not leaving,
Fed by the rivers, but unswelled by those;—
So is the perfect one! to his soul's ocean
    The world of sense pours streams of witchery;
They leave him as they find, without commotion,
    Taking their tribute, but remaining free.
Yea! whoso, shaking off the yoke of flesh
Lives lord, not servant, of his lusts; set free
From pride, from passion, from the sin of "Self,"
Toucheth tranquillity! O Pritha's Son!
That is the state of Brahm! There rests no dread
When that last step is reached! Live where he will,
Die when he may, such passeth from all 'plaining,
To blest Nirvana, with the Gods, attaining.

                        • • •

ARJUNA: Yet, Krishna! at the one time thou dost laud
Surcease of works, and, at another time,
Service through work. Of these twain plainly tell
Which is the better way?

KRISHNA: To cease from works
Is well, and to do works in holiness
Is well; and both conduct to bliss supreme;
But of these twain the better way is his
Who working piously refraineth not.

That is the true Renouncer, firm and fixed,
Who-seeking nought, rejecting nought-dwells proof
Against the "opposites."[1]
      O valiant Prince!
In doing, such breaks lightly from all deed:
'Tis the new scholar talks as they were two,
This Sankhya and this Yoga: wise men know
Who husbands one plucks golden fruit of both!
The region of high rest which Sankhyans reach
Yogins attain. Who sees these twain as one
Sees with clear eyes! Yet such abstraction, Chief
Is hard to win without much holiness.
Whoso is fixed in holiness, self-ruled,
Pure-hearted, lord of senses and of self,
Lost in the common life of all which lives—
A "Yogayukt"—he is a Saint who wends
Straightway to Brahm. Such an one is not touched
By taint of deeds. "Nought of myself I do!"
Thus will he think—who holds the truth of truths—
In seeing, hearing, touching, smelling; when
He eats, or goes, or breathes; slumbers or talks,
Holds fast or loosens, opes his eyes or shuts;
Always assured "This is the sense—world plays
With senses." He that acts in thought of Brahm,
Detaching end from act, with act content,
The world of sense can no more stain his soul
Than waters mar th' enamelled lotus—leaf.
With life, with heart, with mind,—nay, with the help
Of all five senses—letting selfhood go—
Yogins toil ever towards their souls' release.
Such votaries, renouncing fruit of deeds,
Gain endless peace: the unvowed, the passion—bound,
Seeking a fruit from works, are fastened down.
The embodied sage, withdrawn within his soul,
At every act sits godlike in "the town
Which hath nine gateways,"[2] neither doing aught
Nor causing any deed. This world's Lord makes
Neither the work, nor passion for the work,
Nor lust for fruit of work; the man's own self
Pushes to these!

        . . .

The world is overcome—aye! even here!
By such as fix their faith on Unity.
The sinless Brahma dwells in Unity,
And they in Brahma. Be not over—glad
Attaining joy, and be not over—sad
Encountering grief, but, stayed on Brahma, still
Constant let each abide! The sage whose soul
Holds off from outer contacts, in himself
Finds bliss; to Brahma joined by piety,
His spirit tastes eternal peace. The joys
Springing from sense—life are but quickening wombs
Which breed sure griefs: those joys begin and end!
The wise mind takes no pleasure, Kunti's Son!
In such as those! But if a man shall learn,

Even while he lives and bears his body's chain,
To master lust and anger, he is blest!
He is the *Yukta*; he hath happiness,
Contentment, light, within: his life is merged
In Brahma's life; he doth Nirvana touch!
Thus go the Rishis unto rest, who dwell
With sins effaced, with doubts at end, with hearts
Governed and calm. Glad in all good they live,
Nigh to the peace of God; and all those live
Who pass their days exempt from greed and wrath,
Subduing self and senses, knowing the Soul!

The Saint who shuts outside his placid soul
All touch of sense, letting no contact through;
Whose quiet eyes gaze straight from fixed brows,
Whose outward breath and inward breath are drawn
Equal and slow through nostrils still and close;
That one—with organs, heart, and mind constrained,
Bent on deliverance, having put away
Passion, and fear, and rage;—hath, even now,
Obtained deliverance, ever and ever freed.
Yea! for he knows Me Who am He that heeds
The sacrifice and worship, God revealed;
And He who heeds not, being Lord of Worlds,
Lover of all that lives, God unrevealed,
Wherein who will shall find surety and shield!

. . .

               Sequestered should he sit,
Steadfastly meditating, solitary,
His thoughts controlled, his passions laid away,
Quit of belongings. In a fair, still spot
Having his fixed abode,—not too much raised,
Nor yet too low,—let him abide, his goods
A cloth, a deerskin, and the Kusa—grass.
There, setting hard his mind upon The One,
Restraining heart and senses, silent, calm,
Let him accomplish Yoga, and achieve
Pureness of soul, holding immovable
Body and neck and head, his gaze absorbed
Upon his nose—end, rapt from all around,
Tranquil in spirit, free of fear, intent
Upon his Brahmacharya vow, devout,
Musing on Me, lost in the thought of Me.
That Yojin, so devoted, so controlled,
Comes to the peace beyond,—My peace, the peace
Of high Nirvana!
                    But for earthly needs
Religion is not his who too much fasts
Or too much feasts, nor his who sleeps away
An idle mind; nor his who wears to waste
His strength in vigils. Nay, Arjuna! call
That the true piety which most removes
Earth—aches and ills, where one is moderate

In eating and in resting, and in sport;

78

Measured in wish and act; sleeping betimes,
Waking betimes for duty.

                      When the man,
So living, centres on his soul the thought
Straitly restrained—untouched internally
By stress of sense—then is he *Yukta*. See!
Steadfast a lamp burns sheltered from the wind;
Such is the likeness of the Yogi's mind
Shut from sense—storms and burning bright to Heaven.
When mind broods placid, soothed with holy wont;
When Self contemplates self, and in itself
Hath comfort; when it knows the nameless joy
Beyond all scope of sense, revealed to soul—
Only to soul! and, knowing, wavers not,
True to the farther Truth; when, holding this,
It deems no other treasure comparable,
But, harboured there, cannot be stirred or shook
By any gravest grief, call that state "peace",
That happy severance Yoga; call that man
The perfect Yogin!

                      Steadfastly the will
Must toil thereto, till efforts end in ease,
And thought has passed from thinking.
     Shaking off
All longings bred by dreams of fame and gain,
Shutting the doorways of the senses close
With watchful ward; so, step by step, it comes
To gift of peace assured and heart assuaged,
When the mind dwells self-wrapped, and the soul broods
Cumberless. But, as often as the heart
Breaks—wild and wavering—from control, so oft
Let him re—curb it, let him rein it back
To the soul's governance; for perfect bliss
Grows only in the bosom tranquillised,
The spirit passionless, purged from offence,
Vowed to the Infinite. He who thus vows
His soul to the Supreme Soul, quitting sin,
Passes unhindered to the endless bliss
Of unity with Brahma.

           . . .

ARJUNA: And what road goeth he who, having faith,
Fails, Krishna! in the striving; falling back
From holiness, missing the perfect rule?
Is he not lost, straying from Brahma's light,
Like the vain cloud, which floats 'twixt earth and heaven
When lightning splits it, and it vanisheth?
Fain would I hear thee answer me herein,
Since, Krishna! none save thou can clear the doubt.

KRISHNA: He is not lost, thou Son of Pritha! No!
Nor earth, nor heaven is forfeit, even for him,
Because no heart that holds one right desire
Treadeth the road of loss! He who should fail,
Desiring righteousness, cometh at death
Unto the Region of the Just; dwells there

79

Measureless years, and being born anew,
Beginneth life again in some fair home
Amid the mild and happy. It may chance
He doth descend into a Yogin house
On Virtue's breast; but that is rare! Such birth
Is hard to be obtained on this earth, Chief
So hath he back again what heights of heart
He did achieve, and so he strives anew
To perfectness, with better hope, dear Prince!
For by the old desire he is drawn on
Unwittingly; and only to desire
The purity of Yoga is to pass
Beyond the *Sabdabrahm*, the spoken Ved.
But, being Yogi, striving strong and long,
Purged from transgressions, perfected by births
Following on births, he plants his feet at last
Upon the farther path. Such an one ranks
Above ascetics, higher than the wise,
Beyond achievers of vast deeds!

. . .

Learn now, dear Prince! how, if thy soul be set
Ever on Me—still exercising Yog,
Still making Me thy Refuge—thou shalt come
Most surely unto perfect hold of Me.
I will declare to thee that utmost lore,
Whole and particular, which, when thou knowest,
Leaveth no more to know here in this world.

Of many thousand mortals, one, perchance,
Striveth for Truth; and of those few that strive—
Nay, and rise high—one only—here and there—
Knoweth Me, as I am, the very Truth.

Earth, water, flame, air, ether, life, and mind,
And individuality—those eight
Make up the showing of Me, Manifest.

These be my lower Nature; learn the higher,
Whereby, thou Valiant One! this Universe
Is, by its principle of life, produced;
Whereby the worlds of visible things are born
As from a *Yoni*. Know! I am that womb:
I make and I unmake this Universe:
Than me there is no other Master, Prince!
No other Maker! All these hang on me
As hangs a row of pearls upon its string.
I am the fresh taste of the water; I
The silver of the moon, the gold o' the sun,
The word of worship in the Veds, the thrill
That passeth in the ether, and the strength
Of man's shed seed. I am the good sweet smell
Of the moistened earth, I am the fire's red light,
The vital air moving in all which moves,
The holiness of hallowed souls, the root
Undying, whence hath sprung whatever is;

The wisdom of the wise, the intellect
Of the informed, the greatness of the great,
The splendour of the splendid. Kunti's Son!
These am I, free from passion and desire;
Yet am I right desire in all who yearn,
Chief of the Bharatas! for all those moods,
Soothfast, or passionate, or ignorant,
Which Nature frames, deduce from me; but all
Are merged in me—not I in them!

. . .

ARJUNA: Who is that BRAHMA? What that Soul of Souls,
The ADHYATMAN? What, Thou Best of All!
Thy work, the KARMA? Tell me what it is
Thou namest ADHIBHUTA? What again
Means ADHIDAIVA? Yea, and how it comes
Thou canst be ADHLYAJNA in thy flesh?
Slayer of Madhu! Further, make me know
How good men find thee in the hour of death?

KRISHNA: I BRAHMA am! the One Eternal God
And ADHYATMAN is My Being's name,
The Soul of Souls! What goeth forth from Me,
Causing all life to live, is KARMA called:
And, Manifested in divided forms,
I am the ADHIBHUTA, Lord of Lives;
And ADHIDAIVA, Lord of all the Gods,
Because I am PURUSHA, who begets.
And ADHIYAJNA, Lord of Sacrifice,
I—speaking with thee in this body here—
Am, thou embodied one! (for all the shrines
Flame unto Me!) And, at the hour of death,
He that hath meditated Me alone,
In putting off his flesh, comes forth to Me,
Enters into My Being—doubt thou not!
But, if he meditated otherwise
At hour of death, in putting off the flesh,
He goes to what he looked for, Kunti's Son!
Because the Soul is fashioned to its like.

Have Me, then, in thy heart always! and fight!
Thou too, when heart and mind are fixed on Me,
Shalt surely come to Me!

. . .

By Me the whole vast Universe of things
Is spread abroad;—by Me, the Unmanifest!
In Me are all existences contained;
Not I in them!

Yet they are not contained,
Those visible things! Receive and strive to embrace
The mystery majestical! My Being—
Creating all, sustaining all—still dwells
Outside of all!

See! as the shoreless airs
Move in the measureless space, but are not space,
[And space were space without the moving airs];
So all things are in Me, but are not I.

At closing of each Kalpa, Indian Prince!
All things which be back to My Being come:
At the beginning of each Kalpa, all
Issue new-born from Me.
By Energy And help of Prakriti, my outer Self,
Again, and yet again, I make go forth
The realms of visible things—without their will—
All of them—by the power of Prakriti.
Yet these great makings, Prince! involve Me not,
Enchain Me not! I sit apart from them,
Other, and Higher, and Free; nowise attached!

Thus doth the stuff of worlds, moulded by Me,
Bring forth all that which is, moving or still,
Living or lifeless! Thus the worlds go on!
The minds untaught mistake Me, veiled in form;—
Naught see they of My secret Presence, nought
Of My hid Nature, ruling all which lives.
Vain hopes pursuing, vain deeds doing; fed
On vainest knowledge, senselessly they seek
An evil way, the way of brutes and fiends.
But My Mahatmas, those of noble soul
Who tread the path celestial, worship Me
With hearts unwandering,—knowing Me the Source,
Th' Eternal Source, of Life. Unendingly
They glorify Me; seek Me; keep their vows
Of reverence and love, with changeless faith
Adoring Me. Yea, and those too adore,
Who, offering sacrifice of wakened hearts,
Have sense of one pervading Spirit's stress,
One Force in every place, though manifold!
I am the Sacrifice! I am the Prayer!
I am the Funeral—Cake set for the dead!
I am the healing herb! I am the ghee,
The Mantra, and the flame, and that which burns!
I am—of all this boundless Universe—
The Father, Mother, Ancestor, and Guard!
The end of Learning! That which purifies
In lustral water! I am OM! I am
Rig-Veda, Sama-Veda, Yajur-Ved;
The Way, the Fosterer, the Lord, the Judge,
The Witness; the Abode, the Refuge-House,
The Friend, the Fountain and the Sea of Life
Which sends, and swallows up; Treasure of Worlds

And Treasure—Chamber! Seed and Seed—Sower,
Whence endless harvests spring! Sun's heat is mine;
Heaven's rain is mine to grant or to withhold;
Death am I, and Immortal Life I am, Arjuna!

. . .

But to those blessed ones who worship Me,
Turning not otherwise, with minds set fast,
I bring assurance of full bliss beyond.

Nay, and of hearts which follow other gods
In simple faith, their prayers arise to me,
O Kunti's Son! though they pray wrongfully;
For I am the Receiver and the Lord
Of every sacrifice, which these know not
Rightfully; so they fall to earth again!
Who follow gods go to their gods; who vow
Their souls to Pitris go to Pitris; minds
To evil Bhuts given o'er sink to the Bhuts;
And whoso loveth Me cometh to Me.

. . .

KRISHNA: So be it! Kuru Prince! I will to thee unfold
Some portions of My Majesty, whose powers are manifold!
I am the Spirit seated deep in every creature's heart;
From Me they come; by Me they live; at My word they depart!
Vishnu of the Adityas I am, those Lords of Light;
Maritchi of the Maruts, the Kings of Storm and Blight;
By day I gleam, the golden Sun of burning cloudless Noon;
By Night, amid the asterisms I glide, the dappled Moon!
Of Vedas I am Sama—Veda, of gods in Indra's Heaven
Vasava; of the faculties to living beings given
The mind which apprehends and thinks; of Rudras Sankara;
Of Yakshas and of Rakshasas, Vittesh; and Pavaka
Of Vasus, and of mountain-peaks Meru; Vrihas-Pati
Know Me 'mid planetary Powers; 'mid Warriors heavenly
Skanda; of all the water—floods the Sea which drinketh each,
And Bhrigu of the holy Saints, and OM of sacred speech;
Of prayers the prayer ye whisper; of hills Him-ala's snow,
And Aswattha, the fig—tree, of all the trees that grow;
Of the Devarshis, Narada; and Chitrarath of them
That sing in Heaven, and Kapila of Munis, and the gem
Of flying steeds, Uchehaisravas, from Amrit—wave which burst;
Of elephants Airavata; of males the Best and First;
Of weapons Heav'n's hot thunderbolt; of cows white
       Kamadhuk,
From whose great milky udder—teats all hearts' desires are
       strook;
Vasuki of the serpent—tribes, round Mandara en—twined;
And thousand—fanged Ananta, on whose broad coils reclined
Leans Vishnu; and of water—things Varuna; Aryam
Of Pitris, and, of those that judge, Yama the Judge I am;
Of Daityas dread Prahlada; of what metes days and years,

Time's self I am; of woodland—beasts— buffaloes, deers,
    and bears—
The lordly—painted tiger, of birds the vast Garud,
The whirlwind 'mid the winds; 'mid chiefs Rama with blood
    imbrued,
Makar 'mid fishes of the sea, and Ganges 'mid the streams;
Yea! First, and Last, and Centre of all which is or seems
I am, Arjuna! Wisdom Supreme of what is wise,
Words on the uttering lips I am, and eyesight of the eyes,
And "A" of written characters, Dwandwa of knitted speech,
And Endless Life, and boundless Love, whose power sustaineth
    each;
And bitter Death which seizes all, and joyous sudden Birth,
Which brings to light all beings that are to be on earth;
And of the viewless virtues, Fame, Fortune, Song am I,
And Memory, and Patience; and Craft, and Constancy:
Of Vedic hymns the Vrihatsam, of metres Gayatri,
Of months the Margasirsha, of all the seasons three
The flower—wreathed Spring; in dicer's—play the conquering
    Double—Eight;
The splendour of the splendid, and the greatness of the great,
Victory I am, and Action! and the goodness of the good,
And Vasudev of Vrishni's race, and of this Pandu brood
Thyself.—Yea, my Arjuna! thyself; for thou art Mine!
Of poets Usana, of saints Vyasa, sage divine;
The policy of conquerors, the potency of kings,
The great unbroken silence in learning's secret things;
The lore of all the learned, the seed of all which springs.
Living or lifeless, still or stirred, whatever beings be,
None of them is in all the worlds, but it exists by Me!
Nor tongue can tell, Arjuna! nor end of telling come
Of these My boundless glories, whereof I teach thee some;
For wheresoe'er is wondrous work, and majesty, and might,
From Me hath all proceeded. Receive thou this aright!
Yet how shouldst thou receive, O Prince! the vastness of this
    word?
I, who am all, and made it all, abide its separate Lord!

      . . .

ARJUNA: Lord! of the men who serve Thee—true in heart—
As God revealed; and of the men who serve,
Worshipping Thee Unrevealed, Unbodied, Far,
Which take the better way of faith and life?

KRISHNA: Whoever serve Me—as I show Myself—
Constantly true, in full devotion fixed,
Those hold I very holy. But who serve— Worshipping Me The
    One, The Invisible,
The Unrevealed, Unnamed, Unthinkable,
Uttermost, All—pervading, Highest, Sure—
Who thus adore Me, mastering their sense,
Of one set mind to all, glad in all good,
These blessed souls come unto Me.

                        Yet, hard
The travail is for such as bend their minds
To reach th' Unmanifest. That viewless path

Shall scarce be trod by man bearing the flesh!
But whereso any doeth all his deeds
Renouncing self for Me, full of Me, fixed
To serve only the Highest, night and day
Musing on Me—him will I swiftly lift
Forth from life's ocean of distress and death,
Whose soul clings fast to Me. Cling thou to Me!
Clasp Me with heart and mind! so shalt thou dwell
Surely with Me on high. But if thy thought
Droops from such height; if thou be'st weak to set
Body and soul upon Me constantly,
Despair not! give Me lower service! seek
To reach Me, worshipping with steadfast will;
And, if thou canst not worship steadfastly,
Work for Me, toil in works pleasing to Me!
For he that laboureth right for love of Me
Shall finally attain! But, if in this
Thy faint heart fails, bring Me thy failure! find
Refuge in Me! let fruits of labour go,
Renouncing hope for Me, with lowliest heart,
So shalt thou come; for, though to know is more
Than diligence, yet worship better is
Than knowing, and renouncing better still.
Near to renunciation—very near—
Dwelleth Eternal Peace!

                           Who hateth nought
Of all which lives, living himself benign,
Compassionate, from arrogance exempt,
Exempt from love of self, unchangeable
By good or ill; patient, contented, firm
In faith, mastering himself, true to his word,
Seeking Me, heart and soul; vowed unto Me,—
That man I love! Who troubleth not his kind,
And is not troubled by them; clear of wrath,
Living too high for gladness, grief, or fear,
That man I love! Who, dwelling quiet—eyed,
Stainless, serene, well—balanced, unperplexed,
Working with Me, yet from all works detached,
That man I love! Who, fixed in faith on Me,
Dotes upon none, scorns none; rejoices not,
And grieves not, letting good or evil hap
Light when it will, and when it will depart,
That man I love! Who, unto friend and foe
Keeping an equal heart, with equal mind
Bears shame and glory; with an equal peace
Takes heat and cold, pleasure and pain; abides
Quit of desires, hears praise or calumny
In passionless restraint, unmoved by each;
Linked by no ties to earth, steadfast in Me,
That man I love! But most of all I love
Those happy ones to whom 'tis life to live
In single fervid faith and love unseeing,
Drinking the blessed Amrit of my Being!

ARJUNA: Now would I hear, O gracious Kesava!
Of Life which seems, and Soul beyond, which sees,
And what it is we know—or think to know.

KRISHNA: Yea! Son of Kunti! for this flesh ye see
Is *Kshetra*, is the field where Life disports;
And that which views and knows it is the Soul,
Kshetrajna. In all "fields," thou Indian prince!
I am *Kshetrajna*. I am what surveys!
Only that knowledge knows which knows the known
By the knower! What it is, that "field" of life,
What qualities it hath, and whence it is,
And why it changeth, and the faculty
That wotteth it, the mightiness of this,
And how it wotteth—hear these things from Me!

The elements, the conscious life, the mind,
The unseen vital force, the nine strange gates
Of the body, and the five domains of sense;
Desire, dislike, pleasure and pain, and thought
Deep—woven, and persistency of being;
These all are wrought on Matter by the Soul!

Humbleness, truthfulness, and harmlessness,
Patience and honour, reverence for the wise,
Purity, constancy, control of self,
Contempt of sense—delights, self-sacrifice,
Perception of the certitude of ill
In birth, death, age, disease, suffering, and sin;
Detachment, lightly holding unto home,
Children, and wife, and all that bindeth men;
An ever—tranquil heart in fortunes good
And fortunes evil, with a will set firm
To worship Me—Me only! ceasing not;
Loving all solitudes, and shunning noise
Of foolish crowds; endeavours resolute
To reach perception of the Utmost Soul,
And grace to understand what gain it were
So to attain,—this is true Wisdom, Prince!
And what is otherwise is ignorance!

Now will I speak of knowledge best to know—
That Truth which giveth man Amrit to drink,
The Truth of HIM, the Para-Brahm, the All,
The Uncreated; not *Asat*, not *Sat*,
Not Form, nor the Unformed; yet both, and more;—
Whose hands are everywhere, and everywhere
Planted His feet, and everywhere His eyes
Beholding, and His ears in every place
Hearing, and all His faces everywhere
Enlightening and encompassing His worlds.
Glorified in the senses He hath given,
Yet beyond sense He is; sustaining all,
Yet dwells He unattached: of forms and modes
Master, yet neither form nor mode hath He;
He is within all beings—and without—
Motionless, yet still moving; not discerned

For subtlety of instant presence; close
To all, to each; yet measurelessly far!
Not manifold, and yet subsisting still
In all which lives; for ever to be known
As the Sustainer, yet, at the End of Times,
He maketh all to end—and re-creates.
The Light of Lights He is, in the heart of the Dark
Shining eternally. Wisdom He is
And Wisdom's way, and Guide of all the wise,
Planted in every heart.

                             So have I told
Of Life's stuff, and the moulding, and the lore
To comprehend. Whoso, adoring Me,
Perceiveth this, shall surely come to Me!

Know thou that Nature and the Spirit both
Have no beginning! Know that qualities
And changes of them are by Nature wrought;
That Nature puts to work the acting frame,
But Spirit doth inform it, and so cause
Feeling of pain and pleasure. Spirit, linked
To moulded matter, entereth into bond
With qualities by Nature framed, and, thus
Married to matter, breeds the birth again
In good or evil yonis.[3]

                             Yet is this—
Yea! in its bodily prison!—Spirit pure.
Spirit supreme; surveying, governing,
Guarding, possessing; Lord and Master still
PURUSHA, Ultimate, One Soul with Me.

Whoso thus knows himself, and knows his soul
PURUSHA working through the qualities
With Nature's modes, the light hath come for him!
Whatever flesh he bears, never again
Shall he take on its load. Some few there be
By meditation find the Soul in Self
Self-schooled; and some by long philosophy
And holy life reach thither; some by works:
Some, never so attaining, hear of light
From other lips, and seize, and cleave to it
Worshipping; yea! and those—to teaching true—
Overpass Death!

         . . .

                           For in this world
Being is twofold: the Divided, one;
The Undivided, one. All things that live
Are "the Divided." That which sits apart,
"The Undivided."

---

[3] Wombs.

                              Higher still is He,
The Highest, holding all, whose Name is LORD,
The Eternal, Sovereign, First! Who fills all worlds,
Sustaining them. And —dwelling thus beyond
Divided Being and Undivided—I
Am called of men and Vedas, Life Supreme,
The PURUSHOTTAMA.

                              Who knows Me thus,
With mind unclouded, knoweth all, dear Prince!
And with his whole soul ever worshippeth Me.

Now is the sacred, secret Mystery
Declared to thee! Who comprehendeth this
Hath wisdom!

KRISHNA: Fearlessness, singleness of soul, the will
Always to strive for wisdom; opened hand
And governed appetites; and piety,
And love of lonely study; humbleness,
Uprightness, heed to injure nought which lives,
Truthfulness, slowness unto wrath, a mind
That lightly letteth go what others prize;
And equanimity, and charity
Which spieth no man's faults; and tenderness
Towards all that suffer; a contended heart,
Fluttered by no desires; a bearing mild,
Modest, and grave, with manhood nobly mixed,
With patience, fortitude, and purity;
An unrevengeful spirit, never given
To rate itself too high;—such be the signs,
O Indian Prince! of him whose feet are set
On that fair path which leads to heavenly birth!

Deceitfulness, and arrogance, and pride,
Quickness to anger, harsh and evil speech,
And ignorance, to its own darkness blind,—
These be the signs, My Prince! of him whose birth
Is fated for the regions of the vile.

The Heavenly Birth brings to deliverance,
So should'st thou know! The birth with Asuras
Brings into bondage. Be thou joyous, Prince!
Whose lot is set apart for heavenly Birth.

Two stamps there are marked on all living men,
Divine and Undivine; I spake to thee
By what marks thou shouldst know the Heavenly Man,
Hear from me now of the Unheavenly!

They comprehend not, the Unheavenly,
How Souls go forth from Me; nor how they come
Back unto Me: nor is there Truth in these,
Nor purity, nor rule of Life. "This world
Hath not a Law, nor Order, nor a Lord,"
So say they: "nor hath risen up by Cause
Following on Cause, in perfect purposing,

But is none other than a House of Lust."
And, this thing thinking, all those ruined ones—
Of little wit, dark-minded—give themselves
To evil deeds, the curses of their kind.
Surrendered to desires insatiable,
Full of deceitfulness, folly, and pride,
In blindness cleaving to their errors, caught
Into the sinful course, they trust this lie
As it were true—this lie which leads to death—
Finding in Pleasure all the good which is,
And crying "Here it finisheth!"

Ensnared

In nooses of a hundred idle hopes,
Slaves to their passion and their wrath, they buy
Wealth with base deeds, to glut hot appetites;
"Thus much, to-day," they say, "we gained! thereby
Such and such wish of heart shall have its fill;
And this is ours! and th' other shall be ours!
To-day we slew a foe, and we will slay
Our other enemy to-morrow! Look!
Are we not lords? Make we not goodly cheer?
Is not our fortune famous, brave, and great?
Rich are we, proudly born! What other men
Live like to us? Kill, then, for sacrifice!
Cast largesse, and be merry!" So they speak
Darkened by ignorance; and so they fall—
Tossed to and fro with projects, tricked, and bound
In net of black delusion, lost in lusts—
Down to foul Naraka. Conceited, fond,
Stubborn and proud, dead-drunken with the wine
Of wealth, and reckless, all their offerings
Have but a show of reverence, being not made
In piety of ancient faith. Thus vowed
To self-hood, force, insolence, feasting, wrath,
These My blasphemers, in the forms they wear
And in the forms they breed, my foemen are,
Hateful and hating; cruel, evil, vile,
Lowest and least of men, whom I cast down
Again, and yet again, at end of lives,
Into some devilish womb, whence—birth by birth—
The devilish wombs re-spawn them, all beguiled;
And, till they find and worship Me, sweet Prince!
Tread they that Nether Road.

The Doors of Hell

Are threefold, whereby men to ruin pass,—
The door of Lust, the door of Wrath, the door
Of Avarice. Let a man shun those three!

. . .

Whoso performeth-diligent, content—
The work allotted him, whate'er it be,
Lays hold of perfectness! Hear how a man
Findeth perfection, being so content:
He findeth it through worship— wrought by work—

Of HIM that is the Source of all which lives,
Of HIM by Whom the universe was stretched.

Better thine own work is, though done with fault,
Than doing others' work, ev'n excellently.
He shall not fall in sin who fronts the task
Set him by Nature's hand! Let no man leave
His natural duty, Prince! though it bear blame!
For every work hath blame, as every flame
Is wrapped in smoke! Only that man attains
Perfect surcease of work whose work was
With mind unfettered, soul wholly subdued
Desires forever dead, results renounced.

Learn from me, Son of Kunti! also this,
How one, attaining perfect peace, attains
BRAHM, the supreme, the highest height of all!

Devoted—with a heart grown pure, restrained
In lordly self-control, foregoing wiles
Of song and senses, freed from love and hate,
Dwelling 'mid solitudes, in diet spare,
With body, speech, and will tamed to obey,
Ever to holy meditation vowed,
From passions liberate, quit of the Self,
Of arrogance, impatience, anger, pride;
Freed from surroundings, quiet, lacking nought—
Such an one grows to oneness with the BRAHM;
Such an one, growing one with BRAHM, serene,
Sorrows no more, desires no more; his soul,
Equally loving all that lives, loves well
Me, Who have made them, and attains to Me.
By this same love and worship doth he know
Me as I am, how high and wonderful,
And knowing, straightway enters into Me.
And whatsoever deeds he doeth—fixed
In Me, as in his refuge—he hath won
Forever and forever by My grace
Th' Eternal Rest!

Questions:
1. Summarize Krishna's advice to the prince.
2. Does the Bhagavad Gita mandate one code of ethical behavior for all people or different ones for different castes?

3.3 The Foundation of the Kingdom of Righteousness

Buddhism owes its origin to the career of one person-Siddhartha Gautama (563?–483? B.C.), who later came to be called the Buddha (the "Enlightened One"). Buddhism spread throughout the rest of Asia, and beyond, to become one of history's great world religions.

Gautama, the founder of Buddhism, was born in northern India, the son of a local chieftain. Although innumerable legends have grown up about him, the facts apparently are that, as a young man, he became disillusioned with life, as he was living it, and decided to seek salvation through enlightenment. He pursued his goal (it is said for six years), first through philosophical meditation and then through asceticism and the mortification of his body. But neither method produced the result he sought. Finally, in desperation, he sat down under a fig tree (later famous as the "Bo-tree") and reviewed his past, unsuccessful endeavors. There the realization struck him that his efforts must be self-defeating because they were the result of his own desires. From this it followed that he must abandon desires altogether, if he was to gain true peace of mind and blessedness. Here was his great enlightenment; he became the Buddha.

Gautama spent the remainder of his life teaching, preaching, and organizing his growing band of disciples. Each initiate of the Buddhist order subscribed to the following confession: "I take refuge in the Buddha, I take refuge in the Law of Truth, I take refuge in the Order."

Source: Trans. T. W. Rhys Davids.

Reverence to the Blessed One, the Holy One, the Fully-Enlightened One.

Thus have I heard. The Blessed One was once staying at Benares, at the hermitage called Migadaya. And there the Blessed One addressed the company of the five Bhikkhus (monks), and said:

'There are two extremes, O Bhikkhus, which the man who has given up the world ought not to follow—the habitual practice, on the one hand, of those things whose attraction depends upon the passions, and especially of sensuality—a low and pagan way (of seeking satisfaction) unworthy, unprofitable, and fit only for the worldly-minded—and the habitual practice, on the other hand, of asceticism (or self-mortification), which is painful, unworthy, and unprofitable.

'There is a middle path, O Bhikkhus, avoiding these two extremes, discovered by the Tathâgata [Buddha]—a path which opens the eyes, and bestows understanding, which leads to peace of mind, to the higher wisdom, to full enlightenment, to Nirvana.

'What is that middle path, O Bhikkhus, avoiding these two extremes, discovered by the Tathâgata—that path which opens the eyes, and bestows understanding, which leads to peace of mind, to the higher wisdom, to full enlightenment, to Nirvana? Verily! It is this noble eightfold path; that is to say:

'Right views;
Right aspirations;
Right speech;
Right conduct;
Right livelihood;
Right effort;
Right mindfulness; and
Right contemplation.

'This, O Bhikkhus, is that middle path, avoiding these two extremes, discovered by the Tathâgata—that path which opens the eyes, and bestows understanding, which leads to peace of mind, to the higher wisdom, to full enlightenment, to Nirvana.

'Now this, O Bhikkhus, is the noble truth concerning suffering.

'Birth is attended with pain, decay is painful, disease is painful, death is painful. Union with the unpleasant is painful, painful is separation from the pleasant; and any craving that is unsatisfied, that too is painful. In brief, the five aggregates which spring from attachment (the conditions of individuality and their cause) are painful.

'This then, O Bhikkhus, is the noble truth concerning suffering.

'Now this, O Bhikkhus, is the noble truth concerning the origin of suffering.

'Verily, it is that thirst (or craving), causing the renewal of existence, accompanied by sensual delight, seeking satisfaction now here, now there—that is to say, the craving for the gratification of the passions, or the craving for (a future) life, or the craving for success (in this present life).

'This then, O Bhikkhus, is the noble truth concerning the origin of suffering.

'Now this, O Bhikkhus, is the noble truth concerning the destruction of suffering.

'Verily, it is the destruction, in which no passion remains, of this very thirst; the laying aside of, the getting rid of, the being free from, the harbouring no longer of this thirst.

'This then, O Bhikkhus, is the noble truth concerning the destruction of suffering.

'Now this, O Bhikkhus, is the noble truth concerning the way which leads to the destruction of sorrow. Verily! It is the noble eightfold path.'

Question:
1. According to Buddha, what is the essential problem of human existence? What is the solution?

3.4 Dhammapada: Buddhism

This selection, according to tradition, repeats the words of the Buddha himself. The title may be translated in a variety of ways; a good rendition is The Path of Virtue. The work itself consists mainly of a discussion of Buddhist morality; its main goal is to draw distinctions between an evil and a good way of life. More particularly, the author instructs novices in the requirements they must fulfill to become worthy Buddhist monks, wearing "the yellow gown."

Source: Trans. F. Max Müller.

DHAMMAPADA

CHAPTER I

The Twin Verses

All that we are is the result of what we have thought: it is founded on our thoughts, it is made up of our thoughts. If a man speaks or acts with an evil thought . . . , pain follows him, as the wheel follows the foot of the ox that draws the carriage.

All that we are is the result of what we have thought: it is founded on our thoughts, it is made up of our thoughts. If a man speaks or acts with a pure thought, happiness follows him, like a shadow that never leaves him.

'He abused me, he beat me, he defeated me, he robbed me,'—in those who harbour such thoughts hatred will never cease.

'He abused me, he beat me, he defeated me, he robbed me,'—in those who do not harbour such thoughts hatred will cease.

For hatred does not cease by hatred at any time: hatred ceases by love, this is an old rule.

The world does not know that we must all come to an end here;—but those who know it, their quarrels cease at once.

He who lives looking for pleasures only, his senses uncontrolled, immoderate in his food, idle, and weak, Mâra (the tempter) will certainly overthrow him, as the wind throws down a weak tree.

He who lives without looking for pleasures, his senses well controlled, moderate in his food, faithful and strong, him Mâra will certainly not overthrow, any more than the wind throws down a rocky mountain.

He who wishes to put on the yellow dress without having cleansed himself from sin, who disregards also temperance and truth, is unworthy of the yellow dress.

But he who has cleansed himself from sin, is well grounded in all virtues, and regards also temperance and truth, he is indeed worthy of the yellow dress.

They who imagine truth in untruth, and see untruth in truth, never arrive at truth, but follow vain desires.

They who know truth in truth, and untruth in untruth, arrive at truth, and follow true desires.

As rain breaks through an illthatched house, passion will break through an unreflecting mind.

As rain does not break through a well—thatched house, passion will not break through a well—reflecting mind.

The evil—doer mourns in this world, and he mourns in the next; he mourns in both. He mourns and suffers when he sees the evil of his own work.

The virtuous man delights in this world, and he delights in the next; he delights in both. He delights and rejoices, when he sees the purity of his own work.

The evil—doer suffers in this world, and he suffers in the next; he suffers in both. He suffers when he thinks of the evil he has done; he suffers more when going on the evil path.

The virtuous man is happy in this world, and he is happy in the next; he is happy in both. He is happy when he thinks of the good he has done; he is still more happy when going on the good path.

The thoughtless man, even if he can recite a large portion (of the law), but is not a doer of it, has no share in the priesthood, but is like a cowherd counting the cows of others.

The follower of the law, even if he can recite only a small portion (of the law), but, having forsaken passion and hatred and foolishness, possesses true knowledge and serenity of mind, he, caring for nothing in this world or that to come, has indeed a share in the priesthood.

CHAPTER III

Thought

As a fletcher makes straight his arrow, a wise man makes straight his trembling and unsteady thought, which is difficult to guard, difficult to hold back,

As a fish taken from his watery home and thrown on the dry ground, our thought trembles all over in order to escape the dominion of Mâra (the tempter).

It is good to tame the mind, which is difficult to hold in and flighty, rushing wherever it listeth; a tamed mind brings happiness.

Let the wise man guard his thoughts, for they are difficult to perceive, very artful, and they rush wherever they list: thoughts well guarded bring happiness.

Those who bridle their mind which travels far, moves about alone, is without a body, and hides in the chamber (of the heart), will be free from the bonds of Mâra (the tempter).

If a man's thoughts are unsteady, if he does not know the true law, if his peace of mind is troubled, his knowledge will never be perfect.

If a man's thoughts are not dissipated, if his mind is not perplexed, if he has ceased to think of good or evil, then there is no fear for him while he is watchful.

Knowing that this body is (fragile) like a jar, and making this thought firm like a fortress, one should attack Mâra (the tempter) with the weapon of knowledge, one should watch him when conquered, and should never rest.

Before long, alas! this body will lie on the earth, despised, without understanding, like a useless log.

Whatever a hater may do to a hater, or an enemy to an enemy, a wrongly directed mind will do us greater mischief.

Not a mother, not a father will do so much, nor any other relative; a well—directed mind will do us greater service.

CHAPTER V

The Fool

Long is the night to him who is awake; long is a mile to him who is tired; long is life to the foolish who do not know the true law.

If a traveller does not meet with one who is his better, or his equal, let him firmly keep to his solitary journey; there is no companionship with a fool.

'These sons belong to me, and this wealth belongs to me,' with such thoughts a fool is tormented. He himself does not belong to himself; how much less sons and wealth?

The fool who knows his foolishness, is wise at least so far. But a fool who thinks himself wise, he is called a fool indeed.

If a fool be associated with a wise man even all his life, he will perceive the truth as little as a spoon perceives the taste of soup.

If an intelligent man be associated for one minute only with a wise man, he will soon perceive the truth, as the tongue perceives the taste of soup.

Fools of little understanding have themselves for their greatest enemies, for they do evil deeds which must bear bitter fruits.

That deed is not well done of which a man must repent, and the reward of which he receives crying and with a tearful face.

No, that deed is well done of which a man does not repent, and the reward of which he receives gladly and cheerfully.

As long as the evil deed done does not bear fruit, the fool thinks it is like honey: but when it ripens, then the fool suffers grief.

Let a fool month after month eat his food (like an ascetic) with the tip of a blade of Kusa grass, yet is he not worth the sixteenth particle of those who have well weighed the law.

An evil deed, like newly drawn milk, does not turn (suddenly); smouldering, like fire covered by ashes, it follows the fool.

• • •

93

CHAPTER VI

The Wise Man

If you see an intelligent man who tells you where true treasures are to be found, who shows what is to be avoided, and administers reproofs, follow that wise man; it will be better, not worse, for those who follow him.

Let him admonish, let him teach, let him forbid what is improper!—he will be beloved of the good, by the bad he will be hated.

Do not have evil—doers for friends, do not have low people for friends: have virtuous people for friends, have for friends the best of men.

He who drinks in the law lives happily with a serene mind: the sage rejoices always in the law, as preached by the elect (Ariyas).

Well—makers lead the water (wherever they like); fletchers bend the arrow; carpenters bend a log of wood; wise people fashion themselves.

As a solid rock is not shaken by the wind, wise people falter not amidst blame and praise.

Wise people, after they have listened to the laws, become serene, like a deep, smooth, and still lake.

Good people walk on whatever befall, the good do not prattle, longing for pleasure; whether touched by happiness or sorrow wise people never appear elated or depressed.

If, whether for his own sake, or for the sake of others, a man wishes neither for a son, nor for wealth, nor for lordship, and if he does not wish for his own success by unfair means, then he is good, wise, and virtuous.

. . .

CHAPTER IX

Evil

If a man would hasten towards the good, he should keep his thought away from evil; if a man does what is good slothfully, his mind delights in evil.

If a man commits a sin, let him not do it again; let him not delight in sin: pain is the outcome of evil.

If a man does what is good, let him do it again; let him delight in it: happiness is the outcome of good.

Even an evil—doer sees happiness as long as his evil deed has not ripened; but when his evil deed has ripened, then does the evil—doer see evil.

Even a good man sees evil days, as long as his good deed has not ripened; but when his good deed has ripened, then does the good man see happy days.

Let no man think lightly of evil, saying in his heart, It will not come nigh unto me. Even by the falling of water—drops a water—pot is filled; the fool becomes full of evil, even if he gather it little by little.

Let no man think lightly of good, saying in his heart. It will not come nigh unto me. Even by the falling of water—drops a water—pot is filled; the wise man becomes full of good, even if he gather it little by little.

Let a man avoid evil deeds, as a merchant, if he has few companions and carries much wealth, avoids a dangerous road; as a man who loves life avoids poison.

He who has no wound on has hand, may touch poison with his hand; poison does not affect one who has no wound; nor is there evil for one who does not commit evil.

If a man offend a harmless, pure, and innocent person, the evil falls back upon that fool, like light dust thrown up against the wind.

Some people are born again; evildoers go to hell; righteous people go to heaven; those who are free from all worldly desires attain Nirvana.

. . .

CHAPTER XIII

The World

Do not follow the evil law! Do not live on in thoughtlessness! Do not follow false doctrine! Be not a friend of the world.

Rouse thyself! do not be idle! Follow the law of virtue! The virtuous rests in bliss in this world and in the next.

Follow the law of virtue; do not follow that of sin. The virtuous rests in bliss in this world and in the next.

Look upon the world as a bubble, look upon it as a mirage: the king of death does not see him who thus looks down upon the world.

Come, look at this glittering world, like unto a royal chariot; the foolish are immersed in it, but the wise do not touch it.

He who formerly was reckless and afterwards became sober, brightens up this world, like the moon when freed from clouds.

He whose evil deeds are covered by good deeds, brightens up this world, like the moon when freed from clouds.

This world is dark, few only can see here; a few only go to heaven, like birds escaped from the net.

The swans go on the path of the sun, they go through the ether by means of their miraculous power; the wise are led out of this world, when they have conquered Mâra and his train.

If a man has transgressed one law, and speaks lies, and scoffs at another world, there is no evil he will not do.

The uncharitable do not go to the world of the gods; fools only do not praise liberality; a wise man rejoices in liberality, and through it becomes blessed in the other world.

Better than sovereignty over the earth, better than going to heaven, better than lordship over all worlds, is the reward of the first step in holiness.

. . .

CHAPTER XIV

The Buddha

He whose conquest is not conquered again, into whose conquest no one in this world enters, by what track can you lead him, the Awakened, the Omniscient, the trackless?

He whom no desire with its snares and poisons can lead astray, by what track can you lead him, the Awakened, the Omniscient, the trackless?

Even the gods envy those who are awakened and not forgetful, who are given to meditation, who are wise, and who delight in the repose of retirement (from the world).

Difficult (to obtain) is the conception of men, difficult is the life of mortals, difficult is the hearing of the True Law, difficult is the birth of the Awakened (the attainment of Buddhahood).

Not to commit any sin, to do good, and to purify one's mind, that is the teaching of (all) the Awakened.

The Awakened call patience the highest penance, long—suffering the highest Nirvana; for he is not an anchorite who strikes others, he is not an ascetic who insults others.

Not to blame, not to strike, to live restrained under the law, to be moderate in eating, to sleep and sit alone, and to dwell on the highest thoughts,—this is the teaching of the Awakened.

There is no satisfying lusts, even by a shower of gold pieces; he who knows that lusts have a short taste and cause pain, he is wise;

Even in heavenly pleasures he finds no satisfaction, the disciple who is fully awakened delights only in the destruction of all desires.

Men, driven by fear, go to many a refuge, to mountains and forests, to groves and sacred trees.

But that is not a safe refuge, that is not the best refuge; a man is not delivered from all pains after having gone to that refuge.

He who takes refuge with Buddha, the Law, and the Church; he who, with clear understanding, sees the four holy truths:—

Viz, pain, the origin of pain, the destruction of pain, and the eightfold holy way that leads to the quieting of pain;—

That is the safe refuge, that is the best refuge; having gone to that refuge, a man is delivered from all pain.

A supernatural person (a Buddha) is not easily found, he is not born everywhere. Wherever such a sage is born, that race prospers.

Happy is the arising of the awakened, happy is the teaching of the True Law, happy is peace in the church, happy is the devotion of those who are at peace.

He who pays homage to those who deserve homage, whether the awakened (Buddha) or their disciples, those who have overcome the host (of evils), and crossed the flood of sorrow, he who pays homage to such as have found deliverance and know no fear, his merit can never be measured by anybody.

. . .

CHAPTER XVI

Pleasure

He who gives himself to vanity, and does not give himself to meditation, forgetting the real aim (of life) and grasping at pleasure, will in time envy him who has exerted himself in meditation.

Let no man ever look for what is pleasant, or what is unpleasant. Not to see what is pleasant is pain, and it is pain to see what is unpleasant.

Let, therefore, no man love anything; loss of the beloved is evil. Those who love nothing, and hate nothing, have no fetters.

From pleasure comes grief, from pleasure comes fear; he who is free from pleasure knows neither grief nor fear.

From affection comes grief, from affection comes fear; he who is free from affection knows neither grief nor fear.

From lust comes grief, from lust comes fear; he who is free from lust knows neither grief nor fear.

From love comes grief, from love comes fear; he who is free from love knows neither grief nor fear.

From greed comes grief, from greed comes fear; he who is free from greed knows neither grief nor fear.

He who possesses virtue and intelligence, who is just, speaks the truth, and does what is his own business, him the world will hold dear.

. . .

CHAPTER XVII

Anger

Let a man leave anger, let him forsake pride, let him overcome all bondage! No sufferings befall the man who is not attached to name and form, and who calls nothing his own.

He who holds back rising anger like a rolling chariot, him I call a real driver; other people are but holding the reins.

Let a man overcome anger by love, let him overcome evil by good; let him overcome the greedy by liberality, the liar by truth!

Speak the truth, do not yield to anger; give, if thou art asked for little; by these three steps thou wilt go near the gods.

The sages who injure nobody, and who always control their body, they will go to the unchangeable place (Nirvana), where, if they have gone, they will suffer no more.

Those who are ever watchful, who study day and night, and who strive after Nirvana their passions will come to an end.

This is an old saying, O Atula, this is not only of to—day: 'They blame him who sits silent, they blame him who speaks much, they also blame him who says little; there is no one on earth who is not blamed.'

There never was, there never will be, nor is there now, a man who is always blamed, or a man who is always praised.

But he whom those who discriminate praise continually day after day, as without blemish, wise, rich in knowledge and virtue, who would dare to blame him like a coin made of gold from the Gambû river? Even the gods praise him, he is praised even by Brahman.

Beware of bodily anger, and control thy body! Leave the sins of the body, and with thy body practise virtue!

Beware of the anger of the tongue, and control thy tongue! Leave the sins of the tongue, and practise virtue with thy tongue!

Beware of the anger of the mind, and control thy mind! Leave the sins of the mind, and practise virtue with they mind!

The wise who control their body, who control their tongue, the wise who control their mind, are indeed well controlled.

. . .

CHAPTER XVIII

Impurity

Thou art now like a sere leaf, the messengers of death have come near to thee; thou standest at the door of thy departure, and thou hast no provision for thy journey.

Make thyself an island, work hard, be wise! When thy impurities are blown away, and thou art free from guilt, thou wilt enter into the heavenly world of the elect.

Thy life has come to an end, thou art come near to death, there is no resting—place for thee on the road, and thou hast no provision for thy journey.

Make thyself an island, work hard, be wise! When thy impurities are blown away, and thou art free from guilt, thou wilt not enter again into birth and decay.

Let a wise man blow off the impurities of his self, as a smith blows off the impurities of silver, one by one, little by little, and from time to time.

As the impurity which springs from the iron, when it springs from it, destroys it; thus do a transgressor s own works lead him to the evil path.

The taint of prayers is non-repetition; the taint of houses, non-repair; the taint of the body is sloth; the taint of a watchman, thoughtlessness.

Bad conduct is the taint of woman, greediness the taint of a benefactor; tainted are all evil ways, in this world and in the next.

But there is a taint worse than all taints,—ignorance is the greatest taint. O mendicants! throw off that taint, and become taintless!

Life is easy to live for a man who is without shame, a crow hero, a mischief—maker, an insulting, bold, and wretched fellow.

But life is hard to live for a modest man, who always looks for what is pure, who is disinterested, quiet, spotless, and intelligent.

He who destroys life, who speaks untruth, who in this world takes what is not given him, who goes to another man's wife;

And the man who gives himself to drinking intoxicating liquors, he, even in this world, digs up his own root.

O man, know this, that the unrestrained are in a bad state; take care that greediness and vice do not bring thee to grief for a long time!

The world gives according to their faith or according to their pleasure: if a man frets about the food and the drink given to others, he will find no rest either by day or by night.

He in whom that feeling is destroyed, and taken out with the very root, finds rest by day and by night.

There is no fire like passion, there is no shark like hatred, there is no snare like folly, there is no torrent like greed.

The fault of others is easily perceived, but that of oneself is difficult to perceive; a man winnows his neighbour's faults like chaff, but his own fault he hides, as a cheat hides the bad die from the gambler.

· · ·

CHAPTER XXII

The Downward Course

He who says what is not, goes to hell; he also who, having done a thing, says I have not done it. After death both are equal, they are men with evil deeds in the next world.

Many men whose shoulders are covered with the yellow gown are ill—conditioned and unrestrained; such evil—doers by their evil deeds go to hell.

Better it would be to swallow a heated iron ball, like flaring fire, than that a bad unrestrained fellow should live on the charity of the land.

Four things does a reckless man gain who covets his neighbour's wife,—a bad reputation, an uncomfortable bed, thirdly, punishment, and lastly, hell.

There is bad reputation, and the evil way (to hell), there is the short pleasure of the frightened in the arms of the frightened, and the king imposes heavy punishment; therefore let no man think of his neighbour's wife.

As a grass—blade, if badly grasped, cuts the arm, badly—practised asceticism leads to hell.

An act carelessly performed, a broken vow, and hesitating obedience to discipline, all this brings no great reward.

If anything is to be done, let a man do it, let him attack it vigorously! A careless pilgrim only scatters the dust of his passions more widely.

An evil deed is better left undone, for a man repents of it afterwards; a good deed is better done, for having done it, one does not repent.

Like a well—guarded frontier fort, with defences within and without, so let a man guard himself. Not a moment should escape, for they who allow the right moment to pass, suffer pain when they are in hell.

They who are ashamed of what they ought not to be ashamed of, and are not ashamed of what they ought to be ashamed of, such men, embracing false doctrines, enter the evil path.

They who fear when they ought not to fear, and fear not when they ought to fear, such men, embracing false doctrines, enter the evil path.

They who forbid when there is nothing to be forbidden, and forbid not when there is something to be forbidden, such men, embracing false doctrines, enter the evil path.

They who know what is forbidden as forbidden, and what is not forbidden as not forbidden, such men, embracing the true doctrine, enter the good path.

· · ·

CHAPTER XXIV

Thirst

The thirst of a thoughtless man grows like a creeper; he runs from life to life, like a monkey seeking fruit in the forest.

Whomsoever this fierce thirst overcomes, full of poison, in this world, his sufferings increase like the abounding Bîrana grass.

He who overcomes this fierce thirst, difficult to be conquered in this world, sufferings fall off from him, like water—drops from a lotus leaf.

This salutary word I tell you, 'Do ye, as many as are here assembled, dig up the root of thirst, as he who wants the sweet-scented Usîra root must dig up the Bîrana grass, that Mâra (the tempter) may not crush you again and again, as the stream crushes the reeds.'

As a tree, even though it has been cut down, is firm so long as its root is safe, and grows again, thus, unless the feeders of thirst are destroyed, this pain (of life) will return again and again.

He whose thirst running towards pleasure is exceeding strong in the thirty-six channels, the waves will carry away that misguided man, viz, his desires which are set on passion.

The channels run everywhere, the creeper (of passion) stands sprouting; if you see the creeper springing up, cut its root by means of knowledge.

A creature's pleasures are extravagant and luxurious; sunk in lust and looking for pleasure, men undergo (again and again) birth and decay.

Men, driven on by thirst, run about like a snared hare; held in fetters and bonds, they undergo pain for a long time, again and again.

Men, driven on by thirst, run about like a snared hare; let therefore the mendicant drive out thirst, by striving after passionlessness for himself.

He who having got rid of the forest (of lust) (i.e. after having reached Nirvana) gives himself over to forest—life (i.e. to lust), and who, when removed from the forest (i.e. from lust), runs to the forest (i.e. to lust), look at that man! though free, he runs into bondage.

Wise people do not call that a strong fetter which is made of iron, wood, or hemp; far stronger is the care for precious stones and rings, for sons and a wife.

That fetter wise people call strong which drags down, yields, but is difficult to undo; after having cut this at last, people leave the world, free from cares, and leaving desires and pleasures behind.

Those who are slaves to passions, run down with the stream (of desires), as a spider runs down the web which he has made himself; when they have cut this, at last, wise people leave the world, free from cares, leaving all affection behind.

Give up what is before, give up what is behind, give up what is in the middle, when thou goest to the other shore of existence; if thy mind is altogether free, thou wilt not again enter into birth and decay.

If a man is tossed about by doubts, full of strong passions, and yearning only for what is delightful, his thirst will grow more and more, and he will indeed make his fetters strong.If a man delights in quieting doubts, and, always reflecting, dwells on what is not delightful (the impurity of the body, etc.), he certainly will remove, nay, he will cut the fetter of Mâra.

He who has reached the consummation, who does not tremble, who is without thirst and without sin, he has broken all the thorns of life: this will be his last body.

Questions:
1. *What traits to the good— and evil—doer share? Do these similar traits lead to similar results?*
2. *According to Buddha, what is the most beneficial type of companionship? The least?*
3. *Who is a fool's worst enemy?*

3.5 Mahavira: The "Great Hero" of the Jain Religion

As Hinduism became more legalistic and written codes like "Apastamba" reinforced the tendency towards tranforming the faith into a vehicle for perpetuating a rigid social system, there were inevitable reactions against it. One of the earliest and most effective of these was Jainism, founded by Vardhamana Mahavira (c. 540–468 B.C.E), a holy man who is reputed to have wandered for 12 years, observing isolation from human society until he attained spiritual enlightenment. Jain precepts stress nonviolence, vegetarianism, austerity, fasting, and self-denial.

Source: Hermann Jacobi, *Sacred Books of the East* (Oxford:1884, pp. 85–87. Quoted in Mircea Eliade *From Medicine Men to Muhammad* (N.Y: Harper & Row,1974), pp. 43–45.

I. 3. For a year and a month he did not leave off his robe. Since that time the Venerable One, giving up his robe, was a naked, world—relinquishing, houseless (sage).

4. Then he meditated (walking) with his eye fixed on a square space before him of the length of a man. Many people assembled, shocked at the sight; they struck him and cried.

5. Knowing (and renouncing) the female sex in mixed gathering places, he meditated, finding his way himself: I do not lead a worldly life.

6. Giving up the company of all householders whomsoever, he meditated. Asked, he gave no answer; he went and did not transgress the right path.

7. For some it is not easy (to do what he did), not to answer those who salute; he was beaten with sticks, and struck by sinful people....

10. For more than a couple of years he led a religious life without using cold water; he realized singleness, guarded his body, had got intuition, and was calm.

11. Thoroughly knowing the earth-bodies and water-bodies and fire-bodies and wind-bodies, the lichens, seeds, and sprouts,

12. He comprehended that they are, if narrowly inspected, imbued with life, and avoided to injure them; he, the Great Hero.

13. The immovable (beings) are changed to movable ones, and the movable beings to immovable ones; beings which are born in all states become individually sinners by their actions.

14. The Venerable One understands thus: he who is under the conditions (of existenece), that fool suffers pain. Thoroughly knowing (karman), the Venerable One avoids sin.

15. The sage, perceiving the double (karman), proclaims the incomparable activity, he, knowing one; knowing the current of worldliness, the current of sinfulness, and the impulse.

16. Practising the sinless abstinence from killing, he did no acts, neither himself nor with the assistance of others; he to whom woman were known as the causes of all sinful acts, he saw (the true sate of the world)....

III. 7. Ceasing to use the stick (i.e. cruelty) against living beings, abandoning the care of the body, the houseless (Mahāvīa), the Venerable One, endures the thorns of the villages (i.e. the abusive language of the peasants), (being) perfectly enlightened.

8. As an elephant at the head of the battle, so was Mahāvīa victorious. Sometimes he did not reach a village there in Ladha.

9. When he who is free from desires approached the village, the inhabitants met him on the outside, and attacked him, saying, 'Get away from here.'

10. He was struck with a stick, the fist. a lance, hit with a fruit, a clod, a potsherd. Beating him again and again, many cried.

11. When he once (sat) without moving his body, they cut his flesh, tore his hair under pains, or covered him with dust.

12. Throwing him up, they let him fall, or disturbed him in his religious postures; abandoning the care of his body. the Venerable One humbled himself and bore pain, free from desire.

13. As a hero at the head of the battle is surrounded on all sides, so was there Mahāvīa. Bearing all hardships, the Venerable One, undisturbed, proceeded (on the road to NirvAna)....

IV. 1. The Venerable One was able to abstain from indulgence of the flesh, though never attacked by diseases. Whether wounded or not wounded, he desired not medical treatment.

2. Purgatives and emetics, anointing of the body and bathing, shampooing and cleaning of the teeth do not behove him, after he learned (that the body is something unclean).

3. Being averse from the impressions of the senses, the Brāhmana wandered about, speaking but little. Sometimes in the cold season the Venerable One was meditating in the shade.

4. In summer he exposes himself to the heat, he sits squatting in the sun; he lives on rough (food); rice, pounded jujube, and beans.

5. Using these three, the Venerable One sustained himself eight months. Sometimes the Venerable One did not drink for half a month or even for a month.

6. Or he did not drink for more than two months, or even six months, day and night, without desire (for drink). Sometimes he ate stale food.

7. Sometimes he ate only the sixth meal, or the eighth, the tenth, the twelfth; without desires, persevering in meditation.

8. Having wisdom, Mahāvīa committed no sin himself, nor did he induce other to do so, nor did he consent to the sins of others.

Questions:
1. In what ways might Mahāvīa's behavior have provoked such violent responses in others?
2. What did Mahāvīa's diet consist of while he sought enlightenment?
3. What often occurred when Mahāvīa approached a village?
4. What admirable traits does the writer see in Mahāvīa?

3.6 Asoka: How a Life Was Turned Around

Emperor Asoka (c. 274–232 B.C.E.) was the grandson of the Maurya Dynasty's founder, Chandragupta I and, in his early days, acted in the conventional manner of potentates, always seeking to enlarge his personal power and expand his domains through conquest. The sight of the horrendous slaughter and devastation caused by the Battle of Kalinga, however, brought about a spiritual crisis and a change of heart; thereafter Asoka never waged war and tried to atone for his past actions by governing his subjects in as moral and benevolent a manner as possible. A convert to Buddhism, Asoka has been, on up to this day, considered the role model for successive Indian rulers (kings, prime ministers, etc.). His decrees, sometimes inscribed on stone pillars and rocks, set forth his philosophy of government.

Source: N.A. Nikam & Richard McKeon, trans., *The Edicts of Asoka* (Chicago: University of Chicago Press, 1959), pp. 27–30, 51–52. Quoted in Mircea Eliade, *From Medicine Men to Muhammad* (N.Y.: Harper & Row, 1974), pp. 142–145.

('ROCK EDICT' XIII)

The Kalinga country was conquered by King Priyadarshī, Beloved of the Gods, in the eighth year of his reign. One hundred and fifty thousand persons were carried away captive, one hundred thousand were slain, and many times that number died.

Immediately after the Kalingas had been conquered, King Priyadarshī became intensely devoted to the study of Dharma, to the love of Dharma, and to the inculcation of Dharma.

The Beloved of the Gods, conqueror of the Kalingas, is moved to remorse now. For he has felt profound sorrow and regret because the conquest of a people previously unconquered involves slaughter, death, and deportation.

But there is a more important reason for the King's remorse. The Brāhmanas and Shramanas [the priestly and ascetic orders] as well as the followers of other religions and the householders—who all practised obedience to superiors, parents, and teachers, and proper courtesy and firm devotion to friends, acquaintances, companions, relatives, slaves, and servants—all suffer from the injury, slaughter and deportation inflicted on their loved ones. Even those who escaped calamity themselves are deeply afflicted by the misfortunes suffered by those friends, acquaintances, companions, and relatives for whom they feel an undiminished affection. Thus all men share in the misfortune, and this weighs on King Priyadarshī's mind.

[Moreover, there is no country except that of the Yōnas (that the Greeks) where Brahmin and Buddhist ascetics do not exist] there is no place where men are not attached to one faith or another.

Therefore, even if the number of people who were killed died or who were carried away in the Kalinga war had been only one one-hundredth or one one-thousandth of what it actually was, this would still have weighed on the King's mind.

King Priyadarshi now thinks that even a person who wrongs him must be forgiven for wrongs that can be forgiven.

King Priyadarshi seeks to induce even the forest peoples who have come under his dominion [that is, primitive peoples in the sections of the conquered territory] to adopt this way of life and this ideal. He reminds them, however, that he exercises the power to punish, despite his repentance, in order to induce them to desist from their crimes and escape execution.

For King Priyadarshi desires security, self-control, impartiality, and cheerfulness for all living creatures.

King Priyadarshi considers moral conquest [that is, conquest by Dharma, *Dharma vijaya*] the most important conquest. He has achieved this moral conquest repeatedly both here and among the peoples living beyond the borders of his kingdom, even as far away as six hundred *yojanas* [about three thousand miles], where the YOna [Greek] king Antiyoka rules, and even beyond Antiyoka in the realm of the four kings named Turamaya, Antikini, Maka, and Alikasudara and to the south among the Cholas and Pandyas [in the southern tip of the Indian peninsula] as far as Ceylon.

Here in the King's dominion also, among the Yōnas [inhabitants a northwest frontier province, probably Greeks] and the Kambōjas [neighbours of the Yōnas], among the Nābhakas and Nābhapanktis [who probably lived along the Himalayan frontier], among the Bhojas and Paitryanikas, among the Andhras and Paulindas [all peoples of the Indian peninsula], everywhere people heed his instructions in Dharma.

Even in countries which King Priyadarshi's envoys have not reached, people have heard about Dharma and about his Majesty's ordinances and instructions in Dharma, and they themselves conform to Dharma and will continue to do so.

Wherever conquest is achieved by Dharma, it produces satisfaction. Satisfaction is firmly established by conquest by Dharma [since it generates no opposition of conquered and conqueror]. Even satisfaction, however, is of little importance. King Priyadarshi attaches value ultimately to consequences of action in the other world.

This edict on Dharma has been inscribed so that my sons and great-grandsons who may come after me should not think new conquests worth achieving. If they do conquer, let them take pleasure in moderation and mild punishments. Let them consider moral conquest the only true conquest.

That is good, here and hereafter. Let their pleasure be pleasure in [Dharma-rati]. For this alone is good, here and hereafter.

('ROCK EDICT' XII)

King Priyadarshi honours men of all faith, members of religious orders and laymen alike, with gifts and various marks of esteem. Yet he does not value either gifts or honours as much as growth in the qualities essential to religion in men of all faiths.

This growth may take many forms, but its root is in guarding one's speech to avoid extolling one's own faith and disparaging the faith of others improperly or, when the occasion is appropriate, immoderately.

The faiths of others all deserve to be honoured for one reason or another. By honouring them, one exalts one's own faith and at the same time performs a service to the faith of others. By acting otherwise, one injures one's own faith and also does disservice to that of others. For if a man extols his own faith and disparages another because of devotion to his own and because he wants to glorify it, he seriously injures his own faith.

Therefore concord alone is commendable, for through concord men may learn and respect the conception of Dharma accepted by others.

King Priyadarshi desires men of all faiths to know each other's doctrines and to acquire sound doctrines. Those who are attached to their particular faiths should be told that King Priyadarshi does not value gifts or honours as much as growth in the qualities essential to religion in men of all faiths.

Many officials are assigned to tasks bearing on this purpose—the officers in charge of spreading Dharma, the superintendents of women the royal households, the inspectors of cattle and pasture lands, and other officials.

The objective of these measures is the promotion of each man's particular faith and the glorification of Dharma.

('KALINGA EDICT' II)

King Priyadarshi says:

I command that the following instructions be communicated to my official at Samāpā:

Whenever something right comes to my attention, I want it put into practice and I want effective means devised to achieve it. My principal means to do this is to transmit my instructions to you.

All men are my children. Just as I seek the welfare and happiness of my own children in this world and the next, I seek the same things for all men.

Unconquered peoples along the borders of my dominions may wonder what my disposition is towards them. My only wish with respect to them is that they should not fear me, but trust me; that they should expect only happiness from me, not misery; that they should understand further that I will forgive them for offences which can be forgiven; that they should be induced by my example to practise Dharma; and that they should attain happiness in this world and the next.

I transmit these instructions to you in order to discharge my debt [to them] by instructing you and making known to you my will and my unshakable resolution and commitment. You must perform your duties in this way and establish their confidence in the King, assuring them that he is like a father to them, that he loves them as he loves himself, and that they are like his own children.

Having instructed you and informed you of my will and my unshakable resolution and commitment, I will appoint officials to carry out this programme in all the provinces. You are able to inspire the border peoples with confidence in me and to advance their welfare and happiness in this world and the next. By doing so, you will also attain heaven and help me discharge my debts to the people.

This edict has been inscribed here so that my officials will work at all times to inspire the peoples of neighbouring countries with confidence in me and to induce them to practise Dharma.

Questions:

1. *What reasons does Asoka (Priyadarshi) give for his repentence? How does he propose to deal with the forest peoples?*
2. *Taking an overview based on reading all the edicts presented here, precisely what does Asoka's concept of Dharma seem to entail?*
3. *What rationale does Asoka give for his policy of religious tolerance? What benefits does he see in following such a course?*

3.7   "King Milinda": The Greek World's Incursion Into India

The "King Milinda" of the revered Buddhist scripture "The Questions of King Milinda" was based on the historical Greek King Menender of Bactria (c. 160–135 B.C.E.), whose realm was one of the successor-states to the empire of Alexander the Great. Buddhist tradition asserts that Menander converted to Buddhism after exchanging thought and insights with the monk Negasena.

Source: T.W. Rhys Davids, trans., *The Questions of King Milinda* (Delhi, India: Motiles Banarsidass, 1965, first published by Oxford University Press, 1894), pp. 1–10.

THE SECULAR NARRATIVE

1. King Milinda, at Sâgala the famous town of yore,
To Nâgasena, the world famous sage, repaired.
(So the deep Ganges to the deeper ocean flows.)
To him, the eloquent, the bearer of the torch
Of Truth, dispeller of the darkness of men's minds,
Subtle and knotty questions did he put, many,
Turning on many points. Then were solutions given
Profound in meaning, gaining access to the heart,
Sweet to the ear, and passing wonderful and strange.
For Nâgasena's talk plunged to the hidden depths
Of Vinaya and of Abhidhamma (Law and Thought)
Unravelling all the meshes of the Suttas' net,
Glittering the while with metaphors and reasoning
  high.
Come then! Apply your minds, and let your hearts
  rejoice,
And hearken to these subtle questionings, all grounds
Of doubt well fitted to resolve.

2. Thus hath it, been handed down by tradition—There is in the country of the Yonakasa a great centre of trade, a city that is called Sâgala, situate in a delightful country well watered and hilly, abounding in parks and gardens and groves and lakes and tanks a paradise of rivers and mountains and woods. Wise architects have laid it out, and its people know of no oppression, since all their enemies and adversaries have been put down. Brave is its defence, with many and

various strong towers and ramparts, with superb gates and entrance archways; and with the royal citadel in its midst, white walled and deeply moated. Well laid out are its streets, squares, cross roads, and market places. Well displayed are the innumerable sorts of costly merchandise with which its shops are filled. It is richly adorned with hundreds of alms-halls of various kinds; and splendid with hundreds of thousands of magnificent mansions, which rise aloft like the mountain peaks of the Himalayas. Its streets are filled with elephants, horses, carriages, and foot-passengers, frequented by groups of handsome men and beautiful women, and crowded by men of all sorts and conditions, Brahmans, nobles, artificers, and servants. They resound with cries of welcome to the teachers of every creed, and the city is the resort of the leading men of each of the differing sects. Shops are there for the sale of Benares muslin, of Kotumbara stuffs, and of other cloths of various kinds; and sweet odours are exhaled from the bazaars, where all sorts of flowers and perfumes are tastefully set out. Jewels are there in plenty, such as men's hearts desire, and guilds of traders in all sorts of finery display their goods in the bazaars that face all quarters of the sky. So full is the city of money, and of gold and silver ware, of copper and stone ware, that it is a very mine of dazzling treasures. And there is laid up there much store of property and corn and things of value in warehouses—foods and drinks of every sort, syrups and sweetmeats of every kind. In wealth it rivals Uttara-kuru, and in glory it is as Âlakamandâ, the city of the gods.

3. Having said thus much we must now relate the previous birth history of these two persons (Milinda and Nâgasena) and the various sorts of puzzles. This we shall do under six heads:—

1. Their previous history (Pubba-yoga).
2. The Milinda problems.
3. Questions as to distinguishing characteristics.
4. Puzzles arising out of contradictory statements.
5. Puzzles arising out of ambiguity.
6. Discussions turning on metaphor.

And of these the Milinda problems are in divisions—questions as to distinctive characteristics; and questions aiming at the dispelling of doubt; and the puzzles arising out of contradictory statements are in two divisions—the long chapter, and the problems in the life of the recluse.

THEIR PREVIOUS HISTORY (PUBBA-YOGA).

4. By Pubba-yoga is meant their past Karma (their doings in this or previous lives). Long ago, they say, when Kassapa the Buddha was promulgating the faith, there dwelt in one community near the Ganges a great company of members of the Order. There the brethren, true to established rules and duties, rose early in the morning, and taking the long-handled brooms, would sweep out the courtyard and collect the rubbish into a heap, meditating the while on the virtues of the Buddha.

5. One day a brother told a novice to remove the heap of dust. But he, as if he heard not, went about his business; and on being called a second time, and a third, still went his way as if he had not heard. Then the brother, angry with so intractable a novice, dealt him a blow with the broom stick. This time, not daring to refuse, he set about the task crying; and as he did so he muttered to himself this first aspiration: 'May I, by reason of this meritorious act of throwing out the rubbish, in each successive condition in which I may be born up to the time when I attain Nirvâna, be powerful and glorious as the midday sun!'

6. When he had finished his work he went to the river side to bathe, and on beholding the mighty billows of the Ganges seething and surging, he uttered this second aspiration: 'May I, in each successive condition in which I may be born till I attain Nirvâna, possess the power of saying the right thing, and saying it instantly, under any circumstance that may arise, carrying all before me like this mighty surge!'

7. Now that brother, after he had put the broom away in the broom closet, had likewise wandered down to the river side to bathe, and as he walked he happened to overhear what the novice had said. Then thinking: 'If this fellow, on the ground of such an act of merit, which after all was instigated by me, can harbour hopes like this, what may not I attain to?' he too made his wish, and it was thus: 'In each successive condition in which I may be born till I attain Nirvâna, may I too be ready in saying the right thing at once, and more especially may I have the power of unravelling and of solving each problem and each puzzling question this young man may put—carrying all before me like this mighty surge!'

8. Then for the whole period between one Buddha and the next these two people wandered from existence to existence among gods and men. And our Buddha saw them too, and just as he did to the son of Moggall and to Tissa the Elder, so to them also did he foretell their future fate, saying: 'Five hundred years after I have passed away with these two reappear, and the subtle Law and Doctrine taught by me will they two explain, unravelling and disentangling its difficulties by questions put and metaphors adduced.'

103

9. Of the two the novice became the king of the city of Sâgala in India, Milinda by name, learned eloquent, wise, and able; and a faithful observer, and that at the right time, of all the various acts of devotion and ceremony enjoined by his own sacred hymns concerning things past, present, and to come. Many were the arts and sciences he knew—holy tradition and secular law; the Sânkhya, Yoga, Nyâya, and Vaiseshika systems of philosophy; arithmetic; music; medicine; the four Vedas, the Purânas, and the Itihâsas; astronomy, magic, causation, and spells; the art of war; poetry; conveyancing—in a word, the whole nineteen.

As a disputant he was hard to equal, harder still to overcome; acknowledged superior of all the founders of the schools of thought. And as in wisdom so in strength of body, swiftness, and valour there was none equal to Milinda in all India. He was rich too, mighty in wealth and prosperity, and the number of his armed hosts knew no end.

10. Now one day Milinda the king proceeded forth out of the city to pass in review the innumerable host of his mighty army in its fourfold array (of elephants, cavalry, bowmen, and soldiers on foot). And when the numbering of the forces was over, the king, who was fond of wordy disputation, and eager for discussion with casuists, sophists, and gentry of that sort, looked at the sun (to ascertain the time), and then said to his ministers: 'The day is yet young. What would be the use of getting back to town so early? Is there no learned person, whether wandering teacher or Brahman, the head of some school or order, or the master of some band of pupils (even though he profess faith in the Arahat, the Supreme Buddha), who would be able to talk with me, and resolve my doubts?'

11. Thereupon the five hundred Yonakas said to Milinda the king: 'There are the six Masters, O king!—Pûra*n*a Kassapa, Makkhali of the cowshed, the Niga*nth*a of the Nâta clan, Sa*ñ*gaya the son of the Bela*tth*a woman, Agita of the garment of hair, and Pakudha Ka*kk*âyana. These are well known as famous founders of schools, followed by bands of disciples and hearers, and highly honoured by the people. Go, great king! put to them your problems, and have your doubts resolved.

12. So king Milinda, attended by the five hundred Yonakas, mounted the royal car with its splendid equipage, and went out to the dwelling-place of Pûrana Kassapa, exchanged with him the compliments of friendly greeting, and took his seat courteously apart. And thus sitting he said to him: 'Who is it, venerable Kassapa, who rules the world?'

'The Earth, great king, rules the world!'

'But, venerable Kassapa, if it be the Earth that rules the world, how comes it that some men go to the Avîki hell, thus getting outside the sphere of the Earth?'

When he had thus spoken, neither could Pûrana Kassapa swallow the puzzle, nor could he bring it up; crestfallen, driven to silence, and moody, there he sat.

13. Then Milinda the king said to Makkhali of the cowshed: 'Are there, venerable Gosâla, good and evil acts? Is there such a thing as fruit, ultimate result, of good and evil acts?'

'There are no such acts, O king; and no such fruit, or ultimate result. Those who here in the world are nobles, they, O king, when they go to the other world, will become nobles once more. And those who are Brahmans, or of the middle class, or workpeople, or outcasts here, will in the next world become the same. What then is the use of good or evil acts?'

'If, venerable Gosâla, it be as you say then, by parity of reasoning, those who, here in this world have a hand cut off, must in the next world become persons with a hand cut off, and in like manner those who have had a foot cut off or an ear or their nose!'

And at this saying Makkhali was silenced.

14. Then thought Milinda the king within himself: 'All India is an empty thing, it is verily like chaff! There is no one, either recluse or Brahman capable of discussing things with me, and dispelling my doubts.' And he said to his ministers: 'Beautiful is the night and pleasant! Who is the recluse or Brahman we can visit to-night to question him who will be able to converse with us and dispel our doubts?' And at that saying the counsellors remained silent, and stood there gazing upon the face of the king.

Questions:
1. *What can be gleaned from the description of Sagala that sheds light on the city's economic/commercial life?*
2. *What references might tend to bear out Milinda's Greek education and upbringing, and what traits does Milinda demonstrate that might confirm this?*
3. *In what manner does the author tie in Buddhist spiritual ideas to the story?*

3.8 Fa-Hsien: A Chinese Perspective on Gupta India

A comparative paucity of records is one of the main handicaps confronting anyone who studies Gupta India; written documentation is not extensive. Of the intermittent glimpses we have, one of the most intriguing is the account of the Chinese Buddhist monk Fa-Hsien, who undertook a pilgrimmage to sacred sites connected with the Buddha, and made some passing observations about India itself.

Source: Samuel Beal, trans., *Travels of Fa-Hsien and Sung Yun, Buddhist Pilgrims from China to India* (N.Y.: Augustus M. Kelly, 1967), pp. xxxvi–xxxix.

XIV. After remaining here during two months of winter Fa-hian and two companions went south across the Little Snowy Mountains. The Snowy Mountains, both in summer and winter, are covered (*heaped*) with snow. On the north side of the mountains, in the shade, excessive cold came on suddenly, and all the men were struck mute with dread; Hwui-king alone was unable to proceed onwards. The white froth came from his mouth as he addressed Fa-hian and said, "I too have no power of life left; but whilst there is opportunity, do you press on, lest you all perish." Thus he died. Fa-hian, caressing him, exclaimed in piteous voice, "Our purpose was not to produce fortune!" Submitting, he again exerted himself, and pressing forward, they so crossed the range; on the south side they reached the Lo-i country. In this vicinity there are 3,000 priests, belonging both to the Great and Little Vehicle. Here they kept the rainy season. The season past, descending south and journeying for ten days, they reached the Po-na country, where there are also some 3,000 priests or more, all belonging to the Little Vehicle. From this journeying eastward for three days, they again crossed the Sin-tu river. Both sides of it are now level.

XV. The other side of the river there is a country named Pi-t'u. The law of Buddha is very flourishing; they belong both to the Great and Little Vehicle. When they saw pilgrims from China arrive, they were much affected and spoke thus, "How is it that men from the frontiers are able to know the religion of family-renunciation and come from far to seek the law of Buddha?" They liberally provided necessary entertainment according to the rules of religion.

XVI. Going south-east from this somewhat less than 80 *yôjanas*, we passed very many temples one after another, with some myriad of priests in them. Having passed these places, we arrived at a certain country. This country is called Mo-tu-lo. Once more we followed the Pu-na river. On the sides of the river, both right and left, are twenty *sangdârâmas*, with perhaps 3,000 priests. The law of Buddha is progressing and flourishing. Beyond the deserts are the countries of Western India. The kings of these countries are all firm believers in the law of Buddha. They remove their caps of state when they make offerings to the priests. The members of the royal household and the chief ministers personally direct the food-giving; when the distribution of food is over, they spread a carpet on the ground opposite the chief seat (the president's seat) and sit down before it. They dare not sit on couches in the presence of the priests. The rules relating to the almsgiving of kings have been handed down from the time of Buddha till now. Southward from this is the so-called middle-country (Mâklhyadesa). The climate of this country is warm and equable, without frost or snow. The people are very well off, without polltax or official restrictions. Only those who till the royal lands return a portion of profit of the land. If any desire to go, they go; if they like to stop, they stop. The kings govern without corporal punishment; criminals are fined, according to circumstances, lightly or heavily. Even in eases of repeated rebellion they only cut off the right hand. The king's personal attendants, who guard him on the right and left, have fixed salaries. Throughout the country the people kill no living thing nor drink wine, nor do they eat garlic or onions, with the exception of Chandâlas only. The Chandâlas are named "evil men" and dwell apart from others; if they enter a town or market, they sound a piece of wood in order to separate themselves; then men, knowing who they are, avoid coming in contact with them. In this country they do not keep swine nor fowls, and do not deal in cattle; they have no shambles or wine-shops in their market-places. In selling they use cowrie shells. The Chandâlas only hunt and sell flesh. Down from the time of Buddha's *Nirvâna,* the kings of these countries, the chief men and householders, have raised *vihâras* for the priests, and provided for their support by bestowing on them fields, houses, and gardens, with men and oxen. Engraved title-deeds were prepared and handed down from one reign to another; no one has ventured to withdraw them, so that till now there has been no interruption. All the resident priests having chambers (*in these vihâras*) have their beds, mats, food, drink, and clothes provided without stint; in all places this is the case. The priests ever engage themselves in doing meritorious works for the purpose of religious advancement (*karma*—building up their religious character), or in reciting the scriptures, or in meditation. When a strange priest arrives, the senior priests go out to meet him, carrying for him his clothes and alms-bowl. They offer him water for washing his feet and oil for rubbing them; they provide untimely (*vikâla*) food. Having rested awhile, they again ask him as to his seniority in the priesthood, and according to this they give him a chamber and sleeping materials, arranging everything according to the *dharma.* In places where priests reside they make towers in honour of Sâriputra, of Mudgalaputra, of Ânanda, also in honour of the *Abhidharma, Vinaya,* and *Sûtra.* During a month after the season of rest the most pious families urge a collection for an offering to the priests; they prepare an untimely meal for them, and the priests in a great assembly preach the law. The preaching over, they offer to Sâriputra's tower all kinds of scents and flowers; through the night they burn lamps provided by different persons. Sâriputra originally was a Brâhman; on a certain occasion he went to Buddha and requested ordination. The great Mudgala and the great Kâsyapa did likewise. The Bhikshunîs principally honour the tower of Ânanda, because it was Ânanda who requested the lord of the world to let women take orders; Srâmanêras mostly offer to Râhula; the masters of the *Abhidharma* offer to the *Abhidharma;* the masters of the *Vinaya* offer to the *Vinaya.* Every year there is one offering, each according to his own day. Men attached to the Mahâyâna offer to *Prajña-pâramitâ,* Mañjusrî, and Avalôkitêsvara. When the priests have received their yearly dues, then the chief men and

105

householders and Brâhmans bring every kind of robe and other things needed by the priests to offer them; the priests also make offerings one to another. Down from the time of Buddha's death the titles of conduct for the holy priesthood have been (thus) handed down without interruption.

After crossing the Indus, the distance to the Southern Sea of South India is from four to five myriads of li; the land is level throughout, without great mountains or valleys, but still there are rivers.

Questions:
1. *What is Fa-Hsien's impression of the state of Buddhism in India at this time?*
2. *What most impressed Fa-Hsien about the conditions under which people lived and the administration of justice?*
3. *What characteristics does Fa-Hsien observe as related to Chandalas?*

PART 4
Greece and the Hellenistic World

4.1 Homer: The Iliad

Homer's Iliad, the great epic of the Trojan wars, is based on the legend of the seduction and abduction of Helen, wife of King Minolaus of Sparta (in southern Greece), by the young prince Paris of Troy, or Ilium, a city in Asia Minor, not far from present-day Istanbul. Helen, who is considered to have been one of the great beauties of history, fell in love with Paris and gladly accompanied him to Troy. Her husband, understandably, was not pleased so sent a Spartan army to Troy to bring her back home. Once there, however, the Greeks found themselves unable to penetrate the walls of the city. Always ingenious, the Greeks built a wooden horse, the famous "Trojan Horse," and filled it with soldiers. The curious Trojans pulled it inside the city, and the Greek soldiers leaped out, took the city, and recaptured Helen. Prominent in all these activities was the formidable Greek warrior, Achilles.

Little is known of the life of Homer. He lived in the eighth century s.c. and is thought to have been blind. It is probable that he did not actually compose the Iliad and Odyssey in writing but recited them to his disciples who presumably then transcribed them.

Source: Trans. Alexander Pope

BOOK XXII

> To such I call the gods! one constant state
> Of lasting rancour and eternal hate:
> No thought but rage, and never-ceasing strife,
> Till death extinguish rage, and thought, and life.
> Rouse then thy forces this important hour,
> Collect thy soul, and call forth all thy power.
> No further subterfuge, no further chance;
> 'Tis Pallas, Pallas gives thee to my lance.
> Each Grecian ghost, by thee deprived of breath,
> Now hovers round, and calls thee to thy death.
> He spoke, and launch'd his javelin at the foe;
> But Hector shunn'd the mediated blow:
> He stoop'd, while o'er his head the flying spear
> Sang innocent, and spent its force in air.
> Minerva watch'd it falling on the land,
> Then drew, and gave to great Achilles' hand,
> Unseen of Hector, who, elate with joy,
> Now shakes his lance, and braves the dread of Troy.
> 'The life you boasted to that javelin given,
> Prince! you have miss'd. My fate depends on Heaven.
> To thee, presumptuous as thou art, unknown,
> Or what must prove my fortune, or thy own.
> Boasting is but an art, our fears to blind,
> And with false terrors sink another's mind.
> But know, whatever fate I am to try,
> By no dishonest wound shall Hector die.
> I shall not fall a fugitive at least,
> My soul shall bravely issue from my breast.
> But first, try thou my arm; and may this dart
> End all my country's woes, deep buried in thy heart.'
> The weapon flew, its course unerring held,
> Unerring, but the heavenly shield repell'd
> The mortal dart; resulting with a bound
> From off the ringing orb, it struck the ground.

Hector beheld his javelin fall in vain,
Nor other lance, nor other hope remain;
He calls Deïphobus, demands a spear-
In vain, for no Deïphobus was there.
All comfortless he stands: then, with a sigh:
'Tis so-Heaven wills it, and my hour is nigh!
I deem'd Deïphobus had heard my call,
But he secure lies guarded in the wall.
A god deceived me; Pallas, 'twas thy deed,
Death and black fate approach! 'tis I must bleed.
No refuge now, no succour from above,
Great Jove deserts me, and the son of Jove,
Propitious once, and kind! Then, welcome fate!
'Tis true I perish, yet I perish great:
Yet in a mighty deed I shall expire,
Let future ages hear it, and admire!'
        Fierce, at the word, his weighty sword he drew,
And, all collected, on Achilles flew.
So Jove's bold bird, high balanced in the air,
Stoops from the clouds to truss the quivering hare.
Nor less Achilles his fierce soul prepares:
Before his breast the flaming shield he bears,
Refulgent orb! above his fourfold cone
The gilded horse-hair sparkled in the sun,
Nodding at every step: (Vulcanian frame!)
And as he moved, his figure seem'd on flame.
As radiant Hesper shines with keener light,
Far-beaming o'er the silver host of night,
When all the starry train emblaze the sphere:
So shone the point of great Achilles' spear.
In his right hand he waves the weapon round,
Eyes the whole man, and meditates the wound;
But the rich mail Patroclus lately wore
Securely cased the warrior's body o'er.
One space at length he spies, to let in fate,
Where 'twixt the neck and throat the jointed plate
Gave entrance: through that penetrable part
Furious he drove the well-directed dart:
Nor pierced the windpipe yet, nor took the power
Of speech, unhappy! from thy dying hour.
Prone on the field the bleeding warrior lies,
While, thus triumphing, stern Achilles cries:

'At last is Hector stretch'd upon the plain,
Who fear'd no vengeance for Patroclus slain:
Then, prince! you should have fear'd, what now you feel;
Achilles absent was Achilles still: . .

Questions:
1. What seems to be Hector's attitude toward fate?
2. In this passage, does fate seem arbitrary or are there other forces at work? What are these forces?

4.2 Empires and Military Glory: Herodotus Relates the Story of Thermopylae

Imperialism often goes hand-in-hand with a tradition of martial heroism and a glorification of wartime exploits. In rationalizing their future imperial aspirations, the Greek city-states would often hark back to the deeds of valour during the Persian Wars (490–479 B.C.E.), as in this description of the Spartan stand at the pass of Thermopylae by the historian Herodotus.

Source: Bernard Knox, ed.. *The Norton Book of Classical Literature* (N.Y.: W.W. Norton, 1993), p. 288–293.

The Persian army was now close to the pass, and the Greeks, suddenly doubting their power to resist, held a conference to consider the advisability of retreat. It was proposed by the Peloponnesians generally that the army should fall back upon the Peloponnese and hold the Isthmus; but when the Phocians and Locrians expressed their indignation at that suggestion, Leonidas gave his voice for staying where they were and sending, at the same time, an appeal for reinforcements to the various states of the confederacy, as their numbers were inadequate to cope with the Persians.

During the conference Xerxes sent a man on horseback to ascertain the strength of the Greek force and to observe what the troops were doing. He had heard before he left Thessaly that a small force was concentrated here, led by the Lacedaemonians under Leonidas of the house of Heracles. The Persian rider approached the camp and took a thorough survey of all he could see—which was not, however, the whole Greek army; for the men on the further side of the wall which, after its reconstruction, was now guarded, were out of sight. He did, nonetheless, carefully observe the troops who were stationed on the outside of the wall. At that moment these happened to be the Spartans, and some of them were stripped for exercise, while others were combing their hair. The Persian spy watched them in astonishment; nevertheless he made sure of their numbers, and of everything else he needed to know, as accurately as he could, and then rode quietly off. No one attempted to catch him, or took the least notice of him.

Back in his own camp he told Xerxes what he had seen. Xerxes was bewildered; the truth, namely that the Spartans were preparing themselves to kill and to be killed according to their strength, was beyond his comprehension, and what they were doing seemed to him merely absurd. Accordingly he sent for Demaratus, the son of Ariston, who had come with the army, and questioned him about the spy's report, in the hope of finding out what the unaccountable behaviour of the Spartans might mean. "Once before," Demaratus said, "when we began our march against Greece, you heard me speak of these men. I told you then how I saw this enterprise would turn out, and you laughed at me. I strive for nothing, my lord, more earnestly than to observe the truth in your presence; so hear me once more. These men have come to fight us for possession of the pass, and for that struggle they are preparing. It is the common practice of the Spartans to pay careful attention to their hair when they are about to risk their lives. But I assure you that if you can defeat these men and the rest of the Spartans who are still at home, there is no other people in the world who will dare to stand firm or lift a hand against you. You have now to deal with the finest kingdom in Greece, and with the bravest men."

Xerxes, unable to believe what Demaratus said, asked further how it was possible that so small a force could fight with his army. ""My lord," Demaratus replied, "treat me as a liar, if what I have foretold does not take place." But still Xerxes was unconvinced.

For four days Xerxes waited, in constant expectation that the Greeks would make good their escape; then, on the fifth, when still they had made no move and their continued presence seemed mere impudent and reckless folly, he was seized with rage and sent forward the Medes and Cissians with orders to take them alive and bring them into his presence. The Medes charged, and in the struggle which ensued many fell; but others took their places, and in spite of terrible losses refused to be beaten off. They made it plain enough to anyone, and not least to the king himself, that he had in his army many men, indeed, but few soldiers. All day the battle continued; the Medes, after their rough handling, were at length withdrawn and their place was taken by Hydarnes and his picked Persian troops—the King's Immortals—who advanced to the attack in full confidence of bringing the business to a quick and easy end. But, once engaged, they were no more successful than the Medes had been; all went as before, the two armies fighting in a confined space, the Persians using shorter spears than the Greeks and having no advantage from their numbers.

On the Spartan side it was a memorable fight; they were men who understood war pitted against an inexperienced enemy, and amongst the feints they employed was to turn their backs in a body and pretend to be retreating in confusion, whereupon the enemy would come on with a great clatter and roar, supposing the battle won; but the Spartans, just as the Persians were on them, would wheel and face them and inflict in the new struggle innumerable casualties. The Spartans had their losses too, but not many. At last the Persians, finding that their assaults upon the pass, whether by divisions or by any other way they could think of, were all useless, broke off the engagement and withdrew. Xerxes was watching the battle from where he sat; and it is said that in the course of the attacks three times, in terror for his army, he leapt to his feet.

Next day the fighting began again, but with no better success for the Persians, who renewed their onslaught in the hope that the Greeks, being so few in number, might be badly enough disabled by wounds to prevent further resistance. But the Greeks never slackened; their troops were ordered in divisions corresponding to the states from which they came, and each division took its turn in the line except the Phocian, which had been posted to guard the track over the mountains. So when the Persians found that things were no better for them than on the previous day, they once more withdrew.

How to deal with the situation Xerxes had no idea; but while he was still wondering what his next move should be, a man from Malis got himself admitted to his presence. This was Ephialtes, the son of Eurydemus, and he had come, in hope of a rich reward, to tell the king about the track which led over the hills to Thermopylae—and the information he gave was to prove the death of the Greeks who held the pass.

Later on, Ephialtes, in fear of the Spartans, fled to Thessaly, and during his exile there a price was put upon his head at an assembly of the Amphictyons at Pylae. Some time afterwards he returned to Anticyra, where he was killed by Athenades of Trachis. In point of fact, Athenades killed him not for his treachery but for another reason, which I will explain further on; but the Spartans honoured him nonetheless on that account. According to another story, which I do not at all believe, it was Onetes, the son of Phanagoras, a native of Carystus, and Corydallus of Anticyra who spoke to Xerxes and showed the Persians the way round by the mountain track; but one may judge which account is the true one, first by the fact that the Amphictyons, who must surely have known everything about it, set a price not upon Onetes and Corydallus but upon Ephialtes of Trachis, and, secondly, by the fact that there is no doubt that the accusation of treachery was the reason for Ephialtes' flight. Certainly Onetes, even though he was not a native of Malis, might have known about the track, if he had spent much time in the neighbourhood—but it was Ephialtes, and no one else, who showed the Persians the way, and I leave his name on record as the guilty one.

Xerxes found Ephialtes' offer most satisfactory. He was delighted with it, and promptly gave orders to Hydarnes to carry out the movement with the troops under his command. They left camp about the time the lamps are lit.

The track was originally discovered by the Malians of the neighbourhood; they afterwards used it to help the Thessalians, taking them over to attack Phocis at the time when the Phocians were protected from invasion by the wall which they had built across the pass. That was a long time ago, and no good ever came of it since. The track begins at the Asopus, the stream which flows through the narrow gorge, and, running along the ridge of the mountain—which, like the track itself, is called Anopaea—ends at Alpenus, the first Locrian settlement as one comes from Malis, near the rock known as Black-Buttocks' Stone and the seats of the Cercopes. Just here is the narrowest part of the pass.

This, then, was the mountain track which the Persians took, after crossing the Asopus. They marched throughout the night, with the mountains of Oeta on their right hand and those of Trachis on their left. By early dawn they were at the summit of the ridge, near the spot where the Phocians, as I mentioned before, stood on guard with a thousand men, to watch the track and protect their country. The Phocians were ready enough to undertake this service, and had, indeed, volunteered for it to Leonidas, knowing that the pass at Thermopylae was held as I have already described.

The ascent of the Persians had been concealed by the oak-woods which cover this part of the mountain range, and it was only when they reached the top that the Phocians became aware of their approach; for there was not a breath of wind, and the marching feet made a loud swishing and rustling in the fallen leaves. Leaping to their feet, the Phocians were in the act of arming themselves when the enemy was upon them. The Persians were surprised at the sight of troops preparing to resist; they had not expected any opposition—yet here was a body of men barring their way. Hydarnes asked Ephialtes who they were, for his first uncomfortable thought was that they might be Spartans; but on learning the truth he prepared to engage them. The Persian arrows flew thick and fast, and the Phocians, supposing themselves to be the main object of the attack, hurriedly withdrew to the highest point of the mountain, where they made ready to face destruction. The Persians, however, with Ephialtes and Hydarnes paid no further attention to them, but passed on along the descending track with all possible speed.

The Greeks at Thermopylae had their first warning of the death that was coming with the dawn from the seer Megistias, who read their doom in the victims of sacrifice; deserters, too, had begun to come in during the night with news of the Persian movement to take them in the rear, and, just as day was breaking, the look-out men had come running from the hills. At once a conference was held, and opinions were divided, some urging that they must on no account abandon their post, others taking the opposite view. The result was that the army split: some dispersed, the men returning to their various homes, and others made ready to stand by Leonidas.

There is another account which says that Leonidas himself dismissed a part of his force, to spare their lives, but thought it unbecoming for the Spartans under his command to desert the post which they had originally come to guard. I myself am inclined to think that he dismissed them when he realized that they had no heart for the fight and were unwilling to take their share of the danger; at the same time honour forbade that he himself should go. And indeed by remaining at his post he left a great name behind him, and Sparta did not lose her prosperity, as might otherwise have happened; for right at the outset of the war the Spartans had been told by the oracle, when they asked for advice, that either their city must be laid waste by the foreigner or one of their kings be killed. The prophecy was in hexameter verse and ran as follows:

Hear your fate, O dwellers in Sparta of the wide spaces;
Either your famed, great town must be sacked by Perseus'
    sons,
Or, if that be not, the whole land of Lacedaemon
Shall mourn the death of a king of the house of Heracles,
For not the strength of lions or of bulls shall hold him,
Strength against strength; for he has the power of Zeus,
And will not be checked till one of these two he has con-
    sumed.

I believe it was the thought of this oracle, combined with his wish to lay up for the Spartans a treasure of fame in which no other city should share, that made Leonidas dismiss those troops; I do not think that they deserted, or went off without orders, because of a difference of opinion. Moreover, I am strongly supported in this view by the case of Megistias, the seer from Acarnania who foretold the coming doom by his inspection of the sacrificial victims: this man—he was said to be descended from Melampus—was with the army, and quite plainly received orders from Leonidas to quit Thermopylae, to save him from sharing the army's fate. But he refused to go, sending away instead an only son of his, who was serving with the forces.

Thus it was that the confederate troops, by Leonidas' orders, abandoned their posts and left the pass, all except the Thespians and the Thebans who remained with the Spartans. The Thebans were detained by Leonidas as hostages very much against their will—unlike the loyal Thespians, who refused to desert Leonidas and his men, but stayed, and died with them. They were under the command of Demophilus the son of Diadromes.

In the morning Xerxes poured a libation to the rising sun, and then waited till about the time of the filling of the market-place, when he began to move forward. This was according to Ephialtes' instructions, for the way down from the ridge is much shorter and more direct than the long and circuitous ascent. As the Persian army advanced to the assault, the Greeks under Leonidas, knowing that the fight would be their last, pressed forward into the wider part of the pass much further than they had done before; in the previous days' fighting they had been holding the wall and making sorties from behind it into the narrow neck, but now they left the confined space and battle was joined on more open ground. Many of the invaders fell; behind them the company commanders plied their whips, driving the men remorselessly on. Many fell into the sea and were drowned, and still more were trampled to death by their friends. No one could count the number of the dead. The Greeks, who knew that the enemy were on their way round by the mountain track and that death was inevitable, fought with reckless desperation, exerting every ounce of strength that was in them against the invader. By the time most of their spears were broken, and they were killing Persians with their swords.

In the course of that fight Leonidas fell, having fought like a man indeed. Many distinguished Spartans were killed at his side—their names, like the names of all the three hundred, I have made myself acquainted with, because they deserve to be remembered. Amongst the Persian dead, too, were many men of high distinction—for instance, two brothers of Xerxes, Habrocomes and Hyperanthes, both of them sons of Darius by Artanes' daughter Phratagune.

There was a bitter struggle over the body of Leonidas; four times the Greeks drove the enemy off, and at last by their valour succeeded in dragging it away. So it went on, until the fresh troops with Ephialtes were close at hand; and then, when the Greeks knew that they had come, the character of the fighting changed. They withdrew again into the narrow neck of the pass, behind the walls, and took up a position in a single compact body—all except the Thebans—on the little hill at the entrance to the pass, where the stone lion in memory of Leonidas stands today. Here they resisted to the last, with their swords, if they had them, and, if not, with their hands and teeth, until the Persians, coming on from the front over the ruins of the wall and closing in from behind, finally overwhelmed them.

Translated by Aubrey de Sélincourt

Questions:
1. What was the cause for King Xerxes' amazement before the battle took place at Thermopylae?
2. What role was played by Ephialtes?
3. What did the prophecy of the oracle say about Sparta?
4. What was behind Leonidas' decision to fight to the end?

4.3 Thucydides

The period of Athenian greatness, to which the world owes so much, did not last long. Only about seventy-five years lay between the time of the Athenian victory over the Persians and their defeat by the Spartans and their allies in the Peloponnesian War. The two wars were causally connected together through a link that was both political and economic in nature. Even after their repulsion of the Persians, the Greeks were fearful of a return of the invaders so Athens and other city-states of the Aegean Sea and the Ion ian coast formed the Delian League, for mutual self-defense. The League began as a voluntary and equitable association, but, largely under the leadership of the great statesman, Pericles, Athens came to dominate the League, exacting heavy taxes from the other members (much of the money being used to beautify Athens) and refusing to allow any city-state to withdraw from the association. Thus the Delian League was transformed into an Athenian Empire. As a consequence Sparta (as well as other Greek city-states) became alarmed and set out to stem the growing power of Athens.

The result was the Peloponnesian War, which raged intermittently during much of the latter part of the fifth century B.C.

Our great source of information about this war comes from the historian, Thucydides, who was born sometime around 470 B.c. and probably died soon after 400. B.C. Thucydides, a descendant of Miltiades-the victor of the battle of Marathon-was himself a soldier, but not a successful one. Early in the war he failed in his defense of a city against a Spartan force; for this failure he was stripped of his command and sent into exile from Athens for twenty years.

If not an outstanding military leader, Thucydides was a great historian-in the opinion of some scholars the greatest who ever lived. The qualities of his writing that they generally cite in support of this judgment are such attributes as his objectivity, his accuracy, his penetrating analyses of character, his appreciation of the demoralizing effects of warfare on society, and his recognition of the logical connections between events. Finally, he considered history to have a moral value, believing that events like wars, not being chance things but the results of causes, would recur in the future if similar conditions arose. From this one can infer that, if we are acquainted with history, and aware of the mistakes that our predecessors made, we can profit from our knowledge and avoid repeating the past. As Thucydides put it, "My history is an everlasting possession, not a prize composition which is heard and forgotten."

Source: Trans. B. Jowett, 2nd ed.

HISTORY OF THE PELOPONNESIAN WAR
BOOK I

1. Thucydides, an Athenian, wrote the history of the war in which the Peloponnesians and the Athenians fought against one another. He began to write when they first took up arms, believing that it would be great and memorable above any previous war.[1] For he argued that both states were then at the full height of their military power, and he saw the rest of the Hellenes either siding or intending to side with one or the other of them. No movement ever stirred Hellas more deeply than this; it was shared by many of the Barbarians, and might be said even to affect the world at large.

. . .

22. As to the speeches which were made either before or during the war, it was hard for me, and for others who reported them to me, to recollect the exact words. I have therefore put into the mouth of each speaker the sentiments proper to the occasion, expressed as I thought he would be likely to express them, while at the same time I endeavored, as nearly as I could, to give the general purport of what was actually said. Of the events of the war I have not ventured to speak from any chance information, nor according to any notion of my own; I have described nothing but what I either saw myself, or learned from others of whom I made the most careful and particular inquiry. The task was a laborious one, because eye-witnesses of the same occurrences gave different accounts of them, as they remembered or were interested in the actions of one side or the other. And very likely the strictly historical character of my narrative may be disappointing to the ear. But if he who desires to have before his eyes a true picture of the events which have happened, and of the like events which may be expected to happen here-after in the order of human things, shall pronounce what I have written to be useful, then I shall be satisfied. My history is an everlasting possession, not a prize composition which is heard and forgotten.

. . .

---

[1] [Thuycides is here referring to himself in the third person. —*Ed.*]

BOOK II

. . .

34. During the same winter[2], in accordance with an old national custom, the funeral of those who first fell in this war was celebrated by the Athenians at the public charge. The ceremony is as follows: Three days before the celebration they erect a tent in which the bones of the dead are laid out, and every one brings to his own dead any offering which he pleases. At the time of the funeral the bones are placed in chests of cypress wood, which are conveyed on hearses; there is one chest for each tribe. They also carry a single empty litter decked with a pall for all whose bodies are missing, and cannot be recovered after the battle. The procession is accompanied by any one who chooses, whether citizen or stranger, and the female relatives of the deceased are present at the place of interment and make lamentation. The public sepulchre is situated in the most beautiful spot outside the walls; there they always bury those who fall in war; only after the battle of Marathon the dead, in recognition of their preeminent valor, were interred on the field. When the remains have been laid in the earth, some man of known ability and high reputation, chosen by the city, delivers a suitable oration over them; after which the people depart. Such is the manner of interment; and the ceremony was repeated from time to time throughout the war. Over those who were the first buried Pericles was chosen to speak. At the fitting moment he advanced from the sepulchre to a lofty stage, which had been erected in order that he might be heard as far as possible by the multitude, and spoke as follows:-

Funeral Speech

35. "Most of those who have spoken here before me have commended the law-giver who added this oration to our other funeral customs; it seemed to them a worthy thing that such an honor should be given at their burial to the dead who have fallen on the field of battle. But I should have preferred that, when men's deeds have been brave, they should be honored in deed only, and with such an honor as this public funeral, which you are now witnessing. Then the reputation of many would not have been imperilled on the eloquence or want of eloquence of one and their virtues believed or not as he spoke well or ill. For it is difficult to say neither too little nor too much; and even moderation is apt not to give the impression of truthfulness. The friend of the dead who knows the facts is likely to think that the words of the speaker fall short of his knowledge and of his wishes; another who is not so well informed, when he hears of anything which surpasses his own powers, will be envious and will suspect exaggeration. Mankind are tolerant of the praises of others so long as each hearer thinks that he can do as well or nearly as well himself, but, when the speaker rises above him, jealousy is aroused and he begins to be incredulous. However, since our ancestors have set the seal of their approval upon the practice, I must obey, and to the utmost of my power shall endeavor to satisfy the wishes and beliefs of all who hear me.

36. "I will speak first of our ancestors, for it is right and becoming that now, when we are lamenting the dead, a tribute should be paid to their memory. There has never been a time when they did not inhabit this land, which by their valor they have handed down from generation to generation, and we have received from them a free state. But if they were worthy of praise, still more were our fathers, who added to their inheritance, and after many a struggle transmitted to us their sons this great empire. And we ourselves assembled here today, who are still most of us in the vigor of life, have chiefly done the work of improvement, and have richly endowed our city with all things, so that she is sufficient for herself both in peace and war. Of the military exploits by which our various possessions were acquired, or of the energy with which we or our fathers drove back the tide of war, Hellenic or Barbarian, I will not speak; for the tale would be long and is familiar to you. But before I praise the dead, I should like to point out by what principles of action we rose to power, and under what institutions and through what manner of life our empire became great. For I conceive that such thoughts are not unsuited to the occasion, and that this numerous assembly of citizens and strangers may profitably listen to them.

37. "Our form of government does not enter into rivalry with the institutions of others. We do not copy our neighbors, but are an example to them. It is true that we are called a democracy, for the administration is in the hands of the many and not of the few. But while the law secures equal justice to all alike in their private disputes, the claim of excellence is also recognized; and when a citizen is in any way distinguished, he is preferred to the public service, not as a matter of privilege, but as the reward of merit. Neither is poverty a bar, but a man may benefit his country whatever be the obscurity of his condition. There is no exclusiveness in our public life, and in our private intercourse we are not suspicious of one another, nor angry with our neighbor if he does what he likes; we do not put on sour looks at him which, though harmless, are not pleasant. While we are thus unconstrained in our private intercourse, a spirit of reverence pervades our public acts; we are prevented from doing wrong by respect for authority and for the laws, having an especial regard to those which are ordained for the protection of the injured as well as those unwritten laws which bring upon the transgressor of them the reprobation of the general sentiment.

---

[2] [At the end of the first year of the Peloponnesian War, 431 B.C.—*Ed.*]

38. "And we have not forgotten to provide for our weary spirits many relaxations from toil; we have regular games and sacrifices throughout the year; at home the style of our life is refined; and the delight which we daily feel in all these things helps to banish melancholy. Because of the greatness of our city the fruits of the whole earth flow in upon us; so that we enjoy the goods of other countries as freely as of our own.

39. "Then, again, our military training is in many respects, superior to that of our adversaries. Our city is thrown open to the world, and we never expel a foreigner or prevent him from seeing or learning anything of which the secret if revealed to an enemy might profit him. We rely not upon management or trickery, but upon our own hearts and hands. And in the matter of education, whereas they from early youth are always undergoing laborious exercises which are to make them brave, we live at ease, and yet are equally ready to face the perils which they face. And here is the proof. The Lacedaemonians come into Attica not by themselves, but with their whole confederacy following; we go alone into a neighbor's country; and although our opponents are fighting for their homes and we on a foreign soil, we have seldom any difficulty in overcoming them. Our enemies have never yet felt our united strength; the care of a navy divides our attention, and on land we are obliged to send our own citizens everywhere. But they, if they meet and defeat a part of our army, are as proud as if they had routed us all, and when defeated they pretend to have been vanquished by us all.

40. "If then we prefer to meet danger with a light heart but without laborious training, and with a courage which is gained by habit and not enforced by law, are we not greatly the gainers? Since we do not anticipate the pain, although, when the hour comes, we can be as brave as those who never allow themselves to rest; and thus too our city is equally admirable in peace and in war. For we are lovers of the beautiful, yet simple in our tastes, and we cultivate the mind without a loss of manliness. Wealth we employ, not for talk and ostentation, but when there is a real use for it. To avow poverty with us is no disgrace: the true disgrace is in doing nothing to avoid it. An Athenian citizen does not neglect the state because he takes care of his own household; and even those of us who are engaged in business have a very fair idea of politics. We alone regard a man who takes no interest in public affairs, not as a harmless, but as a useless character; and if few of us are originators, we are all sound judges of a policy. The great impediment to action is, in our opinion, not discussion, but the want of that knowledge which is gained by discussion preparatory to action. For we have a peculiar power of thinking before we act and of acting too, whereas other men are courageous from ignorance but hesitate upon reflection. And they are surely to be esteemed the bravest spirits who, having the clearest sense both of the pains and pleasures of life, do not on that account shrink from danger. In doing good, again, we are unlike others; we make our friends by conferring, not by receiving favors. Now, he who confers a favor is the firmer friend, because he would fain by kindness keep alive the memory of an obligation; but the recipient is colder in his feelings, because he knows that in requiting another's generosity he will not be winning gratitude, but only paying a debt. We alone do good to our neighbors not upon a calculation of interest, but in the confidence of freedom and in a frank and fearless spirit.

41. "To sum up: I say that Athens is the school of Hellas, and that the individual Athenian in his own person seems to have the power of adapting himself to the most varied forms of action with the utmost versatility and grace. This is no passing and idle word, but truth and fact; and the assertion is verified by the position to which these qualities have raised the state. For in the hour of trial Athens alone among her contemporaries is superior to the report of her. No enemy who comes against her is indignant at the reverses which he sustains at the hands of such a city; no subject complains that his masters are unworthy of him. And we shall assuredly not be without witnesses; there are mighty monuments of our power which will make us the wonder of this and of succeeding ages; we shall not need the praises of Homer or of any other panegyrist whose poetry may please for the moment, although his representation of the facts will not bear the light of day. For we have compelled every land and every sea to open a path for our valor, and have everywhere planted eternal memorials of our friendship and of our enmity. Such is the city for whose sake these men nobly fought and died; they could not bear the thought that she might be taken from them; and every one of us who survive should gladly toil on her behalf.

42. "I have dwelt upon the greatness of Athens because I want to show you that we are contending for a higher prize than those who enjoy none of these privileges, and to establish by manifest proof the merit of these men whom I am now commemorating. Their loftiest praise has been already spoken. For in magnifying the city I have magnified them, and men like them whose virtues made her glorious. And of how few Hellenes can it be said as of them, that their deeds when weighted in the balance have been found equal to their fame! Methinks that a death such as theirs has been gives the true measure of a man's worth; it may be the first revelation of his virtues, but is at any rate their final seal. For even those who come short in other ways may justly plead the valor with which they have fought for their country; they have blotted out the evil with the good, and have benefited the state more by their public services than they have injured her by their private actions. None of these men were enervated by wealth or hesitated to resign the pleasures of life; none of them put off the evil day in the hope, natural to poverty, that a man, though poor, may one day become rich. But, deeming that the punishment of their enemies was sweeter than any of these things, and that they could fall in no nobler cause, they determined at the hazard of their lives to be honorably avenged, and to leave the rest. They resigned to hope their unknown chance of happiness; but in the face of death they resolved to rely upon themselves alone. And when the moment came they were

minded to resist and suffer, rather than to fly and save their lives; they ran away from the word of dishonor, but on the battle-field their feet stood fast, and in an instant, at the height of their fortune, they passed away from the scene, not of their fear, but of their glory.

43. "Such was the end of these men; they were worthy of Athens, and the living need not desire to have a more heroic spirit, although they may pray for a less fatal issue. The value of such a spirit is not to be expressed in words. Anyone can discourse to you forever about the advantage of a brave defence which you know already. But instead of listening to him I would have you day by day fix your eyes upon the greatness of Athens, until you become filled with the love of her; and when you are impressed by the spectacle of her glory, reflect that this empire has been acquired by men who knew their duty and had the courage to do it, who in the hour of conflict had the fear of dishonor always present to them, and who, if ever they failed in an enterprise, would not allow their virtues to be lost to their country, but freely gave their lives to her as the fairest offering which they could present at her feast. The sacrifice which they collectively made was individually repaid to them; for they received again each one for himself a praise which grows not old, and the noblest of all sepulchres-I speak not of that in which their remains are laid, but of that in which their glory survives, and is proclaimed always and on every fitting occasion both in word and deed. For the whole earth is the sepulchre of famous men; not only are they commemorated by columns and inscriptions in their own country, but in foreign lands there dwells also an unwritten memorial of them, graven not on stone but in the hearts of men. Make them your examples, and esteeming courage to be freedom and freedom to be happiness, do not weigh too nicely the perils of war. The unfortunate who has no hope of a change for the better has less reason to throw away his life than the prosperous who, if he survives, is always liable to a change for the worse, and to whom any accidental fall makes the most serious difference. To a man of spirit, cowardice and disaster coming together are far more bitter than death, striking him unperceived at a time when he is full of courage and animated by the general hope.

44. "Wherefore I do not now commiserate the parents of the dead who stand here; I would rather comfort them. You know that your life has been passed amid manifold vicissitudes; and that they may be deemed fortunate who have gained most honor, whether an honorable death like theirs, or an honorable sorrow like yours, and whose days have been so ordered that the term of their happiness is likewise the term of their life. I know how hard it is to make you feel this, when the good fortune of others will too often remind you of the gladness which once lightened your hearts. And sorrow is felt at the want of those blessings, not which a man never knew, but which were a part of his life before they were taken from him. Some of you are of an age at which they may hope to have other children, and they ought to bear their sorrow better; not only will the children who may hereafter be born make them forget their own lost ones, but the city will be doubly a gainer. She will not be left desolate, and she will be safer. For a man's counsel cannot have equal weight or worth, when he alone has no children to risk in the general danger. To those of you who have passed their prime, I say; 'Congratulate yourselves that you have been happy during the greater part of your days; remember that your life of sorrow will not last long, and be comforted by the glory of those who are gone. For the love of honor alone is ever young, and not riches, as some say, but honor is the delight of men when they are old and useless.'

45. "To you who are the sons and brothers of the departed, I see that the struggle to emulate them will be an arduous one. For all men praise the dead, and, however preeminent your virtue may be, hardly will you be thought, I do not say to equal, but even to approach them. The living have their rivals and detractors, but when a man is out of the way, the honor and goodwill which he receives is unalloyed. And, if I am to speak of womanly virtues to those of you who will henceforth be widows, let me sum them up in one short admonition: To a woman not to show more weakness than is natural to her sex is a great glory, and not to be talked about for good or for evil among men.

46. "I have paid the required tribute, in obedience to the law, making use of such fitting words as I had. The tribute of deeds has been paid in part; for the dead have been honorably interred, and it remains only that their children should be maintained at the public charge until they are grown up; this is the solid prize with which, as with a garland, Athens crowns her sons living and dead, after a struggle like theirs. For where the rewards of virtue are greatest, there the noblest citizens are enlisted in the service of the state. And now, when you have duly lamented, every one his own dead, you may depart."

• • •

BOOK III

• • •

82. For not long afterwards[3] nearly the whole Hellenic world was in commotion; in every city the chiefs of the democracy and of the oligarchy were struggling, the one to bring in the Athenians, the other the Lacedaemonians. Now, in time of peace, men would have had no excuse for introducing either, and no desire to do so, but when they were at war and both sides could easily obtain allies to the hurt of their enemies and the advantage of themselves, the dissatisfied party were only too ready to invoke foreign aid. And revolution brought upon the cities of Hellas many terrible calamities, such as have been and always will be while human nature remains the same, but which are more or less aggravated and differ in character with every new combination of circumstances. In peace and prosperity both states and individuals are actuated by high motives, because they do not fall under the dominion of imperious necessities; but war which takes away the comfortable provision of daily life is a hard master, and tends to assimilate men's characters to their conditions.

When troubles had once begun in the cities, those who followed carried the revolutionary spirit further and further, and determined to outdo the report of all who had preceded them by the ingenuity of their enterprises and the atrocity of their revenges. The meaning of words had no longer the same relation to things, but was changed by them as they thought proper. Reckless daring was held to be loyal courage; prudent delay was the excuse of a coward; moderation was the disguise of unmanly weakness; to know everything was to do nothing. Frantic energy was the true quality of man. A conspirator who wanted to be safe was a recreant in disguise. The lover of violence was always trusted, and his opponent suspected. He who succeeded in a plot was deemed knowing, but a still greater master in craft was he who detected one. On the other hand, he who plotted from the first to have nothing to do with plots was a breaker up of parties and a poltroon who was afraid of the enemy. In a word, he who could outstrip another in a bad action was applauded, and so was he who encouraged to evil one who had no idea of it. The tie of party was stronger than the tie of blood, because a partisan was more ready to dare without asking why. (For party associations are not based upon established law, nor do they seek the public good; they are formed in defiance of the laws and from self-interest.) The seal of good faith was not divine law, but fellowship in crime. If any enemy when he was in the ascendant offered fair words, the opposite party received them, not in a generous spirit, but by a jealous watchfulness of his actions. Revenge was dearer than self-preservation. Any agreements sworn to by either party, when they could do nothing else, were binding as long as both were powerless. But he who on a favorable opportunity first took courage and struck at his enemy when he saw him off his guard, had greater pleasure in a perfidious than he would have had in an open act of revenge; he congratulated himself that he had taken the safer course, and also that he had over-reached his enemy and gained the prize of superior ability. In general, the dishonest more easily gain credit for cleverness than the simple for goodness; men take a pride in the one, but are ashamed of the other.

The cause of all these evils was the love of power originating in avarice and ambition, and the party-spirit which is engendered by them when men were fairly embarked in a contest. For the leaders on either side used specious names, the one party professing to uphold the constitutional equality of the many, the other the wisdom of an aristocracy, while they made the public interests, to which in name they were devoted, in reality their prize. Striving in every way to overcome each other, they committed the most monstrous crimes; yet even these were surpassed by the magnitude of their revenges which they pursued to the very utmost, neither party observing any definite limits either of justice or public expediency, but both alike making the caprice of the moment their law. Either by the help of an unrighteous sentence, or grasping power with the strong hand, they were eager to satiate the impatience of party-spirit. Neither faction cared for religion; but any fair pretence which succeeded in effecting some odious purpose was greatly lauded. And the citizens who were of neither party fell a prey to both; either they were disliked because they held aloof, or men were jealous of their surviving.

83. Thus revolution gave birth to every form of wickedness in Hellas. The simplicity which is so large an element in a noble nature was laughed to scorn and disappeared. An attitude of perfidious antagonism everywhere prevailed; for there was no word binding enough, nor oath terrible enough to reconcile enemies. Each man was strong only in the conviction that nothing was secure; he must look to his own safety, and could not afford to trust others.

• • •

---

[3] [In 427 B.C., or four years after Pericles' Funeral Oration—Ed.]

BOOK V

• • •

84. In the ensuing summer, Alcibiades sailed to Argos with twenty ships, and seized any of the Argives who were still suspected to be of the Lacedaemonian faction, three hundred in number; and the Athenians deposited them in the subject islands near at hand. The Athenians next made an expedition against the island of Melos[4] with thirty ships of their own, six Chian, and two Lesbian, twelve hundred hoplites and three hundred archers besides twenty mounted archers of their own, and about fifteen hundred hoplites furnished by their allies in the islands. The Melians are colonists of the Lacedaemonians who would not submit to Athens like the other islanders. At first they were neutral and took no part. But when the Athenians tried to coerce them by ravaging their lands they were driven into open hostilities. The generals, Cleomedes the son of Lycomedes and Tisias the son of Tisimachus, encamped with the Athenian forces on the island. But before they did the country any harm they sent envoys to negotiate with the Melians. Instead of bringing these envoys before the people, the Melians desired them to explain their errand to the magistrates and to the chief men. They spoke as follows-

85. "Since we are not allowed to speak to the people, lest, forsooth, they should be deceived by seductive and unanswerable arguments which they would hear set forth in a single uninterrupted oration (for we are perfectly aware that this is what you mean in bringing us before a select few), you who are sitting here may as well make assurance yet surer. Let us have no set speeches at all, but do you reply to each several statement of which you disapprove, and criticise it at once. Say first of all how you like this mode of proceeding."

86. The Melian representatives answered:- "The quiet interchange of explanations is a reasonable thing, and we do not object to that. But your warlike movements, which are present not only to our fears but to our eyes, seem to belie your words. We see that, although you may reason with us, you mean to be our judges; and that at the end of the discussion if the justice of our cause prevail and we therefore refuse to yield, we may expect war; if we are convinced by you, slavery."

87. ATHENIAN: Nay, but if you are only going to argue from fancies about the future, or if you meet us with any other purpose than that of looking your circumstances in the face and saving your city, we have done; but if this is your intention we will proceed.

88. MELIAN: It is an excusable and natural thing that men in our position should have much to say and should indulge in many fancies. But we admit that this conference has met to consider the question of our preservation; and therefore let the argument proceed in the manner which you propose.

89. ATHENIAN: Well, then, we Athenians will use no fine words; we will not go out of our way to prove at length that we have a right to rule, because we overthrew the Persians; or that we attack you now because we are suffering any injury at your hands. We should not convince you if we did; nor must you expect to convince us by arguing that, although a colony of the Lacedaemonians, you have taken no part in their expeditions, or that you have never done us any wrong. But you and we should say what we really think, and aim only at what is possible, for we both alike know that into the discussion of human affairs, the question of justice only enters where the pressure of necessity is equal, and that the powerful exact what they can, and the weak grant what they must.

90. MELIAN: Well, then, since you set aside justice and invite us to speak of expediency, in our judgment it is certainly expedient that you should respect a principle which is for the common good; and that to every man when in peril a reasonable claim should be accounted a claim of right, and any plea which he is disposed to urge, even if failing of the point a little, should help his cause. Your interest in this principle is quite as great as ours, inasmuch as you, if you fall, will incur the heaviest vengeance, and will be the most terrible example to mankind.

91. ATHENIAN: The fall of our empire, if it should fall, is not an event to which we look forward with dismay; for ruling states such as Lacedaemon are not cruel to their vanquished enemies. And we are fighting not so much against the Lacedaemonians as against our own subjects who may some day rise up and overcome their former masters. But this is a danger which you may leave to us. And we will now endeavor to show that we have come in the interests of our empire, and that in what we are about to say we are only seeking the preservation of your city. For we want to make you ours with the least trouble to ourselves, and it is for the interests of us both that you should not be destroyed.

92. MELIAN: It may be your interest to be our masters, but how can it be ours to be your slaves?

93. ATHENIAN: To you the gain will be that by submission you will avert the worst; and we shall be all the richer for your preservation.

94. MELIAN: But must we be your enemies? Will you not receive us as friends if we are neutral and remain at peace with you?

---

[4] [In 416 B.C. —*Ed.*]

95. ATHENIAN: No, your enmity is not half so mischievous to us as your friendship; for the one is in the eyes of our subjects an argument of our power, the other of our weakness.

96. MELIAN: But are your subjects really unable to distinguish between states in which you have no concern, and those which are chiefly your own colonies, and in some cases have revolted and been subdued by you?

97. ATHENIAN: Why, they do not doubt that both of them have a good deal to say for themselves on the score of justice, but they think that states like yours are left free because they are able to defend themselves, and that we do not attack them because we dare not. So that your subjection will give us an increase of security, as well as an extension of empire. For we are masters of the sea, and you who are islanders, and insignificant islanders too, must not be allowed to escape us.

98. MELIAN: But do you not recognise another danger? For once more, since you drive us from the plea of justice and press upon us your doctrine of expediency, we must show you what is for our interest, and, if it be for yours also, may hope to convince you:-Will you not be making enemies of all who are now neutrals? When they see how you are treating us they will expect you some day to turn against them; and if so, are you not strengthening the enemies whom you already have, and bringing upon you others who, if they could help, would never dream of being your enemies at all?

99. ATHENIAN: We do not consider our really dangerous enemies to be any of the peoples inhabiting the mainland who, secure in their freedom, may defer indefinitely any measures of precaution which they take against us, but islanders who, like you, happen to be under no control, and all who may be already irritated by the necessity of submission to our empire-these are our real enemies, for they are the most reckless and most likely to bring themselves as well as us into a danger which they cannot but foresee.

100. MELIAN: Surely then, if you and your subjects will brave all this risk, you to preserve your empire and they to be quit of it, how base and cowardly it would be in us, who retain our freedom, not to do and suffer anything rather than be your slaves.

101. ATHENIAN: Not so, if you calmly reflect: for you are not fighting against equals to whom you cannot yield without disgrace, but you are taking counsel whether or not you shall resist an overwhelming force. The question is not one of honor but of prudence.

102. MELIAN: But we know that the fortune of war is sometimes impartial, and not always on the side of numbers. If we yield now all is over; but if we fight there is yet a hope that we may stand upright.

103. ATHENIAN: Hope is a good comforter in the hour of danger, and when men have something else to depend upon, although hurtful, she is not ruinous. But when her spendthrift nature has induced them to stake their all, they see her as she is in the moment of their fall, and not till then. While the knowledge of her might enable them to beware of her, she never fails. You are weak and a single turn of the scale might be your ruin. Do not you be thus deluded; avoid the error of which so many are guilty, who, although they might still be saved if they would take the natural means, when visible grounds of confidence forsake them, have recourse to the invisible, to prophecies and oracles and the like, which ruin men by the hopes which they inspire in them.

104. MELIAN: We know only too well how hard the struggle must be against your power, and against fortune, if she does not mean to be impartial. Nevertheless we do not despair of fortune, for we hope to stand as high as you in the favor of heaven, because we are righteous, and you against whom we contend are unrighteous; and we are satisfied that our deficiency in power will be compensated by the aid of our allies the Lacedaemonians; they cannot refuse to help us, if only because we are their kinsmen, and for the sake of their own honor. And therefore our confidence is not so utterly blind as you suppose.

105. ATHENIAN: As for the Gods, we expect to have quite as much of their favor as you: for we are not doing or claiming anything which goes beyond common opinion about divine or men's desires about human things. For of the Gods we believe, and of men we know, that by a law of their nature wherever they can rule they will. This law was not made by us, and we are not the first who have acted upon it; we did but inherit it, and shall bequeath it to all time, and we know that you and all mankind, if you were as strong as we are, would do as we do. So much for the Gods; we have told you why we expect to stand as high in their good opinion as you. And then as to the Lacedaemonians-when you imagine that out of very shame they will assist you, we admire the simplicity of your idea, but we do not envy you the folly of it. The Lacedaemonians are exceedingly virtuous among themselves, and according to their national standard of morality. But in respect of their dealings with others, although many things might be said, a word is enough to describe them-of all men whom we know they are the most notorious for identifying what is pleasant with what is honorable, and what is expedient with what is just. But how inconsistent is such a character with your present blind hope of deliverance!

106. MELIAN: That is the very reason why we trust them; they will look to their interest, and therefore will not be willing to betray the Melians, who are their own colonists, lest they should be distrusted by their friends in Hellas and play into the hands of their enemies.

107. ATHENIAN: But do you not see the path of expediency is safe, whereas justice and honor involve danger in practice, and such dangers the Lacedaemonians seldom care to face?

108. MELIAN: On the other hand we think that whatever perils there may be, they will be ready to face them for

our sakes, and will consider danger less dangerous where we are concerned. For if they need our aid we are close at hand, and they can better trust our loyal feeling because we are their kinsmen.

109. ATHENIAN: Yes, but what encourages men who are invited to join in a conflict is clearly not the goodwill of those who summon them to their side, but a decided superiority in real power. To this no men look more keenly than the Lacedaemonians; so little confidence have they in their own resources that they only attack their neighbors when they have numerous allies, and therefore they are not likely to find their way by themselves to an island, when we are masters of the sea.

110. MELIAN: But they may send their allies; the Cretan sea is a large place; and the masters of the sea will have more difficulty in overtaking vessels which want to escape than the pursued in escaping. If the attempt should fail, they may invade Attica itself, and find their way to allies of yours whom Brasidas did not reach; and then you will have to fight, not for the conquest of a land in which you have no concern, but nearer home, for the preservation of your confederacy and of your own territory.

111. ATHENIAN: Help may come from Lacedaemon to you as it has come to others, and should you ever have actual experience of it, then you will know that never once have the Athenians retired from a siege through fear of a foe elsewhere. You told us that the safety of your city would be your first care, but we remark that, in this long discussion, not a word has been uttered by you which would give a reasonable man expectation of deliverance. Your strongest grounds are hopes deferred, and what power you have is not to be compared with that which is already arrayed against you. Unless after we have withdrawn you mean to come, as even now you may, to a wiser conclusion, you are showing a great want of sense. For surely you cannot dream of flying to that false sense of honor which has been the ruin of so many when danger and dishonor were staring them in the face. Many men with their eyes still open to the consequences have found the word "honor" too much for them, and have suffered a mere name to lure them on, until it has drawn down upon them real and irretrievable calamities; through their own folly they have incurred a worse dishonor than fortune would have inflicted upon them. If you are wise you will not run this risk; you ought to see that there can be no disgrace in yielding to a great city which invites you to become her ally on reasonable terms, keeping your own land, and merely paying tribute, and that you will certainly gain no honor if, having to choose between two alternatives, safety and war, you obstinately prefer the worse. To maintain our rights against equals, to be politic with superiors, and to be moderate towards inferiors is the path of safety. Reflect once more when we have withdrawn, and say to yourselves over and over again that you are deliberating about your one and only country, which may be saved or may be destroyed by a single decision.

112. The Athenians left the conference: the Melians, after consulting among themselves, resolved to persevere in their refusal, and made answer as follows:- "Men of Athens, our resolution is unchanged; and we will not in a moment surrender that liberty which our city, founded seven hundred years ago, still enjoys; we will trust to the good-fortune which by the favor of the Gods has hitherto preserved us, and for human help to the Lacedaemonians, and endeavor to save ourselves. We are ready however to be your friends, and the enemies neither of you nor of the Lacedaemonians, and we ask you to leave our country when you have made such a peace as may appear to be in the interest of both parties."

113. Such was the answer of the Melians; the Athenians, as they quitted the conference, spoke as follows:-"Well, we must say, judging from the decision at which you have arrived, that you are the only men who deem the future to be more certain than the present, and regard things unseen as already realized in your fond anticipation, and that the more you cast yourselves upon the Lacedaemonians and fortune, and hope, and trust them, the more complete will be your ruin."

114. The Athenian envoys returned to the army, and the generals, when they found that the Melians would not yield, immediately commenced hostilities. They surrounded the town of Melos with a wall, dividing the work among the several contingents. They then left troops of their own and of the allies to keep guard both by land and by sea, and retired with the greater part of their army; the remainder carried on the blockade.

116. . . . The place was now closely invested, and there was treachery among the citizens themselves. So the Melians were induced to surrender at discretion. The Athenians thereupon put to death all who were of military age, and made slaves of the women and children. They then colonised the island, sending thither five hundred settlers of their own.

Questions:
1. What are the main virtues of Athens as described by Pericles?
2. What is his purpose in stating them?

4.4   From Confederacy to Empire: Thucydides

By 479 B.C.E., the combined Greek armies had defeated the Persian forces, which returned home never to invade Greece again. Still, many of the Greek city-states thought it wise to establish an organization intended to protect against any future Persian invasion, to gain booty, and to liberate Greek city-states on the coast of Ionia still under Persian control. Toward this end, many Greek islands pledged their eternal unity to the cause, formed the Delian Confederacy, and contributed money or ships for use against the Persians. Although all members had the same voting weight, the Athenians initially led the organization by supplying the generals and controlling the treasury. Gradually, however, the Athenian allies became Athenian subjects. The historian Thucydides discusses this transition in the following selection.

> **Source:** "From Confederacy to Empire" is from Thucydides, *History of the Peloponnesian War,* 1.97, 1.99, in *A Source-Book of Ancient History,* ed. George W. Botsford (New York: Macmillan, 1912), pp. 177–178.

At first the allies were independent and deliberated in a common assembly under the leadership of Athens. But in the interval between the Persian and Peloponnesian wars, by their military success and by policy in dealing with the barbarian, with their own rebellious allies and with the Peloponnesians [Spartans] who came across their path from time to time, the Athenians made immense strides in power. . . .

The causes which led to the defection of the allies were of different kinds, the principal one being their neglect to pay the tribute or to furnish ships, and, in some cases, failure of military service. For the Athenians were exacting and oppressive, using coercive measures toward men who were neither willing nor accustomed to work hard. And for various reasons they soon began to prove less agreeable leaders than at first. They no longer fought upon an equality with the rest of the confederates, and they had no difficulty in reducing them when they revolted. Now the allies brought all this upon themselves; for the majority of them disliked military service and absence from home, and so they agreed to contribute a regular sum of money instead of ships. Whereby the Athenian navy was proportionately increased, while they themselves were always untrained and unprepared for war when they revolted.

Question:
1. *Consider some of the reasons that Athens became an increasingly dominant power in the Delian League. Who was more to blame, Athens or the allies? Where they equally to blame?*

4.5   The City-State of Sparta

The city-state, or polis, evolved during the period 1200–500 B.C.E. and offered a unique organization for the Greeks. Each polis was independent in its particular form of government, provided for its own defensive arrangements, and conducted its own foreign policy. Thus one city-state might be a monarchy, another a democracy, and a third an oligarchy. One of the most fascinating city-states was Sparta. In the eighth century B.C.E., it had prospered in a rather open political and economic environment. But in the late seventh century, Sparta, under the leadership of Lycurgus, adopted a rigid military system that produced one of the most efficient and feared armies in antiquity. The Spartans enslaved some of the surrounding population (calling them helots) and used them to work the land while Spartan warriors honed their military skills. The following account describes the Spartan way of life. Though they never produced great literature or ideas, the Spartans were admired because they prevented chaos in their society.

> **Source:** "Spartan Discipline" is from Plutarch, Lycurgus, 16–19, in *Readings in Ancient History,* vol. 1, ed. William S. Davis (New York: Allyn and Bacon, 1912), pp. 107–111. Translation modernized by the editor.

SPARTAN DISCIPLINE

PLUTARCH

Nor was it in the power of the father to dispose of the child as he thought fit; he was obliged to carry it before certain officials at a place called Lesche; these were some of the elders of a tribe to which the child belonged; their business it was carefully to view the infant, and, if they found it strong and well formed, they gave order for its rearing, and allowed to it one of the nine thousand shares of land above mentioned for its maintenance, but if they found it puny and ill-shaped, ordered it to be taken to . . . a sort of chasm [and exposed to the elements]; as thinking it neither for the good of the child itself, nor for the public interest, that it should be brought up, if it did not, from the very outset, appear . . . healthy and vigorous. There was much care and art, too, used by the nurses; they had no swaddling bands; the children grew up free and unconstrained in limb and form, and not dainty and fanciful about their food; not afraid in the dark, or of being left alone; without any irritability or ill humor or crying. Upon this account, Spartan nurses were often . . . hired by people of other countries. . . .

Lycurgus would not have tutors brought out of the market for his young Spartans; nor was it lawful, indeed, for the father himself to raise the children after his own fancy; but as soon as they were 7 years old they were to be enrolled in certain companies and classes, where they lived under the same order and discipline, doing their exercises and playing together. Of these, he who showed the most conduct and courage was made captain; they had their eyes always upon him, obeyed his order, and underwent patiently whatsoever punishment he inflicted; so that the whole course of their education was one continued exercise of a ready and perfect obedience. The old men, too, were spectators of their performances, and often raised quarrels and disputes among them, to have a good opportunity of finding out their different characters, and of seeing which would be valiant, which a coward, when they should come to more dangerous encounters. Reading and writing they gave them, just enough to serve their turn; their chief care was to make them good subjects, and to teach them to endure pain and conquer in battle. To this end, as they grew in years, their discipline was proportionably increased; their heads were close clipped, and they were accustomed to go barefoot, and for the most part to play naked.

The Second Stage of the Spartan Education

After they were 12 years old, they were no longer allowed to wear any undergarment; they had one coat to serve them a year; their bodies were hard and dry, with but little acquaintance of baths and unguents; these human indulgences they were allowed only on some few particular days in the year. They lodged together in little bands upon beds made of the reeds which grew by the banks of the river, which they were to break off with their hands without a knife; if it were winter, they mingled some thistledown with their reeds, which it was thought had the property of giving warmth. . . . [Spartan youths were required to steal wood and herbs], which they did by creeping into the gardens, or conveying themselves cunningly and closely into the eating houses: if they were taken in the act, they were whipped without mercy, for thieving so poorly and awkwardly. They stole, too, all other meat they could lay their hands on, looking out and watching all opportunities, when people were asleep or more careless than usual. If they were caught, they were not only punished with whipping, but hunger, too, being reduced to their ordinary allowance, which was very slender, and so contrived on purpose, that they might set about to help themselves, and be forced to exercise their energy and ingenuity. So seriously did the Spartan children go about their stealing, that a youth, having stolen a young fox and hid it under his coat, allowed it to tear out his very guts with its teeth and claws, and died upon the place, rather than let it be seen. What is practiced to this very day in Sparta is enough to gain credit to this story, for I myself have seen several of the youths endure whipping to death. . . .

They taught them, also, to speak in a natural and graceful manner, and to express much in few words. . . . Children in Sparta, by a habit of long silence, came to give just and wise answers; for, indeed, as loose and incontinent livers are seldom fathers of many children, so loose and incontinent talkers seldom originate many sensible words. When some Athenian laughed at their short swords, . . . King Agis answered him, "We find them long enough to reach our enemies"; and as their swords were short and sharp, so, it seems to me, were their sayings. They reach the point and arrest the attention of the hearers better than any other kind.

Question:
1. What was the basis of Spartan achievement?

4.6   The First Philippic: A Great Orator Warns of Macedonian Imperialism

Philip II, King of Macedonia was at first not taken seriously by his Greek adversaries, who considered him uncouth and uncultured and labeled him "Philip the Barbarian." However, the Athenian Demosthenes, arguably the most persuasive speaker of his day, was well aware of the danger, and the growth of Macedonian power confirmed these fears. In a series of impassioned speeches known as the "Philippics," Demosthenes tried to rally his countrymen, as it later proved without avail, to meet the challenge.

Source: J. R. Ellis & R. D. Milne, eds., The Spectre of Philip: Demosthenes' first Phillipic (Sydney, Australia: Sydney University Press, 1970), pp. 16–19; 30–33.

Men of Athens, if some new topic were being proposed for discussion, I would have held back until most of the regular speakers had disclosed their views, and then, if I were satisfied with anything they said, I would have held my peace, and if I were not satisfied, I would have tried to put forward my own point of view. But, since it so happens that the present debate is concerned with matters that these regular speakers have discussed many times, I think that I may reasonably be excused for standing up to speak first of all; for had these men given the requisite advice in the past there would be no need for your deliberations now.

Firstly then, men of Athens, you must not be despondent at the present state of affairs even though they seem to be in a pretty bad way. For the aspect of the situation in the past that is worst is, in fact, the aspect that holds out most hope for the future. And what is this? It is the fact that your affairs are in an evil plight *because* you do none of the things that duty imposes on you; whereas if you were doing all you ought and they were still in such a state, there would be no hope of their improving. Again, it must be borne in mind, both by those hearing the story from others and by those having first-hand knowledge as they recall the occasion, how strong and powerful the Spartans were only a short time ago, yet how nobly and befittingly you did nothing unworthy of the city, but undertook, in defence of the cause of justice, the war against them. And why do I say this? So that you may look and see that when you are on your guard there is nothing that can alarm you, but when you let things slide nothing is the way you would wish it to be. Take as an example to prove this the might of Sparta at that time and the wanton violence of Philip at the present; the former you overcame because you gave your attention to affairs of state, while the latter is throwing us into confusion because we have no concern for the things that matter.

And if anyone thinks that Philip is a tough opponent, as he considers the size of Philip's available resources and the fact that our city has lost all her territories, then he thinks rightly, though he should consider this: that there was a time when we had Pydna, Potidaea and Methone, with all the surrounding area, well disposed towards us, and that many of the tribes that are now with him were then free and autonomous and preferred to be on good terms with us rather than him. If Philip at that time had formed the opinion that waging war on Athens was a hard and difficult task, since the city possessed so many fortresses in his own territory and he himself was without allies, he would never have done any of the things he has now achieved, nor would he have won such great power. But, men of Athens, Philip saw full well that all these places are the prizes of war, ready for the taking, and that the possessions of those who are absent naturally belong to those on the spot, the possessions of the neglectful to those who will endure toil and danger. This is his attitude and because of it he has subdued and possesses all the places in question. Some he now holds by right of conquest, others he has brought into alliance and friendship; for all men are prepared to ally themselves and give attention to those whom they see are ready and willing to do what should be done. Men of Athens, if you are ready to put yourselves in such a frame of mind as this now—for, to date, you have not been—and if each one of you puts aside all his shilly-shallying and shows himself ready to act where he ought to act and where he could be of use to the city (that is, the man with money must pay the property-tax and the man of military age must go on active service); if, I say, to sum up plainly and briefly, you will agree to become your own masters and will cease, each one of you, from expecting to do nothing yourself and your neighbour to do everything on your behalf, then you will redeem what is your own, you will recover what you have let slip through your own carelessness and you will take your revenge upon Philip.

For you must not regard his present position as being invested with an eternal immutability, as though he were a god; he is hated, feared and envied, even by some of the people who now appear to be particularly well disposed towards him. And you must recognize that all the desires and emotions that other men have are present also in the people ranged on Philip's side, although they are all now repressed and have no outlet, thanks to your indolence and indifference-of which I urge you to rid yourselves immediately. Look at the situation, men of Athens, and see what a peak of insolence the fellow has reached. He gives you no choice between action and living at peace, but threatens, utters arrogant statements—so it is said—and cannot be satisfied by his conquests, but is always seeking fresh acquisitions and trying to hedge us in on all sides, while we procrastinate and sit idly by. Men of Athens, when will you do your duty? What must happen before you will do it? 'When' comes the reply, 'the need arises.' But how ought we to regard what is happening now? For my part, I think that for free men a sense of shame over the conduct of their affairs is the most compelling necessity of all. Or, tell me, are you content with going around asking one another: 'Is there any news?' Could there be any hotter news than a Macedonian beating Athenians in war and administering the affairs of the Greeks? 'Is Philip dead?' 'No, but he's ill!' What difference does it make to you? If he dies you will soon make yourselves another Philip, if this is the way you give your attention to your affairs. For Philip has not become great so much by his own strength as by our neglect. And a further point: if anything happens to Philip, if our good fortune—which has always looked after us better than we look after ourselves—should bring this about, I would have you know that if you were close at hand you could take advantage of the general confusion and handle the situation as you wish. But as you now stand, you could not take over Amphipolis even if the opportunity was offered to you, for you are far from ready for it, both in your state of preparations and in your whole outlook....

It seems to me, men of Athens, that some god, ashamed on the city's behalf at what is being done, has inspired Philip with this meddlesome activity of his. For if Philip, holding the places he has already subdued and seized, were willing to keep quiet and do no more, I think that some of you would be quite satisfied with a situation whereby we would stand convicted, as a people, of shameful conduct, of cowardice, of all that is most disgraceful. But as it is, by always making new attempts and always striving for more, he might perhaps stir you to action, if you have not completely given up the struggle. For my part, I am amazed that none of you either takes it to heart or is filled with indignation when he sees that although the war was begun with the object of punishing Philip its end is already concerned with avoiding harm at Philip's hands. And yet it is quite obvious that he will not halt his progress unless he is compelled. Shall we wait for this? Do you think that all is well if you dispatch empty triremes and send off the mere expectations that are being raised by so-and-so? Shall we not embark in our ships? Shall we not set out ourselves with at least part of our own citizen-forces now, even if we have not done so before? Shall we not sail against Philip's territory? But where, somebody asks me, shall we anchor off his coast? The war itself, men of Athens, will discover the weak point in his dispositions, if we make the attempt. But if we sit idly at home listening to the politicians abusing and blaming each other then certainly nothing will ever be done that should be done. For in my opinion, wheresoever any part of our city-even if not the whole-is dispatched in company with the forces there fights along with it the good will of Heaven and of Fortune. But whenever you send out a commander, an empty decree and expressions of hope from the speaker's platform none of the things are done that should be; instead, our enemies laugh at us while our allies stand in mortal fear of such expeditions. For it is not possible, no, quite impossible that one single man could ever achieve for you all that you want achieved. He can, however, make promises, say 'yes' and accuse this man and that man; and the result of this is the ruin of our interests. For when the commander leads miserable, unpaid mercenaries, and when there are men here who glibly give you false information on his activities, when, on the basis of the stories you hear, you pass any decrees that come into your heads, then what must we expect?

How, then, will this situation be ended? It will cease when you, men of Athens, appoint the same men as soldiers and as witnesses what the generals do, and as judges, when they have returned home, of the generals' auditing; in this way you will not only hear about your own affairs but will also be present and see them. As things are, our affairs have reached such a shameful state that each of the commanders is put on trial for his life twice or thrice in your courts, but none of them dares engage in a struggle for life with your enemies even once; they prefer to die the death of a kidnapper or a highwayman rather than the death appropriate to a soldier. For a criminal should die as the result of a court's sentence, a general fighting the enemy. Some of us go about saying that Philip is planning with Sparta the destruction of Thebes and the dissolution of the demo-cratic states, others that he has sent envoys to the Persian king, and still others that he is fortifying cities in Illyria—each one of us goes around inventing his own story.

For my part, men of Athens, I definitely think that Philip is intoxicated with the magnitude of his achievements and has many similar aspirations revolving in his mind; for he sees that there is nobody to stop him and he is buoyed up with his successes. I do not think; however, that he has chosen to act in such a way that the most foolish of our citizens know what he intends to do-for the rumour-mongers are the most foolish of our citizens.

But if we give these tales short shrift and recognize that the fellow is an enemy, that he is depriving us of our possessions, that he has been wantonly outraging and insulting us for a long time, that all we ever expected anyone to do on our behalf has turned out to our detriment, that the future is in our own hands, that if we are not willing to fight Philip there we may perhaps be forced to fight him here—if, I say, we recognize these things then we shall have made the necessary decision and have done with useless talk. For you must not inquire what the future will be; you must fully recognize that it will be bad if you do not give it your attention and are not willing to act appropriately.

I have never chosen on other occasions to speak with a view to pleasing you unless I was fully convinced it would be of benefit, and I have now given you my opinion freely and straightforwardly, with no reservations. I could wish that, just as I know it is beneficial for you to hear the best advice, so I knew that it would also be beneficial to the men who gave it; then I should be much happier. As it is, although it is not clear what will befall me as a result of this advice, I offer it nevertheless, convinced that it is to your benefit if you heed it. May that prevail which is going to be to the advantage of all!

Questions:
1. For what does Demosthenes most criticize his fellow Athenians?
2. What arguments does Demosthenes produce in support of his contention that Philip poses a serious threat?
3. What solutions and course of action does Demosthenes propose?

4.7   The Figure of Alexander

One of the most fascinating and controversial figures of history was Alexander III of Macedon. After Philip's assassination in 336 B.C.E., Alexander was elected to the kingship and continued with his father's plans to invade and conquer Persia. His exploits became legendary and it is difficult to separate fact from fiction. The following selection recounts an early indication of Alexander's special abilities when he tamed a horse too wild for others to control.

> **Source:** "Carve Out A Kingdom Worthy of Yourself!" is from Plutarch, *Life of Alexander,* 5, in *Readings in Ancient History,* vol. 1, ed. William S. Davis (Boston: Allyn and Bacon, 1912), pp. 301–302.

"CARVE OUT A KINGDOM WORTHY OF YOURSELF!"
PLUTARCH

Philonicus the Thessalian brought the horse Bucephalus to Philip, offering to sell him for thirteen talents; but when they went into the field to try him, they found him so very vicious and unmanageable, that he reared up when they endeavored to mount him, and would not so much as endure the voice of any of Philip's attendants. Upon which, as they were leading him away as wholly useless and intractable, Alexander, who stood by, said, "What an excellent horse do they lose, for want of skill and boldness to manage him!" Philip at first took no notice of what he said; but when he heard him repeat the same thing several times, and saw he was very frustrated to see the horse sent away, "Do you criticize," said Philip, "those who are older than yourself, as if you knew more, and were better able to manage him then they?" "I could manage this horse," replied Alexander, "better than others do." "And if you do not," said Philip, "what will you forfeit for your rashness?" "I will pay," answered Alexander, "the whole price of the horse." At this the whole company fell laughing; and as soon as the wager was settled among them, he immediately ran to the horse, and, taking hold of the bridle, turned him directly towards the sun, having, it seems, observed that he was disturbed at and afraid of the motion of his own shadow; then letting him go forward a little, still keeping the reins in his hand, and stroking him gently when he began to grow eager and fiery, . . . with one nimble leap, Alexander securely mounted him, and when he was seated, by little and little drew in the bridle, and curbed him without either striking or spurring him. Presently, when he found him free from all rebelliousness, and only impatient for the course, he let him go at full speed, inciting him now with a commanding voice, and urging him also with his heel. Philip and his friends looked on at first in silence and anxiety for the result, [but when he came] back rejoicing and triumphing for what he had performed, they all burst out into acclamations of applause; and his father, shedding tears, it is said, for joy, kissed him as he came down from his horse, and in his transport said, "O my son, carve out a kingdom equal to and worthy of yourself, for Macedonia is too small for you."

Questions:
1. *Judging by the information given by the sources, what type of man was Alexander?*
2. *Do you think Alexander's actions warrant the epithet "the Great"?*

4.8a   Against Communism

Aristotle (384–322 B.C.E.) was another of the great philosophers of this era who would greatly influence thinkers in the Middle Ages. A student of Plato and tutor to Alexander the Great, Aristotle believed that ideal forms and truths existed but were not found in some abstract world apart from everyday life. In fact, one could discover Truth by observing sensory objects and then logically (through the process of induction) discerning their universal characteristics. Thus Aristotle was very practical and believed that all theories must be abandoned if they could not be observed to be true. Aristotle wrote widely on politics and ethics and is very contemporary in application. Note how many of the following ideas can be applied to our own world.

> **Source:** "Against Communism" is from Aristotle, *Politics,* 2.5, in *The Politics of Aristotle,* trans. Benjamin Jowett (Oxford: Oxford University Press, 1905), pp. 62–64.

ARISTOTLE

Next let us consider what should be our arrangements about property; should the citizens of the perfect state have possessions in common or not? . . .

There is always a difficulty in men living together and having things in common, but especially in their having common property. . . . Property should be in a certain sense common, but, as a general rule, private. For when everyone has his separate interest, men will not complain of one another, and they will make more progress, because everyone will be attending to his own business. Yet among good men, and as regards use, "friends," as the proverb says, "will have all things common." . . . For although every human has his own property, some things he will place at the disposal of his friends, while of others he shares the use of them. . . .

Again, how immeasurably greater is the pleasure, when a man feels a thing to be his own! For love of self is a feeling implanted by nature and not given in vain, although selfishness is rightly condemned. This, however, is not mere love of self, but love of self in excess, like the miser's love of money; for all, or almost all, men love money, and other such objects in a measure. Furthermore, there is the greatest pleasure in doing a kindness or service to friends or guests or companions, which can only be done when a man has private property. These advantages are lost by the excessive unification of the state. . . . No one, when men have all things in common, will any longer set an example of liberality or do any liberal action; for liberality consists in the use a man makes of his own property.

Such [communistic] legislation may have a specious appearance of benevolence. Men readily listen to it, and are easily induced to believe that in some wonderful manner everybody will become everybody's friend, especially when someone is heard denouncing the evils now existing in states, suits about contracts, convictions for perjury, flatteries of rich men and the like, which are said to arise out of the possession of private property. These evils, however, are due to a very different cause—the wickedness of human nature. Indeed, we see that there is much more quarreling among those who have all things in common, though there are not many of them when compared with the vast numbers who have private property.

Again, we ought to reckon, not only the evils from which the citizens will be saved, but also the advantages which they will lose. . . . Unity there should be, both of the family and of the state, but in some respects only. For there is a point at which a state may attain such a degree of unity as to be no longer a state, or at which, without actually ceasing to exist, it will become an inferior state, like harmony passing into unison, or rhythm which has been reduced to a single foot. The state, as I was saying, is a plurality, which should be united and made into a community by education. . . .

Questions:
1. Do you agree with Aristotle's assessment of communism?
2. Define the "Doctrine of the Mean."
3. Why is Aristotle called a "practical philospher"?

4.8b Virtue and Moderation: The Doctrine of the Mean

Aristotle's principle concern in his Ethics is moral virtue, which might best be described as "good character." One obtains a good character by continually doing right acts until they become second nature. In defining "right action," Aristotle offers his Doctrine of the Mean, which serves as a guide toward achieving moral virtue and happiness. Right acts are those that lie between two extremes: courage, therefore, is the mean between the extremes of cowardice and rashness. Aristotle explains this in the following passage.

Source: *Nichomachean Ethics*, Ostwald. Reprinted by permission of Pearson Education, Inc., Upper Saddle River, NJ., pp. 41–44.

ARISTOTLE

It is not sufficient, however, merely to define virtue in general terms as a characteristic: we must also specify what kind of characteristic it is. It must, then, be remarked that every virtue or excellence (1) renders good the thing itself of which it is the excellence, and (2) causes it to perform its function well. For example, the excellence of the eye makes both the eye and its function good, for good sight is due to the excellence of the eye. Likewise, the excellence of a horse makes it both good as a horse and good at running, at carrying its rider, and at facing the enemy. Now, if this is true of all things, the virtue or excellence of man, too, will be characteristic which makes him a good man, and which causes him to perform his own function well. . . .

Of every continuous entity that is divisible into parts it is possible to take the larger, smaller, or equal either in relation to the entity itself, or in relation to us. The "equal" part is something median between excess and deficiency. By the median of an entity I understand a point equidistant from both extremes, and this point is one and the same for everybody. By the median relative to us I understand an amount neither too large nor too small, and this is neither one nor the same for everybody. To take an example. . . if ten pounds of food is much for a man to eat and two pounds little, it does not follow that the trainer will prescribe six pounds, for this may in turn be much or little for him to eat; it may be little for Mile [the wrestler] and much for someone who has just begun to take up athletics. The same applies to running and wrestling. Thus we see that an expert in any field avoids excess and deficiency, but seeks the median and chooses it—not the median of the object but the median relative to us.

If this, then, is the way in which every science perfects its work, by looking to the median and by bringing its work up to that point—and this is the reason why it is usually said of a successful piece of work that it is impossible to detract from it or to add to it, the implication being that excess and deficiency destroy success while the mean safeguards it (good craftsmen, we say, look toward this standard in the performance of their work)—and if virtue, like nature, is more precise and better than any art, we must conclude that virtue aims at the median. I am referring to moral virtue: for it is moral virtue that is concerned with emotions and actions, and it is in emotions and actions that excess, deficiency, and the median are found. Thus we can experience fear, confidence, desire, anger, pity, and generally any kind of pleasure and pain either too much or too little, and in either case not properly. But to experience all this at the right time, toward the right objects, toward the right people, for the right reason, and in the right manner—that is the median and the best course, the course that is a mark of virtue.

Similarly, excess, deficiency, and the median can also be found in actions. Now virtue is concerned with emotions and actions; and in emotions and actions excess and deficiency miss the mark, whereas the median is praised and constitutes success. . . .

We may thus conclude that virtue or excellence is a characteristic involving choice, and that it consists in observing the mean relative to us, a mean which is defined by a rational principle, such as a man of practical wisdom would use to determine it. It is the mean by reference to two vices: the one of excess and the other of deficiency. It is, moreover, a mean because some vices exceed and the others fall short of what is required in emotion and in action, whereas virtue finds and chooses the median.

Questions:
1. *Do you agree with Aristotle's assessment of communism?*
2. *Define the "Doctrine of the Mean."*
3. *Why is Aristotle called a "practical philospher"?*

PART 5
Rome

5.1   A Hero Under Fire: Livy Relates the Trials and Tribulations of Scipio Africanus

Livy (59–17 B.C.E.) wrote the lengthiest account of the formative years of Roman civilization, the "History of Rome." Writing to please the tastes and biases of Caesar Augustus' court, Livy certainly wrote in a great deal of mythology and propaganda concerning the earliest centuries. In his account of later events, however, there is much that rings true, as in his description of the political problems faced by General Scipio Africanus, who had bested the formidable Carthaginian Hannibal at the Battle of Zama (202 B.C.E), and thus secured the Roman triumph over arch-rival Carthage in the Second Punic War.

Source: P. G. Walsh, ed., *Livy* (Warminster, England: Aris and Phillips, 1993), pp. 105–111.

On that day the accusations would have prevailed over the defence if the senators had not drawn out the dispute until a late hour. When the senate was dismissed, the general belief was that it seemed to have been on the point of refusing a triumph. But the following day relatives and friends of Gnaeus Manlius brought all their resources to bear, and in addition the authority of older members was decisive, for they argued that it was unprecedented for a commander who had vanquished the enemies of the state, completed his sphere of duty, and brought back his army, to enter the city without chariot and laurel-wreath as a private citizen deprived of glory. This impression of indignity prevailed over ill-will, and the senators in large numbers voted a triumph.

The entire mention and recollection of this dispute were subsequently overshadowed by the rise of a greater controversy, involving a greater and more celebrated man. Valerius Antias states that the two Qinti Petilii indicted Publius Scipio Africanus; individuals reacted to this according to their temperaments. Some attacked not the plebeian tribunes but the entire state for envisaging the possibility of allowing this. Their argument was that the two greatest cities of the world had been seen to show ingratitude to their leading men at virtually the same time, but that Rome's ingratitude was the greater, for when Carthage exiled Hannibal both city and leader had been conquered, whereas Rome was driving out Africanus when both were victorious. Others claimed that no one citizen should be so outstanding that he could not be subjected to interrogation under the laws; nothing was so important for the impartial application of liberty as that all most powerful men should be liable to defend themselves against indictment. Could any individual be safely entrusted with anything, let alone the direction of the state, if he were not to be accountable? Constraints applied to anyone who could not brook the equality of the law were by no means unjust. These were the issues under discussion until the day of the impeachment came. No-one before that date, even including Scipio himself as consul or censor, was attended on his way to the forum by a greater crowd of people of every rank than was the defendant on that day. When he was ordered to plead his case, he made no mention of the charges. He embarked upon a speech about his own achievements which was so splendid that it was wholly clear that no man had ever been the subject of a better or more truthful panegyric; for he recounted those achievements with the same spirit and genius with which he had performed them, and because they were uttered in the context of his trial and not for vainglory, he did not alienate the ears of his audience.

The plebeian tribunes first resurrected ancient charges of degenerate life in the winter-quarters at Syracuse, and the disturbances associated with Pleminius at Locri, to lend credence to their immediate accusations. Then they charged the defendant with peculation on the basis of suspicions rather than proofs. They stated that his son, previously captured, had been restored without a ransom, and that Scipio had been courted by Antiochus in all other matters, as though the issue of peace and war with Rome rested in the hands of him alone. He had acted not as legate but as dictator towards the consul in his province; his only purpose in going there was so that Greece, Asia, and all the kings and nations facing eastward should recognise the reality of what Spain, Gaul, Sicily and Africa had long been persuaded: namely, that one man was the source and stay of the Roman empire, that the state which was mistress of the world lay hidden under Scipio's shadow, that his nod represented senatorial decrees and the people's commands. They hounded this man, who was untouched by ill-repute, with the spite which was their strength. The speeches were prolonged until nightfall, when the date for resumption of the trial was announced.

When that day came, the tribunes took their seats at dawn on the platform. The defendant was summoned, and he made his way to the Rostra, attended by a large retinue of friends and dependants, through the midst of the gathering. Once silence had been imposed, Scipio spoke: "On this day, plebeian tribunes and you, citizens, I joined battle with Hannibal and the Carthaginians, and fought well and successfully. Since therefore today it is right to renounce disputes and reproaches, I shall at once make my way from here to the Capitol to hail Jupiter greatest and best, Juno, Minerva and the other deities who preside over the Capitol and citadel; and I shall thank them for having granted me, both today and often on other occasions, the intention and capacity to perform public service with distinction. I invite those of you, citizens, who find it convenient, to accompany me and to pray to the gods that you may have leaders like me, with this proviso: if from when I was seventeen up to my old age you have always bestowed your distinctions earlier than my years warranted, and if my achievements have preceded the distinctions you awarded."

He mounted from the Rostra to the Capitol, and at the same moment the entire assembly moved off and followed Scipio, so that finally the clerks and messengers forsook the tribunes, and no-one was left in their company except their slave-retinue and the herald whose job from the platform was to summon the defendant. Scipio, accompanied by the Roman people, toured all the gods' temples not only on the Capitol but throughout the entire city. This day became almost more famous through the citizens' affection and appreciation of his true greatness than the day on which he rode into the city in triumph over king Syphax and the Carthaginians.

This was the last day of glory to shine on Publius Scipio. Since he foresaw following it the onset of odium and struggles with the tribunes, when a quite lengthy adjournment of the trial was announced he retired to his estate at Liternum, for he had made up his mind not to attend to plead his case. His spirit and disposition were too lofty, and he was too accustomed to a loftier fortune, to reconcile himself to undergo a trial, and to abase himself to the humiliation of joining the ranks of defendants. When the day of the resumption came and his name began to be called in his absence, Lucius Scipio entered the excuse of illness for his non-appearance. The tribunes who had indicted him refused to accept this explanation. They maintained that the reason for his non-arrival to plead his case was the same arrogance with which he had previously quitted the trial, the plebeian tribunes, and the assembly; accompanied by those whom he had deprived of the right and freedom of passing judgment on him, he had dragged them along like captives to celebrate a triumph over the Roman people, and on that day he had organized a secession from the plebeian tribunes to the Capitol. "So now you have your reward for that rash gesture. You yourselves have been abandoned by the man who led and induced you to abandon us. Our native spirit has so declined day by day that we do not dare to dispatch men to drag this private citizen from his farmhouse to plead his case, though seventeen years ago, when he commanded an army and a fleet, we steeled ourselves to send plebeian tribunes and an aedile to Sicily to arrest him and bring him back to Rome." Lucius Scipio formally appealed to the plebeian tribunes, who decreed that if the plea of illness was being cited as excuse, their ruling was that this be accepted, and that their colleagues should adjourn the trial to a later date.

One of the plebeian tribunes at that time was Tiberius Sempronius Gracchus; personal enmity existed between him and Publius Scipio. He forbade his name to be appended to his colleagues' decree, and all were anticipating a more hostile proposal. But his resolution was that since Lucius Scipio had pleaded illness as excuse for his brother, he considered this sufficient; he would not allow Publius Scipio to be indicted before he returned to Rome, and even then, if he appealed to him, he would support him in a refusal to plead his case. Publius Scipio, by the general assent of gods and men, had attained such high distinction by his achievements and the honours conferred by the Roman people, that for him to stand indicted beneath the Rostra, and to listen to the reproaches of young men, was more dishonourable for the Roman people than for himself.

To his proposal he appended this expression of anger: "Is Scipio, the man who reduced Africa, to be set beneath your feet, tribunes? Was it for this that he scattered and routed four most illustrious Carthaginian generals and four armies in Spain? Was it for this that he captured Syphax, overthrew Hannibal, made Carthage pay tribute to us, and expelled Antiochus behind the ridges of Taurus (for Lucius Scipio admitted his brother to partnership in that glorious exploit), that he should bow the knee to the two Petilii, and that you should seek the palm of victory over Publius Africanus? Will eminent men never through their own merits, or through the honours bestowed by you, attain a stronghold affording them safety and virtual veneration, in which their old age can find rest—if not with respect, at any rate with immunity from attack?"

This resolution and the speech appended to it affected not only the other listeners but also the accusers themselves, and they said that they would weigh carefully their rights and duties. Then, following the adjournment of the people's council, a meeting of the senate began, in which profuse thanks were offered by the whole order, and especially by those of consular rank and the older senators, to Tiberius Gracchus, because he had put the public interest before private disagreements; and the Petilii were assailed with reproaches for having sought prominence by bringing odium on another, and plunder by triumphing over Africanus. Thereafter no more was heard of Africanus; he spent his life at Liternum without hankering after Rome. They say that as he was dying, he gave instructions that he be buried in that same country area, and that his tombstone should be erected there so that his funeral should not be held in his ungrateful native city. He was a man worthy of remembrance, but for his skills in war rather than in peace. The earlier years of his life were more noteworthy than the later, because wars were waged continually in his young days, whereas with the onset of old age his achievements too lost their bloom, and his talents were offered no scope. His second consulship was as nothing compared with the first, even if you added the censorship as well; similarly his tenure of office as legate in Asia, for it was ineffective through ill-health and disfigured by his son's misfortune, and following his return, by the need either to stand trial or to absent himself from both the trial and his native region. Yet he and no other gained the outstanding glory of bringing to a close the Punic war, and no war which the Romans waged was greater or more hazardous.

Questions:
1. How does the treatment handed out to Scipio compare to that meted out to Hannibal by Carthage, according to the arguments advanced by certain Romans?
2. What decision did Scipio enter into regarding attending his trial, and why?
3. In the final analysis, how does Livy rate the career of Scipio?

5.2 "The War with Catiline": Sallust's Insights Into the Roman Republic's Decline

Gaius Sallustius Crispus, known as Sallust (86–35? B.C.E.) was a plebeian-born historian-public official who witnessed the death throes of Republican Rome and contributed to its demise as an ardent supporter of Julius Caesar. In his account of Catiline's 63 B.C.E. plot to seize control of the state, Sallust lucidly analyses the decay of the old republican spirit and republican institutions that sent Rome down the path of autocracy. While bemoaning the general corruption, Sallust may have been guilty of it himself: he was once expelled from the Senate for alleged immorality and accused of using his position as governor of Africa Nova to commit extortion and embezzlement, but was never brought to trial because of Caesar's intervention.

Source: J. C. Rolfe, trans., *Sallust* (Cambridge, MA: Harvard University Press, 1965), pp.17–23.

…But the Roman people never had that advantage, since their ablest men were always most engaged with affairs; their minds were never employed apart from their bodies; the best citizen preferred action to words, and thought that his own brave deeds should be lauded by others rather than that theirs should be recounted by him.

IXAccordingly, good morals were cultivated at home and in the field; there was the greatest harmony and little or no avarice; justice and probity prevailed among them, thanks not so much to laws as to nature. Quarrels, discord, and strife were reserved for their enemies; citizen vied with citizen only for the prize of merit. They were lavish in their offerings to the gods, frugal in the home, loyal to their friends. By practising these two qualities, boldness in warfare and justice when peace came, they watched over themselves and their country. In proof of these statements I present this convincing evidence: firstly, in time of war punishment was more often inflicted for attacking the enemy contrary to orders, or for withdrawing too tardily when recalled from the field, than for venturing to abandon the standards or to give ground under stress; and secondly, in time of peace they ruled by kindness rather than fear, and when wronged preferred forgiveness to vengeance.

XBut when our country had grown great through toil and the practice of justice, when great kings had been vanquished in war, savage tribes and mighty peoples subdued by force of arms, when Carthage, the rival of Rome's away, had perished root and branch, and all seas and lands were open, then Fortune began to grow cruel and to bring confusion into all our affairs. Those who had found it easy to bear hardship and dangers, anxiety and adversity, found leisure and wealth, desirable under other circumstances, a burden and a curse. Hence the lust for money first, then for power, grew upon them; these were, I may say, the root of all evils. For avarice destroyed honour, integrity, and all other noble qualities; taught in their place insolence, cruelty, to neglect the gods, to set a price on everything. Ambition drove many men to become false; to have one thought locked in the breast, another ready on the tongue; to value friendships and enmities not on their merits but by the standard of self-interest, and to show a good front rather than a good heart. At first these vices grew slowly, from time to time they were punished; finally, when the disease had spread like a deadly plague, the state was changed and a government second to none in equity and excellence became cruel and intolerable.

XIBut at first men's souls were actuated less by avarice than by ambition—a fault, it is true, but not so far removed from virtue; for the noble and the base alike long for glory, honour, and power, but the former mount by the true path, whereas the latter, being destitute of noble qualities, rely upon craft and deception. Avarice implies a desire for money, which no wise man covets; steeped as it were with noxious poisons, it renders the most manly body and soul effeminate; it is ever unbounded and insatiable, nor can either plenty or want make it less. But after Lucius Sulla, having gained control of the state by arms, brought everything to a bad end from a good beginning, all men began to rob and pillage. One coveted a house, another lands; the victors showed neither moderation nor restraint, but shamefully and cruelly wronged their fellow citizens. Besides all this, Lucius Sulla, in order to secure the loyalty of the army which he led into Asia, had allowed it a luxury and license foreign to the manners of our forefathers; and in the intervals of leisure those charming and voluptuous lands had easily demoralized the warlike spirit of his soldiers. There it was that an army of the Roman people first learned to indulge in women and drink; to admire statues, paintings, and chased vases, to steal them from private houses and public places, to pillage shrines, and to desecrate everything, both sacred and profane. These soldiers, therefore, after they had won the victory, left nothing to the vanquished. In truth, prosperity tries the souls even of the wise; how then

129

should men of depraved character like these make a moderate use of victory?

X. As soon as riches came to be held in honour, when glory, dominion, and power followed in their train, virtue began to lose its lustre, poverty to be considered a disgrace, blamelessness to be termed malevolence. Therefore as the result of riches, luxury and greed, united with insolence, took possession of our young manhood. They pillaged, squandered; set little value on their own, coveted the goods of others; they disregarded modesty, chastity, everything human and divine; in short, they were utterly thoughtless and reckless.

It is worth your while, when you look upon houses and villas reared to the size of cities, to pay a visit to the temples of the gods built by our forefathers, most reverent of men. But they adorned the shrines of the gods with piety, their own homes with glory, while from the vanquished they took naught save the power of doing harm. The men of to-day, on the contrary, basest of creatures, with supreme wickedness are robbing our allies of all that those heroes in the hour of victory had left them; they act as though the one and only way to rule were to wrong.

XI. Why, pray, should I speak of things which are incredible except to those who have seen them, that a host of private men have levelled mountains and built upon the seas? To such men their riches seem to me to have been but a plaything; for while they might have enjoyed them honourably, they made haste to squander them shamefully. Nay more, the passion which arose for lewdness, gluttony, and the other attendants of luxury was equally strong; men played the woman, women offered their chastity for sale; to gratify their palates they scoured land and sea; they slept before they needed sleep; they did not await the coming of hunger or thirst, of cold or of weariness, but all these things their self-indulgence anticipated. Such were the vices that incited the young men to crime, as soon as they had run through their property. Their minds, habituated to evil practices, could not easily refrain from self-indulgence, and so they abandoned themselves the more recklessly to every means of gain as well as of extravagance.

Questions:
1. *In Sallust's estimation, which two qualities practiced by the early Romans were most instrumental in maintaining domestic peace and moral strength?*
2. *When, and through what factors, does Sallust see a change as having taken place?*
3. *According to Sallust's assessment, how did the later Romans compare/contrast with those of an earlier era?*

5.3   The Transition from Republic to Principate: Tacitus

After the assassination of Julius Caesar After the assassination of Julius Caesar in 44 B.C.E., a civil war ensued between the forces of Mark Antony, Caesar's chief lieutenant, and Octavian, Caesar's grand nephew and designated heir. By 27 B.C.E., Antony was dead and Octavian, by virtue of his military support, controlled the entire Roman Empire. At this point, he went to the senate and proclaimed that he had restored the Republic. Upon request of the senators, he decided to assume the advisory position of princeps or "first citizen" and the honorary title of "Augustus." The Republic was to function as it had in the past, with voting in the assemblies, election of magistrates, and traditional freedom. But as long as Augustus controlled the army, his "advice" could not be safely ignored. His system of government, called the principate, lasted in the same basic form until 180 C.E. The following accounts describe the powers of the princeps (or emperor, as he was also called). Note especially the cynicism of the historian Tacitus, who saw through the facade of republicanism and decried the loss of liberty.

> **Source:** "The Transition from Republic to Principate" is from Tacitus, *Annals,* 1.2–4, trans. Alfred Church and William Brodribb (New York: Macmillan and Co., 1891).

TACITUS

Augustus won over the soldiers with gifts, the populace with cheap [grain], and all men with the sweets of repose, and so grew greater by degrees, while he concentrated in himself the functions of the Senate, the magistrates, and the laws. He was wholly unopposed, for the boldest spirits had fallen in battle, or in the proscription, while the remaining nobles, the readier they were to be slaves, were raised the higher by wealth and promotion, so that, aggrandised by revolution, they preferred the safety of the present to the dangerous past. Nor did the provinces dislike that condition of affairs, for they distrusted the government of the Senate and the people, because of the rivalries between the leading men and the rapacity of the officials. . . . At home all was tranquil, and there were magistrates with the same titles; there was a younger generation, sprung up since the victory of Actium, and even many of the older men had been born during the civil wars. How few were left who had seen the Republic.

Thus the State had been revolutionized, and there was not a vestige left of the old sound morality. Stripped of equality, all looked up to the commands of a sovereign without the least apprehension for the present, while Augustus in the vigour of life, could maintain his own position, that of his house, and the general tranquility.

Question:
1. What happened to Augustus's opposition?

5.4 "All Roads Lead to Rome!": Strabo

The city of Rome was the vibrant center of this extensive empire. It provided services and entertainment to a teeming population of about one million inhabitants from all over the world. The following excerpts reveal the advantages and disadvantages of city life.

Source: "The Glory of the City" is from Strabo, *Geography,* 5.3.8, in *Readings in Ancient History,* vol. 2, ed. William S. Davis (Boston: Allyn and Bacon, 1913), pp. 179–181.

THE GLORY OF THE CITY
STRABO

[The Romans] paved the roads, cut through hills, and filled up valleys, so that the merchandise may be conveyed by carriage from the ports. The sewers, arched over with hewn stones, are large enough in parts for actual hay wagons to pass through, while so plentiful is the supply of water from the aqueducts, that rivers may be said to flow through the city and the sewers, and almost every house is furnished with water pipes and copious fountains.

We may remark that the ancients [of Republican times] bestowed little attention upon the beautifying of Rome. But their successors, and especially those of our own day, have at the same time embellished the city with numerous and splendid objects. Pompey, the Divine Caesar [i.e., Julius Caesar], and Augustus, with his children, friends, wife, and sister have surpassed all others in their zeal and munificence in these decorations. The greater number of these may be seen in the Campus Martius which to the beauties of nature adds those of art. The size of the plain is remarkable, allowing chariot races and the equestrian sports without hindrance, and multitudes [here] exercise themselves with ball games, in the Circus, and on the wrestling grounds. . . . The summit of the hills beyond the Tiber, extending from its banks with panoramic effect, present a spectacle which the eye abandons with regret.

Near to this plain is another surrounded with columns, sacred groves, three theaters, an amphitheater, and superb temples, each close to the other, and so splendid that it would seem idle to describe the rest of the city after it. For this cause the Romans esteeming it the most sacred place, have erected funeral monuments there to the illustrious persons of either sex. The most remarkable of these is that called the "Mausoleum" [the tomb of Augustus] which consists of a mound of earth raised upon a high foundation of white marble, situated near the river, and covered on the top with evergreen shrubs. On the summit is a bronze statue of Augustus Caesar, and beneath the mound are the funeral urns of himself, his relatives, and his friends. Behind is a large grove containing charming promenades. . . . If then you proceed to visit the ancient Forum, which is equally filled with basilicas, porticoes, and temples, you will there behold the Capitol, the Palatine, and the noble works that adorn them, and the piazza of Livia [Augustus' Empress],—each successive work causing you speedily to forget that which you have seen before. Such then is Rome!

Question:
1. Does this description accurately represent all of Rome? Why or why not?

5.5 Gladiatorial Combat: Seneca

The city of Rome was the vibrant center of this extensive empire. It provided services and entertainment to a teeming population of about one million inhabitants from all over the world. The following excerpts reveal the advantages and disadvantages of city life.

Source: *"Gladiatorial Combat"* is reprinted by permission of the publishers and the Loeb Classical Library from Seneca, *Moral Epistles,* 7.3–5, trans. Richard Gummere, vol. 1 (Cambridge, MA: Harvard University Press, 1917), pp. 31, 33.

SENECA

By chance I attended a mid-day exhibition, expecting some fun, wit, and relaxation—an exhibition at which men's eyes have respite from the slaughter of their fellow-men. But it was quite the reverse. The previous combats were the essence of compassion; but now all the trifling is put aside and it is pure murder. The men have no defensive armour. They are exposed to blows at all points, and no one ever strikes in vain. . . . In the morning they throw men to the lions and the bears; at noon, they throw them to the spectators. The spectators demand that the slayer shall face the man who is to slay him in his turn; and they always reserve the latest conqueror for another butchering. The outcome of every fight is death, and the means are fire and sword. This sort of thing goes on while the arena is empty. You may retort: "But he was a highway robber; he killed a man!" And what of it? Granted that, as a murderer, he deserved this punishment, what crime have you committed, poor fellow, that you should deserve to sit and see this show? In the morning they cried "Kill him! Lash him! Burn him! Why does he meet the sword in so cowardly a way? Why does he strike so feebly? Why doesn't he die game? Whip him to meet his wounds! Let them receive blow for blow, with chests bare and exposed to the stroke!" And when the games stop for the intermission, they announce: "A little throat-cutting in the meantime, so that there may still be something going on!"

Question:
1. What do Seneca's observations tell you about the type of person that attended gladiatorial games? Are there any similarities with modern-day sporting events?

5.6   The Stoic Philosophy

The Romans were never known for their contributions to abstract thought and did not produce a unique philosophy. Still, they borrowed well and adapted ideas that complemented their values. For the Roman, duty and organization were particularly important; consequently, the Stoic philosophy, which had originated in Greece in the third century B.C.E., was especially popular among the aristocracy. According to Stoic tenets, a divine plan ordered the universe, so whatever lot or occupation fell to one in life should be accepted and coped with appropriately. Restraint and moderation characterized the ideal Stoic, and he advocated tolerance as an essential component of the "brotherhood of man." To a Stoic who felt that his honor was somehow compromised, suicide was an acceptable and dutiful way of preserving his dignity. The following selections come from the writings of three Stoics of diverse backgrounds. Epictetus was the slave of a rich freedman; Seneca was tutor to the emperor Nero and finally committed suicide at his command in 66 C.E.; Marcus Aurelius became emperor in 161 C.E., an occupation he did not seek, but dutifully executed.

"HOW WILL I DIE?"
EPICTETUS

> **Source:** "'How Will I Die?'" is from T. W. Higginson, ed., *The Works of Epictetus* (Boston: Little Brown, 1886).

I must die: if instantly, I will die instantly; if in a short time, I will dine first; and when the hour comes, then I will die. How? As becomes one who restores what is not his own.

Do not you know that both sickness and death must overtake us? At what employment? The husbandman at his plough; the sailor on his voyage. At what employment would you be taken? For my own part, I would be found engaged in nothing but in the regulation of my own Will; how to render it undisturbed, unrestrained, uncompelled, free. I would be found studying this, that I may be able to say to God, "Have I transgressed Thy commands? Have I perverted the powers, the senses, the instincts, which Thou hast given me? Have I ever accused Thee, or censured Thy dispensations? I have been sick, because it was Thy pleasure, like others; but I willingly. I have been poor, it being Thy will; but with joy. I have not been in power, because it was not Thy will; and power I have never desired. Hast Thou ever seen me saddened because of this? Have I not always approached Thee with a cheerful countenance; prepared to execute Thy commands and the indications of Thy will? Is it Thy pleasure that I should depart from this assembly? I depart. I give Thee all thanks that Thou hast thought me worthy to have a share in it with Thee; to behold Thy works, and to join with Thee in comprehending Thy administration." Let death overtake me while I am thinking, while I am writing, while I am reading such things as these.

"WHAT IS THE PRINCIPAL THING IN LIFE?"
SENECA

Source: "'What Is the Principal Thing in Life?'" is from Seneca, *Natural Questions,* 3. Preface, 10–17, trans. J. Clarke (London, 1910).

What is the principal thing in human life? . . . To raise the soul above the threats and promises of fortune; to consider nothing as worth hoping for. For what does fortune possess worth setting your heart upon? . . . What is the principal thing? To be able to endure adversity with a joyful heart; to bear whatever occurs just as if it were the very thing you desired to have happen to you. For you would have felt it your duty to desire it, had you known that all things happen by divine decree. Tears, complaints, lamentations are rebellion [against divine order]. . . .

What is the principal thing? To have life on the very lips, ready to issue when summoned. This makes a man free, not by right of Roman citizenship but by right of nature. He is, moreover, the true freeman who has escaped from bondage to self; that slavery is constant and unavoidable —it presses us day and night alike, without pause, without respite. To be a slave to self is the most grievous kind of slavery; yet its fetters may easily be struck off, if you will cease to make large demands upon yourself, if you will cease to seek a personal reward for your services, and if you will set before your eyes your nature and your age, even though it be the bloom of youth; if you will say to yourself, "Why do I rave, and pant, and sweat? Why do I ply the earth? Why do I haunt the Forum? Man needs but little, and that not for long."

Question:
1. Why can this be considered a philosophy compatible with Roman values?

5.7 Sidonius Appolinaris: Rome's Decay, and a Glimpse of the New Order

Sidonius Appolinaris (430?–485? C.E.) descended from an aristocratic family that had, by the time of his birth, completely converted to Christianity. Sidonius would witness the final agonizing years of the western Roman Empire, ending his days as Bishop of Clermont in Southern France. Like many people of his rank and position, Sidonius had to come to terms with the half-civilized Germanic invaders (in his case, the Visigoths). He writes admiringly of the Visigothic king, Theodoric II (first letter); and of wedding of the Frankish prince Sigismer (second letter). All the same, his third letter reflects a pervasive concern over the power of the Germans, and their potential for destruction.

Source: Finley, Hooper & Matthew Schwartz, ed., *Roman Letters: History from a Personal Point of View* (Detriot: Wayne State University, 1991), pp. 272–277.

1

You have often begged a description of Theodoric the Gothic king, whose gentle breeding fame commends to every nation; you want him in his quantity and quality, in his person, and the manner of his existence. I gladly accede, as far as the limits of my page allow, and highly approve so fine and ingenuous a curiosity.

Well, he is a man worth knowing, even by those who cannot enjoy his close acquaintance, so happily have Providence and Nature joined to endow him with the perfect gifts of fortune; his way of life is such that not even the envy which lies in wait for a king can rob him of his proper praise. And first as to his person. He is well set up, in height above the average man, but below the giant. His head is round, with curled hair retreating somewhat from brow to crown. His nervous neck is free from disfiguring knots. The eyebrows are bushy and arched; when the lids droop, the lashes reach almost half-way down the cheeks. The upper ears are buried under overlying locks, after the fashion of his race. The nose is finely aquiline; the lips are thin and not enlarged by undue distention of the mouth. Every day the hair springing from his nostrils is cut back; that on the face springs thick from the hollow of the temples, but the razor has not yet come upon his cheek, and his barber is assiduous in eradicating the rich growth on the lower part of the face. Chin, throat, and neck art full, but not fat, and all of fair complexion; seen close, their colour is fresh as that of youth; they often flush, but from modesty, and not from anger. His shoulders are smooth, the upper- and forearms strong and hard; hands broad, breast prominent; waist receding. The spine dividing the broad expanse of back does not project, and you can see the spring of the ribs; the sides swell with salient muscle, the well-girt flanks are full of vigour. His thighs are like hard horn; the knee-joints firm and masculine; the knees themselves the comeliest and least wrinkled in the world. A full ankle supports the leg, and the foot is small to bear such mighty limbs.

Now for the routine of his public life. Before daybreak he goes with a very small suite to attend the service of his priests. He prays with assiduity, but, if I may speak in confidence, one may suspect more of habit than conviction in this piety. Administrative duties of the kingdom take up the rest of the morning. Armed nobles stand about the royal seat; the mass of guards in their garb of skins are admitted that they may be within call but kept at the threshold for quiet's sake; only a murmur of them comes in from their post at the doors, between the curtain and the outer barrier. And now the foreign envoys are introduced. The king hears them out, and says little; if a thing needs more discussion he puts it off, but accelerates matters ripe for dispatch. The second hour arrives; he rises from the throne to inspect his treasure-chamber or stable. If the chase is the order of the day, he joins it, but never carries his bow at his side, considering this derogatory to royal state. When a bird or beast is marked for him, or happens to cross his path, he puts his hand behind his back and takes the bow from a page with the string all hanging loose; for as he deems it a boy's trick to bear it in a quiver, so he holds it effeminate to receive the weapon ready strung. When it is given him, he sometimes holds it in both hands and bends the extremities towards each other; at others he sets it, knot-end downward, against his lifted heel, and runs his finger up the slack and wavering string. After that, he takes his arrows, adjusts, and lets fly. He will ask you beforehand what you would like him to transfix; you choose, and he hits. If there is a miss through either's error, your vision will mostly be at fault, and not the archer's skill.

On ordinary days, his table resembles that of a private person. The board does not groan beneath a mass of dull and unpolished silver set on by panting servitors; the weight lies rather in the conversation than in the plate; there is either sensible talk or none. The hangings and draperies used on these occasions are sometimes of purple silk, sometimes only of linen; art, not costliness, commends the fare, as spotlessness rather than bulk the silver. Toasts are few, and you will oftener see a thirsty guest impatient, than a full one refusing cup or bowl. In short, you will find elegance of Greece, good cheer of Gaul, Italian nimbleness, the state of public banquets with the attentive service of a private table, and everywhere the discipline of a king's house. What need for me to describe the pomp of his feast days? No man is so unknown as not to know of them. But to my theme again. The siesta after dinner is always slight and sometimes intermitted. When inclined for the board-game, he is quick to gather up the dice, examines them with care, shakes the box with expert hand, throws rapidly, humorously apostrophizes them, and patiently waits the issue. Silent at a good throw, he makes merry over a bad, annoyed by neither fortune, and always the philosopher. He is too proud to ask or to refuse a revenge; he disdains to avail himself of one if offered; and if it is opposed will quietly go on playing. You effect recovery of your man without obstruction on his side; he recovers his without collusion upon yours. You see the strategist when he moves the pieces; his one thought is victory. Yet at play he puts off a little of his kingly rigour, inciting all to good fellowship and the freedom of the game: I think he is afraid of being feared. Vexation in the man whom he beats delights him; he will never believe that his opponents have not let him win unless their annoyance proves him really victor. You would be surprised how often the pleasure born of these little happenings may favour the march of great affairs....I myself am gladly beaten by him when I have a favor to ask, since the loss of my game may mean the gaining of my cause. About the ninth hour, the burden of government begins again. Back come the importunates, back the ushers to remove them; on all sides buzz the voices of petitioners, a sound which lasts till evening, and does not diminish till interrrupted by the royal repast; even then they disperse to attend their various patrons among the courtiers, and are astir till bedtime. Sometimes, though this is rare, supper is enlivened by sallies of mimes, but no guest is ever exposed to the wound of a biting tongue. Withal there is no noise of hydraulic organ, or choir with its conductor intoning a set piece; you will hear no players of lyre of flute, no master of the music, no girls with cithara or tabor; the king cares for no strains but those which no less charm the mind with virtue than the ear with melody. When he rises to withdraw, the treasury watch begins its vigil; armed sentries stand on guard during the first hours of slumber. But I am wandering from my subject. I never promised a whole chapter on the kingdom, but a few words about the king. I must stay my pen; you asked for nothing more than one or two facts about the person and the tastes of Theodoric; and my own aim was to write a letter, not a history.

2

You take such pleasure in the sight of arms and those who wear them, that I can imagine your delight if you could have seen the young prince Sigismer on his way to the palace of his father-in-law in the guise of a bridegroom or suitor in all the pomp and bravery of the tribal fashion. His own steed with its caparisons, other steeds laden with flashing gems, paced before and after; but the conspicuous interest in the procession centred in the prince himself as with a charming modesty he went afoot amid his bodyguard and footmen, in flame-red mantle, with much glint of ruddy gold, and gleam of snowy silken tunic, his fair hair, red cheeks and white skin according with the three hues of his equipment. But the chiefs and allies who bore him company were dread of aspect, even thus on peace intent. Their feet were laced in boots of bristly hide reaching to the heels; ankles and legs were exposed. They wore high tight tunics of varied colour hardly descending to their bare knees, the sleeves covering only the upper arm. Green mantles they had with crimson borders; baldrics supported swords hung from their shoulders, and pressed on sides covered with cloaks of skin secured by brooches. No small part of their adornment consisted of their arms; in their hands they grasped barbed spears and missile axes; their left sides were guarded by shields, which flashed with tawny golden bosses and snowy silver borders, betraying at once their wealth and their good taste. Though the business in hand was wedlock, Mars was no whit less prominent in all his pomp than Venus. Why need I say more? Only your presence was wanting to the full enjoyment of so fine a spectacle. For when I saw you had missed the things you love to see, I longed to have you with me in all the impatience of your longing soul.

3

Rumour has it that the Goths have occupied Roman soil; our unhappy Auvergne is always their gateway on every such incursion. It is our fate to furnish fuel to the fire of a peculiar hatred, for, by Christ's aid, we are the sole obstacle to the fulfilment of their ambition to extend their frontier to the Rhone, and so hold all the country between that river, the Atlantic, and the Loire. Their menacing power has long pressed us hard; it has already swallowed up whole tracts of territory round us, and threatens to swallow more. We mean to resist with spirit, though we know our peril and the risks which we incur. But our trust is not in our poor walls impaired by fire, or in our rotting palisades, or in our ramparts worn by the breasts of the sentries, as they lean on them in continual watch. Our only present help we find in those Rogations which you introduced; and this is the reason why the people of Clermont refuse to recede, though terror surge about them on every side. By inauguration and institution of these prayers we are already new initiates; and if so far we have effected less than you have, our hearts are affected equally with yours. For it is not unknown to us by what portents and alarms the city entrusted to you by God was laid desolate at the time when first you ordained this form of prayer. Now it was earthquake, shattering the outer palace walls with frequent shocks; now fire, piling mounds of glowing ash upon proud houses fallen in ruin; now, amazing spectacle! wild deer grown ominously tame, making their lairs in the very forum. You saw the city being emptied of its inhabitants, rich and poor taking to flight. But you resorted in our latter day to the example shown of old in Nineveh, that you at least might not discredit the divine warning by the spectacle of your despair. And, indeed, you of all men have been least justified in distrusting the providence of God, after the proof of it vouchsafed to your own virtues. Once, in a sudden conflagration, your faith burned stronger than the flames. In full sight of the trembling crowd you stood forth all alone to stay them, and lo! the fire leapt back before you, a sinuous beaten fugitive. It was miracle, a formidable thing, unseen before and unexampled; the element which naturally shrinks from nothing, retired in awe at your approach. You therefore first enjoined a fast upon a few members of our sacred order, denouncing gross offences, announcing punishment, promising relief. You made it clear that if the penalty of sin was nigh, so also was the pardon; you proclaimed that by frequent prayer the menace of coming desolation might be removed. You taught that it was by water of tears rather than water of rivers that the obstinate and raging fire could best be extinguished, and by firm faith the threatening shock of earthquake stayed. The multitude of the lowly forthwith followed your counsel, and this influenced persons of higher rank, who had not scrupled to abandon the town, and now were not ashamed to return to it. By this devotion God was appeased, who sees into all hearts; your fervent prayers were counted to you for salvation; they became an example for your fellow citizens, and a defence about you all, for after those days there were neither portents to alarm, nor visitations to bring disaster.

We of Clermont know that all these ills befell your people of Vienne before the Rogations, and have not befallen them since; and therefore it is that we are eager to follow the lead of so holy a guide, beseeching your Beatitude from your own pious lips to give us the advocacy of those prayers now known to us by the examples which you have transmitted. Since the Confessor Ambrose discovered the remains of Gervasius and Protasius, it has been granted to you alone in the West to translate the relics of two martyrs—all the holy body of Ferteolus, and the head of our martyr Julian, which once the executioner's gory hand brought to the raging persecutor from the place of testimony. It is only fair, then, in compensation for the loss of this hallowed relic, that some part of your patronage should come to us from Vienne, since a part of our patronal saint has migrated thither. Deign to hold us in remembrance, my Lord Bishop.

Questions:
1. *What is the overall impression given by Sidonius in his decription of Theodoric II—admiration or fear? What specific evidence might support either viewpoint?*
2. *On what does Sidonius seem to focus in his description of Sigismer's wedding festivities?*
3. *For what reasons does Sidonius fear for the future of his native region of Auvergne? What does he single out as his peoples' main hope for survival?*
4. *What do the letters reveal about the character, policy, and priorities of Sidonius himself?*

PART 6
The Rise of Christianity

6.1 The Acts of the Apostles

In the province of Judea, tucked away in a far corner of the Roman Empire, was born midway through the reign of Caesar Augustus a man whose influence on world history was far to surpass that of the princeps—Jesus of Nazareth. The selection that follows from the New Testament contains excerpts illustrating the teachings of Jesus and the early history and theological doctrines of his followers. The Acts, written by Luke, is a historical book detailing the activities of the founders of the Christian church in the years immediately following the crucifixion, as seen through the eyes of the early church fathers several years later. Of crucial importance to history is the transformation of Christianity from the exclusive possession of an obscure Jewish sect into a message of salvation open to Gentiles as well as to Jews. This was the first step on Christianity's long road to religious domination of the Western world.

Source: The Scripture quotations contained herein are from the *New Revised Standard Version Bible,* copyright ©1989 by the Division of Christian Education of the National Council of the Churches of Christ in the U.S.A., and are used by permission. All rights reserved.

CHAPTER 1

1-5. The former treatise have I made, O Theophilus, of all that Jesus began both to do and teach, until the day in which he was taken up, after that he through the Holy Ghost had given commandments unto the apostles whom he had chosen. To whom also he shewed himself alive after his passion by many infallible proofs, being seen of them forty days, and speaking of the things pertaining to the kingdom of God: And, being assembled together with them, commanded them that they should not depart from Jerusalem, but wait for the promise of the Father, which, saith he, ye have heard of me. For John truly baptized with water; but ye shall be baptized with the Holy Ghost not many days hence.

6. When they therefore were come together, they asked of him, saying, "Lord, wilt thou at this time restore again the kingdom to Israel?" 7-8. And he said unto them, "It is not for you to know the times or the seasons, which the Father hath put in his own power. But ye shall receive power, after that the Holy Ghost is come upon you: and ye shall be witnesses unto me both in Jerusalem, and in all Judaea, and in Samaria, and unto the uttermost part of the earth." 9. And when he had spoken these things, while they beheld, he was taken up; and a cloud received him out of their sight. 10-11. And while they looked stedfastly toward heaven as he went up, behold, two men stood by them in white apparel; which also said, "Ye men of Galilee, why stand ye gazing up into heaven? This same Jesus, which is taken up from you into heaven, shall so come in like manner as ye have seen him go into heaven."

12. Then returned they unto Jerusalem from the mount called Olivet, which is from Jerusalem a sabbath day's journey.

. . .

CHAPTER 2

1-4. And when the day of Pentecost was fully come, they were all with one accord in one place. And suddenly there came a sound from heaven as of a rushing mighty wind, and it filled all the house where they were sitting. And there appeared unto them cloven tongues like as of fire, and it sat upon each of them. And they were all filled with the Holy Ghost, and began to speak with other tongues, as the Spirit gave them utterance. 5-13. And there were dwelling at Jerusalem Jews, devout men, out of every nation under heaven. Now when this was noised abroad, the multitude came together, and were confounded, because that every man heard them speak in his own language. And they were all amazed and marvelled, saying one to another, "Behold are not all these which speak Galilaeans? And how hear we every man in our own tongue, wherein we were born? Parthians, and Medes, and Elamites, and the dwellers in Mesopotamia, and in Judaea, and Cappadocia, in Pontus, and Asia, Phrygia, and Pamphylia, in Egypt, and in the parts of Libya about Cyrene, and strangers of Rome, Jews and proselytes, Cretes and Arabians, we do hear them speak in our tongues the wonderful works of God." And they were all amazed, and were in doubt, saying one to another, "What meaneth this?" Others mocking said, "These men are full of new wine."

14. But Peter, standing up with the eleven, lifted up his voice, and said unto them, "Ye men of Judaea, and all ye that dwell at Jerusalem, be this known unto you, and hearken to my words. 15-21. For these are not drunken, as ye suppose, seeing it is but the third hour of the day. But this is that which was spoken by the prophet Joel: 'And it shall come

to pass in the last days,' saith God, 'I will pour out of my Spirit upon all flesh: and your sons and your daughters shall prophesy, and your young men shall see visions, and your old men shall dream dreams: And on my servants and on my handmaidens I will pour out in those days of my Spirit; and they shall prophesy. And I will shew wonders in heaven above, and signs in the earth beneath; blood, and fire, and vapour of smoke: The sun shall be turned into darkness, and the moon into blood, before the great and notable day of the Lord come. And it shall come to pass, that whosoever shall call on the name of the Lord shall be saved.' 22. Ye men of Israel, hear these words; Jesus of Nazareth, a man approved of God among you by miracles and wonders and signs, which God did by him in the midst of you, as ye yourselves also know. 23. Him, being delivered by the determinate counsel and foreknowledge of God, ye have taken, and by wicked hands have crucified and slain. 24. Whom God hath raised up, having loosed the pains of death: because it was not possible that he should be holden of it. 25. For David speaketh concerning him, 'I foresaw the Lord always before my face, for he is on my right hand, that I should not be moved. 26-28. Therefore did my heart rejoice, and my tongue was glad; moreover also my flesh shall rest in hope: Because thou wilt not leave my soul in hell, neither wilt thou suffer thine Holy One to see corruption. Thou hast made known to me the ways of life; thou shalt make me full of joy with thy countenance.' 29-31. Men and brethren, let me freely speak unto you of the patriarch David, that he is both dead and buried, and his sepulchre is with us unto this day. Therefore being a prophet, and knowing that God had sworn with an oath to him, that of the fruit of his loins, according to the flesh, he would raise up Christ to sit on his throne; he seeing this before spake of the resurrection of Christ, and his soul was not left in hell neither his flesh did see corruption. 32-33. This Jesus hath God raised up, whereof we all are witnesses. Therefore being by the right hand of God exalted, and having received of the Father the promise of the Holy Ghost, he hath shed forth this, which ye now see and hear. 34-35. For David is not ascended into the heavens: but he saith himself, 'The LORD said unto my Lord, "Sit thou on my right hand, until I make thy foes thy footstool."' 36. Therefore let all the houses of Israel know assuredly, that God hath made that same Jesus, whom ye have crucified, both Lord and Christ."

37. Now when they heard this, they were pricked in their heart, and said unto Peter and to the rest of the apostles, "Men and brethren, what shall we do?" 38-41. Then Peter said unto them, "Repent, and be baptized every one of you in the name of Jesus Christ for the remission of sins, and ye shall receive the gift of the Holy Ghost. For the promise is unto you, and to your children, and to all that are afar off, even as many as the Lord our God shall call." And with many other words did he testify and exhort, saying, "Save yourselves from this untoward generation."

Then they that gladly received his word were baptized; and the same day there were added unto them about three thousand souls.

• • •

CHAPTER 6

7. And the word of God increased; and the number of the disciples multiplied in Jerusalem greatly; and a great company of the priests were obedient to the faith. 8. And Stephen, full of faith and power, did great wonders and miracles among the people.

8-10. Then there arose certain of the synagogue, which is called the synagogue of the Libertines, and Cyrenians, and Alexandrians, and of them of Cilicia and of Asia, disputing with Stephen. And they were not able to resist the wisdom and the spirit by which he spake. 11. Then they suborned men, which said, "We have heard him speak blasphemous words aganist Moses, and against God." 12-15. And they stirred up the people, and the elders, and the scribes, and came upon him, and caught him, and brought him to the council, and set up false witnesses, which said, "This man ceaseth not to speak blasphemous words against this holy place, and the law: For we have heard him say that his Jesus of Nazareth shall destroy this place, and shall change the customs which Moses delivered us." And all that sat in the council, looking stedfastly on him, saw his face as it had been the face of an angel.

CHAPTER 7

1. Then said the high priest, "Are these things so?" 2-50. And he said, "Men, brethren, and fathers, hearken: *[After defending himself by an appeal to the Old Testament, Stephen concludes:]* 51. Ye stiffnecked and uncircumcised in heart and ears, ye do always resist the Holy Ghost: as your fathers did, so shall ye. 52-53. Which of the prophets have not your fathers persecuted? And they have slain them which shewed before of the coming of the Just One; of whom ye have been now the betrayers and murderers: who have received the law by the disposition of angels, and have not kept it."

54. When they heard these things, they were cut to the heart, and they gnashed on him with their teeth. 55-56. But he, being full of the Holy Ghost, looked up stedfastly into heaven, and saw the glory of God, and Jesus standing on the right hand of God, and said, "Behold, I see the heavens opened, and the Son of man standing on the right hand of God." 57-59. Then they cried out with a loud voice, and stopped their ears, and ran upon him with one accord, and cast him out

of the city, and stoned him: and the witnesses laid down their clothes at a young man's feet, whose name was Saul. And they stoned Stephen, calling upon God, and saying, "Lord Jesus, receive my spirit." 60. And he kneeled down, and cried with a loud voice, "Lord, lay not this sin to their charge." And when he had said this, he fell asleep.

CHAPTER 8

1. And Saul was consenting unto his death. And at that time there was a great persecution against the church which was at Jerusalem; and they were all scattered abroad throughout the regions of Judaea and Samaria, except the apostles. 2-3. And devout men carried Stephen to his burial, and made great lamentation over him. As for Saul, he made havoc of the church, entering into every house, and haling men and women committed them to prison.

. . .

CHAPTER 9

1-2. And Saul, yet breathing out threatenings and slaughter against the disciples of the Lord, went unto the high priest, and desired of him letters to Damascus to the synagogues, that if he found any of this way, whether they were men or women, he might bring them bound into Jerusalem. 3-4. And as he journeyed, he came near Damascus: and suddenly there shined round about him a light from heaven. And he fell to the earth, and heard a voice saying unto him, "Saul, Saul, why persecutest thou me?" 5-9. And he said, "Who art thou, Lord?" And the Lord said, "I am Jesus whom thou persecutest: it is hard for thee to kick against the pricks." And he trembling and astonished said, "Lord, what wilt thou have me to do?" And the Lord said unto him, "Arise, and go into the city, and it shall be told thee what thou must do." And the men which journeyed with him stood speechless, hearing a voice, but seeing no man. And Saul arose from the earth; and when his eyes were opened he saw no man: but they led him by the hand, and brought him into Damascus. And he was three days without sight, and neither did eat nor drink. 10. And there was a certain disciple at Damascus, named Ananias; and to him said the Lord in a vision, "Ananias." And he said, "Behold, I am here, Lord." 11-12. And the Lord said unto him, "Arise, and go into the street which is called Straight, and enquire in the house of Judas for one called Saul, of Tarsus: for, behold, he prayeth, and hath seen in a vision, a man named Ananias coming in, and putting his hand on him, that he might receive his sight." 13-14. Then Ananias answered, "Lord, I have heard by many of this man, how much evil he hath done to thy saints at Jerusalem: And here he hath authority from the chief priests to bind all that call on thy name." 15-16. But the Lord said unto him, "Go thy way: for he is a chosen vessel unto me, to bear my name before the Gentiles, and kings, and the children of Israel: For I will shew him how great things he must suffer for my name's sake." 17. And Ananias went his way and entered into the house; and putting his hands on him said, "Brother Saul, the Lord, even Jesus, that appeared unto thee in the way as thou camest, hath sent me, that thou mightest receive thy sight, and be filled with the Holy Ghost." 18. And immediately there fell from his eyes as it had been scales: and he received sight forthwith, and arose, and was baptized. 19-20. And when he had received meat, he was strengthened. Then was Saul certain days with the disciples which were at Damascus. And straightway he preached Christ in the synagogues, that he is the Son of God. 21-22. But all that heard him were amazed, and said; "Is not this he that destroyed them which called on this name in Jerusalem, and came hither for that intent, that he might bring them bound unto the chief priests?" But Saul increased the more in strength, and confounded the Jews which dwelt at Damascus, proving that this is very Christ.

. . .

CHAPTER 10

1-3. There was a certain man in Caesarea called Cornelius, a centurion of the band called the Italian band. A devout man, and one that feared God with all his house, which gave much alms to the people, and prayed to God always. He saw in a vision evidently about the ninth hour of the day an angel of God coming in to him, and saying unto him, "Cornelius." 4-6. And when he looked on him, he was afraid, and said, "What is it, Lord?" And he said unto him, "Thy prayers and thine alms are come up for a memorial before God. And now send men to Joppa, and call for one Simon, whose surname is Peter: He lodgeth with one Simon a tanner, whose house is by the sea side: he shall tell thee what thou oughtest to do." 7-8. And when the angel which spake unto Cornelius was departed, he called two of his household servants, and a devout soldier of them that waited on him continually; and when he had declared all these things unto them, he sent them to Joppa. 9-13. On the morrow, as they went on their journey, and drew nigh into the city, Peter went up upon the housetop to pray about the sixth hour. And he became very hungry, and would have eaten: but while they made ready, he fell into a trance, and saw heaven opened, and a certain vessel descending unto him, as it had been a great sheet knit at the four corners, and let down to the earth: wherein were all manner of four-footed beasts of the earth, and wild beasts, and creeping things, and fowls of the air. And there came a voice to him, "Rise, Peter; kill, and eat." 14. But Peter said, "Not so, Lord; for I have never eaten any thing that is common or unclean." 15-18. And the voice spake unto him again the second time, "What God hath cleansed, that call not thou common." This was done thrice: and the vessel was received up again into heaven. Now while Peter doubted in himself what this vision which he had seen should mean, behold, the men which were sent from Cornelius had made enquiry for Simon's house, and stood before the gate, and called, and asked whether Simon, which was surnamed Peter, were lodged there.

19. While Peter thought on the vision, the Spirit said unto him, "Behold, three men seek thee. 20. Arise therefore, and get thee down, and go with them doubting nothing: for I have sent them." 21. Then Peter went down to the men which were sent unto him from Cornelius; and said, "Behold, I am he whom ye seek: what is the cause wherefore ye are come?" 22. And they said, "Cornelius the centurion, a just man, and one that feareth God, and of good report among all the nation of the Jews, was warned from God by an holy angel to send for thee into his house, and to hear words of thee." 23. Then called he them in, and lodged them. And on the morrow Peter went away with them, and certain brethren from Joppa accompanied him. 24-27. And the morrow after they entered into Caesarea. And Cornelius waited for them, and had called together his kinsmen and near friends. And as Peter was coming in, Cornelius met him, and fell down at his feet, and worshipped him. But Peter took him up, saying, "Stand up; I myself also am a man." And as he talked with him, he went in, and found many that were come together. 28-33. And he said unto them, 'Ye know how that it is an unlawful thing for a man that is a Jew to keep company, or come unto one of another nation; but God hath shewed me that I should not call any man common or unclean. Therefore came I unto you without gain-saying, as soon as I was sent for: I ask therefore for what intent ye have sent for me? And Cornelius said, "Four days ago I was fasting until this hour; and at the ninth hour I prayed in my house, and, behold, a man stood before me in bright clothing. And said, 'Cornelius, thy prayer is heard, and thine alms are had in remembrance in the sight of God. Send therefore to Joppa, and call hither Simon, whose surname is Peter; he is lodged in the house of one Simon a tanner by the sea side: who, when he cometh, shall speak unto thee.' Immediately therefore I sent to thee; and thou hast well done that thou art come. Now therefore are we all here present before God, to hear all things that are commanded thee of God." 34-35. Then Peter opened his mouth, and said, "Of a truth I perceive that God is no respecter of persons: But in every nation he that feareth him, and worketh righteousness, is accepted with him. 36-43. The word which God sent unto the children of Israel, preaching peace by Jesus Christ (He is Lord of all:) The word, I say, ye know, which was published throughout all Judaea, and began from Galilee, after the baptism which John preached; how God anointed Jesus of Nazareth with the Holy Ghost and with power: who went about doing good, and healing all that were oppressed of the devil; for God was with him. And we are witnesses of all things which he did both in the land of the Jews, and in Jerusalem; whom they slew and hanged on a tree: Him God raised up the third day, and shewed him openly; not to all the people, but unto witnesses chosen before of God, even to us, who did eat and drink with him after he rose from the dead. And he commanded us to preach unto the people, and to testify that it is he which was ordained of God to be the Judge of quick and dead. To him give all the prophets witness, that through his name whosoever believeth in him shall receive remission of sins."

44-48. While Peter yet spake these words, the Holy Ghost fell on all them which heard the word. And they of the circumcision which believed were astonished, as many as came with Peter, because that on the Gentiles also was poured out the gift of the Holy Ghost. For they heard them speak with tongues, and magnify God. Then answered Peter, "Can any man forbid water, that these should not be baptized, which have received the Holy Ghost as well as we?" And he commanded them to be baptized in the name of the Lord.

Questions:
1. *Compare Peter's sermon with Stephen's. How do the responses to these sermons differ?*
2. *According to Stephen's sermon, who may or may not receive the gift of the Holy Spirit? How is this confirmed by the crowd's response?*

6.2 Pliny the Younger on the Vesuvius Eruption and the Christian "Controversy"

Gaius Plinius Secondus, or "Pliny the Younger" (62–113 C.E.), has always stood in the shadow of his illustrious uncle and adoptive father, Pliny the Elder, but grew up to be a competent official in his own right. His letters "Epistulae" provide a significant insight into major events and problems in the early Roman Empire. The first of these describes, for the historian Tacitus, the Mount Vesuvius explosion of 79 C.E., and the second is an exchange with the Emperor Trajan over how Pliny, in his capacity as governor of Bithynia, might best deal with members of the illegal sect of Christianity.

Source: Betty Radice, trans., *The Letters of the Younger Pliny* (Baltimore: Penguin, 1963), pp. 166–168, 293–295.

TO CORNELIUS TACITUS

Thank you for asking me to send you a description of my uncle's death so that you can leave an accurate account of it for posterity; I know that immortal fame awaits him if his death is recorded by you. It is true that he perished in a catastrophe which destroyed the loveliest regions of the earth, a fate shared by whole cities and their people, and one so memorable that it is likely to make his name live for ever: and he himself wrote a number of books of lasting value: but you write for all time and can still do much to perpetuate his memory. The fortunate man, in my opinion, is he to whom the gods have granted the power either to do something which is worth recording or to write what is worth reading, and most fortunate of all is the man who can do both. Such a man was my uncle, as his own books and yours will prove. So you set me a task I would choose for myself, and I am more than willing to start on it.

My uncle was stationed at Misenum in active command of the fleet. On 24 August, in the early afternoon, my mother drew attention to a cloud of unusual size and appearance. He had been out in the sun, had taken a cold bath, and lunched while lying down, and was then working at his books. He called for his shoes and climbed up to a place which would give him the best view of the phenomenon. It was not clear at that distance from which mountain the cloud was rising (it was afterwards known to be Vesuvius); its general appearance can best be expressed as being like an umbrella pine, for it rose to a great height on a sort of trunk and then split off into branches, I imagine because it was thrust upwards by the first blast and then left unsupported as the pressure subsided, or else it was borne down by its own weight so that it spread out and gradually dispersed. In places it looked white, elsewhere blotched and dirty, according to the amount of soil and ashes it carried with it. My uncle's scholarly acumen saw at once that it was important enough for a closer inspection, and he ordered a boat to be made ready, telling me I could come with him if I wished. I replied that I preferred to go on with my studies, and as it happened he had himself given me some writing to do.

As he was leaving the house he was handed a message from Rectina, wife of Tascus whose house was at the foot of the mountain, so that escape was impossible except by boat. She was terrified by the danger threatening her and implored him to rescue her from her fate. He changed his plans, and what he had begun in a spirit of inquiry he completed as a hero. He gave orders for the warships to be launched and went on board himself with the intention of bringing help to many more people besides Rectina, for this lovely stretch of coast was thickly populated. He hurried to the place where everyone else was hastily leaving, steering his course straight for the danger zone. He was entirely fearless, describing each new movement and phase of the portent to be noted down exactly as he observed them. Ashes were already falling, hotter and thicker as the ships drew near, followed by bits of pumice and blackened stones, charred and cracked by the flames: then suddenly they were in shallow water, and the shore was blocked by debris from the mountain. For a moment my uncle wondered whether to turn back, but when the helmsman advised this he refused, telling him that Fortune stood by the courageous and that they must make for Pomponianus at Stabiae. He was cut off there by the breadth of the bay (for the shore gradually curves round a basin filled by the sea) so that he was not as yet in danger, though it was clear that this would come nearer as it spread. Pomponianus had therefore already put his belongings on board ship, intending to escape if the contrary wind fell. This wind was of course full in my uncle's favour, and he was able to bring his ship in. He embraced his terrified friend, cheered and encouraged him, and thinking he could calm his fears by showing his own composure, gave orders that he was to be carried to the bathroom. After his bath he lay down and dined; he was quite cheerful, or at any rate he pretended he was, which was no less courageous.

Meanwhile on Mount Vesuvius broad sheets of fire and leaping flames blazed at several points, their bright glare emphasized by the darkness of night. My uncle tried to allay the fears of his companion by repeatedly declaring that these were nothing but bonfires left by the peasants in their terror, or else empty homes on fire in the districts they had abandoned. Then he went to rest and certainly slept, for as he was a stout man his breathing was rather loud and heavy and could be heard by people coming and going outside his door. By this time the courtyard giving access to his room was full of ashes mixed with pumice-stones, so that its level had risen, and if he had stayed in the room any longer he would never have got out. He was wakened, came out and joined Pomponianus and the rest of the household who had sat up all night. They debated whether to stay indoors or take their chance in the open, for the buildings were now shaking with violent shocks, and seemed to be swaying to and fro as if they were torn from their foundations. Outside on the other hand, there was the danger of falling pumice-stones, even though these were light and porous; however, after comparing the risks they chose the latter. In my uncle's case one reason outweighed the other, but for the others it was a choice of fears. As a protection against falling objects they put pillows on their heads tied down with cloths.

Elsewhere there was daylight by this time, but they were still in darkness, blacker and denser than any ordinary night, which they relieved by lighting torches and various kinds of lamp. My uncle decided to go down to the shore and investigate on the spot the possibility of any escape by sea, but he found the waves still wild and dangerous. A sheet was spread on the ground for him to lie down, and he repeatedly asked for cold water to drink. Then the flames and smell of sulphur which gave warning of the approaching fire drove the others to take flight and roused him to stand up. He stood leaning on two slaves and then suddenly collapsed, I imagine because the dense fumes choked his breathing by blocking his windpipe which was constitutionally weak and narrow and often inflamed. When daylight returned on the 26th—two days after the last day he had seen—his body was found intact and uninjured, still fully clothed and looking more like sleep than death.

Meanwhile my mother and I were at Misenum, but this is not of any historic interest, and you only wanted to hear about my uncle's death. I will say no more, except to add that I have described in detail every incident which I either witnessed myself or heard about immediately after the event, when reports were most likely to be accurate. It is for you to select what best suits your purpose, for there is a great difference between a letter to a friend and history written well for all to read.

PLINY TO THE EMPEROR TRAJAN

It is my custom to refer all my difficulties to you, Sir, for no one is better able to resolve my doubts and to inform my ignorance.

I have never been present at an examination of Christians. Consequently, I do not know the nature of the extent of the punishments usually meted out to them, nor the grounds for starting an investigation and how far it should be pressed. Nor am I at all sure whether any distinction should be made between them on the grounds of age, or if young people and adults should be treated alike; whether a pardon ought to be granted to anyone retracting his beliefs, or if he has once professed Christianity, he shall gain nothing by renouncing it; and whether it is the mere name of Christian which is punishable, even if innocent of crime, or rather crimes associated with the name.

For the moment this is the line I have taken with all persons brought before me on the charge of being Christians. I have asked them in person if they are Christians, and if they admit it, I repeat the question a second and a third time, with a warning of punishment awaiting them. If they persist, I order them to be led away for execution; for, whatever the nature of their admission, I am convinced that their stubbornness and unshakeable obstinacy ought not to go unpunished. There have been others similarly fanatical who are Roman citizens. I have entered them on the list of persons to be sent to Rome for trial.

Now that I have begun to deal with this problem, as so often happens, the charges are becoming more widespread and increasing in variety. An anonymous pamphlet has been circulated which contains the names of a number of accused persons. Amongst these I considered that I should dismiss any who denied that they were or had been Christians when they had repeated after me a formula of invocation to the gods and had made offerings of wine and incense to your statue (which I had ordered to be brought into court for this purpose along with the images of the gods), and furthermore had reviled the name of Christ: none of which things, I understand, any genuine Christian can be induced to do.

Others, whose names were given to me by an informer, first admitted the charge and then denied it; they said that they had ceased to be Christiana two or more years previously, and some of them even twenty years ago. They all did reverence to your statue and the images of the gods in the same way as the others, and reviled the name of Christ. They also declared that the sum total of their guilt or error mounted to no more than this: they had met regularly before dawn on a fixed day to chant verses alternately amongst themselves in honour of Christ as if to a god, and also to bind themselves by oath, not for any criminal purpose, but to abstain from theft, robbery, and adultery, to commit no breach of trust and not to deny a deposit when called upon to restore it. After this ceremony it had been their custom to disperse and reassemble later to take food of an ordinary, harmless kind; but they had in fact given up this practice since my edict, issued on your instructions, which banned all political societies. This made me decide it was all the more necessary to extract the truth by torture from two slave-women, whom they call deaconesses. I found nothing but a degenerate sort of cult carried to extravagant lengths.

I have therefore postponed any further examination and hastened to consult you. The question seems to me to be worthy of your consideration, especially in view of the number of persons endangered; for a great many individuals of every age and class, both men and women, are being brought to trial, and this is likely to continue. It is not only the towns, but villages and rural districts too which are infected through contact with this wretched cult. I think though that it is still possible for it to be checked and directed to better ends, for there is no doubt that people have begun to throng the temples which had been almost entirely deserted for a long time; the sacred rites which had been allowed to lapse are being performed again, and flesh of sacrificial victims is on sale everywhere, though up till recently scarcely anyone could be found to buy it. It is easy to infer from this that a great many people could be reformed if they were given an opportunity to repent.

TRAJAN TO PLINY

You have followed the right course of procedure, my dear Pliny, in your examination of the cases of persons charged with being Christians, for it is impossible to lay down a general rule to a fixed formula. These people must not be hunted out; if they are brought before you and the charge against them is proved, they must be punished, but in the case of anyone who denies that he is a Christian, and makes it clear that he is not by offering prayers to our gods, he is to be pardoned as a result of his repentance however suspect his past conduct may be. But pamphlets circulated anonymously must play no part in any accusation. They create the worst sort of precedent and are quite out of keeping with the spirit of our age.

Questions:
1. *What traits exhibited by Pliny's uncle during the crisis of the Vesuvius eruption are held up as being the most admirable, and why?*
2. *From certain comments made by Pliny in his letter to Tacitus, what does he envision as being the historian's task?*
3. *What dilemma was Pliny faced with regarding people accused of practicing Christianity, and what administrative procedures did he follow?*
4. *To what extent and in what manner does the Emperor both praise and criticize Pliny in his letter of reply?*

6.3 Julian Imperator: The Ultimate Pagan

Julian, Emperor of Rome (reigned 361–363 B.C.E.), was a throwback to the Augustan period. Having been baptized and raised a Christian, he reverted to the ancestral paganism of the Civic cult, and was thus labelled by future (Christian) historians with the uncomplimentary term: "the Apostate." Julian was running against the spirit of his age and his attempted pagan revival collapsed upon his death. During his brief reign—as his letters demonstrate—he endeavored to straddle both worlds with a policy of tol- eration. The following excerpts from his letters address: the ironic punishment of Arian Christians; the lin- gering of paganist sentiment and forms, even in Christian settings; admiration for Christian charity; and adminitions for restraint while dealing with Christians ("Galileans").

> **Source:** Finley Hooper & Matthew Schwartz, ed., *Roman Letters: History from a Personal Point of View* (Detroit: Wayne State University Press, 1991), pp. 133, 136, 139, 140, 142.

I have behaved to all the Galilaeans [Christians] with such kindness and benevolence that none of them has suffered vio- lence anywhere or been dragged into a temple or threatened into anything else of the sort against his own will. But the fol- lowers of the Arian church, in the insolence bred by their wealth, have attacked the followers of Valentine [founder of an obscure sect of Gnostics] and have committed in Edessa such rash acts as could never occur in a well-ordered city. There- fore, since by their most admirable law they are bidden to sell all they have and give to the poor that so they may attain more easily to the kingdom of the skies, in order to aid those persons in that effort, I have ordered that all their funds, namely, that belong to the church of the people of Edessa, are to be taken over that they may be given to the soldiers, and that its property be confiscated to my private purse. This is in order that poverty may teach them to behave properly and that they may not be deprived of that heavenly kingdom for which they still hope.

***

I stayed [in Beroea, modern Aleppo in northwest Syria] for a day and saw the Acropolis and sacrificed to Zeus in imper- ial fashion a white bull. Also I conversed briefly with the senate about the worship of the gods. But though they all applauded my arguments very few were converted by them, and these few were men who even before I spoke seemed to me to hold sound views. But they were cautious and would not strip off and lay aside their modest reserve, as though afraid of too frank speech. For it is the prevailing habit of mankind, O ye gods, to blush for their noble qualities, manliness of soul and piety, and to plume themselves, as it were, on what is most depraved, sacrilege and weakness of mind and body.

***

I should never have favoured Pegasius unhesitatingly if I had not had clear proofs even in former days, when he had the title of the Bishop of the Galileans [Christians], he was wise enough to revere and honour the gods....after rising at early dawn I came from Troas to Iliois about the middle of the morning. Pegasius came to meet me, as I wished to explore the city—this was my excuse for visiting the temples—and he was my guide and showed me all the sights. So now let me tell you what he did and said, and from it one may guess that he was not lacking in right sentiments towards the gods.

Hector has a hero's shrine there and his bronze statue stands in a tiny little temple. Opposite this they have set up a figure of the great Achilles in the unroofed court....Now I found that the altars were still alight a I might almost say still blazing, and that the statue of Hector had been anointed till it shone. So I looked at Pegasius and said: "What does this mean? Do the people of Ilios offer sacrifices?" This was to test him cautiously, to find out his own views. He replied: "Is it not natural that they should worship a brave man who was their own citizen, just as we worship the martyrs?" Now the analogy was far from sound; but his point of view and intentions were those of a man of culture, if you consider the times in which we then lived. Observe what followed. "Let us go," said he, "to the shrine of Athene of Ilios." Thereupon with the greatest eagerness he led me there and opened the temple, and as though he were producing evidence he showed me all the statues in perfect preservation, nor did he behave at all as those impious men do usually, I mean when they make the sign on their impious foreheads, nor did he hiss to himself as they do. For these two things are the quintessence of their theology, to hiss at demons and make the sign of the cross on their foreheads....This same Pegasius went with me to the temple of Achilles as well and showed me the tomb in good repair; yet I had been informed that this also had been pulled to pieces by him. But he approached it with great reverence; I saw this with my own eyes.

***

Why...do we not observe that it is their benevolence to strangers, their care for the graves of the dead and the pretended holiness of their lives that have done most to increase atheism [Julian often refers to Christianity this way]? I believe that we ought really and truly to practice every one of these virtues. And it is not enough for you alone to practice them, but so must all the priests in Galatia, without exception...In the second place, admonish them that no priest may enter a theatre or drink in a tavern or control any craft or trade that is base and not respectable. Honour those who obey you, but those who disobey, expel from office. In every city establish frequent hostels in order that strangers may profit by our benevolence; I do not mean for our own people only, but for others also who are in need of money....For it is disgraceful that, when no Jew ever has to beg and the impious Galilaeans [Christians] support not only their own poor but ours as well, all men see that our people lack aid from us.

***

I thought that the leaders of the Galilaeans would be more grateful to me than to my predecessor in the administration of the Empire. For in his reign it happened to the majority of them to be sent into exile, prosecuted, and cast into prison, and moreover, many whole communities of those who are called "heretics" were actually butchered, as at Samosata and Cyzicus, in Paphlagonia, Bithynia, and Galatia, among many other tribes also villages were sacked and completely devastated; whereas, during my reign, the contrary has happened. For those who had been exiled have had their exile remitted, and those whose property was confiscated have, by a law of mine received permission to recover all their possessions. Yet they have reached such a pitch of raving madness and folly that they are exasperated because they are not allowed to behave like tyrants or to persist in the conduct in which they at one time indulged against one another, and afterwards carried on towards us who revered the gods....but do you, the populace, live in agreement with one another, and let no man be quarrelsome or act unjustly. Neither let those of you who have strayed from the truth outrage those who worship the gods duly and justly, according to the beliefs that have been handed down to us from time immemorial; nor let those of you who worship the gods outrage or plunder the houses of those who have strayed rather from ignorance than of set purpose. It is by reason that we ought to persuade and instruct men, not by blows, or insults, or bodily violence. Wherefore, again and often I admonish those who are zealous for true religion not to injure the communities of the Galilaeans or attack or insult them....

***

I affirm by the gods that I do not wish the Galilaeans to be either put to death or unjustly beaten, or to suffer any other injury; but nevertheless I do assert absolutely that the god-fearing must be preferred to them. For through the folly of the Galilaeans almost everything has been overturned, whereas through the grace of the gods are we all preserved. Wherefore we ought to honour the gods and the god-fearing, both men and cities.

Questions:
1. *How does Julian administer an ironic/humorous penalty upon the Arians?*
2. *What do the letters referring to the Emperor's stay in Beroea and his meeting with Bishop Pegasius reveal about the state of pagan worship?*
3. *What significant Christian virtue does Julian grudgingly concede, and how does he describe his administrative policy towards the Christian church?*
4. *How does Julian's attitude contrast with that of Pliny and Trajan in Document 6–4? What inferences can be drawn?*

6.4   Bishop Synesius of Cyrene: A Lukewarm Churchman

In contrast with the steadfast conduct of the martyrs as described by Eusebius, there were some Christians who would not have carried their zeal for the faith to such lengths. Synesius (365?–414), who was born in North Africa, was a worldly-wise, skeptical man who was versed in hermetic studies through the school of Hypatia of Alexandria, and in Neoplatonic philosophy. Though he was named Bishop of Cyrene in 410, he was never that zealous in his faith, as evidenced from this letter to his brother.

Source: Finley Cooper & Matthew Schwartz, eds., *Roman letters: History from a Personal Point of View* (Detroit: Wayne State University, 1991), pp. 264–267.

I should be altogether lacking in sense, if I did not show myself very grateful to the inhabitants of Ptokmais, who consider me worthy of an honour to which I should never have dared to aspire. At the same time I ought to examine, not the importance of the duties with which they desire to entrust me, but merely my own capacity for fulfillng them. To see oneself called to a vocation which is almost divine, when after all one is only a man, is a great source of ioy, if one really deserves it. But if, on the other hand, one is very unworthy of it, the prospects of the future are sombre. It is by no means a recent fear of mine, but a very old one, the fear of winning honour from men at the price of sinning against God.

When I examine myself, I fail to find the capacity necessary to raise me to the sanctity of such a priesthood as this. I will now speak to you of the emotions of my soul: for I cannot speak to any one in preference to you who are so dear to me, and have been brought up with me. It is quite natural that you should share my anxieties, that you should watch with me during the night, and that by day we should search together whatever may bring me joy or turn sorrow away from me. Let me tell you, then, how my circumstances are, ahhough you know in advance most of what I am going to say to you.

I took up a light burden, and up to this moment I think I have borne it well. It is, in a word, philosophy Inasmuch as I have never fallen too far below the level of the duties which it imposed upon me, people have praised me for my work. And I am regarded as capable of better things still, by those who do not know how to estimate in what directions my talents lie. Now, if I frivolously accept the dignity of the position which has been offered to me, I fear I may fail in both causes, slighting the one, without at the same time raising myself to the high level of the other. Consider the situation. All my days are divided between study and recreation. In my hours of work, above all when I am occupied with divine matters, I withdraw into myself. In my leisure hours I give myself up to my friends. For you know that when I look up from my books, I like to enter into every sort of sport. I do not share in the political turn of mind, either by nature or in my pursuits. [That statement seems to be at variance with his own actions, however.] But the priest should be a man above human weaknesses. He should be a stranger to every sort of diversion, even as God Himself. All eyes are keeping watch on him to see that he justifies his mission. He is of little or no use unless he has made himself austere and unyielding towards any pleasure. In carrying out his holy office he should belong no longer to himself, but to all men. He is a teacher of the law, and must utter that which is approved by law. In addition to all this, he has as many calls upon him as all the rest of the world put together, for the affairs of all he alone must attend to, or incur the reproaches of all.

Now, unless he has a great and noble soul, how can he sustain the weight of so many cares without his intellect being submerged? How can he keep the divine flame alive within him when such varied duties claim him on every side? I know well that there are such men l have every admiration for their character, and I regard them as really divine men, whom intercourse with man's affairs does not separate from God. But I know myself also. I go down to the town, and from the town I come up again, always enveloped in thoughts that drag me down to earth, and covered with more stains than anybody could imagine. In a word, I have so many personal defilements of old date, that the slightest addition fills up my measure. My strength fails me I have no strength and there is no health in me. I am not equal to confronting what is without me, and I am far from being able to bear the distress of my own conscience. If anybody asks me what my idea of a bishop is, I have no hesitation in saying explicitly that he ought to be spotless, more than spotless, in all things, he to whom is allotted the purification of others.

In writing to you, my brother, l have still another thing to say You will not be by any means the only one to read this letter. In addressing it to you, I wish above all things to make known to every one what I feel, so that whatever happens hereafter, no one will have a right to accuse me before God or before man, nor, above all, before the venerable Theophilus [the bishop of Alexandria]. In publishing my thoughts, and in giving myself up entirely to his decision, how can I be in the wrong? God himself, the law of the land, and the blessed hand of Theophilus himself have given me a wife. I, therefore, proclaim to all and call them to witness once for all that I will not be separated from her, nor shall I associate with her surrepticiously like an adulterer; for of these two acts, the one is impious, and the other is unlawful. I shall desire and pray to have many virtuous children. This is what I must inform the man upon whom depends my consecration. Let him learn this from his comrades Paul and Dionysius, for I understand that they have become his deputies by the will of the people.

There is one point, however, which is not new to Theophilus, but of which I must remind him. I must press my point here a little more, for beside his difficulty all the others are as nothing. It is difficult, if not quite impossible, that convictions should be shaken, which have entered the soul through knowledge to the point of demonstration. Now you know that philosophy rejects many of those convictions which are cherished by the common people. For my own part, I can never persuade myself that the soul is of more recent origin than the body. Never would l admit that the world and the parts which make it up must perish. This resurrection, which is an object of common belief, is nothing for me but a sacred and mysterious allegory, and I am far from sharing the views of the vulgar crowd thereon. The philosophic mind, albeit the discerner of truth, admits the employment of falsehood, for light is to truth what the eye is to the mind. Just as the eye would be injured by excess of light, and just as darkness is more helpful to those of weak eyesight, even so do I consider that the false may be beneficial to the populace, and the truth injurious to those not strong enough to gaze steadfastly on the radiance of real being. If the laws of the priesthood that obtain with us permit these views to me, I can take over the holy office on condition that I may prosecute philosophy at home and spread legends abroad, so that if I teach no doctrine, at all events I undo no teaching, and allow men to remain in their already acquired convictions. But if anybody says to me that he must be under this influence, that the bishop must belong to the people in his opinions, I shall betray myself very quickly. What can there be in common between the ordinary man and philosophy? Divine truth should remain hidden, but the vulgar need a different system. I shall never cease repeating that I think the wise man, to the extent that necessity allows, should not force his opinions upon others, nor allow others to force theirs upon him.

No, if I am called to the priesthood, I declare before God and man that I refuse to preach dogmas in which I do not believe. Truth is an attribute of God, and I wish in all things to be blameless before Him. This one thing I will not dissimulate. I feel that I have a good deal of inclination for amusements. Even as a child, I was charged with a mania for arms and horses. I shall be grieved, indeed greatly shall I suffer at seeing my beloved dogs deprived of their hunting, and my bow eaten up by worms. Nevertheless I shall resign myself to this, if it is the will of God. Again, I hate all care; nevertheless, whatever it costs, I will endure lawsuits and quarrels, so long as I can fulfil this mission, heavy though it he, according to God's will; but never will I consent to conceal my beliefs, nor shall my opinions be at war with my tongue. l believe that I am pleasing God in thinking and speaking thus. I do not wish to give any one the opportunity of saying that I, an unknown man, grasped at the appointment. But let the beloved of God, the right reverend Theophilus, knowing the situation and giving me clear evidence that he understands it, decide on this issue concerning me. He will then either leave me to myself to lead my own life, and to philosophize, or he will not leave himself any grounds on which hereafter to sit in judgment over me, and to turn me out of the ranks of the priesthood. In comparison with these truths, every opinion is insignificant, for I know well that Truth is dearest to God. I swear it by your sacred head, nay, better still, I swear by God the guardian of Truth that I suffer. How can I fail to suffer, when I must, as it were, remove from one life to another? But if after those things have been made clear which I least desire to conceal, if the man who holds this power from Heaven persists in putting me in the hierarchy of bishops I will submit to the inevitable, and I will accept the token as divine. For I reason thus, that if the emperor or some ill-fated Augustal had given an order, I should have been punished if I disobeyed, but that one must obey God with a willing heart. But even at the expense of God's not admitting me to this service, I must nevertheless place first my love for Truth, the most divine thing of all. And I must not slip into His service through ways most opposed to it—such as falsehood. See then that the scholasti [We would say intellectuals of Alexandria] know well my sentiments, and that they inform Theophilus. (105)

Questions:
1. *In what ways does Synesius believe that he falls short of the priestly requirements?*
2. *What important dogmas of church belief does Synesius doubt? And how so?*
3. *What does Synesius assert that he will not do if he becomes a bishop?*
4. *What individual is dominant in this letter: Synesius the philosopher or Synesius the Christian? Explain.*

6.5   Leo I: The Man Who Laid the Foundations for the Medieval Papacy

There is no evidence that, during the Church's early years, the Bishop of Rome was held in any greater esteem than his colleagues who shepherded the major cities of the time: Antioch, Alexandria, or Jerusalem. It was only after four centuries had elapsed that the leadership claims of the Bishop of Rome (who assumed the title of "Pope), on the basis of Apostolic Succession to St. Peter, and an interpretation of Matthew 16:13–19, were solidified into the Petrine Theory. It was Pope Leo I (440–461) who most effectively asserted these claims of supremacy as representative of Christ on earth. In the following instance, he states some of these claims while attacking an opponent, Bishop Hilary of Aries.

> **Source:** Filey Cooper and Matthew Schwartz. eds., *Roman letters: History from a Personal Point of View* (Detroit: Wayne State University, 1991), pp. 291–292.

Our Lord Jesus Christ, Saviour of the human race, desired to have the observance of divine religion shine out through God's grace unto all nations and races. He established it in such a way that truth, previously contained only in proclamations of the Law and the Prophets, might proceed from the Apostles' trumpet for the salvation of all, as it is written: "Their sound has gone forth unto all the earth: and their words unto the ends of the world." Now, the Lord desired that the dispensing of this gift should be shared as a task by all the Apostles, but in such a way that He put the principal charge on the most blessed Peter, the highest of all the Apostles. He wanted His gifts to flow into the entire body from Peter himself, as it were from the head…But the man who attempts to infringe on its power by furthering his own desires and not following practices received from antiquity is trying with absolutely blasphemous presumption, to destroy this most sacred solidity of that rock, established with God as the builder, as we mentioned. For he believes that he is subject to no law, that he is not restrained by any regulations that the Lord ordained. Being intent on novel assumption of power, he departs from what you and we are accustomed to; he presumes to do what is illegal and neglects traditions that he ought to have maintained…Your Fraternities should, of course, realize with us that the Apostolic See (out of reverence for it) has countless times been reported to in consultation by bishops even in your province. And through the appeal of various cases to it, decisions already made have been either rescinded or confirmed, as dictated by long-standing custom. As a result, with "unity of spirit in the bond of peace" being preserved, with letters being sent and received, what was done in a holy manner has been conducive to abiding charity. For our solicitude, which seeks not its own interests but those of Christ, does not detract from the dignity given by God to the churches and the bishops of the churches. This was the procedure always well observed and profitably maintained by our predecessors. But Hilary has departed from it, aiming to disturb the status of the churches and harmony among the bishops by his novel usurpations of power. He seeks to subject you to his authority while not allowing himself to be under the Jurisdiction of the blessed Apostle Peter. He claims for himself the right to consecrate in all the churches of Gaul and takes as his own the dignity which belongs to the metropolitan bishops. He even lessens the reverence due to the most blessed Peter himself by his quite arrogant statements. And although the power to bind and loose was given to Peter before the others, still, in an even more special way, the pasturing ot the sheep was entrusted to him. Anyone who thinks that the primacy should be denied to Peter cannot in any way lessen the Apostle's dignity: inflated with the wind of his own pride, he buries himself in hell.

Questions:
1. *Of what does Leo accuse Bishop Hilary?*
2. *How does Leo explain his ideas as to why Christ would have placed the Apostle Peter in the position of leadership?*
3. *What consequences does Leo forsee for what he views as Hilary's insubordinate actions?*

6.6 St. Augustine of Hippo, The Just War

St. Augustine was the first father of the church to develop the theory of the just war. His ideas emerged in response to current events, as Christians were required to cope with increasing threats to the security of the empire. Pieced together from numerous topical writings he completed over the years, his theory can be presented in terms of four characteristics that a just war must have: (1) It must be defensive in nature. (2) It must not do more damage than it prevents. (3) Its aim must be the restoration of peace, rather than the expansion of control. (4) It must be waged only by constituted authority.

> **Source:** From *De civitate Dei libri* xxii, ed. Emmanuel Hoffman (Vienna: F. Tempsky, 1899–1900), extracts from Books I–V and XIX, *passim;* and *Contra Faustum libri xxxiii,* ed. Josephus Zycha (Vienna: F. Tempsky, 1891), extracts from Book XXII, chs. 74–75. Trans. Henry A. Myers.

ABOUT THE WAR IN WHICH KING RADAGAIS OF THE GOTHS, A WORSHIPPER OF DEMONS, WAS DEFEATED WITH HIS HUGE ARMY IN A SINGLE DAY

When Radagais, King of the Goths, was already threatening the Romans' very necks with his huge and savage army encamped near the city, he was beaten in one day with such speed and in such a way that not one single Roman was wounded, let alone killed, while well over a hundred thousand of his soldiers were struck down, and he was captured and soon put to a deserved death. For if such a godless man with such equally godless troops had entered Rome, who would have been spared by him? What shrines of the martyrs would he have respected? In dealing with what person would the fear of God have restrained him? Whose blood would he have wanted to leave unshed and whose chastity unravaged?

WHETHER THE SWEEP OF IMPERIAL COMMAND . . . IS AMONG THINGS OF VALUE FOR WISE AND HAPPY MEN

It makes sense that if the true God is worshipped and served with true rites and good morals, it is a benefit for good men to have long reigns over great territories. This is actually not of so much use to themselves as it is to their subjects, because as far as they themselves are concerned their own true faith and righteousness, which are great gifts from God, are enough to give them the true happiness that lets them live this life well and attain eternal life afterwards. Thus the reign of good men here on earth does not serve their own good so much as it does human concerns.

THE HARSH BRUTALITY IN THE SACK OF ROME CORRESPONDED WITH ESTABLISHED CUSTOMS OF WAR, WHEREAS THE MERCY SHOWN REVEALED THE POWER OF CHRIST'S NAME

All the destruction, killing, looting, burning, and suffering which took place in the recent sack of Rome happened in accordance with the customs of waging war. What was altogether new and previously unheard of, however, was that the barbarian brutality [of the Goths] was so tamed that they picked the largest of the basilicas and allowed them to remain sanctuaries, where no one could be struck down and from which no one could be dragged away. Many people were led there to freedom and safety by soldiers showing sympathy for them. . . . Anyone who does not see fit to credit this to the name of Christ—yes, to Christian times—is blind. Anyone who sees this new turn of events but fails to praise it is most ungrateful.

THE SAINTS LOSE NOTHING OF VALUE IN LOSING MATERIAL GOODS

In the sack of Rome faithful and godly men . . . "lost everything they had." How about their faith? How about their godliness? How about the goods of the inner being which make a person rich before God? Listen to what the Apostle Paul says about the riches of Christianity: " . . . Godliness with contentment is great gain, for we brought nothing into this world and certainly we can carry nothing out. If we have food and clothing, let us be content with them. People who want to be rich fall into temptations and traps. They fall into foolish and harmful desires which drown men in destruction and perdition."[1]

THE UNIVERSAL PEACE, WHICH THE LAW OF NATURE PRESERVES THROUGH ALL DISTURBANCES, AND THE CONDITION WHICH EACH PERSON DESERVES TO FIND HIMSELF IN, ACCORDING TO THE WAY HE HAS USED HIS WILL AND ACCORDING TO THE DECISION OF THE JUST JUDGE

Domestic peace is a harmonious arrangement in matters of command and obedience among those of the same household, and the peace of a [normal] city is a similar one among its citizens. The peace of the Heavenly City is the most perfectly and harmoniously designed communal relationship in the enjoyment of God and in the fellowship resulting from union with God. Peace for all beings is tranquility within order. Order is the arrangement of equal and unequal things, with each assigned its proper place.

And so we see that miserable people [lacking faith and godliness] . . . in the very fact that they justly deserve their misery are confined to a condition of misery by the principle of order. This keeps them from being united with saved people. When they live without obvious disturbances they adapt to their bondage, and so there is a bit of tranquil order among them, and so they enjoy a peace of sorts. They still remain miserable, however, since, in spite of not suffering constantly from a total lack of security, they are not within that realm where there is no cause to worry about either suffering or security. . . .

WHERE PEACE AND DISCORD BETWEEN THE HEAVENLY AND EARTHLY CITIES COME FROM

The Earthly City, which does not live by faith, desires an earthly peace, seeking to bring it about through harmony of command and obedience among citizens, even though its scope is limited to uniting people's wills on matters pertaining to this mortal life.

The Heavenly City, however, or, to be more precise, those of its members who are living by faith during their mortal pilgrimages, must make use of this peace, although only until they are through with their transient status on earth, which requires it. For this reason, the Heavenly City sojourning either as a captive or a wandering stranger in the Earthly City does not hesitate to obey earthly authority in matters required by the communal life of mortals. With mortal life common to the people of both Cities, a certain harmony between them may be maintained in relation to its requirements.

While the Heavenly City sojourns on earth, it recruits members from all peoples and forms a pilgrim society of men and women speaking all different languages, which pays no attention to the diversity of customs, laws, and institutions among them, by which earthly peace is established and maintained.

WHETHER WAR IS ALWAYS EVIL OR MAY SOMETIMES BE JUST

Just what is wrong with war? Is it that some people will die in it—people who will die sometime anyway—so that others may live in peace under authority? That is the objection of cowards, not believers. The real evils in war are: a love of inflicting violence, vengeful cruelty, raging and implacable hatred, ferocity in rebelling, lust for power, and similar things. It is normally to punish under law these very things that, at the command of God or some legitimate authority, good men resort to war against violent offenders. . . . Much depends on the reasons for which and the authority by which men commit themselves to waging war. The natural order among mortal men requires the promotion of peace. It justifies the exercise of military force through the authority and direction of the ruler when he decides it is necessary for soldiers to carry out their duties on behalf of the peace and safety of the community. When men wage war in obedience to God, it is not appropriate to doubt that it is waged justly either to deter, or humble, or subdue the pride of men.

Questions:
1. Why does St. Augustine view the sack of Rome as a cause for heightened, rather than diminished, respect for Christianity?
2. Why is a temporary peace observable between the City of God and the Earthly City?

6.7   Paulus Orosius, History Against the Pagans

In writing this dissertation for St. Augustine, Orosius became the first Christian graduate student on record. His work, entitled without the slightest pretense of objectivity, Seven Books of History Against the Pagans, became the Christian textbook of world history, as opposed to plain Church history, from creation to A.D. 417.

> **Source:** From *Historiarum adversum paganos libri* VII, ed. Karl Zangemeister (Vienna: C. Gerold, 1882), excerpts from Books III, viii, 5–8, and V, i, 10–13, ii, 1–8. Trans. Allen C. Myers.

Let us assume there is no doubt about the fact that it was under Augustus Caesar, following the peace treaty with the Parthians, that for the first time the entire world laid down its arms and overcame its disagreements under an all-encompassing peace and new tranquility in obedience of Roman laws. Foreign peoples preferred relying on Roman laws to relying on their own arms. All races, all provinces, innumerable city-states, infinite populations—in fact, the whole world—finally united with a single will in freely and honestly serving the cause of peace, ever mindful of the common good. In earlier days, not even one city-state, nor one group of citizens, nor even (more significantly) one household of brothers could get along with another indefinitely. If we confirm that all this came to pass under Augustus as ruler, it is quite clear that in the same empire of Augustus the birth of our Lord Jesus Christ was beginning to light up the world in a most certain manifestation of His approval.

Although it will be against their will, those driven to blasphemy by jealousy will be forced to admit and acknowledge that this worldwide peace and most tranquil serenity was made possible not by the greatness of Augustus Caesar, but by the Son of God, who appeared at the time of Caesar and who came not just to be the ruler of one city-state but rather as the Creator of the universe, to be recognized by everyone, in order to unite the world. In the same way as the rising sun fills the day with light, upon His arrival he mercifully adorned the world with peace.

We need to take a look at ourselves and the lifestyles we have chosen and gotten used to, in order to get our bearings. Our ancestors waged wars until, exhausted by wars, they sought peace by offering to pay tribute. Tribute is the price of peace: we pay tribute to avoid the suffering of war, and we stop and wait in the same harbor (of tribute-paying) where our ancestors sheltered themselves from storms of evils.

It is in this light that we should judge whether our times are happy ones: surely we find them happier than those of old because we continually enjoy the peace they arrived at only late in their game. We are strangers to the violence of wars which exhausted them. In fact, we are able to enjoy that carefree existence from birth to old age, which they could enjoy only in part after the coming of Augustus Caesar's empire and Christ's birth. What we contribute freely for our defense was simply taken from them earlier, as what they owed in their slave-like status. How different modern times are from past ones can be seen when we compare the way Rome extorted money by force of arms from its subject peoples, in order to support Roman luxury, with the way Rome now allocates funds for the general good of all our communities.

For me my native land is everywhere. I can get away to a safe place at the first hint of any sort of disturbance.

Right now Africa has taken me in with a hospitality commensurate with my confidence in approaching her. Now Africa receives me into its own community with its carefree enjoyment of peace under laws common to us all. That same Africa, of which it was said in olden days and truly said,

> We dare not ask for refuge on her sand:
> The wars they stir up keep us from this land[1]

now opens wide the doors to her hearths for weary bodies and keeps them warm and welcome. The huge expanse of the East, the abundance produced in the North, the expansive diversity of the South, the great and secure strongholds on our large islands now have my law and name because I come to Christians and Romans as a Christian and Roman. I do not fear any gods of my host. I do not fear that his religion will mean my death. I have none of that fear of strange lands where a native gets away with whatever he wants and a traveller cannot tend to his own business in peace or even of lands where the law of foreigners is not mine. One God, loved and feared by all, established this unity of the kingdom at the time He chose to reveal Himself among men: those same laws under one God now rule everywhere. Whenever I arrive unknown, I need not fear sudden violence as if I were alone and deserted. Among Romans, as I was saying, I am a Roman; among Christians, a Christian; among men, a man. I can appeal to the state on the basis of its laws, to the consciences of men on the basis of religion, and to nature on the basis of our common sharing of it. I enjoy time spent in each country, as though it were my own fatherland—keeping in mind that the true fatherland I love most does not have its roots on earth. I have lost nothing where I loved nothing, and I have everything when He whom I do love is with me, particularly since He is the same among all men. He not only gives me an introduction to all men but helps me become a friend of theirs. Nor does He desert me when I am in need, for "The earth is His and the fullness thereof." He instructs that all things from this abundance be made available to all people in common. These are the benefits of our own time, and our ancestors did not enjoy them fully, whether we refer to our present tranquility, or to hope for the future, or to places of refuge for all. Lacking these, they waged wars without end. Since they were not free to move as groups from place to place, they had to cling to their old homes when warfare came and face miserable death or the disgrace of enslavement.

Questions:
1. *In spite of the great optimism of Orosius, he does give a few hints that the Roman Empire in the West is coming apart at the seams. Can you find one or more of them?*
2. *Comparing the excerpts from St. Augustine and Orosius, what similarities do you find? Where is the emphasis different?*

6.8   St. Benedict

St. Benedict (c. 480(?)-543(?)) was one of the earliest of the Christian theologians. Benedict established a monastic order and built a monastery on top of Monte Cassino, in central Italy, which flourished for about fifteen hundred years. During World War II the monastery was occupied by the German army and subsequently bombed to rubble by Allied planes; it can still be seen on top of the mountain, above the town of Cassino.

The selection that follows is taken from the beginning of St. Benedict's Rule, a guidebook for those wishing to enter the Benedictine order. Clearly exhibiting the fervid piety of the early medieval Christians, it was widely studied throughout the Middle Ages. St. Benedict's interpretation of Christianity exerted a profound influence not only on the thinking but also on the lives of medieval Christians. The Benedictine order, like the Franciscan, developed into one of the major institutions of the Catholic Church, of which it is still a part.

Source: Trans. Richard Crotty. (Nedlands: The University of Western Australia Press, 1963).

RULE OF ST. BENEDICT

LISTEN, my son, to the precepts of your master, and incline the ear of your heart: willingly receive and faithfully fulfil the admonition of your loving father, that you may return by the toil of obedience to Him from whom you had departed through the sloth of disobedience. To you, therefore, my words are now addressed, whoever you are that (renouncing your own desires) are taking up the strong and bright weapons of obedience, in order to fight for the Lord Christ, our true King. In the first place, whatever good work you begin to do, beg of Him with most earnest prayer to complete it; that He who has now been good enough to count us in the number of His children may not at any time have to grieve over our evil deeds. For we must always so serve Him with the gifts with which He has endowed us that He will never as an angry Father disinherit His children, and never as a dread Master, incensed by our sins, deliver us to eternal punishment as most wicked servants who were unwilling to follow Him to glory.

Let us then at long last arise, since Scripture stirs us up saying: It is high time for us to awake from sleep. And, our eyes being open to the deifying light, let us hear with attentive ears the Divine Voice warning us, daily crying out: Would you but listen to His voice today! Do not harden your hearts. And again: He that hath ears to hear, let him hear what the Spirit says to Christian communities. And what does He say? Come, my children (He says), listen to Me; I will teach you to be God-fearing folk. Run while you have the light of life, lest the darkness of death overtake you.

And the Lord, seeking His own workman in the multitude of people to whom He thus cries out, says again: Who is the man who wants life, and desires success? And if you, hearing this, answer that you do, God says to you: If you want true, everlasting life, keep your tongue from evil, and your lips from deceit; turn from evil and do good; seek peace, and pursue it. And when you have done these things, My eyes will look favourably on you, and My ears will be open to your prayers; and before you call upon Me, I shall say unto you: Behold, I am here. What can be sweeter to us, dearest brethren, than this voice of the Lord inviting us? See how the Lord, in His loving-kindness, shows us the way of life.

Having our loins girded, therefore, with faith and the performance of good works, let us walk in His paths by the guidance of the Gospel, so that we may deserve to see Him who has called us into His kingdom. And if we wish to dwell in the tabernacle of His kingdom, be sure we shall not reach it unless we run to it by our good deeds. But let us ask the Lord, in the words of the prophet: Lord, who shall dwell in Your tabernacle? Who shall find rest upon Your holy hill? Having asked this question, brethren, let us listen to the Lord answering and showing us the way to His tabernacle in these words: He that lives a pure life and practises virtue, he that is honest at heart and does not deceive with his tongue, he that does not defraud or slander his neighbour. He that has brought Satan and his malice to nought, casting him out of his heart with all his suggestions, taken his temptations, newly born as yet, and dashed them upon the rock that is Christ. Such God-fearing men are not made proud by their own good works:

knowing that the good which is in them comes not from themselves but from the Lord, they magnify Him for what He accomplishes in them, saying with the prophet: Not unto us, Lord, not unto us, but unto Your Name give the glory. Just as the apostle Paul took no credit to himself for his preaching, but said: By the grace of God I am what I am. And the same apostle says elsewhere: He who boasts should make his boast in the Lord.

Hence also the Lord says in the Gospel: He that hears these instructions of mine and carries them out is like a wise man who built his house upon rock; the floods came and the winds blew and beat upon that house, but it did not fall, because it was founded upon rock. And the Lord, in fulfilment of these words, is waiting daily for us to make due response by deeds to His holy warnings. So the number of our days is increased, with a view to the mending of our evil ways, as the apostle says: Do you not know that the patience of God is inviting you to repentance? For in His love the Lord says: I desire not the death of the sinner, but that he be converted, and live.

So, brethren, since we have asked the Lord who are to inhabit His tabernacle, He has told us the duties of an inhabitant: if only we can fulfil those duties! Our hearts and bodies, therefore, must be made ready for the holy warfare which consists of obedience to His commands; and let us ask God to supply by the help of His grace what we cannot do by nature. And if we want to attain eternal life, escaping the penalties of hell, then while there is yet time, while we are still in the flesh and able to fulfil all these things before darkness and death come upon us, let us hasten to do now what will benefit us in eternity.

We must establish, therefore, a school of the Lord's service, in the arrangement of which we hope to order nothing that is harsh or burdensome. But if it does turn out that equity itself, for the amendment of vices or the safeguarding of charity, should dictate some element of strictness, do not thereupon yield to fear and turn aside from a way of salvation whose beginning is inevitably difficult. But as we make progress in our way of life and in faith, our heart becomes more courageous, and with ineffable sweetness of love we run in the way of God's commandments; so that, never departing from His guidance, persevering in His teaching in a monastery until death, we may share by patience in the sufferings of Christ, so as to deserve also to reign with Him in heaven.

CHAPTER I
ON THE VARIOUS KINDS OF MONKS

It is clear that there are four kinds of monks. The first are the Cenobites: those who perform their service in monasteries, under a rule and an abbot. The second are the Anchorites, i.e. the Hermits: not in the first fervour of Religious life, but after long probation in a monastery, they have learned by the help and experience of others to fight against the devil, and going forth well equipped from the ranks of their brethren to the lonely combat of the desert, are not anxious now in being without the support of others, fighting single-handed, with God's aid, against vices of flesh or spirit.

A third kind of monks, but a detestable kind, are the Sarabaites. They have not been tried or taught by the experience of living under a rule, as gold is tried in a furnace; but, being as soft as lead, are still loyal to the world in practice, though by their tonsure they make an obviously false claim of loyalty to God. In twos or threes or even singly without a shepherd, not enclosed in the Lord's sheep-folds but in their own, they make a law for themselves of their own pleasure and desires: whatever they think fit, whatever it pleases them to do, that they call holy; and what they do not desire, that they think unlawful.

The fourth kind of monks are those called Gyrovagues, who spend all their lives wandering about various provinces, staying in different monasteries for three or four days at a time, perpetual vagrants, always unsettled, given up to their own wills and to the snares of gluttony, worse in every way than the Sarabaites. Of the wretched way of life of all these it is better to say nothing than to speak. Leaving them aside, then, let us with God's help set about laying down a rule for the strong breed of Cenobites.

CHAPTER II
WHAT KIND OF MAN THE ABBOT OUGHT TO BE

An Abbot who is worthy to rule over a monastery ought always to remember what he is called, and be superior in deed as well as in name. For he is believed to be the representative of Christ in a monastery, since he is called by a name of His, as the Apostle says: You have received the spirit of adoption, which makes you sons, crying Abba (Father). So the Abbot ought not to reach or arrange or command anything contrary to the law of God; but let his commands and teaching be as a leaven of God-given holiness introduced into the minds of his disciples. Let the Abbot be ever mindful that at the dread judgment of God an account will have to be given both of his own teaching and of the obedience of his disciples. Let him be assured that any failure of the flock discovered by the Head of the Household will be a heavy load of guilt laid upon the shepherd. On the other hand, if he has bestowed all pastoral diligence on a restless and disobedient flock, and taken all possible care to mend their corrupt ways, then it is equally clear that their shepherd will go free at the Lord's judgment, saying to Him with the prophet: I have not hidden Your just dealing in my heart, I have made known Your faithfulness and saving power; but adding that they looked down on and despised him. Then, finally, for souls that refused his care punishment shall prevail: death itself.

So when anyone takes the name of Abbot he ought to rule his disciples by teaching them in two different ways; that is, he should let all that is good and holy be seen in his deeds even more than in his words: declaring to the intelligent disciples by words, but to the hard-hearted and simple-minded by his exemplary deeds what it is that the Lord commands. Whatever he has taught his disciples to be contrary to God's law, let him indicate by his example that it is not to be done; lest while preaching to others he himself become reprobate; and lest God finally say to him in his sins: How is it that you can repeat My commandments by rote, and boast of My covenant with you, and all the while have no love for the amendment of your ways, casting every warning of Mine to the winds? And: You who saw the speck of dust in your brother's eye, did you not see the beam in your own?

Let him have no human preferences in the monastery. Let not one be loved more than another unless he be found better than others in good works or obedience. Let not one who is classified as well-born be put before one who was formerly a slave, unless some other and reasonable cause exist for doing so. If, in the Abbot's judgment, justice requires it, let him make such a promotion, and from any class whatever: otherwise let the monks keep their own places, because, whether slave-born or free, we are all one in Christ, and undertake one and the same service in the army of the one Lord; there are no human preferences with God. Only for one reason are we preferred by Him: if we be found to surpass others in good works and humility. So the Abbot should show equal love to all; and let the same discipline be meted out to them, according to the deserts of each.

In his teaching, the Abbot ought always to observe the rule of the Apostle, which runs: Bring home wrong-doing, comfort the waverer, rebuke the sinner; in other words: there is a time for everything, let your regime be a blend of gentleness and severity, show now the rigour of a master, now the loving affection of a father. That is to say, the Abbot must rebuke the undisciplined and restless, and exhort the obedient, gentle and patient to advance in virtue; and such as are negligent and contemptuous of authority we bid him reprove and correct. Let him not shut his eyes to the faults of offenders; but rather, as soon as they manifest their presence, let him root them out, as he has authority for that (the fate of Heli, priest of Shiloh, is worth remembering). The sensible ones, and those of rather good disposition, at a first or second offence are to be corrected only with words, but such as are impudent, hard of heart and proud, or disobedient, should be chastised with bodily stripes at the first sign of sin. Let the Abbot remember what is written: A fool is not amended by mere words; and: Strike your son with the rod, and you will deliver his soul from death.

The Abbot ought always to remember what he is, and what he is called, knowing that more is expected of him to whom more is entrusted; and he must realize how difficult and arduous a task he is undertaking, that of ruling souls and of being at the service of a variety of characters. Let him accommodate himself to the peculiarities and mentality of each, winning some by kindness, others by reproof, others again by persuasion, in such a way that he may not only keep intact the flock committed to him, but also rejoice over an increase in their numbers and virtue.

Above all, let him not overlook or undervalue the spiritual needs of his charges, taking too much care of fleeting, material and perishable things; rather let him always consider that he has undertaken to govern souls and will have to answer for them. And that there may be no talk of the possibility of want, let him recall the text: Make it your first care to find the Kingdom of God and His approval, and all these things shall be yours without the asking. And again: Those who fear God never go wanting. And let him realize that preparation is necessary, in the case of a ruler of souls, for rendering an account of them. Whatever the number of breathren under his care, let him be well assured that on the Day of Judgment he must account to the Lord for all these souls, and of course for his own as well. And so, ever in fear of the future examination of the shepherd on the state of the flock entrusted to him, ever careful about other men's accounts, he will take exceptional care over his own. So, while correcting others by his warnings, he too will be cured of his defects.

Questions:
1. What is the purpose of the monastic life?
2. Describe the perfect monk.

PART 7
Mediterranean Civilization after the Fall of Rome

7.1   Procopius, History of the Wars

This selection, from the History of the Wars, depicts the causes and results of the a.d. 532 Nika revolt and reveals how Empress Theodora helped to control this uprising.

Source: Reprinted by permission of the publishers and the Trustees of the Loeb Classical Library from Procopius, *History of the Wars,* Book I, pp. 2, 19, 221, 223, 231, 233.

HISTORY OF THE WARS

At this same time an insurrection broke out unexpectedly in Byzantium among the populace, and, contrary to expectation, it proved to be a very serious affair, and ended in great harm to the people and to the senate, as the following account will show. In every city the population has been divided for a long time past into the Blue and the Green factions; but within comparatively recent times it has come about that, for the sake of these names and the seats which the rival factions occupy in watching the games, they spend their money and abandon their bodies to the most cruel tortures, and even do not think it unworthy to die a most shameful death. And they fight against their opponents knowing not for what end they imperil themselves, but knowing well that, even if they overcome their enemy in the fight, the conclusion of the matter for them will be to be carried off straightway to the prison, and finally, after suffering extreme torture, to be destroyed. So there grows up in them against their fellow men a hostility which has no cause, and at no time does it cease or disappear, for it gives place neither to the ties of marriage nor of relationship nor of friendship, and the case is the same even though those who differ with respect to these colours be brothers or any other kin. They care neither for things divine nor human in comparison with conquering in these struggles; and it matters not whether a sacrilege is committed by anyone at all against God, or whether the laws and the constitution are violated by friend or by foe; nay even when they are perhaps ill supplied with the necessities of life, and when their fatherland is in the most pressing need and suffering unjustly, they pay no need if only it is likely to go well with their "faction"; for so they name the bands of partisans. And even women join with them in this unholy strife, and they not only follow the men, but even resist them if opportunity offers, although they neither go to the public exhibitions at all, nor are they impelled by any other cause; so that I, for my part, am unable to call this anything except a disease of the soul. This, then, is pretty well how matters stand among the people of each and every city.

But at this time the officers of the city administration in Byzantium were leading away to death some of the rioters. But the members of the two factions, conspiring together and declaring a truce with each other, seized the prisoners and then straightway entered the prison and released all those who were in confinement there, whether they had been condemned on a charge of stirring up sedition, or for any other unlawful act. And all the attendants in the service of the city government were killed indiscriminately; meanwhile, all of the citizens who were sane-minded were fleeing to the opposite mainland, and fire was applied to the city as if it had fallen under the hand of an enemy. The sanctuary of Sophia and the baths of Zeuxippus, and the portion of the imperial residence from the propylaea as far as the so-called House of Ares were destroyed by fire, and besides these both the great colonnades which extended as far as the market place which bears the name of Constantine, in addition to many houses of wealthy men and a vast amount of treasure. During this time the emperor and his consort with a few members of the senate shut themselves up in the palace and remained quietly there. Now the watchword which the populace passed around to one another was Nika,[1] and the insurrection has been called by this name up to the present time. . . .

Now the emperor and his court were deliberating as to whether it would be better for them if they remained or if they took to flight in the ships. And many opinions were expressed favouring either course. And the Empress Theodora also spoke to the following effect: "As to the belief that a woman ought not to be daring among men or to assert herself boldly among those who are holding back from fear, I consider that the present crisis most certainly does not permit us to discuss whether the matter should be regarded in this or in some other way. For in the case of those whose interests have come into the greatest danger nothing else seems best except to settle the issue immediately before them in the best possible way. My opinion then is that the present time, above all others, is inopportune for flight, even though it brings safety. For while it is impossible for a man who has seen the light not also to die, for one who has been an emperor it is unendurable to be a fugitive. May I never be separated from this purple, and may I not live that day on which those who meet me shall not address me as mistress. If, now, it is your wish to save yourself, O Emperor, there is no difficulty. For we have much money, and there is the sea, here the boats. However consider whether it will not come about after you have been saved that you would gladly exchange that safety for death. For as for myself, I approve a certain ancient saying that royalty is a good burial-shroud." When the queen had spoken thus, all were filled with boldness, and, turning their thoughts towards resistance, they began to consider how they might be able to defend themselves if any hostile force should come against them.

Questions:
1. What caused the Nika revolt, and who did the most to stop it?
2. Who are some of the women in other civilizations we have studied who had great importance?

7.2   Iconoclasm and Orthodoxy: The Second Council of Nicaea (787)

Another primary religious dispute within Eastern Christianity was the tradition of worshiping images of Christ, the Virgin, and the saints. Although this was acceptable practice in Western churches, in 726 the Byzantine emperor Leo IV abolished the cult of images by imperial edict. This was called "iconoclasm," and it is a primary example of Caesaro-papism. In 787, however, the empress Irene, who served as regent to her young son, reestablished the veneration of images at the Second Council of Nicaea, as the following source indicates. This policy remained under dispute for centuries.

> **Source:** "Iconoclasm and Orthodoxy" is from Joseph G. Ayer, Jr., ed. *A Source Book for Ancient Church History* (New York: Charles Scribner's Sons, 1913), pp. 696–697.

We, therefore, following the royal pathway and the divinely inspired authority of our holy Fathers and the traditions of the Catholic Church for, as we all know, the Holy Spirit dwells in her, define with all certitude and accuracy, that just as the figure of the precious and life-giving cross, so also the venerable and holy images, as well in painting and mosaic, as of other fit materials, should be set forth in the holy churches of God. . . . For by so much the more frequently as they are seen in artistic representation, by so much the more readily are men lifted up to the memory of their prototypes, and to a longing after them; and to these should be given due salutation and honorable reverence, not indeed that true worship which pertains alone to the divine nature; but to these, as to the figure of the precious and life—giving cross, and to the book of the Gospels and to other holy objects, incense and lights may be offered according to ancient pious custom. For the honor which is paid to the image passes on to that which the image represents, and he who shows reverence to the image shows reverence to the subject represented in it.

Those, therefore, who dare to think or teach otherwise, or as wicked heretics dare to spurn the traditions of the Church and to invent some novelty, or else to reject some of those things which the Church hath received, to wit, the book of the Gospels, or the image of the cross, or the pictorial icons, or the holy relics of a martyr, or to devise anything subversive of the lawful traditions of the Catholic Church, or to turn to common uses the sacred vessels and the venerable monasteries, if they be bishops or clerics we command that they be deposed [and] be cut off from communion.

Question:
1. What reasons are given to justify the veneration of icons?

7.3   A Western Attitude Toward the Byzantine Greeks (1147): Odo of Deuil

One of the primary obstacles to the eventual success of the Crusades was the lack of trust and cooperation between the Roman Catholic Church in the West and the Greek Orthodox Church in the East.

These two Christian churches had separated in 1054 over doctrinal differences, and this rift fueled a political and economic competition between Western forces and those of the Byzantine emperor. The following selection notes Western disgust for the Byzantine Greeks at the beginning of the Second Crusade.

> **Source:** "A Western Attitude toward the Byzantine Greeks" is from Odo of Deuil, *De Profectione Ludovici VII*, ed. and trans. Virginia G. Berry, p. 57. Copyright © 1948 by Columbia University Press. Reprinted by permission of the publisher.

ODO OF DEUIL

We know other heresies of theirs, both concerning their treatment of the Eucharist and concerning the procession of the Holy Ghost, but none of these matters would mar our page if not pertinent to our subject. Actually, it was for these reasons that the Greeks had incurred the hatred of our men, for their error had become known even among the lay people. Because of this they were judged not to be Christians, and the Franks considered killing them a matter of no importance and hence could with more difficulty be restrained from pillage and plundering.

And then the Greeks degenerated entirely . . . putting aside all manly vigor, both of words and of spirit, they lightly swore whatever they thought would please us, but they neither kept faith with us nor maintained respect for themselves. In general they really have the opinion that anything which is done for the holy empire [that is, Byzantium] cannot be considered perjury.

Question:
1. What does this tell you about how heretics were viewed by the Roman Catholic Church?

7.4 Einhard

Charlemagne (c. 742-814) was a remarkable man. Although only semiliterate himself, he was a patron of learning, as well as of the arts. He made his capital at Aachen (Aix-laChapelle) a cultural center by establishing a palace school there to train both the clergy and the sons of the nobles of his court. He appointed, as director of the school, the English teacher and scholar, Alcuin of York, who was probably the outstanding intellectual of his time. He also brought together a number of other scholars from around Europe, among them Einhard.

Einhard (c. 770-844) was born in what is now southern Germany, of a wealthy family. After studying at the Abbey of Fulda, he went to Aachen as a student of Alcuin in the palace school. He remained in Aachen for nearly forty years, becoming a close friend and advisor of Charlemagne. An individual of many talents, Einhard not only continued the tradition of his mentor, Alcuin, as a teacher but also engaged in diplomatic missions for his lord. In addition he employed his skills as an architect to design the royal palace at Aachen, much of which still stands. But his major contribution to history was his biography of Charlemagne. Even after the death of the emperor in 814, Einhard remained in Aachen, continuing his position as advisor to the next monarch, Louis the Pious. It was during these years that he wrote his famous biography. He finally left the royal household in 830 and retired to a rural location in southern Germany where he founded an abbey.

Einhard's is not a disinterested biography, for the author's admiration for Charlemagne is evident throughout. Still it gives us an informative, if brief, description of the emperor and his times. Einhard used the classical biographer, Suetonius, for his literary model, copying his style and even reproducing the language of his Life of Augustus, Life of Charlemagne.

> **Source:** Einhard, *The Life of Charlemagne,* trans. E. S. Firchow and E. H. Zeydel (Coral Gables:University of Miami Press, 1972). Used by permission of University of Miami Press.

THE LIFE OF CHARLEMAGNE
PROLOGUE

After I had made up my mind to describe the life and habits and, above all, the deeds of my lord and patron, the illustrious and deservedly famous King Charles, I set about doing so as succinctly as possible. I have tried not to omit anything that has come to my notice, and at the same time not to be long-winded and offend those discerning readers who object to the very idea of a modern history. But I also wanted to keep my new work from displeasing those who disapprove even of the masterpieces of the wisest and most learned authors of antiquity. To be sure, I am fully aware that there are many men of letters who do not regard contemporary matters so far beneath their notice as to treat them with contempt and consider them fit only to sink into silence and oblivion. On the contrary, the enthusiasm for things past leads some writers to recount the famous deeds of other men as best they can, and in this way they hope to insure that their own names will be remembered by posterity.

Be this as it may, none of these possible objections can prevent me from writing on the subject, since I am convinced that no one can describe these events better than I can. For I was there when they took place and I know them as an eyewitness, so to speak. Furthermore, I am not entirely sure if they will be recorded by anyone else. And so I thought it would be better to write down what I had to say even at the risk of duplicating what others might write, rather than to allow the illustrious life of the greatest king of the age and his famous deeds, unmatched by his contemporaries, to disappear forever into forgetfulness.

Besides, there was another reason, important enough in itself, I think, to make me compose this book: namely, that Charles educated me and gave me his lifelong friendship and that of his children from the time I came to the court. In this way he attached me to his person and made me so devoted to him in life and death that I might well be called ungrateful if I were to forget everything he did for me and never say a word about his great and magnificent generosity, I, who owe him so much; indeed, that would mean allowing his life to remain unremembered and unpraised, as though he had never lived! To be sure, my abilities, feeble and inadequate as they are-nonexistent even-are incapable of portraying his life as it really ought to be portrayed. Even the eloquence of a Cicero would not have been up to that.

Here, then, is the book containing the life story of a truly great man. You will marvel at his deeds, and probably also at the presumption of a barbarous Frank for imagining that he could write tastefully and elegantly in Latin. For I am not much versed in the Roman tongue. Then, too, you will perhaps be amazed at my temerity in ignoring the words of Cicero when, speaking of Latin writers, he said in the first book of his *Tusculan Disputations* that "whoever puts his thoughts in writing and can not arrange and state them clearly, and delight the reader with a pleasant style, makes a complete mockery of the writer's craft." This remark of the famous orator might have kept me from writing if I had not already made up my mind to brave the judgment of the world and take a chance with my feeble talents. I thought this would be better than to allow the memory of so great a man to perish out of petty concern for my own reputation.

1. THE MEROVINGIANS

The family of the Merovingians from which the Franks customarily chose their kings is believed to have ruled until the time of King Hilderich. Hilderich was deposed, tonsured, and sent to a monastery by the command of the Roman Pope Stephen. Although the royal line apparently ended only with him, it had long before ceased to matter and possessed no more except the empty title of king. The real wealth and power of the kingdom were in the hands of the prefects of the palace, the so-called majordomos, and their word was law. The king had no choice but to sit on the throne with flowing hair and full beard, content with his tide and the semblance of sovereignty. He would listen to messengers coming from all around and, as they left, give them replies as though they were his own, but in reality, they had been dictated to him or even forced on him.

Except for the empty title of king and an intermittent allowance which the prefect of the palace gave or did not give him at his pleasure, the king owned nothing but a single estate, and that was not a very lucrative one. He lived on it and had a few servants there performing the most necessary duties and making a show of obsequiousness. Wherever he had to go, he went like a farmer in a cart drawn by a span of oxen with a carter driving them. That is how he went to the palace and how he went to the meetings of his people, which took place yearly for the good of the realm. And in the same way he returned home. But the administration of the state and all internal and external business was carried out by the prefect of the palace.

2. CHARLES' ANCESTORS

When Hilderich was deposed, the office of majordomo was already hereditarily held by Pepin, the father of King Charles. For Pepin's father, Charles [Charles Martel—*Ed.*], had in his time crushed the rebels who were trying to take over all of Franconia. He had also defeated the Saracens so badly in two great battles, when they attempted to occupy Gaul, that they had to return to Spain. One of these battles had taken place in Aquitaine near Poitiers [in 732—*Ed.*], the other on the Berre River not far from Narbonne. This same Charles had in turn received the office of majordomo from his father Pepin and had administered it extremely well. It was customary for the people to bestow such an honor only on men of noble birth and great wealth.

When Pepin, the father of King Charles, held this office, bequeathed by his grandfather and father to him and to his brother Carloman, the two of them shared it quite amicably for several years, nominally under King Hilderich. But then for some unknown reason Carloman abandoned the burdensome government of the temporal kingdom-possibly because he longed for a more contemplative life-and went into retirement in Rome. There, giving up his worldly garb, he became a monk and built a monastery on Mt. Soracte near the church of St. Sylvester. For a number of years he enjoyed his longed-for seclusion, along with a few monks who had accompanied him. But when a great many noble Franks came on pilgrimages to Rome to fulfill vows and insisted on paying homage to their former lord, it was impossible for him to get any peace, which he cherished more than anything else, and he decided to move elsewhere. When he saw that the crowds of intruders were interfering with his resolve to be alone, he left the mountain and went away to the province of Samnium, to the monastery of St. Benedict on Monte Cassino, where he spent the rest of his life in prayer.

3. CHARLES BECOMES KING

Pepin, no longer majordomo but king by authority of the Roman pontiff, ruled alone over the Franks for fifteen years or more. For nine unbroken years he fought against Waifar, duke of Aquitaine, and then, at the end of the war, he died of dropsy in Paris. His sons Charles and Carloman survived him, and on them, by the will of Providence, the succession devolved. In solemn assembly the Franks appointed them kings on condition that they share the realm equally, Charles ruling the part which had belonged to their father Pepin, Carloman the part formerly controlled by his uncle Carloman. Both accepted these conditions and each one took over that section of the divided kingdom which he had received according to the agreement.

But peace between the two brothers was maintained only with the greatest difficulty since many of Carloman's followers plotted to break up the partnership. A few even tried to provoke a war with their intrigues. The outcome, however, showed that there was more imagined than real danger. When Carloman died, his wife and sons fled to Italy with the most important members of their court. Without any apparent reason she spurned her brother-in-law and placed herself and her children under the protection of Desiderius, king of the Lombards. Carloman had succumbed to an illness after ruling jointly for two years, and at his death Charles was unanimously proclaimed king of the Franks.

4. PLAN OF THIS WORK

Because nothing has been recorded in writing about Charles' birth,[1] infancy, or even boyhood, and because no survivor has been found who claims to know of these matters, I consider it foolish to write about them. So I have decided to skip what we know nothing about and proceed to recount and describe Charles' exploits, habits, and other facts of his life. First I want to tell of his deeds at home and abroad, then describe his habits and interests, his rulership and finally his death, omitting nothing that is worth mentioning or necessary to know.

5. WAR IN AQUITAINE

Of all the wars Charles waged, the first was the Aquitainian campaign, begun but not finished by his father. Charles believed that it would soon be over. He asked his brother, who was still living at the time, to help him. But although his brother disappointed him and failed to provide the promised support, Charles completed the undertaking with great vigor. He was unwilling to give up what he had begun or to abandon a task once taken on until he had carried out his plans and brought them to a happy conclusion by force of perseverance and steadfastness. He even compelled Hunold, who after Waifar's death had tried to seize Aquitaine and revive a war that was almost finished, to leave the country and flee to the land of the Basques. But Charles gave him no respite. He crossed the Garonne River, built Fort Fronsac, and through diplomatic channels let the Basque Duke Lupus know that he had better return the fugitive speedily or he would come and get Hunold by force. Lupus thought better of it and not only handed over Hunold but also submitted himself and the province he ruled to the jurisdiction of Charles.

6. WAR WITH THE LOMBARDS

When the affairs of Aquitaine had been settled and the war ended, and after his brother had died, Charles undertook a campaign against the Lombards at the request and pleading of Bishop Hadrian of Rome. His father had once before fought the Lombards, that time in response to the entreaties of Pope Stephen. Pepin had done so under great difficulties, for certain nobles with whom he usually consulted had opposed his wished so strongly that they openly declared they would desert the king and go home. Nevertheless, arms were taken up against King Aistulf at that time and the war brought to a speedy end. But although the reasons for this conflict seem to have been similar and indeed the same in both Charles' and Pepin's case, the difficulties of seeing it through and settling it varied in each instance. Pepin, after a few days' siege at Pavia, forced Aistulf to give hostages and to return to the Romans the cities and fortresses he had taken. He also made Aistulf swear a sacred oath that he would not try to regain what he had surrendered. Charles, on the other hand, pursued the war more single-mindedly and did not rest until he had forced King Desiderius to surrender unconditionally after weakening him in a lengthy siege. He also ordered Desiderius' son Adalgis, who was the favorite of his people, to leave the kingdom and Italy and to restore everything he had taken from the Romans. Charles then prevented Rotgaud, the duke of Friuli, from starting a revolt. After that he subjected all of Italy to his rule and made his son Pepin king of the conquered Italian territories.

At this point I should describe how difficult it was for Charles to cross the Alps on the way to Italy and how the Franks toiled when crossing the trackless mountain ridges, the rocky cliffs, and the sharp peaks reaching to the sky. But I have decided to describe in this work Charles' way of life rather than the outcome of the wars he waged. Suffice it to say that the end of the campaign resulted in the subjugation of Italy, the deportation of Desiderius into permanent exile, the expulsion of his son Adalgis from Italy, and the restoration of the possessions taken by the Lombard kings to Pope Hadrian of Rome.

7. WAR WITH THE SAXONS

Then the Saxon war-which had merely been interrupted-was taken up again. The Franks have never been involved in any struggle that was more prolonged, more bitter, or more laborious. For the Saxons-like almost all of the nations inhabiting

Germania-are savage by nature, given to the cult of demons, and hostile to our religion. They do not find it dishonorable to violate or break divine or human laws. Hardly a day passed without incidents threatening the peace. The border between our land and theirs runs almost entirely through plains, with the exception of a few areas where large forests or mountain ridges provide the territories with natural boundaries. Thus, murder, robbery, and arson never ceased on both sides. Eventually the Franks became so enraged that it no longer seemed enough to retaliate and so they decided to wage open war. Accordingly, war was declared and fought by both parties with great ferocity. It continued for thirty-three years and cost the Saxons far more than the Franks. To be sure, it could have been concluded sooner if the treachery of the Saxons had allowed it. For it is difficult to say how many times they surrendered to the king and promised to do what they were ordered, how often and without delay they furnished hostages that were demanded, and how often they received legates. Many times they were so badly defeated and weakened that they vowed to give up their cult of demons and indicated their willingness to submit to the Christian faith. But just as they were often ready to do this, just as often were they in a hurry to break their promises. Thus, I cannot say with certainty which of these courses of action they more truthfully favored. It is a fact, however, that after the beginning of the war against the Saxons hardly a year passed without some vacillation on their part. And yet the king in his high purpose and unswerving constancy both in success and failure was not to be frustrated by their fickleness, nor could he be made to abandon what he had begun. He never allowed any of them who perpetrated such perfidy to go unpunished. In these instances he either led an army personally or sent one with his counts to avenge the crimes and mete out proper punishment. After he had defeated all of those who had been offering resistance, he subjected them to his power. Then he took ten thousand Saxons who lived on both banks of the Elbe river, with their wives and children, and resettled them in various contingents here and there throughout Gaul and Germania. And so the war which had dragged on for so many years was concluded under the conditions which the king imposed and the Saxons accepted. The conditions were that they give up the cult of demons, abandon the religious practices of their ancestors, adopt the sacraments of the Christian faith and religion, and become a single nation with the Franks.

8. WAR WITH THE SAXONS
(CONTINUED)

Although this struggle had gone on for many years, the king himself fought the enemy not more than twice during the period, and this within a single month with only a few days intervening: once at the mountain Osning, in a place called Detmold, and once at the river Hase. The enemies were so routed and defeated in these two battles that they subsequently never dared to provoke the king again or to resist him when he approached, unless they were protected by fortifications. In these fights many noblemen and leaders in highest positions were killed, both among the Franks and Saxons. Finally, the strife ended in the thirty-third year. But meanwhile so many other great wars had been declared against the Franks in various parts of the world and were taken up under the king's guidance that anyone considering the matter might justifiably wonder whether Charles' endurance in time of trouble or his good fortune is more to be admired. The Saxon war had begun two years before the Italian, and, although it was carried on without interruption, none of the other pressing duties were set aside nor other equally difficult struggles dropped for its sake. For the king surpassed everyone in his time in prudence and nobility of mind, and he turned down nothing that had to be undertaken or carried out. He did not shy at the difficulties or fear the dangers involved because he had learned to accept and endure everything in accordance with its nature. Neither in adversity did he yield nor was he misled by good fortune when it beckoned deceptively during times of great success.

9. EXPEDITION TO SPAIN

While Charles was engaged in the strenuous and almost incessant struggle with the Saxons and after he had built fortifications at strategic points along the frontier, he decided to invade Spain with as large an army as he could raise. He crossed the Pyrenees successfully and accepted the surrender of all the towns and castles on his way. Finally, he turned back with his forces safe and intact, but when recrossing the mountains he was made to feel the treachery of the Basques. In a densely wooded area well suited for ambush the Basques had prepared to attack the army from the top of the highest mountain. As the troops were proceeding in a long column through the narrow mountain passes, the Basques descended on the baggage train and the protecting rear guard and forced them into the valley. In the ensuing battle the Basques slaughtered them to a man. They seized the baggage and, under cover of the growing darkness, quickly scattered in all directions. In this encounter the Basques had the advantage of light weapons and a favorable terrain; the Franks on the other hand were hampered by their heavy equipment and the unevenness of the battle ground. Ekkehard, the royal steward, Anshelm, the count of the Palace, and Roland the Margrave of Brittany, as well as many others were killed in the engagement.[2] Unfortunately, the incident could not be avenged since the enemies disappeared without a trace after the attack and there were no signs where they might be found.

10. SUBMISSION OF THE BRETONS AND BENEVENTIANS

Charles also conquered the Bretons, who lived in a certain remote part of Gaul along the west coast and were not subject to him. He sent an expedition against them, which forced them to give hostages and made them promise to do what was expected of them.

Then he entered Italy with an army and, marching through Rome, went as far as Capua, a city in Campania. There he set up a camp and threatened to take up arms against the Beneventians unless they surrendered. Aregis, the duke of Benevento, prevented this by sending his sons Rumold and Grimold with a large sum of money asking the king to accept them as hostages. He promised that he and his people would do as Charles demanded, on the condition that he would not be forced to appear before the king in person. Charles was more concerned about the good of the people than about the duke's stubbornness, and so he accepted the hostages and agreed that, in view of the large gift of money, the duke should not be compelled to come. He kept one of the two sons of Aregis, not yet of age, as a hostage and sent the older one back to his father. Charles also dispatched legates to receive oaths of loyalty from the Beneventians and from Aregis himself. After that he returned to Rome, spent several days there in worship at the holy places, and finally went back to Gaul.

11. TASSILO AND THE WAR WITH THE BENEVENTIANS

All at once a war broke out in Bavaria which was, however, swiftly concluded. It was caused by the pride and folly of Duke Tassilo. At the urging of his wife, who was a daughter of King Desiderius and who imagined that she could avenge her father's exile through her husband, he made an alliance with the Huns, the neighbors of the Bavarians to the east. According to its terms, Tassilo not only refused to do the king's bidding but also tried his best to challenge him to war. The dauntless king could not tolerate this outrageous insolence. He therefore collected his troops from all over and personally marched to Bavaria with a large army. He reached the river Lech, which separates the Bavarians from the Alemanni, and established his camp there. Before invading the province, however, he decided to find out about the plans of the duke by sending messengers to him. Tassilo realized that there was no point for him or his people to act stubbornly, and so he presented himself to the king to ask for forgiveness. He furnished the hostages that were demanded, among them also his son Theodo, and swore an oath that he would never again be persuaded by anyone to be disobedient to Charles. Thus a speedy end was made to the war which at first had threatened to become one of major proportions. Tassilo, however, was later summoned to the court and not permitted to return. His province was from that time on ruled not by one duke but by several counts.

12. WAR WITH THE SLAVS

After these problems had been solved arms were taken up against the Slavs, who were known to us as Wiltzes but who call themselves Welatabi in their own language. The Saxons fought as auxiliaries in this war, together with other peoples who followed the standards of the king. To be sure, their loyalty was more perfunctory than real. The conflict was caused by the Wiltzes, who were constantly invading and harassing the Abodrites- long-time allies of the Franks-and could not be intimidated by warnings.

A gulf of undetermined length stretches from the western Ocean toward the East, nowhere exceeding a hundred miles across, though narrower at many points [the Baltic *Sea—Ed.*]. Numerous nations live around its shores. The Danes, for instance, and the Swedes, whom we call Norsemen, occupy the northern shore and all the islands along it. The southern shore, on the other hand, is inhabited by Slavs, Estes, and various other nationalities. Among these are the Wiltzes whom Charles was attacking now. In a single campaign led by himself, he crushed and conquered them so effectively that they never again dared to refuse his order.

13. WAR WITH THE HUNS

Next to the Saxon the war which now followed was the most important of them all: it was directed against the Avars or Huns. Charles undertook it with greater energy and far better equipment than any other before. He made one expedition himself to Pannonia-the Huns were occupying this province at that time-and the execution of the rest of the campaign he assigned to his son Pepin and to his provincial prefects, counts, and representatives. Although the war was carried on most vigorously, it ended only in the eighth year. The deserted palace of the Khan as well as the way in which Pannonia was divested of all its population so that not even a trace of human habitation now remains, testify to the many battles fought and the great amount of blood shed there. The entire Hunnish nobility perished during these struggles and their glory vanished. All the money and treasures they had collected over many years were taken away. There is in memory of man no war ever fought against the Franks in which they became richer and accumulated greater wealth. Indeed, although up to that time the Huns had almost seemed to be paupers, so much gold and silver were found in their palace, and so much precious loot captured in the battles, that one can say with good reason: the Franks justly took away from the Huns what the latter had previously unjustly acquired from other peoples.

Only two leaders of the Franks perished in this campaign. Duke Eric of Friuli was killed through the treachery of the townspeople in the seaport town of Tarsatica in Liburnia. Gerold, the prefect of Bavaria, was slain by an unidentified person in Pannonia when he was about to join the attack against the Huns and was marshaling his lines on horseback. He died together with two others who accompanied him while he was exhorting his soldiers one by one to muster their courage for the battle. Otherwise the conflict was practically bloodless and its outcome highly advantageous for the Franks, although because of its magnitude, it lasted for a long time.

14. WAR WITH THE DANES

At long last the Saxon war, too, came to a proper conclusion befitting its long duration. The following wars in Bohemia and Linonia were bound to be brief. Under the leadership of the young King Charles they were quickly settled. Charles' last campaign was directed against those Norsemen who are called Danes. They first were engaged in piracy; later they invaded and devastated the coasts of Gaul and Germania with a rather large fleet. Godofrid, their king, was so filled with vain ambition that he saw himself as the future master over all of Germania. Already he regarded Frisia and Saxony as his own provinces and had subjugated his neighbors, the Abodrites, forcing them to pay tribute. Furthermore, he bragged that in a short time he would be coming with a very large force to the king's court at Aachen. However empty his boasts were, some people thought that he was about to do something of this kind. But he was prevented by sudden death from carrying out his plans. He was assassinated by his own guard, and this ended his life and the war he had begun.

15. CONQUEST

These were the wars which the mighty King Charles planned so carefully and executed so brilliantly in various parts of the world during his reign of forty-seven years. As a result the kingdom of the Franks, which was already great and powerful when Charles inherited it from his father Pepin, was almost doubled in size. Formerly, the Frankish territory had encompassed only that part of Gaul lying between the Rhine and the Loire, the ocean and the Balearic Sea, as well as that part of Germania inhabited by the so-called East Franconians and bordering on Saxony and the Danube, the Rhine and the Saale-a river separating the Thuringians from the Sorbs-and, finally, the land of the Alemanni and Bavarians.

Through the wars described above Charles conquered first Aquitaine, then Gascony and the entire Pyrenees region as far south as the Ebro River. This river originates in Navarre and flows through the most fertile plains of Spain, emptying into the Balearic Sea beneath the walls of the city of Tortosa. Charles also added to his territory all of Italy from Aosta to Lower Calabria, where the border runs between the Beneventians and the Greeks-an area extending over more than a thousand miles. Furthermore, he incorporated Saxony-no small part of Germania and considered equal in length and twice the width of Franconia-and both Upper and Lower Pannonia, as well as Dacia on the other side of the Danube, Istria, Liburnia, and Dalmatia. Only the coastal towns of the latter countries he left to the emperor of Constantinople out of friendship and in consideration of a treaty he had made with him. Finally, Charles subjugated and forced to pay tribute all of the barbarian and savage nations who inhabit Germania between the Rhine and the Vistula rivers, the ocean and the Danube. They speak almost the same language but have very different customs and habits. The most important of these tribes are the Wiltzes, Sorbs, Abodrites, and Bohemians. With these he was forced to fight, but others, by far the greater number, surrendered without a struggle.

16. FOREIGN RELATIONS

Charles also increased the glory of his empire by establishing friendly relations with many kings and peoples. An example is his close friendship with King Alfons of Galicia and Asturias, who always insisted on calling himself Charles' vassal when sending him letters or ambassadors. Charles also secured the favor of the Scottish kings by his great generosity, so that they always referred to him as their master and called themselves his subjects and servants. To this day there exist letters sent by them which clearly express these feelings.

With King Harun of Persia, who ruled almost all of the Orient except India, he was on such friendly terms that Harun preferred Charles' goodwill to the friendship of all other kings and potentates on earth and considered Charles alone worthy of his respect and homage. At one time the king of the Franks sent messengers with offerings to the most Holy Sepulcher, the site of the Resurrection of our Lord and Savior. When they appeared before Harun to relay their master's wishes, the king not only permitted them to carry out their mission but also gave Charles the jurisdiction over their holy and blessed place. On their return Harun sent along his own messengers with precious gifts, garments, spices, and other riches of the Orient. A few years earlier Charles had asked him for an elephant and Harun had sent him the only one he owned.

The three emperors of Constantinople, Nicephorus, Michael, and Leo, all sought Charles' friendship and alliance and sent numerous legations to his court. Only when Charles assumed the title of emperor did they begin to distrust him out of fear that he would seize their lands. To allay these fears and make sure that there would be no occasion for further trouble, Charles at once concluded a firm treaty with them. But the Greeks and the Romans remained suspicious of Frankish power. Hence a Greek proverb; "Have a Frank as a friend, but not as a neighbor."

17. PUBLIC WORKS

No matter how much time and effort Charles spent on planning and carrying out campaigns to enlarge his realm and subjugate foreign nations, he still was able to begin work on a number of public projects designed to help and beautify his kingdom. Some of them he actually managed to complete. The Basilica of the Holy Mother of God in Aachen, a triumph of the arts in construction, is quite rightly considered among the most remarkable of these. So, too, the bridge spanning the Rhine at Mainz, which is a full five hundred paces long, since the river is that wide at this point [2250 *feet—Ed.*]. The bridge was destroyed by fire and was not rebuilt because Charles died a year later. He had intended to replace the wooden structure with one of stone. He also began building two magnificent palaces, one near the city of Mainz close to his estate at Ingelheim, the other in Nymwegen on the Waal River, which flows south of the island of the Batavians. But his chief concern was for the churches. When he discovered one in any part of his kingdom that was old and ready to collapse he charged the responsible bishops and priests with restoring it. And he made sure that his instructions were carried out by having his agents check up on them.

He also set up a navy to withstand the attacks of the Norsemen and had the necessary ships built on the rivers which flow from Gaul and Germania into the North Sea. Since the Norsemen were continuously invading and devastating the Gallic and Germanic coasts, he placed guards and fortifications in all harbors and large estuaries where ships could enter. In this way he prevented the enemy from landing and looting. He did the same in the south along the shores of Narbonensis, Septimania, and Italy as far south as Rome to ward off the Moors who had just begun to take up piracy. As a consequence Italy was hardly touched during his reign except for the Etruscan town of Civita Vecchia, which was treacherously captured and plundered by the Moors. Gaul and Germania were likewise spared except for a few Frisian islands along the Germanic coast which were laid waste by Norsemen.

18. PRIVATE LIFE

This is how Charles enlarged and defended his empire and at the same time made it beautiful. My subject from this point on will be his intellectual abilities and his extraordinary steadfastness both in success and in adversity; and, further, whatever else concerns his private and domestic life.

After the death of his father, Charles ruled the kingdom together with his brother. Everyone was surprised that he bore the latter's animosity and envy with so much patience that he could never be provoked to anger by him. At his mother's request he married a daughter of the Lombard king Desiderius but repudiated her for unknown reasons after one year. Then he married Hildegard, who came from a very noble Swabian family. With her he had three sons, Charles, Pepin, and Louis, and as many daughters, Rotrud, Bertha, and Gisela. He had three more daughters, Theoderada, Hiltrud, and Rotheid, two of them with his [third] wife Fastrada, who came from Eastern Franconia and was therefore Germanic, the third by a concubine whose name I cannot recall at the moment. When Fastrada died he took Liutgard to wife, who was from Alemannia and with whom he had no children. After her death he had four concubines: Madelgard, who bore him a daughter by the name of Rothild; Gerswinda from Saxony, with whom he had another daughter called Adeltrud; Regnia, who gave him two sons, Drogo and Hugo; and Adelind, who had Theoderic.

His mother Berthrada spent her old age in great honor in his house. He always treated her with the greatest respect; only when he divorced the daughter of King Desiderius, whom he had married to please her, was there any disagreement between them. Berthrada died soon after Hildegard, but she had lived long enough to see three grandsons and three granddaughters in the house of her son. Charles buried her with highest honors in the church of St. Denis, where his father had been laid to rest.

Like his mother, he treated his only sister Gisela, who had entered a convent as a young girl, with the greatest affection. She died a few years before he did in the convent where she had spent most of her life.

19. PRIVATE LIFE (CONTINUED)

For the education of his children Charles made the following provisions: his sons as well as his daughters were to be instructed first in those liberal arts in which he took most interest himself. As soon as the boys were old enough they had to learn how to ride, hunt, and handle weapons in Frankish style. The girls had to get used to carding wool and to the distaff and the spindle. To prevent their becoming bored and lazy he gave orders for them to be taught to engage in these and all other virtuous activities. Of his children, only two sons and one daughter died before him: Charles, who was the oldest; Pepin, whom he had made king of Italy; and his oldest daughter Rotrud, who had been engaged to marry the emperor Constantine of Greece. Pepin was survived by one son, called Bernhard, and five daughters: Adelheid, Atula, Guntrada, Bertheid, and Theoderada. How much Charles cared for his grandchildren was proved after their father's death: he made

Bernhard Pepin's successor and raised the five girls together with his own daughters. When his two sons and daughter died, Charles reacted to their deaths with much less equanimity than might have been expected of so strong-minded a man. Because of his deepseated devotion to them he broke down in tears. Also, when he was told of the death of the Roman Pope Hadrian, who was one of his best friends, he wept as much as if he had lost a brother or a favorite son. For Charles was by nature a man who had a great gift for friendship, who made friends easily and never wavered in his loyalty to them. Those whom he loved could rely on him absolutely.

He supervised the upbringing of his sons and daughters very carefully. When he was at home he never ate his meals without them and when he went away, he always took them along. At such times his sons rode by his side and his daughters followed close behind, protected by a bodyguard of hand-picked men. Although the girls were very beautiful and he loved them dearly, it was odd that he did not permit any of them to get married either to a man of his own nation or to a foreigner. Rather, he kept all of them with him until his death, saying that he could not live without their company. And on account of this, he had to suffer a number of unpleasant experiences, however lucky he was in every other respect. But he never let on that he had heard of any suspicions regarding their chastity or any rumors about them.

20. CONSPIRACIES AGAINST CHARLES

By one of the concubines he had a son whom I have not mentioned along with the others. His name was Pepin and he had a handsome face but was hunchbacked. While his father was wintering in Bavaria during the war against the Huns, Pepin pretended to be ill and became involved with some Frankish nobles in a plot against his father. He had been lured into it by empty promises that they would make him king. But the scheme was discovered and the traitors punished. Pepin was tonsured and allowed, on his own free will, to enter the monastery of Pruem, where he spent the rest of his life as a monk.

But even before this there had been a great conspiracy in Germania against Charles. All of the guilty ones were exiled; some of them only after being blinded, but the others were not harmed physically. Only three were killed because they had drawn their swords and tried to resist being taken prisoners. After they had slaughtered a number of men, they were killed themselves since there was no other way to subdue them. It was generally felt that Queen Fastrada's cruelty was responsible for these uprisings. And in both cases the reason they were aimed at Charles was because he apparently acquiesced in his wife's cruelty and seemed to have lost a good deal of his usual kindness and easy disposition. But for the rest, he was deeply loved and respected by everyone at home and abroad during all of his life, and no one ever accused him of being unnecessarily harsh.

21. TREATMENT OF FOREIGNERS

Charles liked foreigners and made every effort to see that they were well received. Often there were so many of them in his palace and kingdom that they were quite rightly considered a nuisance. But, magnanimous as he was, he was never bothered by such annoyances. For he felt that he would be rewarded for his troubles if they praised his generosity and gave him a good reputation.

22. PERSONAL APPEARANCE

Charles had a big and powerful body and was tall but well-proportioned. That his height was seven times the length of his own feet is well known. He had a round head, his eyes were unusually large and lively, his nose a little longer than average, his gray hair attractive, and his face cheerful and friendly. Whether he was standing or sitting his appearance was always impressive and dignified. His neck was somewhat short and thick and his stomach protruded a little, but this was rendered inconspicuous by the good proportion of the rest of his body. He walked firmly and his carriage was manly, yet his voice, though clear, was not as strong as one might have expected from someone his size. His health was always excellent except during the last four years of his life, when he frequently suffered from attacks of fever. And at the end he also limped with one foot. All the same, he continued to rely on his own judgment more than on that of his physicians, whom he almost hated because they ordered him to give up his customary roast meat and eat only boiled meat instead.

According to Frankish custom, he rode and hunted a great deal. There is probably no nation on earth that can match the Franks in these skills. Charles was also found of the steam of natural hot springs. He swam a great deal and did it so well that no one could compete with him. This was why he built the palace in Aachen and spent there the last years of his life without interruption until he died. He invited not only his sons but also his nobles and friends, sometimes even his retinue and bodyguard, to bathe with him, so that frequently there would be more than a hundred people in the baths.

23. DRESS

He wore the national dress of the Franks. The trunk of his body was covered with a linen shirt, his thighs with linen pants. Over these he put a tunic trimmed at the border with silk. The legs from the knee down-ward were wound with leggings, fastened around the calves with laces, and on his feet he wore boots. In winter he protected his shoulders and chest with a vest made of otter skins or marten fur, and over that he wrapped a blue cloak. He always carried a sword strapped to his side, and the hilt and belt thereof were made either of gold or silver. Only on special holidays or when ambassadors from foreign nations were to be received did he sometimes carry a jewel-studded saber. He disliked foreign clothes no matter how beautiful they were, and would never allow himself to be dressed in them. Only in Rome was he seen on two occasions in a long tunic, chlamys, and Roman shoes: the first time at the entreaty of Pope Hadrian and the second by request of his successor Leo. On high festival days he wore a suit of golden cloth and boots ornamented with jewels. His cloak was fastened by a golden brooch, and on his head he carried a diadem of gold, embellished with gems. On the other days, however, his dress was not much different from that of the common people.

24. HABITS

Charles was a moderate eater and drinker, especially the latter, because he abominated drunkenness in any man, particularly in himself and in his associates. But he could not easily abstain from eating and often complained that fasting was bad for his health. He rarely gave banquets and then only on special feast days for large numbers of guests. His daily dinner consisted of four courses, besides the roast which the hunters used to bring in on spits and which he loved more than any other food. During the meal he either listened to music or to someone reading aloud. Stories and the deeds of the old heroes were recited to him. He also enjoyed the books of St. Augustine, especially *The City of God*.

He was so temperate in drinking wine or other beverages that he rarely drank more than three times during a meal. After his midday meal in the summer he would eat some fruit and take another drink, then remove his clothes and shoes, just as he did at night, and rest for two to three hours. His sleep at night would usually be interrupted four or five times, and as soon as he awoke, he got up. While he was being dressed and having his shoes put on, he would invite his friends to come into the room. If the count of the palace told him of some dispute which could not be settled without his decision, he ordered the litigants brought before him at once and, just as though he were sitting in a court of justice, would hear the case and pronounce judgment. At the same time he would give instructions on what had to be transacted that day, or what his ministers were to be charged with doing.

25. STUDIES

Charles was a gifted speaker. He spoke fluently and expressed whatever he had to say with great clarity. Not only was he proficient in his mother tongue but he also took trouble to learn foreign languages. He spoke Latin as well as his own language, but Greek he understood better than he could speak it. At times he was so eloquent that he almost seemed verbose. He was zealous in his cultivation of the liberal arts, and respected and honored highly those who taught them. He learned grammar from the Deacon Peter of Pisa, who was then already an old man. Another deacon, Albinus, surnamed Alcuin,[3] a man of Saxon origin who came from Britain and was the greatest scholar of his time, taught him the other subjects. Under his direction, the king spent a great deal of time and effort studying rhetoric, logic, and especially astronomy. He learned how to calculate and with great diligence and curiosity investigated the course of the stars. He also tried his hand at writing and to this end always kept writing tablets and notebooks under his pillow in bed in order to practice during spare moments. But since he had only started relatively late in life, he never became very accomplished in this art.

26. PIETY

The king practiced the Christian religion, in which he had been raised since childhood, with the greatest piety and devotion. That is why he built the beautiful basilica in Aachen and decorated it with gold and silver, candelabras, lattices, and portals of solid bronze. Since he was unable to get the columns and marble for the structure from anywhere else, he had them brought from Rome and Ravenna.

As long as his health permitted, the king attended church regularly in the morning and evening and took part in the late-night hours and morning mass. He was especially concerned that everything done in church should be carried out with the greatest possible dignity. Often he admonished the sacristans to see to it that nothing unseemly or unclean was brought into the church or left there. He gave many sacred vessels of gold and silver and so many priestly vestments that when services were held not even the doorkeepers- the humblest in ecclesiastical rank- had to perform their duties in everyday clothes.

Charles also worked very hard at improving the quality of liturgical reading and chanting of the psalms. He himself was well versed in both, although he would never read in public or sing, except in a low voice and together with the congregation.

27. GENEROSITY

Charles was especially interested in helping the poor, and his generosity was of the kind for which the Greeks use the word *eleemosyna* (alms). But his charity was not limited to his own country and kingdom, for wherever he heard of Christians living in poverty, he would send them money out of compassion for their wretched lot, even overseas, to Syria and Egypt, as well as to Africa, Jerusalem, Alexandria, and Carthage. This was also the chief reason why he cultivated friendships with kings across the seas, so that the Christians living in need under their jurisdiction would receive some aid and succor.

Of all sacred and hallowed places, he loved the Cathedral of the Holy Apostle Peter in Rome most of all. He endowed its treasure room with great quantities of gold, silver, and precious stones. He sent its pontiffs many, indeed innumerable, gifts. During his entire reign nothing seemed more important to him than to exert himself to restore the city of Rome to its old splendor and to have the Cathedral of St. Peter not only secured and defended but, through his generosity, adorned and enriched beyond all other churches. Although he favored this church so much, he only visited it four times during his reign of forty-seven years, there to fulfill his vows and offer his prayers.

28. CHARLES BECOMES EMPEROR

But there were also other reasons for Charles' last visit to Rome. The Romans had forced Pope Leo, on whom they had inflicted various injuries, like tearing out his eyes and cutting out his tongue, to beg for the king's assistance. Charles therefore went to Rome to put order into the confused situation and reestablish the status of the Church. This took the whole winter. It was on this occasion that he accepted the titles of Emperor and Augustus, which at first he disliked so much that he said he would never have entered the church even on this highest of holy days[4] if he had beforehand realized the intentions of the Pope. Still, he bore with astonishing patience the envy his imperial title aroused in the indignant Eastern Roman emperors. He overcame their stubborn opposition with magnanimity-of which he unquestionably had far more than they did-and sent frequent embassies to them, always calling them his brothers in his letters.

29. REFORMS

After Charles had accepted the imperial title he noticed that there were many flaws in the legal code of his people, for the Franks have two separate sets of laws differing markedly in many details. He planned to fill in the gaps, to reconcile discrepancies, and to correct what was wrongly and improperly stated. But he was unable to get very much done, except for making a very few additions and even those incomplete. Even so, he did order all the unwritten laws of the nations under his rule collected and written down. He also had the same done for the very old heathen songs which tell of the deeds and wars of former kings, so that they might be preserved for posterity. In addition, he began a grammar of his native language.

Charles gave Frankish names to the months. Before that the Franks had used partly Latin, partly barbarian names for them. He also invited appropriate designations for the twelve winds for which there had previously been barely four words. As for the months, he called January uuintarmanoth, February hornung, March lenzinmanoth, April ostarmanoth, May uuinnemanoth, June brachmanoth, July heuuimanoth, August aranmanoth, September uuitumanoth, October uuindumemanoth, November herbistmanoth, and December heilagmanoth. To the winds he gave the following names: the east wind (subsolanus) he called ostroniuuint, the southeaster (eurus) ostsundroni, the south-southeaster (euroauster) sundostroni, the south wind (auster) sundroni, the south-southwester (austroafricus) sunduuestroni, the southwester (africus) uuestsundroni, the west wind (zephyrus) uuestroni, the northwester (chorus) uuestnordroni, the north-northwester (circius) norduuestroni, the north wind (septentrio) nordroni, the northeaster (aquilo) nordostroni, and the north-northeaster (vulturnus) ostnordroni.

30. CORONATION OF LOUIS AND CHARLES' DEATH

At the end of his life, when he was already beset by illness and old age, Charles summoned Louis, the king of Aquitaine and Hildegard's only surviving son, to his presence. He invited all of the Frankish nobles to a solemn assembly, in which with their consent he appointed Louis coregent over the entire realm and heir to the imperial title. He crowned his son himself by placing the diadem on his head and ordering that he be addressed Emperor and Augustus. His decision was received by all those present with great acclaim since it seemed to be divinely inspired for the good of the kingdom. It increased his reputation as a ruler and instilled considerable respect among foreign nations. After Charles had sent his son back to Aquitaine, he started out as usual for the hunt paying no heed to his advanced age. Thus occupied, he spent what was left of the autumn not far from Aachen and returned to the palace at approximately the beginning of November. While he was wintering there he was attacked by a high fever during the month of January and had to retire to bed. As he always did when he had a temperature, he began to diet in the belief that he could cure or at least alleviate his illness by abstaining from food. In addition to the fever he developed a pain in his side, which the Greeks call pleurisy, but he kept fasting and did not take any sustenance except for an occasional drink. On the seventh day after he had taken to bed he received the Holy Communion and died on 28 January between eight and nine o'clock in the morning. Charles was then in the seventy-second year of his life and in the forty-seventh year of his reign.

31. BURIAL

His body was washed and prepared for burial in the usual way, then brought to the basilica and buried amid the great lamentations of the entire population. At first there was uncertainty about where he should be laid to rest because he had never given any instructions on this point during his lifetime. Finally everyone agreed that there could be no more appropriate place than the basilica which he had built at his own expense in this city out of love for God and our Lord Jesus Christ and in honor of the Holy and Immaculate Virgin. He was interred there on the same day he died. Above his grave a gilded arch was raised with his image and an inscription reading as follows: "In this tomb lies the body of Charles, the great Christian Emperor, who gloriously increased the kingdom of the Franks and ruled successfully for forty-seven years. He died in his seventies in the seventh year of the indiction, on January 28th in the year of our Lord 814."

32. OMENS OF DEATH

There were many omens indicating the approach of his death, so that not only others but even himself took note of the forewarnings. During the last three years of his life there were frequent eclipses of the sun and moon, and black spots were seen on the face of the sun for seven days. On Ascension Day the portico between the cathedral and the palace which he had built with immense effort suddenly came crashing down in complete ruin. The wooden bridge across the Rhine at Mainz, which had taken ten years of hard work to build and which was so cleverly constructed that it seemed as if it would last forever, this bridge accidentally caught fire and burnt to ashes in three hours, so that not a single plank remained except what was under water. During his last campaign in Saxony against Godofrid, the king of the Danes, Charles all at once saw a ball of brilliant fire falling from the sky and flashing from right to left through the clear atmosphere. He had just left his camp before sunrise to start out on the march. While everybody was looking and wondering what his sign meant, his horse fell headfirst and threw him to the ground so violently that the clasp on his cloak broke and his sword belt burst. The attendants who were near him and rushed to his aid helped him up without his weapons and cloak. The lance which he had been holding tightly in his hand was thrown a distance of more than twenty feet.

In addition to all this there were numerous earth tremors in his palace in Aachen, and in the houses which Charles visited the wooden beams in the ceilings creaked constantly. Furthermore, lightning had struck the basilica in which he was later to be buried and the golden ball which decorated the gable was destroyed and hurled onto the roof of the bishop's house next to the church. In the same basilica there was an inscription written in red ochre naming its builder and running along the edge of the circular space which surrounds the interior part of the building between the upper and lower arches. Its last words read: "Karolus Princeps." Several people noticed that during the last year of his life, only a few months before he died, the letters of the word "Princeps" had become so blurred that they could hardly be deciphered.

But Charles took no notice of these omens; in any case he acted as if they had nothing whatever to do with him.

33. LAST WILL

Charles had decided to draw up a will in which he wanted to make his daughters and illegitimate children heirs to some part of his estate. Since he started too late, however, he was unable to complete it. Nevertheless, three years before his death he made a division of his treasures, money, clothing, and other movable property in the presence of his friends and attendants. He called on them to bear witness that the apportionment which he had planned should be executed faithfully after his death. He had a brief statement prepared summarizing what he wanted done with the property he had divided. This document reads as follows: "In the name of the Almighty Lord God, the Father, the Son, and the Holy Ghost. Here is a description of the division which was made by the most glorious and pious Lord Charles, Emperor and Augustus, in the eight hundred and eleventh year after the incarnation of our Lord Jesus Christ, during the forty-third year of his region over the Franks, in the thirty-sixth year of his rule over Italy, in the eleventh year of his imperial sovereignty, and in the fourth indiction. After much pious and prudent deliberation and with the help of God, he has decided to distribute the valuables and money which on this day are on deposit in his treasury. In doing so he wished above all to ensure that in his case the distribution of alms, which among Christians is traditionally made from their own personal belongings, would be carried out in an orderly and reasonable fashion. He also wanted to be certain that his heirs should understand quite clearly and definitely what was to be theirs, so that they could divide up the inheritance properly without any litigation or dispute. Such being his intention and purpose, he first divided all his tangible and movable possessions, consisting of gold and of silver, precious stones and royal vestments, deposited in his treasury on the stipulated day into three main parts. One part he left intact; the other two he subdivided into twenty-one smaller portions, the reason for this being that, as is well known, there are twenty-two capital cities in his realm. One of these portions shall be given for charitable purposes to each of the cities by his heirs and friends. The archbishop responsible for the diocese shall receive the portion and divide it with his suffragans in such a manner that one-third is kept for his church and two-thirds is given to the suffragans. These twenty-one portions into which two-thirds of his property were subdivided to correspond to the number of capital cities in the kingdom have been carefully separated and set aside in individual coffers on which the names of the cities of destination are written. The cities to which these alms and gifts are to be given are as follows: Rome, Ravenna, Milan, Cividale del Friuli, Grado, Cologne, Mainz, Salzburg, Trier, Sens, Besançon, Lyons, Rouen, Rheims, Arles, Vienne, Moûtiers-en-Tarantise, Embrun, Bordeaûx, Tours, and Bourges.

"The third main part which is to be preserved intact shall be dealt with in the following manner: while both of the above-mentioned parts are to be divided in the way stated and are to be kept under seal, the third part is to be used for the defrayment of the daily expenses by the owner and will constitute property of which he cannot be deprived by any sworn obligation whatsoever. This provision shall remain in force for as long as he lives or for as long as he judges that he has need of it. After his death or voluntary withdrawal from the secular world the said part is to be divided into four shares. One of these shall be added to the above-mentioned twenty-one portions; the second share is to go to his sons and daughters and their sons and daughters and shall be distributed in a just and equitable way; the third shall be devoted to the poor in the customary Christian manner; the fourth is to be similarly parceled out in form of a pension, in the name of Christian charity, among the male and female servants of the Palace.

"To this third main part of his fortune, which like the rest consists of gold and silver, he desires that there be added all vessels and utensils made of bronze, iron, and other metal, together with his weapons, clothes, and other movable property, whether valuable or not, and for whatever use intended, such as curtains, coverlets, tapestries, woolens, leather goods, pack saddles, and whatever else might be found that day in the treasury or in his wardrobe. In this way the shares of the third part will be enlarged and the alms distributed among a greater number of people.

"Further, he has given orders that the chapel, that is to say the furnishings which he has donated and collected, or inherited from his father, be kept intact and not be subject to any kind of division. Should there, however, be any vessels, books, or other objects of which it is certainly known that they were not given to the chapel by him, then any person desiring them may buy them, provided a fair price is paid. In the same way he decreed that the large collection of books in his library may be bought by persons who want them and will pay a just price for them. The proceeds shall go to the poor."Among his other treasures and valuables there are known to be three silver tables and one of unusual size and weight made of gold. He has stipulated and decreed that one of them, square in shape and decorated with a plan of the city of Constantinople, be sent to Rome to the Cathedral of the Holy Apostle Peter along with the other gifts thereto intended. The second table, round in shape and engraved with a picture of the city of Rome, shall be given to the bishopric of the church of Ravenna. The third, far superior to the others, both in beauty of craftsmanship and in weight, consists of three concentric circles on which a map of the entire world is skillfully traced in great detail. This table together with the golden one, called the fourth, shall be added to the third main part of his fortune, which he has allotted to his heirs and to those who are to receive alms.

"These arrangements and stipulations were done in the presence of the following bishops, abbots, and counts who were able to attend on that day, and whose names are herein recorded:

Bishops

Hildebald	John
Richolf	Theodolf
Arno	Jesse
Wolfar	Heito
Bernoin	Waltgaud
Laidrad	

Abbots

Fridugis	Angilbert
Adalung	Irmino

Counts

Walach	Uruoch
Meginher	Burchard
Otolf	Meginhard
Stephan	Hatto
Richwin	Bero
Edo	Hildegren
Ercanger	Hroccolf
Gerold	

After Charles' death, his son Louis, who succeeded him by divine ordination, examined this document and had its provisions carried out as speedily as possible and with the utmost scrupulousness.

Questions:
1. According to Einhard, what made Charlemagne a great ruler?
2. Describe Charlemagne's relationship to the Roman church.

7.5 The Missi Dominici (802)

The greatness of a ruler has often been determined not just by how much territory he conquered, but by how well he maintained it. The administration of an empire as vast as Charlemagne's depended on efficient servants of the king. The selections below testify to Charlemagne's organization and efficient rule. The Missi Dominici were members of the church and nobility who traveled throughout the realm administering justice by acting as an appellate court; it was an attempt to inject the presence of the king directly into the law and affairs of the realm.

> **Source:** "The Missi Dominici" is from Dana Munro, ed., *Translations and Reprints from the Original Sources of European History,* vol. 6, pt. 5 (Philadelphia: University of Pennsylvania, 1899), p. 16.

Concerning the embassy sent out by the lord emperor. Therefore, the most serene and most Christian lord emperor Charles has chosen from his nobles the wisest and most prudent men, both archbishops and some of the other bishops also, and venerable abbots and pious laymen, and has sent them throughout his whole kingdom, and through them by all the following chapters has allowed men to live in accordance with the correct law. Moreover, where anything which is not right and just has been enacted in the law, he has ordered them to inquire into this most diligently and to inform him of it; he desires, God granting, to reform it. And let no one, through his cleverness or astuteness, dare to oppose or thwart the written law, as many would like to do, or the judicial sentence passed upon him, or to do injury to the churches of God or the poor or the widows or the wards or any Christian. But all shall live entirely in accordance with God's precept, justly and under a just rule, and each one shall be admonished to live in harmony with his fellows in his business or profession; the canonical clergy ought to observe in every respect a canonical life without seeking base gain, nuns ought to keep diligent watch over their lives, laymen and the secular clergy ought rightly to observe their laws without malicious fraud, and all ought to live in mutual charity and perfect peace.

Question:
1. In what ways does Charlemagne's administration of his empire reflect authority and structure?

7.6 Launching the Crusades (1095): "It Is the Will of God!"

The first expedition to free the Holy Land from the control of the Infidel Muslim was launched in 1095 at the Council of Clermont. Pope Urban II presided and in a rousing speech excited the crowd with this impassioned plea for action. Although we are not sure about the accuracy of the text (we have five contemporary versions), the following account by Robert the Monk is credible and clearly illustrates Urban's justification for the First Crusade as well as his popular appeal.

> **Source:** "Launching the Crusades" is from Oliver Thatcher and Edgar McNeal, eds., *A Source Book of Medieval History* (New York: Charles Scribner's Sons, 1905), pp. 518–520.

ROBERT THE MONK

In 1095 a great council was held in Auvergne, in the city of Clermont. Pope Urban II, accompanied by cardinals and bishops, presided over it. It was made famous by the presence of many bishops and princes from France and Germany. After the council had attended to ecclesiastical matters, the pope went out into a public square, because no house was able to hold the people, and addressed them in a very persuasive speech, as follows: "O race of the Franks, O people who live beyond the mountains [the Alps], O people loved and chosen of God, as is clear from your many deeds, distinguished over all other nations by the situation of your land, your catholic faith, and your regard for the holy church, we have a special message and exhortation for you. For we wish you to know what a grave matter has brought us to your country. The sad news has come from Jerusalem and Constantinople that the people of Persia, an accursed and foreign race, enemies of God, a generation that set not their heart aright, and whose spirit was not steadfast with God [Ps. 78:8], have invaded the lands of those Christians and devastated them with the sword, rapine, and fire. Some of the Christians they have carried away as slaves, others they have put to death. The churches they have either destroyed or turned into mosques. They desecrate and overthrow the altars. They circumcise the Christians and pour the blood from the circumcision on the altars or in the baptismal fonts. Some they kill in a horrible way by cutting open the abdomen, taking out a part of the entrails and tying them to a stake; they then beat them and compel them to walk until all their entrails are drawn out and they fall to the ground. Some they use as targets for their arrows. They compel some to stretch out their necks and then they try to see whether they can cut off their heads with one stroke of the sword. It is better to say nothing of their horrible treatment of the women. They have taken from the Greek empire a tract of land so large that it takes more than two months to walk through it. Whose duty is it to avenge this and recover that land, if not yours? For to you more than to other nations the Lord has given the military spirit, courage, agile bodies, and the bravery to strike down those who resist you. Let your minds be stirred to bravery by the deeds of your forefathers, and by the efficiency and greatness of [Charlemagne], and of Ludwig his son, and of the other kings who have destroyed Turkish kingdoms, and established Christianity in their lands. You should be moved especially by the holy grave of our Lord and Saviour which is now held by unclean peoples, and by the holy places which are treated with dishonor and irreverently befouled with their uncleanness.

"O bravest of knights, descendants of unconquered ancestors, do not be weaker than they, but remember their courage. If you are kept back by your love for your children, relatives and wives, remember what the Lord says in the Gospel: 'He that loveth father or mother more than me is not worthy of me' [Matt. 10:37]; 'and everyone that hath forsaken houses, or brothers, or sisters, or father, or mother, or wife, or children, or lands for my name's sake, shall receive a hundredfold and shall inherit everlasting life' [Matt. 19:29]. Let no possessions keep you back, no solicitude for your property. Your land is shut in on all sides by the sea and mountains, and is too thickly populated. There is not much wealth here, and the soil scarcely yields enough to support you. On this account you kill and devour each other, and carry on war and mutually destroy each other. Let your hatred and quarrels cease, your civil wars come to an end, and all your dissensions stop. Set out on the road to the holy sepulchre, take the land from that wicked people, and make it your own. . . . This land our Saviour made illustrious by his birth, beautiful with his life, and sacred with his suffering; he redeemed it with his death and glorified it with his tomb. This royal city is now held captive by her enemies, and made pagan by those who know not God. She asks and longs to be liberated and does not cease to beg you to come to her aid. She asks aid especially from you because, as I have said, God has given more of the military spirit to you than to other nations. Set out on this journey and you will obtain the remission of your sins and be sure of the incorrigible glory of the kingdom of heaven."

When Pope Urban had said this and much more of the same sort, all who were present were moved to cry out with one accord, "It is the will of God, it is the will of God!" When the pope heard this he raised his eyes to heaven and gave thanks to God, and, commanding silence with a gesture of his hand, he said: "My dear brethren, today there is fulfilled in you that which the Lord says in the Gospel, 'Where two or three are gathered in my name, there am I in the midst' [Matt. 18:20]. For unless the Lord God had been in your minds you would not all have said the same thing. For although you spoke with many voices, nevertheless it was one and the same thing that made you speak. So I say unto you, God, who put those words into your hearts, has caused you to utter them. Therefore let these words be your battle cry, because God caused you to speak them. Whenever you meet the enemy in battle, you shall all cry out, 'It is the will of God! It is the will of God!'"

Questions:
1. What reasons are given for the necessity of a Crusade?
2. How does Urban II justify his reasons?

PART 8
Islam

8.1 The Qur'an

Although of more recent origin than the others, Islam is one of the great world religions; today the number of its adherents is comparable to that of Christianity. The word "Islam" itself means submission or surrender, and a Muslim, or follower of Islam, is one who surrenders or submits himself to the will of Allah (God).

Islam had its beginnings on the Arab peninsula in the seventh century A.D.. Its founder, Muhammad (c. 571-632), was orphaned in early childhood and grew up in poverty. As he matured he became increasingly estranged from the polytheistic religion of his native city of Mecca, with its worship of idols and its practice of female infanticide. He began to absent himself from Mecca for protracted periods, retiring to a cave in the mountains to meditate. There, one night, he had a vision in which the angel Gabriel appeared before him, telling him he was a messenger, transmitting to him the word of God. On later occasions Gabriel reappeared with more messages, which Muhammad memorized and repeated to his disciples. These were collected together and became the Qur'an. Opposed by the traditional religious functionaries in Mecca, Muhammad was forced to flee for his life to the city of Medina, where he consolidated his forces, finally returning in triumph to Mecca. By the time of his death in 632, Muhammad and Islam had achieved both religious and political control over Arabia.

The Qur'an is the sacred book of Islam; it is held by Muslims to be the infallible word of God, directly revealed to Muhammad. Although it was written in part during the prophet's lifetime it was completed and arranged in its present form shortly after his death. The Islamic creed rests on two central articles of faith. The first is "There is no god but God (Allah)." Thus Islam is a strict monotheism; as such it rejects not only the traditional Arabian polytheism that it supplanted but the trinitarianism of Christianity as well. The second article of faith is "Muhammad is the messenger, or prophet, of Allah." Islam recognizes other important prophets, like Abraham, Moses, and Jesus, and frequent references to them appear in the Qur'an, but it insists that Muhammad is the ultimate, authoritative prophet. Yet he is a human and not a divine being. Although Muslims believe that on one occasion Muhammad actually ascended to the throne of God and conversed with him, he lived and died as an ordinary mortal.

As an elaborated religion the Muslim faith rests on "Five Pillars," which are obligatory on its adherents: (1) Repetition of the creed "There is no god but Allah, and Muhammad is the prophet of Allah"; (2) prayer, normally done five times daily while bowing toward Mecca; (3) alms-giving, for the support of the poor and needy; (4) the fast, for a full day during the sacred month of Ramadan; and (5) the pilgrimage, to Mecca, which every Muslim is expected to make once in a lifetime.

To one outside of the Muslim community the organization of the Qur'an may appear baffling because it seems to lack any recognizable logical coherence. To give the Qur'an's message greater structure and continuity, the contents of the selection that follows have been rearranged. The numbers of the "Suras" or chapters of the Qur'an from which the excerpts have been taken are given in parentheses at the end of each quotation. Also, headings describing the contents of each of these have been added.

Source: Trans. J.M. Rodwell

THE QUR'AN

PREAMBLE

> In the Name of God, The
> Compassionate, the Merciful
>
> Praise be to God, Lord of the worlds!
> The compassionate, the merciful!
> King on the day of reckoning!
> Thee *only* do we worship, and to Thee do we cry for help.
> Guide Thou us on the straight path,

The path of those to whom Thou hast been gracious;-with
whom thou are not angry, and who go not astray. (1)

GOD

He is God alone;
God the eternal!
He begetteth not, and He is not begotten;
And there is none like unto Him. (112)

MUHAMMAD THE PROPHET

Muhammad is not more than an apostle; other apostles have already passed away before him. If he die, therefore, or be slain, will ye turn upon your heels? But he who turneth on his heels shall not injure God at all, and God will certainly reward the thankful! (3)

THE QUR'AN

This Book is without a doubt a revelation sent down from the Lord of the Worlds.

Will they say, he [Muhammad] hath forged it? Nay, it is the truth from thy Lord that thou mayest warn a people to whom no warner hath come before thee, that haply they may be guided.

God it is who hath created the heavens and the earth and all that is between them in six days, then ascended his throne. Save Him ye have no patron, and none to plead for you. Will ye not then reflect?

From the heaven to the earth He governeth all things; hereafter shall they come up to him on a day, whose length shall be a thousand of such years as ye reckon.

This is He who knoweth the unseen and the seen; the Mighty, the Merciful. Who hath made everything which he hath created most good; and began the creation of man with clay;

Then ordained his progeny from germs of life, from sorry water;

Then shaped him and breathed of His Spirit into him, and gave you hearing and seeing and hearts: What little thanks do ye return? (32)

By the star when it setteth,
Your compatriot [Muhammad] erreth not, nor is he led
astray,
Neither speaketh he from mere impulse.
The Qur'an is no other than a revelation revealed to him.
One terrible in power [Gabriel] taught it him,
Endued with wisdom. With even balance stood he
In the highest part of the horizon
Then came he nearer and approached,
And was at the distance of two bows, or even closer,—
And he revealed to his servant what he revealed. (53)

GOD'S CREATION AND CREATURES

Verily God causeth the grain and the date stone to put forth. He bringeth forth the living from the dead, and dead from the living! This is God! Why, then, are ye turned aside from Him?

He causeth the dawn to appear, and hath ordained the night for rest, and the sun and the moon for computing time! The ordinance of the Mighty, the Wise!

And it is He who hath ordained the stars for you that ye may be guided thereby in the darknesses of the land and of the sea! Clear have we made our signs to men of knowledge.

And it is He who hath produced you from one man, and hath provided for you an abode and resting place! Clear have we made our signs for men of insight.

And it is He who sendeth down rain from heaven; and we bring forth by it the buds of all the plants, and from them bring we forth the green foliage, and the close growing grain, and palm trees with sheaths of clustering dates, and gardens of grapes, and the olive and the pomegranate, like and unlike. Look ye on their fruits when they fruit and ripen. Truly herein are signs unto people who believe. (6)

Now of fine clay have we created man;

Then we placed him a moist germ, in a safe abode;

Then made we the moist germ a clot of blood; then made the clotted blood into a piece of flesh; then made the piece of flesh into bones; and we clothed the bones with flesh; then brought forth man of yet another make-Blessed therefore be God, the most excellent of makers-

Then after this ye shall surely die;

Then shall ye be waked up on the
day of resurrection.

And we have created over you seven heavens:-and we are not careless of the creation.

And we send down water from the heaven in its due degree, and we cause it to settle on the earth;-and we have power for its withdrawal;—

And by it we cause gardens of palm trees, and vineyards to spring forth for you, in which ye have plenteous fruits, and whereof ye eat;

And the tree that groweth up on Mount Sinai; which yieldeth oil and a juice for those who eat.

And there is a lesson for you in the cattle. We give you to drink of what is in their bellies, and many advantages do ye derive from them, and for food they serve you;

And on them and on ships are ye borne. (23)

Nay! but it (the Qur'an) is a warning; (And whoso is
willing beareth it in mind)

Written on honored pages,

Exalted, purified,

By the hands of scribes, honored, righteous.

Cursed be man! What hath made him unbelieving?

Of what thing did God create him?

Out of moist germs,

He created him and fashioned him,

Then made him an easy passage from the womb,

Then causeth him to die and burieth him;

Then, when he pleaseth, will raise him again to life.

Aye! but man hath not yet fulfilled the bidding of his
Lord.

Let man look at his food;

It was We who rained down the copious rains,

Then cleft the earth with clefts,

And caused the upgrowth of the grain,

And grapes and healing herbs,

And the olive and the palm,

And enclosed gardens thick with trees,

And fruits and herbage,

For the service of yourselves and of your cattle. (80)

GOD'S PROVIDENCE

And with Him are the keys of the secret things; none knoweth them but He. He knoweth whatever is on the land and in the sea; and no leaf falleth but He knoweth it; neither is there a grain in the darknesses of the earth, nor a thing green or sere, but it is noted in a distinct writing.

It is He who taketh your souls at night, and knoweth what ye have merited in the day; then he awaketh any one of you, our messengers take his soul, and fail not.

Then are they returned to God their Lord, the True. Is not judgment His? (6)

Thus unto thee as unto those who preceded thee doth God, the Mighty, the Wise, reveal!

All that is in the heavens and all that is in the earth is His, and He is the High, the Great!

Ready are the heavens to cleave asunder from above for very awe, and the angels celebrate the praise of their Lord, and ask forgiveness for the dwellers on earth. Is not God the Indulgent, the Merciful?

But whoso take aught beside Him as lords-God watcheth them! But thou hast them not in thy charge.

It is thus moreover that we have revealed to thee an Arabic Qur'an, that thou mayest warn the mother city [Mecca] and all around it, and that thou mayest warn them of that day of the Gathering, of which there is no doubt-when part shall be in Paradise and part in the flame.

Had God so pleased, He had made them one people and of one creed, but He bringeth whom He will within His mercy; and as for the doers of evil, no patron, no helper shall there be for them.

Will they take other patrons than Him? But God is man's only Lord. He quickeneth the dead, and He is mighty over all things.

And whatever the subject of your disputes, with God doth its decision rest. This is God, my Lord; in Him do I put my trust, and to Him do I turn in penitence.

Creator of the heavens and of the earth! He giveth with open hand, or sparingly, to whom He will; He knoweth all things.

To you hath He prescribed the faith which He commanded unto Noah, and which we have revealed to thee, and which we commanded unto Abraham and Moses and Jesus, saying, "Observe this faith, and be not divided into sects therein." Intolerable to those who worship idols jointly with God is that faith to which thou dost call them. Whom He pleaseth will God choose for it, and whosoever shall turn to Him in penitence will He guide to it. (42)

ESCHATOLOGY

By the night when she spreads her veil;
By the day when it brightly shineth;
By Him who made male and female;
At different ends truly do ye aim!
But as to him who giveth alms and feareth
    God,
And yieldeth assent to the good,
To him will we make easy the path to happi-
    ness.
But as to him who is covetous and bent on
    riches,
And calleth the good a lie,
To him will we make easy the path to misery,
And what shall his wealth avail him when he
    goeth down?
Truly man's guidance is with Us,
And ours, the future and the past.
I warn you therefore of the flaming fire;
None shall be cast to it but the most
    wretched,-
Who hath called the truth a lie and turned his
    back.
But the God-fearing shall escape it,-
Who giveth away his substance that he may
    become pure;
And who offereth not favors to any one for the
    sake of recompense,
But only as seeking the face of his Lord the
    Most High.
And surely in the end he shall be well
    content. (92)

Of what ask they of one another?
Of the great news.
The theme of their disputes.
Nay! they shall certainly know its truth!
Again. Nay! they shall certainly know it.
Have we not made the earth a couch?
And the mountains its tent-stakes?
We have created you of two sexes,

And ordained you sleep for rest,
And ordained the night as a mantle,
And ordained the day for gaining livelihood.
And built above you seven solid heavens,
And placed therein a burning lamp;
And we send down water in abundance from
    the rain-clouds,
That we may bring forth by it corn and herbs,
And gardens thick with trees.
Lo! the day of Severance is fixed;
The day when there shall be a blast on the
    trumpet, and ye shall come in crowds,
And the heaven shall be opened and be full of
    portals,
And the mountains shall be set in motion, and
    melt into thin vapor.
Hell truly shall be a place of snares,
The home of transgressors,
To abide therein ages.
No coolness shall they taste therein nor any
    drink,
Save boiling water and running sores;
Meet recompense!
For they looked not forward to their account;
And they gave the lie to our signs, charging
    them with falsehood.
But we noted and wrote down all.

"Taste this then, and we will give you increase
    of nought but torment."
But for the God-fearing is a blissful abode,
Enclosed gardens and vineyards;
And damsels with swelling breasts, their peers
    in age,
And a full cup.
There shall they hear no vain discourse nor
    any falsehood;
A recompense from thy Lord-sufficing gift!—

Lord of the heavens and of the earth, and of all that between them lieth-the God of Mercy! But not a word shall they obtain from Him.

On the day whereon the Spirit and the Angels shall be ranged in order, they shall not speak; save he whom the God of Mercy shall permit, and who shall say that which is right.

This is the sure day. Whoso then will, let him take the path of return to his Lord.

Verily, we warn you of a chastisement close at hand.

The day on which a man shall see the deeds which his hands have sent before him; and when the unbeliever shall say, "Oh! would I were dust!" (78)

O children of Adam! There shall come to you apostles from among yourselves, rehearsing my signs to you; and whoso shall fear God and do good works, no fear shall be upon them, neither shall they be put to grief.

But they who charge our signs with falsehood, and turn away from them in their pride, shall be inmates of the fire; for ever shall they abide therein. And who is worse than he who deviseth a lie of God, or treateth our signs as lies? To them shall a portion here below be assigned in accordance with the Book of our decrees, until the time when our messengers, as they receive their souls, shall say, "Where are they on whom ye called beside God?" They shall say, "Gone from us." And they shall witness against themselves that they were infidels.

He shall say, "Enter ye into the Fire with the generations of Djinn and men who have preceded you. So oft as a fresh generation entereth, it shall curse its sister, until when they have all reached it, the last comers shall say to the former, "O our Lord! these are they who led us astray; assign them therefore a double torment of the fire." He will say, "Ye shall all have double." But of this are ye ignorant.

And the former of them shall say to the latter, "What advantage have ye over us? Taste ye therefore the torment for that which ye have done."

Verily, they who have charged our signs with falsehood and have turned away from them in their pride, heaven's gates shall not be opened to them, nor shall they enter Paradise, until the camel passeth through the eye of the needle. After this manner will we recompense the transgressors.

They shall make their bed in hell, and above them shall be coverings of fire! And this way will we recompense the evil doers.

But as to those who have believed and done the things which are right (we will lay on no one a burden beyond his power)—these shall be inmates of Paradise, for ever shall they abide therein.

And we will remove whatever rancor was in their bosoms; rivers shall roll at their feet, and they shall say, "Praise be to God who hath guided us hither! We had not been guided had not God guided us! Of a surety the apostles of our Lord came to us with truth." And a voice shall cry to them, "This is Paradise, of which, as the meed of your works, ye are made heirs."

And the inmates of Paradise shall cry to the inmates of the fire, "Now have we found what our Lord promised us to be true. Have ye too found what your Lord promised you to be true?" And they shall answer, "Yes." And a herald shall proclaim between them, "The curse of God be upon the evil doers.

"Who turn men aside from the way of God, and seek to make it crooked, and who believe not in the life to come!"

And between them shall be a partition, and on the wall Al Araf [between heaven and hell] shall be men who will know all, by their tokens, and they shall cry to the inmates of Paradise, "Peace be on you!" but they shall not yet enter it, although they long to do so.

And when their eyes are turned towards the inmates of the fire they shall say, "O our Lord! place us not with the offending people."

And they who upon Al Araf shall cry to those whom they shall know by their tokens, "Your amassings and your pride have availed you nothing.

"Are these they on whom ye sware God would not bestow mercy? Enter ye into Paradise! where no fear shall be upon you, neither shall ye be put to grief."

And the inmates of the fire shall cry to the inmates of Paradise, "Pour upon us some water, or of the refreshments God hath given you." They shall say, "Truly God hath forbidden both to unbelievers, who made their religion a sport and pastime, and whom the life of the world hath deceived." This day therefore will we forget them. . . . (71)

MORAL PRECEPTS

Kill not your children for fear of want; for them and for you will we provide. Verily, the killing them is a great wickedness.

Have nought to do with adultery; for it is a foul thing and an evil way.

Neither slay any one whom God hath forbidden you to slay, unless for a just cause; and whosoever shall be slain wrongfully, to his heir have we given powers; but let him not outstep bounds in putting the manslayer to death, for he too, in his turn, will be assisted and avenged.

And touch not the substance of the orphan, unless in an upright way, till he attain his age of strength. And perform your covenant; verily the covenant shall be inquired of.

And give full measure when you measure, and weigh with just balance. This will be better, and fairest for settlement.

And follow not that of which thou hast no knowledge; because the hearing and the sight and the heart- each of these shall be inquired of.

And walk not proudly on the earth, for thou canst not cleave the earth, neither shalt thou reach to the mountains in height. (17)

There is no piety in turning your faces toward the east or the west, but he is pious who believeth in God, and the last day, and the angels, and the scriptures, and the prophets; who for the love of God disburseth his wealth to his kindred, and to the orphans, and the needy, and the wayfarer, and those who ask, and for ransoming; who observeth prayer, and payeth the legal alms, and who is of those who are faithful to their engagements when they have engaged in them, and patient under ills and hardships, and in time of trouble. These are they who are just, and these are they who fear the Lord.

O believers! retaliation for blood-shedding is prescribed to you; the free man for the free, and the slave for the slave, and the woman for the woman. But he to whom his brother shall make any remission is to be dealt with equitably, and to him should he pay a fine with liberality.

This is a relaxation from your Lord and a mercy. For him who after shall transgress a sore punishment!

But in this law of retaliation is your security for life, O men of understanding! to the intent that ye may fear God.

It is prescribed to you, when any one of you is at the point of death, if he leave goods, that he bequeath equitably to his parents and kindred. This is binding on those who fear God. But as for him who after he hath heard the bequest shall change it, surely the wrong of this shall be on those who change it; verily, God heareth, knoweth.

But he who feareth from the testator any mistake or wrong, and shall make a settlement between the parties-that shall be no wrong in him; verily, God is Lenient, Merciful.

O believers! a Fast is prescribed to you as it was prescribed to those before you, that ye may fear God, for certain days.

But he among you who shall be sick, or on a journey shall fast that same number of other days; and as for those who are able to keep it and yet break it, the expiation of this shall be the maintenance of a poor man. And he who of his own accord performeth a good work shall derive good from it, and good shall it be for you to fast-if ye knew it.

As to the month Ramadhan in which the Qur'an was sent down to be man's guidance, and an explanation of that guidance, and of that illumination, as soon as any one of you observeth the moon, let him set about the fast; but he who is sick, or upon a journey, shall fast a like number of other days. God wisheth you ease, but wisheth not your discomfort and that you fulfil the number of days, and that you glorify God for his guidance, and that you be thankful.

And when my servants ask thee concerning me, then will I be nigh unto them. I will answer the cry of him that crieth, when he crieth unto me; but let them hearken unto me, and believe in me, that they may proceed aright.

You are allowed on the night of the fast to approach your wives; they are your garment and ye are their garment. God knoweth that ye defraud yourselves therein, so He turneth unto you and forgiveth you! Now, therefore, go in unto them with full desire for that which God hath ordained for you; and eat and drink until ye can discern a white thread from a black thread by the daybreak, then fast strictly till night, and go not in unto them, but rather pass the time in the Mosque.

• • •

The likeness of those who expend their wealth for the cause of God is that of a grain of corn which produceth seven ears, and in each ear a hundred grains; and God will multiply to whom He pleaseth. God is Liberal, Knowing!

They who expend their wealth for the cause of God, and never follow what they have laid out with reproaches or harm, shall have their reward with their Lord; no fear shall come upon them, neither shall they be put to grief.

A kind speech and forgiveness is better than alms followed by injury. God is Rich, Clement.

O ye who believe! make not your alms void by reproaches and injury, like him who spendeth his substance to be seen of men, and believeth not in God and in the latter day. The likeness of such an one is that of a rock with a thin soil upon it, on which a heavy rain falleth but leaveth it hard. No profit from their works shall they be able to gain; for God guideth not the unbelieving people.

And the likeness of those who expend their substance from a desire to please God, and for the stablishing of their souls, is as a garden on a hill, on which the heavy rain falleth, and it yieldeth its fruits twofold; and even if a heavy rain fall not on it, yet is there a dew. God beholdeth your actions.

• • •

Ye may divorce your wives twice. Keep them honorably or put them away with kindness. But it is not allowed you to appropriate to yourselves aught of what ye have given to them, unless both fear that they cannot keep within the bounds set up by God. And if ye fear that they cannot observe the ordinances of God, no blame shall attach to either of you for what the wife shall herself give for her redemption. These are the bounds of God; therefore overstep them not, for whoever oversteppeth the bounds of God, they are evildoers.

But if the husband divorce her a third time, it is not lawful for him to take her again, until she shall have married another husband; and if he also divorce her, then shall no blame attach to them if they return to each other, thinking that they can keep within the bounds fixed by God. (2)

O men! fear your Lord, who hath created you of one man (soul), and of him created his wife, and from these twain hath spread abroad so many men and women. And fear ye God, in whose name ye ask mutual favors,- and reverence the wombs that bare you. Verily is God watching over you!

And give to the orphans their property; substitute not worthless things of your own for their valuable ones, and devour not their property after adding it to your own, for this is a great crime.

And if ye are apprehensive that ye shall not deal fairly with orphans, then of other women who seem good in your eyes, marry but two, or three, or four; and if ye still fear that ye shall not act equitably, then one only; or the slaves whom ye have acquired. This will make justice on your part easier. Give women their dowry freely; but if of themselves they give up aught thereof to you, then enjoy it as convenient, and profitable.

And entrust not to the incapable the substance which God hath placed with you for their support; but maintain them therewith, and clothe them, and speak to them with kindly speech.

. . .

And if ye be desirous to exchange one wife for another, and have given one of them a talent, make no deduction from it. Would ye take it by slandering her, and with manifest wrong?

How, moreover, could ye take it, when one of you hath gone in unto the other, and they have received from you a strict bond of union?

And marry not women whom your fathers have married; for this is a shame, and hateful, and an evil way:-though what is past may be allowed.

Forbidden to you are your mothers, and your daughters, and your sisters, and your aunts, both on the father and mother's side, and your nieces on the brother and sister's side, and your foster-mothers, and your foster-sisters, and the mothers of your wives, and your step-daughters who are your wards, born of your wives to whom ye have gone in; (but if ye have not gone in unto them, it shall be no sin in you to marry them); and the wives of your sons who proceed out of your loins; and ye may not have two sisters, except where it is already done. Verily, God is Indulgent, Merciful!

Forbidden to you also are married women, except those who are in your hands as slaves. This is the law of God for you. And it is allowed you, beside this, to seek out wives by means of your wealth, with modest conduct, and without fornication. And give those with whom ye have cohabited their dowry. This is the law. But it shall be no crime in you to make agreements over and above the law.

. . .

Men are superior to women on account of the qualities with which God hath gifted the one above the other, and on account of the outlay they make from their substance for them. Virtuous women are obedient, careful, during the husband's absence, because God hath of them been careful. But chide those for whose refractoriness ye have cause to fear; remove them into beds apart, and scourge them. But if they are obedient to you, then seek not occasion against them. (4)

WARFARE

Fight for the cause of God against those who fight against you; but commit not the injustice of attacking them first. God loveth not such injustice.

And kill them wherever ye shall find them, and eject them from whatever place they have ejected you; for civil discord is worse than carnage. Yet attack them not at the sacred Mosque, unless they attack you therein; but if they attack you, slay them. Such is the reward of the infidels.

But if they desist, then verily God is Gracious, Merciful.

Fight therefore against them until there be no more civil discord, and the only worship be that of God. But if they desist, then let there be no hostility, save against the wicked. (2)

CHRISTIANS AND JEWS

We believe in God, and in what hath been sent down to us, and what hath been sent down to Abraham, and Ismael, and Isaac, and Jacob, and the tribes, and in what was given to Moses, and Jesus, and the Prophets, from their Lord. We make no difference between them. And to Him are we resigned (Muslims).

Whoso desireth any other religion than Islam, that religion shall never be accepted from him, and in the next world he shall be among the lost. (3)

Verily, they who believe (Muslims), and they who follow the Jewish religion, and the Christians, and the Sabeites-whoever of these believeth in God and the last day, and doeth that which is right, shall have their reward with their Lord. Fear shall not come upon them, neither shall they be grieved. (2)

Make war upon such of those to whom the Scriptures have been given as believe not in God, or in the last day, and who forbid not that which God and His Apostle have forbidden, and who profess not the profession of the truth, until they pay tribute out of hand, and they be humbled.

The Jews say, "Ezra is a son of God," and the Christians say, "The Messiah is a son of God." Such the sayings in their mouths! They resemble the saying of the infidels of old! God do battle with them! How are they misguided!

They take their teachers, and their monks, and the Messiah, son of Mary, for Lords beside God, though bidden to worship one God only. There is no God but He! Far from His glory be what they associate with Him! (9)

Questions:
1. *Summarize the message of the Qur'an. How is it similar to. Or different from, the central message of the Christian Scriptures? The Hebrew Scriptures?*
2. *What sort of social structures (class, gender, ethnicity, etc.) are assumed in the Qur'an?*

8.2 Al-Tabari: an Early biography of Islam's Prophet

Though the Q'uran itself provides hints about Muhammad's past and his personal life, biographies of the Prophet, which drew upon various (usually oral) accounts and recollections, came out shortly after his death in 632 C.E. One of the most revered of the early Muslim chroniclers was Al-Tabari, who made it a habit to cite his souces whenever possible. Here he has left us an account of a crucial event: the first call of Muhammad to prophesy (note: Aisha was Muhamad's second wife; Khadija his first).

> **Source:** Arthur Jeffrey, trans., *Islam, Muhammad and His Religion* (N.Y.: Liberal Arts Press, 1958), pp. 15–17. Quoted in Mircea Eliade, *From Medicine Men to Muhammad* (N.Y.: Harper & Row, 1974), pp. 63–64.

Ahmad b. 'Uthman, who is known as Abu'l-jawza', has related to me on the authority of Wahb b. Jarir, who heard his father say that he had heard from an-Nu'man b. Rashid, on the authority of az-Zuhri from 'Urwa, from 'A'isha, who said: The way revelation (*wahy*) first began to come to the Apostle of Allah—on whom be Allah's blessing and peace—was by means of true dreams which would come like the morning dawn. Then he came to love solitude, so he used to go off to a cave in Hira where he would practise *tahannuth* certain nights before returning to his family. Then he would come back to his family and take provisions for the like number [of nights] until unexpectedly the truth came to him.

He (i.e., Gabriel) came to him saying: 'O Muhammad, thou art Allah's Apostle (rasUl).' Said the Apostle of Allah—upon whom be Allah's blessing and peace: 'Thereat I fell to my knees where I had been standing, and then with trembling limbs dragged myself along till I came in to Khadija, saying: "Wrap ye me up! Wrap ye me up!" till the terror passed from me. Then [on another occasion] he came to me again and said: "O Muhammad, thou art Allah's Apostle," [which so disturbed me] that I was about to cast myself down from some high mountain cliff. But he appeared before me as I was about to do this, and said: "O Muhammad, I am Gabriel, and thou art Allah's Apostle." Then he said to me: "Recite!"; but I answered: "What should I recite?"; whereat he seized me and grievously treated me three times, till he wore me out. Then he said: "Recite, in the name of thy Lord who has created" (SUra XCVI, 1). So I recited it and then went to Khadija, to whom I said: "I am worried about myself." Then I told her the whole story. She said: "Rejoice, for by Allah, Allah will never put thee to shame. By Allah, thou art mindful of thy kinsfolk, speakest truthfully, renderest what is given thee in trust, bearest burdens, art ever hospitable to the guest, and dost always uphold the right against any wrong." Then she took me to Waraqua b. Naufal b. Asad [to whom] she said: "Give ear to what the son of thy brother [has to report]." So he questioned me, and I told him [the whole] story. Said he: "This is the *nAmUs* which was sent down upon Moses the son of Amram. Would that I might be a stalwart youth [again to take part] in it. Would that I might still be alive when your people turn you out." "And will they turn me out?" I asked. "Yes," said he, "never yet has a man come with that with which you come but has been turned away. Should I be there when your day comes I willlend you mighty assistance."'

Questions:
1. *How did Muhammad react to the first visitations from Gabriel?*
2. *What role did Khadija play?*
3. *What form of suffering does Muhammad's uncle foresee will occur to the Prophet on account of his visions?*

8.3 Orations: The Words of the Prophet Through His Speeches

Muhammad was more than a religious leader; he was a political figure who had, by the time of his death, united most of the Arab peoples into a centralized government based on "Shariah" (Islamic law), and which encompassed both the secular and religious. Church-state separation is a concept that is foreign to Orthodox Islam: the two were originally viewed as inseparable. Collections of Muhammad's "Orations" reveal the Prophet in his role of charismatic messenger. The excerpt is Muhammad's last oration and was delivered, while he was ill, only five days prior to his death.

Source: Mohammad Ubaidul Akbar, *Orations of Muhammad, the Prophet of Islam* (New Delhi, India: Nusrat Ali Nasri for Kitab Bhanan, 1979), pp. 101–106.

He praised Allah, thanked Him, sought forgiveness for the martyrs of the battle of Uhad and prayed for them. Then he said: "O people, (draw near) to me." So they gathered round him.

Then he said: "Well, there is a man whose Lord has given him option between living in this world as long as he wishes to live and eating from this world as much as he likes to eat, or meeting his Lord."

(Hearing it) Abu Bakr wept and said: "Nay, may our fathers, mothers and properties be your ransom…"

Then the Apostle of Allah—may Allah send him bliss and peace!—said: "There is none more bountiful to us for his company and wealth than the son of Abu QuhAfa (Abu Bakr). Had I taken any intimate friend except my Lord, I would have taken the son of Abu QuhAfa as my intimate friend. But there is love and brotherhood of Faith"—He said it twice or thrice).

"The fact is that your companion is the intimate friend of Allah. There should not remain in the mosque any door (open) except the door of Abu Bakr."

"O people, it has reached me that you are afraid of your Prophet's death. Has any previous prophet lived for ever among those to whom he was sent: so that I would live for ever among you?

"Behold, I am going to my Lord and you will be going to Him. I recommend you to do good to the First Emigrants and I recommend the Emigrants to do good among themselves.

"Lo, Allah, the Exalted, says: 'By the time, Man is in loss'—to the end of the Sura (ciii.).

"Verily the things run with the permission of Allah, the Exalted, and verily delay in a matter should not urge you on its hastening in demand. Allah,—the Mighty and the Great—does not hasten for the hastiness of anybody.

"He who contends with Allah, He overcomes him. He who tries to deceive Allah, He outwits him. In a near future if you get the authority then do no mischief on the earth and do not cut off your blood relations.

"I recommend you to do good to the Helpers. They are those who prepared the lodging and faith for you. So you should behave them well.

"Did they not divide with you their fruits equally? Did they not make space for you in their houses? Did they not prefer you to themselves while poverty was with them?'

"Lo, men will increase in number, but the Helpers will decrease to the extent that they will be among men as salt in food. They are my family with whom I took my shelter; they are my sandals; and they are my paunch in which I eat. So observe me in them.

"By Him in Whose hand is my life, verily I love you; verily the Helpers have done what was on them and there remains what is on you.

"So he who from among you gets power in any matter and becomes able to do harm to people therein or to do good to other therein, then he should appreciate one of them who does well and should overlook one of them who does bad. Lo, do not be selfish about them.

"Behold, I shall precede you; I will be your witness and you are to meet me. Lo, the 'Haud' is your meeting place. By Allah, just now, I see my 'Haud' from here.

"Beware, he who likes to come to it along with me to-morrow, should hold back his hand and tongue except from necessary matters."

"Lo, I have, indeed, been given the keys of the treasures of the earth. By Allah, I do not fear for you that you will turn polytheists after me. But I fear for you that you will be entangled in them, then you will fight one another and will perish like those who perished before you.

"O people, verily the sins spoil the blessings and change the lots. When the people are good, their rulers do good to them and when the people are bad, they oppress them."

"Then he said: "There may be some rights which I owe to you and I am nothing but a human being. So if there be any man whose honour I have injured a bit, here is my honour; he may retaliate.

"Whosoever he may be if I have wounded a bit of his skin, here is my skin; He may retaliate.

"Whosoever he may be, if I have taken anything from his property, here is my property; so he may take. Know that he, among you, is more loyal to me who has got such a thing and takes it or absolves me; then I meet my Lord while I am absolved.

"Nobody should say, I fear enmity and grudge of the Apostle of Allah. Verily these things are not in my nature and character. He whose passion has overcome him in aught, should seek help from me so that I may pray for him."

Questions:

1. In what ways does Muhammad foster solidarity amongst his followers?
2. How does Muhammad attempt to encourage and comfort his people against the eventuality of his death?
3. From this last oration, how does it appear that Muhammad wishes to be remembered?

8.4   Islam in the Prophet's Absence: Continuation Under the Caliphate

The sudden demise of Muhammad in 632 left his state in disarray; he had never specified procedures for designating a successor. How was the Muslim state he had forged to be governed? A debate ensued and its results had far-reaching implications, as related by the respective chroniclers Al-Tabari and Ibn Hisham.

> **Source:** Bernard Lewis, ed., *Islam from the Prophet to the Capture of Constantinople*, Vol. I (N.Y.: Walker & Co.,1974), pp. 2–6.

THE FOUNDING OF THE CALIPHATE (632)

An account of what happened between the Emigrants and the Helpers concerning the leadership, in the porch of the Banu Sa'ida[1]

Hishām ibn Muhammad told me on the authority of Abū Mikhnaf, who said: 'Abdallāh ibn 'Abd al-Rahmān ibn Abī 'Umra, the Helper, told me:

When the Prophet of God, may God bless and save him, died, the Helpers assembled in the porch of the Banu Sā'ida and said, "Let us confer this authority, after Muhammad, upon him be peace, on Sa'd ibn 'Ubāda." Sa'd, who was ill, was brought to them, and when they assembled Sa'd said to his son or to one of his nephews, "I cannot, because of my sickness, speak so that all the people can hear my words. Therefore, hear what I say and then repeat it to them so that they may hear it." Then he spoke and the man memorized his words and raised his voice so that the others could hear.

He said, after praising God and lauding Him, "O company of the Helpers! You have precedence in religion and merit in Islam which no other Arab tribe has. Muhammad, upon him be peace, stayed for more than ten years amid his people, summoning them to worship the Merciful One and to abandon false gods and idols. But among his own people only a few men believed in him, and they were not able to protect the Prophet of God or to glorify his religion nor to defend themselves against the injustice which beset them. God therefore conferred merit on you and brought honor to you and singled you out for grace and vouchsafed to you faith in Him and in His Prophet and protection for Him and His companions and glorification to Him and His religion and holy war against His enemies. It was you who fought hardest against His enemy and weighed more heavily on His enemy than any other, until the Arabs obeyed the command of God willy-nilly and the distant ones gave obedience, humbly and meekly; until Almighty God, through you, made the world submit to His Prophet, and through your swords the Arabs drew near to him. And when God caused him to die, he was content with you and delighted with you. Therefore, keep this authority for yourselves alone, for it is yours against all others."

They all replied to him, "Your judgment is sound and your words are true. We shall not depart from what you say and we shall confer this authority on you. You satisfy us and you will satisfy the right believer."

Then they discussed it among themselves and some of them said, "What if the Emigrants of Quraysh refuse, and say: 'We are the Emigrants and the first Companions of the Prophet of God; we are his clan and his friends. Why therefore do you dispute the succession to his authority with us?'" Some of them said, "If so, we would reply to them, 'An amir from us and an amir from you! And we shall never be content with less than that.'" Sa'd ibn 'Ubāda, when he heard this, said, "This is the beginning of weakness."

News of this reached 'Umar, and he went to the house of the Prophet, may God bless and save him. He sent to Abū Bakr, who was in the Prophet's house with 'Alī ibn Abī Tālib, upon him be peace, preparing the body of the Prophet, may God bless and save him, for burial. He sent asking Abū Bakr to come to him, and Abū Bakr sent a message in reply saying that he was busy. Then 'Umar sent saying that something had happened which made his presence necessary, and he went to him and said, "Have you not heard that the Helpers have gathered in the porch of the Banu Sā'ida? They wish to confer this authority on Sa'd ibn 'Ubāda, and the best they say is, 'an amir from among us and an amir from among Quraysh.'" They made haste toward them, and they met Abū 'Ubayda ibn al-Jarrāh. The three of them went on together, and they met 'Asim ibn 'Adī and 'Uwaym ibn Sā'ida, who both said to them: "Go back, for what you want will not happen." They said, "We shall not go back," and they came to the meeting.

'Umar ibn al-Khattāb said: We came to the meeting, and I had prepared a speech which I wished to make to them. We reached them, and I was about to begin my speech when Abū Bakr said to me, "Gently! Let me speak first, and then afterwards say whatever you wish." He spoke. 'Umar said, "He said all I wanted to say, and more."

'Abdallāh ibn 'Abd al-Rahmān said: Abū Bakr began. He praised and lauded God and then he said, "God sent Muhammad as a Prophet to His creatures and as a witness to His community that they might worship God and God alone, at a time when they were worshipping various gods beside Him and believed that they were intercessors for them with God and could be of help to them, though they were only of hewn stone and carved wood. Then he recited to them, 'And they worship apart from God those who could neither harm them nor help them, and they say these are our intercessors with God' [Qur'ān x, 19/18]. And they said, 'We worship them only so that they may bring us very near to God' [Qur'ān xxxix, 4/3]. It was a tremendous thing for the Arabs to abandon the religion of their fathers. God distinguished the first Emigrants of his people by allowing them to recognize the truth and believe in him and console him and suffer with him from the harsh persecution of his people when they gave them the lie and all were against them and reviled them. Yet they were not affrighted because their numbers were few and the people stared at them and their tribe was joined against them. They were the first in the land who worshipped God and who believed in God and the Prophet. They are his friends and his clan and the best entitled of all men to this authority after him. Only a wrongdoer would dispute this with them. And as for you, O company of the Helpers, no one can deny your merit in the faith or your great precedence in Islam. God was pleased to make you Helpers to His religion and His Prophet and caused him to migrate to you, and the honor of sheltering his wives and his Companions is still yours, and after the first Emigrants there is no one we hold of equal standing with you. We are the amirs and you are the viziers. We shall not act contrary to your advice and we shall not decide things without you."

Abū Bakr said, "Here is 'Umar and here is Abū 'Ubayda. Swear allegiance to whichever of them you choose." The two of them said, "No, by God, we shall not accept this authority above you, for you are the worthiest of the Emigrants and the second of the two who were in the cave and the deputy [khalifa] of the Prophet of God in prayer, and prayer is the noblest part of the religion of the Muslims. Who then would be fit to take precedence of you or to accept this authority above you? Stretch out your hand so that we may swear allegiance to you."

And when they went forward to swear allegiance to him, Bashir ibn Sa'd went ahead of them and swore allegiance to him…and when the tribe of Aws saw what Bashir ibn Sa'd had done…they came to him and swore allegiance to him.…

Hishām said on the authority of Abū Mikhnaf: 'Abdallāh ibn 'Abd al-Rahmān said: People came from every side to swear allegiance to Abū Bakr.

2. The Accession Speech of Abū Bakr (632)

Then Abū Bakr spoke and praised and lauded God as is fitting, and then he said: O people, I have been appointed to rule over you, though I am not the best among you. If I do well, help me, and if I do ill, correct me. Truth is loyalty and falsehood is treachery; the weak among you is strong in my eyes until I get justice for him, please God, and the strong among you is weak in my eyes until I exact justice from him, please God. If any people holds back from fighting the holy war for God, God strikes them with degradation. If weakness spreads among a people, God brings disaster upon all of them. Obey me as long as I obey God and His Prophet. And if I disobey God and His Prophet, you do not owe me obedience. Come to prayer, and may God have mercy on you.

Questions:
1. What was the nature of the split between the Helpers and the Emigrants after the Prophet's death?
2. What was Abū Bakr's perspective on the difference in prestige and authority between the two?
3. In his accession speech, how does Abu Bakr personally set limits on his own authority as Caliph?

8.5 Harun al-Rashid and the Zenith of the Caliphate

The Caliphate endured as a political entity until 1258. After the rule of the first four ("Orthodox") Caliphs, all of whom had been directly associated with Muhammad, the Ummayyad family assumed control and maintained a dynasty from 661–750. They were then overturned by the Abbasid clan, who claimed descent from the Prophet's uncle, Abbas. The Abbasids established the Islamic capital at Baghdad, and it was there, during the reign of Caliph Harun al-Rashid (786–809), that the Empire attained its peak of power and prestige.

Source: Bernard Lewis., ed., *Islam from the Prophet to the Capture of Constantinople,* vol. I (N.Y.: Walker & Co., 1974), pp. 27–30

A woman came to rule over the Romans because at the time she was the only one of their royal house who remained. She wrote to the Caliphs al-Mahdī and al-Hādī and to al-Rashīd at the beginning of his Caliphate with respect and deference and showered him with gifts. When her son [Constantine VI] grew up and came to the throne in her place, he brought trouble and disorder and provoked al-Rashīd. The empress, who knew al-Rashīd and feared his power, was afraid lest the kingdom of the Romans pass away and their country be ruined. She therefore overcame her son by cunning and put out his eyes so that the kingdom was taken from him and returned to her. But the people of their kingdom disapproved of this and hated her for it. Therefore Nikephoros, who was her secretary, rose against her, and they helped and supported him so that he seized power and became the ruler of the Romans.

When he was in full control of his kingdom, he wrote to al-Rashīd, "From Nikephoros, the king of Romans, to al-Rashīd, the king of the Arabs, as follows: That woman put you and your father and your brother in the place of kings and put herself in the place of a commoner. I put you in a different place and am preparing to invade your lands and attack your cities, unless you repay me what that woman paid you. Farewell!"

When his letter reached al-Rashīd, he replied, "In the name of God, the Merciful and the Compassionate, from the servant of God, Hārūn, Commander of the Faithful, to Nikephoros, the dog of the Romans, as follows: I have understood your letter, and I have your answer. You will see it with your own eye, not hear it." Then he at once sent an army against the land of the Romans of a size the like of which was never heard before and with commanders unrivaled in courage and skill. When news of this reached Nikephoros, the earth became narrow before him and he took counsel. Al-Rashid advanced relentlessly into the land of the Romans, killing, plundering, taking captives, destroying castles, and obliterating traces, until they came to the narrow roads before Constantinople, and when they reached there, they found that Nikephoros had already had trees cut down, thrown across these roads, and set on fire. The first who put on the garments of the naphtha-throwers was Muhammad ibn Yazīd ibn Mazyad. He plunged boldly through, and then the others followed him.

Nikephoros sent gifts to al-Rashīd and submitted to him very humbly and paid him the poll tax for himself as well as for his companions.

On this Abu'l-'Atāhiya said:

> *O Imam of God's guidance, you have become the*
> *guardian of religion, quenching the thirst of all who*
> *pray for rain.*
> *You have two names drawn from righteousness*
> *[rashād] and guidance [hudā], for you are the one*
> *called Rashīd and Mahdī,*
> *Whatever displeases you becomes loathsome; if any*
> *thing pleases you, the people are well pleased with*
> *it.*
> *You have stretched out the hand of nobility to us, east*
> *and west, and bestowed bounty on both easterner*
> *and westerner.*
> *You have adorned the face of the earth with generosi-*
> *ty and munificence, and the face of the earth is*
> *adorned with generosity.*
> *O, Commander of the Faithful, brave and pious, you*
> *have opened that part of benevolence which was*
> *closed!*
> *God has destined that the kingdom should remain to*

Hārūn, and, God's destiny is binding on mankind.
The world submits to Hārūn, the favored of God, and
Nikepharos has become the dhimmI of Hārūn.

Then al-Rashīd went back, because of what Nikephoros had given him, and got as far as Raqqa. When the snow fell and Nikephoros felt safe from attack, he took advantage of the respite and broke the agreement between himself and al-Rashīd and returned to his previous posture. Yahyā ibn Khālid [the vizier], let alone any other, did not dare to inform al-Rashīd of the treachery of Nikephoros. Instead, he and his sons offered money to the poets to recite poetry and thereby inform al-Rashīd of this. But they all held back and refrained, except for one poet from Jedda, called Abū Muhammad, who was very proficient, strong of heart and strong of poetry, distinguished in the days of al-Ma'mūn and of very high standing. He accepted the sum of 100,000 dirhams from Yahyā and his sons and then went before al-Rashīd and recited the following verses:

> *Nikephoros has broken the promise he gave you, and*
> *now death hovers above him.*
> *I bring good tidings to the Commander of the*
> *Faithful, for Almighty God is bringing you a great*
> *victory.*
> *Your subjects hail the messenger who brings the good*
> *news of his treachery*
> *Your right hand craves to hasten to that battle which*
> *will assuage our souls and bring a memorable*
> *punishment.*
> *He paid you his poll tax and bent his cheek in fear of*
> *sharp swords and in dread of destruction.*
> *You protected him from the blow of swords which we*
> *brandished like blazing torches.*
> *You brought all your armies back from him and he to*
> *whom you gave your protection was secure and*
> *happy.*
> *Nikephoros! If you played false because the Imam*
> *was far from you, how ignorant and deluded you*
> *were!*
> *Did you think you could play false and escape? May*
> *your mother mourn you! What you thought is delu-*
> *sion.*
> *Your destiny will throw you into its brimming depths;*
> *seas will envelop you from the Imam.*
> *The Imam has power to overwhelm you, whether your*
> *dwelling be near or far away.*
> *Though we may be neglectful the Imam does not*
> *neglect that which he rules and governs with his*
> *strong will.A king who goes in person to the holy war! His*
> *enemy is always conquered by him.*
> *O you who seek God's approval by your striving,*
> *nothing in your inmost heart is hidden from God.*
> *No counsel can avail him who deceives his Imam, but*
> *counsel from loyal counsellers deserves thanks.*
> *Warning the Imam is a religious duty, an expiation*
> *and a cleansing for those who do it.*

When he recited this, al-Rashīd asked, "Has he done that?" and he learned that the viziers had used this device to inform him of it. He then made war against Nikephoros while the snow still remained and conquered Heraclea at that time.

Questions:

1. Under what circumstances did Nikephoros become ruler of the (Byzantine) Romans, and how did his attitude to the Caliph differ from his predecessor's?

2. What was Harun's response, and the consequences?

3. Why did no one wish to inform Harun of Nikephoros' treachery and what device was ultimately employed to alert him?

8.6   Al-Farabi: The Perfect State

One of the most important Muslim thinkers during the Golden Age of Islam was Abu Nasr Muhammad al-Farabi (c. 870-950). Of Turkish descent al-Farabi was born in Turkestan, in the interior of southern Asia. For most of his life he lived in the city of Baghdad, where he became a student of philosophy, taught by Christians steeped in the classical Greek tradition as it had been developed during the Hellenistic age and later in the school of Alexandria in Egypt. Although he was a noted philosopher in his own time, al-Farabi shunned fame and publicity, preferring to live a secluded and austere life.

The influence of classical Greek philosophy on al-Farabi, particularly of Plato, Aristotle, and the neo-Platonists, is evident throughout his writings, including his book The Perfect State. Although the title of this work indicates its subject to be politics, al-Farabi turns to his description of the ideal state only in Chapter 15, after he has grounded his views in a full theory both of metaphysics (including theology and natural science) and psychology, employing arguments from analogy as the basis for his political conclusions. His use of this kind of philosophical generalization and integration reveals the influence of Aristotle, as does the opening paragraph of the following selection, in which he reiterates the Aristotelian view that "man is a political animal." In his description of the ideal ruler, whom al-Farabi conceives to be a philosopher-king, can be found a strong echo of the central theme of Plato's Republic.

But al-Farabi's thought was not just derivative from the Greeks. As a Muslim he added a further dimension to the philosopher-king concept. The ideal ruler must also be a prophet. Not only is such a ruler an individual of high intelligence but one of an intellect of "divine quality" who can look into the future and warn "of things to come."

Source: *Al-Farabi on the Perfect State,* trans. Richard Walzer (Oxford: Clarendon Press, 1985). Reprinted by permission of Oxford University Press.

SECTION V

Chapter 15 Perfect Associations and Perfect Ruler; Faulty Associations

1. In order to preserve himself and to attain his highest perfections every human being is by his very nature in need of many things which he cannot provide all by himself he is indeed in need of people who each supply him with some particular need of his. Everybody finds himself in the same relation to everybody in this respect. Therefore man cannot attain the perfection, for the sake of which his inborn nature has been given to him, unless many (societies of) people who co-operate come together who each supply everybody else with some particular need of his, so that as result of the contribution of the whole community all the things are brought together which everybody needs in order to preserve himself and to attain perfection. Therefore human individuals have come to exist in great numbers, and have settled in the inhabitable (inhabited?) region of the earth, so that human societies have come to exist in it, some of which are perfect, others imperfect.

2. There are three kinds of perfect society, great, medium and small. The great one is the union of all the societies in the inhabitable world; the medium one the union of one nation in one part of the inhabitable world; the small one the union of the people of a city in the territory of any nation whatsoever. Imperfect are the union of people in a village, the union of people in a quarter, then the union in a street, eventually the union in a house, the house being the smallest union of all. Quarter and village exist both for the sake of the city, but the relation of the village to the city is one of service whereas the quarter is related to the city as a part of it; the street is a part of the quarter, the house a part of the street. The city is a part of the territory of a nation, the nation a part of all the people of the inhabitable world.

3. The most excellent good and the utmost perfection is, in the first instance, attained in a city, not in a society which is less complete than it. But since good in its real sense is such as to be attainable through choice and will, and evils are also due to will and choice only, a city may be established to enable its people to cooperate in attaining some aims that are evil. Hence felicity is not attainable in every city. The city, then, in which people aim through association at co-operating for the things by which felicity in its real and true sense can be attained, is the excellent city, and the society in which

there is a co-operation to acquire felicity is the excellent society; and the nation in which all of its cities co-operate for those things through which felicity is attained is the excellent nation. In the same way, the excellent universal state will arise only when all the nations in it co-operate for the purpose of reaching felicity.

4. The excellent city resembles the perfect and healthy body, all of whose limbs co-operate to make the life of the animal perfect and to preserve it in this state. Now the limbs and organs of the body are different and their natural endowments and faculties are unequal in excellence, there being among them one ruling organ, namely the heart, and organs which are close in rank to that ruling organ, each having been given by nature a faculty by which it performs its proper function in conformity with the natural aim of that ruling organ. Other organs have by nature faculties by which they perform their functions according to the aims of those organs which have no intermediary between themselves and the ruling organ; they are in the second rank. Other organs, in turn, perform their functions according to the aim of those which are in the second rank, and so on until eventually organs are reached which only serve and do not rule at all.

The same holds good in the case of the city. Its parts are different by nature, and their natural dispositions are unequal in excellence: there is in it a man who is the ruler, and there are others whose ranks are close to the ruler, each of them with a disposition and a habit through which he performs an action in conformity with the intention of that ruler; these are the holders of the first ranks. Below them are people who perform their actions in accordance with the aims of those people; they are in the second rank. Below them in turn are people who perform their actions according to the aims of the people mentioned in the second instance, and the parts of the city continue to be arranged in this way, until eventually parts are reached which perform their actions according to the aims of others, while there do not exist any people who perform their actions according to their aims; these, then, are the people who serve without being served in turn, and who are hence in the lowest rank and at the bottom of the scale.

But the limbs and organs of the body are natural, and the dispositions which they have are natural faculties, whereas, although the parts of the city are natural, their dispositions and habits, by which they perform their actions in the city, are not natural but voluntary-notwithstanding that the parts of the city are by nature provided with endowments unequal in excellence which enable them to do one thing and not another. But they are not parts of the city by their inborn nature alone but rather by the voluntary habits which they acquire such as the arts and their likes; to the natural faculties which exist in the organs and limbs of the body correspond the voluntary habits and dispositions in the parts of the city.

5. The ruling organ in the body is by nature the most perfect and most complete of the organs in itself and in its specific qualification, and it also has the best of everything of which another organ has a share as well; beneath it, in turn, are other organs which rule over organs inferior to them, their rule being lower in rank than the rule of the first and indeed subordinate to the rule of the first; they rule and are ruled.

In the same way, the ruler of the city is the most perfect part of the city in his specific qualification and has the best of everything which anybody else shares with him; beneath him are people who are ruled by him and rule others.

The heart comes to be first and becomes then the cause of the existence of the other organs and limbs of the body, and the cause of the existence of their faculties in them and of their arrangement in the ranks proper to them, and when one of its organs is out of order, it is the heart which provides the means to remove that disorder. In the same way the ruler of this city must come to be in the first instance, and will subsequently be the cause of the rise of the city and its parts and the cause of the presence of the voluntary habits of its parts and of their arrangement in the ranks proper to them; and when one part is out of order he provides it with the means to remove its disorder.

The parts of the body close to the ruling organ perform of the natural functions, in agreement-by nature-with the aim of the ruler, the most noble ones; the organs beneath them perform those functions which are less noble, and eventually the organs are reached which perform the meanest functions. In the same way the parts of the city which are close in authority to the ruler of the city perform the most noble voluntary actions, and those below them less noble actions, until eventually the parts are reached which perform the most ignoble actions. The inferiority of such actions is sometimes due to the inferiority of their matter, although they may be extremely useful-like the action of the bladder and the action of the lower intestine in the body; sometimes it is due to their being of little use; at other times it is due to their being very easy to perform. This applies equally to the city and equally to every whole which is composed by nature of well ordered coherent parts: they have a ruler whose relation to the other parts is like the one just described.

6. This applies also to all existents. For the relation of the First Cause to the other existents is like the relation of the king of the excellent city to its other parts. For the ranks of the immaterial existents are close to the First. Beneath them are the heavenly bodies, and beneath the heavenly bodies the material bodies. All these existents act in conformity with the First Cause, follow it, take it as their guide and imitate it; but each existent does that according to its capacity, choosing its aim precisely on the strength of its established rank in the universe: that is to say the last follows the aim of that which is slightly above it in rank, equally the second existent, in turn, follows what is above itself in rank, and in the same way the third existent has an aim which is above it. Eventually existents are reached which are linked with the First Cause without any intermediary whatsoever. In accordance with this order of rank all the existents permanently follow the aim of the First Cause. Those which are from the very outset provided with all the essentials of their existence are made to imitate the First (Cause) and its aim from their very outset, and hence enjoy eternal bliss and hold the highest ranks; but those which

are not provided from the outset with all the essentials of their existence, are provided with a faculty by which they move towards the expected attainment of those essentials and will then be able to follow the aim of the First (Cause). The excellent city ought to be arranged in the same way: all its parts ought to imitate in their actions the aim of their first ruler according to their rank.

7. The ruler of the excellent city cannot just be any man, because rulership requires two conditions: (a) he should be predisposed for it by his inborn nature, (b) he should have acquired the attitude and habit of will for rulership which will develop in a man whose inborn nature is predisposed for it. Nor is every art suitable for rulership; most of the arts, indeed, are rather suited for service within the city, just as most men are by their very nature born to serve. Some of the arts rule certain (other) arts while serving others at the same time, whereas there are other arts which, not ruling anything at all, only serve. Therefore the art of ruling the excellent city cannot just be any chance art, nor due to any chance habit whatever. For just as the first ruler in a genus cannot be ruled by anything in that genus-for instance the ruler of the limbs cannot be ruled by any other limb, and this holds good for any ruler of any composite whole-so the art of the ruler in the excellent city of necessity cannot be a serving art at all and cannot be ruled by any other art, but his art must be an art towards the aim of which all the other arts tend, and for which they strive in all the actions of the excellent city.

8. That man is a person over whom nobody has any sovereignty whatsoever. He is a man who has reached his perfection and has become actually intellect and actually being thought (intelligized), his representative faculty having by nature reached its utmost perfection in the way stated by us; this faculty of his is predisposed by nature to receive, either in waking life or in sleep, from the Active Intellect the particulars, either as they are or by imitating them, and also the intelligibles, by imitating them. His Passive Intellect will have reached its perfection by [having apprehended] all the intelligibles, so that none of them is kept back from it, and it will have become actually intellect and actually being thought. Indeed any man whose Passive Intellect has thus been perfected by [having apprehended] all the intelligibles and has become actually intellect and actually being thought, so that the intelligible in him has become identical with that which thinks in him, acquires an actual intellect which is superior to the Passive Intellect and more perfect and more separate from matter (immaterial?) than the Passive Intellect. It is called the 'Acquired Intellect' and comes to occupy a middle position between the Passive Intellect and the Active Intellect, nothing else being between it and the Active Intellect. The Passive Intellect is thus like matter and substratum for the Acquired Intellect, and the Acquired Intellect like matter and substratum for the Active Intellect, and the rational faculty, which is a natural disposition, is a matter underlying the Passive Intellect which is actually intellect.

9. The first stage, then, through which man becomes man is the coming to be of the receptive natural disposition which is ready to become actually intellect; this disposition is common to all men. Between this disposition and the Active Intellect are two stages, the Passive Intellect which has become actually intellect, and [the rise of] the Acquired Intellect. There are thus two stages between the first stage of being a man and the Active Intellect. When the perfect Passive Intellect and the natural disposition become one thing in the way the compound of matter and form is one-and when the form of the humanity of this man is taken as identical with the Passive Intellect which has become actually intellect, there will be between this man and the Active Intellect only one stage. And when the natural disposition is made the matter of the Passive Intellect which has become actually intellect, and the Passive Intellect the matter of the Acquired Intellect, and the Acquired Intellect the matter of the Active Intellect, and when all this is taken as one and the same thing, then this man is the man on whom the Active Intellect has descended.

10. When this occurs in both parts of his rational faculty, namely the theoretical and the practical rational faculties, and also in his representative faculty, then it is this man who receives Divine Revelation, and God Almighty grants him Revelation through the mediation of the Active Intellect, so that the emanation from God Almighty to the Active Intellect is passed on to his Passive Intellect through the mediation of the Acquired Intellect, and then to the faculty of representation. Thus he is, through the emanation from the Active Intellect to his Passive Intellect, a wise man and a philosopher and an accomplished thinker who employs an intellect of divine quality, and through the emanation from the Active Intellect to his faculty of representation a visionary prophet: who warns of things to come and tells of particular things which exist at present.

11. This man holds the most perfect rank of humanity and has reached the highest degree of felicity. His soul is united as it were with the Active Intellect, in the way stated by us. He is the man who knows every action by which felicity can be reached. This is the first condition for being a ruler. Moreover, he should be a good orator and able to rouse [other people's] imagination by well chosen words. He should be able to lead people well along the right path to felicity and to the actions by which felicity is reached. He should, in addition, be of tough physique, in order to shoulder the tasks of war.

This is the sovereign over whom no other human being has any sovereignty whatsoever; he is the Imam; he is the first sovereign of the excellent city, he is the sovereign of the excellent nation, and the sovereign of the universal state.

12. But this state can only be reached by a man in whom twelve natural qualities are found together, with which he is endowed by birth. (1) One of them is that he should have limbs and organs which are free from deficiency and strong, and that they will make him fit for the actions which depend on them; when he intends to perform an action with one of them, he

accomplishes it with ease. (2) He should by nature be good at understanding and perceiving everything said to him, and grasp it in his mind according to what the speaker intends and what the thing itself demands. (3) He should be good at retaining what he comes to know and see and hear and apprehend in general, and forget almost nothing. (4) He should be well provided with ready intelligence and very bright; when he sees the slightest indication of a thing, he should grasp it in the way indicated. (5) He should have a fine diction, his tongue enabling him to explain to perfection all that is in the recess of his mind. (6) He should be fond of learning and acquiring knowledge, be devoted to it and grasp things easily, without finding the effort painful, nor feeling discomfort about the toil which it entails. (7) He should by nature be fond of truth and truthful men and hate falsehood and liars. (8) He should by nature not crave for food and drink and sexual intercourse, and have a natural aversion to gambling and hatred of the pleasures which these pursuits provide. (9) He should be proud of spirit and fond of honour, his soul being by his (?) nature above everything ugly and base, and rising naturally to the most lofty things. (10) Dirham and dinar and the other worldly pursuits should be of little amount in his view. (11) He should by nature be fond of justice and of just people, and hate oppression and injustice and those who practice them, giving himself and others their due, and urging people to act justly and showing pity to those who are oppressed by injustice; he should lend his support to what he considers to be beautiful and noble and just; he should not be reluctant to give in nor should he be stubborn and obstinate if he is asked to do justice; but he should be reluctant to give in if he is asked to do injustice and evil altogether. (12) He should be strong in setting his mind firmly upon the thing which, in his view, ought to be done, and daringly and bravely carry it out without fear and weak-mindedness.

13. Now it is difficult to find all these qualities united in one man, and, therefore, men endowed with this nature will be found one at a time only, such men being altogether very rare. Therefore if there exists such a man in the excellent city who, after reaching maturity, fulfils the six aforementioned conditions-or five of them if one excludes the gift of visionary prophecy through the faculty of representation-he will be the sovereign. Now when it happens that, at a given time, no such man is to be found but there was previously an unbroken succession of sovereigns of this kind, the laws and the customs which were introduced will be adopted and eventually firmly established.

The next sovereign, who is the successor of the first sovereigns, will be someone in whom those [twelve] qualities are found together from the time of his birth and his early youth and who will, after reaching his maturity, be distinguished by the following six qualities: (1) He will be a philosopher. (2) He will know and remember the laws and customs (and rules of conduct) with which the first sovereigns had governed the city, conforming in all his actions to all their actions. (3) He will excel in deducing a new law by analogy where no law of his predecessors has been recorded, following for his deductions the principles laid down by the first Imams. (4) He will be good at deliberating and be powerful in his deductions to meet new situations for which the first sovereigns could not have laid down any law; when doing this he will have in mind the good of the city. (5) He will be good at guiding the people by his speech to fulfil the laws of the first sovereigns as well as those laws which he will have deduced in conformity with their principles after their time. (6) He should be of tough physique in order to shoulder the tasks of war, mastering the serving as well as the ruling military art.

14. When one single man who fulfils all these conditions cannot be found but there are two, one of whom is a philosopher and the other fulfils the remaining conditions, the two of them will be the sovereigns of this city.

But when all these six qualities exist separately in different men, philosophy in one man and the second quality in another man and so on, and when these men are all in agreement, they should all together be the excellent sovereigns.

But when it happens, at a given time, that philosophy has no share in the government, though every other condition may be present in it, the excellent city will remain without a king, the ruler actually in charge of this city will not be a king, and the city will be on the verge of destruction; and if it happens that no philosopher can be found who will be attached to the actual ruler of the city, then, after a certain interval, this city will undoubtedly perish.

Questions:
1. *To what extent has al-Farabi adopted the philosophy of the Central Mediterranean?*
2. *To what extent does this selection reflect Islamic ideas and assumptions?*

8.7   Islamic Science and Mathematics

The Islamic community during the Middle Ages and beyond was not simply concerned with matters of faith and obedience to doctrine. As Muslim armies covered North Africa and the Middle East, even venturing into Europe, they carried with them some of the great advancements of Islamic civilization. Muslim learning was embraced in such academic centers as Córdoba, Spain, where Jewish scholars were central in establishing a conduit of knowledge to the West by translating Arabic science and medical texts into Spanish and Latin. Many of these ideas in astronomy, medicine, advanced mathematics, law, literature, poetry, philosophy, and history fell on deaf ears in the West because of the fear of doctrinal contamination. Indeed, for Western Christians, the followers of Allah were the "Infidel," to be feared and opposed through Crusades to recapture the Holy Land for the glory of a Christian God.

The following selections attest to the framework of learning and inquiry that was a most impressive benefit of Islamic civilization.

ON THE SEPARATION OF MATHEMATICS AND RELIGION
AL-GHAZZALI

> **Source:** "On the Separation of Mathematics and Religion" is from Al-Ghazzali, *The Confession of Al-Ghazzali,* trans. Claud Field, The Wisdom of the East Series (London: John Murray Publishers Ltd., 1908), pp. 33–34.

Mathematics comprises the knowledge of calculation, geometry, and cosmography: it has no connection with the religious sciences, and proves nothing for or against religion; it rests on a foundation of proofs which, once known and understood, cannot be refuted. Mathematics tend, however, to produce two bad results.

The first is this: Whoever studies this science admires the subtlety and clearness of its proofs. His confidence in philosophy increases, and he thinks that all its departments are capable of the same clearness and solidity of proof as mathematics. But when he hears people speak on the unbelief and impiety of mathematicians, of their professed disregard for the Divine Law, which is notorious, it is true that, out of regard for authority, he echoes these accusations, but he says to himself at the same time that, if there was truth in religion, it would not have escaped those who have displayed so much keenness of intellect in the study of mathematics.

Next, when he becomes aware of the unbelief and rejection of religion on the part of these learned men, he concludes that to reject religion is reasonable. How many of such men gone astray I have met whose sole argument was that just mentioned. . . .

It is therefore a great injury to religion to suppose that the defence of Islam involves the condemnation of the exact sciences. The religious law contains nothing which approves them or condemns them, and in their turn they make no attack on religion. The words of the Prophet, "The sun and the moon are two signs of the power of God; they are not eclipsed for the birth or the death of any one; when you see these signs take refuge in prayer and invoke the name of God"—these words, I say, do not in any way condemn the astronomical calculations which define the orbits of these two bodies, their conjunction and opposition according to particular laws.

Questions:
1. *What do the selections on mathematics and the scientific description of smallpox tell you about Islamic values?*
2. *According to Al-Ghazzali, should mathematics and religion be separated? Why or why not?*

ON THE CAUSES OF SMALL-POX
AL-RAZI

> **Source:** "On the Causes of Small-Pox" is from Abu Bekr Muhammad Ibn Zacariya Al-Razi, *A Treatise on Small-Pox and Measles,* trans. William A. Greenhill (London, 1848), pp. 28–31.

Although [scholars] have certainly made some mention of the treatment of the Small-Pox (but without much accuracy and distinctness), yet there is not one of them who has mentioned the cause of the existence of the disease, and how it comes to pass that hardly any one escapes it, or who has disposed the modes of treatment in their right places. And for this reason I . . . have mentioned whatever is necessary for the treatment of this disease, and have arranged and carefully disposed everything in its right place, by god's permission. . . .

I say then that every man, from the time of his birth until he arrives at old age, is continually tending to dryness; and for this reason the blood of children and infants is much moister than the blood of young men, and still more so than that of old men. . . . Now the Small-Pox arises when the blood putrefies and ferments, so that the superfluous vapors are thrown out of it, and it is changed from the blood of infants, which is like must, into the blood of young men, which is like wine perfectly ripened: and the Small-Pox itself may be compared to the fermentation and the hissing noise which takes place in must at that time. And this is the reason why children, especially males, rarely escape being seized with this disease, because it is impossible to prevent the blood's changing from this state into its second state. . . .

As to young men, whereas their blood is already passed into the second state, its maturation is established, and the superfluous particles of moisture which necessarily cause putrefaction are now exhaled; hence it follows that this disease only happens to a few individuals among them, that is, to those whose vascular system abounds with too much moisture, or is corrupt in quality with a violent inflammation. . . .

And as for old men, the Small-Pox seldom happens to them, except in pestilential, putrid, and malignant constitutions of the air, in which this disease is chiefly prevalent. For a putrid air, which has an undue proportion of heat and moisture, and also an inflamed air, promotes the eruption of this disease.

Question:
1. According to this document, should math and religion be separate? Why or why not?

8.8   The Caliphate in Decline: Al-Matawwakil's Murder

In the years following Harun al-Rashid's death, conflicts surfaced and, in many respects, the ethical qualities of those who held the Caliphate deteriorated to the point that the ruler openly violated the strictures of the Q'uran—notably those against alcohol consumption—and increasingly relied on brutal methods to enforce their authority. The last effective Caliph was al-Mutawwakil (847–861), whose celebrated Mosque at Samarra is among the greatest masterpieces of Muslim architecture. His assassination, related here by Al-Tabari, was followed by the disintegration of the Empire, a lengthy period of decline, and the burning of Baghdad by the Mongols in 1258.

> **Source:** Bernard Lewis, ed., *Islam from the Prophet to the Capture of Constantinople,* Vol. I (N.Y.: Walker & Co., 1974), pp. 30–34.

It is said that on the feast of 'Id al-Fitr [247/861], al-Mutawakkil rode on horseback between two lines of soldiers four miles long. Everybody walked on foot in front of him. He conducted the public prayer and then returned to his palace, where he took a handful of earth and put it on his head. They asked him why and he replied, "I have seen the immensity of this gathering, I have seen them subject to me, and it pleased me to humble myself before Almighty God." The day after the feast he did not send for any of his boon companions. The third day, Tuesday, 3 ShawwAl [December 10] he was lively, merry, and happy....

The singer Ibn al-Hafsi, who was present at the party, said: The Commander of the Faithful was never merrier than on that day. He began his party and summoned his boon companions and singers, who came. Qabiha, the mother of al-Mu'tazz, presented him with a square cape of green silk, so splendid that no one had ever seen its like. Al-Mutawakkil looked at it for a long time, praised it and admired it greatly and then ordered that it be cut in two and taken back to her, saying to her messenger, "She can remember me by it." Then he added, "My heart tells me that I shall not wear it, and I do not want anyone else to wear it after me; that is why I had it torn." We said to him, "Master, today is a day of joy. God preserve you, O Commander of the Faithful from such words." He began to drink and make merry, but he repeated, "By God, I shall soon leave you." However, he continued to amuse and enjoy himself until nightfall.

Some said that al-Mutawakkil had decided, together with al-Fath [ibn Khāqān], to call next day, Thursday 5th Shawwāh [December 12], on 'Abdallāh ibn 'Umar al-Baziyār to ask him to murder al-Muntasir and to kill Wasif, Bughā, and other commanders and leaders of the Turks.

On the previous day, Tuesday, according to Ibn al-Hafsi, the Caliph subjected his son al-Muntasir to heavy horseplay, sometimes abusing him, sometimes forcing him to drink more than he could hold, sometimes having him slapped, and sometimes threatening him with death.

It is reported, on the authority of Hārūn ibn Muhammad ibn Sulaymān al-Hashimī, who said that he had heard it from one of the women behind the curtain, that al-Mutawakkil turned toward al-Fath and said to him, "I shall renounce God and my kinship with the Prophet of God (may God bless and save him) if you don't slap him (that is, al-Muntasir)." Al-Fath rose and slapped the back of his neck twice. Then al-Mutawakkil said to those present, "Be witnesses, all of you, that I declare al-Musta'jil-al-Muntasir—deprived of his rights to my succession." Then he turned to him and said, "I gave you the name of al-Muntasir [the triumphant] but people called you al-Muntazir [the expectant] because of your foolishness. Now you have become al-Musta'jil [the urgent]."

"O, Commander of the Faithful," replied al-Muntasir, "If you were to give the orders to behead me, it would be more bearable than what you are doing to me!"

"Give him a drink!" cried al-Mutawakkil and called for supper, which was brought. It was late at night. Al-Muntasir went out and ordered Bunan, the page of Ahmad ibn Yahyā, to follow him. When he had gone the table was placed before al-Mutawakkil who began to eat and gobble. He was drunk.

It is related on the authority of Ibn al-Hafsi that when al-Muntasir left to return to his own quarters, he took the hand of Zurāfa and asked him to accompany him. "But my Lord," said Zurāfa, "the Commander of the Faithful has not yet risen." "The Commander of the Faithful," said al-Muntasir, "is overcome by drink, and Bughā and the boon companions will soon leave. I would like to talk to you about your son. Utamish has asked me to marry his son to your daughter and your son to his daughter."

"We are your slaves, my lord," replied Zurāfa, "and at your orders." Al-Muntasir then took him by the hand and led him away. Zurāfa had earlier said to me, "Be calm, for the Commander of the Faithful is drunk and will soon recover. Tamra called me and asked me to ask you to go to him. Let us therefore go together to his quarters." "I shall go there ahead of you," I said, and Zurāfa left with al-Muntasir for his quarters.

Bunān, the page of Ahmād ibn Yahyā, related that al-Muntasir said to him, "I have united Zurāfa's son to Utamish's daughter and Utamish's son to Zurāfa's daughter."

"My lord," asked Bunān, "where are the confetti, for in that lies the beauty of such a union."

"Tomorrow, please God!" he said, "for today has already passed."

Zurāfa had gone to Tamra's quarters. He entered and called for food, which was brought to him, but he had hardly begun to eat when we heard a noise and shouting. We stood up. "It is only Zurāfa leaving Tamra's quarters," said Bunān. Suddenly Bughā appeared before al-Muntasir, who asked, "What is this noise?"

"Good tidings, O, Commander of the Faithful," said Bughā.

"What are you saying, wretch?" said al-Muntasir.

"May God give you a great reward in return for our master the Commander of the Faithful. He was God's slave. God called him, and he went."

Al-Muntasir held an audience and gave orders to close the door of the room in which al-Mutawakkil had been murdered, as well as that of the audience chamber. All the doors were closed. He then sent for Wasif and ordered him to summon al-Mu'tazz and al-Mu'ayyad, in the name of al-Mutawakkil.

It is reported, on the authority of 'Ath'ath, that when al-Muntasir had risen and gone, taking Zurāfa with him, al-Mutawakkil had sent for his table. Bughā the younger, known as al-Sharābī, was standing by the curtain. On that day it was the turn of Bughā the elder to be on duty in the palace, but as he was in Sumaysāt at the time he had himself replaced by his son Mūsā, whose mother was al-Mutawakkil's maternal aunt. Bughā the younger entered the gathering and ordered the boon companions of the Caliph to return to their quarters.

"It is not yet time for them to go," al-Fath said to him, "the Commander of the Faithful has not yet risen."

"The Commander of the Faithful," said Bughā, "has ordered me to leave no one in the room after he has drunk seven pints [ratl], and he has already drunk fourteen." Al-Fath objected to their going, but Bughā said, "The Commander of the Faithful is drunk, and his women are behind this curtain. Get up and go!" They all went out, leaving only al-Fath, 'Ath'ath, and four of the Caliph's servants, Shafi, Faraj the younger, Mu'nis, and Abū 'Isā Mārid al-Muhrizī. 'Ath'ath said: The cook placed the table in front of al-Mutawakkil, who began to eat and gobble, and invited Marid to eat with him. He was drunk, and after eating, he drank again.

'Ath'ath said that Abū Ahmād, the son of al-Mutawakkil and uterine brother of al-Mu'ayyad, who was present in the hall, came out to go to the lavatory. Bughā al-Sharābī had closed all the doors except that which opened to the river bank. It was by this door that those who had been appointed to murder the Caliph entered. Abū Ahmad saw them enter, and cried out, "What is this, villains?" Then suddenly they drew their swords. Leading the murderers were Baghlun the Turk, Baghir, Musa ibn Bughā, Hārūn ibn Suwārtagin, and Bughā al-Shārābī.

When al-Mutawakkil heard Abū Ahmad shout, he raised his head and saw them and asked, "What is it, Bughā?" And Bughā answered, "These are the men of the night watch, who will guard the gate of my lord, the Commander of the Faithful." When they heard al-Mutawakkil speak to Bughā, they turned back. Neither Wajin and his men nor the sons of Wasif were with them. 'Ath'ath said: I heard Bughā say to them, "Villains! You are all dead men without escape; at least die with honor." They then came back into the hall, and Baghūn attacked first, giving the Caliph a blow which cut off his ear and struck his shoulder. "Ho!" cried al-Mutawakkil. Hārūn ran him through with his sword, and he throw himself at his attacker, who, however, fended him off with his arm, and Bāghir joined them.

"Wretches!" cried al-Fath, "this is the Commander of the Faithful!"

"Be quiet!" said Bughā, and al-Fath threw himself over al-Mutawakkil. Hārūn ran him through with his sword, and he screamed "Death!" Hārūn and Bughā ibn Mūsā, striking him in turn with their swords, killed him, and cut him to pieces. 'Ath'ath was wounded in the head. A young eunuch who was with al-Mutawakkil hid behind the curtain and was saved. The others fled.

Questions:
1. What conclusions can one draw as to al-Mutawwakil's character, and his relationship with his son?
2. What role did Bugha and the Turks play in this story?
3. Where was al-Muntasir and was he allegedly doing while his father was being murdered?

8.9 Shiism and Caliph Ali: Controversy Over the Prophetic Succession

Shiism, the most substantial dissenting denomination within the Islamic faith (as opposed to the Sunni majority), was born out of the issue over who should succeed Muhammad in his leadership over the Muslim world. Shiites demand that true authority must be vested in an Imam, who must be a physical descendent of the Prophet through his daughter Fatima and her husband (Muhammad's nephew), Ali. Within the Shiite community, Ali, who from 656–661 was the fourth successor to Muhammad, is mainly considered to have been the sole legitimate Caliph. The following document is excerpted from Ali's instructions to Malik al-Ashtar, whom he had just appointed governor of Egypt.

Source: William C. Chittick, ed., *A Shiite Anthology* (Albany, N.Y.: State University of New York Press, 1981, copyright: Muhammadi Trust of Great Britain and Northern Ireland), pp.68–72.

ᶜAlī wrote these instructions to al-Ashtar al-Nakhaᶜt when he appointed him governor of Egypt and its provinces at the time the rule of Muhammad ibn Abī Bakr was in turmoil. It is the longest set of instructions (in the *Nahj al-bal-āghah*). Among all his letters it embraces the largest number of good qualities.

PART ONE: INTRODUCTION

In the Name of God, the Merciful, the Compassionate

This is that with which ᶜAlī, the servant of God and Commander of the Faithful, charged Malik ibn al-Hārith al-Ashtar in his instructions to him when he appointed him governor of Egypt: to collect its land tax, to war against its enemies, to improve the condition of the people and to engender prosperity in its regions. He charged him to fear God, to prefer obedience to Him (over all else) and to follow what He has directed in His Book—both the acts He has made obligatory and those He recommends—for none attains felicity but he who follows His directions, and none is overcome by wretchedness but he who denies them and lets them slip by. (He charged him) to help God—glory be to Him—with his heart, his hand and his tongue, for He—majestic is His Name—has promised to help him who exalts Him. And he charged him to break the passions of his soul and restrain it in its recalcitrance, for the soul incites to evil, except inasmuch as God has mercy.

PART TWO: COMMANDS AND INSTRUCTIONS CONCERNING RIGHTEOUS ACTION IN THE AFFAIRS OF THE STATE

Know, O Mālik, that I am sending you to a land where governments, just and unjust, have existed before you. People will look upon your affairs in the same way that you were wont to look upon the affairs of the rulers before you. They will speak about you as you were wont to speak about those rulers. And the righteous are only known by that which God causes to pass concerning them on the tongues of His servants. So let the dearest of your treasuries be the treasury of righteous action. Control your desire and restrain your soul from what is not lawful to you, for restraint of the soul is for it to be equitous in what it likes and dislikes. Infuse your heart with mercy, love and kindness for your subjects. Be not in face of them a voracious animal, counting them as easy prey, for they are of two kinds: either they are your brothers in religion or your equals in creation. Error catches them unaware, deficiencies overcome them, (evil deeds) are committed by them intentionally and by mistake. So grant them your pardon and your forgiveness to the same extent that you hope God will grant you His pardon and His forgiveness. For you are above them, and he who appointed you is above you, and God is above him who appointed you. God has sought from you the fulfillment of their requirements and He is trying you with them.

Set yourself not up to war against God, for you have no power against His vengeance, nor are you able to dispense with His pardon and His mercy. Never be regretful of pardon or rejoice at punishment, and never hasten (to act) upon an impulse if you can find a better course. Never say, "I am invested with authority, I give orders and I am obeyed," for surely that is corruption in the heart, enfeeblement of the religion and an approach to changes (in fortune). If the authority you possess engender in you pride or arrogance, then reflect upon the tremendousness of the dominion of God above you and His power over you in that in which you yourself have no control. This will subdue your recalcitrance, restrain your violence and restore in you what has left you of the power of your reason. Beware of vying with God in His tremendousness and likening yourself to Him in His exclusive power, for God abases every tyrant and humiliates all who are proud.

See that justice is done towards God and justice is done towards the people by yourself, your own family and those whom you favor among your subjects. For if you do not do so, you have worked wrong. And as for him who wrongs the servants of God, God is his adversary, not to speak of His servants. God renders null and void the argument of whosoever contends with Him. Such a one will be God's enemy until he desists or repents. Nothing is more conducive to the removal of God's blessing and the hastening of His vengeance than to continue in wrongdoing, for God harkens to the call of the oppressed and He is ever on the watch against the wrongdoers.

Let the dearest of your affairs be those which are middlemost in rightfulness, most inclusive in justice and most comprehensive in (establishing) the content of the subjects. For the discontent of the common people invalidates the content of favorites, and the discontent of favorites is pardoned at (the achievement of) the content of the masses. Moreover, none of the subjects is more burdensome upon the ruler in ease and less of a help to him in trial than his favorites. (None are) more disgusted by equity, more importunate in demands, less grateful upon bestowal, slower to pardon (the ruler upon his) withholding (favor) and more deficient in patience at the misfortunes of time than the favorites. Whereas the support of religion, the solidarity of Muslims and preparedness in the face of the enemy lie only with the common people of the community, so let your inclination and affection be toward them.

Let the farthest of your subjects from you and the most hateful to you be he who most seeks out the faults of men. For men possess faults, which the ruler more than anyone else should conceal. So do not uncover those of them which are hidden from you, for it is only encumbent upon you to remedy what appears before you. God will judge what is hidden from you. So veil imperfection to the extent you are able; God will veil that of yourself which you would like to have veiled from your subjects. Loose from men the knot of every resentment, sever from yourself the cause of every animosity, and ignore all that which does not become your station. Never hasten to believe the slanderer, for the slanderer is a deceiver, even if he seems to be a sincere advisor.

Bring not into your consultation a miser, who might turn you away from liberality and promise you poverty; nor a coward, who might enfeeble you in your affairs; nor a greedy man, who might in his lust deck out oppression to you as something fair. Miserliness, cowardliness and greed are diverse temperaments which have in common distrust in God.

Truly the worst of your viziers are those who were the viziers of the evil (rulers) before you and shared with them in their sins. Let them not be among your retinue, for they are aides of the sinners and brothers of the wrongdoers. You will find the best of substitutes for them from among those who possess the like of their ideas and effectiveness but are not encumbranced by the like of their sins and crimes; who have not aided a wrongdoer in his wrongs nor a sinner in his sins. These will be a lighter burden upon you, a better aid, more inclined toward you in sympathy and less intimate with people other than you. So choose these men as your special companions in privacy and at assemblies. Then let the most influential among them be he who speaks most to you with the bitterness of the truth and supports you least in activities which God dislikes in His friends, however this strikes your pleasure. Cling to men of piety and veracity. Then accustom them not to lavish praise upon you nor to (try to) gladden you by (attributing to you) a vanity you did not do, for the lavishing of abundant praise causes arrogance and draws (one) close to pride.

Never let the good-doer and the evil-doer possess an equal station before you, for that would cause the good-doer to abstain from his good-doing and habituate the evil-doer to his evil-doing. Impose upon each of them what he has imposed upon himself.

Know that there is nothing more conducive to the ruler's trusting his subjects than that he be kind towards them, lighten their burdens and abandon coercing them in that in which they possess not the ability. So in this respect you should attain a situation in which you can confidently trust your subjects, for trusting (them) will sever from you lasting strain. And surely he who most deserves your trust is he who has done well when you have tested him, and he who most deserves your mistrust is he who has done badly when you have tested him.

Abolish no proper custom (*sunnah*) which has been acted upon by the leaders of this community, through which harmony has been strengthened and because of which the subjects have prospered. Create no new custom which might in any way prejudice the customs of the past, lest their reward belong to him who originated them, and the burden be upon you to the extent that you have abolished them.

Study much with men of knowledge (*ʿulamā'*) and converse much with sages (*hukanā'*) concerning the consolidation of that which causes the state of your land to prosper and the establishment of that by which the people before you remained strong.

PART THREE: CONCERNING THE CLASSES OF MEN

Know that subjects are of various classes, none of which can be set aright without the others and none of which is independent from the others. Among them are (1.) the soldiers of God, (2.) secretaries for the common people and the people of distinction, executors of justice, and administrators of equity and kindness, (3.) payers of *jizyah* and land tax, namely the people of protective covenants~and the Muslims, (4.) merchants and craftsmen and (5.) the lowest class, the needy and wretched. For each of them God has designated a portion, and commensurate with each portion He has established obligatory acts (*farīdah*) in His Book and the Sunnah of His Prophet—may God bless him and his household and give them peace—as a covenant from Him maintained by us.

Now soldiers, by the leave of God, are the fortresses of the subjects, the adornment of rulers, the might of religion and the means to security. The subjects have no support but them, and the soldiers in their turn have no support but the land tax which God has extracted for them, (a tax) by which they are given the power to war against their enemy and upon which they depend for that which puts their situation in order and meets their needs. Then these two classes (soldiers and tax-payers) have no support but the third class, the judges, administrators and secretaries, for they draw up contracts, gather yields, and are entrusted with private and public affairs. And all of these have no support but the merchants and craftsmen, through the goods which they bring together and the markets which they set up. They provide for the needs (of the first three classes) by acquiring with their own hands those (goods) to which the resources of others do not attain. Then there is the lowest class, the needy and wretched, those who have the right to aid and assistance. With God there is plenty for each (of the classes). Each has a claim upon the ruler to the extent that will set it aright. But the ruler will not truly accomplish what God has enjoined upon him in this respect except by resolutely striving, by recourse to God's help, by reconciling himself to what the truth requires and by being patient in the face of it in what is easy for him or burdensome.

Questions:
1. *What advice does Ali give the al-Ashtar about policy towards the proper customs of the subject peoples?*
2. *What does Ali recommend as a cure for pride generated by power?*
3. *What five classes does Ali designate whose well-being is essential for conducting a successful administration, and what claims do each of them have on those who govern them?*

PART 9
Imperial China and the Diffusion of East Asian Civilization

9.1   The Tang Dynasty (618–907): The Art of Government

In the following document, Tang Daizong, a founder of the Tang dynasty, set the tone for his new administration to his chosen officials. His emphasis on honesty and open communication contrasts the single-minded and obsessive rule of the former Sui dynasty.

Source: Reprinted with the permission of Scribner, a Division of Simon & Schuster, Inc., from *The Civilization of China*, translated by Dun J. Li. Copyright © 1975 by Dun J. Li.

TANG DAIZONG

Different people are bound to have different opinions; the important thing is that differences in opinion should not degenerate into personal antagonism. Sometimes to avoid the possibility of creating personal grievances or causing embarrassment to a colleague, an official might decide to go ahead with the implementation of a policy even though he knows that the policy is wrong. Let us remember that preservation of a colleague's prestige, or the avoidance of embarrassment to him, cannot be compared with the welfare of the nation in importance, and to place personal consideration above the well-being of the multitude will lead to defeat for the government as a whole. I want all of you to understand this point and act accordingly.

During the Sui dynasty, all officials, in the central as well as the local governments, adopted an attitude of conformity to the general trend in order to be amiable and agreeable with one another. The result was disaster as all of you well know. Most of them did not understand the importance of dissent and comforted themselves by saying that as long as they did not disagree, they could forestall harm to themselves that might otherwise cross their path. When the government, as well as their families, finally collapsed in a massive upheaval, they were severely but justifiably criticized by their contemporaries for their complacency and inertia, even if they themselves may have been fortunate enough to escape death through a combination of circumstances. This is the reason that I want all of you to place public welfare above private interest and hold steadfastly the principle of righteousness, so that all problems, whatever they are, will be resolved in such a way as to bring about a most beneficial result. Under no circumstances are you allowed to agree with one another for the sake of agreement.

As for Sui Wenti, I would say that he was politically inquisitive, but mentally closed. Being close-minded, he could not see truth even if it were spotlighted for him; being over inquisitive, he was suspicious even when there was no valid reason for his suspicion. He rose to power by trampling on the rights of orphans and widows and was consequently not so sure that he had the unanimous support of his own ministers. Being suspicious of his own ministers, he naturally did not trust them and had to make a decision on every matter himself. He became a hard worker out of necessity and, having overworked, could not make the right decision every time. Knowing the kind of man he was, all his ministers, including the prime minister, did not speak as candidly as they should have and unanimously uttered "Yes, sir" when they should have registered strong dissent.

I want all of you to know that I am different. The empire is large and its population enormous. There are thousands of matters to be taken care of, each of which has to be closely coordinated with the others in order to bring about maximum benefit. Each matter must be thoroughly investigated and thought out before a recommendation is submitted to the prime minister, who, having consulted all the men knowledgeable in this matter, will then present the commendation, modified if necessary, to the emperor for approval and implementation. It is impossible for one person, however intelligent and capable, to be able to make wise decisions by himself. . . .

I want all of you to know that whenever an imperial decree is handed down you should carefully study its content and decide for yourselves whether all or part of it is or is not wise or feasible. If you have any reservations, postpone the enforcement and petition me immediately. You can do no less as my loyal ministers.

Governing a country is like taking care of a patient. The better the patient feels, the more he should be looked after, lest in a moment of complacency and neglect one irrevocably reverse the recovery process and send him to death. Likewise, when a country has only recently recovered from chaos and war, those responsible for running the country should be extremely diligent in their work, for false pride and self-indulgence will inevitably return the country to where it used to be and perhaps make it worse.

I realize that the safety of this nation relies to a great extent on what I can or may do and consequently I have not relaxed for a moment in doing the best I can. But I cannot do it alone. You gentlemen are my eyes and ears, legs and arms, and should do your best to assist me. If anything goes wrong anywhere in the empire, you should let me know immediately.

If there is less than total trust between you and me and consequently you and I cannot do the best we can, the nation will suffer enormous damage.

Questions:
1. What mistakes did Sui Wenti make?
2. What were the responsibilities of Tang government officials?

9.2 Sung (Song) China: Imperial Examination System

One of the unique features of the imperial government of China was the imperial examination system. Through it, the Chinese government recruited the members of its bureaucracy from the general populace, rather than leaving the imperial administration to the hereditary nobles. This system evolved gradually, starting in the second century b.c. during the former Han dynasty (206 b.c.–a.d. 8), becoming more elaborate and institutionalized during the early part of the Sung [Song] dynasty (960–1279), and continuing with only slight modifications down to the early years of this century. The last imperial examinations were held in 1905.

Millions of young men in China during the imperial period invested their time, energy, money, and passion in an effort to pass the examination, since this was the road to power and wealth. Aspirants for imperial bureaucratic posts usually spent ten or more years preparing for the examination, primarily by reading, analyzing, and memorizing the voluminous Confucian classics. During the Sung period, prospective candidates for imperial administrative posts were expected to pass three levels of highly competitive examinations—prefectural, metropolitan, and palace—and attain the Presented Scholar (Chin-shih [Jinshi]) degree, which was the most coveted degree, roughly comparable to a Ph.D. in the West. The candidates in the palace examination were ranked in order of their achievements in the examination. The higher the rank the candidates achieved, the better the chances were that they would receive more powerful and prestigious imperial appointments. The candidate for the Chin-shih degree was required to produce, among other things, poems in various styles, a rhyme prose piece, a policy essay, answers to five policy questions, and answers to ten "written elucidation" questions on Confucian classics such as the Spring and Autumn Annals and the Book of Rites. The following selection is an example of an essay question on policy matters.

Source: Copyright © 1985 Thomas H.C. Lee. From *Government Education and Examinations* in Sung China by Thomas H.C. Lee, pp. 150–51. Reprinted with permission of St. Martin's Press and The Chinese University Press.

It is stated in the Book of Kuan-tzu [Guan Zi][1]: "the method by which a sage rules the world is this: he does not let the four classes of people live together. Therefore, there are no complaints, and things run smoothly. As a result, scholars know how to spend their leisure, laborers abide with the orders of officials, merchants go to the marketplaces and farmers go to the fields. Everyone goes to his appropriate place and lives there satisfactorily. Young children are sent to study; their wills are satisfied and they do not change their minds when they see strange things." The Kuan-tzu Book further states: "Children of scholars and farmers must always be scholars and farmers and children of merchants and laborers must also always be merchants and laborers, so that a scholar can give instructions and take care of his proper status, and a farmer can work attentively in cultivating his crops to feed the people. Everyone is satisfied with his occupation and does not seek to change. This is truly good! Otherwise, hundreds of laborers might all go to the marketplaces and ten thousand merchants might all try to work in the same [most profitable] business; they would all become cunning, deceitful, eager to play tricks, and they would also become capricious, greedy and seek only profits."

Now, to fit people in their occupations is not to improve morals. To see something better and change—what harm is there in this? Take the example of Tuan-mu [Duanmu] who became a merchant [after being a disciple of Confucius], Chiao Li [Jiao Li] who became a fisherman [after being an important official] and Wang Meng who went to sell dust-baskets [after being a prime minister]; these men responded to their times and changed in myriad ways, why should they have been restricted to their fixed occupations? Similarly, Huang Hsien [Huang Xian] was originally a lowly veterinarian, Sang Hung-yang [Sang Hongyang] a merchant, Sun Shu-ao a wood-cutter, and yet they all were able to preserve their intelligence and help strengthen their states. How can we accuse them of responding to their times and of going to take up responsibilities other than their own occupations! We now have a regulation keeping the descendants of those in despised occupations from taking the civil service examinations. Although this rule has been in force for some time, I consider that it still is a good time to examine this regulation. You candidates have excelled yourselves in knowledge of the past, and in debating various problems; I would like you to spend time considering the issue I have just outlined above.

Questions:
1. What do you think are the merits and demerits of the Chinese imperial examination system?
2. How does this system compare with the way the Ottoman Empire recruited Janissaries?

9.3 Record of Ancient Matters: Futo No Yasumaro

The Kojiki, or Records of Ancient Matters, filled as it is with inconsistencies and anomalies, is a document that is next to impossible for us today to disentangle, let alone comprehend. But it is of great historical importance because it is the earliest attempt made by the Japanese to give a written account of their beginnings, including the birth of the islands themselves and the descent of the imperial rulers. It would be gratuitous to suggest, as its author Yasumaro presumably believed, that the episodes he describes constitute authentic history, for they obviously are an amalgam of mythology and fantasy. Yet they provide us with valuable insights not only into ways of early thinking but also, in the special case of Japan, into a set of beliefs that has persisted in the national consciousness for millennia.

The history of the composition of the Kojiki is worthy of note. In the seventh century, A.D., as Yasumaro explains in his preface, the Emperor Temmu decided, probably following the precedent of China, to produce an accurate history of early Japan and the imperial line. So he appointed a young man of exceptional memory to carry out the project. But the emperor died before the task was completed and it was not renewed until the following century under the Empress Gemmyo, who commissioned Yasumaro to put the Records in writing, an undertaking he completed in a few months.

The selection that follows details the generation and activities of the innumerable gods who preceded human occupation of Japan, as well as of the origin of the Japanese islands themselves. Passages have been chosen in an attempt to provide a maximum amount of coherence to an often-unintelligible sequence of events. Many of the gods named are of relatively minor significance except for the fact that they indicate that the early Japanese were prepared to deify almost everything. Of particular significance is the description near the end of the generation of the early leaders of Japan, who culminated in the imperial line, from gods descended from heaven. The myth of the divine descent of the emperors persisted throughout Japanese history until 1946 when Emperor Hirohito, bowing to pressure from the American army of occupation, acknowledged in an official proclamation to his people that he was not really a divine descendant of the sun goddess but only an ordinary human being.

It should be noted that the Kojiki is of relatively late origin historically. As the first written records of early Japanese "history," thus an important symbol of the beginnings of that civilization, it appeared around a thousand years after the classics of ancient Chinese civilization.

Source: Trans. *Basil Hall Chamberlain*

THE *KOJIKI* OR RECORDS OF ANCIENT MATTERS

PREFACE

. . .

The Heavenly Sovereign [Emperor Temmu] commanded, saying "I hear that the chronicles of the emperors and likewise the original words in the possession of the various families deviate from exact truth, and are most amplified by empty falsehoods. If at the present time these imperfections be not amended, ere many years shall have elapsed, the purport of this, the great basis of the country, the grand foundation of the monarchy, will be destroyed. So now I desire to have the chronicles of the emperors selected and recorded, and the old words examined and ascertained, falsehoods being erased and truth determined, in order to transmit the latter to after ages." At that time there was a retainer whose surname was Hiyeda and his personal name Are. He was twenty-eight years old, and of so intelligent a disposition that he could repeat with his mouth whatever met his eyes, and record in his heart whatever struck his ears. Forthwith Are was commanded to learn by heart the genealogies of the emperors, and likewise the words of former ages. Nevertheless, time elapsed and the age changed, and the thing was not yet carried out.

     Prostrate I consider how Her Majesty the Empress [Gemmyo], having obtained Unity, illumines the empire. . . Regretting the errors in the old words, and wishing to correct the misstatements in the former chronicles, She, on the eighteenth day of the ninth moon of the fourth year of Wado [A.D. 711], commanded me Yasumaro to select and record the old words learnt by heart by Hiyeda no Are according to the Imperial Decree, and dutifully to lift them up to Her.

In reverent obedience to the contents of the Decree, I have made a careful choice. . . . Altogether the things recorded commence with the separation of Heaven and Earth, and conclude with the august reign at Woharida [in 628, when Empress Sui-ko died]. . . . Altogether I have written three volumes, which I reverently and respectfully present. I Yasumaro, with true trembling and true fear, bow my head, bow my head.

Reverently presented by the Court Noble Futo no Yasumaro, an Officer of the Upper Division of the First Class of the Fifth Rank and of the Fifth Order of Merit, on the 28th day of the first moon of the fifth year of Wado [March 10, 712].

SECTION 1. THE BEGINNING OF HEAVEN AND EARTH*

The names of the Deities** that were born in the Plain of High Heaven when the Heaven and Earth began were the Deity Master-of-the-August-Centre-of-Heaven, next the High-August-Producing-Wondrous-Deity, next the Divine-Producing-Wondrous-Deity. These three Deities were all Deities born alone, and hid their persons [i.e., died]. The names of the Deities that were born next from a thing [that sprouted up like unto a reed-shoot when the earth, young and like unto floating oil, drifted about medusa-like, were the Pleasant-Reed-Shoot-Prince-Elder-Deity, next the Heavenly-Eternally-Standing-Deity. These two Deities were likewise born alone, and hid their persons.

SECTION II. THE SEVEN DIVINE GENERATIONS

The names of the Deities that were born next were the Earthly-Eternally-Standing-Deity, next the Luxuriant-Integrating-Master-Deity. These two Deities were likewise Deities born alone, and hid their persons. The names of the Deities that were born next were the Deity Mud-Earth-Lord, next his younger sister the Deity Mud-Earth-Lady, next the Germ-Integrating-Deity, next his younger sister the Life-Integrating-Deity, next the Deity Elder-of-the-Great-Place, next his younger sister the Deity Elder-Lady-of-the-Great-Place, next the Deity Perfect-Exterior, next his younger sister the Deity Oh-Awful-Lady, next the Deity Male-Who-Invites [also named Izanagi], next his younger sister the Deity Female-Who-Invites [also named Izanami]. From the Earthly-Eternally-Standing-Deity down to the Deity Female-Who-Invites [Izanami] in the previous list are what are termed the Seven Divine Generations.

SECTION III. THE ISLAND OF ONOGORO

Hereupon all the Heavenly Deities commanded the two Deities His Augustness Izanagi and Her Augustness Izanami, ordering them to "make, consolidate, and give birth to this drifting land [Japan]." Granting to them a heavenly jewelled spear, they thus deigned to charge them. So the two Deities, standing upon the Floating Bridge of Heaven, pushed down the jewelled spear and stirred with it, whereupon when they had stirred the brine till it went curdle-curdle, and drew the spear up, the brine that dripped down from the end of the spear was piled up and became an island. This is the Island of Onogoro [a Japanese islet].

SECT1ON IV. COURTSHIP OF THE DEITIES THE MALE-WHO-INVITES AND THE FEMALE-WHO-INVITES

Having descended from Heaven onto this island, they saw to the erection of a heavenly august pillar, they saw to the erection of a hall of eight fathoms. [They then produced a child.] This child they placed in a boat of reeds, and let it float away. Next they gave birth to the Island of Aha [another islet]. .

SECTION V. BIRTH OF THE EIGHT GREAT 1SLANDS

Hereupon the two Deities took counsel, saying: "The children to whom we have now given birth are not good. It will be best to announce this in the august place of the Heavenly Deities." They ascended forthwith to Heaven and inquired of Their Augustnesses the Heavenly Deities. Then the Heavenly Deities commanded and found out by grand divination, and ordered them, saying: "They were not good because the woman spoke first. Descend back again and amend your words." So thereupon descending back, they again went round the heavenly august pillar as before. Thereupon his Augustness Izanagi spoke first: "Ah! what a fair and lovely maiden!" Afterwards his younger sister Her Augustness Izanami spoke: "Ah! what a fair and lovely youth!" [They gave birth to another child.] Next they gave birth to the Island of Futa-na in Iyo. This island has one body and four faces, and each face has a name. So the Land of Iyo is called Lovely-Princess, the Land of Sanuki is called Prince-Good-Boiled-Rice, the Land of Aha is called the Princess-of-Great-Food, the Land of Tosa is called Brave-Good-Youth. Next they gave birth to the Islands of Mitsu-go near Oki, another name for which islands is Heavenly-Great-Heart-Youth. Next they gave birth to the island of Tsukushi. This island likewise has one body and four faces, and each face has a name. So the Land of Tsukushi is called White-Sun-Youth, the Land of Toyo is called Luxuriant-Sun-Youth, the Land of Hi is called Brave-Sun-Confronting-Luxuriant-Wondrous-Lord-Youth, the Land of Kumaso is called Brave-Sun-Youth. Next they gave birth to the Island of Iki, another name for which is Heaven's-One-Pillar. Next they gave birth to the Island of Tsu, another name for which is Heavenly-Hand-net-Good-Princess. Next they gave birth to the Island of Sado. Next they gave birth to Great-Yamato-the-Luxuriant-Island-of-the-Dragon-Fly, another name for which is Heavenly-August-Sky-Luxuriant-Dragon-Fly-Lord-Youth. The name of "Land-of-the-Eight-Great-Islands" therefore originated in these eight islands having been born first. [They then completed giving birth to the islands of Japan.]

SECTION VI. BIRTH OF THE VARIOUS DEITIES

When they had finished giving birth to countries, they began afresh giving birth to Deities. [There follows a long list of deities to whom Izanagi and Izanami give birth, and who in turn give birth to further deities, and so on. Many of these deities have names descriptive of natural phenomena like rocks, wind, sea, autumn, trees, mountains, and moors.]

SECTION VII. RETIREMENT OF HER AUGUSTNESS THE PRINCESS WHO-INVITES

Through giving birth to this child her august private parts were burnt, and she [Izanami] sickened and lay down. . . . So the Deity Izanami, through giving birth to the Deity-of-Fire, at length divinely retired [died]. The total number of islands given birth to jointly by the two Deities Izanagi and Izanami was fourteen, and of Deities thirty-five.

So then His Augustness Izanagi said: "Oh! Thine Augustness my lovely younger sister! Oh! that I should have exchanged thee for this single child!" And as he crept round her august pillow, and as he crept round her august feet and wept, there was born from his august tears the Deity that dwells at Konomoto near Unewo on Mount Kagu, and whose name is the Crying-Weeping-Female-Deity. So he buried the divinely retired Deity Izanami on Mount Hiba at the boundary of the Land of Idzumo and the Land of Hahaki.

. . .

SECTION IX. THE LAND OF HADES

Thereupon His Augustness Izanagi, wishing to meet and see his younger sister Her Augustness Izanami, followed after her to the Land of Hades. So when from the palace she raised the door and came out to meet him, His Augustness Izanagi spoke, saying: "Thine Augustness my lovely younger sister! the lands that I and thou made are not yet finished making, so come back." Then Her Augustness Izanami answered, saying: "Lamentable indeed that thou camest not sooner! I have eaten of the furnace of Hades. Nevertheless, as I reverence the entry here of Thine Augustness my lovely elder brother, I wish to return. Moreover I will discuss it particularly with the Deities of Hades. Look not at me!" Having thus spoken, she went back inside the palace; and as she tarried there very long, he could not wait. So having taken and broken off one of the end-teeth of the multitudinous and close-toothed comb stuck in the august left bunch of his hair, he lit one light and went in and looked. Maggots were swarming, and she was rotting, and in her head dwelt the Great-Thunder, in her breast dwelt the Fire-Thunder, in her belly dwelt the Black-Thunder, in her private parts dwelt the Cleaving-Thunder, in her left hand dwelt the Young-Thunder, in her right hand dwelt the Earth-Thunder, in her left foot dwelt the Rumbling-Thunder, in her right foot dwelt the Couchant-Thunder-altogether eight Thunder-Deities had been born and dwelt there. Hereupon His Augustness Izanagi, overawed at the sight, fled back, whereupon his younger sister Her Augustness Izanami said: "Thou hast put me to shame," and at once sent the Ugly-Female-of-Hades to pursue him. So His Augustness Izanagi took his black august headdress and cast it down, and it instantly turned into grapes. While she picked them up and ate them, he fled on; but as she still pursued him, he took and broke the multitudinous and close-toothed comb in the right bunch of his hair and cast it down, and it instantly turned into bamboo-sprouts. While she pulled them up and ate them, he fled on. Again later his younger sister sent the eight Thunder-Deities with a thousand and five hundred warriors of Hades to pursue him. So he, drawing the ten-grasp sabre that was augustly girded on him, fled forward brandishing it in his back hand; and as they still pursued, he took, on reaching the base of the Even Pass of Hades, three peaches that were growing at its base, and waited and smote his pursuers therewith, so that they all fled back. Then His Augustness Izanagi announced to the peaches: "Like as ye have helped me, so much ye help all living people in the Central Land of Reed-Plains [Japan] when they shall fall into troublous circumstances and be harassed!" -and he gave to the peaches the designation of Their Augustnesses Great-Divine-Fruit. Last of all his younger sister Her Augustness Izanami came out herself in pursuit. So he drew a thousand-draught rock, and with it blocked up the Even Pass of Hades, and placed the rock in the middle; and they stood opposite to one another and exchanged leave-takings; and Her Augustness Izanami said: "My lovely elder brother, thine Augustness! If thou do like this, I will in one day strangle to death a thousand of the folks of thy land." Then His Augustness Izanagi replied: "My lovely younger sister, Thine Augustness! If *thou* do this I will in one day set up a thousand and five hundred parturition-houses. In this manner each day a thousand people would surely die, and each day a thousand and five hundred people would surely be born." So Her Augustness Izanami is called the Great-Deity-of-Hades.

Again it is said that, owing to her having pursued and reached her elder brother, she is called the Road-Reaching-Great-Deity. Again the rock with which he blocked up the Pass of Hades is called the Great-Deity-of-the-Road-Turning-Back, and again it is called the Blocking-Great-Deity-of-the-Door-of-Hades. .

SECTION X. THE PURIFICATION OF THE AUGUST PERSON

Therefore the Great Deity Izanagi said: "Nay! hideous! I have come to a hideous and polluted land, I have! So I will perform the purification of my august person." So he went out to a plain covered with bushclover at a small river mouth near Tachibana in Himuka [probably on Honshu] in the island of Tsukushi and purified and cleansed himself. [Izanagi removes his clothing and begins to bathe; as by-products of these activities he creates a sizeable number of diverse deities, of which only the last three are significant.] The name of the Deity that was born as he thereupon washed his left august eye was the Heaven-Shining-Great-August-Deity. The name of the Deity that was next born as he washed his right august eye was His Augustness Moon-Night-Possessor. The name of the Deity that was next born as he washed his august nose was His Brave-Swift-Impetuous-Male-Augustness (or Susanoo). .

SECTION XI. INVESTITURE OF THE THREE DEITIES, THE ILLUSTRIOUS AUGUST CHILDREN

At this time His Augustness Izanagi greatly rejoiced, saying: "I, begetting child after child, have at my final begetting gotten three illustrious children," with which words, at once jinglingly taking off and shaking the jewel-string forming his august necklace, he bestowed it on the Heaven- Shining-Great-August-Deity, saying:

"Do Thine Augustness rule the Plain-of-High-Heaven." With this charge he bestowed it on her. Now the name of this august necklace was the August-Storehouse-Shelf-Deity. Next he said to His Augustness Moon-Night-Possessor: "Do Thine Augustness rule the Dominion of the Night." Thus he charged him. Next he said to Susanoo: "Do Thine Augustness rule the Sea-Plain."

SECTION XII. THE CRYING AND WEEPING OF HIS IMPETUOUS-MALE-AUGUSTNESS

So while the other two Deities each assumed his and her rule according to the command with which their father had deigned to charge them, Susanoo did not assume the rule of the dominion with which he had been charged, but cried and wept till his eight-grasp beard reached to the pit of his stomach. The fashion of his weeping was such as by his weeping to wither the green mountains into withered mountains and by his weeping to dry up all the rivers and seas. For this reason the sound of bad Deities was like unto the flies in the fifth moon as they all swarmed, and in all things every portent of woe arose. So the Great August Deity Izanagi said to Susanoo: "How is it that, instead of ruling the land with which I charged thee, thou dost wail and weep?" He replied, saying: "I wail because I wish to depart to my deceased mother's land, to the Nether Distant Land [Hades] ." Then the Great August Deity Izanagi was very angry and said: "If that be so, thou shalt not dwell in this land," and forthwith expelled him with a divine expulsion…

SECTION XIII. THE AUGUST OATH

So thereupon Susanoo said: "If that be so, I will take leave of the Heaven-Shining-Great-August-Deity, and depart." With these words he forthwith went up to Heaven, whereupon all the mountains and rivers shook, and every land and country quaked. So the Heaven-Shining-Great-August-Deity, alarmed at the noise, said: "The reason of the ascent hither of His Augustness my elder brother is surely no good intent. It is only that he wishes to wrest my land from me." And she forthwith, unbinding her august hair, twisted it into august bunches, and both into the left and into the right august bunch, as likewise into her august head-dress and likewise on to her left and her right august arm, she twisted an augustly complete string of curved jewels eight feet long, of five hundred jewels, and, slinging on her back a quiver holding a thousand arrows, and adding thereto a quiver holding five hundred arrows, she likewise took and slung at her side a mighty and high-sounding elbow-pad, and brandished and stuck her bow upright so that the top shook, and she stamped her feet into the hard ground up to her opposing thighs, kicking away the earth like rotten snow, and stood valiantly like unto a mighty man, and waiting, asked: "Wherefore ascendest thou hither?"

Then Susanoo replied, saying: "I have no evil intent. It is only that when the Great-August-Deity our father spoke, deigning to inquire the cause of my wailing and weeping, I said: 'I wail because I wish to go to my deceased mother's land,' whereupon the Great-August-Deity said: 'Thou shalt not dwell in this land,' and deigned to expel me with a divine expulsion. It is therefore solely with the thought of taking leave of thee and departing, that I have ascended hither. I have no strange intentions" [The two deities then engage in a contest of producing children, the sun goddess begetting five male deities and Susanoo begetting three female deities.]

SECTION XV. THE AUGUST RAVAGES OF HIS IMPETUOUS—MALE-AUGUSTNESS

Then Susanoo said to the Heaven-Shining-Great-August-Deity: "Owing to the sincerity of my intentions I have, in begetting children, gotten delicate females. Judging from this, I have undoubtedly gained the victory." With these words, and impetuous with victory, he broke down the divisions of the ricefields laid out by the Heaven-Shining-Great-August-Deity, filled up the ditches, and moreover strewed excrements in the palace where she partook of the great food. So, though he did thus, the Heaven-Shining-Great-August-Deity upbraided him not, but said: "What looks like excrements must be something that His Augustness mine elder brother has vomited through drunkenness. Again, as to his breaking down the divisions of the rice-fields and filling up the ditches, it must be because he grudges the land they occupy that His Augustness mine elder brother acts thus." But notwithstanding these apologetic words, he still continued his evil acts, and was more and more violent. As the Heaven-Shining-Great-August-Deity sat in her awful [sacred] weaving-hall seeing to the weaving of the august garments of the Deities, he broke a hole in the top of the weaving-hall, and through it let fall a heavenly piebald horse which he had flayed. . .

SECTION XVI. THE DOOR OF THE HEAVENLY ROCK DWELLING

So thereupon the Heaven-Shining-Great-August-Deity, terrified at the sight, closed behind her the door of the Heavenly Rock-Dwelling, made it fast, and retired. Then the whole Plain of High Heaven was obscured and all the Central Land of Reed-Plains [Japan] darkened. Owing to this, eternal night prevailed. Hereupon the voices of the myriad Deities were like unto the flies in the fifth moon as they swarm and a myriad portents of woe arose. Therefore did the eight hundred myriad Deities assemble in a divine assembly in the bed of the Tranquil River of Heaven, and bid the Deity Thought-Includer, child of the High-August-Producing-Wondrous-Deity, think of a plan, assembling the long-singing birds of eternal night and making them sing, taking the hard rocks of Heaven from the river-bed of the Tranquil River of Heaven, and taking the iron from the Heavenly Metal-Mountains, calling in the smith Ama-tsu-ma-ra, charging Her Augustness I-shi-ko-ri-do-me to make a mirror, and charging His Augustness Jewel-Ancestor to make an augustly complete string of curved jewels eight feet long, of five hundred jewels, and summoning His Augustness Heavenly-Beckoning-Ancestor-Lord and His Augustness Grand-Jewel, and causing them to pull out with a complete pulling the shoulder-blade of a true stag from the Heavenly Mount Kagu, and take cherry-bark from the Heavenly Mount Kagu, and perform divination, and pulling up by pulling its roots a true Cleyera japonica with five hundred branches from the Heavenly Mount Kagu, and taking and putting upon its upper branches the augustly complete string of curved jewels eight feet long, of five hundred jewels, and taking and tying to the middle branches the mirror eight feet long, and taking and hanging upon its lower branches the white pacificatory offerings and the blue pacificatory offerings, His Augustness Grand-Jewel taking these divers things and holding them together with the grand august offerings, and His Augustness Heavenly-Beckoning-Ancestor-Lord prayerfully reciting grand liturgies, and the Heavenly-Hand-Strength-Male-Deity standing hidden beside the door, and Her Augustness Heavenly-Alarming-Female hanging round her the heavenly clubmoss from the Heavenly Mount Kagu as a sash, and making the heavenly spindle-tree her headdress, and binding the leaves of the bamboo-grass of the Heavenly Mount Kagu in a posy for her hands, laying a sounding-board before the door of the Heavenly Rock-Dwelling, and stamping till she made it resound and doing as if possessed by a Deity, and pulling out the nipples of her breasts, pushing down her skirt-string to her private parts. Then the Plain of High Heaven shook, and the eight hundred myriad Deities laughed together. Hereupon the Heaven-Shining-Great-August-Deity was amazed, and, slightly opening the door of the Heavenly Rock-Dwelling, spoke thus from the inside: "Methought that owing to my retirement the Plain of Heaven would be dark, and likewise the Central Land of Reed-Plains would all be dark: how then is it that the Heavenly-Alarming-Female makes merry, and that likewise the eight hundred myriad Deities all laugh?" Then the Heavenly-Alarming-Female spoke, saying: "We rejoice and are glad because there is a Deity more illustrious than Thine Augustness." While she was thus speaking, His Augustness Heavenly-Beckoning-Ancestor-Lord and His Augustness Grand-Jewel pushed forward the mirror and respectfully showed it to the Heaven-Shining-Great-August-Deity, whereupon the Heaven-Shining-Great-August-Deity, more and more astonished, gradually came forth from the door and gazed upon it, whereupon the Heavenly-Hand-Strength-Male-Deity, who was standing hidden, took her august hand and drew her out, and then His Augustness Grand-Jewel drew the bottom-tied rope along at her august back, and spoke, saying: "Thou must not go back further in than this!" So when the Heaven-Shining-Great-August-Deity had come forth, both the Plain of High Heaven and the Central-Land-of-Reed-Plains of course again became light.

• • •

SECTION XXXIII. THE AUGUST DESCENT FROM HEAVEN OF HIS AUGUSTNESS THE AUGUST GRANDCHILD

Then the Heaven-Shining-Great-August-Deity and the High-Integrating-Deity commanded and charged the Heir Apparent His Augustness Truly-Conqueror-I-Conquer-Shift-Heavenly-Great-Great-Ears saying: "The Brave-Awful-Possessing-Male-

Deity says that he has now finished pacifying the Central Land of Reed-Plains. So do thou, in accordance with our gracious charge, descend to and dwell in and rule over it." Then the Heir Apparent His Augustness Truly-Conqueror-I-Conquer-Con-quering-Swift-Heavenly-Great-Great-Ears replied, saying: "While I have been getting ready to descend, there has been born to me a child whose name is His Augustness Heaven-Plenty-Earth-Plenty-Heaven's-Sun-Height-Prince-Rice-ear-Ruddy-Plenty. This child should be sent down." Therefore, in accordance with these words, they laid their command on His Augustness Prince-Rice-ear-Ruddy-Plenty, deigning to charge him with these words: "This Luxuriant Reed-Plain-Land-of-Fresh-Rice-ears [Japan] is the land over which thou shalt rule." So he replied: "I will descend from Heaven according to your commands."

Then ... they sent him down from Heaven. Thereupon they joined to him the eight-feet-long curved jewels and mirror that had allured the Heaven-Shining-Great-August-Deity from the Rock-Dwelling and also the Herb-Quelling-Great-Sword, and likewise the Deity Thought-Includer, the Hand-Strength-Male-Deity, and the Deity Heavenly-Rock-Door-Opener of Eternal Night, and charged him thus: "Regard this mirror exactly as if it were our august spirit, and reverence it as if reverencing us." Next did they say: "Let the Deity Thought-Includer take in hand our affairs, and carry on the government." These two Deities are worshipped at the temple of Isuzu [at Ise]. The next, the Deity of Luxuriant-Food, is the Deity dwelling in the outer temple of Watarahi. The next, the Deity Heavenly-Rock-Door-Opener, another name for whom is the Wondrous-Rock-True-Gate-Deity, and another name for whom is the Luxuriant-Rock-True-Gate-Deity- this Deity is the Deity of the August Gate [of the Imperial Palace]. The next, the Deity Hand-Strength-Male dwells in Sanagata. Now His Augustness the Heavenly-Beckoning-Ancestor-Lord is the ancestor of the Nakatomi Chieftains, His Augustness Grand Jewel is the ancestor of the Imibe Headmen, Her Augustness the Heavenly-Alarming-Female is the ancestress of the Duchesses of Saru, Her Augustness I-shi-ko-ri-do-me is the ancestress of the Mirror-Making Chieftains, His Augustness-Jewel-Ancestor is the ancestor of the Jewel-Ancestor Chieftains.

Questions:
1. How are the gods depicted in this text? What are their functions?
2. This text was created to legitimize the authority of the imperial dynasty. How does it do that? How is this approach different from Chinese writings with the same purpose?

9.4 Prince Shotoku's Seventeen Article Constitution

During the reign of the Japanese Empress Suiko, the true power behind the throne and chief adminis-trator was her nephew, Prince Shotoku (574–622 B.C.E.). Japan was just recovering from a bitter and sometimes bloody power struggle between court traditionalists and nobles like Shotoku, who desired to reform the government along the lines of Chinese administrative methods morally buttressed with Bud-dhist precepts. The main purpose was, of course, to centralize and bureaucratize authority along Chinese Confucian lines, but the idea of a moral responsibility was stated explicitly.

> **Source:** Ryusaku Tsunoda, ed., *Sources of the Japanese Tradition,* Vol.1 (N.Y.: Columbia University Press, 1964), pp. 49–51.

12th year [604], Summer, 4th month, 3rd day. The Prince Imperial in person prepared for the first time laws. There were seventeen clauses, as follows:

I. Harmony is to be valued and an avoidance of wanton opposition to be honored. All men are influenced by par-tisanship, and there are few who are intelligent. Hence there are some who disobey their lords and fathers, or who main-tain feuds with the neighboring villages. But when those above are harmonious and those below are friendly, and there is concord in the discussion of business, right views of things spontaneously gain acceptance. Then what is there which cannot be accomplished?

II. Sincerely reverence the three treasures. The three treasures, viz. Buddha, the Law, and the Monastic orders, are the final refuge of the four generated beings, and are the supreme objects of faith in all countries. Few men are utterly bad. They may be taught to follow it. But if they do not betake them to the three treasures, wherewithal shall their crookedness be made straight?

III. When you receive the imperial commands, fail not scrupulously to obey them. The lord is Heaven, the vassal is Earth. Heaven overspreads, and Earth upbears. When this is so, the four seasons follow their due course, and the powers of Nature obtain their efficacy. If the Earth attempted to overspread, Heaven would simply fall in ruin. Therefore is it that when the lord speaks, the vassal listens; when the superior acts, the inferior yields compliance. Consequently when you receive the imperial commands, fail not to carry them out scrupulously. Let there be a want of care in this matter, and ruin is the natural consequence.

IV. The ministers and functionaries should make decorous behavior their leading principle, for the leading principle of the government of the people consists in decorous behavior. If the superiors do not behave with decorum, the inferiors are disorderly: if inferiors are wanting in proper behavior, there must necessarily be offenses. Therefore it is that when lord and vassal behave with decorum, the distinctions of rank are not confused: when the people behave with decorum, the government of the commonwealth proceeds of itself.

V. Ceasing from gluttony and abandoning covetous desires, deal impartially with the suits which are submitted to you. Of complaints brought by the people there are a thousand in one day. If in one day there are so many, how many will there be in a series of years? If the man who is to decide suits at law makes gain his ordinary motive, and hears cases with a view to receiving bribes, then will the suits of the rich man be like a stone flung into water, while the plaints of the poor will resemble water cast upon a stone. Under these circumstances the poor man will not know whither to betake himself. Here too there is a deficiency in the duty of the minister.

VI. Chastise that which is evil and encourage that which is good. This was the excellent rule of antiquity. Conceal not, therefore, the good qualities of others, and fail not to correct that which is wrong when you see it. Flatterers and deceivers are a sharp weapon for the overthrow of the State, and a pointed sword for the destruction of the people. Sycophants are also fond, when they meet, of dilating to their superiors on the errors of their inferiors; to their inferiors, they censure the faults of their superiors. Men of this kind are all wanting in fidelity to their lord, and in benevolence towards the people. From such an origin great civil disturbances arise.

VII. Let every man have his own charge, and let not the spheres of duty be confused. When wise men are entrusted with office, the sound of praise arises. If unprincipled men hold office, disasters and tumults are multiplied. In this world, few are born with knowledge: wisdom is the product of earnest meditation. In all things, whether great or small, find the right man, and they will surely be well managed: on all occasions, be they urgent or the reverse, meet but with a wise man, and they will of themselves be amenable. In this way will the State be lasting and the Temples of the Earth and of Grain will be free from danger. Therefore did the wise sovereigns of antiquity seek the man to fill the office, and not the office for the sake of the man.

VIII. Let the ministers and functionaries attend the court early in the morning, and retire late. The business of the State does not admit of remissness, and the whole day is hardly enough for its accomplishment. If, therefore, the attendance at court is late, emergencies cannot be met: if officials retire soon, the work cannot be completed.

IX. Good faith is the foundation of right. In everything let there be good faith, for in it there surely consists the good and the bad, success and failure. If the lord and the vassal observe good faith one with another, what is there which cannot be accomplished? If the lord and the vassal do not observe good faith towards one another, everything without exception ends in failure.

X. Let us cease from wrath, and refrain from angry looks. Nor let us be resentful when others differ from us. For all men have hearts, and each heart has its own leanings. Their right is our wrong, and our right is their wrong. We are not unquestionably sages, nor are they unquestionably fools. Both of us are simply ordinary men. How can any one lay down a rule by which to distinguish right from wrong? For we are all, one with another, wise and foolish, like a ring which has no end. Therefore, although others give way to anger, let us on the contrary dread our own faults, and though we alone may be in the right, let us follow the multitude and act like them.

XI. Give clear appreciation to merit and demerit, and deal out to each its sure reward or punishment. In these days, reward does not attend upon merit, nor punishment upon crime. Ye high functionaries who have charge of public affairs, let it be your task to make clear rewards and punishments.

XII. Let not the provincial authorities or the Kuni no Miyakko levy exaction on the people. In a country there are not two lords; the people have not two masters. The sovereign is the master of the people of the whole country. The officials to whom he gives charge are all his vassals. How can they, as well as the Government, presume to levy taxes on the people?

XIII. Let all persons entrusted with office attend equally to their functions. Owing to their illness or to their being sent on missions, their work may sometimes be neglected. But whenever they become able to attend to business, let them be as accommodating as if they had had cognizance of it from before, and not hinder public affairs on the score of their not having had to do with them.

XIV. Ye ministers and functionaries! Be not envious. For if we envy others, they in turn will envy us. The evils of envy know no limit. If others excel us in intelligence, it gives us no pleasure; if they surpass us in ability, we are envious. Therefore it is not until after a lapse of five hundred years that we at last meet with a wise man, and even in a thousand years we hardly obtain one sage. But if we do not find wise men and sages, wherewithal shall the country be governed?

XV. To turn away from that which is private, and to set our faces towards that which is public—this is the path of a minister. Now if a man is influenced by private motives, he will assuredly feel resentments, and if he is influenced by resentful feelings, he will assuredly fail to act harmoniously with others. If he fails to act harmoniously with others, he will assuredly sacrifice the public interests to his private feelings. When resentment arises, it interferes with order, and is subversive of law. Therefore in the first clause it was said, that superiors and inferiors should agree together. The purport is the same as this.

XVI. Let the people be employed [in forced labor] at seasonable times. This is an ancient and excellent rule. Let them be employed, therefore, in the winter months, when they are at leisure. But from Spring to Autumn, when they are engaged in agriculture or with the mulberry trees, the people should not be so employed. For if they do not attend to agriculture, what will they have to eat? if they do not attend to the mulberry trees, what will they do for clothing?

XVII. Decisions on important matters should not be made by one person alone. They should be discussed with many. But small matters are of less consequence. It is unnecessary to consult a number of people. It is only in the case of the discussion of weighty affairs, when there is a suspicion that they may miscarry, that one should arrange matters in concert with others, so as to arrive at the right conclusion.

Questions:
1. Which element of the "Seventeen Articles is the more dominant, the political or the ethical? Why?
2. What particular areas of deficiency of the old system does Shotoku imply are in need of reform?
3. Are there passages that seem to express sympathy for, and a wish to alleviate the burden of, ordinary people? Explain.

9.5 Pilgrimage to China (840): Ennin

Ennin (793–864) was a Buddhist monk who traveled in Tang China from 838–847 in search of knowledge about his religion. In this letter to the regional magistrate, Ennin asked for permission to visit several monasteries and shrines. In just this way, the Japanese imported ideas and institutions from China before adapting them to their own culture.

> **Source:** Reischauer, Edwin O., trans., *Ennin's Diary: The Record of a Pilgrimage to China in Search of the Law,* 1955, pp. 179–180.

To the Magistrate, His Honor, Jiexia, with humble respect:

In order to seek the Buddha's teachings, Ennin has come here from afar, moved by your virtue, and has tarried in your region. . . . Humbly he presents this letter, stating his thanks. Respectfully written in brief.

The said Ennin and [his disciples and servant] are solely devoted to the Buddhist teaching and to practicing the Buddha's Way. From afar they heard of Wutai and other places in China. These are the sources of the Buddhist Law, the places where the great saints have manifested themselves. Eminent monks of India have come there from afar, crossing precipitous slopes; famous patriarchs of China have there obtained enlightenment. Ennin and the others of old have admired these places and, crossing the sea, have come to visit them, but they have of yet accomplished their long-cherished wish. . . . Separated by the ocean wastes from the land of their birth and forgetting their beloved land on this ocean shore, they reached the Korean Cloister at Mt. Qia. Fortunately, they were free to travel and were able to come to the Magistrate's enlightened territory.

They now wish to go to various regions to worship at the holy sites and to seek teachers and to study the Law [the tenets of Buddhism], but they fear that everywhere in the prefectures and subprefectures, the barriers and fords, the passes and market places, and the monasteries and temples, their reasons for traveling will not be honored, so they humbly hope that the Magistrate, out of his magnanimity, will especially grant them official credentials to serve as verification, and they humbly ask for a decision regarding this. The said matter is as stated above. Humbly written.

Question:
1. What is the tone of this letter?

9.6 Thai Civilization: Southeast Asia

The Thai people originally dwelt in what is now southern China. Driven south by Chinese and Mongol expansion in the twelfth and thirteen centuries, they built a powerful empire in Southeast Asia in the thirteenth and fourteenth centuries. The following selection commemorates the reign of Rām Khamhāēng, a powerful and influential Thai king who died in 1307.

> **Source:** Benda & Larkin, *The World of Southeast Asia: Selected Historical Readings,* (New York: Harper & Row). Out of print. Could not find rights holder.

My father was named Sī Intharāthit, my mother was named Nāng Süang, and my elder brother was named Bān Müang. There were five of us children, born of the same womb: three boys and two girls. Our first-born brother died when he was still small. When I had grown up and attained the age of nineteen, Khun Sām Chon, chieftain of the city of Chŏt, came to attack the city of Tāk. My father went into combat on Khun Sām Chon's left. Khun Sām Chon made a massive charge; my father's men fled and dispersed in a complete rout. But as for me, I did not take flight. I mounted the elephant "Anekphon" and I urged it on before my father. I engaged Khun Sām Chon in an elephant duel: I rode in quickly against Khun Sām Chon's elephant. "Māt Müang," and put him out of combat. Khun Sām Chon fled. Then my father conferred upon me the title Phra Rām Khamhaēng because I had defeated Khun Sām Chon's elephant.

During my father's life I served my father and I served my mother. If I got a bit of meat or a bit of fish, I took it to my father; if I had any sort of fruit, sour or sweet, anything delicious and good to eat; I took it to my father. If I went on an elephant hunt and caught any, I took them to my father. If I went to attack a village or a city and collected some elephants and ivory, men and women, silver and gold, I gave them to my father. Then my father died-only my elder brother remained. I continued to serve my elder brother, as I had served my father. When my elder brother died the kingdom in its entirety fell to me.

During the life of King Rām Khamhaēng this city of Sukhōthai has prospered. In the water there are fish; in the fields there is rice. The lord of the country levies no tolls on his subjects as they travel along the roads, driving cattle to go trade, riding horses to go sell. Whoever desires to trade elephants does so; whoever desires to trade horses, does so; whoever desires to trade silver or gold does so. If a commoner, a nobleman, a chieftain, or anyone at all falls ill, dies, and disappears, the house of his ancestors, his clothing, his elephants, his family, his granaries, his servants, his ancestors' areca and betel orchards are transmitted as a whole to his children. If some commoners, nobles, or chieftains are in disagreements, (the king) makes a true inquiry, and settles the matter for his subjects in an equitable fashion; he is never in collusion with practicers of thievery and deceit. If he sees someone else's wealth he does not interfere. He accords aid and assistance to whomever comes riding an elephant to find him, requesting his protection for their country. If they have neither elephants nor horses, neither male servants nor female, neither silver nor gold, he gives them some and helps them to layout their Own villages and cities. If he captures some enemy soldiers or warriors he neither kills them nor beats them. In the (palace) doorway a bell is suspended-if an inhabitant of the kingdom has any complaint or any matter which irritates his stomach and torments his mind, and he desires to expose it to the king it is not difficult: he has only to ring the bell that the king has hung there. Every time that King Rām Khamhaēng hears the sound of the bell he questions (the complainant) on his case and settles it in an equitable fashion. Consequently the inhabitants of this city of Sukhōthai admire him.

There are areca and betel orchards in all areas of the country. There are many coconut orchards in this country, many jack-fruit orchards in this country, many mango orchards in this country, and many tamarind orchards in this country. Whoever starts an orchard is permitted to do so by the king. In the middle of this city of Sukhōthai there is a marvelous well, with clean and delicious water like that of the Mekong during the dry season. Around this city of Sukhōthai there is a triple rampart measuring 3,400 wā (= 20,400 feet). The inhabitants of this city of Sukhōthai are fond of almsgiving, charity, and the maintenance of the precepts. King Rām Khamhaēng, the sovereign of this city of Sukhōthai, the princes as well as the princesses, the men as well as the women, the nobles, and the chieftains, all without exception, without distinction of rank or of sex, practice the religion of the Buddha with devotion and observe the precepts during the rainy season retreat. At the close of the rainy season, the Kathin ceremonies take place, lasting one month. At the time of the Kathin ceremonies offerings are made of stacks of cowry shells, of stacks of areca, of stacks of flowers, of cushions, and of pillows. The Kathin offerings made each year amount to two million. Chanting, (the people) go off to perform the Kathin ceremonies at the monastery of the Aranyik, and when they return to the city the procession forms at the monastery of the Aranyik and stretches as far as the border of the plain. There everyone prostrates himself, while lutes and guitars, hymns and songs resound. Whoever wants to play, plays; whoever wants to laugh laughs; whoever wants to sing, sings. This city of Sukhōthai has four main gates-each year a great crowd presses against them in order to enter and see the king light candles and gesture with the fire. And this city of Sukhōthai is filled with people to the bursting point!

In the middle of this city of Sukhōthai there are sanctuaries. There are some gold statues of the Buddha, there is a statue of the Buddha which measures eighteen cubits, there are some statues of the Buddha which are large, and there are some which are of moderate size. There are large sanctuaries, and there are moderate-sized ones; there are monks, both theras and mahatheras.

To the west of this city of Sukhōthai is found the monastery of Aranyik. King Rām Khamhaēng founded it and offered it to the patriarch, to the chief monk, a scholar who has studied completely the Three Scriptures and who is more learned than all other monks of the country, having come from Nakhon Si Thammarat. In the middle of this monastery of the Aranyik there is a great, lofty sanctuary, beautifully situated, which contains a statue of the standing Buddha, with a height of eighteen cubits.

To the east of this city of Sukhōthai there are sanctuaries ands monks. There is a large lake, areca and betel orchards, dry fields and paddy fields, hamlets, large and small villages, and there are mango and tamarind orchards. All of this is as beautiful as in a picture.

To the north of this city of Sukhōthai there is a market, there is a Buddha image, and there is a prasat. There are areca and jackfruit orchards, dry fields and paddy fields, hamlets, and villages large and small.

To the south of this city of Sukhōthai there are hermitages and sanctuaries, and monks who live there. There is a dam; coconut, jack-fruit, mango and areca orchards; and there is a spring from a hillside. There is Phra Khaphung—the spirit of divinity of this mountain, superior to all the spirits of the country. If a prince, whoever he might be, governing this city of Sukhōthai deals with (the spirit's) cult in a dignified way and presents ritual offerings to him, then this country is stable and prospers; but if (the sovereign) does not follow the prescribed cult and does not present ritual offerings properly then the spirit of this mountain no longer protects nor respects this country which [consequently] falls into decadence.

In 1214, the year of the dragon, King Rām Khamhāeng, sovereign of the cities of Si Satchanalay and Sukhōthai who had had sugar palms planted fourteen years earlier, ordered some artisans to cut a stone slab (a dais) and place it in the midst of these sugar palms. On the day of the new moon, the eighth day of the waxing moon, the day of the full moon, and the eighth day of the waning moon a group of monks, theras and mahatheras, mounts and sits down upon that dais, and recites the Law there to the laity and to the assembly of the faithful, observing the precepts. On days other than those for the recitation of the Law, King Rām Khamhāeng, sovereign of the cities of Si Satchanalay and Sukhōthai, mounts the stone dais and sits down, and together with the assembled nobles and dignitaries governs the affairs of the country. On the days of the new moon and the full moon the king has the white elephant Rucasi harnessed ... and the right (and left) tusks all decorated with gold and ivory. The king then mounts it and goes to make his devotions to the venerable chief of the Aranyik, then he returns.

There is an inscription in the city of Chaliang situated near the holy Si Ratanathat relic, (Also) there is an inscription in the cave called "King's Cave" situated on the bank of the Samphay River. (In addition) there is an inscription in the Ratanathan Cave.

In the middle of the sugar palm (grove) there are two pavilions: One is called "The Pavilion of the Gold Buddha," the other "The Pavilion of the Buddha." The stone dais is called Manangkhasilabat—it has been put in that place so that everyone can see (it).

King Rām Khamhāeng, the son of King Si Intharathit, is the sovereign of the cities of Si Satchanalay and Sukhōthai, as well as the Ma, the Kaw, the Lao, and the Thai who live under the celestial vault. Both the river Thai of the U River and the river people of the Khohg have Submitted and pay him homage. In 1207, the year of the pig, he had the holy relics exhumed so that everyone could contemplate them. He worshiped and venerated these relics for; one month and six days, then he had them buried in the middle of the city of Si Satchanalay; there he erected a cetiya (or "chadi") which was finished in six years; he surrounded the Great Relic with a stone fort which was built in three years.

This alphabet for writing Thai did not exist previously. In 1205, the year of the goat, King Rām Khamhāeng with great concentration and meditation devised this alphabet for writing Thai, and this Thai alphabet exists because the king developed it.

This king, Rām Khamhāeng, seeks to be the chief and the sovereign of all the Thai. He is the master who instructs all of the Thai so that they may know about merit and the true Law. Among all the men who live in this Thai country none is his equal in knowledge and in wisdom, in bravery and in hardiness, in force and in energy. He has vanquished the crowd of his enemies who possess broad cities and numerous elephants. . . .

Questions:
1. For what accomplishments does the king want to be remembered?
2. To what extent do you trunk Sukhōthai has been influenced by the ideal of the Buddhist ruler exemplified by Ashoka?

PART 10
The Formation of European Civilization

10.1 St. Hildegard of Bingen, Know the Ways

As was true of their male contemporaries, women served in the formative years of the Christian Church as deaconesses or later helped to convert relatives or barbarian peoples. A few, such as St. Teresa of Avila and St. Catherine of Siena, became famous for their teaching roles and were sometimes even called "Doctors," but for the most part female mystics remained relatively unknown, although their writings would be gathered and recopied over the centuries. It is only in the twentieth century that their important contributions are being recognized.

A notable exception to the general rule that female mystics received little attention was St. Hildegard (1098–1179), mother superior of a community of Benedictine nuns at Rupertsburg near Bingen on the Rhine. Over a period of many years, she spoke and wrote of experiencing large-scale, highly detailed visions with figures or voices explaining the significance of their related parts. She also wrote on medical subjects and the world of nature; occasionally she brought her natural-scientific observations to bear on the interpretation of her visions. In 1150, she finished recording her visions of the preceding nine years in a book, Scivias (Sci Vias means Know the Ways), which enhanced her contemporary recognition. As long as she lived after that, people from all walks of life sought her out for advice and help with prophecy, which she freely gave.

Source: From *Scivias in S. Hildegardis Abbatissae Opera Omnia, Patrologia,* Vol. CXCVII (Paris: J.P. Migne, 1853), columns 427–28, 453–57, 625–33, passim. Trans. Henry A. Myers.

BODY AND SOUL

The body is a tent and the resting place of all spiritual powers, for the soul, who lives outside the body, works with it—and it with her—for both good and evil. . . . The soul is the lady in charge, the flesh truly is her serving-maid. In what way? The soul rules the body in giving life to it; the body submits to the soul's governance for living, since the body dissolves when the soul no longer sustains life in it. When a person does an evil deed with the soul conscious of it, it is as bitter for the soul as if the body knowingly took some poison, but then the soul rejoices at a good deed in the way that the body finds delight in a tasty dish.

The soul flows through the body as sap through a tree. What is that? The sap enables the tree to send forth green leaves, to blossom and to bear fruit. But what makes the fruit of the tree ripen? The weather gives it sunny days with their warmth and rainy ones with water, and so it ripens under the influence of the weather. What does that mean? That, like the sun, the merciful grace of God gives light to man, the breath of the Holy Spirit, like the rain, gives him the water of encouragement and, like the weather elements in turn, they bring good fruit in him to full development.

The soul is thus for the body what the sap is for the tree, applying its powers to the tree as it grows into its ordained form. How so? Gathering knowledge is like unto the greening of the tree's twigs and leaves, directing the will is like unto its blossoming, while feelings resemble the fruit in its early stages and reason the fully developed fruit. Finally, the development of understanding is like unto the spreading growth of the tree to its full dimensions.

And so in this way the soul strengthens and sustains the body. Therefore, o man, recognize what you are in your soul, you who reject the good of knowledge as if wanting to put yourself on the same level as cattle!

HOLY MOTHER CHURCH

After this I saw a female image, so huge that it was like looking at a large city. She wore a wonderfully decorated crown on her head. Bright rays of light, beaming from Heaven to earth, fell from her arms like flowing sleeves. Her lower abdomen resembled a net, full of open spaces through which a great throng of humanity entered. . . . And this image spread her radiance out like a garment and spoke: "I must conceive and bear!"

Then I saw black children swimming through the air, close to the ground, like fish in water. Through the openings they entered the womb of the great figure. She then took a deep breath, drawing them up to her head, from whence they came out of her mouth. She herself was not hurt by all this.

And behold: there appeared a bright light and within it a human figure, surrounded by a fiery red glow. This apparition pulled the black skin off every child and threw it aside, clothed every single one of them with a garment of blinding white and caused a bright light to beam upon them all. "Take off," she said to each of them, "your old clothing of unrighteousness and put on the new garment of holiness, for the gates to your inheritance have been opened. . . ."

And again, I heard the voice from Heaven, saying to me: "The edifice of living souls is built in Heaven to its perfection. It receives the virtues of its sons, which become its building stones of priceless gems, like a huge city absorbs throngs of people and a wide net pulls up great numbers of fish together. . . . The woman you see, so tall that she resembles a large city when you look at her, is my Son's bride, who keeps on giving him new children, those born again from the spirit and the water. The most stout-hearted warrior of all has chosen her to gather in the great throng of His chosen ones . . . and make them perfect. No attacking enemy can storm her towers, for she hurls unbelief into flight, and through the faith of believers she continues to grow. . . .

Her head is crowned with wonderful adornments. When the Church first came into being, awakened in the blood of the Lamb, the apostles and martyrs fittingly crowned her the true bride wed to my Son with their deeds. From the blood of His wounds she went through faith into the world, where she builds her own structure with hallowed souls. For this reason, bright rays of light descend from her arms like flowing sleeves. This signifies the working of divine power in the priests, who present the holiest of sacrifices at the consecrated altar in the mystery of the flesh and blood of their Redeemer. . . .

Like a net, the lower abdomen of the woman is open in many places through which a great crowd of people enter: this is her maternal love, opening for a catch of believing souls. . . . You see black children swimming through the air close to the ground, like fish in water. Through the openings they enter the figure's womb. . . . Their blackness signifies the foolishness of people who are not yet washed in the bath of redemption. Although they love earthly things, run about in the world and set up their dwellings in it, they have finally succeeded in reaching the mother of holiness. . . .

It is for this reason that the figure takes a deep breath, drawing them up inside her head, where they come out through her mouth. The process does not hurt her in the least. As often as a baptism is carried out . . . the Holy Mother [Church] takes a deep breath—her breath is the Holy Spirit—so that the human being is drawn up to the highest bestower of blessedness, the Head of all, and becomes a member of Christ[1] when he is born again, this time to salvation, calling upon the Holy Trinity through the mouth of the Holy Mother. . . .

The human figure shimmering in the fiery red glow . . . pulls the black skin off each individual child and casts it aside, then clothes all of them in garments of blinding white and reveals a brightly shining light to them with words of salvation bringing admonition. The divine power, which looks into the hearts of men, mercifully takes away all sinful unbelief with the bath of baptism, for in Christ there is no death but rather life through the righteous acknowledgment of Him and the washing away of sins.

THE WALLS OF AUTHORITY

And then I was looking from inside the great building between the north and west corners out at the surrounding walls. The inner wall was one of arches filled with lattice work, but filled in solidly and not with any empty space in the usual fashion of lattice work. . . . Out from this inner wall, I saw two lesser walls running parallel to it from the north corner to the west corner. . . . On both ends they turned towards the inner wall, joining at the top in the way that plates on a turtle's shell come together. Both of these walls were a yard and a half high. Half a yard's distance separated the middle wall from the inner one with only the width of a child's palm between it and the outer one. . . .

While I was attentively observing, He who was sitting on the throne spoke to me again: "Let no believer who wants to serve God humbly withhold in doubt his submission to earthly authority. For the Holy Spirit has established government over the people, to further the people's wellbeing. . . .

"These two outer walls, each a yard and a half high, signify that, following the division into two estates on earth—those situated high and those low[2]—three groups make up the second estate: those leaders with exalted ruling powers, those who are free and not bound in [manorial] service, and those who are obedient to lords to whom they owe [manorial] services. And so the reason that there is a distance of half a yard from the middle wall to the inner one of arches is that this signifies the distance in dignity between those who rank higher because of their spiritual office and those who are assigned lesser titles because their occupations are earthly ones. They enjoy one faith together, but the differentiation still exists according to God's will until the final gathering together of His subjects. But between the outer and middle wall the space is only the width of a child's palm, because between the power of secular rulership, with its inferior ranking, and those who are bound to serve their higher-ups the distance—justly considered—is very limited, so that with the single-minded, simple devotion of innocent children they can touch each other and carry out the chores hand in hand.

Questions:
1. *How does St. Hildegard relate body and soul to each other?*
2. *What are the main attributes of Holy Mother Church, as she appears in a vision?*
3. *Why does Hildegard refer to secular authority, even in its royal ruling form, as "inferior"?*

10.2 St. Francis of Assisi, "The Rule of St. Francis"

Francis of Assisi (1182–1226), founder of the Franciscan Order, is one of the most celebrated saints of medieval Europe. As the son of a prosperous merchant, young Francis enjoyed a carefree life of pleasure and paid little attention to religion. But in 1206, he underwent a conversion experience and committed the rest of his life to ministering to the poorest of the poor living in the burgeoning cities of his native Italy. In imitation of the first apostles, Francis accepted a life of absolute poverty. He gave away all of his property and made his way by begging. Francis was an open, joyful man who loved animals and loved to laugh. Despite the hardships of his ministry, he naturally drew people to him. Francis was loath to establish detailed regulations for his followers, but by 1210, so many people had joined in his work that he was compelled to organize a rule for his followers. To underscore the virtue of humility, Francis called his followers the Order of Friars Minor. Unlike monks, who retreated from the world to live in monasteries, his "little brothers" or friars were to live among the people.

The Franciscan Friars, and the women's order of the Poor Clare nuns that he inspired, were to own nothing. Like Francis, they were to earn their way by manual labor or by begging. The focus of their ministry was the poor of the inner cities. Soon the Franciscans had established hospitals for lepers, orphanages for abandoned children, and shelters for the homeless. By 1217, Franciscan missionaries had been sent to France, Germany, Hungary, Spain, and North Africa and would soon be in China and Japan (see Reading 93). By the end of the thirteenth century, fourteen hundred Franciscan convents and friaries had been established. Because of the tremendous growth of the Franciscan movement, Francis was forced to revise his rule of 1210, and in 1223, three years before his death, he produced a more detailed rule to guide his Franciscans.

Source: From Oliver J. Thatcher and Edgar J. McNeal, eds., *A Source Book for Medieval History: Selected Documents* (New York: Charles Scribner's Sons, 1905), pp. 499–504.

1. This is the rule and life of the Minor Brothers, namely, to observe the holy gospel of our Lord Jesus Christ by living in obedience, in poverty, and in chastity. Brother Francis promises obedience and reverence to pope Honorius and to his successors who shall be canonically elected, and to the Roman Church. The other brothers are bound to obey brother Francis, and his successors.

2. If any, wishing to adopt this life, come to our brothers [to ask admission], they shall be sent to the provincial ministers, who alone have the right to receive others into the order. The provincial ministers shall carefully examine them in the catholic faith and the sacraments of the church. And if they believe all these and faithfully confess them and promise to observe them to the end of life, and if they have no wives, or if they have wives, and the wives have either already entered a monastery, or have received permission to do so, and they have already taken the vow of chastity with the permission of the bishop of the diocese [in which they live], and their wives are of such an age that no suspicion can rise against them, let the provincial ministers repeat to them the word of the holy gospel, to go and sell all their goods and give to the poor [Matt. 19:21]. But if they are not able to do so, their good will is sufficient for them. And the brothers and provincial ministers shall not be solicitous about the temporal possessions of those who wish to enter the order; but let them do with their possessions whatever the Lord may put into their minds to do. Nevertheless, if they ask the advice of the brothers, the provincial ministers may send them to God-fearing men, at whose advice they may give their possessions to the poor. Then the ministers shall give them the dress of a novice, namely: two robes without a hood, a girdle, trousers, a hood with a cape reaching to the girdle. But the ministers may add to these if they think it necessary. After the year of probation is ended they shall be received into obedience [that is, into the order], by promising to observe this rule and life forever. And according to the command of the pope they shall never be permitted to leave the order and give up this life and form of religion. For according to the holy gospel no one who puts his hand to the plough and looks back is fit for the kingdom of God [Luke 9:62]. And after they have promised obedience, those who wish may have one robe with a hood and one without a hood. Those who must may wear shoes, and all the brothers shall wear common clothes, and they shall have God's blessing if they patch them with coarse cloth and pieces of other kinds of cloth. But I warn and exhort them not to despise nor judge other men who wear fine and gay clothing, and have delicious foods and drinks. But rather let each one judge and despise himself.

3. The clerical brothers shall perform the divine office according to the rite of the holy Roman church, except the psalter, from which they may have breviaries. The lay brothers shall say 24 Paternosters at matins, 5 at lauds, 7 each at primes, terces, sexts, and nones, 12 at vespers, 7 at completorium, and prayers for the dead. And they shall fast for All

Saints' day [November 1] to Christmas. They may observe or not, as they choose, the holy Lent which begins at epiphany [January 6] and lasts for 40 days, and which our Lord consecrated by his holy fasts. Those who keep it shall be blessed of the Lord, but those who do not wish to keep it are not bound to do so. But they shall all observe the other Lent [that is, from Ash-Wednesday to Easter]. The rest of the time the brothers are bound to fast only on Fridays. But in times of manifest necessity they shall not fast. But I counsel, warn, and exhort my brothers in the Lord Jesus Christ that when they go out into the world they shall not be quarrelsome or contentious, nor judge others. But they shall be gentle, peaceable, and kind, mild and humble, and virtuous in speech, as is becoming to all. They shall not ride on horseback unless compelled by manifest necessity or infirmity to do so. When they enter a house they shall say, "Peace be to this house." According to the holy gospel, they may eat of whatever food is set before them.

4. I strictly forbid all the brothers to accept money or property either in person or through another. Nevertheless, for the needs of the sick, and for clothing the other brothers, the ministers and guardians may, as they see that necessity requires, provide through spiritual friends, according to the locality, season, and the degree of cold which may be expected in the region where they live. But, as has been said, they shall never receive money or property.

5. Those brothers to whom the Lord has given the ability to work shall work faithfully and devotedly, so that idleness, which is the enemy of the soul, may be excluded and not extinguish the spirit of prayer and devotion to which all temporal things should be subservient. As the price of their labors they may receive things that are necessary for themselves and the brothers, but not money or property. And they shall humbly receive what is given them, as is becoming to the servants of God and to those who practise the most holy poverty.

6. The brothers shall have nothing of their own, neither house, nor land, nor anything, but as pilgrims and strangers in this world, serving the Lord in poverty and humility, let them confidently go asking alms. Nor let them be ashamed of this, for the Lord made himself poor for us in this world. This is that highest pitch of poverty which has made you, my dearest brothers, heirs and kings of the kingdom of heaven, which has made you poor in goods, and exalted you in virtues. Let this be your portion, which leads into the land of the living. Cling wholly to this, my most beloved brothers, and you shall wish to have in this world nothing else than the name of the Lord Jesus Christ. And wherever they are, if they find brothers, let them show themselves to be of the same household, and each one may securely make known to the other his need. For if a mother loves and nourishes her child, how much more diligently should one nourish and love one's spiritual brother? And if any of them fall ill, the other brothers should serve them as they would wish to be served.

7. If any brother is tempted by the devil and commits a mortal sin, he should go as quickly as possible to the provincial minister, as the brothers have determined that recourse shall be had to the provincial ministers for such sins. If the provincial minister is a priest, he shall mercifully prescribe the penance for him. If he is not a priest, he shall, as may seem best to him, have some priest of the order prescribe the penance. And they shall guard against being angry or irritated about it, because anger and irritation hinder love in themselves and in others.

8. All the brothers must have one of their number as their general minister and servant of the whole brotherhood, and they must obey him. At his death the provincial ministers and guardians shall elect his successor at the chapter held at Pentecost, at which time all the provincial ministers must always come together at whatever place the general minister may order. And this chapter must be held once every three years, or more or less frequently, as the general minister may think best. And if at any time it shall be clear to the provincial ministers and guardians that the general minister is not able to perform the duties of his office and does not serve the best interests of the brothers, the aforesaid brothers, to whom the right of election is given, must, in the name of the Lord, elect another as general minister. After the chapter at Pentecost, the provincial ministers and guardians may, each in his own province, if it seems best to them, once in the same year, convoke the brothers to a provincial chapter.

9. If a bishop forbids the brothers to preach in his diocese, they shall obey him. And no brother shall preach to the people unless the general minister of the brotherhood has examined and approved him and given him the right to preach. I also warn the brothers that in their sermons their words shall be chaste and well chosen for the profit and edification of the people. They shall speak to them of vices and virtues, punishment and glory, with brevity of speech, because the Lord made the word shortened over the earth [Rom. 9:28].

10. The ministers and servants shall visit and admonish their brothers and humbly and lovingly correct them. They shall not put any command upon them that would be against their soul and this rule. And the brothers who are subject must remember that for God's sake they have given up their own wills. Wherefore I command them to obey their ministers in all the things which they have promised the Lord to observe and which shall not be contrary to their souls and this rule. And whenever brothers know and recognize that they cannot observe this rule, let them go to their ministers, and the ministers shall lovingly and kindly receive them and treat them in such a way that the brothers may speak to them freely and treat them as lords speak to, and treat, their servants. For the ministers ought to be the servants of all the brothers. I warn and exhort the brothers in the Lord Jesus Christ to guard against all arrogance, pride, envy, avarice, care, and solicitude for this world, detraction, and murmuring. And those who cannot read need not be anxious to learn. But above all things let them desire to have the spirit of the Lord and his holy works, to pray always to God with a pure heart, and to have humility, and patience in persecution and in infirmity, and to love those who persecute us and reproach us and blame us. For the Lord says, "Love your enemies, and pray

for those who persecute and speak evil of you" [cf. Matt. 5:44]. "Blessed are they who suffer persecution for righteousness' sake, for theirs is the kingdom of heaven" [Matt. 5:10]. He that endureth to the end shall be saved [Matt. 10:22].

11. I strictly forbid all the brothers to have any association or conversation with women that may cause suspicion. And let them not enter nunneries, except those which the pope has given them special permission to enter. Let them not be intimate friends of men or women, lest on this account scandal arise among the brothers or about brothers.

12. If any of the brothers shall be divinely inspired to go among Saracens and other infidels they must get the permission to go from their provincial minister, who shall give his consent only to those who he sees are suitable to be sent. In addition, I command the ministers to ask the pope to assign them a cardinal of the holy Roman church, who shall be the guide, protector, and corrector of the brotherhood, in order that, being always in subjection and at the feet of the holy church, and steadfast in the catholic faith, they may observe poverty, humility, and the holy gospel of our Lord Jesus Christ, as we have firmly promised to do. Let no man dare act contrary to this confirmation. If anyone should, and so on.

Questions:
1. Why would the Rule of St. Francis be so attractive to thousands of men and women throughout medieval Europe?
2. Why did Francis exempt his followers from certain periods of fasting and permit them to "eat whatever food is set before them"?
3. What does the success of the Franciscan order suggest about social conditions in thirteenth-century Europe?

10.3   The Goodman of Paris

Written late in the fourteenth century by an elderly, anonymous author ("The Goodman of Paris") to his much younger new wife, these instructions center on the importance of a tidy house and good relations between husband and wife. In this communication to her, the Goodman of Paris indicates that he loves his young wife so much that he not only wants her to manage his house efficiently but, after his death, if she should marry again, he wants her to please her new husband by performing properly all of her domestic responsibilities.

> **Soruce:** From Jérôme Pichon, ed., *Le Ménagier de Paris: Traité de Morale et d' Économie domestique composé vers* 1393 *par un Bourgeois Parisien.* 2 vols. (Paris: Imprimerie Crapelet, 1847), 1:169–76; trans. Philip F. Riley.

Indeed fair sister, certain services make a man love and want to return home to see his good wife, and keep away from others. Therefore I advise you to comfort your husband all the while, persevere and be at peace with him. Remember the rustic proverb that says there are three things that drive a goodman from home: a leaking roof, a smoking chimney, and a scolding woman.

Dear sister I beg you, if you want to keep the love and good will of your husband, be gentle, loving, and sweet. Do for him what the good, simple women of our country say other people have done to their own sons, when these sons give their love elsewhere, and their own mothers cannot win them back. For it is certain that when fathers and mothers are dead and stepfathers and stepmothers scold their stepsons, rebuke them, or pay no attention to where they sleep, what they eat or drink, to their stockings, to their shirts, or other needs, these children will find a good home and counsel with some other woman, one who gives them warm shelter, soup, a bed, keeps them clean, mends their stockings, breeches, shirts, and other clothes. These children follow her, they want to be with her and to sleep and be cradled between her breasts. Soon they will be completely estranged from their step parents who neglected them, but now want them back.

But it is too late, for now these children prefer the company of strangers who care for them, rather than their own relatives who cared so little for them. These step parents lament and cry and say that these women have bewitched their children and have used spells to turn their children against them. But, no matter what they say, this is not witchcraft. For it is done for the sake of the love, the care, the intimacies, the joys and pleasures that these women have shown them in all things and, on my soul, there is no witchcraft. For whoever gives pleasure to a bear, a wolf, or a lion, that same bear, wolf, or lion will follow them. And so the other beasts might say, if they could speak, that those tamed animals must be bewitched. And, by my soul, I believe that this is not witchcraft; it is simply doing good. One does not bewitch a man by doing what pleases him.

Therefore dear sister, I ask that you bewitch and bewitch again your husband. Protect him from a poorly roofed house, a smoky chimney, and do not scold him, but be sweet, gentle, amiable and peaceable. See to it that in winter he has a good, smokeless fire. Be certain that he rests well between your breasts, and bewitch him there!

And in summer ensure that there be no fleas in your room nor in your bed. I have heard you may do this in six ways. Some suggest that if the room be strewn with alder leaves, the fleas will be caught on them. Also I have heard that at night if you set out in your room one or two slices of bread spread with glue or turpentine, along with a lighted candle, the fleas will come stick to the bread. Another way I have tried that works, is to take a rough cloth: spread it about your room and over your bed; then all the fleas that land on it will be caught, and you can whisk them away with the cloth. Also sheepskins or white wool set on the straw or on the bed works well, for when the black fleas land on this white background they can be seen and killed. But the best way is to be mindful that there are fleas in the coverlets, the furs, and the clothing you wear. One way I have tried to get rid of fleas is to take the infested coverlets, furs, or dresses, fold them and shut them tightly up in a chest, that is cinched tightly with straps. Another way is to put all the clothing in an air-tight bag so that the fleas will not have any light or air and will eventually die. Occasionally I have seen rooms full of mosquitoes, which were attracted by the sleeper's breath, so that they sat on their face, stung them so hard, that they were forced to awake, light a fire of hay to make a smoke to drive the mosquitoes away. Certainly this can be done in daytime as well. Also, if you have a mosquito net use it.

If you have a chamber or a passage where there are many flies, take little cuttings of fern and tie them together and hang them up in the evening so that the flies will land on them; then take down the cuttings and throw them out. In the evening close off all your room save a little opening in the wall towards the east. At first light, all the flies will go through this opening; afterwards close the opening.

Take a bowl of milk and a hare's gall;[1] mix them together and then set out two or three bowls in places where the flies light so that all the flies that drink this mixture will die.

Tie a piece of linen to the bottom of a pot with an opening in its neck, and set that pot in the place where the flies gather and smear it within with honey, apples, or pears; when it is full of flies, cover it and shake it.

Take raw red onions, dice them and pour the juice into a bowl and set it where the flies are so that when they drink it they will die. Have fly swatters to kill them by hand. Have little twigs covered with glue in a bowl of water. Shut your windows tightly with oil cloth, parchment or something else, so that no fly can enter, and those that do can be killed with a fly swatter. Soak a string in honey, and after the flies land on it, gather them up each evening in a bag. Remember that flies will not stop in a room where there are no standing tables, dressers or other things they can light on and rest. For if they have nothing but broad, flat surfaces to settle and cling to, they will not settle. Nor will they light in a place that is watered and shut up. Therefore, it seems to me that if the room is well watered, closed and sealed, and if nothing is left on the floor, no fly will settle there.

Protect your husband from all discomforts, give him all the comforts you can think of, serve him and have him well served in your house. You can expect him to take care of matters outside the home, for if he is good, he will do even more than you could wish. Do what I have said and he will treasure you and give his heart to you. He will avoid all other houses, all other women, and all other services and households. None of these will interest him, but follow the example of horsemen who as soon as they return from a journey give their horses fresh bedding up to their bellies. These horses are unharnessed and made comfortable. They are given hay and oats, and they are well cared for in their own stables. If the horses are treated this way, the same should be done for persons, especially the masters when they return home. Upon returning from the woods and from hunting, the master gives his dogs fresh litter and a place before the fire. Their feet are greased with soft cream, they are given treats and are made as comfortable as possible.

Wives should do at least as much for their husbands as men do for their horses, dogs, asses, mules, and other beasts. If this is the case, all other houses, where their husbands have been served, will seem like dark prisons and strange places, when compared to their own home, which will be a restful haven for them. And so, when traveling, husbands will think only of their wives. No burden will be too heavy, for they will think only of their wives, whom they want to see again, just as the poor hermits and penitents wish to see the face of Jesus Christ. If cared for in this way, these husbands will never be content to live elsewhere. For all other places will seem to them to be a bed of stones compared to their home. Never stop loving: do it honestly and with a good heart.

Questions:

1. *What does this reading tell you about the character and quality of domestic life in fourteenth-century Parisian homes?*
2. *According to the Goodman of Paris, how should a wife keep the love of her husband and of her children? What does the author mean when he urges wives to "bewitch and bewitch again your husband"? Do you agree with his advice?*

10.4   The Love of God

The twelfth century was truly remarkable for its intellectual focus and development of thought. The new commitment to learning was reflected in a system of argument and study called Scholasticism. Scholars edited and commented on ancient writers, methodically arguing for the acceptance or rejection of such philosophers as Aristotle and Plato. No longer was it enough simply to accept the existence of God without a rational argument of proof. Saint Bernard's passage on the love of God reflects the argument of faith.

Source: "The Love of God" is from E. G. Gardner, trans., *On the Love of God* (London: J. M. Dent and Sons, 1916), p. 27. Reprinted by permission of the publisher.

SAINT BERNARD OF CLAIRVAUX

You would hear from me, then, why and how God is to be loved? I answer: The cause of loving God is God; the manner is to love without measure. Is this enough? Yes, perhaps, for the wise. But I am debtor to the unwise as well; where enough is said for the wise, we must comply with the others also. Therefore I will not refuse to repeat it, more fully rather than more deeply, for the sake of the slower in apprehension. I may say that God is to be loved for His own sake for a double reason: because nothing can be loved more justly, nothing more fruitfully. . . . Assuredly I find no other worthy cause of loving Him, save Himself. . . .

Question:
1. Sum up Saint Bernard's rules. Are they compelling? Why or why not?

10.5   St. Thomas Aquinas

St. Thomas Aquinas (1225-1274) was one of the greatest synthesizers in European thought. The task he undertook was to reconcile the philosophy of Aristotle, rediscovered by European scholars through their contacts with the Muslims in Spain and elsewhere, with Christian theology. During a relatively short lifetime, he succeeded in combining these two disparate elements into a single system capable in principle of explaining everything in the universe that people could know. Questions have been raised about the logical consistency of the Thomistic synthesis, but, whether successful or not, it still stands as a substantial intellectual achievement.

Beyond their general historical importance, the writings of Thomas have a special significance in the history of Catholicism. Although Thomas was opposed during his lifetime by various religious leaders because of his heavy reliance on the pagan Aristotle, and although his writings were even condemned at several theological centers in the years immediately after his death, within a century his system was generally accepted as the basis for orthodox Roman Catholic philosophy. The authoritativeness of Thomistic doctrine was formally recognized by the church in 1879 in the encyclical Aeterni Patris of Pope Leo XIII, which ordered all Catholic schools to teach Thomas's position as the true philosophy. Leo's order was reiterated in 1923 by Pius X, who wrote, "The following canon of the church's code should be held as a sacred command: In the study of rational philosophy and theology and in the instruction of students the professor should follow entirely the method, doctrine and principles of the Angelic Doctor [Thomas], and hold them religiously."

Of noble Italian lineage, Thomas decided early in life to become a Dominican monk, much to the displeasure of his family. As a student, he was nicknamed "the dumb ox" because of his quietness and ponderous bulk. Later, as a teacher at the University of Paris, he was so popular that it was difficult to find a hall large enough to accommodate the students who flocked to his lectures.

The selection that follows illustrates Thomas's attempt to establish the consonance between the philosophers' quest for truth based on reason and the Christians' acceptance of divine truth based on revelation. It is clear from the nature of his argument that, however much we should rely on reason, in the final analysis revelation is the arbiter of truth.

Source: *The "Summa Contra Gentiles" of St. Thomas Aquinas,* trans. Fathers of the English Dominican Province (New York: Benziger Brothers, Inc., 1924). Courtesy of Benziger Publishing Co.

SUMMA CONTRA GENTILES
CHAPTER III

In What Way It Is Possible to Make Known the Divine Truth

Since, however, not every truth is to be made known in the same way,

and it is the part of an educated man to seek for conviction in each subject, only so far

as the nature of the subject allows, as the Philosopher[1] most rightly observes as quoted by Boethius, it is necessary to show first of all in what way it is possible to make known the aforesaid truth.

Now in those things which we hold about God there is truth in two ways. For certain things that are true about God wholly surpass the capability of human reason, for instance that God is three and one: while there are certain things to which even natural reason can attain, for instance that God is, that God is one, and others like these, which even the philosophers proved demonstratively of God, being guided by the light of natural reason.

That certain divine truths wholly surpass the capability of human reason, is most clearly evident. For since the principle of all the knowledge which the reason acquires about a thing, is the understanding of that thing's essence, because according to the Philosopher's teaching the principle of a demonstration is *what a thing is*, it follows that our knowledge about a thing will be in proportion to our understanding of its essence. Wherefore, if the human intellect comprehends the essence of a particular thing, for instance a stone or a triangle, no truth about that thing will surpass the capability of human reason. But this does not happen to us in relation to God, because the human intellect is incapable by its natural power of attaining to the comprehension of His essence: since our intellect's knowledge, according to the mode of the present life, originates from the senses: so that things which are not objects of sense cannot be comprehended by the human intellect, except in so far as knowledge of them is gathered from sensibles. Now sensibles cannot lead our intellect to see in them what God is, because they are effects unequal to the power of their cause. And yet our intellect is led by sensibles to the divine knowledge so as to know about God that He is, and other such truths, which need to be ascribed to the first principle. Accordingly some divine truths are attainable by human reason, while others altogether surpass the power of human reason.

Again. The same is easy to see from the degrees of intellects. For if one of two men perceives a thing with his intellect with greater subtlety, the one whose intellect is of a higher degree understands many things which the other is altogether unable to grasp; as instanced in a yokel who is utterly incapable of grasping the subtleties of philosophy. Now the angelic intellect surpasses the human intellect more than the intellect of the cleverest philosopher surpasses that of the most uncultured. For an angel knows God through a more excellent effect than does man, for as much as the angel's essence, through which he is led to know God by natural knowledge, is more excellent than sensible things, even than the soul itself, by which the human intellect mounts to the knowledge of God. And the divine intellect surpasses the angelic intellect much more than the angelic surpasses the human. For the divine intellect by its capacity equals the divine essence, wherefore God perfectly understands of Himself what He is, and He knows all the things that can be understood about Him: whereas the angel knows not what God is by his natural knowledge, because the angel's essence, by which he is led to the knowledge of God, is an effect unequal to the power of its cause. Consequently an angel is unable by his natural knowledge to grasp all that God understands about Himself: nor again is human reason capable of grasping all that an angel understands by his natural power. Accordingly just as a man would show himself to be a most insane fool if he declared the assertions of a philosopher to be false because he was unable to understand them, so, and much more, a man would be exceedingly foolish, were he to suspect of falsehood the things revealed by God through the ministry of His angels, because they cannot be the object of reason's investigations.

Furthermore. The same is made abundantly clear by the deficiency which every day we experience in our knowledge of things. For we are ignorant of many of the properties of sensible things, and in many cases we are unable to discover the nature of those properties which we perceive by our senses. Much less therefore is human reason capable of investigating all the truths about the most sublime existence.

With this the saying of the Philosopher is in accord where he says *that our intellect in relation to those primary things which are most evident in nature is like the eye of a bat in relation to the sun.*

To this truth Holy Writ also bears witness. For it is written (Job xi. 7):

Peradventure thou wilt comprehend the steps of God and wilt find out the Almighty perfectly? and (xxxvi. 26) *Behold God is great, exceeding our knowledge,* and (I Cor. xiii. 9): *We know in part.*

Therefore all that is said about God, though it cannot be investigated by reason, must not be forthwith rejected as false, as the Manicheans and many unbelievers have thought.

CHAPTER IV

That the Truth about Divine Things Which Is Attainable by Reason Is Fittingly Proposed to Man as an Object of Belief

While then the truth of the intelligible things of God is twofold, one to which the inquiry of reason can attain, the other which surpasses the whole range of human reason, both are fittingly proposed by God to man as an object of belief. We must first show this with regard to that truth which is attainable by the inquiry of reason, lest it appears to some, that since it can be attained by reason, it was useless to make it an object of faith by supernatural inspiration. Now three disadvantages would result if this truth were left solely to the inquiry of reason. One is that few men would have knowledge of God: because very many are hindered from gathering the fruit of diligent inquiry, which is the discovery of truth, for three reasons. Some indeed on account of an indisposition of temperament, by reason of which many are naturally indisposed to knowledge: so that no efforts of theirs would enable them to reach to the attainment of the highest degree of human knowledge, which consists in knowing God. Some are hindered by the needs of household affairs. For there must needs be among men some that devote themselves to the conduct of temporal affairs, who would be unable to devote so much time to the leisure of contemplative research as to reach the summit of human inquiry, namely the knowledge of God. And some are hindered by laziness. For in order to acquire the knowledge of God in those things which reason is able to investigate, it is necessary to have a previous knowledge of many things: since almost the entire consideration of philosophy is directed to the knowledge of God: for which reason metaphysics, which is about divine things, is the last of the parts of philosophy to be studied. Wherefore it is not possible to arrive at the inquiry about the aforesaid truth except after a most laborious study: and few are willing to take upon themselves this labour for the love of a knowledge, the natural desire for which has nevertheless been instilled into the mind of man by God.

The second disadvantage is that those who would arrive at the discovery of the aforesaid truth would scarcely succeed in doing so after a long time. First, because this truth is so profound, that it is only after long practice that the human intellect is enabled to grasp it by means of reason. Secondly, because many things are required beforehand, as stated above. Thirdly, because at the time of youth, the mind, when tossed about by the various movements of the passions, is not fit for the knowledge of so sublime a truth, whereas *calm gives prudence and knowledge,* as stated in 7 Phys. Hence mankind would remain in the deepest darkness of ignorance, if the path of reason were the only available way to the knowledge of God: because the knowledge of God which especially makes men perfect and good, would be acquired only by the few, and by these only after a long time.

The third disadvantage is that much falsehood is mingled with the investigations of human reason, on account of the weakness of our intellect in forming its judgments, and by reason of the admixture of phantasms. Consequently many would remain in doubt about those things even which are most truly demonstrated, through ignoring the force of the demonstration: especially when they perceive that different things are taught by the various men who are called wise. Moreover among the many demonstrated truths, there is sometimes a mixture of falsehood that is not demonstrated, but assumed for some probable or sophistical reason which at times is mistaken for a demonstration. Therefore it was necessary that definite certainty and pure truth about divine things should be offered to man by the way of faith.

Accordingly the divine clemency has made this salutary commandment, that even some things which reason is able to investigate must be held by faith: so that all may share in the knowledge of God easily, and without doubt or error.

Hence it is written (Eph. iv. 17, 18): That *henceforth you walk not as also the Gentiles walk in the vanity of their mind, having their understanding darkened;* and (Isa. liv. 13): *All thy children shall be taught of the Lord.*

CHAPTER V

That Those Things Which Cannot Be Investigated by Reason Are Fittingly Proposed to Man as an Object of Faith

It may appear to some that those things which cannot be investigated by reason ought not to be proposed to man as an object of faith: because divine wisdom provides for each thing according to the mode of its nature. We must therefore prove that it is necessary also for those things which surpass reason to be proposed by God to man as an object of faith.

For no man tends to do a thing by his desire and endeavour unless it be previously known to him. Wherefore since man is directed by divine providence to a higher good than human frailty can attain in the present life, as we shall show in the sequel, it was necessary for his mind to be bidden to something higher than those things to which our reason can reach in the present life, so that he might learn to aspire, and by his endeavors to tend to something surpassing the whole state of the present life. And this is especially competent to the Christian religion, which alone promises goods spiritual and eternal: for which reason it proposes many things surpassing the thought of man: whereas the old law which contained promises of temporal things, proposed few things that are above human inquiry. It was with this motive that the philosophers, in order to wean men from sensible pleasures to virtue, took care to show that there are other goods of greater account than those which appeal to the senses, the taste of which things affords much greater delight to those who devote themselves to active or contemplative virtues.

Again it is necessary for this truth to be proposed to man as an object of faith in order that he may have truer knowledge of God. For then alone do we know God truly, when we believe that He is far above all that man can possibly think of God, because the divine essence surpasses man's natural knowledge, as stated above. Hence by the fact that certain things about God are proposed to man, which surpass his reason, he is strengthened in his opinion that God is far above what he is able to think.

There results also another advantage from this, namely, the checking of presumption which is the mother of error. For some there are who presume so far on their wits that they think themselves capable of measuring the whole nature of things by their intellect, in that they esteem all things true which they see, and false which they see not. Accordingly, in order that man's mind might be freed from this presumption, and seek the truth humbly, it was necessary that certain things far surpassing his intellect should be proposed to man by God.

Yet another advantage is made apparent by the words of the Philosopher (10 *Ethic*). For when a certain Simonides maintained that man should neglect the knowledge of God, and apply his mind to human affairs, and declared that *a man ought to relish human things, and a mortal, mortal things:* the Philosopher contradicted him, saying that *a man ought to devote himself to immortal and divine things as much as he can.* Hence he says (11 *De Anima.*) that though it is but little that we perceive of higher substances, yet that little is more loved and desired than all the knowledge we have of lower substances. He says also (2 *De Coelo et Mundo*) that when questions about the heavenly bodies can be answered by a short and probable solution, it happens that the hearer is very much rejoiced. All this shows that however imperfect the knowledge of the highest things may be, it bestows very great perfection on the soul: and consequently, although human reason is unable to grasp fully things that are above reason, it nevertheless acquires much perfection, if at least it hold things, in any way whatever, by faith.

Wherefore it is written (Eccles, iii. 25): *Many things are shown to thee above the understanding of men,* and (I Cor. ii. 10, 11): *The things. . . that are of God no man knoweth, but the Spirit of God: but to us God hath revealed them by His Spirit.*

CHAPTER VI

That It Is Not a Mark of Levity to Assent to the Things That Are of Faith, Although They Are Above Reason

Now those who believe this truth, *of which reason affords a proof* believe not lightly, as though *following foolish fables* (2 Pet. i. 16). For divine Wisdom Himself, Who knows all things most fully, designed to reveal to man *the secrets of God's wisdom:* and by suitable arguments proves His presence, and the truth of His doctrine and inspiration, by performing works surpassing the capability of the whole of nature, namely, the wondrous healing of the sick, the raising of the dead to life, a marvellous control over the heavenly bodies, and what excites yet more wonder, the inspiration of human minds, so that unlettered and simple persons are filled with the Holy Ghost, and in one instant are endowed with the most sublime wisdom and eloquence. And after considering these arguments, convinced by the strength of the proof, and not by the force of arms, nor by the promise of delights, but-and this is the greatest marvel of all-amidst the tyranny of persecutions, a countless crowd of not only simple but also of the wisest men, embraced the Christian faith, which inculcates things surpassing all human understanding, curbs the pleasures of the flesh, and teaches contempt of all worldly things. That the minds of mortal beings should assent to such things, is both the greatest of miracles, and the evident work of divine inspiration, seeing that they despise visible things and desire only those that are invisible. And that this happened not suddenly nor by chance, but by the disposition of God, is shown by the fact that God foretold that He would do so by the manifold oracles of the prophets, whose books we hold in veneration as bearing witness to our faith. This particular kind of proof is alluded to in the words of Heb. ii, 3, 4: *Which,* namely the salvation of mankind, *having begun to be declared by the Lord, was confirmed with us by them that heard Him, God also bearing witness by signs and wonders, and divers . . . distributions of the Holy Ghost.*

Now such a wondrous conversion of the world to the Christian faith is a most indubitable proof that such signs did take place, so that there is no need to repeat them, seeing that there is evidence of them in their result. For it would be the most wondrous sign of all if without any wondrous signs the world were persuaded by simple and lowly men to believe things so arduous, to accomplish things so difficult, and to hope for things so sublime. Although God ceases not even in our time to work miracles through His saints in confirmation of the faith.

On the other hand those who introduced the errors of the sects proceeded in contrary fashion, as instanced by Mohammed, who enticed people with the promise of carnal pleasures, to the desire of which the concupiscence of the flesh instigates. He also delivered commandments in keeping with his promises, by giving the reins to carnal pleasure, wherein it is easy for carnal men to obey: and the lessons of truth which he inculcated were only such as can be easily known to any man of average wisdom by his natural powers: yea, rather the truths which he taught were mingled by him with many fables and most false doctrines. Nor did he add any signs of supernatural agency, which alone are a fitting witness to divine inspiration, since a visible work that can be from God alone, proves the teacher of truth to be invisibly inspired: but he asserted that he was sent in the power of arms, a sign that is not lacking even to robbers and tyrants. Again, those who believed in him from the outset were not wise men practised in things divine and human, but beastlike men who dwelt in the wilds, utterly ignorant of all divine teaching; and it was by a multitude of such men and the force of arms that he impelled others to submit to his law.

Lastly, no divine oracles or prophets in a previous age bore witness to him; rather he did corrupt almost all the teaching of the Old and New Testaments by a narrative replete with fables, as one may see by a perusal of his law. Hence by a cunning device, he did not commit the reading of the Old and New Testament Books to his followers, lest he should thereby be convicted of falsehood. Thus it is evident that those who believe his words believe lightly.

CHAPTER VII

That the Truth of Reason Is Not in Opposition to the Truth of the Christian Faith

Now though the aforesaid truth of the Christian faith surpasses the ability of human reason, nevertheless those things which are naturally instilled in human reason cannot be opposed to this truth. For it is clear that those things which are implanted in reason by nature, are most true, so much so that it is impossible to think them to be false. Nor is it lawful to deem false that which is held by faith, since it is so evidently confirmed by God. Seeing then that the false alone is opposed to the true, as evidently appears if we examine their definitions, it is impossible for the aforesaid truth of faith to be contrary to those principles which reason knows naturally.

Again. The same thing which the disciple's mind receives from its teacher is contained in the knowledge of the teacher, unless he teach insincerely, which it were wicked to say of God. Now the knowledge of naturally known principles is instilled into us by God, since God Himself is the author of our nature. Therefore the divine Wisdom also contains these principles. Consequently whatever is contrary to these principles, is contrary to the divine Wisdom; wherefore it cannot be from God. Therefore those things which are received by faith from divine revelation cannot be contrary to our natural knowledge.

Moreover. Our intellect is stayed by contrary arguments, so that it cannot advance to the knowledge of truth. Wherefore if conflicting knowledges were instilled into us by God, our intellect would thereby be hindered from knowing the truth. And this cannot be ascribed to God.

Furthermore. Things that are natural are unchangeable so long as nature remains. Now contrary opinions alone cannot be together in the same subject. Therefore God does not instil into man any opinion or belief contrary to natural knowledge.

Hence the Apostle says (Rom. x. 8):

Thy word is nigh thee even in thy heart and in thy mouth. This is the word of faith which we preach. Yet because it surpasses reason some look upon it as though it were contrary thereto; which is impossible.

This is confirmed also by the authority of Augustine who says *That which truth shall make known can nowise be in apposition to the holy books whether of the Old or of the New Testament.*

From this we may evidently conclude that whatever arguments are alleged against the teachings of faith, they do not rightly proceed from the first self-evident principles instilled by nature. Wherefore they lack the force of demonstration, and are either probable or sophistical arguments, and consequently it is possible to solve them.

Questions:
1. *What aspects of Classical Mediterranean philosophy has Thomas adopted?*
2. *According to Thomas, what is the relationship between faith and reason?*

10.6 Unam Sanctam (1302): Pope Boniface VIII

This selection, "Unam Sanctam," was a decree wherein Boniface promulgated the famous "Doctrine of the Two Swords," designed to promote the unity of Christianity and the supremacy of the pope. This policy eventually failed, as Boniface was attacked, captured, and humiliated by agents of the French king, Philip IV; Boniface died soon after. The days of papal supremacy were over.

> **Source:** "Unam Sanctam" is from Oliver Thatcher and Edgar McNeal, eds., *A Source Book of Medieval History* (New York: Charles Scribner's Sons, 1905), pp. 314–317.

POPE BONIFACE VIII

The true faith compels us to believe that there is one holy catholic apostolic church, and this we firmly believe and plainly confess. And outside of her there is no salvation or remission of sins. . . . In this church there is "one Lord, one faith, one baptism" [Eph. 4:5]. . . . Therefore there is one body of the one and only church, and one head, not two heads, as if the church were a monster. And this head is Christ and his vicar, Peter and his successor. . . . If therefore Greeks or anyone else say that they are not subject to Peter and his successors, they thereby necessarily confess that they are not of the sheep of Christ. For the Lord says in the Gospel of John, that there is one fold and only one shepherd [John 10:16]. By the words of the gospel we are taught that the two swords, namely, the spiritual authority and the temporal are in the power of the church. . . . Both swords, . . . the spiritual and the temporal, are in the power of the church. The former is to be used by the church, the latter for the church; the one by the hand of the priest, the other by the hand of kings and knights, but at the command and permission of the priest. Moreover, it is necessary for one sword to be under the other, and the temporal authority to be subjected to the spiritual; for the apostle says, "For there is no power but of God: and the powers that are ordained of God" [Rom. 13:1]; but they would not be ordained [i.e., arranged or set in order] unless one were subjected to the other, and, as it were, the lower made the higher by the other. . . . And we must necessarily admit that the spiritual power surpasses any earthly power in dignity and honor, because spiritual things surpass temporal things. We clearly see that this is true from the paying of tithes, from the benediction, from the sanctification, from the receiving of the power, and from the governing of these things. For the truth itself declares that the spiritual power must establish the temporal power and pass judgment on it if it is not good. Thus the prophecy of Jeremiah concerning the church and the ecclesiastical power is fulfilled: "See, I have this day set thee over the nations and over the kingdoms, to root out, and to pull down, and to destroy, and to throw down, to build, and to plant" [Jer. 1:10]. Therefore if the temporal power errs, it will be judged by the spiritual power, and if the lower spiritual power errs, it will be judged by its superior. But if the highest spiritual power errs, it can not be judged by men, but by God alone. For the apostle says: "But he that is spiritual judgeth all things, yet he himself is judged of no man" [1 Cor. 2:15]. Now this authority, although it is given to man and exercised through man, is not human, but divine. For it was given by the word of the Lord to Peter, and the rock was made firm to him and his successors, in Christ himself, whom he had confessed. For the Lord said to Peter: "Whatsoever thou shalt bind on earth shall be bound in heaven: and whatsoever thou shalt loose on earth shall be loosed in heaven" [Matt. 16:19]. Therefore, whosoever resisteth this power thus ordained of God, resisteth the ordinance of God [Rom. 13:2]. . . . We therefore declare, say, and affirm that submission on the part of every man to the bishop of Rome is altogether necessary for his salvation.

Question:
1. What concepts was Boniface trying to promote?

10.7 "A Most Terrible Plague": Giovanni Boccaccio

Giovanni Boccaccio is best known as a humanist of the Italian Renaissance. The following excerpt is from his most famous work, The Decameron. Written during the plague years between 1348 and 1353, it is a collection of stories told intimately between friends while they passed the time away from Florence in the solitude and safety of the country. It begins with a detailed description of the pestilence. Over two-thirds of the population of Florence died of the plague.

> **Source:** "'A Most Terrible Plague'" is from Giovanni Boccaccio, *The Decameron, in Stories of Boccaccio,* trans. John Payne (London: Bibliophilist Library, 1903), pp. 1–6.

GIOVANNI BOCCACCIO

In the year then of our Lord 1348, there happened at Florence, the finest city in all Italy, a most terrible plague; which, whether owing to the influence of the planets, or that it was sent from God as a just punishment for our sins, had broken out some years before in the Levant, and after passing from place to place, and making incredible havoc all the way, had now reached the west. There, in spite of all the means that art and human foresight could suggest, such as keeping the city clear from filth, the exclusion of all suspected persons, and the publication of copious instructions for the preservation of health; and notwithstanding manifold supplications offered to God in processions and otherwise, it began to show itself in the spring of the aforesaid year, in a sad and wonderful manner. Unlike what had been seen in the east, where bleeding from the nose is the fatal prognostic, here there appeared certain tumours in the groin or under the armpits, some as big as a small apple, others as an egg; and afterwards purple spots in most parts of the body; in some cases large and but few in number, in others smaller and more numerous—both sorts the usual messengers of death. To the cure of this malady, neither medical knowledge nor the power of drugs was of any effect; whether because the disease was in its own nature mortal, or that the physicians (the number of whom, taking quacks and women pretenders into the account, was grown very great) could form no just idea of the cause, nor consequently devise a true method of cure; whichever was the reason, few escaped; but nearly all died the third day from the first appearance of the symptoms, some sooner, some later, without any fever or accessory symptoms. What gave the more virulence to this plague, was that, by being communicated from the sick to the healthy, it spread daily, like fire when it comes in contact with large masses of combustibles. Nor was it caught only by conversing with, or coming near the sick, but even by touching their clothes, or anything that they had before touched. . . .

These facts, and others of the like sort, occasioned various fears and devices amongst those who survived, all tending to the same uncharitable and cruel end; which was, to avoid the sick, and every thing that had been near them, expecting by that means to save themselves. And some holding it best to live temperately, and to avoid excesses of all kinds, made parties, and shut themselves up from the rest of the world; eating and drinking moderately of the best, and diverting themselves with music, and such other entertainments as they might have within doors; never listening to anything from without, to make them uneasy. Others maintained free living to be a better preservative, and would baulk no passion or appetite they wished to gratify, drinking and revelling incessantly from tavern to tavern, or in private houses (which were frequently found deserted by the owners, and therefore common to every one), yet strenuously avoiding, with all this brutal indulgence, to come near the infected. And such, at that time, was the public distress, that the laws, human and divine, were no more regarded; for the officers, to put them in force, being either dead, sick, or in want of persons to assist them, every one did just as he pleased. A third sort of people chose a method between these two: not confining themselves to rules of diet like the former, and yet avoiding the intemperance of the latter; but eating and drinking what their appetites required, they walked everywhere with [fragrances and nose-coverings], for the whole atmosphere seemed to them tainted with the stench of dead bodies, arising partly from the distemper itself, and partly from the fermenting of the medicines within them. Others with less humanity, but . . . with more security from danger, decided that the only remedy for the pestilence was to avoid it: persuaded, therefore, of this, and taking care for themselves only, men and women in great numbers left the city, their houses, relations, and effects, and fled into the country; as if the wrath of God had been restrained to visit those only within the walls of the city. . . .

I pass over the little regard that citizens and relations showed to each other; for their terror was such, that a brother even fled from his brother, a wife from her husband, and, what is more uncommon, a parent from his own child. Hence numbers that fell sick could have no help but what the charity of friends, who were very few, or the avarice of servants supplied; and even these were scarce and at extravagant wages, and so little used to the business that they were fit only to reach what was called for, and observe when their employer died; and this desire of getting money often cost them their lives. . . .

It fared no better with the adjacent country, for . . . you might see the poor distressed labourers, with their families, without either the aid of physicians, or help of servants, languishing on the highways, in the fields, and in their own houses, and dying rather like cattle than human creatures. The consequence was that, growing dissolute in their manners like the citizens, and careless of everything, as supposing every day to be their last, their thoughts were not so much employed how to improve, as how to use their substance for their present support.

What can I say more, if I return to the city, unless that such was the cruelty of Heaven, and perhaps of men, that between March and July following, according to authentic reckonings, upwards of a hundred thousand souls perished in the city only; whereas, before that calamity, it was not supposed to have contained so many inhabitants. What magnificent dwellings, what noble palaces were then depopulated to the last inhabitant! What families became extinct! What riches and vast possessions were left, and no known heir to inherit them! What numbers of both sexes, in the prime and vigour of youth . . . breakfasted in the morning with their living friends, and supped at night with their departed friends in the other world!

Question:
1. According to Boccaccio, to what lengths did some people go to avoid the plague?

PART 11
Eurasian Connections before European Expansion

11.1   Mansa Musa: The "King Who Sits on a Mountain of Gold"

Control of the Trans-Saharan trade from the cities of the Sahel to the North African ports was a certain guarantee to enormous wealth. During the medieval period, three great empires: Ghana, Mali, and Song-hay, dominated this traffic in gold, salt, slaves, and ivory. The most fabulous of the West African emperors was Mansa Musa of Mall (1312–1337), whose lavish display and largess while on a his pilgrimmage to Mecca drew international attention. The following description is from Al' Umari, an Arab traveller.

Source: N. Levtzion & J. F. P. Hopkins, eds., *Corpus of Early Arabic Sources for West African History* (Cambridge, England: Cambridge University Press, 1981), pp. 267–272.

The king of this country imports Arab horses and pays high prices for them. His army numbers about 100,000, of whom about 10,000 are cavalry mounted on horses and the remainder infantry without horses or other mounts. They have camels but do not know how to ride them with saddles.

Barley is quite lacking; it does not grow there at all.

The emirs and soldiers of this king have fiefs (*iqtā'at*) and benefices (*in'āmāt*). Among their chiefs are some whose wealth derived from the king reaches 50,000 mithqāls of gold every year, besides which he keeps them in horses and clothes. His whole ambition is to give them fine clothes and to make his towns into cities. Nobody may enter the abode of this king save barefooted, whoever he may be. Anyone who does not remove his shoes, inadvertently or purposely, is put to death without mercy. Whenever one of the emirs or another comes into the presence of this king he keeps him standing before him for a time. Then the newcomer makes a gesture with his right hand like one who beats the drum of honour (*jūk*) in the lands of Tūrān and Irān. If the king bestows a favour upon a person or makes him a fair promise or thanks him for some deed the person who has received the favour grovels before him from one end of the room to the other. When he reaches there the slaves of the recipient of the favour or some of his friends take some of the ashes which are always kept ready at the far end of the king's audience chamber for the purpose and scatter it over the head of the favoured one, who then returns grovelling until he arrives before the king. Then he makes the drumming gesture as before and rises.

As for this gesture likened to beating the *jūk*, it is like this. The man raises his right hand to near his ear. There he places it, it being held up straight, and places it in contact with his left hand upon his thigh. The left hand has the palm extended so as to receive the right elbow. The right hand too has the palm extended with the fingers held close beside each other like a comb and touching the lobe of the ear.

The people of this kingdom ride with Arab saddles and in respect of most features of their horsemanship resemble the Arabs, but they mount their horses with the right foot, contrary to everybody else.

It is their custom not to bury their dead unless they be people of rank and status. Otherwise those without rank and the poor and strangers are thrown into the bush like other dead creatures.

It is a country where provisions go bad quickly, especially [clarified] butter (*samn*), which is rotten and stinks after two days. This is not to be wondered at, for their sheep go scavenging over the garbage heaps and the country is very hot, which hastens decomposition.

When the king of this kingdom comes in from a journey a parasol (*jitr*) and a standard are held over his head as he rides, and drums are beaten and guitars (*tunbūr*) and trumpets well made of horn are played in front of him. And it is a custom of theirs that when one whom the king has charged with a task or assignment returns to him he questions him in detail about everything which has happened to him from the moment of his departure until his return. Complaints and appeals against administrative oppression (*mazālim*) are placed before this king and he delivers judgement on them himself. As a rule nothing is written down; his commands are given verbally. He has judges, scribes, and government offices (*dīwān*). This is what al-Dukkālī related to me.

The emir Abū 'l-Hasan 'Alī b. Amīr Hājib told me that he was often in the company of sultan Mūsā the king of this country when he came to Egypt on the Pilgrimage. He was staying in [the] Qarāfa [district of Cairo] and Ibn Amīr Hājib was governor of Old Cairo and Qarāta at that time. A friendship grew up between them and this sultan Mūsā told him a great deal about himself and his country and the people of the Sūdān who were his neighbours. One of the things which he told him was that his country was very extensive and contiguous with the Ocean. By his sword and his armies he had conquered 24 cities each with its surrounding district with villages and estates. It is a country rich in livestock—cattle, sheep, goats, horses, mules—and different kinds of poultry—geese, doves, chickens. The inhabitants of his country are numerous, a vast concourse, but compared with the peoples of the Sūdān who are their neighbours and penetrate far to the south they are like a white birthmark on a black cow. He has a truce with the gold-plant people, who pay him tribute.

Ibn Amīr Hājib said that he asked him about the gold-plant, and he said: "It is found in two forms. One is found in the spring and blossoms after the rains in open country (*sahārā*). It has leaves like the *najīl* grass and its roots are gold (*tibr*). The other kind is found all the year round at known sites on the banks of the Nīl and is dug up. There are holes there and roots of gold are found like stones or gravel and gathered up. Both kinds are known as *tibr* but the first is of superior fineness (*afhal fī 'l-'iyār*) and worth more." Sultan Mūsā told ibn āmir Hājib that gold was his prerogative and he collected the crop as a tribute except for what the people of that country took by theft.

But what al-Dukkālī says is that in fact he is given only a part of it as a present by way of gaining his favour, and he makes a profit on the sale of it, for they have none in their country; and what Dukkālī says is more reliable.

Ibn Amīr Hājib said also that the blazon (*shi'ār*) of this king is yellow on a red ground. Standards ('alam) are unfurled over him wherever he rides on horseback; they are very big flags (liwā'). The ceremonial for him who presents himself to the king or who receives a favour is that he bares the front of his head and makes the *jūk*-beating gesture towards the ground with his right hand as the Tatars do; if a more profound obeisance is required he grovels before the king. "I have seen this (says Ibn Amīr Hājib) with my own eyes." A custom of this sultan is that he does not eat in the presence of anybody, be he who he may, but eats always alone. And it is a custom of his people that if one of them should have reared a beautiful daughter he offers her to the king as a concubine (*ama mawtū' a*) and he possesses her without a marriage ceremony as slaves are possessed, and this in spite of the fact that Islam has triumphed among them and that they follow the Malikite school and that this sultan Mūsā was pious and assiduous in prayer, Koran reading, and mentioning God [*dhikr*].

"I said to him (said Ibn Amīr Hājib) that this was not permissible for a Muslim, whether in law (*shar'*) or reason ('aql), and he said: 'Not even for kings?' and I replied: 'No! not even for kings! Ask the scholars!' He said: 'By God, I did not know that. I hereby leave it and abandon it utterly!'

"I saw that this sultan Mūsā loved virtue and people of virtue. He left his kingdom and appointed as his deputy there his son Muhammad and emigrated to God and His Messenger. He accomplished the obligations of the Pilgrimage, visited [the tomb of] the Prophet [at Medina] (God's blessing and peace be upon him!) and returned to his country with the intention of handing over his sovereignty to his son and abandoning it entirely to him and returning to Mecca the Venerated to remain there as a dweller near the sanctuary (*mujāwir*); but death overtook him, may God (who is great) have mercy upon him.

"I asked him if he had enemies with whom he fought wars and he said: 'Yes, we have a violent enemy who is to the Sūdān as the Tatars are to you. They have an analogy with the Tatars in various respects. They are wide in the face and flat-nosed. They shoot well with [bow and] arrows (*nushshāb*). Their horses are cross-bred (*kadīsh*) with slit noses. Battles take place between us and they are formidable because of their accurate shooting. War between us has its ups and downs.'"

(Ibn Sa'īd, in the Mughrib, mentions the Damādim tribe who burst upon various peoples of the Sūdān and destroyed their countries and who resemble the Tatars. The two groups appeared upon the scene at the same moment.)

Ibn Amīr Hājib continued: "I asked sultan Mūsā how the kingdom fell to him, and he said: 'We belong to a house which hands on the kingship by inheritance. The king who was my predecessor~ did not believe that it was impossible to discover the furthest limit of the Atlantic Ocean and wished vehemently to do so. So he equipped 200 ships filled with men and the same number equipped with gold, water, and provisions enough to last them for years, and said to the man deputed to lead them: "Do no return until you reach the end of it or your provisions and water give out." They departed and a long time passed before anyone came back. Then one ship returned and we asked the captain what news they brought. He said: "Yes, O Sultan, we travelled for a long time until there appeared in the open sea [as it were] a river with a powerful current. Mine was the last of those ships. The [other] ships went on ahead but when they reached that place they did not return and no more was seen of them and we do not know what became of them. As for me, I went about at once and did not enter that river." But the sultan disbelieved him.

"'Then that sultan got ready 2,000 ships, 1,000 for himself and the men whom he took with him and 1,000 for water and provisions. He left me to deputize for him and embarked on the Atlantic Ocean with his men. That was the last we saw of him and all those who were with him, and so I became king in my own right.'

"This sultan Mūsā, during his stay in Egypt both before and after his journey to the Noble Hijāz, maintained a uniform attitude of worship and turning towards God. It was as though he were standing before Him because of His continual presence in his mind. He and all those with him behaved in the same manner and were well-dressed, grave, and dignified. He was noble and generous and performed many acts of charity and kindness. He had left his country with 100 loads of gold which he spent during his Pilgrimage on the tribes who lay along his route from his country to Egypt, while he was in Egypt, and again from Egypt to the Noble Hijāz and back. As a consequence he needed to borrow money in Egypt and pledged his credit with the merchants at a very high rate of gain so that they made 700 dinars profit on 300. Later he paid them back amply (?: *bi-'l-rājih*). He sent to me 500 mithqals of gold by way of honorarium.

"The currency in the land of Takrūr consists of cowries and the merchants, whose principal import these are, make big profits on them." Here ends what Ibn Amīr Hājib said.

From the beginning of my coming to stay in Egypt I heard talk of the arrival of this sultan Mūsā on his Pilgrimage and found the Cairenes eager to recount what they had seen of the Africans' prodigal spending. I asked the emir Abū 'l-'Abbās Ahmad b. al-Hāk the *mihmandar* and he told me of the opulence, manly virtues, and piety of this sultan. "When I went out to meet him (he said), that is, on behalf of the mighty sultan al-Malik al-Nāsir, he did me extreme honour and treated me with the greatest courtesy. He addressed me, however, only through an interpreter despite his perfect ability to speak in the Arabic tongue. Then he forwarded to the royal treasury many loads of unworked native gold and other valuables. I tried to persuade him to go up to the Citadel to meet the sultan, but he refused persistently, saying: 'I came for the Pilgrimage and nothing else. I do not wish to mix anything else with my Pilgrimage.' He had begun to use this argument but I realized that the audience was repugnant to him because he would be obliged to kiss the ground and the sultan's hand. I continued to cajole him and he continued to make excuses but the sultan's protocol demanded that I should bring him into the royal presence, so I kept on at him till he agreed.

"When we came in the sultan's presence we said to him: 'Kiss the ground!' but he refused outright saying: 'How may this be?' Then an intelligent man who was with him whispered to him something we could not understand and he said: 'I make obeisance to God who created me!' then he prostrated himself and went forward to the sultan. The sultan half rose to greet him and sat him by his side. They conversed together for a long time, then sultan Mūsā went out. The sultan sent to him several complete suits of honour for himself, his courtiers, and all those who had come with him, and saddled and bridled horses for himself and his chief courtiers. His robe of honour consisted of an Alexandrian open-fronted cloak (*muftaraj*) embellished with tard wahsh cloth containing much gold thread and miniver fur, bordered with beaver fur and embroidered with metallic thread, along with golden fastenings, a silken skull-cap with caliphal emblems, a gold-inlaid belt, a damascened sword, a kerchief [embroidered] with pure gold, standards, and two horses saddled and bridled and equipped with decorated mule[-type] saddles. He also furnished him with accommodation and abundant supplies during his stay.

"When the time to leave for the Pilgrimage came round the sultan sent to him a large sum of money with ordinary and thoroughbred camels complete with saddles and equipment to serve as mounts for him, and purchased abundant supplies for his entourage and others who had come with him. He arranged for deposits of fodder to be placed along the road and ordered the caravan commanders to treat him with honour and respect.

"On his return I received him and supervised his accommodation. The sultan continued to supply him with provisions and lodgings and he sent gifts from the Noble Hijāz to the sultan as a blessing. The sultan accepted them and sent in exchange complete suits of honour for him and his courtiers together with other gifts, various kinds of Alexandrian cloth, and other precious objects. Then he returned to his country.

"This man flooded Cairo with his benefactions. He left no court amIr (*amir muqarrab*) nor holder of a royal office without the gift of a load of gold. The Cairenes made incalculable profits out of him and his suite in buying and selling and giving and taking. They exchanged gold until they depressed its value in Egypt and caused its price to fall."

The *mihmandAr* spoke the truth, for more than one has told this story. When the *mihmandār* died the' tax office (*dīwān*) found among the property which he left thousands of dinars' worth of native gold (al-dhahab al-ma'dini) which he had given to him, still just as it had been in the earth (*fī turābih*), never having been worked.

Merchants of Misr and Cairo have told me of the profits which they made from the Africans, saying that one of them might buy a shirt or cloak (*thawb*) or robe (*izār*) or other garment for five dinars when it was not worth one. Such was their simplicity and trustfulness that it was possible to practice any deception on them. They greeted anything that was said to them with credulous acceptance. But later they formed the very poorest opinion of the Egyptians because of the obvious falseness of everything they said to them and their outrageous behaviour in fixing the prices of the provisions and other goods which were sold to them, so much so that were they to encounter today the most learned doctor of religious science and he were to say that he was Egyptian they would be rude to him and view him with disfavour because of the ill treatment which they had experienced at their hands.

Muhanna' b. 'Abd al-Bāqī al-'Ujrumī the guide informed me that he accompanied sultan Mūsā when he made the Pilgrimage and that the sultan was very open-handed towards the pilgrims and the inhabitants of the Holy Places. He and his companions maintained great pomp and dressed magnificently during the journey. He gave away much wealth in alms. "About 200 mithqals of gold fell to me" said Muhanna' "and he gave other sums to my companions."' Muhanna' waxed eloquent in describing the sultan's generosity, magnanimity, and opulence.

Gold was at a high price in Egypt until they came in that year. The mithqal did not go below 25 *dirharns* and was generally above, but from that time its value fell and it cheapened in price and has remained cheap till now. The mithqal does not exceed 22 *dirhams* or less. This has been the state of affairs for about twelve years until this day~ by reason of the large amount of gold which they brought into Egypt and spent there.

A letter came from this sultan to the court of the sultan in Cairo. It was written in the MaghribI style of handwriting on paper with wide lines. In it he follows his own rules of composition although observing the demands of propriety (*yumsik fī h nāmūsan li-nafsih ma'a murā'āt qawānī n al-adab*). It was written by the hand of one of his courtiers who had come on the Pilgrimage. Its contents comprised greetings and a recommendation for the bearer. With it he sent 5,000 mithqals of gold by way of a gift.

The countries of Mālī and Ghāna and their neighbours are reached from the west side of Upper Egypt. The route passes by way of the Oases (*Wāhāt*) through desert country inhabited by Arab and then Berber communities (*tawā'if*) until cultivated country is reached by way of which the traveller arrives at Mālī and Ghāna. These are on the same meridian as the mountains of the Berbers to the south of Marrakech and are joined to them by long stretches of wilderness and extensive desolate deserts.

The learned faqih Abi 'l-Rūb 'lsā al-Zawāwī informed me that sultan Mūsā Mansā told him that the length of his kingdom was about a year's journey, and Ibn Amīr Hājib told me the same. Aī-Dukkālī's version, already mentioned, is that it is four months' journey long by the same in breadth. What al-Dukkālī says is more to be relied on, for Mūsā Mansā possibly exaggerated the importance of his realm.

Al-Zāwāwi also said: "This sultan Mūsā told me that at a town called ZKRY he has a copper mine from which ingots are brought to BYTY. "There is nothing in my kingdom (he said) on which a duty is levied (*shay' mumakkas*) except this crude copper which is brought in. Duty is collected on this and on nothing else. We send it to the land of the pagan Sūdān and sell it for two-thirds of its weight in gold, so that we sell 100 mithqals of this copper for 66⅔ mithqals of gold." He also stated that there are pagan nations (*umam*) in his kingdom from whom he does not collect the tribute (*jizya*) but whom he simply employs in extracting the gold from its deposits. The gold is extracted by digging pits about a man's height in depth and the gold is found embedded in the sides of the pits or sometimes collected at the bottom of them.

The king of this country wages a permanently Holy War on the pagans of the Sūdān who are his neighhours. They are more numerous than could ever be counted.

Questions:
1. What light does Al' Umari's account shed on the Malian army? On the treatment of the corpses of the dead?
2. In what way was Musa's conduct found to be contrary to Muslim law, and how did the Emperor react upon being informed of this?
3. According to Musa, what happened to his predecessor, and under what circumstances did Musa himself come to the throne?
4. What economic and/or other effects did Musa's pilgrimmage have in Egypt?

11.2 The Cities of the Zanj and The Indian Ocean Trade

The Indian Ocean was, long before the Atlantic was opened by European navigators, one of the world's major maritime commercial arteries. The east coast of Africa was a prime component of this trade, and ships from Egypt, Arabia, India, and as far afield as China plied their way to the Swahili Cities of the Zanj (Africans). These cities, chief among them: Kilwa; Mogadishu; Mombasa; Tanga; Malindi; Sofala, and Zanzibar, developed the language from whose name they are collectively known (Swahili was originally concieved as a commercial language). The cities were known to travellers of varied backgrounds, as evidenced in the following selections.

Source: G. S. P. Freeman-Grenvillem, *The East African Coast: Selected Documents from the 1st to the 19th Century* (London: Rex Collins, 1975), pp. 19–24.

AL-IDRISI: THE FIRST WESTERN NOTICE OF EAST AFRICA

The Zanj of the East African coast have no ships to voyage in, but use vessels from Oman and other. countries which sail to the islands of Zanj which depend on the Indies. These foreigners sell their goods there, and buy the produce of the country. The people of the Djawaga islands go to Zanzibar in large and small ships, and use them for trading their goods, for they understand each others' language. Opposite the Zanj coasts are the Djawaga islands; they are numerous and vast; their inhabitants are very dark in colour, and everything that is cultivated there, fruit, sorghum, sugar-cane and camphor trees, is black in colour. Among the number of the islands is Sribuza, which is said to be 1,200 miles round; and pearl fisheries and various kinds of aromatic plants and perfumes are to be found there, which attract the merchants.

Among the islands of Djawaga included in the present section is Andjuba [Anjouan-Johanna], whose principal town is called Unguja in the language of Zanzibar, and whose people, although mixed, are actually mostly Muslims. The distance from it to Banas on the Zanj coast is 100 miles. The island is 400 miles round; bananas are the chief food. There are five kinds, as follows: the bananas called kundi; fill whose weight is sometimes twelve ounces; omani, muriani, sukari. It is a healthy, sweet, and pleasant food. The island is traversed by a mountain called Wabra. The vagabonds who are expelled from the town flee there, and form a brave and numerous company which frequently infests the surroundings of the town, and which lives at the top of the mountain in a state of defence against the ruler of the island. They are courageous, and feared for their arms and their number. The island is very populous; there are many villages and cattle. They grow rice. There is a great trade in it, and each year various products and goods are brought for exchange and consumption.

From Medouna [on the Somali coast] to Malindi, a town of the Zanj, one follows the coast for three days and three nights by sea. Malindi lies on the shore, at the mouth of a river of sweet water. It is a large town, whose people engage in hunting and fishing. On land they hunt the tiger [*sic*] and other wild beasts. They obtain various kinds of fish from the sea, which they cure and sell.

They own and exploit iron mines; for them iron is an article of trade and the source of their largest profits. They pretend to know how to bewitch the most poisonous snakes so as to make them harmless to everyone except those for whom they wish evil or on whom they wish to take vengeance. They also pretend that by means of these enchantments the tigers and lions cannot hurt them. These wizards are called *al-Musnafu* in the language of the people.

It is two days' journey along the coast to Mombasa. This is a small place and a dependency of the Zanj. Its inhabitants work in the iron mines and hunt tigers. They have red coloured dogs which fight every kind of wild beast and even lions. This town lies on the sea shore near a large gulf up which ships travel two days' journey; its banks are uninhabited because of the wild beasts that live in the forests where the Zanj go and hunt, as we have already said. In this town lives the King of Zanzibar. His guards go on foot because they have no mounts: horses cannot live there.

CHAO JU-KUA: ZANZIBAR AND SOMALIA IN THE THIRTEENTH CENTURY

Zanguebar (Ts'ong-Pa)

The Ts'ong-pa country is an island of the sea south of Hu-ch'a-la. To the west it reaches a great mountain. The inhabitants are of Ta-shi [Arab] stock and follow the Ta-shi religion. They wrap themselves in blue foreign cotton stuffs and wear red leather shoes. Their daily food consists of meal, baked cakes and mutton.

There are many villages, and a succession of wooded hills and terraced rocks. The climate is warm, and there is no cold season. The products of the country consist of elephants' tusks, native gold, amber-gris and yellow sandal-wood.

Every year Hu-ch'a-la and the Ta-shi localities along the sea-coast send ships to this country with white cotton cloth, porcelain, copper and red cotton to trade.

BERBERA COAST (PI-P'A-LO)

The country of Pi-p'a-lo contains four cities; the other places are all villages which are constantly at feud and fighting with each other. The inhabitants pray to Heaven and not to the Buddha. The land produces many camels and sheep, and the people feed themselves with the flesh and milk of camels and with baked cakes.

The other products are ambergris, big elephants' tusks and big rhinoceros' horns. There are elephants' tusks which weigh over 100 carries and rhinoceros' horns of over ten catties weight. The land is also rich in putchuk, liquid storax gum, myrrh, and tortoise-shell of extraordinary thickness, for which there is great demand in other countries. The country also brings forth the so-called 'camel-crane' [ostrich], which measures from the ground to its crown from six to seven feet. It has wings and can fly, but not to any great height.

There is also in this country a wild animal called tsu-la [giraffe]; it resembles a camel in shape, an ox in size, and is of a yellow colour. Its fore legs are five feet long, its hind legs only three feet. Its head is high up and turned upwards. Its skin is an inch thick.

There is also in this country a kind of mule [zebra] with brown, white, and black stripes around its body. These animals wander about in mountain wilds; they are a variety of camel. The inhabitants of this country, who are great huntsman, hunt these animals with poisoned arrows.

ABU-AL-FIDA: MALINDI, MOMBASA, AND SOFALA

Malindi is a town of the land of the Zanj, 81⅒° long., 2° 50' lat. West of the town is a great gulf into which flows a river which comes down from the mountain of Komr. On the banks of this gulf are very large dwellings belonging to the Zanj; the houses of the people of Komr are on the south side. East of Malindi is al-Kerany, the name of a mountain very famous among travellers; this runs out into the sea for a distance of about 100 miles in a north-east direction; at the same time it extends along the continent in a straight line north for a distance of about fifty miles. Among other things which we might say about this mountain are the iron mine which is on the continental side and the lodestone in the part which is in the sea, which attracts iron.

At Malindi is the tree of zendj (the ginger tree) (or at Mallndi there are many Zanjian sorcerers). The King of the Zanj lives at Malindi. Between Mombasa and Mnllndi is about a degree. Mombasa is on the coast. On the west is a gulf along which buildings stand as far as 300 miles. Nearby to the east is the desert which separates the land of the Zanj from Sofaia.

Among the towns of the country of Sofala is Batyna (*or* Banyna). It is situated at the end of a great gulf, away from the equinoctial line, under 2½° lat., 87° long. According to Ibn Said, on the West of Batyna is Adjued, the name of a mountain which projects into the sea towards the north-east for a distance of 100 miles. The waves of the sea make a great noise here. The people of Sofala live to the east of this mountain: their capital is Seruna, under 99° long., 2½° lat. [south]. The town is built on a large estuary where a river, which rises in the mountain of Komr, flows out. There the King of Sofala resides.

Then one arrives at the town of Leirana. Ibn Fathuma, who visited the town, said that it was a seaport where ships put in and whence they set out. The inhabitants profess Islam. Leirana is on long. 102°, lat. 0° 30' [south]. It is on a great gulf.

The town of Daghuta is the last one of the country of Sofala and the furthest of the inhabited part of the continent towards the south. It is on long. 109°, lat. 12°, south of the equator.

Sofala. According to the Canon it is on 50° 3' long., 2° lat., south of the equator. Sofala is in the land of the Zanj. According to the author of the Canon, the inhabitants are Muslims. Ibn Said says that their chief means of existence are mining gold and iron, and that they dress in leopard skins. According to Masudi, horses do not reproduce in the land of the Zanj, so that the warriors go on foot or fight from the backs of oxen.

Questions:
1. Do the three accounts agree on any one (or more) points? Explain.
2. How do the three accounts shed light on the religious life of the Eastern Africans?
3. What are the chief products for trade and consumption?

11.3 Ibn Battuta in Mali

Born in Algiers, Ibn Battuta (1304–1368) was the premier world traveler of the Middle Ages. Although Marco Polo's adventures are better known in the West, never did Polo travel as far or see as many different countries as this indefatigable Berber did. In 1325, Ibn Battuta made the first of four visits to the Holy City of Mecca, thereby beginning an itinerary of 75,000 miles. Later in life, this devout Muslim would dictate to a Moroccan scribe an account of his journeys.

For nearly thirty years, Ibn Battuta traveled continuously throughout Africa, the Middle East, Persia, Russia, India, China, and Spain. He made it a rule, if possible, never to travel the same road twice, and he frequently paid the price of taking the less-traveled road. He often was stranded or overcome by disease. His African editors note: "He seems to have experienced most travellers' diseases from Lahore sore to Delhi belly. Only the fact that the New World had not been discovered saved him from Montezuma's revenge."[1]

The following selection illustrates the range of Ibn Battuta's travels and also suggests that, by the fourteenth century, Islamic civilization, spanning four continents, was truly the "world" civilization. In 1344, Ibn Battuta left the Malabar coast of India and sailed south to the Maldive Islands, where for eighteen months he served as a judge of Islamic sacred law.

Later, after journeys to Ceylon, China, and Syria, he returned to Algiers. In 1352, on his last journey, he set off on foot across the Sahara to visit the African kingdoms of the Niger basin. His account of this experience is one of the primary records of the social customs in the Kingdom of Mali, particularly the city of Iwalatan (Walata).

In reporting on Black Africa, Ibn Battuta's accounts are basically favorable, but his enthusiasm over the devout acceptance of Islam is offset by reservations about non-Islamic elements in living customs.

> **Source:** From *Ibn Battuta, Voyages D'Ibn Batoutah,* trans. from the Arabic by C. Defrémery and B.R. Sanguinétti (Paris: Imprimerie Impériale, 1858), IV, 387–90, 421–24. Trans. Philip F. Riley.

The condition of these people [of Iwalatan] is strange and their manners are bizarre. As for their men, there is no sexual jealousy about them. None of them is named after his father, but each traces his genealogy from his maternal uncle. A man's inheritance is not passed to his own sons but to the sons of his sister. I have never seen such a thing in any other part of the world except among the infidels who live on the Malabar coast of India. These people are Muslims who follow exactly the prescribed laws for prayer, study the laws of Islam, and know the Koran by heart. Their women are not modest in the presence of men; despite reciting their prayers punctually, they do not veil their faces. Any male who wishes to marry one of them can do so very easily, but the women do not travel with their husbands for her family would not allow it. In this country, the women are permitted to have male friends and companions among men who are not members of her family. So too for men; they are permitted to have female companions among women who are not members of his family. It happens quite often that a man would enter his own house and find his wife with one of her own friends and would not rebuke her.

ANECDOTE

One day I entered the home of a judge in Iwalatan after he had given his permission, and I found him with a very young and beautiful woman. Immediately I thought it best to leave, but she laughed at me and was not at all embarrassed. The judge asked me "Why would you want to leave? She is my friend." I was astonished at the conduct of these two. He was a judge and had made a pilgrimage to Mecca. Later I learned that he has asked permission of the Sultan to go on a pilgrimage to Mecca that year with his female friend. Whether it was this one or another I do not know, but the Sultan refused to let him go.

A SIMILAR ANECDOTE

One day I entered the home of Aboû Mohammed Yandecán, a man of the Mesoûfah tribe. He was sitting on a rug while in the middle of his house was a bed covered with a canopy. On it was his wife in conversation with another man sitting at her side. I said to Aboû Mohammed "Who is this woman?"—"She is my wife," he responded—"And who is the man with her?" I asked. "He is her friend," replied the judge. I asked how he, who knew the divine law on such matters, could permit such a thing. He replied that "The companionship of women with men in this country is proper and honorable: It does not inspire suspicion. Our women are not like the women of your country." I was shocked at his stupid answer and immediately left his home and never returned. . . .

GOOD AND BAD QUALITIES

Among their good qualities we can cite the following:
1. There is a small amount of crime, for these people obey the law. Their sultan does not pardon criminals.
2. Travelers and natives alike are safe from brigands, robbers, and thieves.
3. The natives do not confiscate the property of white men who die in this country, even if they are very wealthy; instead they entrust it to another, respected white man to dispose of it properly.
4. The prayers are offered punctually and with fervor. Children who neglect their prayers are beaten. If you do not come to the mosque early on a Friday you cannot find a place to pray because the crowds are so large. Quite often they send their slaves to the mosque with a prayer rug to find and hold a place for their masters. These prayer rugs are made from the leaves of trees similar to palm trees, but one that bears no fruit.
5. White garments are worn on Fridays. If by chance one does not have a proper white garment, regular clothing is washed and cleaned to wear for public prayer.
6. They are committed to learn by heart the sublime Koran. Children who fail to learn the Koran by heart have their feet shackled and these shackles are not removed until they memorize the Koran. On a feast day I visited a judge who had his children in chains. I said to him, "Why don't you release them?" He said,"I will not do so until they know the Koran by heart." Another day I passed a handsome young black man dressed superbly, but shackled by a heavy chain on his feet. I asked my companion, "What has this young man done? Is he a murderer?" The handsome young black man laughed and my companion told me, "He has been chained so that he will learn the Koran by heart."

Among their bad qualities we can cite the following:
1. Their female servants, slave women and small daughters appear before men completely naked, exposing their private parts. Even during the month of Ramadan [a period of fast], military commanders broke their fast in the palace of the Sultan. Twenty or more naked servant girls served them food.
2. Nude women without veils on their faces enter the palace of the Sultan. On the twenty-seventh night of Ramadan, I saw about a hundred naked female slaves coming out of the palace of the Sultan with food. Two of the Sultan's daughters, who have large breasts, were with them and they were naked.
3. These natives put dust and ashes on their head to show their education and as a sign of respect.

4. They laugh when poets recite their verse before the Sultan.

5. Finally, they eat impure meat such as dogs and donkeys.

Questions:
1. Why was Ibn Battuta so troubled by his African hosts' methods of tracing genealogy? Are there political implications of this genealogical system?
2. How would you compare Ibn Battuta's observations of Africa with those of Gomes Eannes de Azurara?

11.4   The Mongol Khan's Ultimatum to the Nations of Europe

Contact between the Mongol Empire of Genghis Khan and his successors and Western Europeans was slight, although detachments of the Mongol forces had stationed themselves in Russia at the doorstep of Eastern European states and had gone so far as to raid and devastate parts of Poland and Hungary. These Tartars (as the Mongols were often called) would maintain a lengthy presence in Russia under the designation of "The Golden Horde." From time to time popes would dispatch emissaries with letters to the Khan. That the Khan was not particularly impressed is made clear in his imperious reply.

> **Source:** Christopher Dawson, ed., *Mission to Asia* (Toronto: University of Toronto Press, for the Medieval Academy of America, 1980), pp. 83–84. (First published by Sheed & Ward, London, 1955, as *The Mongol Mission;* reprinted by Harper & Row 1966).

The Strength of God, the Emperor of all men, to the Great Pope, Authentic and True Letters

Having taken counsel for making peace with us, You Pope and all Christians have sent an envoy to us, as we have heard from him and as your letters declare. Wherefore, if you wish to have peace with us, You Pope and all kings and potentates, in no way delay to come to me to make terms of peace and then you shall hear alike our answer and our will. The contents of your letters stated that we ought to be baptized and become Christians. To this we answer briefly that we do not understand in what way we ought to do this. To the rest of the contents of your letters, viz: that you wonder at so great a slaughter of men, especially of Christians and in particular Poles, Moravians and Hungarians, we reply likewise that this also we do not understand. However, lest we may seem to pass it over in silence altogether, we give you this for our answer.

Because they did not obey the word of God and the command of Chingis Chan and the Chan, but took council to slay our envoys, therefore God ordered us to destroy them and gave them up into our hands. For otherwise if God had not done this, what could man do to man? But you men of the West believe that you alone are Christians and despise others. But how can you know to whom God deigns to confer His grace? But we worshipping God have destroyed the whole earth from the East to the West in the power of God. And if this were not the power of God, what could men have done? Therefore if you accept peace and are willing to surrender your fortresses to us, You Pope and Christian princes, in no way delay coming to me to conclude peace and then we shall know that you wish to have peace with us. But if you should not believe our letters and the command of God nor hearken to our counsel then we shall know for certain that you wish to have war. After that we do not know what will happen, God alone knows.

Chingis Chan, first Emperor, second Ochoday Chan, third Cuiuch Chan.

Questions:
1. What is the Khan's response to requests that he be baptized?
2. How does the Khan justify the slaying and seizure of the land of Eastern European Christians?
3. What is the letter's general tone? What does the Khan command and what consequences does he state could arise from noncompliance?

11.5   William of Rubruck: Impressions of The Medieval Mongols

One of the mere handful of Europeans who did willingly take the trek into the Mongolian ("Tartar") heartland was the monk, William of Rubruck. William was dispatched on a diplomatic Church mission to see the Great Khan Mongke (1251–1259), grandson of Ghengis Khan. Though this attempt proved to be just as fruitless as similar expeditons from the diplomatic and religious points of view, William's descriptions of the Mongol peoples and their culture has proven to be an invaluable resource for scholars of this period.

Source: Christopher Dawson, ed., *Mission to Asia* (Toronto: University of Toronto Press, for the Medieval Academy of America, 1980), pp. 93-104. (First published by Sheed & Ward, London, 1955 as The Mongol Mission; reprinted by Harper & Row, 1966.)

THE TARTARS AND THEIR DWELLINGS

THE Tartars have no abiding city nor do they know of the one that is to come. They have divided among themselves Scythia, which stretches from the Danube as far as the rising of the sun. Each captain, according to whether he has more or fewer men under him, knows the limits of his pasturage and where to feed his flocks in winter, summer, spring and autumn, for in winter they come down to the warmer districts in the south, in summer they go up to the cooler ones in the north. They drive their cattle to graze on the pasture lands without water in winter when there is snow there, for the snow provides them with water.

The dwelling in which they sleep has as its base a circle of interlaced sticks, and it is made of the same material; these sticks converge into a little circle at the top and from this a neck juts up like a chimney; they cover it with white felt and quite often they also coat the felt with lime or white clay and powdered bone to make it a more gleaming white, and sometimes they make it black. The felt round the neck at the top they decorate with lovely and varied paintings. Before the doorway they also hang felt worked in multicoloured designs; they sew coloured felt on to the other, making vines and trees, birds and animals. They make these houses so large that sometimes they are thirty feet across; for I myself once measured the width between the wheel tracks of a cart, and it was twenty feet, and when the house was on the cart it stuck out at least five feet beyond the wheels on each side. I have counted to one cart twenty-two oxen drawing one house, eleven in a row across the width of the cart, and the other eleven in front of them. The axle of the cart was as big as the mast of a ship, and a man stood at the door of the house on the cart, driving the oxen.

In addition they make squares to the size of a large coffer out of slender split twigs; then over it, from one end to the other, they build up a rounded roof out of similar twigs and they make a little entrance at the front end; after that they cover this box or little house with black felt soaked in tallow or ewes' milk so that it is rain-proof, and this they decorate in the same way with multi-coloured handwork. Into these chests they put all their bedding and valuables; they bind them onto high carts which are drawn by camels so that they can cross rivers. These chests are never removed from the carts. When they take down their dwelling houses, they always put the door facing the south; then afterwards they draw up the carts with the chests on each side, half a stone's throw from the house, so that it stands between two rows of carts, as it were between two walls.

The married women make for themselves really beautiful carts which I would not know how to describe for you except by a picture; in fact I would have done you paintings of everything if I only knew how to paint. A wealthy Mongol or Tartar may well have a hundred or two hundred such carts with chests. Baatu has twenty-six wives and each of these has a large house, not counting the other small ones which are placed behind the large one and which are, as it were, chambers in which their attendants live; belonging to each of these houses are a good two hundred carts. When they pitch their houses the chief wife places her dwelling at the extreme west end and after her the others according to their rank, so that the last wife will be at the far east end, and there will bc the space of a stone's throw between the establishment of one wife and that of another. And so the orda of a rich Mongol will look like a large town and yet there will be very few men in it.

One woman will drive twenty or thirty carts, for the country is flat. They tie together the carts, which are drawn by oxen or camels, one after the other, and the woman will sit on the front one driving the ox while all the others follow in step. If they happen to come on a bad bit of track they loose them and lead them across it one by one. They go at a very slow pace, as a sheep or an ox might walk.

When they have pitched their houses with the door facing south, they arrange the master's couch at the northern end. The women's place is always on the east side, that is, on the left of the master of the house when he is sitting on his couch looking towards the south; the men's place is on the west side, that is, to his right.

On entering a house the men would by no means hang up their quiver in the women's section. Over the head of the master there is always an idol like a doll or little image of felt which they call the master's brother, and a similar one over the head of the mistress, and this they call the mistress's brother; they are fastened on to the wall. Higher up between these two is a thin little one which is, as it were, the guardian of the whole house. The mistress of the house places on her right side, at the foot of the couch, in a prominent position, a goat-skin stuffed with wool or other material, and next to it a tiny image turned towards her attendants and the women. By the entrance on the women's side is still another idol with a cow's udder for the women who milk the cows, for this is the women's job. On the other side of the door towards the men is another image with a mare's udder for the men who milk the mares.

When they have foregathered for a drink they first sprinkle with the drink the idol over the master's head, then all the other idols in turn; after this an attendant goes out of the house with a cup and some drinks; he sprinkles thrice towards the south, genuflecting each time; this is in honour of fire; next towards the east in honour of the air, and after that to the west in honour of water; they cast it to the north for the dead. When the master is holding his cup in his hand and is about to drink, before he does so he first pours some out on the earth as its share. If he drinks while seated on a horse, before he drinks he pours some over the neck or mane of the horse. And so when the attendant has sprinkled towards the four quarters of the earth he returns into the house; two servants with two cups and as many plates are ready to carry the drink to the master and the wife sitting beside him upon his couch. If he has several wives, she with whom he sleeps at night sits next to him during the day, and on that day all the others have to come to her dwelling to drink, and the court is held there, and the gifts which are presented to the master are placed in the treasury of that wife. Standing in the entrance is a bench with a skin of milk or some other drink and some cups.

In the winter they make an excellent drink from rice, millet, wheat and honey, which is clear like wine. Wine, too, is conveyed to them from distant regions. In the summer they do not bother about anything except cosmos. Cosmos [koumiss] is always to be found inside the house before the entrance door, and near it stands a musician with his instrument. Our lutes and viols I did not see there but many other instruments such as are not known among us. When the master begins to drink, then one of the attendants cries out in a loud voice "Ha!" and the musician strikes his instrument. And when it is a big feast they are holding, they all clap their hands and also dance to the sound of the instrument, the men before the master and the women before the mistress. After the master has drunk, then the attendant cries out as before and the instrument-player breaks off. Then they drink all round, the men and the women, and sometimes vie with each other in drinking in a really disgusting and gluttonous manner.

When they want to incite anyone to drink they seize him by the ears and pull them vigorously to make his gullet open, and they clap and dance in front of him. Likewise when they want to make a great feast and entertainment for anyone, one man takes a full cup and two others stand, one on his right and one on his left, and in this manner the three, singing and dancing, advance right up to him to whom they are to offer the cup, and they sing and dance before him; when he stretches out his hand to take the cup they suddenly leap back, and then they advance again as before; and in this way they make fun of him, drawing back the cup three or four times until he is in a really lively mood and wants it: then they give him the cup and sing and clap their hands and stamp with their feet while he drinks.

THE FOOD OF THE TARTARS

As for their food and victuals I must tell you they eat all dead animals indiscriminately and with so many flocks and herds you can be sure a great many animals do die. However, in the summer as long as they have any cosmos, that is mare's milk, they do not care about any other food. If during that time an ox or a horse happens to die, they dry the flesh by cutting it into thin strips and hanging it in the sun and the wind, and it dries immediately without salt and without any unpleasant smell. Out of the intestines of horses they make sausages which are better than pork sausages and they eat these fresh; the rest of the meat they keep for the winter. From the hide of oxen they make large jars which they dry in a wonderful way in the smoke. From the hind part of horses' hide they make very nice shoes.

They feed fifty or a hundred men with the flesh of a single sheep, for they cut it up in little bits in a dish with salt and water, making no other sauce; then with the point of a knife or a fork especially made for this purpose—like those with which we are accustomed to eat pears and apples cooked in wine—they offer to each of those standing round one or two mouthfuls, according to the number of guests. Before the flesh of the sheep is served, the master first takes what pleases him; and also if he gives anyone a special portion then the one receiving it has to eat it himself and may give it to no one else. But if he cannot eat it all he may take it away with him or give it to his servant, if he is there to keep for him; otherwise he may put it away in his *captargac,* that is, a square bag which they carry to put all such things in: in this they also keep bones when they have not the time to give them a good gnaw, so that later they may gnaw them and no food be wasted.

HOW THEY MAKE COSMOS

COSMOS, that is mare's milk, is made in this way: they stretch along the ground a long rope attached to two stakes stuck into the earth, and at about nine o'clock they tie to this rope the foals of the mares they want to milk. Then the mothers stand near their foals and let themselves be peacefully milked; if any one of them is too restless, then a man takes the foal and, placing it under her, lets it suck a little, and he takes it away again and the milker takes its place.

And so, when they have collected a great quantity of milk, which is as sweet as cow's milk when it is fresh, they pour it into a large skin or bag and they begin churning it with a specially made stick which is as big as a man's head at its lower end, and hollowed out; and when they beat it quickly it begins to bubble like new wine and to turn sour and ferment, and they churn it until they can extract the butter. Then they taste it and when it is fairly pungent they drink it. As long as one is drinking, it bites the tongue like vinegar; when one stops, it leaves on the tongue the taste of milk of almonds and greatly delights the inner man; it even intoxicates those who have not a very good head. It also greatly provokes urine.

For use of the great lords they also make caracosmos, that is black cosmos, in this wise. Mare's milk does not curdle. Now it is a general rule that the milk of any animal, in the stomach of whose young rennet is not found, does not curdle; it is not found in the stomach of a young horse, hence the milk of a mare does not curdle. And so they churn the milk until everything that is solid in it sinks right to the bottom like the lees of wine, and what is pure remains on top and is like whey or white must. The dregs are very white and are given to the slaves and have a most soporific effect. The clear liquid the masters drink and it is certainly a very pleasant drink and really potent.

Baatu has thirty men within a day's journey of his camp, each one of whom provides him every day with such milk from a hundred mares—that is to say, the milk of three thousand mares every day, not counting the other white milk which other men bring. For, just as in Syria the peasants give a third part of their produce, so these men have to bring to the orda of their lords the mare's milk of every third day.

From cow's milk they first extract the butter and this they boil until it is completely boiled down; then they store it in sheep's paunches which they keep for this purpose; they do not put salt into the butter; however it does not go bad owing to the long boiling. They keep it against the winter. The rest of the milk which is left after the butter has been extracted they allow to turn until it is as sour as it can be, and they boil it, and in boiling, it curdles; they dry the curd in the sun and it becomes as hard as iron slag, and this they keep in bags against the winter. During the winter months when there is a scarcity of milk, they put this sour curd, which they call grut, into a skin and pour hot water on top of it and beat it vigorously until it melts in the water, which, as a result, becomes completely sour, and this water they drink instead of milk. They take the greatest care never to drink plain water.

THE ANIMALS THEY EAT, THEIR CLOTHES, AND THEIR HUNTING

THE great lords have villages in the south from which millet and flour are brought to them for the winter; the poor provide for themselves by trading sheep and skins; and the slaves fill their bellies with dirty water and are content with this. They also catch mice, of which many kinds abound there; mice with long tails they do not eat but give to their bards; they eat dormice and all kinds of mice with short tails. There are also many marmots there which they call *sogur* and these congregate in one burrow in the winter, twenty or thirty of them together, and they sleep for six months; these they catch in great quantities.

Also to be found there are comes with a long tail like a cat and having at the tip of the tail black and white hairs. They have many other little animals as well which are good to eat, and they are very clever at knowing the difference. I saw no deer there, I saw few hares, many gazelles; wild asses I saw in great quantifies and these are like mules. I also saw another kind of animal which is called *arcali* and which has a body just like a ram's and horns twisted like a ram's but of such a size that I could scarce lift the two horns with one hand; and they make large cups out of these horns.

They have hawks, gerfalcons and peregrine falcons in great numbers and these they carry on their right hand, and they always put a little thong round the hawk's neck. This thong hangs down the middle of its breast and by it they pull down with the left hand the head and breast of the hawk when they cast it at its prey, so that it is not beaten back by the wind or carried upwards. They procure a large part of their food by the chase.

When they want to hunt wild animals they gather together in a great crowd and surround the district in which they know the animals to be, and gradually they close in until between them they shut in the animals in a circle and then they shoot at them with their arrows.

I will tell you about their garments and their clothing. From Cathay and other countries to the east, and also from Persia and other districts of the south, come cloths of silk and gold and cotton materials which they wear in the summer. From Russia, Moxel, Great Bulgaria and Pascatu, which is Greater Hungarys and Kerkis, which are all districts towards the north, and full of forests, and from many other regions in the north which are subject to them, valuable furs of many kinds are brought for them, such as I have never seen in our part of the world; and these they wear in winter. In the winter they always make at least two fur garments, one with the fur against the body, the other with the fur outside to the wind and snow, and these are usually of the skins of wolves or foxes or monkeys, and when they sitting in their dwelling they have another softer one. The poor make their outer ones of dog and goat.

They also make trousers out of skins. Moreover, the rich line their garments with silk stuffing which is extraordinarily soft and light and warm. The poor line their clothes with cotton material and with the softer wool which they are able to pick out from the coarser. With the coarse they make felt to cover their dwellings and coffers and also for making bedding. Also with wool mixed with a third part horse-hair they make their ropes. From felt they make saddle pads, saddle cloths and rain cloaks, which means they use a great deal of wool. You have seen the men's costume.

HOW THE MEN SHAVE AND THE WOMEN ADORN THEMSELVES

THE men shave a square on the top of their heads and from the front corners of this they continue the shaving in strips along the sides of the head as far as the temples. They also shave their temples and neck to the top of the cervical cavity and their forehead in front to the top of the frontal bone, where they leave a tuft of hair which hangs down as far as the eyebrows. At the sides and the back of the head they leave the hair, which they make into plaits, and these they braid round the head to the ears.

The costume of the girls is no different from that of the men except that it is somewhat longer. But on the day after she is married a woman shaves from the middle of her head to her forehead, and she has a tunic as wide as a nun's cowl, and in every respect wider and longer, and open in front, and this they tie on the right side. Now in this matter the Tartars differ from the Turks, for the Turks tie their tunics on the left, but the Tartars always on the right.

They also have a head-dress which they call *bocca*, which is made out of the bark of a tree or of any other fairly light material which they can find; it is large and circular and as big as two hands can span around, a cubit and more high and square at the top like the capital of a column. This *bocca* they cover with costly silk material, and it is hollow inside, and on the capital in the middle or on the side they put a rod of quills or slender canes, likewise a cubit and more in length; and they decorate this rod at the top with peacock feathers and throughout its length all round with little feathers from the mallard's tail and also with precious stones. The wealthy ladies wear such an ornament on the top of their head and fasten it down firmly with a hood which has a hole in the top for this purpose, and in it they stuff their hair, gathering it up from the back on to the top of the head in a kind of knot and putting over it the *bocca* which they then tie firmly under the chin. So when several ladles ride together and are seen from a distance, they give the appearance of soldiers with helmets on their heads and raised lances; for the *bocca* looks like a helmet and the rod on top like a lance.

All the women sit on their horses like men, astride, and they tie their cowls with a piece of sky-blue silk round the waist, and with another strip they bind their breasts, and they fasten a piece of white stuff below their eyes which hangs down to the breast.

The women are wondrous fat and the less nose they have the more beautiful they are considered. They disfigure themselves hideously by painting their faces. They never lie down on a bed to give birth to their children.

THE DUTIES OF THE WOMEN AND THEIR WORK

IT is the duty of the women to drive the carts, to load the houses on to them and to unload them to milk the cows, to make the butter and *grut*, to dress the skins and to sew them, which they do with thread made out of tendons. They split the tendons into very thin threads and then twist these into one long thread. They also sew shoes and socks and other garments. They never wash their clothes, for they say that that makes God angry and that it would thunder if they hung them out to dry; they even beat those who do wash them and take them away from them. They are extraordinarily afraid of thunder. At such a time they turn all strangers out of their dwellings and wrap themselves in black felt in which they hide until it has passed over. They never wash their dishes, but when the meat is cooked, they wash out the bowl in which they are going to put it with some boiling broth from the cauldron which they afterwards pour back. The women also make the felt and cover the houses.

The men make bows and arrows, manufacture stirrups and bits and make saddles; they build the houses and carts, they look after the horses and milk the mares, churn the cosmos, that is the mares' milk, and make the skins in which it is kept, and they also look after the camels and load them. Both sexes look after the sheep and goats, and sometimes the men, sometimes the women, milk them. They dress skins with the sour milk of ewes, thickened and salted.

When they want to wash their hands or their head, they fill their mouth with water and, pouring this little by little from their mouth into their hands, with it they wet their hair and wash their head.

As for their marriages, you must know that no one there has a wife unless he buys her, which means that sometimes girls are quite grown up before they marry, for their parents always keep them until they sell them. They observe the first and second degrees of consanguinity, but observe no degrees of affinity; they have two sisters at the same time or one after the other. No widow among them marries, the reason being that they believe that all those who serve them in this life will serve them in the next, and so of a widow they believe that she will always return after death to her first husband. This gives rise to a shameful custom among them whereby a son sometimes takes to wife all his father's wives, except his own mother; for the orda of a father and mother always falls to the youngest son and so he himself has to provide for all his father's wives who come to him with his father's effects; and then, if he so wishes, he uses them as wives, for he does not consider an injury has been done to him if they return to his father after death.

And so when anyone has made an agreement with another to take his daughter, the father of the girl arranges a feast and she takes flight to relations where she lies hid. Then the father declares: "Now my daughter is yours; take her wherever you find her." Then he searches for her with his friends until he finds her; then he has to take her by force and bring her, as though by violence, to his house.

Questions:
1. *As described by William Rubruck, in a culture such as that of the Mongols, what items would have been held in the greatest value?*
2. *What was cosmos, and what role did it play in Mongolian popular culture?*
3. *Why did the Mongols not believe in washing clothes?*
4. *What had to occur before a Mongol could take a wife? How was he expected to take her following the wedding feast?*

11.6   The Book of Ser Marco Polo

Early in the thirteenth century a powerful Mongolian chieftain, Genghis Khan, mounted an attack against northern China and its ruling Chin dynasty. This marked the beginning of a long process that led eventually to the occupation of China by the Mongolians, a process that was completed only toward the end of the century when the grandson of Genghis , Kublai Khan, finally broke the resistance of the Sung dynasty, which had dominated southern China, and proclaimed the Yuan dynasty, which then ruled China for the next hundred years.

The center of Chinese civilization in the Yuan period became the city of Cambaluc (now Beijing), where the emperor had his winter palace. To this imperial city came merchants from all parts of the civilized world, to trade goods and merchandise. Among the thousands of traders to arrive about the year 1275 were two brothers from Venice, Maffeo and Nicolo Polo. Accompanying them was Nicolo's son Marco, who was then a teenager. Marco Polo was to remain in China for nearly a quarter of a century. During this time he entered the Chinese bureaucracy, later performing a number of tasks for the emperor that led him to travel extensively throughout China and thus become well acquainted with the land and its people.

The Book of Ser Marco Polo, which is an account of his travels, paints a vivid picture of Chinese civilization in the thirteenth century, a civilization significantly more advanced than that of Europe. The origin of the book is an interesting story. When he finally returned home in 1295 Polo became involved in a war between the Venetians and the Genoese. He was captured in battle and thrown into prison. While incarcerated he passed the time telling stories of his travels and adventures to his cellmate, who in turn transcribed them. The selection that follows gives a description of the person of Kublai Khan, his palace and court, the city of Cambaluc, and something of the imperial machinery for the rule of China.

Source: Trans. Henry Yule.

BOOK II

I. Of Cublay Kaan, the Great Kaan now Reigning, and of his Great Puissance

Now am I come to that part of our Book in which I shall tell you of the great and wonderful magnificence of the Great Kaan now reigning, by name Cublay Kaan; Kaan being a title which signifyeth "The Great Lord of Lords," or Emperor. And of a surety he hath good right to such a title, for all men know for a certain truth that he is the most potent man, as regards forces and lands and treasure, that existeth in the world, or ever hath existed from the time of our first father Adam until this day. All this I will make clear to you for truth, in this book of ours, so that every one shall be fain to acknowledge that he is the greatest Lord that is now in the world, or ever hath been.

. . .

VIII. Concerning the Person of the Great Kaan

The personal appearance of the Great Kaan, Lord of Lords, whose name is Cublay, is such as I shall now tell you. He is of a good stature, neither tall nor short, but of a middle height. He has a becoming amount of flesh, and is very shapely in all his limbs. His complexion is white and red, the eyes black and fine, the nose well formed and well set on. He has four wives, whom he retains permanently as his legitimate consorts; and the eldest of his sons by those four wives ought by rights to be emperor;-I mean when the father dies. Those four ladies are called em-presses, but each is distinguished also by her proper name. And each of them has a special court of her own, very grand and ample; no one of them having fewer than 300 fair and charming damsels. They have also many pages and eunuchs, and a number of other attendants of both sexes; so that each of these ladies has not less than 10,000 persons attached to her court.

When the Emperor desires the society of one of these four consorts, he will sometimes send for the lady to his apartment and sometimes visit her at her own. He has also a great number of concubines, and I will tell you how he obtains them.

You must know that there is a tribe of Tartars called Ungrat, who are noted for their beauty. Now every year an hundred of the most beautiful maidens of this tribe are sent to the Great Kaan, who commits them to the charge of certain elderly ladies dwelling in his palace. And these old ladies make the girls sleep with them, in order to ascertain if they have sweet breath and do not snore, and are sound in all their limbs. Then such of them as are of approved beauty, and are good and sound in all respects, are appointed to attend on the Emperor by turns. Thus six of these damsels take their turn for three days and nights, and wait on him when he is in his chamber and when he is in his bed, to serve him in any way, and to be entirely at his orders. At the end of the three days and nights they are relieved by other six. And so throughout the year, there are reliefs of maidens by six and six, changing every three days and nights.

IX. Concerning the Great Kaan's Sons

The Emperor hath, by those four wives of his, twenty-two male children; the eldest of whom was called Chinkin for the love of the good Genghis Khan, the first Lord of the Tartars. And this Chinkin, as the eldest son of the Kaan, was to have reigned after his father's death; but, as it came to pass, he died. He left a son behind him, however, whose name is Temur, and he is to be the Great Kaan and Emperor after the death of his grandfather, as is but right; he being the child of the Great Kaan's eldest son. And this Temur is an able and brave man, as he hath already proven on many occasions.

The Great Kaan hath also twenty-five other sons by his concubines; and these are good and valiant soldiers, and each of them is a great chief. I tell you moreover that of his children by his four lawful wives there are seven who are kings of vast realms or provinces, and govern them well; being all able and gallant men, as might by expected....

X. Concerning the Palace of the Great Kaan

You must know that for three months of the year, to wit December, January, and February, the Great Kaan resides in the capital city of Cathay [China], which is called Cambaluc [now Beijing], and which is at the northeastern extremity of the country. In that city stands his great palace and now I will tell you what it is like.

It is enclosed all round by a great wall forming a square, each side of which is a mile in length; that is to say, the whole compass thereof is four miles. This you may depend on; it is also very thick, and a good ten paces in height, white-washed and loop-holed all round. At each angle of the wall there is a very fine and rich palace in which the war-harness of the Emperor is kept, such as bows and quivers, saddles and bridles, and bowstrings, and everything needful for an army. Also midway between every two of these corner palaces there is another of the like; so that taking the whole compass of the enclosure you find eight vast palaces stored with the Great Lord's harness of war. And you must understand that each palace is assigned to only one kind of article; thus one is stored with bows, a second with saddles, a third with bridles, and so on in succession right round.

The great wall has five gates on its southern face, the middle one being the great gate which is never opened on any occasion except when the Great Kaan himself goes forth or enters. Close on either side of this great gate is a smaller one by which all other people pass; and then towards each angle is another great gate, also open to people in general; so that on that side there are five gates in all.

Inside of this wall there is a second, enclosing a space that is somewhat greater in length than in breadth. This enclosure also has eight palaces corresponding to those of the outer wall, and stored like them with the Lord's harness of war. This wall also hath five gates on the southern face, corresponding to those in the outer wall, and hath one gate on each of the other faces, as the outer wall hath also. In the middle of the second enclosure is the Lord's great palace, and I will tell you what it is like.

You must know that it is the greatest palace that ever was. Towards the north it is in contact with the outer wall, while towards the south there is a vacant space which the barons and the soldiers are constantly traversing. The palace itself hath no upper story, but is all on the ground floor, only the basement is raised some ten palms above the surrounding soil and this elevation is retained by a wall of marble raised to the level of the pavement, two paces in width and projecting beyond the base of the palace so as to form a kind of terrace-walk, by which people can pass round the building, and which is exposed to view, while on the outer edge of the wall there is a very fine pillared balustrade; and up to this the people are allowed to come. The roof is very lofty, and the walls of the palace are all covered with gold and silver. They are also adorned with representations of dragons sculptured and gilt, beasts and birds, knights and idols, and sundry other subjects. And on the ceiling too you see nothing but gold and silver and painting. On each of the four sides there is a great marble staircase leading to the top of the marble wall, and forming the approach to the palace.

The hall of the palace is so large that it could easily dine 6000 people; and it is quite a marvel to see how many rooms there are besides. The building is altogether so vast, so rich, and so beautiful, that no man on earth could design anything superior to it. The outside of the roof also is all colored with vermilion and yellow and green and blue and other hues, which are fixed with a varnish so fine and exquisite that they shine like crystal, and lend a resplendent luster to the palace as seen for a great way round. This roof is made too with such strength and solidity that it is fit to last for ever.

On the interior side of the palace are large buildings with halls and chambers, where the Emperor's private property is placed, such as his treasures of gold, silver, gems, pearls, and gold plate, and in which reside the ladies and concubines. There he occupies himself at his own convenience, and no one else has access.

Between the two walls of the enclosure which I have described, there are fine parks and beautiful trees bearing a variety of fruits. There are beasts also of sundry kinds, such as white stags and fallow deer, gazelles and roebucks, and fine squirrels of various sorts, with numbers also of the animal that gives the musk, and all manner of other beautiful creatures, insomuch that the whole place is full of them, and no spot remains void except where there is traffic of people going and coming. The parks are covered with abundant grass; and the roads through them being all paved and raised two cubits above the surface, they never become muddy, nor does the rain lodge on them, but flows off into the meadows, quickening the soil and producing that abundance of herbage.

From that corner of the enclosure which is towards the northwest there extends a fine lake, containing foison of fish of different kinds which the Emperor hath caused to be put in there, so that whenever he desires any he can have them at his pleasure. A river enters this lake and issues from it, but there is a grating of iron or brass put up so that the fish cannot escape in that way.

Moreover on the north side of the palace, about a bow-shot off, there is a hill which has been made by art from the earth dug out of the lake; it is a good hundred paces in height and a mile in compass. This hill is entirely covered with trees that never lose their leaves, but remain ever green. And I assure you that wherever a beautiful tree may exist, and the Emperor gets news of it, he sends for it and has it transported bodily with all its roots and the earth attached to them, and planted on that hill of his. No matter how big the tree may be, he gets it carried by his elephants; and in this way he has got together the most beautiful collection of trees in all the world. And he has also caused the whole hill to be covered with the ore of azure, which is very green. And thus not only are the trees all green, but the hill itself is all green likewise; and there is nothing to be seen on it that is not green; and hence it is called the Green Mount; and in good sooth 'tis named well.

On the top of the hill again there is a fine big palace which is all green inside and out; and thus the hill, and the trees, and the palace form together a charming spectacle; and it is marvellous to see their uniformity of color. Everybody who sees them is delighted. And the Great Kaan had caused this beautiful prospect to be formed for the comfort and solace and delectation of his heart.

You must know that beside the palace (that we have been describing), i.e. the great palace, the Emperor has caused another to be built just like his own in every respect, and this he hath done for his son when he shall reign and be Emperor after him. Hence it is made just in the same fashion and of the same size, so that everything can be carried on in the same manner after his own death. It stands on the other side of the lake from the Great Kaan's palace, and there is a bridge crossing the water from one to the other. The Prince in question holds now a Seal of Empire, but not with such complete authority as the Great Kaan, who remains supreme as long as he lives.

Now I am going to tell you of the chief city of Cathay, in which these palaces stand, and why it was built, and how.

XI. Concerning the City of Cambaluc

Now there was on that spot in old times a great and noble city called Cambaluc, which is as much as to say in our tongue "The city of the Emperor." But the Great Kaan was informed by his astrologers that this city would prove rebellious and raise great disorders against his imperial authority. So he caused the present city to be built close beside the old one, with only a river between them. And he caused the people of the old city to be removed to the new town that he had founded, and this is called Taidu. However, he allowed a portion of the people which he did not suspect to remain in the old city because the new one could not hold the whole of them, big as it is.

As regards the size of this new city you must know that it has a compass of 24 miles, for each side of it hath a length of 6 miles, and it is foursquare. And it is all walled round with walls of earth which have a thickness of full ten paces at bottom and a height of more than 10 paces; but they are not so thick at top for they diminish in thickness as they rise so that at top they are only about 3 paces thick. And they are provided throughout with loop-holed battlements which are all whitewashed.

There are 12 gates and over each gate there is a great and handsome palace, so that there are on each side of the square three gates and five palaces for (I ought to mention) there is at each angle also a great and handsome palace. In those palaces are vast halls in which are kept the arms of the city garrison.

The streets are so straight and wide that you can see right along them from end to end and from one gate to the other. And up and down the city there are beautiful palaces and many great and fine hostelries and fine houses in great numbers. All the plots of ground on which the houses of the city are built are foursquare and laid out with straight lines, all the plots being occupied by great and spacious palaces with courts and gardens of proportionate size. All these plots were assigned to different heads of families. Each square plot is encompassed by handsome streets for traffic and thus the whole city is arranged in squares just like a chess board and disposed in a manner so perfect and masterly that it is impossible to give a description that should do it justice.

Moreover, in the middle of the city there is a great clock-that is to say, a bell-which is struck at night. And after it has struck three times no one must go out in the city, unless it be for the needs of a woman in labor, or of the sick. And those who go about on such errands are bound to carry lanterns with them. Moreover, the established guard at each gate of the city is 1000 armed men, not that you are to imagine the guard is kept up for fear of any attack, but only as a guard of honor for the sovereign, who resides there, and to prevent thieves from doing mischief in the town.

• • •

XIII. The Fashion of the Great Kaan's Table at his High Feasts

And when the Great Kaan sits at table on any great court occasion, it is in this fashion. His table is elevated a good deal above the others, and he sits at the north end of the hall, looking towards the south, with his chief wife besides him on the left. On his right sit his sons and his nephews, and other kinsmen of the blood imperial, but lower, so that their heads are on a level with the Emperor s feet. And then the other barons sit at other tables lower still. So also with the women; for all the wives of the Lord's sons, and of his nephews and other kinsmen, sit at the lower table to his right; and below them again the ladies of the other barons and knights, each in the place assigned by the Lord's orders. The tables are so disposed that the Emperor can see the whole of them from end to end, many as they are. Further, you are not to suppose that everybody sits at table; on the contrary, the greater part of the soldiers and their officers sit at their meal in the hall on the carpets. Outside the hall will be found more than 40,000 people; for there is a great concourse of folk bringing presents to the Lord, or come from foreign countries with curiosities.

In a certain part of the hall near where the Great Kaan holds his table, there is set a large and very beautiful piece of workmanship in the form of a square coffer, or buffet, about three paces each way, exquisitely wrought with figures of animals, finely carved and gilt. The middle is hollow, and in it stands a great vessel of pure gold, holding as much as an ordinary butt; and at each corner of the great vessel is one of smaller size of the capacity of a firkin, and from the former the wine or beverage flavored with fine and costly spices is drawn off into the latter. And on the buffet aforesaid are set all the Lord's drinking vessels, among which are certain pitchers of the finest gold, which are called verniques, and are big enough to hold drink for eight or ten persons. And one of these is put between every two persons, besides a couple of golden cups with handles, so that every man helps himself from the pitcher that stands between him and his neighbor. And the ladies are supplied in the same way. The value of these pitchers and cups is something immense; in fact, the Great Kaan has such a quantity of this kind of plate, and of gold and silver in other shapes, as no one ever before saw or heard tell of, or could believe.

There are certain barons specially deputed to see that foreigners who do not know the customs of the court are provided with places suited to their rank and these barons are continually moving to and fro in the hall, looking to the wants of the guests at table and causing the servants to supply them promptly with wine, milk, meat, or whatever they lack. At every door of the hall (or, indeed, wherever the Emperor may be) there stand a couple of big men like giants, one on each side, armed with staves. Their business is to see that no one steps upon the threshold in entering, and if this does happen they strip the offender of his clothes and he must pay a forfeit to have them back again, or in lieu of taking his clothes they give him a certain number of blows. If they are foreigners ignorant of the order, then there are barons appointed to introduce them and explain it to them. They think, in fact, that it brings bad luck if any one touches the threshold. Howbeit, they are not expected to stick at this in going forth again, for at that time some are like to be the worse for liquor and incapable of looking to their steps.

And you must know that those who wait upon the Great Kaan with his dishes and his drink are some of the great barons. They have the mouth and nose muffled with fine napkins of silk and gold, so that no breath nor odor from their persons should taint the dish or the goblet presented to the Lord. And when the Emperor is going to drink, all the musical instruments, of which he has vast store of every kind, begin to play. And when he takes the cup all the barons and the rest of the company drop on their knees and make the deepest obeisance before him, and then the Emperor doth drink. But each time that he does so the whole ceremony is repeated.

I will say nought about the dishes, as you may easily conceive that there is a great plenty of every possible kind. But you should know that in every case where a baron or knight dines at those tables, their wives also dine there with the other ladies. And when all have dined and the tables have been removed, then come in a great number of players and jugglers, adepts at all sorts of wonderful feats, and perform before the Emperor and the rest of the company, creating great diversion and mirth, so that everybody is full of laughter and enjoyment. And when the performance is over, the company breaks up and every one goes to his quarters.

XIV. Concerning the Great Feast Held by the Grand Kaan Every Year on his Birthday

You must know that the Tartars keep high festival yearly on their birthdays. And the Great Kaan was born on the 28th day of the September moon, so on that day is held the greatest feast of the year at the Kaan's court, always excepting that which he holds on New Year's Day, of which I shall tell you afterwards. Now, on his birthday the Great Kaan dresses in the best of his robes, all wrought with beaten gold; and full 12,000 barons and knights on that day come forth dressed in robes of the same color and precisely like those of the Great Kaan, except that they are not so costly, but still they are all of the same color as his and are also of silk and gold. Every man so clothed has also a girdle of gold and this as well as the dress is given him by the sovereign. And I will aver that there are some of these decked with so many pearls and precious stones that a single suit shall be worth full 10,000 golden bezants.

And of such raiment there are several sets. For you must know that the Great Kaan thirteen times in the year presents to his barons and knights such suits of raiment as I am speaking of. And on each occasion they wear the same color that he does, a different color being assigned to each festival. Hence you may see what a huge business it is and that there is no prince in the world but he alone who could keep up such customs as these.

On his birthday also all the Tartars in the world and all the countries and governments that owe allegiance to the Kaan offer him great presents according to their several ability and as prescription or orders have fixed the amount. And many other persons also come with great presents to the Kaan, in order to beg for some employment from him. And the Great Kaan has chosen twelve barons on whom is laid the charge of assigning to each of these supplicants a suitable answer.

On this day likewise all the idolaters, all the Saracens, and all the Christians and other descriptions of people make great and solemn devotions with much chanting and lighting of lamps and burning of incense, each to the God whom he doth worship, praying that he would save the Emperor and grant him long life and health and happiness.

And thus, as I have related, is celebrated the joyous feast of the Kaan's birthday.

Now I will tell you of another festival which the Kaan holds at the New Year and which is called the White Feast.

XV. Of the Great Festival which the Kaan Holds on New Year's Day

The beginning of their New Year is the month of February, and on that occasion the Great Kaan and all his subjects made such a Feast as I now shall describe.

It is the custom that on this occasion the Kaan and all his subjects should be clothed entirely in white so that day everybody is in white, men and women, great and small. And this is done in order that they may thrive all through the year for they deem that white clothing is lucky. On that day also all the people of all the provinces and governments and kingdoms and countries that owe allegiance to the Kaan bring him great presents of gold and silver, and pearls and gems, and rich textures of divers kinds. And this they do that the Emperor throughout the year may have abundance of treasure and enjoyment without care. And the people also make presents to each other of white things and embrace and kiss and make merry and wish each other happiness and good luck for the coming year. On that day, I can assure you, among the customary presents there shall be offered to the Kaan from various quarters more than 100,000 white horses, beautiful animals, and richly caparisoned. And you must know 'tis their custom in offering presents to the Great Kaan (at least when the province making the present is able to do so), to present nine times nine articles. For instance, if a province sends horses, it sends nine times nine or 81 horses; of gold, nine times nine pieces of gold, and so with stuffs or whatever else the present may consist of.

On that day also the whole of the Kaan's elephants, amounting fully to 5000 in number, are exhibited, all covered with rich and gay housings of inlaid cloth representing beasts and birds, while each of them carries on his back two splendid coffers, all of these being filled with the Emperor's plate and other costly furniture required for the court on the occasion of the White Feast. And these are followed by a vast number of camels which are likewise covered with rich housings and laden with things needful for the Feast. All these are paraded before the Emperor and it makes the finest sight in the world.

Moreover, on the morning of the Feast, before the tables are set, all the kings and all the dukes, marquesses, counts, barons, knights, and astrologers, and philosophers, and leeches, and falconers, and other officials of sundry kinds from all the places round about present themselves in the Great Hall before the Emperor, while those who can find no room to enter stand outside in such a position that the Emperor can see them all well. And the whole company is marshalled in this wise. First are the Kaan's sons, and his nephews, and the other princes of the blood imperial; next to them all kings; then dukes, and then all others in succession according to the degree of each. And when they are all seated, each in his proper place, then a great prelate rises and says with a loud voice: "Bow and adore!" And as soon as he has said this the company bow down until their foreheads touch the earth in adoration towards the Emperor as if he were a god. And this adoration they repeat four times, and then go to a highly decorated altar on which is a vermilion tablet with the name of the Grand Kaan inscribed thereon, and a beautiful censer of gold. So they incense the tablet and the altar with great reverence and then return each man to his seat.

When all have performed this then the presents are offered, of which I have spoken as being so rich and costly. And after all have been offered and been seen by the Emperor the tables are set and all take their places at them with perfect order as I have already told you. And after dinner the jugglers come in and amuse the court as you have heard before and when that is over every man goes to his quarters.

· · ·

XXII. Concerning the City of Cambaluc and its Great Traffic and Population

You must know that the city of Cambaluc hath such a multitude of houses, and such a vast population inside the walls and outside, that it seems quite past all possibility. There is a suburb outside each of the gates, which are twelve in number; and these suburbs are so great that they contain more people than the city itself for the suburb of one gate spreads in width till it meets the suburb of the next, while they extend in length some three or four miles. In those suburbs lodge the foreign merchants and travellers, of whom there are always great numbers who have come to bring presents to the Emperor, or to sell articles at court, or because the city affords so good a mart to attract traders. There are in each of the suburbs, to a distance of a mile from the city, numerous fine hostelries for the lodgement of merchants from different parts of the world, and a special hostelry is assigned to each description of people, as if we should say there is one for the Lombards, another for the Germans, and a third for the Frenchmen. And thus there are as many good houses outside of the city as inside, without counting those that belong to the great lords and barons, which are very numerous.

You must know that it is forbidden to bury any dead body inside the city. If the body be that of an idolater it is carried out beyond the city and suburbs to a remote place assigned for the purpose, to be burnt. And if it be of one belonging to a religion the custom of which is to bury, such as the Christian, the Saracen, or what not, it is also carried out beyond the suburbs to a distant place assigned for the purpose. And thus the city is preserved in a better and more healthy state.

Moreover, no public woman resides inside the city, but all such abide outside in the suburbs. And 'tis wonderful what a vast number of these there are for the foreigners; it is a certain fact that there are more than 20,000 of them living by prostitution. And that so many can live in this way will show you how vast is the population.

Guards patrol the city every night in parties of 30 or 40, looking out for any persons who may be abroad at unseasonable hours, i.e. after the great bell hath stricken thrice. If they find any such person he is immediately taken to prison, and examined next morning by the proper officers. If these find him guilty of any misdemeanor they order him a proportionate beating with the stick. Under this punishment people sometimes die; but they adopt it in order to eschew bloodshed; for their Bacsis say that it is an evil thing to shed man's blood.

To this city also are brought articles of greater cost and rarity, and in greater abundance of all kinds, than to any other city in the world. For people of every description, and from every region, bring things including all the costly wares of India, as well as the fine and precious goods of Cathay itself with its provinces, some for the sovereign, some for the court, some for the city which is so great, some for the crowds of barons and knights, some for the great hosts of the Emperor which are quartered round about; and thus between court and city the quantity brought in is endless.

As a sample, I tell you, no day in the year passes that there do not enter the city 1000 cart loads of silk alone, from which are made quantities of cloth of silk and gold, and of other goods. And this is not to be wondered at; for in all the countries round about there is no flax, so that everything has to be made of silk. It is true, indeed, that in some parts of the country there is cotton and hemp, but not sufficient for their wants. This, however, is not of much consequence, because silk is so abundant and cheap, and is a more valuable substance than either flax or cotton.

Round about this great city of Cambaluc there are some 200 other cities at various distances, from which traders come to sell their goods and buy others for their lords; and all find means to make their sales and purchases, so that the traffic of the city is passing great.

· · ·

XXIV. How the Great Kaan Causeth the Bark of Trees, Made into Something like Paper, to Pass for Money over all His Country

Now that I have told you in detail of the splendor of the city of the Emperor's, I shall proceed to tell you of the mint which he hath in the same city, in which he hath his money coined and struck, as I shall relate to you. And in doing so I shall make manifest to you how it is that the Great Lord may well be able to accomplish even much more than I have told you, or am going to tell you, in this Book. For, tell it how I might, you never would be satisfied that I was keeping within truth and reason.

The Emperor's mint then is in this same city of Cambaluc and the way it is wrought is such that you might say he hath the secret of alchemy in perfection, and you would be right. For he makes his money after this fashion.

He makes them take of the bark of a certain tree, in fact of the mulberry tree, the leaves of which are the food of the silkworms,-these trees being so numerous that whole districts are full of them. What they take is a certain fine white bast or skin which lies between the wood of the tree and the thick outer bark, and this they make into something resembling sheets of paper, but black. When these sheets have been prepared they are cut up into pieces of different sizes. The smallest of these sizes is worth a half tornesel; the next, a little larger, one tornesel; one, a little larger still, is worth half a silver groat of Venice; another a whole groat; others yet two groats, five groats, and ten groats. There is also a kind worth one bezant of gold, and others of three bezants, and so up to ten. All these pieces of paper are issued with as much solemnity and authority as if they were of pure gold or silver; and on every piece a variety of officials, whose duty it is, have to write their names, and to put their seals. And when all is prepared duly, the chief officer deputed by the Kaan smears the seal entrusted to him with vermilion, and impresses it on the paper, so that the form of the seal remains printed upon it in red; the money is then authentic. Any one forging it would be punished with death. And the Kaan causes every year to be made such a vast quantity of this money, which costs him nothing, that it must equal in amount all the treasure in the world.

With these pieces of paper, made as I have described, he causes all payments on his own account to be made; and he makes them to pass current universally over all his kingdoms and provinces and territories, and whithersoever his power and sovereignty extends. And nobody, however important he may think himself, dares to refuse them on pain of death. And indeed everybody takes them readily, for wheresoever a person may go throughout the Great Kaan's dominions he shall find these pieces of paper current, and shall be able to transact all sales and purchases of goods by means of them just as well as if they were coins of pure gold. And all the while they are so light that ten bezants' worth does not weigh one golden bezant.

. . .

XXVI. How the Kaan's Posts and Runners are Sped through Many Lands and Provinces

Now you must know that from this city of Cambaluc proceed many roads and highways leading to a variety of provinces, one to one province, another to another; and each road receives the name of the province to which it leads; and it is a very sensible plan. And the messengers of the Emperor in travelling from Cambaluc, be the road whichsoever they will, find at every twenty-five miles of the journey a station which they call Yamb, or, as we should say, the "Horse-Post-House." And at each of those stations used by the messengers, there is a large and handsome building for them to put up at, in which they find all the rooms furnished with fine beds and all other necessary articles in rich silk, and where they are provided with everything they can want. If even a king were to arrive at one of these, he would find himself well lodged.

At some of these stations, moreover, there shall be posted some four hundred horses standing ready for the use of the messengers; at others there shall be two hundred, according to the requirements, and to what the Emperor has established in each case. At every twenty-five miles, as I said, or anyhow at every thirty miles, you find one of these stations, on all the principal highways leading to the different provincial governments; and the same is the case throughout all the chief provinces subject to the Great Kaan. Even when the messengers have to pass through a roadless tract where neither house nor hostel exists, still there the station houses have been established just the same, excepting that the intervals are somewhat greater and the day's journey is fixed at thirty-five to forty-five miles, instead of twenty-five to thirty. But they are provided with horses and all the other necessaries just like those we have described, so that the Emperor's messengers, come they from what region they may, find everything ready for them.

And in sooth this is a thing done on the greatest scale of magnificence that ever was seen. Never had emperor, king, or lord such wealth as this manifests. For it is a fact that on all these posts taken together there are more than 300,000 horses kept up, specially for the use of the messengers. And the great buildings that I have mentioned are more than 10,000 in number, all richly furnished, as I told you. The thing is on a scale so wonderful and costly that it is hard to bring oneself to describe it.

But now I will tell you another thing that I had forgotten, but which ought to be told while I am on this subject. You must know that by the Great Kaan's orders there has been established between those post-houses, at every interval of three miles, a little fort with some forty houses round about it, in which dwell the people who act as the Emperor's foot-runners. Every one of those runners wears a great wide belt, set all over with bells, so that as they run the three miles from post to post their bells are heard jingling a long way off. And thus on reaching the post the runner finds another man similarly equipt, and all ready to take his place, who instantly takes over whatsoever he has in charge, and with it receives a slip of paper from the clerk, who is always at hand for the purpose; and so the new man sets off and runs his three miles. At the next station he finds his relief ready in like manner; and so the post proceeds, with a change at every three miles.

And in this way the Emperor, who has an immense number of these runners, receives despatches with news from places ten day's journey off in one day and night; or, if need be, news from a hundred days off in ten days and nights; and that is no small matter. In fact in the fruit season many a fine fruit shall be gathered one morning in Cambaluc and the evening of the next day it shall reach the Great Kaan in Chandu, a distance of ten days' journey. The clerk at each of the posts notes the time of each courier s arrival and departure; and there are often other officers whose business it is to make monthly visitations of all the posts, and to punish those runners who have been slack in their work. The Emperor exempts these men from all tribute, and pays them besides.

Moreover, there are also at those stations other men equipt similarly with girdles hung with bells, who are employed for expresses when there is a call for great haste in sending despatches to any governor of a province, or to give news when any baron has revolted, or in other such emergencies; and these men travel a good two hundred or two hundred and fifty miles in the day and as much in the night. I'll tell you how it stands. They take a horse from those at the station which are standing ready saddled, all fresh and in wind, and mount and go at full speed, as hard as they can ride in fact. And when those at the next post hear the bells they get ready another horse and a man equipt in the same way, and he takes over the letter or whatever it be, and is off full-speed to the third station, where again a fresh horse is found all ready, and so the despatch speeds along from post to post, always at full gallop, with regular change of horses. And the speed at which they go is marvellous.

. . .

XXVIII. How the Great Kaan Causes Trees to be Planted by the Highways

The Emperor moreover hath taken order that all the highways travelled by his messengers and the people generally should be planted with rows of great trees a few paces apart; and thus these trees are visible a long way off, and no one can miss the way by day or night. Even the roads through uninhabited tracts are thus planted, and it is the greatest possible solace to travellers. And this is done on all the ways, where it can be of service. The Great Kaan plants these trees all the more readily, because his astrologers and diviners tell him that he who plants trees lives long.

But where the ground is so sandy and desert that trees will not grow, he causes other landmarks, pillars or stones, to be set up to show the way.

XXIX. Concerning the Rice Wine Drunk by the People of Cathay

Most of the people of Cathay drink wine of the kind that I shall now describe. It is a liquor which they brew of rice with a quantity of excellent spice, in such fashion that it makes better drink than any other kind of wine; it is not only good, but clear and pleasing to the eye. And being very hot stuff, it makes one drunk sooner than any other wine.

XXX. Concerning the Black Stones that are Dug in Cathay and are Burnt for Fuel

It is a fact that all over the country of Cathay there is a kind of black stones existing in beds in the mountains, which they dig out and burn like firewood. If you supply the fire with them at night, and see that they are well kindled, you will find them still alight in the morning; and they make such capital fuel that no other is used throughout the country. It is true that they have plenty of wood also, but they do not burn it, because those stones burn better and cost less.

Moreover with that vast number of people, and the number of hot baths that they maintain-for every one has such a bath at least three times a week, and in winter if possible every day, while every nobleman and man of wealth has a private bath for his own use-the wood would not suffice for the purpose.

XXXI. How the Great Kaan Causes Stores of Corn to be Made, to Help His People Withal in Time of Dearth

You must know that when the Emperor sees that corn is cheap and abundant, he buys up large quantities, and has it stored in all his provinces in great granaries, where it is so well looked after that it will keep for three or four years.

And this applies, let me tell you, to all kinds of corn, whether wheat, barley, millet, rice, panic, or what not, and when there is any scarcity of a particular kind of corn, he causes that to be issued. And if the price of the corn is at one bezant the measure, he lets them have it at a bezant for four measures, or at whatever price will produce general cheapness; and every one can have food in this way. And by this providence of the Emperor's, his people can never suffer from dearth. He does the same over his whole Empire; causing these supplies to be stored everywhere, according to calculation of the wants and necessities of the people.

XXXII. On the Charity of the Emperor to the Poor

I have told you how the Great Kaan provides for the distribution of necessaries to his people in time of dearth, by making store in time of cheapness. Now I will tell you of his alms and great charity to the poor of his city of Cambaluc.

You see he causes selection to be made of a number of families in the city which are in a state of indigence, and of such families some may consist of six in the house, some of eight, some of ten, more or fewer in each as it may hap, but the whole number being very great. And each family he causes annually to be supplied with wheat and other corn sufficient for the whole year. And this he never fails to do every year. Moreover, all those who choose to go to the daily dole at the court receive a great loaf apiece, hot from the baking, and nobody is denied; for so the Lord hath ordered. And so some 30,000 people go for it every day from year's end to year's end. Now this is a great goodness in the Emperor to take pity of his poor people thus. And they benefit so much by it that they worship him as he were God.

He also provides the poor with clothes. For he lays a tithe upon all wool, silk, hemp, and the like from which clothing can be made and he has these woven and laid up in a building set apart for the purpose and as all artisans are bound to give a day's labor weekly, in this way the Kaan has these stuffs made into clothing for those poor families, suitable for summer or winter, according to the time of year. He also provides the clothing for his troops and has woolens woven for them in every city, the material for which is furnished by the tithe aforesaid. You should know that the Tartars, before they were converted to the religion of the idolaters, never practised almsgiving. Indeed, when any poor man begged of them they would tell him, "Go with God's curse, for if he loved you as he loves me he would have provided for you." But the sages of the idolaters told the Great Kaan that it was a good work to provide for the poor and that his idols would be greatly pleased if he did so. And since then he has taken to do so for the poor so much as you have heard.

XXXIII. Concerning the Astrologers in the City of Cambaluc

There are in the city of Cambaluc, what with Christians, Saracens, and Cathayans, some five thousand astrologers and soothsayers, whom the Great Kaan provides with annual maintenance and clothing, just as he provides the poor of whom we have spoken, and they are in the constant exercise of their art in this city.

They have a kind of astrolabe on which are inscribed the planetary signs, the hours and critical points of the whole year. And every year these Christian, Saracen, and Cathayan astrologers, each sect apart, investigate by means of this astrolabe the course and character of the whole year, according to the indications of each of its Moons, in order to discover by the natural course and disposition of the planets and the other circumstances of the heavens what shall be the nature of the weather, and what peculiarities shall be produced by each Moon of the year as, for example, under which Moon there shall be thunderstorms and tempests, under which there shall be disease, murrain, wars, disorder, and treasons, and so on, according to the indications of each, but always adding that it lies with God to do less or more according to his pleasure. And they write down the results of their examination in certain little pamphlets for the year, which are called Tacuin, and these are sold for a groat to all who desire to know what is coming. Those of the astrologers, of course, whose predictions are found to be most exact are held to be the greatest adepts in their art and get the greater fame.

And if any one have some great matter in hand, or proposing to make a long journey for traffic or other business, desires to know what will be the upshot, he goes to one of these astrologers and says: "Turn up your books and see what is the present aspect of the heavens for I am going away on such and such a business." Then the astrologer will reply that the applicant must also tell the year, month, and hour of his birth, and when he has got that information he will see how the horoscope of his nativity combines with the indications of the time when the question is put, and then he predicts the result, good or bad, according to the aspect of the heavens.

You must know, too, that the Tartars reckon their years by twelves, the sign of the first year being the Lion, of the second the Ox, of the third the Dragon, of the fourth the Dog, and so forth up to the twelfth, so that when one is asked the year of his birth he answers that it was in the year of the Lion (let us say), on such a day or night, at such an hour, and such a moment. And the father of a child always takes care to write these particulars down in a book. When the twelve yearly symbols have been gone through then they come back to the first and go through with them again in the same succession.

XXXIV. Concerning the Religion of the Cathayans, Their Views as to the Soul, and Their Customs

As we have said before, these people are idolaters and, as regards their gods, each has a tablet fixed high up on the wall of his chamber on which is inscribed a name which represents the most high and heavenly God, and before this they pay daily worship, offering incense from a thurible, raising their hands aloft and gnashing their teeth three times, praying him to grant them health of mind and body, but of him they ask nought else. And below on the ground there is a figure which they call Natigai, which is the god of things terrestrial. To him they give a wife and children and they worship him in the same manner, with incense and gnashing of teeth and lifting up of hands, and of him they ask seasonable weather and the fruits of the earth, children, and so forth.

Their view of the immortality of the soul is after this fashion. They believe that as soon as a man dies his soul enters into another body, going from a good to a better, or from a bad to a worse, according as he hath conducted himself well or ill. That is to say, a poor man, if he have passed through life good and sober, shall be born again of a gentlewoman, and shall be a gentleman, and on a second occasion shall be born of a princess and shall be a prince, and so on, always rising, til he be absorbed into the Deity. But if he have borne himself ill he who was the son of a gentleman shall be reborn as the son of a boor, and from a boor shall become a dog, always going down lower and lower.

The people have an ornate style of speech; they salute each other with a cheerful countenance and with great politeness; they behave like gentlemen, and eat with great propriety. They show great respect to their parents and should there be any son who offends his parents or fails to minister to their necessities there is a public office which has no other charge but that of punishing unnatural children, who are proved to have acted with ingratitude towards their parents.

Criminals of sundry kinds who have been imprisoned are released at a time fixed by the Great Kaan (which occurs every three years), but on leaving prison they are branded on one cheek that they may be recognized.

The Great Kaan hath prohibited all gambling and sharping, things more prevalent there than in any other part of the world. In doing this he said: "I have conquered you by force of arms and all that you have is mine; if, therefore, you gamble away your property it is in fact my property that you are gambling away." Not that he took anything from them however.

I must not omit to tell you of the orderly way in which the Kaan's barons and others conduct themselves in coming to his presence. In the first place, within a half mile of the place where he is, out of reverence for his exalted majesty, everybody preserves a mien of the greatest meekness and quiet, so that no noise of shrill voices or loud talk shall be heard. And every one of the chiefs and nobles carries always with him a handsome little vessel to spit in while he remains in the Hall of Audience- for no one dares spit on the floor of the hall-and when he hath spitten he covers it up and puts it aside. So also they all have certain handsome buskins of white leather, which they carry with them, and, when summoned by the sovereign, on arriving at the entrance to the hall they put on these white buskins, and give their others in charge to the servants, in order that they may not foul the fine carpets of silk and gold and divers colors.

Questions:

1. *Ghengis Khan was the leader of a group of warrior-nomads and despised civilized, urban life. To what extent has his grandson, Kublai Khan, been influenced by the civilization he has conquered?*
2. *What do we learn about Chinese society during the time of Mongol domination from this document?*

11.7 John Pian del Carpini, The Tartars

John (Giovanni) del Carpini (1182?–1252) had been a companion and disciple of St. Francis of Assisi (see Reading 68). He led the Franciscan expedition sent by Pope Innocent IV to Kuyuk Khan and wrote extensively of his travels and experiences at the Mongol court. It is not known how he entitled his work, which is often called the History of the Mongols, even though there is relatively little history in it. One of the surviving manuscripts has the simple title A Book About the Tartars, which seems more accurate. The following excerpts from it are fairly typical in showing his admiration for the hardiness and capacity for cooperation the Mongols exhibited among themselves, coupled with his revulsion at their ferocity and lack of scruples in dealing with foreign peoples. John was less hopeful of converting the Mongols to Christianity than were most of the explorer-missionaries who followed him; both his travel book and the letter he brought to the pope from Kuyuk Khan indicate why. His Franciscan successors who visited China under Mongol conquest had better experiences, however; they and Venetian traders, particularly the very observant Marco Polo, who became a Mongol administrator in China, were beginning to acquaint Europe with some of the real East Asia.

Source: From *Historia Mongalorum,* in *Studi Italiani di Filologia Indo-Iranica,* Vol. IX (Firenze: Carnesecchi e Figli, 1913), pp. 54–101, passim. Trans. Henry A. Myers.

The Tartars have a very different appearance from other peoples. There is more space between their eyes and between their cheekbones than is true of other men. . . . They have flat noses and rather small eyes. . . . Almost all of them are of medium height. Their men have only sparse growths of beard, some letting their wispy moustaches droop long. . . .

I will tell something of their good characteristics and then of their bad ones. . . . They show greater respect to their superiors than any other people in the world. . . . They deceive their own masters rarely or never with words and never at all with deeds. . . . They do not fight among themselves: Internal warfare, brawls and assaults do not occur. . . . If a large animal strays, whoever finds it either lets it go or leads it to men of authority from whom the owner can get it back with no difficulty at all simply by asking for it. They respect each other quite well enough and . . . throw frequent banquets in spite of the scarcity of good things to eat among them. At the same time, they are so hardy that they can go a day or even two without eating and still sing and joke around as if they had had plenty to eat. . . . Tartar women are chaste: There are not even rumors of immodest female behavior among them, although the women do sometimes use filthy language. . . . Even though the Tartars get quite drunk often, this does not lead to hostile words or actions among them.

Having said this much about their good side, let me go on to their bad one. Their pride is terrible when they confront non-Tartars—nobles and commoners alike—whom they are apt to despise. . . . They show their angry and totally condescending natures to foreigners, to whom they habitually lie. When Tartars speak to non-Tartars the truth is seldom in them. When they start off, their conversation is nice enough, but they sting like scorpions before they are through talking. They are cunning, crafty, and very elusive with their falsehoods. When they have hostile plans toward foreigners, they are experts in concealing them so that the foreigners will not know to be on guard. . . . They are very greedy and shameless with their outrageous demands, while they hold fast to what is theirs and are unbelievably stingy givers. Killing off foreign peoples simply does not bother them.

Chinghiz Khan arranged their order of battle by putting ten men under the command of a squad leader, ten squad leaders under one centurion, ten centurions under a battalion commander, thus giving him a thousand men, ten battalion commanders under a colonel and the whole army under two or three generals, but with one of them clearly the theater commander. If in battle, one, two, or three—any number—of men flee from a squad, the whole squad is executed; if the whole squad flees, then the hundred soldiers with the centurion over them are all executed; and, to summarize this point briefly, units with men in them who flee are wiped out. . . . If members of a squad are captured and not rescued by the rest, the rest are executed. The minimum arms they are required to carry are: two bows . . . , three quivers full of arrows, one ax, and ropes to pull along machines of war. To be sure, their nobles carry . . . slightly curved swords with sharp points, and their horses wear armor of multiple thickness of leather shaped to fit their bodies. . . .

Some of them have a hook attached to the necks of their lances with which they will pull a rider off his saddle if they can. Their arrows are about two feet, eight inches long . . . and each man carries a file in his quiver to sharpen their heads. . . .

When they come to a river, they cross it with the higher-ups using large, lightweight leather bags with loops and drawstrings to seal up their clothes and necessary equipment for the crossing. The resulting pack floats. Tied to the tails of their horses, who swim over, the pack serves as a sort of boat. . . . Even the common soldiers have nearly waterproof leather bags, into which they stuff their things . . . and then hang them securely on the bases of their horses' tails before crossing.

You should know that the Tartar emperor told me in person that he wanted to send his armies into Livonia [on the Baltic Sea] and Prussia and that he intended to destroy the whole countryside or reduce it to servitude. They enslave people in a way which we find intolerable. . . . Their tactics include using captives from lands just conquered to fight against a province still holding out against them. They put these captives in the front ranks: If they fight poorly, they kill them; if they fight well, they encourage them with cheering words and promise to make them great lords so that they will not escape. However, once the dangers of battle are passed, they keep these people in line by making hapless serfs out of them, while taking the women they want for serving maids and concubines. Their use of men from one defeated country after another against the next country makes it impossible for any single country to resist them, unless God chooses to fight for them. . . .

Thus, if Christians wish to defend themselves, their countries, and Christianity, it will be necessary for kings, princes, barons, and other chiefs of the lands to cooperate as one and to send men under a consolidated command into battle against them before they have so drained the earth of men that there will be nowhere to draw aid from. . . . This army should be ordered as they do it, from officers commanding a thousand through officers commanding a hundred and overall commanders of the army. These generals should never enter the fighting themselves, just as Tartar commanders do not enter it, but they should be able to observe the army's action and direct it. Our people should make it a regulation that the soldiers advance into battle together or elsewhere in the order established.

Questions:
1. Why does John consider the Mongol threat a real one?
2. What does John think Westerners could learn from the Mongols?

11.8   Kuyuk Khan, Letter to Pope Innocent IV

Kuyuk Khan, who ruled the Mongols for a brief period beginning in 1246, participated in the Mongol invasion of Europe in the 1230s and quite possibly was planning another invasion at the time he died in 1248.

> **Source:** *"Lettre del Gran Can al Sommo Pontefece"*, appended to *Friar John's Historia Mongolorum, in Studi Italiani Filologia Indo-Iranica,* Vol. IX (Firenze: Carnesecchi e Figli, 1913), p. 125. Translated by Henry A. Myers.

Courage. Kuyuk Khan, Emperor of all men, whose courage is God-given, sends a letter of his own to the great Pope in reply to the message sent to us in which you express your desire to have peace and friendship with us, as we have understood from your emissary.

Your letter to us contains a number of things we must do: We must be baptized and must become Christians. To this we answer that we do not understand how you seek to require us to do anything. Then, as for what you have in your letter showing great surprise at such thorough slaughter of men, for the most part Hungarian Christians, as well as some Polish or Moravian ones, we have not heard of anything that would require us to answer you about that either; however, so that you will not think that we wish to lull you through our silence [into feeling secure], we will answer you in this way:

No khan can heed more apt advice than comes from the command of God and the recorded words of Jenghiz Khan. Khans have been inspired to do some killing all right, because—once God has decided upon the destruction of men—what God does not do Himself He will enable man to do to man. Consequently, with our God-inspired courage we have wrought massive destruction on every land from the East to the West.

You Christians do worship God, but then—believing yourselves to be the only true ones—you despise nations other than those you consider worthy of having your grace bestowed upon them.

You now, Pope: If you want to have peace and friendship with us, come with all the kings and potentates who serve you to our court. You should listen to this response of ours: Subject your will to us and bring us tribute, for if you do not obey our instructions and do not journey to us we are certain that you will have war with us. After that, to be sure, we do not know what the future holds. Only God knows that.

Question:
1. How did Kuyuk Khan assess the relationship between Mongols and the Christian world?

PART 12
Islamic Empires

12.1   Sunni versus Shi'ite: "We Exhort You to Embrace the True Faith!"

This selection is a letter from the Ottoman ruler, Selim I to his Persian rival, Isma'il I, leader of the Shi'ite Safavid state. Ismail had entered Ottoman territory and had demanded that Ottoman subjects accept Shi'ism. This response by Selim I, a committed Sunni, reveals the divisive competition among Islamic religious sects and political leaders. Selim I won the battle of Chaldiran in 1514 and protected his territory from Shi'ite encroachment.

Source: "Sunni versus Shi'ite" is from C. T. Foster and F. H. Blackburne Daniell, *The Life and Letters of Ogier Ghiselin de Busbecq,* vol. 1 (London: Hakluyt Society, 1881), pp. 152-156; 219-221.

SULTAN SELIM I

Keep in Mind . . .

- What is the purpose of this warning to Amir Isma'il from Sultan Selim I?
- How does Selim use the *Qur'an* to justify his actions?

The Supreme Being who is at once the sovereign arbiter of the destinies of men and the source of all light and knowledge, declares in the *Qur'an* that the true faith is that of the Muslims, and that whoever professes another religion, far from being hearkened to and saved, will on the contrary be cast out among the rejected on the great day of the Last Judgment; He says further, this God of truth, that His designs and decrees are unalterable, that all human acts are perforce reported to Him, and that he who abandons the good way will be condemned to hell-fire and eternal torments. Place yourself, O Prince, among the true believers, those who walk in the path of salvation, and who turn aside with care from vice and infidelity. May the purest and holiest blessings be upon Muhammad, the master of the two worlds, the prince of prophets, as well as upon his descendants and all who follow his Law!

I, sovereign chief of the Ottomans, master of the heroes of the age . . . I, the exterminator of idolaters, destroyer of the enemies of the true faith, the terror of the tyrants and pharaohs of the age; I, before whom proud and unjust kings have humbled themselves . . . and whose hand breaks the strongest scepters; . . . I address myself graciously to you, Amir Isma'il, chief of the troops of Persia . . . and predestined to perish . . . in order to make known to you that the works emanating from the Almighty are not the fragile products of caprice or folly, but make up an infinity of mysteries impenetrable to the human mind. The Lord Himself says in His holy book: "We have not created the heavens and the earth in order to play a game" [*Qur'an,* 21:16]. Man, who is the noblest of the creatures and the summary of the marvels of God, is in consequence on earth the living image of the Creator. It is He who has set up Caliphs on earth, because, joining faculties of soul with perfection of body, man is the only being who can comprehend the attributes of the divinity and adore its sublime beauties; but because he possesses this rare intelligence, he attains this divine knowledge only in our religion, and by observing the precepts of the prince of prophets, the Caliph of Caliphs, the right are of the God of Mercy; it is then only by practicing the true religion that man will prosper in this world and merit eternal life in the other. As to you, Amir Isma'il, such a recompense will not be your lot; because you have denied the sanctity of the divine laws; because you have deserted the path of salvation and the sacred commandments; because you have impaired the purity of the dogmas of Islam; because you have dishonored, soiled, and destroyed the altars of the Lord, usurped the scepter of the East by unlawful and tyrannical means; because coming forth from the dust, you have raised yourself by odious devices to a place shining with splendor and magnificence; because you have opened to Muslims the gates of tyranny and oppression; because you have joined iniquity, perjury, and blasphemy to your sectarian impiety; because under the cloak of the hypocrite, you have sowed everywhere trouble and sedition; because you have raised the standard of irreligion and heresy; because yielding to the impulse of your evil passions, and giving yourself up without rein to the most infamous disorders, you have dared to throw off the control of Muslim laws and to permit lust and rape, the massacre of the most virtuous and respectable men, the destruction of pulpits and temples . . . the repudiation of the *Qur'an,* the cursing of the legitimate Caliphs. Now as the first duty of a Muslim and above all of a pious prince is to obey the commandment, "O, you faithful who believe, be the executors of the decrees of God!" the ulama [religious leadership] and our doctors have pronounced sentence of death against you, perjurer and blasphemer, and have imposed on every Muslim the sacred obligation to arm in defense of religion and destroy heresy and impiety in your person and that of all your partisans.

Animated by this [religious decree], conforming to the *Qur'an*, the code of divine laws, and wishing on one side to strengthen Islam, on the other to liberate the lands and peoples who writhe under your yoke, we have resolved to lay aside our imperial robes in order to put on the shelf and coat of mail, to raise our ever victorious banner, to assemble our invincible armies, to take up the gauntlet of the avenger, to march with our soldiers, whose sword strikes mortal blows. . . . In pursuit of this noble resolution, we have entered upon the campaign, and guided by the hand of the Almighty, we hope soon to strike down your tyrannous arm, blow away the clouds of glory and grandeur which trouble your head and cause your fatal blindness, release from your despotism your trembling subjects, smother you in the end in the very mass of flames which your infernal [spirit] raises everywhere along your passage, accomplishing in this way on you the maxim which says: "He who sows discord can only reap evils and afflictions." However, anxious to conform to the spirit of the law of the Prophet, we come, before commencing war, to set out before you the words of the *Qur'an*, in place of the sword, and to exhort you to embrace the true faith; this is why we address this letter to you. . . .

But if, to your misfortune, you persist in your past conduct; if, puffed up with the idea of your power and your foolish bravado, you wish to pursue the course of your iniquities, you will see in a few days your plains covered with our tents and inundated with our battalions. Then prodigies of valor will be done, and we shall see the decrees of the Almighty, Who is the God of Armies, and sovereign judge of the actions of men, accomplished. For the rest, victory to him who follows the path of salvation!

Consider This:

- Aren't Sunnis and Shi'ites both Muslims? What was the reason for this confrontation?
- Why was Selim I so sure that he embodied the "true religion" and that this justified his military threat?

Questions:

1. What is the purpose of this warning to Amir Isma'il from Sultan Selim I.
2. How does Selim use the Qur'an to justify his actions?

12.2 Süleyman "The Lawgiver" and the Advantages of Islam: Oigier de Busbecq

The energy of the Ottoman Empire perhaps reached its zenith under the direction of Sultan Süleyman "the Lawgiver" (r. 1520–1566). One of the most important assessments of Süleyman's influence came from Ogier Ghiselin de Busbecq, the ambassador from Austria to Süleyman's court at Istanbul from 1554–1562. Busbecq had been dispatched in the recent wake of the unsuccessful Ottoman siege of Vienna in 1529. His mission was to use his diplomatic skills to prevent another possible attack on the city. Busbecq's letters reveal much about Süleyman, his court, capital, Islamic traditions, and treatment of women.

Source: "Süleyman "the Lawgiver" is from C. T. Foster and F. H. Blackburne Daniell, *The Life and Letters of Ogier Ghiselin de Busbecq,* vol. 1 (London: Hakluyt Society, 1881), pp. 152-156.

Keep in Mind . . .

- What are the most important qualities for success and advancement in the Ottoman empire?

The Sultan [Süleyman "The Lawgiver"] was seated on a very low ottoman, not more than a foot from the ground, which was covered with a quantity of costly rugs and cushions of exquisite workmanship; near him lay his bow and arrows. . . . The Sultan then listened to what I had to say; but the language I used was not at all to his taste, for the demands of his Majesty breathed a spirit of independence and dignity, which was by no means acceptable to one who deemed that his wish was law; and so he made no answer beyond saying in an impatient way, "Giusel, giusel," that is, well, well. After this we were dismissed to our quarters.

The Sultan's hall was crowded with people, among whom were several officers of high rank. Besides these, there were all the troopers of the Imperial guard, and a large force of Janissaries [the elite infantry corps], but there was not in all that great assembly a single man who owed his position to anything save his valor and his merit. No distinction is attached to birth among the Turks; the respect to be paid to a man is measured by the position he holds in the public service. There is no fighting for precedence; a man's place is marked out by the duties he discharges. . . . It is by merit that men rise in the service, a system which ensures that posts should only be assigned to the competent. Each man in Turkey carries in his own hand his ancestry and his position in life, which he may make or mar as he will. Those who receive the highest offices from the Sultan are for the most part the sons of shepherds or herdsmen, and so far from being ashamed of their parentage, they actually glory in it, and consider it a matter of boasting that they owe nothing to the accident of birth; for they do not believe that high qualities are either natural or hereditary, nor do they think that they can be handed down from father to son, but that they are partly the gift of God, and partly the result of good training, great industry, and unwearied zeal; arguing that high qualities do not descend from a father to his son or heir, any more than a talent for music, mathematics, or the like. . . . Among the Turks, therefore, honors, high posts, and judgeships are the rewards of great ability and good service. If a man is dishonest, or lazy, or careless, he remains at the bottom of the ladder, an object of contempt; for such qualities there are no honors in Turkey!

This is the reason that they are successful in their undertakings, that they lord it over others, and are daily extending the bounds of their empire. These are not our ideas, with us there is no opening left for merit; birth is the standard for everything; the prestige of birth is the sole key to advancement in the public service.

The Turkish monarch going to war takes with him over 40,000 camels and nearly as many baggage mules, of which a great part, when he is invading Persia, are loaded with rice and other kinds of grain. These mules and camels also serve to carry tents and armor, and likewise tools and munitions for the campaign. . . . The invading army carefully abstains from encroaching on its supplies at the outset, as they are well aware that, when the season for campaigning draws to a close, they will have to retreat over districts wasted by the enemy, or scraped as bare by countless hordes of men and droves of baggage animals, as if they had been devastated by locusts; accordingly they reserve their stores as much as possible for this emergency. . . .

From this you will see that it is the patience, self denial, and thrift of the Turkish soldier that enable him to face the most trying circumstances, and come safely out of the dangers that surround him. What a contrast to our men! . . .

For each man is his own worst enemy, and has no foe more deadly than his own intemperance, which is sure to kill him, if the enemy be not quick. It makes me shudder to think of what the result of a struggle between such different systems must be; one of us must prevail and the other be destroyed, at any rate we cannot both exist in safety. On their side is the vast wealth of their empire, unimpaired resources, experience and practice in arms, a veteran soldiery, an uninterrupted series of victories, readiness to endure hardships, union, order, discipline, thrift, and watchfulness. On ours are found an empty exchequer, luxurious habits, exhausted resources, broken spirits, a raw and insubordinate soldiery, and greedy generals; there is no regard for discipline, license runs riot, the men indulge in drunkenness and debauchery, and, worst of all, the enemy are accustomed to victory, we, to defeat. Can we doubt what the result must be?

Consider This:

- Busbecq maintained that between Christians and Muslims, "one of us must prevail and the other be destroyed." Why did he think Christian nations were at a disadvantage? By painting such a picture, was Busbecq hoping to frighten European nations into reform?

Question:
1. *What are the most important qualities for success and advancement in the Ottoman Empire?*

12.3   Women in Ottoman Society: Oigier de Busbecq

The energy of the Ottoman Empire perhaps reached its zenith under the direction of Sultan Süleyman "the Lawgiver" (r. 1520–1566). One of the most important assessments of Süleyman's influence came from Ogier Ghiselin de Busbecq, the ambassador from Austria to Süleyman's court at Istanbul from 1554–1562. Busbecq had been dispatched in the recent wake of the unsuccessful Ottoman siege of Vienna in 1529. His mission was to use his diplomatic skills to prevent another possible attack on the city. Busbecq's letters reveal much about Süleyman, his court, capital, Islamic traditions, and treatment of women.

Source: "Women in Ottoman Society" is from C. T. Foster and F. H. Blackburne Daniell, *The Life and Letters of Ogier Ghiselin de Busbecq*, vol. 1 (London: Hakluyt Society, 1881), pp. 219-221.

Keep in Mind . . .

- What is the role of woman in Ottoman society?

The Turks are the most careful people in the world of the modesty of their wives, and therefore keep them shut up at home and hide them away, so that they scarce see the light of day. But if they have to go into the streets, they are sent out so covered and wrapped up in veils that they seem to those who meet them mere gliding ghosts. They have the means of seeing men through their linen or silken veils, while no part of their own body is exposed to men's view. For it is a received opinion among them, that no woman who is distinguished in the very smallest degree by her figure or youth, can be seen by a man without his desiring her, and therefore without her receiving some contamination; and so it is the universal practice to confine the women to the harem. Their brothers are allowed to see them, but not their brothers-in-law. Men of the richer classes, or of higher rank, make it a condition when they marry, that their wives shall never set foot outside the threshold, and that no man or woman shall be admitted to see them for any reason whatever, not even their nearest relations, except their fathers and mothers, who are allowed to pay a visit to their daughters at the [festival of Bairam].

On the other hand, if the wife has a rather high rank, or has brought a larger dowry than usual, the husband promises on his part that he will take no concubine, but will keep to her alone. Otherwise, the Turks are not forbidden by any law to have as many concubines as they please in addition to their lawful wives. Between the children of wives and those of concubines there is no distinction, and they are considered to have equal rights. As for concubines, they either buy them for themselves or win them in war; when they are tired of them there is nothing to prevent their bringing them to market and selling them; but they are entitled to their freedom if they have borne children to their master. . . . The only distinction between the lawful wife and the concubine, is that the former has a dowry, while the slaves have none. A wife who has a portion settled on her [a dowry] is mistress of her husband's house, and all the other women have to obey her orders. The husband, however, may choose which of them shall spend the night with him. He makes known his wishes to the wife, and she sends to him the slave he has selected. . . . Only Friday night . . . is supposed to belong to the wife; and she grumbles if her husband deprives her of it. On all the other nights he may do so as he pleases.

Divorces are granted among them for many reasons which it is easy for the husbands to invent. The divorced wife receives back her dowry, unless the divorce has been caused by some fault on her part. There is more difficulty in a woman's getting a divorce from her husband.

Consider This:

* Why are women completely covered in Ottoman society? What were the expectations for women at this time and what distinctions were made between wives and concubines?

Question:
1. What is the role of women in Ottoman society?

12.4 The Ottomans: Empire-builders at the Crossroads of Three Continents

Militarily speaking, the strongest force in the West during the 16th and 17th centuries was that of the Ottoman Turks. From being an obscure Muslim nation, the Ottomans emerged with a vengeance in the 15th century, capturing Constantinople in 1453, and ultimately establishing hegemony over the Balkans, North Africa, the Arabian penninsula, and the western portion of the Near East. Ottoman armies kept European powers under constant pressure, besieging Vienna in 1527 and 1683. Few Westerners were permitted to observe conditions within the mysterious Ottoman state; the following observations date from 1668.

Source: Harry Schwartz, ed., *Paul Rycaut: The Present State of the Ottoman Empire* (N.Y.: Arno Press & New York Times, 1971), pp 3–5, 167, 190–191.

In this Government, severity, violence, and cruelty are natural to it; and it were as great an errour to begin to loose the reigns, and ease the people of that oppression to which they and their fore-fathers have since their first original have been accustomed, as it would be in a nation free-born, and used to live under the protection of good laws, and the clemency of a virtuous and Christian Prince, to exercise a Tyrannical power over their estates and lives, and change their liberty into servitude and slavery. The *Turks* had the original of their Civil Government founded in the time of war: for when they first came out of *Scythia,* and took arms in their hands, and submitted unto one General, it is to be supposed, that they had no Laws but what were Arbitrary and Martial, and most agreeable to the enterprise and design they had then in hand, when *Tangrolipix* overthrew the *Persian Sultan;* possessed himself of his Dominions and Power, and called and opened the way for his companions out of *Armenia;* when *Cutlumuses* revolted from him, and made a distinct kingdom in *Arabia:* when other Princes of the *Selcuccian* family in the infancy of Turkish power had by wars among themselves, or by Testament made division of their possessions; when *(Anno 1300) Ottoman,* by strange fortunes, and from small beginnings swallowed up all the other Governments into the *Ogusian* Tribe, and united them under one head, untill at last it arrived to that greatness and power it now enjoys. The whole condition of this people was but a continued state of war; wherefore it is not strange, if their laws are severe, and in most things arbitrary; that the Emperor should be absolute and above law, and that most of their customs should run in a certain channel and course not answerable to the height and unlimited power of the Governour, and consequently to the oppression and subjection of the people: and that they should thrive most by servitude, be most happy, prosperous and contented under Tyranny, is as natural to them, as to a body to be nourished with that diet, which it had from its infancy or birth been acquainted with. But not only is Tyranny requisite for this people, and a stiff rein to curb them, left by an unknown liberty, they grow mutinous and unruly, but likewise the large territories and remote parts of the Empire require speedy preventions, without processes of law, or formal indictment: jealousie and suspition of mis-government being license and authority enough for the Emperour to inflict his severest punishments: all which depends on the absoluteness of the Prince; which because it is that whereby the *Turks* are principally supported in their greatness, and is the prime Maxim and Foundation of their State, we shall make it the discourse and subject of the following Chapter.

***

The *Turks* having (as is before declared) laid the first foundation of their Government with the principles most agreeable to Military Discipline, their Generals or Princes, whose will and lusts they served, became absolute Masters of their Lives and Estates; so that what they gained and acquired by the Sword with labours, perils, and sufferings, was appropriated to the use and benefit of their Great Master. All the delightful fields of *Asia,* the pleasant plains of *Tempe* and *Thrace,* all the plenty of *Ægypt* and fruitfulness of the *Nile,* the luxury of *Corinth,* the substance of *Peleponesus, Athens, Lemnos, Scio,* and *Mitylen,* with other Isles of the *Ægean Sea,* the Spices of *Arabia,* and the riches of a great part of *Persia,* all *Armenia,* the Provinces of *Pontus, Galatia, Bythinia, Phrygia, Lycia, Pamphylia, Palestine, Cœlostria,* and *Phœnicia, Colchis,* and a great part of *Georgia,* the tributary principalities of *Moldavia* and *Valachia, Romania, Bulgaria* and *Servia,* and the best part of *Hungary,* concur all together to satisfise the appetite of one single person; all the extent of this vast territory, the Lands and Houses, as well as the Castles and Arms, are the proper goods of the Grand Grand Signior, in his sole disposal and gift they remain, whose possession and right they are; only to lands dedicated to religious uses…

***

Those who would appear of a compassionate and tender nature, hold it a pious work to buy a Bird from a cage to give him his liberty; and hold it a merciful action to buy bread and feed the Dogs, of which there is a great number of diseased Curs in all streets appropriate to no Master, but are mangy and foul, and no small causes of breeding the Plague, so frequent in *all* the Cities of the *Turks.* And this care of Dogs is accounted so charitable, that there are certain laws made for the protection and maintenance of them: and it is a lighter offense to deny bread to a poor Christian who is famished in his chains, then to the Dogs of their street, which are fit for nothing but to breed Infection; and some bind themselves by a vow to give such a quantity of bread a day to the Dogs of such a street, others bequeath it by Testament; for they maintain their quarters from other wandring Curs, and joyn together in a strange manner to preserve certain limits free from others that are not whelped and bred amongst them.

    The *Camel* is another sort of Beast to which the *Turks* bear not only a love, but a Religious reverence, accounting it a greater sin to over-burthen and tyre them with too much labour than the Horse, because it is the Beast most common to the Holy parts of *Arabia,* and carries the *Alchoran* in Pilgrimage; so that I have observed those who have the government of the *Camels,* when they have given water to them in a Bason, to take of the foam or froth that comes from the mouth of the Beast, and with that, as if it were some rare Balsome, with a singular devotion to anoint their Beards…

***

    The next main sinew of the *Ottoman* Power is the order of the *Janizaries,* which is as much as to say, the new Militia; and yet their Antiquity may be deduced from *Ottoman* the first King of the Turks; but because they received honours and priviledges from *Amurath* their third King; our Turkish History accounts that to be the time of the first original: it is certain that in his time they were modelized, and certain Laws prescribed both for their education and maintenance; when by the counsel of *Catradin,* otherwise called *Kara Rustbenes, Amurath's* prime Vizier, it was ordained that for the augmentation of this Militia, every fifth Captive taken from the Christians, above the age of 15 years, should be the dues of the *Sultan* who at first were to be distributed amongst the Turkish Husbandmen in *Asia,* to learn and be instructed in the Turkish Language and Religion.

    Their number at first was not accounted above 6 or 7000, now with time they are encreased to the number of twenty thousand effective men; but were there a list taken of all those who assume this title of *Janizary,* and enjoy their priviledges though not their pay, there would be found above a hundred thousand; six or seven go under the name of one *Janizary,* for gaining by this means a priviledge of being free from all Duties and Taxes, they bestow a certain summe of money or annual presents on the Officers, in consideration of which they are owned and countenanced as *Janizaries*. Their Habit is as the Picture represents, wearing alwaies the beard of their Chin and underlip shaven, which some say they learned from the *Italians;* but certain it is, that this Custom is more ancient, than since the time of their Neighbourhood unto *Italy:* this manner of their shaving being generally used as a token of their subjection, and so all the Pages and Officers in the *Seraglio* of great men, orders of the Gardeners, *Baltagees* or Hatchetmen and others are distinguished by this mark to be in service and obliged to the attendance of a Master: But when they are either licensed from the War, or promoted to Office, or freed to their own disposal, they immediately suffer their Beards to grow as a signe of their liberty and gravity.

In former times this Militia consisted only of the Sons of Christians, educated in the Mahometan Rights; but of late that politick Custom hath been disused, the reason of which some attribute to the abundance of people the *Turks* having of their own to supply all their occasions: but I am rather induced to another opinion, having not observed the multitude which Histories and Travellers tell us, that the Turks swarm with; and rather assigne the neglect of this practice, so prejudicial to Christian Interest in these parts, to the corruption of the Officers, and the carelesness in their Discipline.

Questions:
1. *What conclusions does Rycaut reach as to the tyrannical slant of Ottoman government? Does he envision the possibilty or desirability of reform?*
2. *What attitude do the Turks assume towards dogs and camels?*
3. *Who are the Jannisaries and how are they recruited ?*

12.5 The Safavid Shi'ite Empire of Persia

The Safavid state in Persia had been built upon a fervent commitment to the Shi'ite sect of Islam. The greatest Safavid ruler, Shah Abbas I (r. 1588–1629) had inherited his throne at a difficult time. His father had been forced to abdicate and much of his empire was on the brink of disintegration. Ottoman invaders from the west and Uzbecs from the east had placed tremendous pressure on the new monarch. But within fifteen years, Abbas I had defeated both groups and the Mughals in India as well by 1621, securing more territory and trading posts in the Persian Gulf. He then focused on international trade and manufacturing and on protecting his territories through diplomatic contacts.

In executing this strategy, Shah Abbas I cultivated relations with several European countries whose skills in war and technology were of the highest importance. Abbas was more interested in European gun-smiths than in the vagaries of Muslim doctrine. As a result, he allowed European missionaries to visit his realm and openly seek converts among his Muslim population. The following accounts are from Fathers Simon and Vincent, Carmelite friars dispatched to Abbas's capital at Isfahan in 1605. They spent six months gathering information and then made their report to Pope Paul V.

> **Source:** "Shah Abbas I" is from Robert Simon, *A Chronicle of the Carmelites in Persia and the Papal Mission of the Seventeenth and Eighteenth Centuries* (London: Eyre and Spottiswoode, 1939), pp. 158-161.

SHAH ABBAS I
FATHER SIMON

Keep in Mind . . .

* What qualities made Shah Abbas I an effective leader?

The king, Shah Abbas . . . is [43] years old . . . of medium height, rather thin than fat, his face round and small, tanned by the sun, with hardly any beard; very vivacious and alert, so that he is always doing something or other. He is sturdy and healthy, accustomed to much exercise and toil: many times he goes about on foot, and recently he had been forty days on pilgrimage, which he made on foot the whole time. He has extraordinary strength, and with his scimitar can cut a man in two and a sheep with its wool on at a single blow—and the Persian sheep are of large size. He has done many other feats and has found no one to come up to him in them. In his food he is frugal, as also in his dress, and this to set an example to his subjects; and so in public he eats little else than rice, and that cooked in water only. His usual dress is of linen, and very plain: similarly the nobles and others in his realm follow suit, whereas formerly they used to go out dressed in brocade with jewels and other fopperies: and if he sees anyone who is overdressed, he takes him to task, especially if it be a soldier. But in private, he eats what he likes.

He is sagacious in mind, likes fame and to be esteemed: he is courteous in dealing with everyone and at the same time very serious. For he will go through the public streets, eat from what they are selling there and other things, speak at ease freely with the lower classes, cause his subjects to remain sitting while he himself is standing, or will sit down beside this man and that. He says that is how to be a king, and that the king of Spain and other Christians do not get any pleasure out of ruling, because they are obliged to comport themselves with so much pomp and majesty.

He causes foreigners to sit down beside him and to eat at his table. With that and accompanying all such informality he requires that people shall not [lack] respect toward him and, should anyone fail in this regard, he will punish the individual severely. So the more he demonstrates kindliness to his subjects and the more familiarly he talks with them, they tremble before him, even the greatest among them, for, while joking, he will have their heads cut off. He is very strict in executing justice and pays no regard to his own favorites in this respect; but rather is the stricter with them in order to serve an example to others. So he has no private friends, nor anyone who has influence with him. . . . While we were at Court, he caused the bellies of two of his favorites to be ripped open, because they behaved improperly to an ordinary woman. From this it comes about that there are so very few murderers and robbers. In all the time I was at Isfahan, there was never a case of homicide.

He is very speedy in dispatching business: when he gives audience, which he does at the gate of his palace, . . . he finishes off all the cases that are brought to him. The parties stand present before him, the officers of justice, and his own council, with whom he consults when it pleases him. The sentence which he gives is final and is immediately executed. If the guilty party deserves death, they kill him at once. . . .

Because of the great obedience [the nobles] pay the Shah, when he wills to have one of the nobles killed, he dispatches one of his men to fetch the noble's head: the man goes off to the grandee, and says to him: "The Shah wants your head." The noble replies: "Very well," and lets himself be decapitated—otherwise he would lose it and with it, all his family would become extinct. But, when [the nobles] allow themselves to be decapitated, [the Shah] aggrandizes the children. . . .

Regarding the religion of the king, I think that no one knows what he believes: he does not observe the Muslim law in many things, nor is he a Christian. Six or seven years ago he displayed many signs of not being averse to our Faith: God knows whether they were feigned, or came from his heart. In his [harem] he has many Christian Armenian, Georgian, and Circassian women. I think that he lets them live as they wish, because when I enquired what the Shah did with so many [holy] pictures that were presented to him as gifts and some relics of the Saints, for which he asked, the answer was made to me that he used to give them to the women in his harem. Besides that he is well informed regarding the mysteries of our holy Faith and discourses on the mystery of the most holy Trinity: he knows many examples and allusions which the Saints give in order to prove it, and discourses about the other mysteries—which we know from a man who had the opportunity of hearing him—if he does not talk about the women in his harem or about some demon or other. On account of the many disappointments which he asserts the Christians have caused him all this fervor has cooled. With all that he does not detest them. For he converses and eats with them, he suffers us to say frankly what we believe about our Faith and his own: sometimes he asks us about this. To us he has given a house: he knows that we say Mass publicly, he allows whoever may wish among the Persians to come to it, and we can teach them freely regarding our holy Faith, whenever they make inquiries about it. . . . I believe that the king realizes the objective with which our friars go out there. Till now none of them has been converted: I think they are waiting for one of the nobles or of their [religious leaders] to break the ice. . . .

Compare and Contrast:

- According to Father Simon, why was Shah Abbas I both loved and feared?
- Father Simon noted that "no one knows what [Shah Abbas I] believes." Was the Shah a devout Muslim? Why did he provide Christian churchmen with such flexibility in trying to convert Muslims in his realm? What does this say about Shah Abbas I as a political and religious leader?

THE WORSHIP OF IDOLS
FATHER VINCENT

Keep in Mind . . .

- What was Father Vincent's argument in rejecting the charge that Catholics were idolaters?

Two days previously the English had been with the king and discoursed at great length on the matter of religion and spoken ill of the Catholics saying that they were idolaters, who adored pictures and images, and made the sign of the cross, etc. The Shah had said that he would bring the Fathers together with them, so that they might hold a disputation on these matters.

This was the motive why the king of Persia asked the Fathers about the difference there is between Catholics and English. The Father Visitor answered that the English are heretics and false Christians and that Roman Catholics are the true Christians. . . .

In order to convince him, the Fathers put the question to the king: "Because your Highness and your people prostrate yourselves and worship seals and beads made of earth, would it be right for us to call your Highness and your people idolaters? Certainly not, because we know that, when you perform that act of adoration, you do not mean by it that the seal and stone are God, but do it out of piety and reverence for that soil, as it comes from the places of sepulture of your ancestors and that great men whom you consider saints." The Shah answered: "That is not the chief reason and intention we have for worshiping on earthen seals and beads, but rather in that act of veneration we make an act of recognizing that we are clay, and that from earth God created us, and we adore the Creator of this: and the reason why in the mosques and in our houses while we say our prayers on matting and carpets, our prayers would not be lawful and acceptable, unless we said them [touching] the earth. With this in view, for more convenience and cleanliness we use the earthen medallions [to touch with our foreheads during prayer] and beads: and that they are of this or that soil is an accidental matter: it suffices that it be earth. And so, when we have any other sort of stone, even if it be a piece of rock, we have no need of a seal. It is also true that we venerate it (the seal) as a memorial and a pious object, as you say, but no mainly for that reason."

To this the Fathers replied: "Very good! And thus our Christian religion does not adore nor serve images, as if they were gods, nor does it expect from them the future judgment (God preserve us from such a thing!), but it venerates images for the things they represent. They serve us also as memorials to remind us of the virtues of those saints they represent, in order that we may imitate them and beg them to intercede by their prayers with our Lord God, that He will grant us what we ask and that we may be good and his servants, as they have been, so that we may attain the glory which they now enjoy. So that, just as your Highness and your people do not say that the earthen medallion is God, no more do we say that the statues of the saints are gods, nor do we adore them as such." With these reasonings the Shah and his courtiers remained content.

Question:

1. Father Vincent stated that "the English are heretics and False Christians and that Roman Catholics are the true Christians." Compare this with Sultan Selim I's argument in rejecting the Shi'ite sect that Sunni Muslims were the "true religion." What does this tell you about sectarian disputes within a religion? Which is the "true religion"?

12.6 Shah Abbas the Great: The Resurgence of the Persian Empire

Persia, under the remarkable Safavid Dynasty, was the sole Middle Eastern power able to meet the Ottomans on equal terms—and the two great Islamic states were often in conflict. Persia was Shiite in its religious orientation while the Ottomans adhered to the Sunni variety of Islam. The most outstanding Safavid Emperor was Shah Abbas the Great (1587–1629), whose capital at Isfahan was fabled to be one of the wealthiest and most beautiful cities of the East. A portrait of Shah Abbas has been bequeathed to us through the biography written by his secretary, Eskander Bey Monshi (1560–1632?).

Source: Roger M. Savory, trans., *Eskander Bey Monshi: History of Shah Abbas the Great,* Vol. I (Boulder, CO.: Westview Press, 1978), pp. 523, 527–529, 531, 533.

DISCOURSE 5

On Shah 'Abbas's Justice, Concern for the Security of the Roads, and Concern for the Welfare of His Subjects

The greater part of governing is the preservation of stability within the kingdom and security on the roads. Prior to the accession of Shah 'abbas, this peace and security had disappeared in Iran, and it had become extremely difficult for people to travel about the country. As soon as he came to the throne, Shah 'abbas turned his attention to this problem. He called for the principal highway robbers in each province to be identified, and he then set about eliminating this class of people. Within a short space of time, most of their leaders had been arrested. Some of them, who had been driven by misfortune to adopt this way of life, were pardoned by Shah 'abbas and their troubles solved by various forms of royal favor. Overwhelmed by this display of royal clemency, these men swore to serve the king and to behave as law-abiding citizens. Others, however, were handed over to the *sahna* (a police official) for punishment, and society was rid of this scourge. With security restored to the roads, merchants and tradesmen traveled to and from the Safavid empire.

The welfare of his people was always a prime concern of the Shah, and he was at pains to see that the people enjoyed peace and security, and that oppression by officialdom, the major cause of anxiety on the part of the common man, was totally stamped out in his kingdom. Substantial reductions were made in the taxes due to the *dīvān*: first, the tax on flocks in Iraq, amounting to nearly fifteen thousand Iraqi *tomān*, was remitted to the people of that province, and the population of Iraq, which is the flourishing heart of Iran and the seat of government, by this gift was preferred above the other provinces. Second, all *dīvān* levies were waived for all Shi'ites throughout the empire during the month of Ramazān. The total revenues for one month, which according to the computation of the *dīvān* officials amounted to some twenty thousand *tomān*, were given to the people as alms. The object was that they should be free from demands for taxes during this blessed month, which is a time to be devoted to the service and worship of God.

DISCOURSE 7

On Shah 'Abbas's Policy-making and Administration

If scholars consider Sha 'Abbas to be the founder of the laws of the realm and an example in this regard to the princes of the world, they have justification for this opinion, for he has been responsible for some weighty legislation in the field of administration.

One of his principal pieces of legislation has been his reform of the army. Because the rivalries of the *qezelbās* tribes had led them to commit all sorts of enormities, and because their devotion to the Safavid royal house had been weakened by dissension, Shah 'Abbas decided (as the result of divine inspiration, which is vouchsafed to kings but not to ordinary mortals), to admit into the armed forces groups other than the *qezelbās*. He enrolled in the armed forces large numbers of Georgian, Circassian, and other *gōlāms*, and created the office of *qollar-āqāsī* commander-in-chief of the *gōlām* regiments), which had not previously existed under the Safavid regime. Several thousand men were drafted into regiments of musketeers from the Cāgatāy tribe, and from various Arab and Persian tribes in Khorasan, Azerbaijan, and TabarestAn. Into the regiments of musketeers, too, were drafted all the riff-fall from every province—sturdy, serviceable men who were unemployed and preyed on the lower classes of society. By this means the lower classes were given relief from their lawless activities, and the recruits made amends for their past sins by performing useful service in the army. All these men were placed on the *gōlām* muster rolls. Without question, they were an essential element in 'Abbas's conquests, and their employment had many advantages.

Shah 'Abbas tightened up provincial administration. Any emir or noble who was awarded a provincial governorship, or who was charged with the security of the highways, received his office on the understanding that he discharge his duties in a proper manner. If any merchant or traveler or resident were robbed, it was the duty of the governor to recover his money for him or replace it out of his own funds. This rule was enforced throughout the Safavid empire. As a result, property was secure, and people could travel without hindrance to and from Iran.

Another of Shah 'Abbas's policies has been to demand a truthful reply whenever he asked anyone for information. Lying, he said, is forbidden and considered a sin by God, so why should it not be a sin to lie to him who is one's king, one's spiritual director, and one's benefactor? Is not falsehood to such a one ingratitude? In the opinion of Shah 'Abbas, lying to one's benefactor constituted the rankest ingratitude. If he detected anyone in a lie, he visited punishment upon him. The effects of this policy have been felt at all levels of society. For example, if someone has committed various acts that merit the death penalty and the king questions him on his conduct, the poor wretch has no option but to tell the truth. In fact, the opinion is commonly held that, if a person tells a lie to the Shah, the latter intuitively knows he is lying. The result is that the biggest scoundrel alive hesitates to allow even a small element of falsehood to creep into any story he is telling the Shah. The beneficial effects of this on government and the administration of justice need no elaboration.

DISCOURSE 8

On His Simplicity of Life, Lack of Ceremony, and Some Contrary Qualities

The character of the Shah contains some contradictions; for instance, his fiery temper, his imperiousness, his majesty, and regal splendor are matched by his mildness, leniency, his ascetic way of life, and his immortality. His is equally at home on the dervish's mat and the royal throne. When he is in good temper, he mixes with the greatest informality with the members of his household, his close friends and retainers with others, and treats them like brothers. In contrast, when he is in a towering rage, his aspect is so terrifying that the same man who, shortly before, was his boon companion and was treated with all the informality of a close friend, dares not to speak a word out of turn for fear of being accused of insolence or discourtesy. At such times, the emirs, sultans, and even the court wits and his boon companions keep silent, for fear of the consequences. The Shah, then, posesses these two contrasting natures, each of which is developed to the last degree.

DISCOURSE 9

On Shah 'Abbas's Concern for the Rights of His Servants and His Avoiding Laying Hands on Their Possessions

One of the most agreeable qualities of this monarch is his compassionate treatment of his servants, which is coupled with a concern that faithful service should receive its just reward. His record in this regard is so outstanding that it is not matched by that of any other chivalrous prince. As long as his servants are constant in their loyalty, the royal favor is lavished upon them, nor is it withdrawn for any trifling offense committed out of ignorance or from negligence. If any of his servants dies from natural causes, or gives his life in battle in the defense of the faith and the state, the Shah is generous in his treatment of their dependents. In the case of officeholders, even if their sons are too young at the time of their father's death to be fit for office, nevertheless, in order to resuscitate their families, he confers the same office on the sons out of his natural generosity and magnanimity.

Moreover, since the Shah considers the possessions and treasures of this world of little value, even if the deceased has left substantial sums of money, such is the Shah's magnanimity and concern to follow the prescripts of canon law that he (unlike the majority of princes) does not lay covetous eyes on the inheritance, but divides it among the heirs in the proportions ordained by God. This is regarded by some as his most praiseworthy characteristic, for most of the princes of the world consider it impossible for them to show greater appreciation for their servants than by following this practice, which brings with it heavenly rewards.

DISCOURSE 10

On Shah 'Abbas's Breadth of Vision, and His Knowledge of World Affairs and of the Classes of Society

After he has dealt with the affairs of state, Shah 'Abbas habitually relaxes. He has always been fond of conviviality and, since he is still a young man, he enjoys wine and the company of women. But this does not affect the scrupulous discharge of his duties, and he knows in minute detail what is going on in Iran and also in the world outside. He has a well-developed intelligence system, with the result that no one, even if he is sitting at home with his family, can express opinions which should not be expressed without running the risk of their being reported to the Shah. This has actually happened on numerous occasions.

As regards his knowledge of the outside world, he possesses information about the rulers (both Muslim and non-Muslim) of other countries, about the size and composition of their armies, about their religious faith and the organization of their kingdoms, about their highway systems, and about the prosperity or otherwise of their realms. He has cultivated diplomatic relations with most of the princes of the world, and the rulers of the most distant parts of Europe, Russia, and India are on friendly terms with him. Foreign ambassadors bearing gifts are never absent from his court, and the Shah's achievements in the field of foreign relations exceed those of his predecessors.

Shah 'Abbas mixes freely with all classes of society, and in most cases is able to converse with people in their own particular idiom. He is well versed in Persian poetry; he understands it well, indulges in poetic license, and sometimes utters verses himself. He is a skilled musician, an outstanding composer of rounds, rhapsodies, and part-songs; some of his compositions are famous. As a conversationalist, he is capable of elegant and witty speech.

Questions:
1. *To what extent was clemency a part of Shah Abbas' policy? To what degree was severity employed? Which predominated?*
2. *What novelties in policy does Eskander seem to indicate derived their inspiration from the Shah?*
3. *What does Eskander indicate about the Shah's personality?*
4. *Reading between the lines of Eskander's biography of the Shah, what would it be like to live in the state administered by Shah Abbas? Do the positives outweigh the negatives, or vice-versa? Explain.*

12.7 Moghul Apogee: Akbar the Enlightened

Though he was the grandson of Muslim conquerors from Central Asia, Emperor Akbar of India (1556–1605) broke the ancestral mold by espousing policies of religious toleration which would be remarkable by the standards of any age, let alone the latter 16th century. He went so far as to attempt a synthesis of all major faiths, from Islam to Hinduism to Christianity to Buddhism, around his principle of "Sulahku," or tolerance for all shades of belief. Though, administratively speaking, he must go down as one of India's most able monarchs, the faith he launched did not long survive his death; his son and successor Jahangir soon reversed many of his innovations. Akbar's biographer, Abu I'Fazl Allami (1551–1602), served in various capacities at the imperial court.

> **Source:** H. Blochmann, trans., *Abu'Fazl Allami: The Aini Alcbari* (Delhi, India: Naresh C. Jain, 1965), pp. 46–47, 59–61, 162–165.

THE IMPERIAL HAREM

His Majesty is a great friend of good order and propriety in business. Through order, the world becomes a meadow of truth and reality; and that which is but external, receives through it a spiritual meaning. For this reason, the large number of women—a vexatious question even for great statesmen—furnished his Majesty with an opportunity to display his wisdom, and to rise from the low level of worldly dependence to the eminence of perfect freedom. The imperial palace and household are therefore in the best order.

His majesty forms matrimonial alliances With princes of Hindustan, and of other countries; and secures by these ties of harmony the peace of the world.

As the sovereign, by the light of his Wisdom, has raised fit persons from the dust of obscurity, and appointed them to various offices, so does he also elevate faithful persons to the several ranks in the service of the seraglio. Short-sighted men think of impure gold, which will gradually turn into pure gold; but the farsighted know that his Majesty understands how to use elixirs and chemical processes. Any kind of growth will alter the constitution of a body; copper and iron will turn to gold, and tin and lead to silver; hence it is no matter of astonishment if an excellent being changes the worthless into men. "The saying of the wise is true that the eye of the exalted is the elixir for producing goodness." Such also are the results flowing from the love of order of his Majesty, from his wisdom, insight, regard to rank, his respect for others, his activity, his patience. Even when he is angry, he does not deviate from the right path; he looks at everything with kindly feelings, weighs rumours well, and is free from all prejudice; he considers it a great blessing to have the good wishes of the people, and does not allow the intoxicating pleasures of this world to overpower his calm judgment.

His Majesty has made a large enclosure with fine buildings inside, where he reposes. Though there are more than five thousand women, he has given to each a separate apartment. He has also divided them into sections, and keeps them attentive to their duties. Several chaste women have been appointed as *daroghas,* and superintendents over each section, and one has been selected for the duties of writer. Thus, as in the imperial offices, everything is here also in proper order. The salaries are sufficiently liberal. Not counting the presents, which his Majesty most generously bestows, the women of the highest rank receive from 1610 to 1028 Rs. *per mensem.* Some of the servants have from 51 to 20, others from 40 to 2 Rs. Attached to the private audience hall of the palace is a clever and zealous writer, who superintends the expenditure of the Harem, and keeps an account of the cash and the stores. If a woman wants anything, within the limit of her salary, she applies to one of the *Tahwĭldārs* (cash-keepers) of the seraglio. The TahwIldAr then sends a memorandum to the writer, who checks it, when the General Treasurer makes the payment in cash, as for claims of this nature no cheques are given.

The writer also makes out an estimate of the annual expenditure, writes out summarily a receipt, which is countersigned by the ministers of the state. It is then stamped with a peculiar imperial seal, which is only used in grants connected with the Harem, when the receipt becomes payable. The money itself is paid by the cash-keeper of the General Treasury to the General *Tahwĭldār,* who on the order of the writer of the Harem, hands it over to the several Sub-*Tahwĭldārs* for distribution among the servants of the seraglio. All moneys are reckoned in their salaries at the current rate.

The inside of the Harem im guarded by sober and active women; the most trustworthy of them are placed about the apartments of his Majesty. Outside the enclosure the eunuchs are placed; and at a proper distance, there is a guard of faithful *RAjpUts,* beyond whom are the porters of the gates. Besides, on all four sides, there are guards of Nobles, *Ahadĭs,* and other troops, according to their ranks.

Whenever *Begams,* or the wives of nobles, or other women of chaste character, desire to be presented, they first notify their wish to the servants of the seraglio, and wait for a reply. From thence they send their request to the officers of the palace, after which those who are eligible are permitted to enter the Harem. Some women of rank, obtain permission to remain there for a whole month.

Notwithstanding the great number of faithful guards, his Majesty does not dispense with his own vigilance, but keeps the whole in proper order.

THE IMPERIAL KITCHEN

His Majesty even extends his attention to this department, and has given many wise regulations for it; nor can a reason be given why he should not do so, as the equilibrium of man's nature, the strength of the body, the capability of receiving external and internal blessings, and the acquisition of Worldly and religious advantages, depend ultimately on proper care being shown for appropriate food. This knowledge distinguishes man from beasts, with whom, as far as mere eating is concerned, he stands upon the same level. If his Majesty did not possess so lofty a mind, so comprehensive an understanding, so universal a kindness, he would have chosen the path of solitude, and given up sleep and food altogether; and even now, when he has taken upon himself the temporal and spiritual leadership of the people, the question, "What dinner has been prepared to-day?" never passes over his tongue. In the course of twenty-four hours his Majesty eats but Once, and leaves off before he is fully satisfied; neither is there any fixed time for this meal, but the servants have always things so far ready, that in the space of an hour, after the order has been given, a hundred dishes are served up. The food allowed to the women of the seraglio commences to be taken from the kitchen in the morning, and goes on till night.

Trustworthy and experienced people are appointed to this department; and all good servants attached to the court, are resolved to perform well whatever service they have undertaken. Their head is assisted by the Prime Minister himself. His Majesty has entrusted to the latter the affairs of the state, but especially this important department. Notwithstanding all this, his Majesty is not unmindful of the conduct of the servants. He appoints a zealous and sincere man as *Mīr Bakāwal*, or Master of the Kitchen, upon whose insight the success of the department depends, and gives him several upright persons as assistants. There are also treasurers for the cash and the stores, several tasters, and a clever writer. Cooks from all countries prepare a great variety of dishes of all kinds of grains, greens, meats; also oily, sweet, and spicy dishes. Every day such dishes are prepared as the nobles can scarcely command at their feasts, from which you may infer how exquisite the dishes are which are prepared for his Majesty.

In the beginning of the year the Sub-treasurers make out an animal estimate, and receive the amount; the money bags and the door of the store-house being sealed with the seals of the *Mīr Bakāwal* and the writer; and every month a correct statement of the daily expenditure is drawn up, the receipt for which is sealed by the same two officers, when it is entered under the head of the expenditure. At the beginning of every quarter, the *Dīwān-i buyūtāt* and the *Mīr Bakāwal*, collect whatever they think will be necessary; e.g. *Sukhdās* rice from Bharāji, *Dewzīra* rice from Gwāliar, *Jinjin* rice from Rājórī and Nīmlah, *ghī* from *Hisār Fīrūza*; ducks, water-fowls, and certain vegetables from Kashmīr. Patterns are always kept. The sheep, goats, berberies, fowls, ducks, etc., are fattened by the cooks; fowls are never kept less than a month. The slaughter-house is without the city or the camp, in the neighbourhood of rivers and tanks, where the meat is washed, when it is sent to the kitchen in sacks sealed by the cooks. There it is again washed, and thrown into the pots. The water-carriers pour the water out of their leather bags into earthen vessels, the mouths of which are covered with pieces of cloth, and sealed up; and the water is left to settle before it is used. A place is also told off as a kitchen garden, that there may be a continual supply of fresh greens. The *Mīr Bakāwal* and the writer determine the price of every eatable, which becomes a fixed rule; and they sign the day-book, the estimates, the receipts for transfers, the list of wages of the servants, etc., and watch every transaction. Bad characters, idle talkers, unknown persons are never employed; no one is entertained without a personal security, nor is personal acquaintance sufficient.

The victuals are served up in dishes of gold and silver, stone and earthenware; some of the dishes being in charge of each of the *Sub-Bakāwals*. During the time of cooking, and when the victuals are taken out, an awning is spread, and lookers-on kept away. The cooks tuck up their sleeves, and the hems of their garments, and hold their hands before their mouths and noses when the food is taken out; the cook and the *Bakāwal* taste it, after which it is tasted by the *Mīr Bakāwal*, and then put into the dishes. The gold and silver dishes are tied up in red cloths, and those of copper and china in white ones. The *Mīr Bakāwal* attaches his seal, and writes on it the names of the contents, whilst the clerk of the pantry writes out on a sheet of paper a list of all vessels and dishes, which he sends inside, with the seal of the *Mīr Bakāwal*, that none of the dishes may be changed. The dishes are carried by the *Bakāwals*, the cooks, and the other servants, and macebearers precede and follow, to prevent people from approaching them. The servants of the pantry send at the same time, in bags containing the seal of the *Bakāwal*, various kinds of bread, saucers of curds piled up, and small stands containing plates of pickles, fresh ginger, limes, and various greens. The servants of the palace again taste the food, spread the table cloth on the ground, and arrange the dishes; and when after some time his Majesty commences to dine, the table servants sit opposite him in attendance; first, the share of the derwishes is put apart, when his Majesty commences with milk or curds. After he has dined, he prostrates himself in prayer. The *Mīr Bakāwal* is always in attendance. The dishes are taken away according to the above list. Some victuals are also kept half ready, should they be called for.

The copper utensils are tinned twice a month; those of the princes, etc., once; whatever is broken is given to the braziers, who make new ones.

THE MANNER IN WHICH HIS MAJESTY SPENDS HIS TIME

The success of the three branches of the government, and the fulfilment of the wishes of the subjects, whether great or small, depend upon the manner in which a king spends his time. The care with which His Majesty guards over his motives, and watches over his emotions, bears on its face the sign of the Infinite, and the stamp of immortality; and though thousands of important matters occupy, at one and the same time, his attention, they do not stir up the rubbish of confusion in the temple of his mind, nor do they allow the dust of dismay to settle on the vigour of his mental powers, or the habitual earnestness with which His Majesty contemplates the charms of God's world. His anxiety to do the will of the Creator is ever increasing; and thus his insight and wisdom are ever deepening. From his practical knowledge, and capacity for everything excellent, he can sound men of experience, though rarely casting a glance on his own ever extending excellence. He listens to great and small, expecting that a good thought, or the relation of a noble deed, may kindle in his mind a new lamp of wisdom, though ages have passed without his having found a really great man. Impartial statesmen, on seeing the sagacity of His Majesty, blotted out the book of their own wisdom, and commenced a new leaf. But with the magnanimity which distinguishes him, and with his wonted zeal, he continues his search for superior men, and finds a reward in the care with which he selects such as are fit for his society.

Although surrounded by every external pomp and display, and by every inducement to lead a life of luxury and ease, he does not allow his desires, or his wrath, to renounce allegiance to Wisdom, his sovereign—how much less would he permit them to lead him to a bad deed! Even the telling of stories, which ordinary people use as a means of lulling themselves into sleep, serves to keep His Majesty awake.

Ardently feeling after God, and searching for truth, His Majesty exercises upon himself both inward and outward austerities, though he occasionally joins public worship, in order to hush the slandering tongues of the bigots of the present age. But the great object of his life is the acquisition of that sound morality, the sublime loftiness of which captivates the hearts of thinking sages, and silences the taunts of zealots and sectarians.

Knowing the value of a lifetime, he never wastes his time, nor does he omit any necessary duty, so that in the light of his upright intentions, every action of his life may be considered as an adoration of God.

It is beyond my power to describe in adequate terms His Majesty's devotions. He passes every moment of his life in self-examination or in adoration of God. He especially does so at the time, when morning spreads her azure silk, and scatters abroad her young, golden beams; and at noon, when the light of the world-illuminating sun embraces the universe, and thus becomes a source of joy for all men; in the evening when that fountain of light withdraws from the eyes of mortal man, to the bewildering grief of all who are friends of light; and lastly at midnight, when that great cause of life turns again to ascend, and to bring the news of renewed cheerfulness to all who, in the melancholy of the night, are stricken with sorrow. All these grand mysteries are in honor of God, and in adoration of the Creator of the world; and if dark-minded, ignorant men cannot comprehend their signification, who is to be blamed, and whose loss is it? Indeed, every man acknowledges that we owe gratitude and reverence to our benefactors; and hence it is incumbent on us, though our strength may fail, to show gratitude for the blessings we receive from the sun, the light of all lights, and to enumerate the benefits which he bestows. This is essentially the duty of kings, upon whom, according to the opinion of the wise, this sovereign of the heavens sheds an immediate light. And this is the very motive which actuates His Majesty to venerate fire and reverence lamps.

But why should I speak of the mysterious blessings of the sun, or of the transfer of his greater light to lamps? Should I not rather dwell on the perverseness of those weak-minded zealots, who, with much concern, talk of His Majesty's religion as of a deification of the Sun, and the introduction of fire-worship? But I shall dismiss them with a smile.

The compassionate heart of His Majesty finds no pleasure in cruelties, or in causing sorrow to others; he is ever sparing of the lives of his subjects, wishing to bestow happiness upon all.

His Majesty abstains much from flesh, so that whole months pass away without his touching any animal food, which, though prized by most, is nothing thought of by the sage. His august nature cares but little for the pleasures of the world. In the Course of twenty-four hours he never makes more than one meal. He takes a delight in spending his time in performing whatever is neceseary and proper. He takes a little repose in the evening, and again for a short time in the morning; but his sleep looks more like waking.

His Majesty is accustomed to spend the hours of the night profitably ; to the private audience hall are then admitted eloquent philosophers and virtuous SUfIs, who are seated according to their rank and entertain His Majesty with wise discourses. On such occasions His Majesty fathoms them, and tries them on the touch-stone of knowledge. Or the object of an ancient institution is disclosed, or new thoughts are hailed with delight. Here young men of talent learn to revere and adore His Majesty, and experience the happiness of having their wishes fulffilled, whilst old men of impartial judgment see themselves on the expanse of sorrow, finding that they have to pass through a new course of instruction.

There are also present in these assemblies, unprejudiced historians, who do not mutilate history by adding or suppressing facts, and relate the impressive events of ancient times. His Majesty often makes remarks wonderfully shrewd, or starts a fitting subject for conversation. On other occasions matters referring to the empire and the revenue are brought up, when His Majesty gives orders for whatever is to be done in each case.

About a watch before daybreak, musicians of all nations are introduced, who recreate the assembly with music and songs, and religious strains; and when four *gharīs* are left till morning His Majesty retires to his private apartments, brings his external appearance in harmony with the simplicity of his heart, and launches forth into the ocean of contemplation. In the meantime, at the close of night, soldiers, merchants, peasants, tradespeople, and other professions gather round the palace, patiently waiting to catch a glimpse of His Majesty. Soon after daybreak, they are allowed to make the *kornish* (*vide* A^e in 74). After this, His Majesty allows the attendants of the Harem to pay their compliments. During this time various matters of worldly and religious import are brought to the notice of His Majesty. As soon as they are settled, he returns to his private apartments and reposes a little.

The good habits of His Majesty are so numerous that I cannot adequately describe them. If I were to compile dictionaries on this subject they would not be exhaustive.

Questions:

1. What does Abu's description of the Imperial harem indicate about the status and treatment of women at Akbar's court?
2. What were the duties and functions of the imperial functionary known as the "Mir Bakawal"?
3. What traits does Abu seem to set forward as Akbar's most commendable? Is it fair to dismiss these descriptions as shameless attempts at flattery on the part of Abu? Why or why not?

PART 13
Renaissance and Reformation in Europe

13.1 Oration on the Dignity of Man (1486)

Perhaps the supreme statement of the Renaissance idolization of man is an extended essay by Pico della Mirandola, a linguist and philosopher who lived from 1463 to 1494. Note Pico's conception of man's relationship to God in this excerpt from the Oration on the Dignity of Man.

Source: E. Cassirer, P.O. Kristeller, and J.H. Randall, Jr., eds., *The Renaissance Philosohy of Man.* Copyright © 1948 bythe University of Chicago Press. Reprinted with permission.

PICO DELLA MIRANDOLA

At last it seems to me I have come to understand why man is the most fortunate of creatures and consequently worthy of all admiration and what precisely is that rank which is his lot in the universal chain of Being—a rank to be envied not only by brutes but even by the stars and by minds beyond this world. It is a matter past faith and a wondrous one. Why should it not be? For it is on this very account that man is rightly called and judged a great miracle and wonderful creature indeed. . . .God the Father, the supreme Architect, had already built this cosmic home we behold, the most sacred temple of His godhead, by the laws of His mysterious wisdom. The region above the heavens He had adorned with Intelligences, the heavenly spheres He had quickened with eternal souls, and the . . . filthy parts of the lower world He had filled with a multitude of animals of every kind. But, when the work was finished, the Craftsman kept wishing that there were someone to ponder the plan of so great a work, to love its beauty, and to wonder at its vastness. Therefore, when everything was done . . . He finally took thought concerning the creation of man. But there was not among His archetypes that from which He could fashion a new offspring, nor was there in His treasure houses anything which He might bestow on His new son as an inheritance, nor was there in the seats of all the world a place where the latter might sit to contemplate the universe. All was now complete; all things had been assigned to the highest, the middle, and the lowest orders. But in its final creation it was not the part of the Father's power to fail as though exhausted. It was not the part of His wisdom to waver in a needful matter through poverty of counsel. It was not the part of His kindly love that he who was to praise God's divine generosity in regard to others should be compelled to condemn it in regard to himself. At last the best of artisans ordained that the creature to whom He had been able to give nothing proper to himself should have joint possession of what ever had been peculiar to each of the different kinds of being. He therefore took man as a creature of indeterminate nature and, assigning him a place in the middle of the world, addressed him thus: . . . "The nature of all other beings is limited and constrained within the bounds of laws prescribed by Us. Thou, constrained by no limits, in accordance with thine own free will, in whose hand We have placed thee, shalt ordain for thyself the limits of thy nature. We have set thee at the world's center that thou mayest from thence more easily observe whatever is in the world. We have made thee neither of heaven nor of earth, neither mortal nor immortal, so that with freedom of choice and with honor, as though the maker and molder of thyself, thou mayest fashion thyself in whatever shape thou shalt prefer. Thou shalt have the power to degenerate into the lower forms of life, which are brutish. Thou shalt have the power, out of thy soul's judgment, to be reborn into the higher forms, which are divine." O supreme generosity of God the Father, O highest and most marvelous felicity of man! To him it is granted to have whatever he chooses, to be whatever he wills.

Question:
1. According to Mirandola, what is man's relationship to God?

13.2 The Soul of Man (1474)

The ideas of the Greek philosopher Plato were revived during the Renaissance by Neoplatonists who applied his theory on transmigration of the soul to Christian concepts of resurrection. The leading exponent of this philosophy was Marsilio Ficino. Some of his ideas on God and man follow.

Source: Burroughs, Josephine, trans. "Marsilio Ficino's Platonic Theology," *Journal of the History of Ideas* 5 (1944), 234–236. © Journal of the History of Ideas, Inc. Reprinted by permission of the Johns Hopkins University Press.

MARSILIO FICINO

Man is really the vicar of God, since he inhabits and cultivates all elements and is present on earth without being absent from the ether. He uses not only the elements, but also all the animals which belong to the elements, the animals of the earth, of the water, and of the air, for food, convenience, and pleasure, and the higher celestial beings for knowledge and the miracles of magic. Not only does he make use of the animals, he also rules them. It is true, with the weapons received from nature some animals may at times attack man or escape his control. But with the weapons he has invented himself man avoids the attacks of wild animals, puts them to flight and tames them. Who has ever seen any human beings kept under the control of animals, in such a way as we see everywhere herds of both wild and domesticated animals obeying men throughout their lives? Man not only rules the animals by force, he also governs, keeps and teaches them. Universal providence belongs to God, who is the universal cause. Hence man who provides generally for all things, both living and lifeless, is a kind of god. Certainly he is the god of the animals, for he makes use of them all, and instructs many of them. It is also obvious that he is the god of the elements for he inhabits and cultivates all of them. Finally, he is the god of all materials for he handles, changes and shapes all of them. He who governs the body in so many and so important ways, and is the vicar of the immortal God, he is no doubt immortal. . . .

Individual animals are hardly capable of taking care of themselves or their young. Man alone abounds in such a perfection that he first rules himself, something that no animals do, and thereafter rules the family, administers the state, governs nations and rules the whole world. . . .

We have shown that our soul in all its acts is trying with all its power to attain the first gift of God, that is, the possession of all truth and all goodness. Does it also seek His second attribute? Does not the soul try to become everything just as God is everything? It does in a wonderful way; for the soul lives the life of a plant when it serves the body in feeding it; the life of an animal, when it flatters the senses; the life of a man, when it deliberates through reason on human affairs; the life of the heroes, when it investigates natural things; . . . the life of the angels, when it enquires into the divine mysteries; the life of God, when it does everything for God's sake. Every man's soul experiences all these things in itself in some way, although souls do it in different ways, and thus the human species strives to become all things by living the lives of all things. . . . Man is a great miracle, a living creature worthy of reverence and adoration, for he . . . transforms himself into God as if he were God himself.

Question:
1. In his opinion, what is man's position with respect to God?

13.3   Castiglione's "Courtier": Prosperity Makes a Gentleman

The increase in mercantile contact from Asia and Africa with Europe revitalized the latter's moribund markets, and helped generate the Renaissance, wherein Europe broke the bond of manorialism in favor of a capitalist economy. A rising standard of living, most pronounced among the noble and upper-middle classes, and increasing literacy levels and intellectual sophistication had, as one byproduct, the conceptualization of the courtly "gentleman." The new breed of noble, the courtier, was not expected to be one-dimensional as his predecessor, the feudal knight. While the courtly Renaissance noble still had a military function, he was expected to be versatile and as much at home with the arts of peace (music, art, letters, politics, etc.) as those of war. This new type of aristocrat is depicted in "The Book of the Courtier" by Baldassaro Castiglione (1478–1529), which was meant to serve as a handbook for genteel conduct.

> **Source:** Friench Simpson, ed., *Baldassare Castiglione: The Book of the Courtier* (N.Y.: Frederick Ungar, 1959), pp. 34–40, 46–47.

41. The Courtier must be a man of virtue and integrity.

You can appreciate how contrary and fatal affectation is to the grace of every function not only of the body, but likewise of the mind, concerning which we have as yet said little, though we should not therefore pass it over. For as the mind is much more noble than the body, so also it deserves to be more cultivated and enriched. And as to how this should be accomplished in our Courtier, let us leave aside the precepts of so many wise philosophers who write on this subject and define the powers of the mind and so subtly dispute about their worth, and let us, keeping to our subject, say in few words that it is enough he should be, as they say, a man of virtue and integrity; for in this are com- prehended the practical wisdom, justice, fortitude, and temperance of mind and all the other qualifies which attend upon so honored a name. And I feel that he alone is the true moral philosopher who wishes to be good; and for that purpose he needs few precepts other than that wish....

42–44. Next in importance to virtue comes knowledge of humane letters.

"But with the exception of goodness, the true and chief ornament of the mind in each of us is, I think, letters....

I desire that in letters [our Courtier] should be more than passably learned, at least in these studies which men call humanities, and that he be acquainted not only with Latin but also with Greek, for the sake of the numerous and varied works which have been superbly written in that language. Let him be versed in the poets, and no less in the orators and historians. Let him also be trained in the writing of verse and prose, especially in our vernacular tongue. For in addition to the private enjoyment which he will derive, he will, thanks to this, never find himself at a loss for pleasing pastime with women, who for the most part love such things.

"And if, either because of other employment or because of lack of study he does not arrive at such perfection that his compositions are worthy of much praise, let him take the precaution of concealing them in order not to make others laugh at him and let him show them only to a friend whom he can trust, because they will benefit him to this extent at least that through that training he will know how to judge the works of others, for indeed it rarely happens that a person not accustomed to writing, however learned he be, can ever fully appreciate the labor and ingenuity of writers or enjoy the sweetness and excellence of styles and those latent niceties which are often found in the ancients. And besides that, these studies make him fluent and, as Aristippus replied to that tyrant, bold enough to speak with confidence to everyone. I greatly desire furthermore that our Courtier hold fixed in his mind one precept, namely, that in this and in every other thing he always be attentive and cautious rather than daring, and that he guard against persuading himself mistakenly that he knows what he does not know; for we are all by nature much more eager for praise than we should be, and our ears love the melody of the words which sing our praises more than any other song or sound, however sweet; and yet often, like the Siren's voices, these words bring shipwreck to any man who does not stop his ears against music so deceiving. Recognizing this danger, some among the sages of antiquity have written books telling us how we may distinguish the true friend from the flatterer. But what benefit has come of this if many, nay innumerable, are those who clearly realize that they are being flattered and yet love the flatterer and loathe the man who tells them the truth? And often it appears to them that the man who praises is too niggardly in what he says; so they themselves come to his aid and say such things about themselves as make the most shameless flatterer blush.

"Let us leave these blind men in their error and see to it that our Courtier is so sound of judgment that he cannot be made to take black for white or think highly of himself except in such measure as he clearly knows to be just....On the contrary, in order not to err, even if he knows very well that the praises that are given him are just, let him not concur in them too openly or confirm them without some show of opposition, but rather let him modestly come near to denying them, always claiming and actually considering arms as his chief calling and all the other good attributes as ornaments of them. Let him observe this caution especially among soldiers, in order not to behave like those who in their studies wish to appear men of war and among men of war wish to appear men of letters. In this fashion and for the reasons which we have given, he will avoid affectation, and even the commonplace things that he does will appear very impressive."

45. Bembo objects that letters rather than arms ought to be the Courtier's chief glory.

At this point Messer Pietro Bembo said in reply: "I do not know, Count, why you should desire that this Courtier, accomplished in letters and possessed of so many other qualities, should consider everything an ornament of arms and not arms and the rest an ornament of letters, which in and for themselves are as much superior to arms in worth as the mind is to the body, since the pursuit of letters belongs properly to the mind, as that of arms does to the body."

The Count then replied:

"Rather, the pursuit of arms belongs to the mind and to the body. But I am not desirous of having you, Messer Pietro, as judge of this dispute, because you would be too suspect of bias in the eyes of one of the parties; and since this debate has long been carried on by the most learned men, there is no need to renew it. However, I consider it settled in favor of arms and I stipulate that our Courtier, since I can shape him according to my will, shall also consider the matter so. And if you are of contrary opinion, wait until you hear of a dispute over it in which those who defend the case for arms may as lawfully use arms as those who defend letters use those same letters in their defence. For if each can avail himself of his own instruments, you will see that the men of letters will lose...."

47. The Courtier should be an accomplished musician.

"My lords..., you must know that I am not satisfied with the Courtier if he is not also a musician and if besides understanding music and reading notes readily he does not know a variety of instruments; for if we consider the matter carefully, we can find no repose from toil or medicine for ailing minds more wholesome and commendable for leisure time than this; and especially at courts, where much is done not only to provide the relief from vexations that music offers all of us but also to please the women, whose delicate and impressionable spirits are easily penetrated by harmony and filled with sweetness. Therefore it is no wonder if in ancient and in modern times women have always been favorably disposed toward musicians and have found music a most welcome food for the spirit."

Thereupon Lord Gaspar said:

"Music, along with many other follies, I consider suitable indeed for women and perhaps also for some who possess the appearance of men, but not for those who truly are men and who ought not to unman their minds with pleasures and thus incline them to be afraid of death."

"Do not say such a thing," answered the Count; "for I will here set forth on a vast sea of praise of music, and I will recall to what a degree among the ancients it was always extolled and regarded as something holy and how widely the wisest philosophers held that the world is fashioned of music and that the heavens produce harmony as they move and, moreover, that our soul was formed according to the same principles and therefore awakens and, as it were, quickens its powers through music. For this reason it is recorded that Alexander was so warmly aroused by it on a certain occasion that almost against his will he was obliged to rise from the banquet and rush to arms; then, as the musician altered the quality of the tone, to grow mild and return from arms to banqueting…

"Have you not read that music was one of the first disciplines that the good old Chiron taught Achilles, when Achilles, whom he reared from the time of milk and cradle, was at a tender age; and the wise master desired that the hands which were to spill so much Trojan blood should be often busied with the music of the cithara? What soldier, pray, will there be who is ashamed to imitate Achilles, not to mention many other famous commanders whom I could name? Therefore do not be disposed to deprive our Courtier of music, which not only softens the minds of men but often makes the fierce become gentle; and one can be certain that if a man does not enjoy music his spirits are all out of tune."

48. Giuliano de' Medici wishes to know how the Courtier is to apply his attributes in actual practice.

Since the Count was silent for a little while at this point, the Magnifico Giuliano said: "I am not at all of Lord Gaspat's opinion; on the contrary I believe, for the reasons that you state and for many others, that music is not only an ornament but a necessity for the Courtier. I should greatly like you to declare in what way this and the other attributes which you assign to him are to be put into practice, both at what time and after what fashion. For many things which in themselves deserve praise frequently become highly unsuitable when done at the wrong time. And by way of contrast, some things which appear of small weight are much valued when they are properly managed."

49. Before answering Giuliano the Count recommends that the Courtier be taught to draw and to understand painting.

Then the Count said:

"Before we enter into this subject I want to talk of another matter which, since I consider it of great importance, should, I think, by no means be left out by our Courtier. And this is knowing how to draw and possessing an understanding of the true art of painting. Do not marvel if I desire this skill which today perhaps is judged to be a craft and little fitting for a gentleman; for I recall having read that the ancients, especially through the whole of Greece, used to require that children of noblemen give attention to painting in school, as something wholesome and requisite; and that this subject was admitted into the first rank of the liberal arts and subsequently by public edict was forbidden to be taught to slaves. Among the Romans also it was held in the highest honor.…

"And to tell the truth I think that anyone who does not value this art is very much a stranger to reason; for the universe in its structure, with the wide heaven of bright stars surrounding it and in the middle the earth girdled by the seas, figured with mountains, valleys, and rivers, and embellished by trees of many different kinds and by lovely flowers and plants, one can call a noble and magnificent picture executed by the hand of nature and of God; and the man who can imitate it I consider worthy of great praise; nor can one succeed in this without the knowledge of many things, as anyone who tries it well knows.

BOOK THREE

The Attributes of the Court Lady and the Character of Women in General

The Court Lady as described by the Magnifico is to possess the same virtues as the Courtier and undergo the same training in letters, music, painting, dancing and other graces; also she should avoid affectation and cultivate *sprezzatura*. She is to avoid manly exercises and manners and preserve a feminine sweetness and delicacy. For example, she should not play on drums or trumpets, or take part in tennis or hunting. Above all she should acquire a pleasant affability in entertaining men, being neither too bashful nor too bold in company.

Gaspar Pallavicino declares such a woman impossible; women are imperfect creatures. The Magnifico answers this with the proposition that since two members of the same species have the same essential substance, one cannot be essentially less perfect than the other. Pallavicino counters with the claim that man is to woman as form is to matter; woman is imperfect without man. The argument follows these metaphysical lines for a while; then the Magnifico undertakes to show that for every great man there are equally admirable women to be cited, both in ancient and in modern times.

Lord Gaspar Pallavicino continues to insist that women are chaste only through fear of punishment, Cesare Gonzaga then takes up the defense of women, citing cases of women who defended their chastity to the death and describing the wiles which men use to overcome female chastity; then, passing on to the Courtly Love tradition, he asserts that all the refinements of life are cultivated in order to please women.

Finally the discussion turns to the way the Court Lady should respond to talk of love. The Magnitieo's opinion is that only unmarried women should allow themselves to fall in love, and then only when love is likely to end in marriage. All physical gratification outside marriage is forbidden. Federico Fregoso suggests that where there is no possibility of divorce a woman whose husband hates her should be permitted to bestow her love elsewhere. The Magnifico replies that she may bestow only spiritual love. Pallavicino denounces women because they love to drive a lover mad by refusing their favors for a very long while and then, when the lover's appetite is dulled by exasperation, at last bestowing favors that can no longer be fully enjoyed by him.

Questions:
1. For what reasons should a courtly man possess knowledge of the "humane letters" and what should he do if he has not had the time to acquire this knowledge?
2. In what light should the courtier consider the noble ladies?
3. Why should the courtier be versed in music and painting?
4. What virtues, in and of herself, is the court lady expected to possess that differs from the expectations of a courtly gentleman?

13.4 Martin Luther

The theory that all events are interrelated receives dramatic confirmation in the relationship between the Renaissance and the Reformation. To raise money to build St. Peter's Cathedral in Rome, the greatest monument of Renaissance art, Pope Leo X authorized the granting of papal indulgences in return for suitable donations to the church. In 1517, one of the papal agents, a Dominican friar named John Tetzel, appeared in central Germany to grant these indulgences. Martin Luther (1483–1546), a professor at the University of Wittenberg, responded by posting on the door of the Castle Church a list of Ninety-Five Theses, in which he attacked the entire theory and practice of indulgences. Luther's act, in turn, set in motion a series of events that resulted finally in the Protestant Reformation.

Although Tetzel's activities had set him off, Luther based his opposition to the church on grounds far deeper than the problem of indulgences. Basically, the question centered on the salvation of people's souls. From his studies of St. Paul and St. Augustine, Luther, who was himself a Catholic monk, became convinced that, since all people are utterly condemned and lost as a result of original sin, it is impossible for them to achieve salvation by any works of their own. Rather, salvation is the free gift of God's grace through faith. This doctrine of justification by faith rather than by works undercut the position of the Catholic Church, which maintained that since the works necessary to salvation (such as the sacraments) could be performed only with the aid of the priesthood, the church provided the sole means to salvation. In place of the priestly hierarchy, Luther substituted the notion of the priesthood of all believers, an idea that was to become a cornerstone of Protestantism. In the selection that follows he defends his "heretical" views, largely through a vigorous attack on both the theology and the practices of the church.

Source: Trans. C. M. Jacobs.

AN OPEN LETTER TO THE CHRISTIAN NOBILITY OF THE GERMAN NATION CONCERNING THE REFORM OF THE CHRISTIAN ESTATE, 1520

To His Most Illustrious and Mighty Imperial Majesty, and to the Christian Nobility of the German Nation.

Doctor Martin Luther

Grace and power from God, Most illustrious Majesty, and most gracious and dear Lords.

It is not out of sheer forwardness or rashness that I, a single, poor man, have undertaken to address your worships. The distress and oppression which weigh down all the Estate of Christendom, especially of Germany, and which move not me alone, but everyone to cry out time and again, and to pray for help, have forced me even now to cry aloud that God may inspire some one with His Spirit to lend this suffering nation a helping hand. Oft times the councils have made some pretence at reformation, but their attempts have been cleverly hindered by the guile of certain men and things have gone from bad to worse. I now intend, by the help of God, to throw some light upon the wiles and wickedness of these men, to the end that when they are known, they may not henceforth be so hurtful and so great a hindrance. God has given us a noble youth to be our head and thereby has awakened great hopes of good in many hearts; wherefore it is meet that we should do our part and profitably use this time of grace.

In this whole matter the first and most important thing is that we take earnest heed not to enter on it trusting in great might or in human reason, even though all power in the world were ours; for God cannot and will not suffer a good work to be begun with trust in our own power or reason. Such works He crushes ruthlessly to earth, as it is written in the xxxiii Psalm, "There is no king saved by the multitude of an host: a mighty man is not delivered by much strength." On this account, I fear, it came to pass of old that the good Emperors Frederick I and II, and many other German emperors were shamefully oppressed and trodden under foot by the popes, although all the world feared them. It may be that they relied on their own might more than on God, and therefore they had to fall. In our own times, too, what was it that raised the blood-thirsty Julius II to such heights? Nothing else, I fear, except that France, the Germans, and Venice relied upon themselves. The children of Benjamin slew forty-two thousand Israelites because the latter relied on their own strength.

That it may not so fare with us and our noble young Emperor Charles, we must be sure that in this matter we are dealing not with men, but with the princes of hell, who can fill the world with war and bloodshed, but whom war and bloodshed do not overcome. We must go at this work despairing of physical force and humbly trusting God; we must seek God's help with earnest prayer, and fix our minds on nothing else than the misery and distress of suffering Christendom, without regard to the deserts of evil men. Otherwise we may start the game with great prospect of success, but when we get well into it the evil spirits will stir up such confusion that the whole world will swim in blood, and yet nothing will come of it. Let us act wisely, therefore, and in the fear of God. The more force we use, the greater our disaster if we do not act humbly and in God's fear. The popes and the Romans have hitherto been able, by the devil's help, to set kings at odds with one another, and they may well be able to do it again, if we proceed by our own might and cunning, without God's help.

I. The Three Walls of the Romanists

The Romanists, with great adroitness, have built three walls about them, behind which they have hitherto defended themselves in such wise that no one has been able to reform them; and this has been the cause of terrible corruption throughout all Christendom.

First, when pressed by the temporal power, they have made decrees and said that the temporal power has no jurisdiction over them, but, on the other hand, that the spiritual is above the temporal power. Second, when the attempt is made to reprove them out of the Scriptures, they raise the objection that the interpretation of the Scriptures belongs to no one except the pope. Third, if threatened with a council, they answer with the fable that no one can call a council but the pope.

In this wise they have slyly stolen from us our three rods, that they may go unpunished, and have ensconced themselves within the safe stronghold of these three walls, that they may practise all the knavery and wickedness which we now see. Even when they have been compelled to hold a council they have weakened its power in advance by previously binding the princes with an oath to let them remain as they are. Moreover, they have given the pope full authority over all the decisions of the council, so that it is all one whether there are many councils-except that they deceive us with puppet-shows and sham-battles. So terribly do they fear for their skin in a really free council! And they have intimidated kings and princes by making them believe it would be an offence against God not to obey them in all these knavish, crafty deceptions.

Now God help us, and give us one of the trumpets with which the walls of Jericho were overthrown, that we may blow down these walls of straw and paper, and may set free the Christian rods for the punishment of sin, bringing to light the craft and deceit of the devil, to the end that through punishment we may reform ourselves, and once more attain God's favor.

Against the first wall we will direct our first attack.

It is pure invention that pope, bishops, priests, and monks are to be called the "spiritual estate"; princes, lords, artisans, and farmers the "temporal estate." That is indeed a fine bit of lying and hypocrisy. Yet no one should be frightened by it; and for this reason- viz., that all Christians are truly of the "spiritual estate," and there is among them no difference at all but that of office, as Paul says in I Corinthians xii, "We are all one body, yet every member has its own work, whereby it serves every other, all because we have one baptism, one Gospel, one faith, and are all alike Christians"; for baptism, Gospel and faith alone make us "spiritual" and a Christian people.

But that a pope or a bishop anoints, confers, tonsures, ordains, consecrates, or prescribes dress unlike that of the laity,-this may make hypocrites, and graven images, but it never makes a Christian or "spiritual" man. Through baptism all of us are consecrated to the priesthood, as St. Peter says in I Peter ii, "Ye are a royal priesthood, a priestly kingdom," and the book of Revelation says, "Thou hast made us by Thy blood to be priests and kings." For if we had no higher consecration than pope or bishop gives, the consecration by pope or bishop would never make a priest, nor might anyone either say mass or preach a sermon or give absolution. Therefore when the bishop consecrates it is the same thing as if he, in the place and stead of the whole congregation, all of whom have like power, were to take one out of their number and charge him to use this power for the others; just as though ten brothers, all king's sons and equal heirs, were to choose one of themselves to rule the inheritance for them all,-they would all be kings and equal in power, though one of them would be charged with the duty of ruling.

To make it still clearer. If a little group of pious Christian laymen were taken captive and set down in a wilderness, and had among them no priest consecrated by a bishop, and if there in the wilderness they were to agree in choosing one of themselves, married or unmarried, and were to charge him with the office of baptising, saying mass, absolving, and preaching, such a man would be as truly a priest as though all bishops and popes had consecrated him. That is why in cases of necessity any one can baptise and give absolution, which would be impossible unless we were all priests. This great grace and power of baptism and of the Christian Estate they have well-nigh destroyed and caused us to forget through the canon law. It was in the manner aforesaid that Christians in olden days chose from their number bishops and priests, who were afterwards confirmed by other bishops, without all the show which now obtains. It was thus that Sts. Augustine, Ambrose, and Cyprian became bishops.

Since, then, the temporal authorities are baptised with the same baptism and have the same faith and Gospel as we, we must grant that they are priests and bishops, and count their office one which has a proper and a useful place in the Christian community. For whoever comes out of the water of baptism can boast that he is already consecrated priest, bishop, and pope, though it is not seemly that every one should exercise the office. Nay, just because we are all in like manner priests, no one must put himself forward and undertake, without our consent and election, to do what is in the power of all of us. For what is common to all, no one dare take upon himself without the will and the commands of the community; and should it happen that one chosen for such an office were deposed for malfeasance, he would then be just what he was before he held office. Therefore a priest in Christendom is nothing else than an office-holder. While he is in office, he has precedence; when deposed, he is a peasant or a townsman like the rest. Beyond all doubt, then, a priest is no longer a priest when he is deposed. But now they have invented *characters indelebiles*, and prate that a deposed priest is nevertheless something different from a mere layman. They even dream that a priest can never become a layman, or be anything else than a priest. All this is mere talk and man-made law.

From all this it follows that there is really no difference between laymen and priests, princes and bishops, "spirituals" and "temporals," as they call them, except that of office and work, but not of "estate"; for they are all of the same estate,-true priests, bishops, and popes,-though they are not all engaged in the same work, just as all priests and monks have not the same work. This is the teaching of St. Paul in Romans xii and I Corinthians xii, and of St. Peter in I Peter ii, as I have said above, viz., that we are all one body of Christ, the Head, all members one of another. Christ has not two different bodies, one "temporal," the other "spiritual." He is one Head, and He has one Body.

Therefore, just as those who are now called "spiritual"-priests, bishops or popes-are neither different from other Christians nor superior to them, except that they are charged with the administration of the Word of God and the sacraments, which is their work and office, so it is with the temporal authorities,-they bear sword and rod with which to punish the evil and to protect the good. A cobbler, a smith, a farmer, each has the work and office of his trade, and yet they are all alike consecrated priests and bishops, and every one by means of his own work or office must benefit and serve every other, that in this way many kinds of work may be done for the bodily and spiritual welfare of the community, even as all the members of the body serve one another.

See, now, how Christian is the decree which says that the temporal power is not above the "spiritual estate" and may not punish it. That is as much as to say that the hand shall lend no aid when the eye is suffering. Is it not unnatural, not to say unchristian, that one member should not help another and prevent its destruction? Verily, the more honorable the member, the more should the others help. I say then, since the temporal power is ordained of God to punish evildoers and to protect them that do well, it should therefore be left free to perform its office without hindrance through the whole body of Christendom without respect of persons, whether it affect pope, bishops, priests, monks, nuns or anybody else. For if the mere fact that the temporal power has a smaller place among the Christian offices than has the office of preachers or confessors, or of the clergy, then the tailors, cobblers, masons, carpenters, potboys, tapsters, farmers, and all the secular tradesmen, should also be prevented from providing pope, bishops, priests and monks with shoes, clothing, houses, meat and drink, and from paying them tribute. But if these laymen are allowed to do their work unhindered, what do the Roman scribes mean by their laws, with which they withdraw themselves from the jurisdiction of the temporal Christian power, only so that they may be free to do evil and to fulfill what St. Peter has said: "There shall be false teachers among you, and through covetousness shall they with feigned words make merchandise of you."

On this account the Christian temporal power should exercise its office without let or hindrance, regardless whether it be pope, bishop, or priest whom it affects; whoever is guilty, let him suffer. All that the canon law has said to the contrary is sheer invention of Roman presumption. For thus saith St. Paul to all Christians: "Let every soul (I take that to mean the pope's soul also) be subject unto the higher powers; for they bear not the sword in vain, but are the ministers of God for the punishment of evildoers, and for the praise of them that do well." St. Peter also says: "Submit yourselves unto every ordinance of man for the Lord's sake, for so is the will of God." He has also prophesied that such men shall come as will despise the temporal authorities, and this has come to pass through the canon law.

So then, I think this first paper-wall is overthrown, since the temporal power has become a member of the body of Christendom, and is of the "spiritual estate," though its work is of a temporal nature. Therefore its work should extend freely and without hindrance to all the members of the whole body; it should punish and use force whenever guilt deserves or necessity demands, without regard to pope, bishops, and priests,-let them hurl threats and bans as much as they will.

This is why guilty priests, if they are surrendered to the temporal law, are first deprived of their priestly dignities, which would not be right unless the temporal sword had previously had authority over them by divine right.

Again, it is intolerable that in the canon law so much importance is attached to the freedom, life, and property of the clergy, as though the laity were not also as spiritual and as good Christians as they, or did not belong to the Church. Why are your life and limb, your property and honor so free, and mine not? We are all alike Christians, and have baptism, faith, Spirit, and all things alike. If a priest is killed, the land is laid under interdict,-why not when a peasant is killed? Whence comes this great distinction between those who are equally Christians? Only from human laws and inventions!

Moreover, it can be no good spirit who has invented such exceptions and granted to sin such license and impunity. For if we are bound to strive against the works and words of the evil spirit, and to drive him out in whatever way we can, as Christ commands and His Apostles, ought we, then, to suffer it in silence when the pope or his satellites are bent on dev-ilish words and works? Ought we for the sake of men to allow the suppression of divine commandments and truths which we have sworn in baptism to support with life and limb? Of a truth we should then have to answer for all the souls that would thereby be abandoned and led astray.

It must therefore have been the very prince of devils who said what is written in the canon law: "If the pope were so scandalously bad as to lead souls in crowds to the devil, yet he could not be deposed." On this accursed and devilish foundation they build at Rome, and think that we should let all the world go to the devil, rather than resist their knavery. If the fact that one man is set over others were sufficient reason why he should escape punishment, then no Christian could punish another, since Christ commands the lowliest and the least.

Where sin is, there is no escape from punishment; as St. Gregory also writes that we are indeed all equal, but guilt puts us in subjection one to another. Now we see how they whom God and the Apostles have made subject to the tempo-ral sword deal with Christendom, depriving it of its liberty by their own wickedness, without warrant of Scripture. It is to be feared that this is a game of Antichrist or a sign that he is close at hand.

The second wall is still more flimsy and worthless. They wish to be the only Masters of the Holy Scriptures, even though in all their lives they learn nothing from them. They assume for themselves sole authority, and with insolent juggling of words they would persuade us that the pope, whether he be a bad man or a good man, cannot err in matters of faith; and yet they cannot prove a single letter of it. Hence it comes that so many heretical and unchristian, nay, even unnatural ordi-nances have a place in the canon law, of which, however, there is no present need to speak. For since they think that the Holy Spirit never leaves them, be they ever so unlearned and wicked, they make bold to decree whatever they will. And if it were true, where would be the need or use of the Holy Scriptures? Let us burn them, and be satisfied with the unlearned lords at Rome, who are possessed of the Holy Spirit,-although He can possess only pious hearts! Unless I had read it myself, I could not have believed that the devil would make such clumsy pretensions at Rome, and find a following.

But, not to fight them with mere words, we will quote the Scriptures. St. Paul says in I Corinthians xiv: "If to anyone something better is revealed, though he be sitting and listening to another in God's Word, then the first, who is speaking, shall hold his peace and give place." What would be the use of this commandment, if we were only to believe him who does the talking or who has the highest seat? Christ also says in John vi, that all Christians shall be taught of God. Thus it may well happen that the pope and his followers are wicked men, and no true Christians, not taught of God, not having true understanding. On the other hand, an ordinary man may have true understanding; why then should we not follow him? Has not the pope erred many times? Who would help Christendom when the pope errs, if we were not to believe another, who had the Scriptures on his side, more than the pope?

Therefore it is a wickedly invented fable, and they cannot produce a letter in defence of it, that the interpretation of Scripture or the confirmation of its interpretation belongs to the pope alone. They have themselves usurped this power; and although they allege that this power was given to Peter when the keys were given to him, it is plain enough that the keys were not given to Peter alone, but to the whole community. Moreover, the keys were not ordained for doctrine or gov-ernment, but only for the binding and loosing of sin, and whatever further power of the keys they arrogate to themselves is mere invention. But Christ's word to Peter, "I have prayed for thee that thy faith fail not," cannot be applied to the pope, since the majority of the popes have been without faith, as they must themselves confess. Besides, it is not only for Peter that Christ prayed, but also for all Apostles and Christians, as he says in John xvii: "Father, I pray for those whom Thou has given Me, and not for these only, but for all who believe on Me through their word." Is not this clear enough?

Only think of it yourself! They must confess that there are pious Christians among us, who have the true faith, Spirit, understanding, word, and mind of Christ. Why, then, should we reject their word and understanding and follow the pope, who has neither faith nor Spirit? That would be to deny the whole faith and the Christian Church. Moreover, it is not the pope alone who is always in the right, if the article of the Creed is correct: "I believe in one holy Christian Church"; otherwise the prayer must run: "I believe in the pope at Rome," and so reduce the Christian Church to one man,-which would be nothing else than a devilish and hellish error.

Besides, if we are all priests, as was said above, and all have one faith, one Gospel, one sacrament, why should we not also have the power to test and judge what is correct or incorrect in matters of faith? What becomes of the words of Paul in I Corinthians ii: "He that is spiritual judgeth all things, yet he himself is judged of no man," and II Corinthians iv: "We have all the same Spirit of faith"? Why, then, should not we perceive what squares with faith and what does not, as well as does an unbelieving pope?

All these and many other texts should make us bold and free, and we should not allow the Spirit of liberty, as Paul calls Him, to be frightened off by the fabrications of the popes, but we ought to go boldly forward to test all that they do or leave undone, according to our interpretation of the Scriptures, which rests on faith, and compel them to follow not their own interpretation, but the one that is better. In the olden days Abraham had to listen to his Sarah, although she was in more complete subjection to him than we are to anyone on earth. Balaam's ass, also, was wiser than the prophet himself. If God then spoke by an ass against a prophet, why should He not be able even now to speak by a righteous man against the pope? In like manner St. Paul rebukes St. Peter as a man in error. Therefore it behooves every Christian to espouse the cause of the faith, to understand and defend it, and to rebuke all errors.

The third wall falls of itself when the first two are down. For when the pope acts contrary to the Scriptures, it is our duty to stand by the Scriptures, to reprove him, and to constrain him, according to the word of Christ in Matthew xviii: "If thy brother sin against thee, go and tell it him between thee and him alone; if he hear thee not, then take with thee one or two more; if he hear them not, tell it to the Church; if he hear not the Church, consider him a heathen." Here every member is commanded to care for every other. How much rather should we do this when the member that does evil is a ruling member, and by his evil-doing is the cause of much harm and offence to the rest! But if I am to accuse him before the Church, I must bring the Church together.

They have no basis in Scripture for their contention that it belongs to the pope alone to call a council or confirm its actions; for this is based merely upon their own laws, which are valid only in so far as they are not injurious to Christendom or contrary to the laws of God. When the Pope deserves punishment, such laws go out of force, since it is injurious to Christendom not to punish him by means of a council.

Thus we read in Acts xv that it was not St. Peter who called the Apostolic Council, but the Apostles and elders. If, then, that right had belonged to St. Peter alone, the council would not have been a Christian council, but an heretical *conciliabulum*. Even the Council of Nicaea-the most famous of all-was neither called nor confirmed by the Bishop of Rome, but by the Emperor Constantine, and many other emperors after him did the like, yet these councils were the most Christian of all. But if the pope alone had the right to call councils, then all these councils must have been heretical. Moreover, if I consider the councils which the pope has created, I find that they have done nothing of special importance.

Therefore, when necessity demands, and the pope is an offence to Christendom, the first man who is able should, as a faithful member of the whole body, do what he can to bring about a truly free council. No one can do this so well as the temporal authorities, especially since now they also are fellow-Christians, fellow-priests, "fellow-spirituals," fellow-lords over all things, and whenever it is needful or profitable, they should give free course to the office and work in which God has put them above every man. Would it not be an unnatural thing, if a fire broke out in a city, and every body were to stand by and let it burn on and on and consume everything that could burn, for the sole reason that nobody had the authority of the burgomaster, or because, perhaps, the fire broke out in the burgomaster's house? In such case is it not the duty of every citizen to arouse and call the rest? How much more should this be done in the spiritual city of Christ, if a fire of offence breaks out, whether in the papal government, or anywhere else? In the same way, if the enemy attacks a city, he who first rouses the others deserves honour and thanks; why then should he not deserve honour who makes known the presence of the enemy from hell, and awakens the Christians, and calls them together?

But all their boasts of an authority which dare not be opposed amount to nothing after all. No one in Christendom has authority to do injury, or to forbid the resisting of injury. There is no authority in the Church save for edification. Therefore, if the pope were to use his authority to prevent the calling of a free council, and thus became a hindrance to the edification of the Church, we should have regard neither for him nor for his authority; and if he were to hurl his bans and thunderbolts, we should despise his conduct as that of a madman, and relying on God, hurl back the ban on him, and coerce him as best we could. For this presumptuous authority of his is nothing; he has no such authority; and he is quickly overthrown by a text of Scripture; for Paul says to the Corinthians: "God has given us authority not for the destruction, but for the edification of Christendom." Who is ready to overleap this text? It is only the power of the devil and of Antichrist which resists the things that serve for the edification of Christendom; it is, therefore, in no wise to be obeyed, but is to be opposed with life and goods and all our strength.

Even though a miracle were to be done in the pope's behalf against the temporal powers, or though someone were to be stricken with a plague-which they boast has sometimes happened-it should be considered only the work of the devil, because of the weakness of our faith in God. Christ Himself prophesied in Matthew xxiv: "There shall come in My Name false Christs and false prophets, and do signs and wonders, so as to deceive even the elect," and Paul says in II Thessalonians ii, that Antichrist shall, through the power of Satan, be mighty in lying wonders.

Let us, therefore, hold fast to this: No Christian authority can do anything against Christ; as St. Paul says, "We can do nothing against Christ, but for Christ." Whatever does aught against Christ is the power of Antichrist and of the devil, even though it were to rain and hail wonders and plagues. Wonders and plagues prove nothing, especially in these evil times, for which all the Scriptures prophesy false wonders. Therefore we must cling with firm faith to the words of God, and then the devil will cease from wonders.

Thus I hope that the false, lying terror with which the Romans have this long time made our conscience timid and stupid, has been allayed. They, like all of us, are subject to the temporal sword; they have no power to interpret the Scriptures by mere authority, without learning; they have no authority to prevent a council or, in sheer wantonness, to pledge it, bind it, or take away its liberty; but if they do this, they are in truth in the communion of Antichrist and of the devil, and have nothing at all of Christ except the name.

II. Abuses to be Discussed in Councils

We shall now look at the matters which should be discussed in the councils, and with which popes, cardinals, bishops, and all the scholars ought properly to be occupied day and night if they love Christ and His Church. But if they neglect this duty, then let the laity and the temporal authorities see to it, regardless of bans and thunders; for an unjust ban is better than ten just releases, and an unjust release worse than ten just bans. Let us, therefore, awake, dear Germans, and fear God rather than men, that we may not share the fate of all the poor souls who are so lamentably lost through the shameful and devilish rule of the Romans, in which the devil daily takes a larger and larger place-if indeed, it were possible that such a hellish rule could grow worse, a thing I can neither conceive nor believe.

1. It is a horrible and frightful thing that the ruler of Christendom, who boasts himself vicar of Christ and successor of St. Peter, lives in such worldly splendor that in this regard no king nor emperor can equal or approach him, and that he who claims the title of "most holy" and "most spiritual" is more worldly than the world itself. He wears a triple crown, when the greatest kings wear but a single crown; if that is like the poverty of Christ and of St. Peter, then it is a new kind of likeness. When a word is said against it, they cry out "Heresy!" but that is because they do not wish to hear how unchristian and ungodly such a practice is. I think, however, that if the pope were with tears to pray to God he would have to lay aside these crowns, for our God can suffer no pride, and his office is nothing else than this,- daily to weep and pray for Christendom, and to set an example of all humility.

However that may be, this splendour of his is an offence, and the pope is bound on his soul's salvation to lay it aside, because St. Paul says, "Abstain from all outward shows, which give offence," and in Rom. xii, "We should provide good, not only in the sight of God, but also in the sight of all men." An ordinary bishop's crown would be enough for the pope; he should be greater than others in wisdom and holiness, and leave the crown of pride to Antichrist, as did his predecessors several centuries ago. They say he is a lord of the world; that is a lie; for Christ, Whose vicar and officer he boasts himself to be, said before Pilate, "My kingdom is not of this world," and no vicar's rule can go beyond his lord's. Moreover, he is not the vicar of the glorified, but of the crucified Christ, as Paul says, "I was willing to know nothing among you save Christ, and Him only as the Crucified"; and in Philippians ii, "So think of yourselves as ye see in Christ. Who emptied Himself and took upon Him the appearance of a servant"; and again in I Corinthians i, "We preach Christ, the Crucified." Now they make the pope a vicar of the glorified Christ in heaven, and some of them have allowed the devil to rule them so completely that they have maintained that the pope is above the angels in heaven and has authority over them. These are indeed the very works of the very Antichrist.

2. What is the use in Christendom of these people who are called the cardinals? I shall tell you. Italy and Germany have many rich monasteries, foundations, benefices, and livings. No better way has been discovered to bring all these to Rome than by creating cardinals and giving them the bishoprics, monasteries, and prelacies, and so overthrowing the worship of God. For this reason we now see Italy a very wilderness- monasteries in ruins, bishoprics devoured, the prelacies and the revenues of all the churches drawn to Rome, cities decayed, land and people laid waste, because there is no more worship or preaching. Why? The cardinals must have the income. No Turk could have so devastated Italy and suppressed the worship of God.

Now that Italy is sucked dry, they come into Germany, and begin oh so gently. But let us beware, or Germany will soon become like Italy. Already we have some cardinals; what the Romans seek by that the "drunken Germans are not to understand until we have not a bishopric, a monastery, a living, a benefice, a *heller* or a *pfennig* left. Antichrist must take the treasures of the earth, as it was prophesied. So it goes on. They skim the cream off the bishoprics, monasteries, and benefices, and because they do not yet venture to turn them all to shameful use, as they have done in Italy, they only practise for the present the sacred trickery of coupling together ten or twenty prelacies and taking a yearly portion from each of them, so as to make a tidy sum after all. The priory of Würzburg yields a thousand *gulden*; that of Bamberg, something;

Mainz, Trier and the others, something more; and so from one to ten thousand *gulden* might be got together, in order that a cardinal might live at Rome like a rich king.

"After they are used to this, we will create thirty or forty cardinals in a day, and give to one Mount St. Michael at Bamberg and the bishopric of Würzburg to boot, hang on to these a few rich livings, until churches and cities are waste, and after that we will say, 'We are Christ's vicars and shepherds of Christ's sheep; the mad, drunken Germans must put up with it.'"

I advise, however, that the number of cardinals be reduced, or that the pope be made to keep them at his own expense. Twelve of them would be more than enough, and each of them might have an income of a thousand *gulden* a year. How comes it that we Germans must put up with such robbery and such extortion of our property, at the hands of the pope? If the Kingdom of France has prevented it, why do we Germans let them make such fools and apes of us? It would all be more bearable if in this way they only stole our property; but they lay waste the churches and rob Christ's sheep of their pious shepherds, and destroy the worship and the Word of God. Even if there were not a single cardinal, the Church would not go under. As it is they do nothing for the good of Christendom; they only wrangle about the incomes of bishoprics and prelacies, and that any robber could do.

3. If ninety-nine parts of the papal court were done away and only the hundredth part allowed to remain, it would still be large enough to give decisions in matters of faith. Now, however, there is such a swarm of vermin yonder in Rome, all boasting that they are "papal," that there was nothing like it in Babylon. There are more than three thousand papal secretaries alone: who will count the other offices, when they are so many that they scarcely can be counted? And they all lie in wait for the prebends and benefices of Germany as wolves lie in wait for the sheep. I believe that Germany now gives much more to the pope at Rome than it gave in former times to the emperors. Indeed, some estimate that every year more than three hundred thousand *gulden* find their way from Germany to Rome, quite uselessly and fruitlessly; we get nothing for it but scorn and contempt. And yet we wonder that princes, nobles, cities, endowments, land, and people are impoverished! We should rather wonder that we still have anything to eat!

Questions:
1. According to Luther, what authority do political leaders have to enact religious reform?
2. What role do the Christian Scriptures play in Luther's argument?

13.5   Luther vs. Erasmus: A Reformer's Attack on Free Will

Martin Luther's defiance of the Papacy in 1517 had been an act of great spiritual and physical courage and, although many factors went into assuring the success of the Lutheran Reformation, the character of Luther himself was not the least of them. Once Luther actually came to a commitment regarding a belief or principle, it was impossible to shake him and he would pursue his defense of his conviction with an emotional, aggressive intensity that few could match. One of Luther's most skilled adversaries was Desiderius Erasmus of Rotterdam (1469–1536), an advocate of Church reform in his own right but one who had reservations about abandoning allegiance to the Catholic faith (he would remain in the Church until his death). Here, Luther attempts to counter Erasmus' arguments regarding free will: the complete freedom of the individual to make moral choices.

Source: J.I. Packer & O.R. Johnson, trans., *Martin Luther: The Bondage of the Will* (Westwood, N.J.: Fleming H. Revell, copyright James Clarke & Co., 1957), pp. 312–315, 317–320.

…To sum up: Since Scripture everywhere proclaims Christ categorically and antithetically, as I said, and thereby subjects all that is without the Spirit of Christ to Satan, ungodliness error, darkness, sin, death and the wrath of God, every statement concerning Christ is a direct testimony against 'free-will' And such statements are innumerable; indeed, they constitute the whole of Scripture. If, therefore, we conduct our argument with Scripture as judge, the victory in every respect belongs to me; for there is not one jot or tittle of Scripture left that does not condemn the doctrine of 'free-will'!

Though the great theologians who guard 'free-will' may not know, or pretend not to know, that Scripture proclaims Christ categorically and antithetically, all Christians know it, and commonly confess it. They know that there are in the world two kingdoms at war with each other. In the one, Satan reigns (which is why Christ calls him 'the prince of this world' (John 12.31), and Paul 'the god of this world' (2 Cor. 4.4). He, so Paul again tells us, holds captive at his will all that are not wrested from him by the Spirit of Christ; nor does he allow them to be plucked away by any other power but the Spirit of God, as Christ tells us in the parable of the strong man armed keeping his palace in peace. In the other kingdom, Christ reigns. His kingdom continually resists and wars against that of Satan; and we are translated into His kingdom, not by our own power, but by the grace of God, which delivers us from this present evil world and tears us away from the power of darkness. The knowledge and confession of these two kingdoms ever warring against each other with all their might and power would suffice by itself to confute the doctrine of 'free-will', seeing that we are compelled to serve in Satan's kingdom if we an not plucked from it by Divine power. The common man, I repeat, knows this, and confesses it plainly enough by his proverbs, prayers, efforts and entire life.

(xvii) *Rom. 7; Gal. 5: the power of the 'flesh' in the saints disproves 'free-will' (783)*

I forbear to insist on the Achilles of my arguments, which the Diatribe proudly passes by without notice—I mean, Paul's teaching in Rom. 7 and Gal. 5, that there is in the saints and the godly such a mighty warfare between the Spirit and the flesh that they cannot do what they would. From this I would argue as follows: If human nature is so bad that in those who are born again of the Spirit it not only fails to endeavour after good, but actually fights against and opposes good, how could it endeavour after good in those who are not yet born again of the Spirit, but serve under Satan in the old man? And Paul is not here speaking of gross affections only (which is the universal expedient by which the Diatribe regularly parries the thrust of every Scripture); but he lists among the works of the flesh heresy, idolatry, contentions, divisions, etc., which reign in what you call the most exalted faculties, that is, reason and will. If, now, the flesh with these affections wars against the Spirit in the saints, much more will it war against God in the ungodly and in their 'free-will'! Hence in Rom. 8 he calls it 'enmity against God' (v. 7). May I say that I should be interested to see *this* argument punctured, and 'free-will' safeguarded from its attack!

(xviii) *Of the comfort of knowing that salvation does not depend on 'free-will' (783)*

I frankly confess that, for myself, even if it could be, I should not want 'free-will' to be given me, nor anything to be left in my own hands to enable me to endeavour after salvation; not merely because in face of so many dangers, and adversities, and assaults of devils, I could not stand my ground and hold fast my 'free-will' (for one devil is stronger than all men, and on these terms no man could be saved); but because, even were there no dangers, adversities, or devils, I should still be forced to labour with no guarantee of success, and to beat my fists at the air. If I lived and worked to all eternity, my conscience would never reach comfortable certainty as to how much it must do to satisfy God. Whatever work I had done, there would still be a nagging doubt as to whether it pleased God, or whether He required something more. The experience of all who seek righteousness by works proves that; and I learned it well enough myself over a period of many years, to my own great hurt. But now that God has taken my salvation out of the control of my own will, and put it under the control of His, and promised to save me, not according to my working or running, but according to His own grace and mercy, I have the comfortable certainty that He is faithful and will not lie to me, and that He is also great and powerful, so that no devils or opposition can break Him or pluck me from Him. 'No one,' He says, 'shall pluck them out of my hand, because my Father which gave them me is greater than all' (John 10.28–29). Thus it is that, if not all, yet some, indeed many, are saved; whereas, by the power of 'free-will' none at all could be saved, but every one of us would perish.

Furthermore, I have the comfortable certainty that I please God, not by reason of the merit of my works, but by reason of His merciful favour promised to me; so that, if I work too little, or badly, He does not impute it to me, but with fatherly compassion pardons me and makes me better. This is the glorying of all the saints in their God.

(xix) *Of faith in the justice of God in His dealings with men* (784–786)

You may be worried that it is hard to defend the mercy and equity of God in damning the undeserving, that is, ungodly persons, who, being born in ungodliness, can by no means avoid being ungodly, and staying so, and being damned, but are compelled by natural necessity to sin and perish; as Paul says: 'We were all the children of wrath, even as others' (Eph. 2.3), created such by God Himself from a seed that had been corrupted by the sin of the one man, Adam. But here God must be reverenced and held in awe, as being most merciful to those whom He justifies and saves in their own utter unworthiness; and we must show some measure of deference to His Divine wisdom by believing Him just when to us He seems unjust. If His justice were such as could be adjudged just by human reckoning, it clearly would not be Divine; it would in no way differ from human justice. But inasmuch as He is the one true God, wholly incomprehensible and inaccessible to man's anderstanding, it is reasonable, indeed inevitable, that His justice also should be incomprehensible; as Paul cries, saying: 'O the depth of the riches both of the wisdom and knowledge of God! How unsearchable are His judgments, and His ways past finding out!' (Rom. 11.33). They would not, however, be 'unsearchable' if we could at every point grasp the grounds on which they are just. What is man compared with God? How much can our power achieve compared with His power? What is our strength compared with His strength? What is our knowledge compared with His wisdom? What is our substance compared with His substance? In a word, what is all that we are compared with all that He is?...

***

I shall here end this book, ready though I am to pursue the matter further, if need be; but I think that abundant satisfaction has here been afforded for the godly man who is willing to yield to truth without stubborn resistance. For if we believe it to be true that God foreknows and foreordains all things; that He cannot be deceived or obstructed in His foreknowledge and predestination; and that nothing happens but at His will (which reason itself is compelled to grant); then, on reason's own testimony, there can be no 'free-will' in man, or angel, or in any creature.

So, if we believe that Satan is the prince of this world, ever ensnaring and opposing the kingdom of Christ with all his strength, and that he does not let his prisoners go unless he is driven out by the power of the Divine Spirit, it is again apparent that there can be no 'free-will'.

So, if we believe that original sin has ruined us to such an extent that even in the godly, who are led by the Spirit, it causes abundance of trouble by striving against good, it is clear that in a man who lacks the Spirit nothing is left that can turn itself to good, but only to evil.

Again, if the Jews, who followed after righteousness with all their powers, fell into unrighteousness instead, while the Gentiles, who followed after unrighteousness, attained to an un-hoped-for righteousness, by God's free gift, it is equally apparent from their very works and experience that man without grace can will nothing but evil.

And, finally, if we believe that Christ redeemed men by His blood, we are forced to confess that all of man was lost; otherwise, we make Christ either wholly superfluous, or else the redeemer of the least valuable part of man only; which is blasphemy, and sacrilege.

VIII

CONCLUSION (W.A. 786–787)

Now, my good Erasmus, I entreat you for Christ's sake to keep your promise at last. You promised that you would yield to him who taught better than yourself. Lay aside respect of persons! I acknowledge that you are a great man, adorned with many of God's noblest gifts—wit, learning and an almost miraculous eloquence, to say nothing of the rest; whereas I have and am nothing, save that I would glory in being a Christian. Moreover, I give you hearty praise and commendation on this further account—that you alone, in contrast with all others, have attacked the real thing, that is, the essential issue. You have not wearied me with those extraneous issues about the Papacy, purgatory, indulgences and such like—trifles, rather than issues—in respect of which almost all to date have sought my blood (though without success); you, and you alone, have seen the hinge on which all turns, and aimed for the vital spot. For that I heartily thank you; for it is more gratifying to me to deal with this issue, insofar as time and leisure permit me to do so. If those who have attacked me in the past had done as you have done, and if those who now boast of new spirits and revelations would do the same also, we should have less sedition and sects and more peace and concord. But thus it is that God, through Satan, has punished our unthankfulness.

However, if you cannot treat of this issue in a different way from your treatment of it in this Diatribe, it is my earnest wish that you would remain content with your own gift, and confine yourself to pursuing, adoming and promoting the study of literature and languages; as hitherto you have done, to great advantage and with much credit. By your studies you have rendered me also some service, and I confess myself much indebted to you; certainly, in that regard, I unfeignedly honour and sincerely respect you. But God has not yet willed nor granted that you should be equal to the subject of our present debate. Please do not think that any arrogance lies behind my words when I say that I pray that the Lord will speedily make you as much my superior in this as you already are in all other respects. It is no new thing for God to instruct a Moses by a Jethro, or to teach a Paul by an Ananias. You say that *'you have wandered far from the mark, if you are ignorant of Christ.'* I think that you yourself see how the matter stands. But not all will go astray if you or I go astray. God is One Who is proclaimed as wonderful among His saints, so that we may regard as saints persons that are very far from sanctity. Nor is it hard to believe that you, as being a man, should fail to understand aright, and to note with sufficient care, the Scriptures, or the sayings of the fathers, under whose guidance you think that you are holding to the mark. That you have thus failed is clear enough from your saying that *you assert nothing, but have 'made comparisons'.* He who sees to the heart of the matter and properly understands it does not write like that. Now I, in this book of mine, HAVE NOT 'MADE COMPARISONS', BUT HAVE ASSERTED, AND DO ASSERT; and I do not want judgment to rest with anyone, but I urge all men to submit! May the Lord, whose cause this is, enlighten you and make you a vessel to honour and glory. *Amen.*

Questions:
1. How does Luther say that the conflict between the Kingdoms of Chist and of Satan disproves free will?
2. Why would Luther not want free will for himself?
3. What is the tone of Luther's conclusion? What can be discerned about his attitude towards Erasmus?

13.6   John Calvin and the Genevan Reformation

Although Lutheranism formed the basis of the Reformation, by the mid-sixteenth century it had lost much of its energy and was confined to Germany and Scandinavia. The movement was spread throughout Europe by other reformers, the most influential of whom was John Calvin (1509–1564).

A trained lawyer and classical scholar, Calvin had been a convert to Luther's ideas and was forced to leave France, eventually settling in Geneva in the 1530s. There in the 1540s he established a very structured society that can best be described as a theocracy. Calvin's strict adherence to biblical authority and his singular strength of personality can be seen in his treatise, On the Necessity of Reforming the Church. In it he defines the church as "a society of all the saints, a society spread over the whole world, and existing in all ages, yet bound together by the one doctrine and the one Spirit of Christ." In the words of Saint Cyprian, which Calvin often quoted, "We cannot have God for our Father without having the Church for our mother." The importance of this idea cannot be overestimated in Calvin's understanding of doctrine and of the reform of the church. In the following excerpt from his famous treatise, which was addressed to the Holy Roman Emperor Charles V in 1544, Calvin expressed disgust that the church had become divorced from the society of saints it was supposed to serve. The continuity of the church as a universal embodiment of all believers had to be reestablished through clerical reform and a reconceptualization of Spirit.

> **Source:** "On the Necessity of Reforming the Church" is from John Calvin, *Tracts and Treatises on the Reformation of the Church,* trans. by Henry Beveridge, vol. 1 (Edinburgh: Calvin Translation Society, 1844), pp. 231-234.

ON THE NECESSITY OF REFORMING THE CHURCH (1544)
JOHN CALVIN

In the present condition of the empire, your Imperial Majesty, and you, Most Illustrious Princes, necessarily involved in various cares, and distracted by a multiplicity of business, are agitated, and in a manner tempest-tossed. . . . I feel what nerve, what earnestness, what urgency, what ardor, the treatment of this subject requires. . . . First, call to mind the fearful calamities of the Church, which might move to pity even minds of iron. Nay, set before your eyes her squalid and unsightly form, and the sad devastation which is everywhere beheld. How long, pray, will you allow the spouse of Christ, the mother of you all, to lie thus protracted and afflicted—thus, too, when she is imploring your protection, and when the means of relief are at hand? Next, consider how much worse calamities impend. Final destruction cannot be far off, unless you interpose with the utmost speed. Christ will, indeed, in the way which to him seems good, preserve his Church miraculously, and beyond human expectation; but this I say, that the consequence of a little longer delay on your part will be, that in Germany we shall not have even the form of a Church. Look round, and see how many indications threaten that ruin which it is your duty to prevent, and announce that it is actually at hand. These things speak loud enough, though I were silent. . . .

Divine worship being corrupted by so many false opinions, and perverted by so many impious and foul superstitions, the sacred Majesty of God is insulted with atrocious contempt, his holy name profaned, his glory only not trampled under foot. Nay, while the whole Christian world is openly polluted with idolatry, men adore, instead of Him, their own fictions. A thousand superstitions reign, superstitions which are just so many open insults to Him. The power of Christ is almost obliterated from the minds of men, the hope of salvation is transferred from him to empty, frivolous, and insignificant ceremonies, while there is a pollution of the Sacraments not less to be execrated. Baptism is deformed by numerous additions, the Holy Supper [communion] is prostituted to all kinds of ignominy, religion throughout has degenerated into an entirely different form. . . .

In the future, therefore, as often as you shall hear the croaking note—"The business of reforming the Church must be delayed for the present"—"there will be time enough to accomplish it after other matters are transacted"— remember, Most Invincible Emperor, that the matter on which you are to deliberate is, whether you are to leave to your posterity some empire or none. Yet, why do I speak of posterity? Even now, while your own eyes behold, it is half bent, and totters to its final ruin. . . .

But be the issue what it may, we will never repent of having begun, and of having proceeded thus far. The Holy Spirit is a faithful and unerring witness to our doctrine. We know, I say, that it is the eternal truth of God that we preach. We are, indeed, desirous, as we ought to be, that our ministry may prove salutary to the world; but to give it this effect belongs to God, not to us. If, to punish, partly the ingratitude, and partly the stubbornness of those to whom we desire to do good, success must prove desperate, and all things go to worse, I will say what it befits a Christian man to say, and what all who are true to this holy profession will subscribe: We will die, but in death even be conquerors, not only because through it we shall have a sure passage to a better life, but because we know that our blood will be as seed to propagate the Divine truth which men now despise.

Question:
1. What is Calvin's primary message to the Holy Roman Emperor?

13.7 Council of Trent: The Catholic-Reformation

The Catholic Reformation expressed itself in three main institutions: the Society of Jesus (usually called the Jesuits), the Inquisition (or Holy Office), and the Council of Trent. The Society of Jesus was founded by St. Ignatius of Loyola (1491-1 556), an unlettered Spanish soldier who, as the result of a religious experience he underwent after being wounded in battle, resolved to become a "soldier of Christ." Once he had recovered, he set about educating himself, starting with elementary school and continuing through the University of Paris, where he began organizing the Jesuit order. Loyola's new society was established along military lines: An iron discipline demanded that each member show complete obedience to his immediate superiors and ultimately to his supreme commander, the pope. During the religious conflicts of the sixteenth and seventeenth centuries the Jesuits were always to be found on the side of the papal forces, in opposition primarily to the Protestants but to Catholic liberals as well.

The Inquisition was an old organization developed by the Dominican order in the thirteenth century primarily to combat the Albigensian heresy in southern France. It gained its greatest strength, however, in Spain. There it was used, particularly under the leadership of Torquemada, as the prime agent of persecution of the Moors and the Jews. After the Reformation the Inquisition joined forces with the Jesuits to combat the "Protestant heresy."

The Council of Trent, called originally by Pope Paul III in 1545, met at irregular intervals over a period of nearly twenty years under three different popes in the northern Italian city of Trent. Although the council reaffirmed the central doctrines of the Catholic church against what it considered to be the heretical views of Protestantism, it also called for the elimination of abuses that had crept into the church. The selection that follows includes some of the more important decrees, concerning both doctrine and practice, adopted by the council.

Source: Trans. J. Waterworth

THE CANONS AND DECREES OF THE COUNCIL OF TRENT

Decree Touching the Opening of the Council

Doth it please you,-unto the praise and glory of the holy and undivided Trinity, Father, and Son, and Holy Ghost; for the increase and exaltation of the Christian faith and religion; for the extirpation of heresies; for the peace and union of the Church; for the reformation of the Clergy and Christian people; for the depression and extinction of the enemies of the Christian name,-to decree and declare that the sacred and general council of Trent do begin, and hath begun?

They answered: It pleaseth us.

Decree Concerning the Canonical Scriptures

The sacred and holy, œcumenical, and general Synod of Trent,-lawfully assembled in the Holy Ghost, the same three legates of the Apostolic See presiding therein,-keeping this always in view, that, errors being removed, the purity itself of the Gospel be preserved in the Church; which [Gospel], before promised through the prophets in the holy Scriptures, our Lord Jesus Christ, the Son of God, first promulgated with His own mouth, and then commanded to be preached by His Apostles to every creature, as the fountain of all, both saving truth, and moral discipline; and seeing clearly that this truth and books, and the unwritten traditions which, received by the Apostles from the mouth of Christ himself, or from the Apostles themselves, the Holy Ghost dictating, have come down even unto us, transmitted as it were from hand to hand; [the Synod] following the examples of the orthodox Fathers, receives and venerates with an equal affection of piety, and reverence, all the books both of the Old and the New Testament-seeing that one God is the author of both-as also the said traditions, as well those appertaining to faith as to morals, as having been dictated, either by Christ's own word of mouth, or by the Holy Ghost, and preserved in the Catholic Church by a continuous succession.

Decree Concerning the Edition, and the Use, of the Sacred Books

Moreover, the same sacred and holy Synod,-considering that no small utility may accrue to the Church of God, if it be made known which out of all the Latin editions, now in circulation, of the sacred books, is to be held as authentic,-ordains and declares, that the said old and vulgate edition, which, by the lengthened usage of so many ages, has been approved of in the Church, be, in public lectures, disputations, sermons and expositions, held as authentic; and that no one is to dare, or presume to reject it under any pretext whatever.

Furthermore, in order to restrain petulant spirits, It decrees, that no one, relying on his own skill, shall,- in matters of faith, and of morals pertaining to the edification of Christian doctrine ,-wresting the sacred Scripture to his own senses, presume to interpret the said sacred Scripture contrary to that sense which holy mother Church,-whose it is to judge of the true sense and interpretation of the holy Scriptures,-hath held and doth hold;-or even contrary to the unanimous consent of the Fathers; even though such interpretations were never [intended] to be at any time published....

Decree Concerning Original Sin

That our *Catholic faith, without which it is impossible to please God,* may, errors being purged away, continue in its own perfect and spotless integrity, and that the Christian people may not *be carried about with every wind of doctrine;* whereas that old serpent, the perpetual enemy of mankind, amongst the very many evils with which the Church of God is in these our times troubled, has also stirred up not only new, but even old, dissensions touching original sin, and the remedy thereof; the sacred and holy, œcumenical and general Synod of Trent,-lawfully assembled in the Holy See presiding therein,-wishing now to come to the reclaiming of the erring, and the confirming of the wavering-following the testimonies of the sacred Scriptures, of the holy Fathers, or the most approved councils, and the judgment and consent of the Church itself, ordains, confesses, and declares these things touching the said original sin:

1. If any one does not confess that the first man, Adam, when he had transgressed the commandment of God in Paradise, immediately lost the holiness and justice wherein he had been constituted; and that he incurred, through the offense of that prevarication, the wrath and indignation of God, and consequently death, with which God had previously threatened him, and, together with death, captivity under his power who thenceforth *had the empire of death, that is to say, the devil,* and that the entire Adam, through that offence of prevarication, was changed, in body and soul, for the worse; let him be anathema.

2. If any one asserts, that the prevarication of Adam injured himself alone, and not his posterity; and that the holiness and justice, received of God, which he lost, he lost for himself alone, and not for us also; or that he, being defiled by the sin of disobedience, has only transfused death, and pains of the body, into the whole human race, but not sin also, which is the death of the soul; let him be anathema:-whereas he contradicts the apostle who says; *By one man sin entered into the world, and by sin death, and so death passed upon all men, in whom all have sinned.*

3. If any one asserts, that this sin of Adam,-which in its origin is one, and being transfused into all by propagation, not by imitation, is in each one as his own,-is taken away either by the powers of human nature, or by any other remedy than the merit of the *one mediator our Lord Jesus Christ, who had reconciled us to God in his own blood, made unto us justice, sanctification, and redemption;* or if he denies that the said merit of Jesus Christ is applied, both to adults and to infants, by the sacrament of baptism rightly administered in the form of the Church; let him be anathema: *For there is no other name under heaven given to men, whereby we must be saved.* Whence that voice; *Behold the lamb of God, behold him who taketh away the sins of the world; and that other; As many as have been baptized, have put on Christ.*

. . .

That a Rash Presumptuousness in the Matter of Predestination Is to Be Avoided

No one, moreover, so long as he is in this mortal life, ought so far to presume as regards the secret mystery of divine predestination, as to determine for certain that he is assuredly in the number of the predestinate; as if it were true, that he that is justified, either cannot sin any more, or, if he do sin, that he ought to promise himself an assured repentance; for except by special revelation, it cannot be known whom God hath chosen unto Himself.

. . .

On the Sacraments in General

Canon I

If any one saith, that the sacraments of the New Law were not all instituted by Jesus Christ, our Lord; or, that they are more, or less, than seven, to wit, Baptism, Confirmation, the Eucharist, Penance, Extreme Unction, Order, and Matrimony; or even that any one of these seven is not truly and properly a sacrament; let him be anathema.

Canon II

If any one saith, that these said sacraments of the New Law do not differ from the sacraments of the Old Law, save that the ceremonies are different, and different the outward rites; let him be anathema.

Canon III

If any one saith, that these seven sacraments are in such wise equal to each other, as that one is not in any way more worthy than another; let him be anathema.

Canon IV

If any one saith, that the sacraments of the New Law are not necessary unto salvation, but superfluous; and that, without them, or without the desire thereof, men obtain of God, through faith alone, the grace of justification;-though all [the sacraments] are not indeed necessary for every individual; let him be anathema.

Canon V

If any one saith, that these sacraments were instituted for the sake of nourishing faith alone; let him be anathema.

Canon VI

If any one saith, that the sacraments of the New Law do not contain the grace which they signify; or, that they do not confer that grace on those who do not place an obstacle there-unto; as though they were merely outward signs of grace or justice received through faith, and certain marks of the Christian profession, whereby believers are distinguished amongst men from unbelievers; let him be anathema.

Canon VII

If any one saith, that grace, as far as God's part is concerned, is not given through the said sacraments, always, and to all men, even though they receive them rightly, but [only] sometimes, and to some persons; let him be anathema.

Canon VIII

If any one saith, that by the said sacraments of the New Law grace is not conferred through the act performed, but that faith alone in the divine promise suffices for the obtaining of grace; let him be anathema.

Canon IX

If any one saith, that, in the three sacraments, Baptism, to wit, Confirmation, and Order, there is not imprinted in the soul a character, that is, a certain spiritual and indelible sign, on account of which they cannot be repeated; let him be anathema.

Canon X

If any one saith, that all Christians have power to administer the word, and all the sacraments; let him be anathema.

Canon XI

If any one saith, that, in ministers, when they effect, and confer the sacraments, there is not required the intention at least of doing what the Church does; let him be anathema.

Canon XII

If any one saith, that a minister, being in mortal sin,-if so be that he observe all the essentials which belong to the effecting, or conferring of, the sacrament,-neither effects, nor confers the sacrament; let him be anathema.

Canon XIII

If any one saith, that the received and approved rites of the Catholic Church, wont to be used in the solemn administration of the sacraments, may be condemned, or without sin be omitted at pleasure by the ministers, or be changed, by every pastor of the churches, into other new ones; let him be anathema.

• • •

On the Real Presence of Our Lord Jesus Christ in the Most Holy Sacrament of the Eucharist

In the first place, the holy Synod teaches, and openly and simply professes, that, in the august sacrament of the holy Eucharist, after the consecration of the bread and wine, our Lord Jesus Christ, true God and man, is truly, really, and substantially contained under the species of those sensible things. For neither are these things mutually repugnant,-that our Saviour Himself always sitteth at the right hand of the Father in heaven, according to the natural mode of existing, and that, nevertheless, He be, in many other places, sacramentally present to us in his own substance, by a manner of existing, which, though we can scarcely express it in words, yet can we, by the understanding illuminated by faith, conceive, and we ought most firmly to believe, to be possible unto God: for thus all our forefathers, as many as were in the true Church of Christ, who have treated of his most holy Sacrament have most openly professed, that our Redeemer instituted this so admirable a sacrament at the last supper, when, after the blessing of the bread and wine, He testified, in express and clear words, that He gave them His own very Body, and His own Blood; words which,- recorded by the holy Evangelists, and afterwards repeated by Saint Paul, whereas they carry with them that proper and most manifest meaning in which they were understood by the Fathers,-it is indeed a crime the most unworthy that they should be wrested, by certain contentious and wicked men, to fictitious and imaginary tropes, whereby the verity of the flesh and blood of Christ is denied, contrary to the universal sense of the Church, which, as *the pillar and ground of truth*, has detested, as satanical, these inventions devised by impious men; she recognising, with a mind ever grateful and unforgetting, this most excellent benefit of Christ.

• • •

On the Most Holy Sacrament of the Eucharist

Canon I

If any one denieth, that, in the sacrament of the most holy Eucharist, are contained truly, really, and substantially, the body and blood together with the soul and divinity of our Lord Jesus Christ, and consequently the whole Christ; but saith that He is only therein as in a sign, or in figure, or virtue; let him be anathema.

Canon II

If any one saith, that, in the sacred and holy sacrament of the Eucharist, the substance of the bread and wine remains conjointly with the body and blood of our Lord Jesus Christ, and denieth that wonderful and singular conversion of the whole substance of the bread into the Body, and of the whole substance of the wine into the Blood-the species only of the bread and wine remaining which-conversion indeed the Catholic Church most aptly calls Transubstantiation; let him be anathema.

• • •

Canon IX

If any one denieth, that all and each of Christ's faithful of both sexes are bound, when they have attained to years of discretion, to communicate every year, at least at Easter, in accordance with the precept of the holy Mother Church; let him be anathema.

• • •

Canon XI

If any one saith, that faith alone is a sufficient preparation for receiving the sacrament of the most holy Eucharist; let him be anathema. And for fear lest so great a sacrament may be received unworthily, and so unto death and condemnation, this holy Synod ordains and declares, that sacramental confession, when a confessor may be had, is of necessity to be made beforehand, by those whose conscience is burthened with mortal sin, how contrite evensoever they may think themselves.

But if any one shall presume to teach, preach, or obstinately to assert, or even in public disputation to defend the contrary, he shall be thereupon excommunicated.

. . .

On the Ecclesiastical Hierarchy, and on Ordination

But, forasmuch as in the sacrament of Order, as also in Baptism, and Confirmation, a character is imprinted, which can neither be effaced nor taken away; the holy Synod with reason condemns the opinion of those, who assert that the priests of the New Testament have only a temporary power; and that those who have once been rightly ordained, can again become laymen, if they do not exercise the ministry of the word of God. And if any one affirm, that all Christians indiscriminately are priests of the New Testament, or that they are all mutually endowed with an equal spiritual power, he clearly does nothing but confound the ecclesiastical hierarchy, which is *as an army set in array;* as if, contrary to the doctrine of blessed Paul, *all* were *apostles, all prophets, all evangelists, all pastors, all doctors.* Wherefore, the holy Synod declares that, besides the other ecclesiastical degrees, bishops, who have succeeded to the place of the apostles, principally belong to this hierarchical order; that they are placed, as the same apostle says *by the Holy Ghost, to rule the Church of God;* that they are superior to priests; administer the sacrament of Confirmation; ordain the ministers of the Church; and that they can perform very many other things; over which functions others of an inferior order have no power. Furthermore, the sacred and holy Synod teaches, that, in the ordination of bishops, priests, and of the other orders, neither the consent, nor vocation, nor authority, whether of the people, or of any civil power or magistrate whatsoever, is required in such wise as that, without this, the ordination is invalid; yea rather doth It decree, that all those who, being only called and instituted by the people, or by the civil power and magistrate, ascend to the exercise of these ministrations, and those who of their own rashness assume them to themselves, are not ministers of the Church, but are to be looked upon as *thieves and robbers, who have not entered by the door.* These are the things which it hath seemed good to the sacred Synod to teach the faithful of Christ, in general terms, touching the sacrament of Order.

. . .

On the Sacrament of Matrimony

Canon IX

If anyone saith, that clerics constituted in sacred orders or Regulars, who have solemnly professed chastity, are able to contract marriage, and that being contracted it is valid, notwithstanding the ecclesiastical law, or vow; and that the contrary is nothing else than to condemn marriage; and, that all who do not feel that they have the gift of chastity, even though they have made a vow thereof, may contract marriage; let him be anathema; seeing that God refuses not that gift to those who ask for it rightly, neither does *He suffer us to be tempted above that which we are able.*

Canon X

If any one saith, that the marriage state is to be placed above the state of virginity, or of celibacy, and that it is not better and more blessed to remain in virginity, or in celibacy, than to be united in matrimony; let him be anathema.

. . .

On the Invocation, Veneration, and Relics, of Saints, and on Sacred Images

The holy Synod enjoins on all bishops, and others who sustain the office and charge of teaching, that, agreeably to the usage of the Catholic and Apostolic Church, received from the primitive times of the Christian religion, and agreeably to the consent of the holy Fathers, and to the decrees of sacred Councils, they especially instruct the faithful diligently concerning the intercession and invocation of saints; the honour [paid] to relics; and the legitimate use of images: teaching them, that the saints, who reign together with Christ, offer up their own prayers to God for men; that it is good and useful suppliantly to invoke them, and to have recourse to their prayers, aid, [and] help for obtaining benefits from God, through His Son, Jesus Christ our Lord, who is our alone Redeemer and Saviour; but that they think impiously, who deny that the saints, who enjoy eternal happiness in heaven, are to be invocated; or who assert either that they do not pray for men; or, that the invocation of them to pray for each of us even in particular, is idolatry: or that it is repugnant to the word of God; and is opposed to the honour of the *one mediator of God and men, Christ Jesus;* or, that it is foolish to supplicate, vocally, or mentally, those who reign in heaven. Also, that the holy bodies of holy martyrs, and of others now living with Christ- which bodies were the living members of Christ, and *the temple of the Holy Ghost,* and which are by Him to be raised unto eternal life, and to be glorified-are to be venerated by the faithful; through which [bodies] many benefits are bestowed by God on men; so that they who affirm that veneration and honour are not due to the relics of saints; or, that these, and other sacred monuments, are uselessly honoured by the faithful; and that the places dedicated to the memories of the saints are in vain visited with the view of obtaining their aid; are wholly to be condemned, as the Church has already long since condemned, and now also condemns them.

Moreover, that the images of Christ, of the Virgin Mother of God, and of the other saints, are to be had and retained particularly in temples, and that due honour and veneration are to be given them; not that any divinity, or virtue, is believed to be in them, on account of which they are to be worshipped; or that anything is to be asked of them; or, that trust is to be reposed in images, as was of old done by the Gentiles who placed their hope in idols; but because the honour which is shown them is referred to the prototypes which those images represent; in such wise that by the images which we kiss, and before which we uncover the head, and prostrate ourselves, we adore Christ; and we venerate the saints, whose similitude they bear: as by the decrees of Councils, and especially of the second Synod of Nicaea, has been defined against the opponents of images.

. . .

Cardinals and All Prelates of the Churches Shall Be Content with Modest Furniture and a Frugal Table: They Shall Not Enrich Their Relatives or Domestics Out of the Property of the Church

It is to be wished, that those who undertake the office of a bishop should understand what their portion is; and comprehend that they are called, not to their own convenience, not to riches or luxury, but to labours and cares for the glory of God. For it is not to be doubted, that the rest of the faithful also will be more easily excited to religion and innocence, if they shall see those who are set over them, not fixing their thoughts on the things of this world, but on the salvation of souls, and on their heavenly country. Wherefore the holy Synod, being minded that these things are of the greatest importance toward restoring ecclesiastical discipline, admonishes all bishops, that, often meditating thereon, they show themselves conformable to their office, by their actual deeds, and the actions of their lives; which is a kind of perpetual sermon; but above all that they so order their whole conversation, as that others may thence be able to derive examples of frugality, modesty, continency, and of that holy humility which so much recommends us to God.

Wherefore, after the example of our fathers in the Council of Carthage, it not only orders that bishops be content with modest furniture, and a frugal table and diet, but that they also give heed that in the rest of their manner of living, and in their whole house, there be nothing seen that is alien from this holy institution, and which does not manifest simplicity, zeal toward God, and a contempt of vanities. Also, it wholly forbids them to strive to enrich their own kindred or domestics out of the revenues of the church: seeing that even the canons of the Apostles forbid them to give to their kindred the property of the church, which belongs to God: but if their kindred be poor, let them distribute to them thereof as poor, but not misapply, or waste, it for their sakes: yea, the holy Synod with the utmost earnestness, admonishes them completely to lay aside all this human and carnal affection toward brothers, nephews, and kindred, which is the seed-plot of many evils in the Church. And what has been said of bishops, the same is not only to be observed by all who hold ecclesiastical benefices, whether Secular or Regular, each according to the nature of his rank, but the Synod decrees that it also regards the cardinals of the holy Roman Church; for whereas, upon their advice to the most holy Roman Pontiff, the administration of the universal Church depends, it would seem to be a shame, if they did not at the same time shine so pre-eminent in virtue and in the discipline of their lives, as deservedly to draw upon themselves the eyes of all men.

. . .

Decree Concerning Indulgences

Whereas the power of conferring Indulgences was granted by Christ to the Church; and she has, even in the most ancient times, used the said power, delivered unto her of God; the sacred holy Synod teaches, and enjoins, that the use of Indulgences, for the Christian people most salutary, and approved of by the authority of sacred Councils, is to be retained in the Church; and It condemns with anathema those who either assert, that they are useless; or who deny that there is in the Church the power of granting them. In granting them, however, It desires that, in accordance with the ancient and approved custom in the Church, moderation be observed; lest, by excessive facility, ecclesiastical discipline be enervated. And being desirous that the abuses which have crept therein, and by occasion of which this honourable name of Indulgences is blasphemed by heretics, be amended and corrected, It ordains generally by this decree, that all evil gains for the obtaining thereof,-whence a most prolific cause of abuses amongst the Christian people has been derived,-be wholly abolished. But as regards the other abuses which have proceeded from superstition, ignorance, irreverence, or from whatsoever other source, since, by reason of the manifold corruptions in the places and provinces where the said abuses are committed, they cannot conveniently be specially prohibited; it commands all bishops, diligently to collect, each in his own church, all abuses of this nature, and to report them in the first provincial Synod; that, after having been reviewed by the opinions of the other bishops also, they may forthwith be referred to the Sovereign Roman Pontiff, by whose authority and prudence that which may be expedient for the universal Church will be ordained; that thus the gift of holy Indulgences may be dispensed to all the faithful, piously, holily, and incorruptly.

Questions:
1. What aspects of the Reformation did the Council of Trent rejoice?
2. What are the sacraments? What role do they play in Tridentine Roman Catholicism?

13.8   The Society of Jesus

During the Protestant movement, the Catholic church was active in its own efforts to reform from within. The Society of Jesus (Jesuits) was a religious order founded by Ignatius Loyola in 1540.

Loyola (1491–1556) was a soldier who had turned to religion while recovering from wounds. Under Loyola's firm leadership, the Jesuits became a disciplined organization that was dedicated to serving the pope with unquestioned loyalty. The next two selections from the constitution of the society and the famous spiritual exercises of Loyola demonstrate the purity and determination of these Catholic reformers.

CONSTITUTION (1540)

Source: "Constitution" is from James H. Robinson, ed., *Readings in European History,* vol. 1 (Boston: Ginn and Company, 1904), pp. 162–163.

He who desires to fight for God under the banner of the cross in our society,—which we wish to distinguish by the name of Jesus,—and to serve God alone and the Roman pontiff, his vicar on earth, after a solemn vow of perpetual chastity, shall set this thought before his mind, that he is a part of a society founded for the especial purpose of providing for the advancement of souls in Christian life and doctrine and for the propagation of faith through public preaching and the ministry of the word of God, spiritual exercises and deeds of charity, and in particular through the training of the young and ignorant in Christianity and through the spiritual consolation of the faithful of Christ in hearing confessions; and he shall take care to keep first God and next the purpose of this organization always before his eyes. . . .

All the members shall realize, and shall recall daily, as long as they live, that this society as a whole and in every part is fighting for God under faithful obedience to one most holy lord, the pope, and to other Roman pontiffs who succeed him. And although we are taught in the gospel and through the orthodox faith to recognize and steadfastly profess that all the faithful of Christ are subject to the Roman pontiff as their head and as the vicar of Jesus Christ, yet we have adjudged that, for the special promotion of greater humility in our society and the perfect mortification of every individual and the sacrifice of our own wills, we should each be bound by a peculiar vow, in addition to the general obligation, that whatever the present Roman pontiff, or any future one, may from time to time decree regarding the welfare of souls and the propagation of the faith, we are pledged to obey without evasion or excuse, instantly, so far as in us lies, whether he send us to the Turks or any other infidels, even to those who inhabit the regions men call the Indies; whether to heretics or schismatics, or, on the other hand, to certain of the faithful.

SPIRITUAL EXERCISES (1548)
IGNATIUS LOYOLA

Source: Bettenson, Henry, ed., *Documents of the Christian Church,* Second Edition. Copyright © 1963. Reprinted by permission of Oxford University Press.

1. Always to be ready to obey with mind and heart, setting aside all judgement of one's own, the true spouse of Jesus Christ, our holy mother our infallible and orthodox mistress, the Catholic Church, whose authority is exercised over us by the hierarchy.

2. To commend the confession of sins to a priest as it is practised in the Church; the reception of the Holy Eucharist once a year, or better still every week, or at least every month, with the necessary preparation.

4. To have a great esteem for the religious orders, and to give the preference to celibacy or virginity over the married state.

5. To approve of the religious vows of chastity, poverty, perpetual obedience, as well as the other works of perfection and supererogation. Let us remark in passing, that we must never engage by vow to take a state (such e.g. as marriage) that would be an impediment to one more perfect. . . .

6. To praise relics, the veneration and invocation of Saints: also the stations, and pious pilgrimages, indulgences, jubilees, the custom of lighting candles in the churches, and other such aids to piety and devotion. . . .

9. To uphold especially all the precepts of the Church, and not censure them in any manner; but, on the contrary, to defend them promptly, with reasons drawn from all sources, against those who criticize them.

10. To be eager to commend the decrees, mandates, traditions, rites and conduct; although there may not always be the uprightness of conduct that there ought to be, yet to attack or revile them in private or in public tends to scandal and disorder. Such attacks set the people against their princes and pastors; we must avoid such reproaches and never attack superiors before inferiors. The best course is to make private approach to those who have power to remedy the evil.

Question:

1. What does Loyola demand from the Catholic faithful?

PART 14
European Explorations and Expansion

14.1   Kilwa, Mombasa, and the Portuguese: Realities of Empire

The heroic depiction of Portuguese exploration in the "Lusiads" is countered by accounts of the acquis-
itive brutality which became part-and-parcel of all colonial enterprises. It did not take the Portuguese long
to realize their superiority in military technology, and to employ this to their advantage. The prosperous
Swahili cities were obvious targets, and moreover held the key to the linkage of Portugal to its com-
mercial concessions in India. The colonial soldier-administrator followed closely on the heels of the mer-
chant-explorer and the missionary, in this instance, in the person of Francisco d'Almeida. D'Almeida's
no-nonsense approach included brute force, and in 1505 the cities of Kilwa and Mombasa were sacked.
The following account is believed to have been written by Hans Mayr, a German seaman in the service
of the Portuguese.

> **Source:** E. Axelson, "South East Africa," 1940; pp. 231–238. Quoted in G.S.P. Freeman-Grenville, *The East*
> *African Coast: Selected Documents* (London: Rex Collings, 1974), pp. 105–112.

The Voyage and Acts of Dom Francisco, Viceroy of India, written in the ship *Sam Rafael* of Oporto, captained by Fernan Suarez.

In the year 1505, on 25 March, Tuesday, the feast of the Annunciation of Our Lady, Dom Francisco d'Almeida sailed with a fleet of twenty vessels. There were fourteen large men-of-war and six caravels.

They rounded the Cape of Good Hope on 20 June and were driven away from it seventy leagues. On 2 July there were great storms with thunder, and two men from the flagship and one from the *Lyomarda* fell overboard. On 18 July they sighted land for the first time, 369 leagues beyond the Cape of Good Hope, near the Ylhas Darradeiras, which are thirty leagues from the island of Mozambique. On 19 July they were in sight of Mozambique, and on 2I July they were cross-ing the shallow waters of Sam Rafael, which are thirty leagues from Kilwa.

On Tuesday, 22 July, they entered the harbour of Kilwa at noon, with a total of eight ships. Immediately on their arrival the Grand-Captain, Dom Francisco d'Almeida, sent Bona Ajuta Veneziano to summon the king. He excused him-self from coming, but sent the Grand-Captain gifts instead; They were five goats, a small cow and a large number of coconuts and other fruit.

Next flay the Grand-Captain ordered the ships to have their artillery in readiness. Then the captains, each in his best clothes, and full armour, went in his own boat to lie off the town in the hope that the king would decide to come out. The sheikh, however, sent a message to say that he could not come since he had guests, but, if required, he would send the tribute due to the King of Portugal. This message was brought by a party of five Moors, who were immediately seized.

At dawn on Thursday, 24 July, the vigil of the feast of St. James the Apostle, all went in their boats to the shore. The first to land was the Grand-Captain, and he was followed by the others. They went straight to the royal palace, and on the way only those Moors who did not fight were granted their lives. At the palace there was a Moor leaning out of the window with a Portuguese flag in his hand, shouting: 'Portugal! Portugal!' This flag had been left behind by the admiral [Vasco da Gama] when he had arranged for Kilwa to pay a tribute of 1,500 ounces of gold a year. The Moor was asked to open the door, and, when he did not do so, the door was broken down with axes. They found neither the Moor nor anyone else in the Palace, which was deserted.

In Kilwa there are many strong houses several storeys high. They are built of stone and mortar and plastered with various designs. As soon as the town had been taken without opposition, the Vicar-General and some of the Franciscan fathers came ashore carrying two crosses in procession and singing the Te Deum. They went to the palace, and there the cross was put down and the Grand-Captain prayed. Then everyone started to plunder the town of all its merchandise and provisions.

The town of Kilwa lies on an island around which ships of 500 tons can sail. The island and town have a popu-lation of 4,000 people. It is very fertile and produces maize similar to that of Guinea, butter, honey, and wax. On the trees hang beehives like jars of three *almudes* capacity, each closed with woven palm leaves. There are holes through which the bees go in and come out.

There are many trees and palms here and on the mainland, some of them different from those of Portugal. From the island to the mainland the distance is in some places two leagues and in others one.

There are sweet oranges, lemons, vegetables, small onions, and aromatic herbs. They are grown in gardens and watered with water from the wells. Here also grows betel which has leaves like ivy and is grown like peas with sticks at the root for support. The leaf is used by the wealthy Arabs for chewing together with specially prepared limes which look like an ointment. They keep the leaves as if they were to be put on wounds. These leaves make the mouth and teeth very red, but are said to be most refreshing.

There are more black slaves than white Moors here: they are engaged on farms growing maize and other things. There are various types of peas which are produced by plants as high as large pepper trees; when they are ripe, they are gathered and stored. The soil is red, the top layer being sandy; the grass is always green. There are many fat beasts, oxen, cows, sheep, and goats and also plenty of fish; there are also whales which swim round the ships. There is no running drinking water on the island. Near the island there are other small islands which are inhabited. There are many boats as large as a caravel of fifty tons and other smaller ones. The large ones lie aground on the shore and are dragged down to the sea when the people wish to sail them. They are built without nails: the planks are sewn together with rope made from knotted coir from the coconut palm. The same kind of rope is used for the rudder. The boats are caulked with black pitch made from crude incense and resin. They sail from here to Sofala, 255 leagues away.

The palms here do not produce dates but from some of them wine and vinegar are obtained. These come from the palm trees which do not produce coconuts. The coconuts are the size of large melons, and from the fibres inside the shell all kinds of rope are made. Inside the shell is a fruit the size of a large pineapple. It contains half a pint of milk which is very pleasant to drink. When the milk has been drunk the nut is broken and eaten; the kernel tastes like a walnut which is not fully ripe. They dry it and it yields a large quantity of oil.

People here sleep raised above the ground in hammocks made of palm leaves in which only one person can lie.

The Portuguese found here a large quantity of pure drinking water. Flasks of very good perfume are exported from here and a large quantity of glass of all types and all kinds of cotton piece-goods, incense, resin, gold, silver, and pearls. The Grand-Captain ordered the loot to be deposited under seal in a house.

The fortress of Kilwa was built out of the best house there was there. All the other houses round it were pulled down. It was fortified and guns were set in place with everything else a fort needs. Pero Ferreira was left in command of it with eighty men.

The country is not very hot. The men are armed with bows and large arrows, strong shields of palm leaves bound with cotton, and pikes better than those of Guinea. Few swords were seen. They have four catapults for hurling stones but do not yet know the use of gunpowder.

The sea laps the entrance of the fortress at high water near where the ships enter.

When the king fled from Kilwa, the Grand-Captain appointed another, a local Moor beloved by all, whom they took in procession on horseback through the town.

Lime is prepared here in this manner: large logs of wood are piled in a circle and inside them coral limestone is placed; then the wood is burnt. The process after that is the same as in Portugal.

Cotton is found in abundance. It is of good quality and is planted and grows well in the island. The sheep have wool no better than goats. The slaves wear a cotton cloth round the waist and down to the knees; the rest of the body is naked. The white Arabs and slave owners wear two pieces of cotton cloth, one round the waist down to the feet and the other thrown over the shoulders and reaching down as far as where the first cloth is tied.

They have copper coins like our *ceptis,* four being equal to one *real;* Portuguese coins have the same value there as at home. There are no gold coins but the weight of their *mitical* is equal to 460 *reis* in Portugal.

The winter season in Kilwa is from April to September. It is not cold and for this reason the people wear scanty clothes.

The Grand-Captain twice went from one side of the town to the other. Once he saw twenty-five gazelle which had been let loose on the island. There are also many wild cats in the bush.

There are many vaulted mosques, one of which is like that of Cordova. All the upper-class Moors carry a rosary.

MOMBASA

On 9 August the ships left Kilwa for Mombasa, sixty leagues up the coast. The ship Sam Rafael reached there on 14 August, but the Grand-Captain arrived with the other ten ships a day earlier.

The Moors of Mombasa had built a strongpoint with many guns at the entrance of the harbour, which is very narrow. When we entered, the first ship, which was under the command of Gonzalo de Paiva, who was going in front to explore the channel, was fired on by the Moors from both sides. We promptly replied to the fire, and with such intensity that the gunpowder in their strongpoint caught fire. It started burning and the Moors fled, thus allowing the whole fleet to enter and lie at anchor in front of the town. And on that day, the vigil of the feast of the Assumption, the town was bombarded with all the guns on the ships, while the guns of the town replied to our fire.

When the Grand-Captain went ashore he seized a Moor who happened to be a member of the royal household. The Portuguese obtained good information from him.

The first night the fleet arrived in Mombasa there came out on the shore a Spanish Christian who was living there, a gunner by profession and a convert to Islam. He told the Christians to go away and that Mombasa was not like

Kilwa: they would not find people with hearts that could be eaten like chickens as they had done in Kilwa, but that if they were keen to come ashore the people were ready to set about them for their supper. The Grand-Captain, however, offered him his protection and pardon, but he refused.

Mombasa is a very large town and lies on an island from one and a half to two leagues round. The town is built on rocks on the higher part of the island and has no walls on the side of the sea; but on the land side it is protected by a wall as high as the fortress. The houses are of the same type as those of Kilwa: some of them are three storeyed and all are plastered with lime. The streets are very narrow, so that two people cannot walk abreast in them: all the houses have stone seats in front of them, which makes the streets yet narrower.

The Grand-Captain met with the other captains and decided to burn the town that evening and to enter it the following morning. But when they went to burn the town they were received by the Moors with a shower of arrows and stones. The town has more than 600 houses which are thatched with palm leaves: these are collected green for this purpose. In between the stone dwelling-houses there are wooden houses with porches and stables for cattle. There are very few dwelling houses which have not these wooden houses attached.

Once the fire was started it raged all night long, and many houses collapsed and a large quantity of goods was destroyed. For from this town trade is carried on with Sofala and with Cambay by sea. There were three ships from Cambay and even these did not escape the fury of the attack. It was a moonless night.

On Friday 25 August, the feast of the Assumption of Our Lady, the Grand-Captain drew up eight ships on one side of Mombasa. On the other side was his son, Dom Lourenço d'Almeida, with three ships. Early in the morning they all prepared their arms and had breakfast. The Grand-Captain had ordered that all should land as soon as a shot from a big gun was fired. Thus all the boats were waiting ready on the water: when the shot was fired all got quickly on to the shore in very good order. The archers and gunners went ahead of everyone else, all going up the steep ascent into the town. When they entered, they found that some of the houses had been deserted as a result of the fire of the previous night. Further on they found three storeyed houses from which stones were thrown at them. But the stones which were thrown fell against the walls of the very narrow streets, so that much of the force of their fall was lost. There were also many balconies projecting over the streets under which one could shelter.

The Grand-Captain went straight to the royal palace: he was led by the Moor who had been captured on the previous day. He had ordered that no one should enter any of the houses, and that anyone who did so should die. When the Grand-Captain arrived at the palace, Captain Verraudez immediately climbed up the wall and hoisted our flag, shouting: Portugal, Portugal. And there were many Moors killed on the way there.

They saw from there some sixty Moors leaving the town, all dressed in gowns and turbans; they were going towards a palm grove and did not seem in any hurry. Some said that the king was among them. The Christians, however, did not follow them. All the people of the town were taken to this palm grove, and the entrance to it was guarded by more than 500 archers. These archers were all negro slaves of the white Moors, and obedient to their masters in their captivity like those of Kilwa.

The Grand-Captain ordered that the town should be sacked and that each man should carry off to his ship whatever he found: so that at the end there would be a division of the spoil, each man to receive a twentieth of what he found. The same rule was made for gold, silver, and pearls. Then everyone started to plunder the town and to search the houses, forcing open the doors with axes and iron bars. There was a large quantity of cotton cloth for Sofala in the town, for the whole coast gets its cotton cloth from here. So the Grand-Captain got a good share of the trade of Sofala for himself. A large quantity of rich silk and gold embroidered clothes was seized, and carpets also; one of these, which was without equal for beauty, was sent to the King of Portugal together with many other valuables.

When night came the Grand-Captain ordered all the men to a field which lay between the town and the sea. A section of it was allotted to each captain and a watch was set for the night. They were at a distance of a gun shot from the palm grove where the Moors were with their king. On the morning of the 16th they again plundered the town, but because the men were tired from fighting and from lack of sleep, much wealth was left behind apart from what each man took for himself. They also carried away provisions, rice, honey, butter, maize, countless camels and a large number of cattle, and even two elephants. They paraded these elephants in front of the people of the town before they took it, in order to frighten them. There were many prisoners, and white women among them and children, and also some merchants from Cambay.

On Saturday evening the Grand-Captain ordered that all should return to the ships in a disciplined manner, keeping a watch for the Moors as they went on their way. And as the Christians left by one way, so the Moors entered by the other to see what destruction had been done. For the streets and houses were full of dead, who were estimated to be about 1,500.

Dom Fernando de Sà was wounded with an arrow which did not have an iron point. Some of their arrows are made of wood with iron points, others of burnt wood soaked in an unknown poison. Some say the wood itself is poisonous. The arrows with iron points have herbs at the tip, but these are not dangerous, as was evident from those wounded by them.

According to the Moors this town is the most famous of all the coast of Abyssinia. The island is very fertile, and produces a large quantity of sweet oranges, pomegranates, lemons, and sugar cane; all these things are more abundant here than at Kilwa.

All the guns belonging to the town were taken to the ships. They found one old cannon lying in the street which five men could not lift. It was said to have belonged to a ship called *Rey* which had been lost nearby. They also found an anchor which had been stolen from the Admiral Vasco da Gama. Because the Portuguese could not take it the Arabs pointed it out to each other. There were only five Portuguese dead in the battle and many wounded—more by the grace of God than by any act of man.

After returning to the ships they weighed anchor and moved inshore so that the anchors were exposed on dry land at low water. They remained there for ten days. It was very difficult to go out through the narrow entrance and also because there were strong contrary winds blowing. The ship *Lyomarda* lost its rudder and they could not find it again. So they were obliged to make a new one, for which each ship had to give up one of its hooks.

The ship *San Gabriel* arrived on 20 August with its mainmast broken, but the whereabouts of the supply ships was still not known.

Now the King of Mombasa and the King of Malindi were at war, and many of their people had been killed on both sides, the cause of the war being the friendship of the King of Malindi with the King of Portugal. Eventually the King of Mombasa had been defeated by the King of Malindi, and for the present they were friends. So the King of Mombasa wrote the following letter to the King of Malindi:

May God's blessing be upon you, Sayyid Ali! This is to inform you that a great lord has passed through the town, burning it and laying it waste. He came to the town in such strength and was of such cruelty, that he spared neither man nor woman, old nor young, nay, not even the smallest child. Not even those who fled escaped from his fury. He not only killed and burnt men but even the birds of the heavens were shot down. The stench of the corpses is so great in the town that I dare not go there; nor can I ascertain nor estimate what wealth they have taken from the town. I give you these sad news for your own safety.

There were more than 10,000 people in Mombasa, of whom 3,700 were men of military age.

MALINDI

Thence they sailed to Malindi, twenty-five leagues further north. Five leagues outside Malindi they were halted by strong currents and there they met the caravel of Johan Homere, which had captured two islands for Portugal. One of them was 450 leagues beyond the Cape of Good Hope and was uninhabited. They took in firewood and water there.

The other island lies between Kilwa and Mombasa and is known as Zanzibar. As the Moors of this island already knew of the destruction of Kilwa, they presented the captain with provisions and said they were at the service of the King of Portugal. The ship had arrived there on 24 August, and they had taken in water, firewood and meat.

Mogadishu lies on this coast and is 100 leagues from Malindi. It is a large town with plenty of horses....

Questions:
1. What was the apparent reason for the attack on Kilwa? What were the results? How did d'Almeida change Kilwa's government?
2. How did the situation at Mombasa differ from that at Kilwa?
3. What orders did d'Almeida give at Mombasa?
4. What was Malindi's decision?

14.2   Vasco da Gama, Journey to India

Vasco da Gama (1460?–1524) was one of the great mariners who helped Portugal take the lead in the era of explorations. In 1497, with four ships and 168 men, da Gama sailed down the west coast of Africa, rounded the Cape of Good Hope, fought Muslims along the way, and reached India. He did not return to Lisbon until 1499, after a voyage of two years and two months, but he brought back pepper, cloves, nutmeg, cinnamon, and precious stones. Shortly after da Gama's return, another explorer, Pedro Cabral, assembled a fleet and set out for India. According to the official account, his ships were blown far off their course and on April 22, 1500, they sighted the coast of Brazil. Although with this discovery the Portuguese Crown could then boast of an empire and stake out its claim in America, Portugal devoted far more interest and attention to its growing empire in the East. The following reading is an excerpt from da Gama's journal of his voyage to India in 1497–1499.

Source: From *Portuguese Voyages*, 1498–1663, ed. Charles David Ley (London: J. M. Dent & Sons Ltd; New York: E. P. Dutton & Co., 1947), pp. 27–38, passim. Reprinted by permission.

The city of Calicut is inhabited by Christians. They are of tawny complexion. Some of them have big beards and long hair, whilst others clip their hair short or shave the head, merely allowing a tuft to remain on the crown as a sign that they are Christians. They also wear moustaches. They pierce the ears and wear much gold in them. They go naked down to the waist, covering their lower extremities with very fine cotton stuffs. But it is only the most respectable who do this, for the others manage as best they are able.[1]

The women of this country, as a rule, are ugly and of small stature. They wear many jewels of gold around the neck, numerous bracelets on their arms, and rings set with precious stones on their toes. All these people are well disposed and apparently of mild temper. At first sight they seem covetous and ignorant.

When we arrived at Calicut, the captain-major sent two men to the King with a message, informing him that an ambassador had arrived from the King of Portugal with letters.

The king presented the bearers of this message with much fine cloth. He sent word to the captain bidding him welcome.

A pilot accompanied our two men, with orders to take us to a place called Pandarani, below the place [Capua] where we anchored at first. At this time we were actually in front of the city of Calicut. We were told that the anchorage at the place to which we were to go was good, whilst at the place we were then it was bad, with a stony bottom, which was quite true; and, moreover, that it was customary for the ships which came to this country to anchor there for the sake of safety. We ourselves did not feel comfortable, and the captain-major had no sooner received this royal message than he ordered the sails to be set, and we departed. We did not, however, anchor as near the shore as the king's pilot desired.

When we were at anchor, a message arrived informing the captain-major that the king was already in the city. At the same time the king sent a bale [governor], with other men of distinction, to Pandarani, to conduct the captain-major to where the king awaited him. This bale is always attended by two hundred men armed with swords and bucklers. As it was late when this message arrived, the captain-major deferred going.

On the following morning, they took us to a large church, and this is what we saw:

The body of the church is as large as the monastery, all built of hewn stone and covered with tiles. At the main entrance rises a pillar of bronze as high as a mast, on the top of which was perched a bird, apparently a cock. In addition to this, there was another pillar as high as a man, and very stout. In the center of the body of the church rose a chapel, all built of hewn stone, with a bronze door sufficiently wide for a man to pass, and stone steps leading up to it. Within this sanctuary stood a small image which they said represented Our Lady. Along the walls, by the main entrance, hung seven small bells. In this church the captain-major said his prayers, and we with him.

We did not go within the chapel, for it is custom that only certain servants of the church should enter. These men wore some threads passing over the left shoulder and under the right arm, in the same manner as our deacons wear the stole. They threw holy water over us, and gave us some white earth, which the Christians of this country are in the habit of putting on their foreheads, breasts, around the neck, and on the forearms. They threw holy water upon the captain-major and gave him some of the earth, which he gave in charge of someone, giving them to understand that he would put it on later.

Many other saints were painted on the walls of the church, wearing crowns. They were painted variously, with teeth protruding an inch from the mouth, and four or five arms.

The captain, on entering, saluted in the manner of the country: by putting the hands together, then raising them towards Heaven, as is done by Christians when addressing God, and immediately afterwards opening them and shutting the fists quickly.

And the captain told the king that he was the ambassador of a king of Portugal, who was lord of many countries and the possessor of great wealth of every description, exceeding that of any king of these parts; that for a period of sixty years his ancestors had annually sent out vessels to make discoveries in the direction of India, as they knew that there were Christians kings there like themselves. This, he said, was the reason which induced them to order this country to be discovered, not because they sought for gold or silver, for of this they had such abundance that they needed not what was to be found in this country. He further stated that the captains sent out traveled for a year or two, until their provisions were exhausted, and then returned to Portugal, without having succeeded in making the desired discovery. There reigned a king now whose name was Dom Manuel, who ordered him not to return to Portugal until he should have discovered the king of the Christians, on pain of having his head cut off. That a letter had been entrusted to him to be presented in case he succeeded in discovering him, and, finally, he had been instructed to say by word of mouth that he [the king of Portugal] desired to be his friend and brother.

In reply to this the king said that he was welcome; that, on his part, he held him as a friend and brother, and would send ambassadors with him to Portugal. This latter had been asked as a favor, the captain pretending that he would not dare to present himself before his king and master unless he was able to present, at the same time, some men of this country.

On Tuesday the captain got ready the following things to be sent to the king: twelve pieces of lambel, four scarlet hoods, six hats, four strings of coral, a case containing six washstand basins, a case of sugar, two casks of oil, and two of honey. And as it is the custom not to send anything to the king without the knowledge of the Moor [who advised him on commercial matters], and of the bale, the captain informed them of his intention. They came, and when they saw the present they laughed at it, saying that it was not a thing to offer to a king, that the poorest merchant from Mecca, or any other part of India, gave more, and that if he wanted to make a present it should be in gold, as the king would not accept such things. When the captain heard this he grew sad, and said he had brought no gold, that, moreover, he was no merchant, but an ambassador; that he gave of that which he had, which was his own [private gift] and not the king's; that if the King of Portugal ordered him to return he would entrust him with far richer presents; and that if King Samolin would not accept these things he would send them back to the ships. Upon this they declared that they would not forward his presents, nor consent to his forwarding them himself. When they had gone there came certain Moorish merchants, and they all depreciated the present which the captain desired to be sent to the king.

When the captain saw that they were determined not to forward his present, he said that he would go to speak to the king, and would then return to the ships. They approved of this, and told him that if he would wait a short time they would return and accompany him to the palace. And the captain waited all day, but they never came back. The captain was very wroth at being among so phlegmatic and unreliable a people, and intended, at first, to go to the palace without them. On further consideration, however, he thought it best to wait until the following day. As to us others, we diverted ourselves, singing and dancing to the sound of trumpets, and enjoyed ourselves much.

On Wednesday morning the Moors returned, and took the captain to the palace. The palace was crowded with armed men. Our captain was kept waiting for fully four long hours, outside a door, which was only opened when the king sent word to admit him, attended by two men only, whom he might select. It seemed to him, as it did to us, that this separation portended no good.

When he had entered, the king said that he had expected him on Tuesday. The captain said that the long road had tired him, and that for this reason he had not come to see him. The king then said that he had told him that he came from a very rich kingdom, and yet had brought him nothing; that he had also told him that he was the bearer of a letter, which had not yet been delivered. To this the captain rejoined that he had brought nothing, because the object of his voyage was merely to make discoveries, but that when other ships came he would then see what they brought him; as to the latter, it was true that he had brought one, and would deliver it immediately.

The king then asked what kind of merchandise was to be found in his country. The captain said that there was much corn, cloth, iron, bronze, and many other things. The king asked whether he had any merchandise with him. The captain replied that he had a little of each sort, as samples, and that if permitted to return to the ships he would order it to be landed, and that meantime four or five men would remain at the lodgings assigned them. The king said no. He might take all his people with him, securely moor his ships, land his merchandise, and sell it to the best advantage. Having taken leave of the king the captain returned to his lodgings, and we with him. As it was already late no attempt was made to depart that night.

The next morning the captain asked for boats to take him to his ships. They began to whisper among themselves, and said that we should have them if we would order our vessels to come nearer to the shore. The captain said that if he ordered his vessels to approach his brother would think that he was being held a prisoner, and that he gave this order on compulsion, and would hoist the sails to return to Portugal. They said that if we refused to order the ships to come nearer we should not be permitted to embark. The captain said that King Samolin had sent him back to his ships, and that as they would not let him go, as ordered by the king, he should return to the king, who was a Christian like himself. If the king would not let him go, and wanted him to remain in his country, he would do so with much pleasure. They agreed that he should be permitted to go, but afforded him no opportunity for doing so, for they immediately closed all the doors, and many armed men entered to guard us, none of us being allowed to go outside without being accompanied by several of these guards.

On the following day, these gentlemen [i.e., the bale and others] came back, and this time they "wore better faces." They told the captain that as he had informed the king that he intended to land his merchandise, he should now give orders to have this done. The captain consented, and said that he would write to his brother to see it being done. They said this was well, and that immediately after the arrival of the merchandise he would be permitted to return to his ship. The captain at once wrote to his brother to send certain things, and he did so at once. On their receipt the captain was allowed to go on board, two men remaining behind with the things that had been landed.

At this we rejoiced greatly, and rendered thanks to God for having extricated us from the hands of the people who had no more sense than beasts, for we knew well that once the captain was on board those who had been landed would have nothing to fear. When the captain reached his ship he ordered that no more merchandise should be sent.

Questions:
1. Describe the Portuguese impressions of the inhabitants of Calicut.
2. Compare and contrast da Gama's historic voyage with that of the other explorers in this section.
3. Do you sense some deception or self-deception in the reporting of strong Christian influences in Calicut (modern Ko*z*hihode)?
4. What were the consequences of the discovery of an ocean route to India at the close of the fifteenth century?

14.3   The Portuguese in Africa and India: Duarte Barbosa

In the following selection the establishment of these commercial colonies came at a distinct price for the inhabitants of those regions. In the following selection, Duarte Barbosa (ca. 1480–1521), an agent of the Portuguese government who helped establish commercial contacts along the east African coast, gives a description of the people and products of the area and of Portuguese methods for controlling trade.

Source: "The East Coast of Africa" is from *The Book of Duarte Barbosa: An Account of the Countries Bordering the Indian Ocean,* 2 vols. (London: Hakluyt Society, 1918, 1921).

THE EAST COAST OF AFRICA
DUARTE BARBOSA

Sofala

Going forward in the direction of India there is a river of no great size upon which up the stream is a town of the Moors [African Muslims] which they call Sofala, close to which the King our Lord [Portuguese King Manuel I] possesses a fort. These Moors have dwelt there a long time by reason of the great traffic which they carried on with the heathen of the mainland. The Moors of this place speak Arabic and have a king over them who is subject to the King our Lord.

And the manner of their traffic was this: they came in small vessels named zambucos from the kingdoms of Kilwa, Mombasa, and Malindi, bringing many cotton cloths, some spotted and others white and blue; also some of silk, and many small beads, grey, red, and yellow, which things come to the said kingdoms from the great kingdom of Cambay [on the coast of northwest India] in other greater ships. And these wares the said Moors who came from Malindi and Mombasa paid for in gold at such a price that those merchants departed well pleased. . . .

Kilwa

Going along the coast from the town of Mozambique, there is an island hard by the mainland which is called Kilwa, in which is a Moorish town with many fair houses of stone and mortar, with many windows after our fashion, very well arranged in streets, with many flat roofs. The doors are of wood, well carved, with excellent joinery. Around it are streams and orchards and fruit-gardens with many channels of sweet water. It has a Moorish king over it. . . . Before the King our Lord sent out his expedition to discover India, the Moors of Sofala, Cuama, Angoya and Mozambique were all subject to the King of Kilwa, who was the most mighty king among them. And in this town was great plenty of gold, as no ships passed toward Sofala without first coming to this island. . . .

This town was taken by force from its king by the Portuguese, as, moved by arrogance, he refused to obey the King our Lord. There took many prisoners and the king fled from the island, and His Highness ordered that a fort should be built there, and kept it under his rule and governance. . . .

Mombasa

Further on, an advance along the coast toward India, there is an isle hard by the mainland, on which is a town called Mombasa. . . . This Mombasa is a land very full of food. Here are found many very fine sheep with round tails, cows and other cattle in great plenty, and many fowls, all of which are exceedingly fat. There is much millet and rice, sweet and bitter oranges, lemons, pomegranates, Indian figs, vegetables of diverse kinds, and much sweet water. The men are often times at war . . . but at peace with those of the mainland, and they carry on trade with them, obtaining great amounts of honey, wax, and ivory.

The king of this city refused to obey the commands of the King our Lord, and through this arrogance he lost it, and our Portuguese took it from him by force. He fled away, and they slew many of his people and also took captive many, both men and women, in such sort that it was left ruined and plundered and burned. Of gold and silver great booty was taken here, bangles, bracelets, earrings and gold beads, also great store of copper with other rich wares in great quantity, and the town was left in ruins.

The City of Brava

Yet further along the coast, beyond these places, is a great town of Moors, of very fine stone and mortar houses, called Brava. It has no king, but is ruled by elders, and ancients of the land, who are the persons held in the highest esteem, and who have the chief dealings in merchandise of diverse kinds. And this place was destroyed by the Portuguese, who slew many of its people and carried many into captivity, and took great spoil of gold and silver and goods. Thenceforth many of them fled away toward the inland country, forsaking the town; yet after had been destroyed the Portuguese again settled and peopled it, so that now it is as prosperous as it was before.

Questions:
1. What does Barbosa find most important and impressive about the east coast of Africa?
2. How does he justify the destruction of African cities?

14.4 "Cut Off Their Ears, Hands and Noses!": Gaspar Correa

The following selection is an excerpt from the journals of Gaspar Correa, who sailed with Vasco da Gama in 1502. This incident occurred after a group of Portuguese had been killed in the trading station of Calcutta. Vasco da Gama sought to control the situation by exacting a bloody vengeance.

> **Source:** "Cut Off Their Ears, Hands and Noses!" is from H.E.J. Stanley, ed., *The Three Voyages of Vasco da Gama* (London: The Hakluyt Society, 1869), pp. 328-332.

The captain-major [Vasco da Gama], on arriving at Calecut, was in the passion because he found the port cleared, and in it there was nothing to which he could do harm, because the Moors, knowing of his coming, had all fled, and hid their vessels and sambuks in the rivers. . . . The King of Calecut thought that he might gain time, so that the captain-major should not do him harm; and when his fleet arrived he sent him a Brahman [religious official] of his in a boat with a white cloth fastened to a pole, as a sign of peace. This Brahman came dressed in the habit of a friar, one of those who had been killed in the country; and on reaching the ship, he asked for a safe conduct to enter. When it was known that he was not a friar—for the captain-major and everyone had been joyful, thinking that he was one of our friars—seeing that he was not, the captain-major gave him a safe conduct, and bade him enter the ship. . . . He then ordered all the fleet to draw in close to the shore, and all day, till night, he bombarded the city, by which he made a great destruction. . . .

While they were doing this business, there came in from the offing two large ships and twenty-two sambuks and Malabar vessels, which came from Coromandel laden with rice, which the Moors of Calecut had ordered to be laden there; . . . but our fleet having sighted them, the [Portuguese] caravels went to them, and the Moors could not fly, as they were laden, and the caravels brought them to the captain-major, and all struck their sails. . . .

Then, the captain-major commanded them to cut off the hands and ears and noses of all the crews, and put all that into one of the small vessels, into which he ordered them to put the friar, also without ears, or nose, or hands, which he ordered to be strung round his neck, with a palm-leaf for the King, on which he told him to have a curry made to eat of what his friar brought him. When all the Indians had been thus executed, he ordered their feet to be tied together, as they had no hands with which to untie them: and in order that they should not untie them with their teeth he ordered them to strike upon their teeth with staves, and they knocked them down their throats; and they were thus put on board, heaped up upon the top of each other, mixed up with the blood which streamed from them; and he ordered mats and dry leaves to be spread over them, and the sails to be set for the shore, and the vessel set on fire; and there were more than eight hundred Moors; and the small vessel with the friar, with all the hands and ears, was also sent on shore under sail, without being fired. These vessels went at once on shore, where many people flocked together to put out the fire, and draw out those whom they found alive, upon which they made great lamentations.

Question:
1. What does this selection say about how control was maintained over Portuguese colonies?

14.5 Christopher Columbus

It is easily forgotten that when Christopher Columbus (1451-1506) set sail across the "Western Ocean" with his three tiny ships on August 3, 1492, he was bound not for a new world but for "the Indies" (India, China, and the islands of East Asia). His venture was a prosaic even though a hazardous one. He hoped to discover a sea route that would make trade with the East-with its highly desired silks, rugs, jewelry, drugs, and spices-easier than the long and arduous caravan treks across Asia. According to Columbus's (mis)calculations, his destination could be reached by sailing some three thousand miles due west around the world. As it turned out, this was the distance to the islands of the Western Hemisphere that he encountered.

In 1484 Columbus had submitted his proposal of reaching the East by sailing west to the king of Portugal, hoping to receive financial support for the project. But the Portuguese were already deeply committed to an attempt to reach the same destination by sailing south around Africa and thence east to India and beyond, so Columbus's appeal was rejected. From there he went to Spain and after two years of effort he gained an audience with King Ferdinand and Queen Isabella. After six more years in negotiations, the monarchs finally agreed to underwrite the venture, and Columbus set off on his epochal voyage. The crossing of the Atlantic, from the Canary Islands (the last port of call on the European side) to an island in the Bahamas group (northeast of Cuba), where Columbus landed on October 12 and took possession in the name of Ferdinand and Isabella, took thirty-six days.

Over a period of twelve years Columbus made four voyages, exploring many of the Caribbean islands and establishing several colonies. His voyages took him to the mainland of South and Central America as well. And although he heard tales of a great ocean farther to the west, he never realized that the lands he had reached belonged not to the Orient but to another continent.

The two selections that follow consist of the initial entry in a journal Columbus kept of his first voyage and a letter he wrote as he neared the end of that voyage, describing some of what he had seen and done. Of special interest is his description of the people who lived on the Caribbean islands, particularly his account of their character, style of life, and reception of the Europeans.

Source: Trans. J. B. Thacher

JOURNAL AND LETTER

Prologue

Because, most Christian and very exalted and very excellent and very powerful Princes, King and Queen of the Spains and of the Islands of the Sea, our Lords, in this present year of 1492 after your Highnesses had made an end to the war of the Moors, who were reigning in Europe, and having finished the war in the very great city of Granada, where in this present year on the 2nd day of the month of January, I saw the Royal banners of your Highnesses placed by force of arms on the towers of the Alhambra, which is the fortress of the said City: and I saw the Moorish King come out to the gates of the City and kiss the Royal hands of your Highnesses, and the hands of the Prince, my Lord: and then in that present month, because of the information which I had given your Highnesses about the lands of India, and about a Prince who is called Great Khan, which means in our Romance language, King of Kings,- how he and his predecessors had many times sent to Rome to beg for men learned in our Holy Faith that they might be instructed therein, and that the Holy Father had never furnished them, and so, many people believing in idolatries and receiving among themselves sects of perdition, were lost:-your Highnesses, as Catholic Christians and Princes, loving the Holy Christian faith and the spreading of it, and enemies of the sect of Mahomet and of all idolatries and heresies, decided to send me, Christopher Columbus, to the said regions of India, to see the said Princes and the peoples and lands, and learn of their disposition, and of everything, and the measures which could be taken for their conversion to our Holy Faith: and you ordered that I should not go to the east by land, by which it is customary to go, but by way of the west, whence until to-day we do not know certainly that any one has gone. So that, after having banished all the Jews from all your Kingdoms and realms, in the same month of January, your Highnesses ordered me to go with a sufficient fleet to the said regions of India: and for that purpose granted me great favours and ennobled me, that from then hence-forward I might entitle myself Don and should be High Admiral of the Ocean-Sea [Atlantic—*Ed.*] and Viceroy and perpetual Governor of all the islands and continental land which I might discover and acquire, and which from now henceforward might be discovered and acquired in the Ocean-Sea, and that my eldest son should succeed in the same manner, and thus from generation to generation for ever after: and I started from the city of Granada on Saturday, the 12th day of the month of May in the same year 1492: I came to the village of Palos, which is a seaport, where I fitted out three vessels, very suitable for a similar undertaking: and I left the said port, well supplied with a large quantity of provisions and with many seamen, on the 3rd day of the month of August in the said year on a Friday at the half hour before sunrise, and took my way to the Canary Islands of your Highnesses, which are in the said Ocean-Sea, in order to set out on my voyage from there and sail until I arrived at the Indies, and make known the message of your Highnesses to those Princes, and fulfil the commands which had thus been given me: and for this purpose, I decided to write everything I might do and see and which might take place on this voyage, very punctually from day to day, as will be seen henceforth. Also, Lords and Princes, besides describing each night what takes place during the day, and during the day, the sailings of the night, I propose to make a new chart for navigation, on which I will locate all the sea and the lands of the Ocean-Sea, in their proper places, under their winds; and further, to compose a book and show everything by means of drawing, by the latitude from the equator and by longitude from the west, and above all, it is fitting that I forget sleep, and study the navigation diligently, in order to thus fulfil these duties, which will be a great labour.

LETTER

Sir:

As I know that you will have pleasure of the great victory which our Lord hath given me in my voyage, I write you this, by which you shall know that, in twenty days I passed over to the Indies with the fleet which the most illustrious King and Queen, our Lords, gave me: where I found very many islands peopled with inhabitants beyond number. And, of them all, I have taken possession for their Highnesses, with proclamation and the royal standard displayed; and I was not gainsaid. On the first which I found, I put the name San Salvador, in commemoration of His high Majesty, who marvellously hath given all this: the Indians call it Guanahani. The second I named the Island of Santa Maria de Concepcion, the third Ferrandina, the fourth Isabella, the fifth La Isla Juana [Cuba]; and so for each one a new name. When I reached Juana, I followed its coast west-wardly, and found it so large that I thought it might be the mainland province of Cathay. And as I did not thus find any towns and villages on the sea-coast, save small hamlets with the people whereof I could not get speech, because they all fled away forthwith, I went on farther in the same direction, thinking I should not miss of great cities or towns. And at the end of many leagues, seeing that there was no change, and that the coast was bearing me northwards, whereunto my desire was contrary since the winter was already confronting us, I formed the purpose of making from thence to the South, and as the wind also blew against me, I determined not to wait for other weather and turned back as far as a port agreed upon; from which I sent two men into the country to learn if there were a king, or any great cities. They travelled for three days, and found interminable small villages and a numberless population, but nought of ruling authority; wherefore they returned. I understood sufficiently from other Indians whom I had already taken, that this land, in its continuousness, was an island; and so I followed its coast eastwardly for a hundred and seven leagues as far as where it terminated; from which headland I saw another island to the east, ten or eight leagues distant from this, to which I at once gave the name La Spañola. And I proceeded thither, and followed the northern coast, as with La Juana, east-wardly for a hundred and seventy-eight great leagues in a direct easterly course, as with La Juana. The which, and all the others, are very large to an excessive degree, and this extremely so. In it, there are many havens on the seacoast, incomparable with any others that I know in Christendom, and plenty of rivers so good and great that it is a marvel. The lands thereof are high, and in it are very many ranges of hills, and most lofty mountains incomparably beyond the Island of Centrefrei; all most beautiful in a thousand shapes, and all accessible, and full of trees of a thousand kinds, so lofty that they seem to reach the sky. And I am assured that they never lose their foliage; as may be imagined, since I saw them as green and as beautiful as they are in Spain during May. And some of them were in flower, some in fruit, some in another stage according to their kind. And the nightingale was singing, and other birds of a thousand sorts, in the month of November, round about the way that I was going. There are palm-trees of six or eight species, wondrous to see for their beautiful variety; but so are the other trees, and fruits, and plants therein. There are wonderful pine-groves, and very large plains of verdure, and there is honey, and many kinds of birds, and many various fruits. In the earth there are many mines of metals; and there is a population of incalculable number. Spañola is a marvel; the mountains and hills, and plains and fields, and land, so beautiful and rich for planting and sowing, for breeding cattle of all sorts, for building of towns and villages. There could be no believing, without seeing, such harbours as are here, as well as the many and great rivers, and excellent waters, most of which contain gold. In the trees and fruits and plants, there are great differences from those of Juana. In this, there are many spiceries, and great mines of gold and other metals. The people of this island, and of all the others that I have found and seen or not seen, all go naked, men and women, just as their mothers bring them forth; although some women cover a single place with the leaf of a plant, or a cotton something which they make for that purpose. They have no iron or steel, nor any weapons; nor are they fit there-unto; not because they be not a well-formed people and of fair stature, but that they are most wondrously timorous. They have no other weapons than the stems of reeds in their seeding state, on the end of which they fix little sharpened stakes. Even these, they dare not use; for many times has it happened that I sent two or three men ashore to some village to parley, and countless numbers of them sallied forth, but as soon as they saw those approach, they fled away in such wise that even a father would not wait for his son. And this was not because any hurt had ever been done to any of them:-on the contrary, at every headland where I have gone and been able to hold speech with them, I gave them of everything which I had, as well cloth as many other things, without accepting aught therefor; but such they are, incurably timid. It is true that since they have become more assured, and are losing that terror, they are artless and generous with what they have, to such a degree as no one would believe but he who had seen it. Of anything they have, if it be asked for, they never say no, but do rather invite the person to accept it, and show as much lovingness as though they would give their hearts. And whether it be a thing of value, or one of little worth, they are straightways content with whatsoever trifle of whatsoever kind may be given them in return for it. I forbade that anything so worthless as fragments of broken platters, and pieces of broken glass, and strap-buckles, should be given them; although when they were able to get such things they seemed to think they had the best jewel in the world, for it was the hap of a sailor to get, in exchange for a strap, gold to the weight of two and a half castellanos, and others much more for other things of far less value; while for new blancas they gave every thing they had, even though it were the worth of two or three gold castellanos, or one or two arrobas of spun cotton. They took even pieces of broken barrelhoops, and gave whatever they had,

287

like senseless brutes; insomuch that it seemed to me ill. I forbade it, and I gave gratuitously a thousand useful things that I carried, in order that they may conceive affection, and furthermore may be made Christians; for they are inclined to the love and service of their Highnesses and of all the Castilian nation, and they strive to combine in giving us things which they have in abundance, and of which we are in need. And they know no sect, or idolatry; save that they all believe that power and goodness are in the sky, and they believed very firmly that I, with these ships and crew, came from the sky; and in such opinion, they received me at every place where I landed, after they had lost their terror. And this comes not because they are ignorant; on the contrary, they are men of very subtle wit, who navigate all those seas, and who give a marvellously good account of everything-but because they never saw men wearing clothes or the like of our ships. And as soon as I arrived in the Indies, in the first island that I found, I took some of them by force, to the intent that they should learn our speech and give me information of what there was in those parts. And so it was, that very soon they understood us and we them, what by speech or what by signs; and those Indians have been of much service. To this day I carry them with me who are still of the opinion that I come from heaven, as appears from much conversation which they have had with me. And they were the first to proclaim it wherever I arrived; and the others went running from house to house and to the neighbouring villages, with loud cries of "Come! come to see the people from heaven!" Then, as soon as their minds were reassured about us, every one came, men as well as women, so that there remained none behind, big or little; and they all brought something to eat and drink, which they gave with wondrous lovingness. They have in all the islands very many canoes, after the manner of rowing-galleys, some larger, some smaller; and a good many are larger than a galley of eighteen benches. They are not so wide, because they are made of a single log of timber, but a galley could not keep up with them in rowing, for their motion is a thing beyond belief. And with these, they navigate through all those islands which are numberless, and ply their traffic. I have seen some of those canoes with seventy and eighty men in them, each one with his oar. In all those islands, I saw not much diversity in the looks of the people, or in their manners and language; but they all understand each other, which is a thing of singular towardness for what I hope their Highnesses will determine, as to making them conversant with our holy faith, unto which they are well disposed. I have already told how I had gone a hundred and seven leagues, in a straight line from West to East, along the seacoast of the Island of Juana; according to which itinerary, I can declare that that island is larger than England and Scotland combined; as, over and above those hundred and seven leagues, there remains for me, on the western side, two provinces whereto I did not go-one of which they call Anan, where the people are born with tails-which provinces cannot be less in length than fifty or sixty leagues, according to what may be understood from the Indians with me, who know all the islands. This other, Española, has a greater circumference than the whole of Spain from Colibre in Catalunya, by the seacoast, as far as Fuente Ravia in Biscay; since, along one of its four sides, I went for a hundred and eighty-eight great leagues in a straight line from West to East. This is a land to be desired,-and once seen, never to be relinquished-in which-although, indeed, I have taken possession of them all for their Highnesses, and all are more richly endowed than I have skill and power to say, and I hold them all in the name of their Highnesses who can dispose thereof as much and as completely as of the kingdoms of Castile-in this Española, in the place most suitable and best for its proximity to the gold mines, and for traffic with the continent, as well on this side as on the further side of the Great Can, where there will be great commerce and profit, I took possession of a large town which I named the city of Navidad. And I have made fortifications there, and a fort which by this time will have been completely finished and I have left therein men enough for such a purpose, with arms and artillery, and provisions for more than a year, and a boat, and a man who is master of all sea-craft for making others; and great friendship with the King of that land, to such a degree that he prided himself on calling and holding me as his brother. And even though his mind might change towards attacking those men, neither he nor his people know what arms are, and go naked. As I have already said, they are the most timorous creatures there are in the world, so that the men who remain there are alone sufficient to destroy all that land, and the island is without personal danger for them if they know how to behave themselves. It seems to me that in all those islands, the men are all content with a single wife; and to their chief or king they give as many as twenty. The women, it appears to me, do more work than the men. Nor have I been able to learn whether they held personal property, for it seemed to me that whatever one had, they all took shares of, especially of eatable things. Down to the present, I have not found in those islands any monstrous men, as many expected, but on the contrary all the people are very comely; nor are they black like those in Guinea, but have flowing hair; and they are not begotten where there is an excessive violence of the rays of the sun. It is true that the sun is there very strong, notwithstanding that it is twenty-six degrees distant from the equinoctial line. In those islands, where there are lofty mountains, the cold was very keen there, this winter; but they endure it by being accustomed thereto, and by the help of the meats which they eat with many and inordinately hot spices. Thus I have not found, nor had any information of monsters, except of an island which is here the second in the approach to the Indies, which is inhabited by a people whom, in all the islands, they regard as very ferocious, who eat human flesh. These have many canoes with which they run through all the islands of India, and plunder and take as much as they can. They are no more illshapen than the others, but have the custom of wearing their hair long, like women; and they use bows and arrows of the same reedstems, with a point of wood at the top, for lack of iron which they have not. Amongst those other tribes who are excessively cowardly, these are ferocious; but I hold them as nothing more than the others. These are they who have to do with the women of Matremonio-which is the first island that is encountered in the passage from

Spain to the Indies-in which there are no men. Those women practise no female usages, but have bows and arrows of reeds such as above mentioned; and they arm and cover themselves with plates of copper of which they have much. In another island, which they assure me is larger than Española, the people have no hair. In this, there is incalculable gold; and concerning these and the rest I bring Indians with me as witnesses. And in conclusion, to speak only of what has been done in this voyage, which has been so hastily performed, their Highnesses may see that I shall give them as much gold as they may need, with very little aid which their Highnesses will give me; spices and cotton at once, as much as their Highnesses will order to be shipped, and as much as they shall order to be shipped of mastic-which till now has never been found except in Greece, in the island of Xio, and the Seignory sells it for what it likes; and aloe-wood as much as they shall order to be shipped; and slaves as many as they shall order to be shipped-and these shall be from idolaters. And I believe that I have discovered rhubarb and cinnamon, and I shall find that the men whom I am leaving there will have discovered a thousand other things of value; as I made no delay at any point, so long as the wind gave me an opportunity of sailing, except only in the town of Navidad till I had left things safely arranged and well established. And in truth I should have done much more if the ships had served me as well as might reasonably have been expected. This is enough; and thanks to eternal God our Lord who gives to all those who walk His way, victory over things which seem impossible; and this was signally one such, for although men have talked or written of those lands, it was all by conjecture, without confirmation from eyesight, importing just so much that the hearers for the most part listened and judged that there was more fable in it than anything actual, however trifling. Since thus our Redeemer has given to our most illustrious King and Queen, and to their famous kingdoms, this victory in so high a matter, Christendom should take gladness therein and make great festivals, and give solemn thanks to the Holy Trinity for the great exaltation they shall have by the conversion of so many peoples to our Holy faith; and next for the temporal benefit which will bring hither refreshment and profit, not only to Spain, but to all Christians. This briefly, in accordance with the facts. Dated on the caravel, off the Canary Islands, the 15 February of the year 1493.

At your command,

The Admiral

Questions:
1. Which aspects of the land and people most interested Columbus?
2. Describe Columbus' attitude towards the Native Americans he encountered.

14.6   Bernal Díaz del Castillo

Bernal Díaz del Castillo, the author of the selection that follows, was born in the Spanish town of Medina del Campo in the year of Columbus's epochal voyage, 1492. Like many of his contemporaries, he was excited by the tales that soon began to circulate through Spain of the gold to be had in the lands recently discovered beyond the great "Western Ocean," so he decided to seek his fortune there. He left his home in 1514, crossing first to Cuba, where he spent about three years, before going on two exploratory trips farther west. In 1519 he joined the historic expedition of the conquistador Hernando Cortés (1485-1547) that was to lead to the subjugation of Mexico and part of Central America and the annexation of these lands to the Spanish crown. Except for two trips he made back to his native land in later years Bernal Díaz remained in the Western Hemisphere for the remainder of his long life, dying in Guatemala around the year 1581. He wrote his book, which he called The True History of the Conquest of New Spain, in his old age, many years after the events he describes in it.

According to Bernal Díaz's account, Cortés, after landing on the east coast of what is now Mexico and burning his ships (so he could not retreat), marched with a small band of soldiers, fighting his way inland and arriving at the capital city of the Aztec civilization, Tenochtitlán (or Mexico City), in November 1519. There he was received by the great cacique (king) Montezuma. The selection that follows begins with the meeting between these two warriors. Its central figure, however, is the Aztec, Montezuma. Bernal Díaz describes his person at some length, as well as his family and court. He gives a detailed account of the personal and physical environment in which the Aztec chief lived, from the architecture of his palaces to the contents of his storehouses to the ritual surrounding his meals. The selection ends with a more general description of the society and commerce of Mexico City, in particular its great marketplace. It is obvious from his comments that Bernal Díaz was greatly impressed by many of the sights he beheld in this strange land and realized that in some ways its civilization equaled or even surpassed that of his native Spain.

Source: Trans. A. P. Maudslay.

THE CONQUEST OF NEW SPAIN

About the Great and Solemn Reception which the Great Montezuma Gave Cortés and all of us at the Entering of the Great City of Mexico.

EARLY next day we left Iztapalapa with a large escort of those great Caciques whom I have already mentioned. We proceeded along the Causeway which is here eight paces in width and runs so straight to the City of Mexico that it does not seem to me to turn either much or little, but, broad as it is, it was so crowded with people that there was hardly room for them all, some of them going to and others returning from Mexico, besides those who had come out to see us, so that we were hardly able to pass by the crowds of them that came; and the towers and cues were full of people as well as the canoes from all parts of the lake. It was not to be wondered at, for they had never before seen horses or men such as we are.

Gazing on such wonderful sights, we did not know what to say, or whether what appeared before us was real, for on one side, on the land, there were great cities, and in the lake ever so many more, and the lake itself was crowded with canoes, and in the Causeway were many bridges at intervals, and in front of us stood the great City of Mexico, and we,- we did not even number four hundred soldiers! and we well remembered the words and warnings given us by the people of Huexotzingo and Tlaxcala and Tlamanalco, and the many other warnings that had been given that we should beware of entering Mexico, where they would kill us, as soon as they had us inside.

Let the curious readers consider whether there is not much to ponder over in this that I am writing. What men have there been in the world who have shown such daring? But let us get on, and march along the Causeway. When we arrived where another small causeway branches off (leading to Coyoacan, which is another city) where there were some buildings like towers, which are their oratories, many more chieftains and Caciques approached clad in very rich mantles, the brilliant liveries of one chieftain differing from those of another, and the causeways were crowded with them. The Great Montezuma had sent these great Caciques in advance to receive us, and when they came before Cortés they bade us welcome in their language, and as a sign of peace, they touched their hands against the ground, and kissed the ground with the hand.

There we halted for a good while, and Cacamatzin, the Lord of Texcoco, and the Lord of Iztapalapa and the Lord of Tacuba and the Lord of Coyoacan went on in advance to meet the Great Montezuma, who was approaching in a rich litter accompanied by other great Lords and Caciques, who owned vassals. When we arrived near to Mexico, where there were some other small towers, the Great Montezuma got down from his litter, and those great Caciques supported him with their arms beneath a marvellously rich canopy of green coloured feathers with much gold and silver embroidery and with pearls and chalchihuites suspended from a sort of bordering, which was wonderful to look at. The Great Montezuma was richly attired according to his usage, and he was shod with sandals. For so they call what they wear on their feet, the soles were of gold and the upper part adorned with precious stones. The four Chieftains who supported his arms were also richly clothed according to their usage, in garments which were apparently held ready for them on the road to enable them to accompany their prince, for they did not appear in such attire when they came to receive us. Besides these four Chieftains, there were four other great Caciques, who supported the canopy over their heads, and many other Lords who walked before the Great Montezuma, sweeping the ground where he would tread and spreading cloths on it, so that he should not tread on the earth. Not one of these chieftains dared even to think of looking him in the face, but kept their eyes lowered with great reverence, except those four relations, his nephews, who supported him with their arms.

When Cortés was told that the Great Montezuma was approaching, and he saw him coming, he dismounted from his horse, and when he was near Montezuma, they simultaneously paid great reverence to one another. Montezuma bade him welcome and our Cortés replied through Doña Marina wishing him very good health. And it seems to me that Cortés, through Doña Marina, offered him his right hand, and Montezuma did not wish to take it, but he did give his hand to Cortés and then Cortés brought out a necklace which he had ready at hand, made of glass stones, which I have already said are called Margaritas, which have within them many patterns of diverse colours, these were strung on a cord of gold and with musk so that it should have a sweet scent, and he placed it round the neck of the Great Montezuma and when he had so placed it he was going to embrace him, and those great Princes who accompanied Montezuma held back Cortés by the arm so that he should not embrace him, for they considered it an indignity.

Then Cortés through the mouth of Doña Marina told him that now his heart rejoiced at having seen such a great Prince, and that he took it as a great honour that he had come in person to meet him and had frequently shown him such favour.

Then Montezuma spoke other words of politeness to him, and told two of his nephews who supported his arms, the Lord of Texcoco and the Lord of Coyoacan, to go with us and show us to our quarters, and Montezuma with his other two relations, the Lord of Cuitlahuac and the Lord of Tacuba who accompanied him, returned to the city, and all those grand companies of Caciques and chieftains who had come with him returned in his train. As they turned back after their Prince we stood watching them and observed how they all marched with their eyes fixed on the ground without looking at him, keeping close to the wall, following him with great reverence. Thus space was made for us to enter the streets of

Mexico, without being so much crowded. But who could now count the multitude of men and women and boys w
in the streets and on the azoteas, and in canoes on the canals, who had come out to see us.

. . .

They took us to lodge in some large houses, where there were apartments for all of us, for they had belonged to
the father qf the Great Montezuma, who was named Axayaca, and at that time Montezuma kept there the great oratories
for his idols, and a secret chamber where he kept bars and jewels of gold, which was the treasure that he had inherited from
his father Axayaca, and he never disturbed it. They took us to lodge in that house, because they called us Teules, and took
us for such, so that we should be with the Idols or Teules which were kept there. However, for one reason or another, it was
there they took us, where there were great halls and chambers canopied with the cloth of the country for our Captain, and
for every one of us beds of matting with canopies above, and no better bed is given, however great the chief may be, for
they are not used. And all these palaces were coated with shining cement and swept and garlanded.

As soon as we arrived and entered into the great court, the Great Montezuma took our Captain by the hand, for
he was there awaiting him, and led him to the apartment and saloon where he was to lodge, which was very richly adorned
according to their usage, and he had at hand a very rich necklace made of golden crabs, a marvellous piece of work, and
Montezuma himself placed it round the neck of our Captain Cort6s, and greatly astonished his own Captains by the great
honour that he was bestowing on him. When the necklace had been fastened, Cortés thanked Montezuma through our
interpreters, and Montezuma replied-"Malinche you and your brethren are in your own house, rest awhile," and then he
went to his palaces which were not far away, and we divided our lodgings by companies, and placed the artillery pointing
in a convenient direction, and the order which we had to keep was clearly explained to us, and that we were to be much
on the alert, both the cavalry and all of us soldiers. A sumptuous dinner was provided for us according to their use and
custom, and we ate it at once. So this was our lucky and daring entry into the great city of Tenochtitlan Mexico on the 8th
day of November the year of our Savior Jesus Christ 1519.

. . .

How on the Following Day our Captain Cortés went to See the Great Montezuma, and About a certain Conversation that Took Place

THE next day Cortés decided to go to Montezuma's palace, and he first sent to find out what he intended doing and to let
him know that we were coming. He took with him four captains, namely Pedro de Alvarado, Juan Velásquez de Leon,
Diego de Ordás, and Gonzalo de Sandoval, and five of us soldiers also went with him.

When Montezuma knew of our coming he advanced to the middle of the hall to receive us, accompanied by
many of his nephews, for no other chiefs were permitted to enter or hold communication with Montezuma where he then
was, unless it were on important business. Cortés and he paid the greatest reverence to each other and then they took one
another by the hand and Montezuma made him sit down on his couch on his right hand, and he also bade all of us to be
seated on seats which he ordered to be brought.

Then Cortés began to make an explanation through our interpreters Doña Marina and Aguilar, and said that he and
all of us were rested, and that in coming to see and converse with such a great Prince as he was, we had completed the journey and fulfilled the command which our great King and Prince had laid on us. But what he chiefly came to say on behalf
of our Lord God had already been brought to his [Montezuma's] knowledge through his ambassadors, Tendile, Pitalpitoque
and Quintalbor, at the time when he did us the favour to send the golden sun and moon to the sand dunes; for we told them
then that we were Christians and worshipped one true and only God, named Jesus Christ, who suffered death and passion
to save us, and we told them that a cross (when they asked us why we worshipped it) was a sign of the other Cross on
which our Lord God was crucified for our salvation, and that the death and passion which He suffered was for the salvation of the whole human race, which was lost, and that this our God rose on the third day and is now in heaven, and it is
He who made the heavens and the earth, the sea and the sands, and created all the things there are in the world, and He
sends the rain and the dew, and nothing happens in the world without His holy will. That we believe in Him and worship
Him, but that those whom they look upon as gods are not so, but are devils, which are evil things, and if their looks are
bad their deeds are worse, and they could see that they were evil and of little worth, for where we had set up crosses such
as those his ambassadors had seen, they dared not appear before them, through fear of them, and that as time went on they
would notice this.

The favour he now begged of him was his attention to the words that he now wished to tell him; then he explained
to him very clearly about the creation of the world, and how we are all brothers, sons of one father and one mother who
were called Adam and Eve, and how such a brother as our great Emperor, grieving for the perdition of so many souls, such
as those which their idols were leading to Hell, where they burn in living flames, had sent us, so that after what he [Mon-

*Part*w heard he would put a stop to it and they would no longer adore these Idols or sacrifice Indian men and
~m, for we were all brethren, nor should they commit sodomy or thefts. He also told them that, in course of
~ord and King would send some men who among us lead very holy lives, much better than we do, who will
~ them all about it, for at present we merely came to give them due warning, and so he prayed him to do what he
~ed and carry it into effect.

As Montezuma appeared to wish to reply, Cortés broke off his argument, and to all of us who were with him he
~d: "with this we have done our duty considering it is the first attempt."

Montezuma replied-"Señor Malinche, I have understood your words and arguments very well before now, from
what you said to my servants at the sand dunes, this about three Gods and the Cross, and all those things that you have
preached in the towns through which you have come. We have not made any answer to it because here throughout all time
we have worshipped our own gods, and thought they were good, as no doubt yours are, so do not trouble to speak to us
any more about them at present. Regarding the creation of the world, we have held the same belief for ages past, and for
this reason we take it for certain that you are those whom our ancestors predicted would come from the direction of the sunrise. As for your great King, I feel that I am indebted to him, and I will give him of what I possess."

. . .

While this conversation was going on, Montezuma secretly sent a great Cacique, one of his nephews who was in
his company, to order his stewards to bring certain pieces of gold, which it seems must have been put apart to give to
Cortés, and ten loads of fine cloth, which he apportioned, the gold and mantles between Cortés and the four captains, and
to each of us soldiers he gave two golden necklaces, each necklace being worth ten pesos, and two loads of mantles. The
gold that he then gave us was worth in all more than a thousand pesos and he gave it all cheerfully and with the air of a
great and valiant prince. As it was now past midday, so as not to appear importunate, Cort6s said to him: "Señor Montezuma, you always have the habit of heaping load upon load in every day conferring favours on us, and it is already your
dinner time." Montezuma replied that he thanked us for coming to see him, and then we took our leave with the greatest
courtesy and we went to our lodgings.

And as we went along we spoke of the good manners and breeding which he showed in everything, and that we
should show him in all ways the greatest respect, doffing our quilted caps when we passed before him, and this we always
did, but let us leave this subject here, and pass on.

Of the Manner and Appearance of the Great Montezuma and What a Great Prince He Was

THE Great Montezuma was about forty years old, of good height and well proportioned, slender, and spare of flesh, not
very swarthy, but of the natural colour and shade of an Indian. He did not wear his hair long, but so as just to cover his ears,
his scanty black beard was well shaped and thin. His face was somewhat long, but cheerful, and he had good eyes and
showed in his appearance and manner both tenderness and, when necessary, gravity. He was very neat and clean and
bathed once every day in the afternoon. He had many women as mistresses, daughters of Chieftains, and he had two great
Cacicas as his legitimate wives, and when he had intercourse with them it was so secretly that no one knew anything
about it, except some of his servants. He was free from unnatural offences. The clothes that he wore one day, he did not
put on again until four days later. He had over two hundred chieftains in his guard, in other rooms close to his own, not
that all were meant to converse with him, but only one or another, and when they went to speak to him they were obliged
to take off their rich mantles and put on others of little worth, but they had to be clean, and they had to enter barefoot with
their eyes lowered to the ground, and not to look up in his face. And they made him three obeisances, and said: "Lord, my
Lord, my Great Lord," before they came up to him, and then they made their report and with a few words he dismissed
them, and on taking leave they did not turn their backs, but kept their faces toward him with their eyes to the ground, and
they did not turn their backs until they left the room. I noticed another thing, that when other great chiefs came from distant lands about disputes or business, when they reached the apartments of the Great Montezuma, they had to come barefoot and with poor mantles, and they might not enter directly into the Palace, but had to loiter about a little on one side of
the Palace door, for to enter hurriedly was considered to be disrespectful.

For each meal, over thirty different dishes were prepared by his cooks according to their ways and usage, and they
placed small pottery brasiers beneath the dishes so that they should not get cold. They prepared more than three hundred
plates of the food that Montezuma was going to eat, and more than a thousand for the guard. When he was going to eat,
Montezuma would sometimes go out with his chiefs and stewards, and they would point out to him which dish was best,
and of what birds and other things it was composed, and as they advised him, so he would eat, but it was not often that he
would go out to see the food, and then merely as a pastime.

I have heard it said that they were wont to cook for him the flesh of young boys, but as he had such a variety of
dishes, made of so many things, we could not succeed in seeing if they were of human flesh or of other things, for they

daily cooked fowls, turkeys, pheasants, native partridges, quail, tame and wild ducks, venison, wild boar, reed birds, pigeons, hares and rabbits, and many sorts of birds and other things which are bred in this country, and they are so numerous that I cannot finish naming them in a hurry; so we had no insight into it, but I know for certain that after our Captain censured the sacrifice of human beings, and the eating of their flesh, he ordered that such food should not be prepared for him thenceforth.

Let us cease speaking of this and return to the way things were served to him at meal times. It was in this way: if it was cold they made up a large fire of live coals of a firewood made from the bark of trees which did not give off any smoke, and the scent of the bark from which the fire was made was very fragrant, and so that it should not give off more heat than he required, they placed in front of it a sort of screen adorned with figures of idols worked in gold. He was seated on a low stool, soft and richly worked, and the table, which was also low, was made in the same style as the seats, and on it they placed the table cloths of white cloth and some rather long napkins of the same material. Four very beautiful cleanly women brought water for his hands in a sort of deep basin which they call "xicales," and they held others like plates below to catch the water, and they brought him towels. And two other women brought him tortilla bread, and as soon as he began to eat they placed before him a sort of wooden screen painted over with gold, so that no one should watch him eating. Then the four women stood aside, and four great chieftains who were old men came and stood beside them, and with these Montezuma now and then conversed, and asked them questions, and as a great favour he would give to each of these elders a dish of what to him tasted best. They say that these elders were his near relations, and were his counsellors and judges of law suits, and the dishes and food which Montezuma gave them they ate standing up with much reverence and without looking at his face. He was served on Cholula earthenware either red or black. While he was at his meal the men of his guard who were in the rooms near to that of Montezuma, never dreamed of making any noise or speaking aloud. They brought him fruit of all the different kinds that the land produced, but he ate very little of it. From time to time they brought him, in cupshaped vessels of pure gold, a certain drink made from cacao which they said he took when he was going to visit his wives, and at the time he took no heed of it, but what I did see was that they brought over fifty great jugs of good cacao frothed up, and he drank of that, and the women served this drink to him with great reverence.

Sometimes at meal-times there were present some very ugly hump-backs, very small of stature and their bodies almost broken in half, who are their jesters, and other Indians, who must have been buffoons, who told him witty sayings, and others who sang and danced, for Montezuma was fond of pleasure and song, and to these he ordered to be given what was left of the food and the jugs of cacao. Then the same four women removed the table cloths, and with much ceremony they brought water for his hands. And Montezuma talked with those four old chieftains about things that interested him, and they took leave of him with the great reverence in which they held him, and he remained to repose.

As soon as the Great Montezuma had dined, all the men of the Guard had their meal and as many more of the other house servants, and it seems to me that they brought out over a thousand dishes of the food of which I have spoken, and then over two thousand jugs of cacao all frothed up, as they make it in Mexico, and a limitless quantity of fruit, so that with his women and female servants and bread makers and cacao makers his expenses must have been very great.

Let us cease talking about the expenses and the food for his household and let us speak of the Stewards and the Treasurers and the stores and pantries and of those who had charge of the houses where the maize was stored. I say that there would be so much to write about, each thing by itself, that I should not know where to begin, but we stood astonished at the excellent arrangements and the great abundance of provisions that he had in all, but I must add what I had forgotten, for it is as well to go back and relate it, and that is, that while Montezuma was at table eating as I have described, there were waiting on him two other graceful women to bring him tortillas, kneaded with eggs and other sustaining ingredients, and these tortillas were very white, and they were brought on plates covered with clean napkins, and they also brought him another kind of bread, like long balls kneaded with other kinds of sustaining food, and "pan pachol" for so they call it in this country, which is a sort of wafer. There were also placed on the table three tubes much painted and gilded, which held liquidambar mixed with certain herbs which they call tabaco, and when he had finished eating, after they had danced before him and sung and the table was removed, he inhaled the smoke from one of those tubes, but he took very little of it and with that he fell asleep.

. . .

Montezuma had two houses full of every sort of arms, many of them richly adorned with gold and precious stones. There were shields great and small, and a sort of broadswords, and others like two handed swords set with stone knives which cut much better than our swords, and lances longer than ours are, with a fathom of blade with many knives set in it, which even when they are driven into a buckler or shield do not come out, in fact they cut like razors so that they can shave their heads with them. There were very good bows and arrows and double-pointed lances and others with one point, as well as their throwing sticks, and many slings and round stones shaped by hand, and some sort of artful shields which are so made that they can be rolled up, so as not to be in the way when they are not fighting, and when they are needed for fighting they let them fall down, and they cover the body from top to toe. There was also much quilted cotton armour, richly ornamented on the outside with many coloured feathers, used as devices and distinguishing marks, and there were casques or helmets made of wood and bone, also highly decorated with feathers on the outside, and there were other arms of other makes which, so as to avoid prolixity, I will not describe, and there were artizans who were skilled in such things and worked at them, and stewards who had charge of the arms.

Let us leave this and go on to another great house, where they keep many Idols, and they say that they are their fierce gods, and with them many kinds of carnivorous beasts of prey, tigers and two kinds of lions, and animals something like wolves which in this country they call jackals and foxes, and other smaller carnivorous animals, and all these carnivores they feed with flesh, and the greater number of them breed in the house. They give them as food deer and fowls, dogs and other things which they are used to hunt, and I have heard it said that they feed them on the bodies of the Indians who have been sacrificed. It is in this way: you have already heard me say that when they sacrifice a wretched Indian they saw open the chest with stone knives and hasten to tear out the palpitating heart and blood, and offer it to their Idols in whose name the sacrifice is made. Then they cut off the thighs, arms and head and eat the former at feasts and banquets, and the head they hang up on some beams, and the body of the man sacrificed is not eaten but given to these fierce animals. They also have in that cursed house many vipers and poisonous snakes which carry on their tails things that sound like bells. These are the worst vipers of all, and they keep them in jars and great pottery vessels with many feathers, and there they lay their eggs and rear their young, and they give them to eat the bodies of the Indians who have been sacrificed, and the flesh of dogs which they are in the habit of breeding.

. . .

Let us go on and speak of the skilled workmen he [Montezuma] employed in every craft that was practised among them. We will begin with lapidaries and workers in gold and silver and all the hollow work, which even the great goldsmiths in Spain were forced to admire, and of these there were a great number of the best in a town named Atzcapotzalco, a league from Mexico. Then for working precious stones and chalchihuites, which are like emeralds, there were other great artists. Let us go on to the great craftsmen in feather work, and painters and sculptors who were most refined; from what we see of their work to-day we can form a judgment of what they did then, for there are three Indians to-day in the City of Mexico named Marcos de Aquino, Juan de la Cruz and El Crespillo, so skilful in their work as sculptors and painters, that had they lived in the days of the ancient and famous Apelles, or of Michael Angelo Buonarotti, in our times, they would be placed in the same company. Let us go on to the Indian women who did the weaving and the washing, who made such an immense quantity of fine fabrics with wonderful feather work designs; the greater part of it was brought daily from some towns of the province on the north coast near Vera Cruz called Cotaxtla, close by San Juan de Ulua, where we disembarked when we came with Cortés.

In the house of the Great Montezuma himself, all the daughters of chieftains whom he had as mistresses always wore beautiful things, and there were many daughters of Mexican citizens who lived in retirement and wished to appear to be like nuns, who also did weaving but it was wholly of feather work. These nuns had their houses near the great Cue of Huichilobos and out of devotion to it, or to another idol, that of a woman who was said to be their mediatrix in the matter of marriage, their fathers placed them in that religious retirement until they married, and they were [only] taken out thence to be married.

Let us go on and tell about the great number of dancers kept by the Great Montezuma for his amusement, and others who used stilts on their feet, and others who flew when they danced up in the air, and others like Merry-Andrews, and I may say that there was a district full of these people who had no other occupation. Let us go on and speak of the workmen that he had as stone cutters, masons and carpenters, all of whom attended to the work of his houses, I say that he had as many as he wished for. We must not forget the gardens of flowers and sweet-scented trees, and the many kinds that there were of them, and the arrangement of them and the walks, and the ponds and tanks of fresh water where the water entered at one end and flowed out at the other; and the baths which he had there, and the variety of small birds that nested in the branches, and the medicinal and useful herbs that were in the gardens. It was a wonder to see, and to take care of it there were many gardeners. Everything was made in masonry and well cemented, baths and walks and closets, and apartments like summer houses where they danced and sang. There was as much to be seen in these gardens as there was everywhere else, and we could not tire of witnessing his great power. Thus as a consequence of so many crafts being practised among them, a large number of skilled Indians were employed.

. . .

How our Captain went out to See the City of Mexico and Tlaltelolco, Which is the Great Market Place and the Great Cue of Huichilobos, and What else Happened

As we had already been four days in Mexico and neither the Captain nor any of us had left our lodgings except to go to the houses and gardens, Cortés said to us that it would be well to go to the great Plaza and see the great Temple of

Huichilobos, and that he wished to consult the Great Montezuma and have his approval. For this purpose he sent Jerónimo de Aguilar and the Doña Marina as messengers, and with them went our Captain's small page named Orteguilla, who already understood something of the language. When Montezuma knew his wishes he sent to say that we were welcome to go; on the other hand, as he was afraid that we might do some dishonour to his Idols, he determined to go with us himself with many of his chieftains. He came out from his Palace in his rich litter, but when half the distance had been traversed and he was near some oratories, he stepped out of the litter, for he thought it a great affront to his idols to go to their house and temple in that manner. Some of the great chieftains supported him with their arms, and the tribal lords went in front of him carrying two staves like sceptres held on high, which was the sign that the Great Montezuma was coming. (When he went in his litter he carried a wand half of gold and half of wood, which was held up like a wand of justice). So he went on and ascended the great Cue accompanied by many priests, and he began to burn incense and perform other ceremonies to Huichilobos.

Let us leave Montezuma, who had gone ahead as I have said, and return to Cortés and our captains and soldiers, who according to our custom both night and day were armed, and as Montezuma was used to see us so armed when we went to visit him, he did not look upon it as anything new. I say this because our Captain and all those who had horses went to Tlaltelolco on horseback, and nearly all of us soldiers were fully equipped, and many Caciques whom Montezuma had sent for that purpose went in our company. When we arrived at the great market place, called Tlaltelolco, we were astounded at the number of people and the quantity of merchandise that it contained, and at the good order and control that was maintained, for we had never seen such a thing before. The chieftains who accompanied us acted as guides. Each kind of merchandise was kept by itself and had its fixed place marked out. Let us begin with the dealers in gold, silver, and precious stones, feathers, mantles, and embroidered goods. Then there were other wares consisting of Indian slaves both men and women; and I say that they bring as many of them to that great market for sale as the Portuguese bring negroes from Guinea; and they brought them along tied to long poles, with collars round their necks so that they could not escape, and others they left free. Next there were other traders who sold great pieces of cloth and cotton, and articles of twisted thread, and there were cacahuateros who sold cacao. In this way one could see every sort of merchandise that is to be found in the whole of New Spain, placed in arrangement in the same manner as they do in my own country, which is Medina del Campo, where they hold the fairs, where each line of booths has its particular kind of merchandise, and so it is in this great market. There were those who sold cloths of henequen and ropes and the cotaras with which they are shod, which are made from the same plant, and sweet cooked roots, and other tubers which they get from this plant, all were kept in one part of the market in the place assigned to them. In another part there were skins of tigers and lions, of otters and jackals, deer and other animals and badgers and mountain cats, some tanned and others untanned, and other classes of merchandise.

Let us go on and speak of those who sold beans and sage and other vegetables and herbs in another part, and to those who sold fowls, cocks with wattles, rabbits, hares, deer, mallards, young dogs and other things of that sort in their part of the market, and let us also mention the fruiterers, and the women who sold cooked food, dough and tripe in their own part of the market; then every sort of pottery made in a thousand different forms from great water jars to little jugs, these also had a place to themselves; then those who sold honey and honey paste and other dainties like nut paste, and those who sold lumber, boards, cradles, beams, blocks and benches, each article by itself, and the vendors of ocote firewood, and other things of a similar nature. I must furthermore mention, asking your pardon, that they also sold many canoes full of human excrement, and these were kept in the creeks near the market, and this they use to make salt or for tanning skins, for without it they say that they cannot be well prepared. I know well that some gentlemen laugh at this, but I say that it is so, and I may add that on all the roads it is a usual thing to have places made of reeds or straw or grass, so that they may be screened from the passers by, into these they retire when they wish to purge their bowels so that even that filth should not be lost. But why do I waste so many words in recounting what they sell in that great market, for I shall never finish if I tell it all in detail. Paper, which in this country is called Amal, and reeds scented with liquidambar, and full of tobacco, and yellow ointments and things of that sort are sold by themselves, and much cochineal is sold under the arcades which are in that great market place, and there are many vendors of herbs and other sorts of trades. There are also buildings where three magistrates sit in judgment, and there are executive officers like Alguacils who inspect the merchandise. I am forgetting those who sell salt, and those who make the stone knives, and how they split them off the stone itself; and the fisherwomen and others who sell some small cakes made from a sort of ooze which they get out of the great lake, which curdles, and from this they make a bread having a flavour something like cheese. There are for sale axes of brass and copper and tin, and gourds and gaily painted jars made of wood. I could wish that I had finished telling of all the things which are sold there, but they are so numerous and of such different quality and the great market place with its surrounding arcades was so crowded with people, that one would not have been able to see and inquire about it all in two days.

Then we went to the great Cue, and when we were already approaching its great courts, before leaving the market place itself, there were many more merchants, who, as I was told, brought gold for sale in grains, just as it is taken from the mines. The gold is placed in thin quills of the geese of the country, white quills, so that the gold can be seen through, and according to the length and thickness of the quills they arrange their accounts with one another, how much so many mantles or so many gourds full of cacao were worth, or how many slaves, or whatever other thing they were exchanging.

Questions:
1. What impresses Díaz most about Aztec civilization? What is he most critical of?
2. How are the Aztecs different from the Caribbean people Columbus encountered?

14.7   Bartolome De Las Casas: Persecutor Turns Protector

The Spaniard who was to ultimately be awarded the title "Apostle to the Indies," Bartolome De Las Casas (1474–1566), first sailed to the Americas in Christopher Columbus' third expedition. He soon settled in the Caribbean and, for the first few years, became a planter/slave-owner. In 1510, appalled by what he had seen and perhaps done, he released his Indian slaves and became a Catholic priest, and later, Bishop of Chiapas in Mexico (1644–47). Las Casas became an indefatigable advocate of Indian rights and freedom. His "The Devastation of the Indies: A Brief Account" is considered the most hard-hitting and accurate indictment of the murderous treatment of Caribbean natives in the aftermath of the Columbian voyages.

> **Source:** Herma Briffault, trans., *Batolome De Las Casas: The Devastation of the Indies: A Brief Account*
> (Baltimore: Johns Hopkins University Press, 1992), pp. 27–33, 48–53, 128–132.

THE INDIES were discovered in the year one thousand four hundred and ninety-two. In the following year a great many Spaniards went there with the intention of settling the land. Thus, forty-nine years have passed since the first settlers penetrated the land, the first so-claimed being the large and most happy isle called Hispaniola, which is six hundred leagues in circumference. Around it in all directions are many other islands, some very big, others very small, and all of them were, as we saw with our own eyes, densely populated with native people called Indians. This large island was perhaps the most densely populated place in the world. There must be close to two hundred leagues of land on this island, and the seacoast has been explored for more than ten thousand leagues, and each day more of it is being explored. And all the land so far discovered is a beehive of people; it is as though God had crowded into these lands the great majority of mankind.

And of all the infinite universe of humanity, these people are the most guileless, the most devoid of wickedness and duplicity, the most obedient and faithful to their native masters and to the Spanish Christians whom they serve. They are by nature the most humble, patient, and peaceable, holding no grudges, free from embroilments, neither excitable nor quarrelsome. These people are the most devoid of rancors, hatreds, or desire for vengeance of any people in the world. And because they are so weak and complaisant, they are less able to endure heavy labor and soon die of no matter what malady. The sons of nobles among us, brought up in the enjoyments of life's refinements, are no more delicate than are these Indians, even those among them who are of the lowest rank of laborers. They are also poor people, for they not only possess little but have no desire to possess worldly goods. For this reason they are not arrogant, embittered, or greedy. Their repasts are such that the food of the holy fathers in the desert can scarcely be more parsimonious, scanty, and poor. As to their dress, they are generally naked, with only their pudenda covered somewhat. And when they cover their shoulders it is with a square cloth no more than two varas in size. They have no beds, but sleep on a kind of matting or else in a kind of suspended net called *hamacas*. They are very clean in their persons, with alert, intelligent minds, docile and open to doctrine, very apt to receive our holy Catholic faith, to be endowed with virtuous custom: and to behave in a godly fashion. And once they begin to hear the tidings of the Faith, they are so insistent on knowing more and on taking the sacraments of the Church and on observing the divine cult that, truly, the missionaries who are here need to be endowed by God with great patience in order to cope with such eagerness. Some of the secular Spaniards who have been here for many years say that the goodness of the Indians is undeniable and that if this gifted people could be brought to know the one true God they would be the most fortunate people in the world.

Yet into this sheepfold, into this land of meek outcast there came some Spaniards who immediately behaved like ravening wild beasts, wolves, tigers, or lions that had been starved for many days. And Spaniards have behaved in no other way during the past forty years, down to the present time, for they are still acting like ravening beasts, killing, terrorizing, afflicting, torturing, and destroying the native peoples, doing all this with the strangest and most varied new methods of cruelty, never seen or heard of before, and to such a degree that this Island of Hispaniola, once so populous (having a population that I estimated to be more than three millions), has now a population of barely two hundred persons.

The island of Cuba is nearly as long as the distance between Valladolid and Rome; it is now almost completely depopulated. San Juan and Jamaica are two of the largest, most productive and attractive islands; both are now deserted and devastated. On the northern side Cuba and Hispaniola lie the neighboring Lucayos comprising more than sixty islands including those called *Gigantes*, beside numerous other islands, some small some large. The least felicitous of them were more fertile and beautiful than the gardens of the King of Seville. They have the healthiest lands in the world, where lived more than five hundred thousand souls; they are now deserted, inhabited by not a single living creature. All the people were slain or died after being taken into captivity and brought to the Island of Hispaniola to be sold as slaves. When the Spaniards saw that some of these had escaped, they sent a ship to find them, and it voyaged for three years among the islands searching for those who had escaped being slaughtered, for a good Christian had helped them escape, taking pity on them and had won them over to Christ; of these there were eleven persons and these I saw.

More than thirty other islands in the vicinity of Juan are for the most part and for the same reason depopulated, and the land laid waste. On these islands I estimate there are 2,100 leagues of land that have been ruined and depopulated, empty of people.

As for the vast mainland, which is ten times larger than all Spain, even including Aragon and Portugal, containing more land than the distance between Seville and Jerusalem, or more than two thousand leagues, we are sure that our Spaniards, with their cruel and abominable acts, have devastated the land and exterminated the rational people who fully inhabited it. We can estimate very surely and truthfully that in the forty years that have passed, with the infernal actions of the Christians, there have been unjustly slain more than twelve million men, women, and children. In truth, I believe without trying to deceive myself that the number of the slain is more like fifteen million.

The common ways mainly employed by the Spaniards who call themselves Christian and who have gone there to extirpate those pitiful nations and wipe them off the earth is by unjustly waging cruel and bloody wars. Then, when they have slain all those who fought for their lives or to escape the tortures they would have to endure, that is to say, when they have slain all the native rulers and young men (since the Spaniards usually spare only the women and children, who are subjected to the hardest and bitterest servitude ever suffered by man or beast), they enslave any survivors. With these infernal methods of tyranny they debase and weaken countless numbers of those pitiful Indian nations.

Their reason for killing and destroying such an infinite number of souls is that the Christians have an ultimate aim, which is to acquire gold, and to swell themselves with riches in a very brief time and thus rise to a high estate disproportionate to their merits. It should be kept in mind that their insatiable greed and ambition, the greatest ever seen in the world, is the cause of their villainies. And also, those lands are so rich and felicitous, the native peoples so meek and patient, so easy to subject, that our Spaniards have no more consideration for them than beasts. And I say this from my own knowledge of the acts I witnessed. But I should not say "than beasts" for, thanks be to God, they have treated beasts with some respect; I should say instead like excrement on the public squares. And thus they have deprived the Indians of their lives and souls, for the millions I mentioned have died without the Faith and without the benefit of the sacraments. This is a well-known and proven fact which even the tyrant Governors, themselves killers, know and admit. And never have the Indians in all the Indies committed any act against the Spanish Christians, until those Christians have first a many times committed countless cruel aggressions against them or against neighboring nations. For in the beginni the Indians regarded the Spaniards as angels from Heaven. Only after the Spaniards had used violence against them, killing, robbing, torturing, did the Indians ever rise up against them.

HISPANIOLA

On the Island Hispaniola was where the Spaniards first landed, as I have said. Here those Christians perpetrated their first ravages and oppressions against the native peoples. This was the first land in the New World to destroyed and depopulated by the Christians, and here they began their subjection of the women and children, taking them away from the Indians to use them and ill use them, eating the food they provided with their sweat and toil. The Spaniards did not content themselves with what the Indians gave them of their own free will, according to their ability, which was always too little to satisfy enormous appetites, for a Christian eats and consumes in one day an amount of food that would suffice to feed three houses inhabited by ten Indians for one month. And they committed other acts of force and violence and oppression which made the Indians realize that these men had not come from Heaven. And some of the Indians concealed their foods while others concealed their wives and children and still others fled to the mountains to avoid the terrible transactions of the Christians....

...This tyrant-Governor who had gone to the mainland along with a large company of Spaniards invented new cruelties, new methods of torture to force the Indians to reveal and hand over their stores of gold. One captain, at the orders of the Governor, slew in a single attack more than forty thousand Indians. This massacre was witnessed by a Franciscan religious who was with him, by name Fray Francisco de San Romàn. The people were killed by the sword, by fire, by being torn to pieces by the fierce dogs kept by the Spaniards, and by being tortured to death in various ways.

And because of the pernicious blindness that has always afflicted those who have ruled in the Indies, nothing was done to *incline* the Indians to embrace the one true Faith, they were rounded up and in large numbers *forced* to do so. Inasmuch as the conversion of the Indians to Christianity was stated to be the principal aim of the Spanish conquerors, they have dissimulated the fact that only with blood and fire have the Indians been brought to embrace the Faith and to swear obedience to the kings of Castile, or by threats of being slain or taken into captivity. As if the Son of God who died for each one of them would have countenanced such a thing! For He commanded His Apostles: "Go ye to all the people" (*Euntes docete omnes gentes*). Christ Jesus would have made no such demands of these peaceable infidels who cultivate the soil of their native lands. Yet they are told they must embrace the Christian Faith immediately, without hearing any sermon preached and without any indoctrination. They are told to subject themselves to a King they have never heard of nor seen and are told this by the King's messengers who are such despicable and cruel tyrants that deprive them of their liberty, their possessions, their wives and children. This is not only absurd but worthy of scorn.

This wretch of a Governor thus gave such instructions in order to justify his and their presence in the Indies, they themselves being absurd, irrational, and unjust when he sent the thieves under his command to attack and rob a settlement of Indians where he had heard there was a store of gold, telling them to go at night when the inhabitants were securely in their houses and that, when half a league away from the settlement, they should read in a loud voice his order: "Caciques and Indians of this land, hark ye! We notify you that there is but one God and one Pope and one King of Castile who is the lord of these lands. Give heed and show obedience!" Etcetera, etcetera. "And if not, be warned that we will wage war against you and will slay you or take you into captivity." Etc., etc.

Then, in the early dawn, when these innocents are asleep with their wives and children, the Spaniards attack and enter the town and set fire to the houses, which, being commonly made of straw, burn rapidly with all who are within them.

Thus they proceeded, killing as many as they liked, and torturing those they took alive, because they had been told of other settlements where there was gold, more than there was in this one, and then they took a number of survivors in chains to sell them as slaves.

They always searched for gold in the ruins of the towns they burned. In this manner and with such acts, that Godforsaken Governor busied himself and his company from the year fourteen until the year twenty-one or twenty-two, sending into those actions five or six of his officers, giving each of them such and such an amount of the booty. The major part of the gold, the pearls, the enslaved Indians falling to himself as their captain-general. The representatives of the King acted in the same way, each one sending out as many underlings as they could, and the first Bishop of that kingdom also sent out his underlings so as to have his share of the treasure-trove. I believe I underestimate when I say they robbed more gold in that time and in that kingdom than was worth one million castellanos, of which amount they sent to the King only three thousand castellanos. And during these actions they killed some eight hundred thousand souls.

The other tyrant who succeeded this one on the mainland until the year one thousand five hundred and twenty-three, killed and allowed to be killed by his henchmen in the wars that followed all the native peoples that survived.

That wretch of a Governor who first penetrated the mainland committed countless vile deeds, of which I shall mention a few. A cacique (as a native ruler was called) had given the tyrant, either of his own accord or impelled by fear, gold worth nine thousand castellanos. Not content with this amount, the Governor had the cacique bound to a stake in a sitting posture, his legs extended, and set a fire to burn the soles of his feet, demanding more gold. The cacique sent to his house for more gold and the servant brought back three thousand castellanos' worth. Not content with this, more gold was demanded of the cacique. And, either because there was no more or else he was unwilling to give more, he continued to be tortured until the bone marrow came out of the soles of his feet and he died. Such things were done to the Indians countless times, always with the aim of getting as much gold as possible from them.

Another instance of such cruelty was when a company of Spaniards made an attack on a mountain refuge where some Indians were hiding from the pestilential acts of the Christians. Falling upon this numerous band, the Spaniards captured some women and maidens, sixty or eighty of them, holding them captive while they killed most of the men. Next day, some of the surviving Indians, anxious about the captive women, came upon the Christians from the rear and attacked them. Seeing they were hard-pressed, the Christians, who hesitated to bring up their cavalry, set their swords against the bodies of the women and maids, leaving not one of them alive. At sight of this, the Indians screamed in an access of grief and horror: "Oh, vile men! Oh, cruel Christians! So you kill women? (In their language their word for women is *iras*, meaning wrath, or vengeance.)

At a distance of ten or fifteen leagues from Panama was a great chief named Paris, who was very rich in gold. The Spaniards went there and he received them as if they were brothers, presenting the captain with gold worth fifty thousand castellanos, giving this of his own free will. It seemed to the captain of the Christian troops that anyone who could give that amount freely must possess a very great quantity (and discovering such treasures of gold was their sole aim and consolation). They dissimulated and made as if to depart. But in the early dawn they turned back and fell upon the town, setting fire to it, killing and burning many people. When the fires died down, they found and took away gold worth fifty or sixty thousand castellanos.

The cacique managed to escape, was neither killed nor captured, and very quickly he assembled as many surviving Indians as he could, and by the end of two or three days caught up with the Christians who were carrying away his gold, and valiantly attacked them, killing fifty Christians and taking the gold from them. The others, badly wounded, fled. But later on they marched against that cacique with a large company and killed him, along with a great many of his troops, taking captives and subjecting them to slavery in the usual way. In short, at the present time there remains no vestige of the large town where once ruled a great chieftain. And this does not take into account the killings and destructions that wretch of a Governor carried out which resulted in the extinction of those kingdoms....

***

...I will finish at this point and shall write no more until more news comes of still more egregious wickedness (if that is possible) or until we return to the Indies and see these things with our own eyes as we constantly did for twenty-two years, constantly protesting before God and my conscience. For I believe, no, I am sure that what I have said about such perditions, injuries, and horrible cruelties and all kinds of ugliness, violence, injustice, thefts, and massacres that those men have perpetrated in these parts of the Indies (and are still perpetrating), I am sure that what I have described is only the ten-thousandth part of what has been done, in quality and quantity, by the Spaniards in the Indies, from the beginning until today.

And so that any Christian may have more compassion for those innocent and ruined nations and their plight, so they may feel the pain of guilt and detest still more the greed and ambition and cruelty of the Spaniards in the Indies, let all that I have said be taken for the real truth, along with what I have affirmed, which is that from the discovery of the Indies until today, never in any part of that New World have the Indians done wrong to the Christians without first having been hurt and robbed and betrayed by them. For in the beginning they thought the Christians were immortals who had come down from Heaven, and they welcomed them, until they saw by their works what these Christians were and what they wanted.

Another thing must be added: from the beginning to the present time the Spaniards have taken no more care to have the Faith of Jesus Christ preached to those nations than they would to have it preached to dogs or other beasts. Instead, they have prohibited the religious from carrying out this intention, and have afflicted them and persecuted them in many ways, because such preaching would, they deemed, have hindered them from acquiring gold and other wealth they coveted. And today in all the Indies there is no more knowledge of God, whether He be of wood or sky, or earth, and this after one hundred years in the New World, except in New Spain, where some religious have gone, and which is but a very small part of the Indies. And thus all the nations have perished and are perishing without the sacraments of the Faith.

I, Fray Bartolomé de Las Casas (or Casaus), a Dominican friar, through the mercy of God, was induced to come to this court of Spain to bring about the ending of that inferno in the Indies and the irremediable destruction of souls that were redeemed by the blood of Jesus Christ; and to set up a work that would bring those souls to know their Creator and Savior. I am also here because of the compassion I have for my native land, Castile, that it not be destroyed by God as punishment for the great sins committed by Spaniards devoid of faith. I am also here because there reside in this court certain persons who are zealous for the honor of God and have compassion for the afflictions of their fellow men.

Finished in Valencia this eighth day of December, one thousand five hundred and forty-two, when actually all the force and violence are at their peak, when conditions in the Indies are at their worst, with all the anguish and disasters, all the massacres, looting, and destruction, outrages, and exterminations I have described. They are the lot of the native peoples in every part of the Indies where there are Christian conquerors. Although in some parts the Christian Spaniards are more ferocious and abominable in their behavior, they are a little less so in Mexico, or at least there they dare not commit their vile acts as openly as in other parts of the Indies. And although some justice does prevail there, all the same, an infernal amount of killing is done. I have great hope that our Emperor Charles V will harken to and comprehend the evils and betrayals that afflict that land and its peoples, against the will of God and against the will of His Majesty, deeds still being perpetrated, because until now the truth has industriously been concealed, and it is my hope that His Majesty will abolish the evils and remedy conditions in the New World that God has entrusted to him, as the lover and motivator of justice that he is, and may God protect his glorious and felicitous life and the Imperial State that all-powerful God has given him, to heal the universal Church. And may his royal soul be saved at last, and may he prosper for many years to come on this earth. Amen.

After writing the above, there were promulgated certain laws and ordinances which His Majesty issued from the city of Barcelona, in the year one thousand five hundred and forty-two, the month of November, and from the palace in Madrid, the following year, by which it was ordained that henceforth such evil deeds and sins against God and our fellow men would cease in the New World. And finally, after having made these laws, His Majesty held many councils and conferences with persons of great authority, learning, and conscience and there were debates in the palace of Valladolid and the votes cast were set down in writing, the Counselors keeping close to the law of Jesus Christ, being good Christians. It was ordained that the Spanish conquerors should cease the corruption and the soiling of their hands and souls in robbing the Indians of their treasures.

The laws being published, the makers of the tyrants who were at the court had many transcriptions made of them, and these were sent to diverse parts of the Indies. (They did this unwillingly, for the laws seemed to shut them out of participating in the robberies and tyrannies.)

And those who, in the Indies, had charge of the ruin and the robberies have continued, as if no orders had been issued, being inspired by Lucifer, when they saw the transcriptions, to engage in still more disorders before the new judges should arrive to execute the laws. And the tyrants rioted and rebelled when the new judges did come to supplant those who had aided and abetted the tyrants (since they had lost all love and all fear of God, and lost all shame and all obedience to the King). And thus they agreed to adopt the fame of traitors, their extreme cruelties and tyrannies were now unleashed, especially in the kingdom of Peru, where today in the year one thousand five hundred and forty-six they are committing such horrible, frightful, nefarious acts as were never before committed in the Indies or anywhere else in the world.

And these acts were committed not only against the Indians, most of the Indians having been killed and their lands destroyed, but against each other, and since the laws of the King no longer operated, punishment came from Heaven, allowing each tyrant to be the executioner of the other.

In imitation of this rebellion against the King in this part of the Indies, the tyrants in other parts of the New World have disregarded the new laws and are behaving in the same way. For they cannot bring themselves to relinquish the estates and properties they have usurped, or let go their hold on the Indians, whom they maintain in perpetual subjection. And wherever killing with the sword has come to an end, they are killing the Indians little by little through subjecting them to servitude. And until now the King has been powerless to check them, for all the Spaniards, young and old, in the Indies, are occupied in pillage, some openly, others secretly and stealthily. And with the pretense of serving the King they are dishonoring God and robbing and destroying the King.

Questions:
1. *How favorably does Las Casas describe the Caribbean natives? What traits of theirs seem to particularly impress him?*
2. *To what overriding cause did Las Casas ascribe the Europeans' motivation to slaughter?*
3. *What role did the first Bishop play?*
4. *What, according to Las Casas' attestations, was the situation at the time of his writing his accounts? What were the results of his petition to King Charles V?*

14.8 The British Encounter Maoris: A Sailor's Impressions

Captain James Cook of Yorkshire was without doubt the greatest seafarer of the 18th century, circumnavigating the globe and opening the Pacific regions to the knowledge of the outside world. All too often, this eventually worked to the detriment of the native cultures of the islands. One of the most resilient nations of Oceania, however, were the Maori of New Zealand, first encountered during Cook's 1772–73 voyage. James Burney (1750–1821), a seaman with Cook who later became an admiral, left these impressions in his journals.

> **Source:** Beverly Hooper, ed., *James Burney: With Captain James Cook in the Pacific.* (Canberra, Australia: National Library of Australia), pp. 67–68, 72–74.

These Islands have been described in so satisfactory a manner, that there is no room left for me to hold forth without making frequent repetitions of what has before been said never the less I will venture a word or two & attempt to draw their characters according to my own opinions—

I must confess I was a little disappointed on my first coming here as I expected to find People nearly as white as Europeans. Some of the better sort are tolerably white, more so than a Spaniard or Portugueze, but the generality are of a dark olive Colour. the men are something larger than the common run in England—

The Similitude of Customs & Language scarce admits any doubt of these Islanders being sprung from the same stock as the Zealanders though from the difference of climate & country they are as opposite in their characters as the enervated, luxurious Italians & the rude unpolished Northern Nations of Europe—the Heavoh & Tattow are common to both though practised in different manners—the Islanders have I think, the Advantage of the Zealanders, in their persons, they are likewise very cleanly, washing both before & after every meal, & take a great deal of Pride in their Dress—any thing showy or Ornamental is much more esteemed here than at Zealand—especially by the girls who have almost as much Vanity as the Women of Europe—Hospitality & a love of Society reigns through all these Islands; I never in any of my Rambles met with an unwelcome reception—In short they are a friendly humane people, superior to the Zealanders in many aspects—I mean the men as to the women, they must not be mentiond together unless by way of contrast—they are reckon'd smaller here than the English Women & not in proportion to the men, but take away our high heads & high heels, the difference of Size would not be perceptible—there are much handsomer women in England & many, more ordinary. I mean as to the face—but for fine turned Limbs & well made persons I think they cannot be excelled—I only speak from my own notions, which are not infallible, for I have not the least pretence to set up for a Judge in this case—the Children are in general exceeding beautifull—as they grow up they lose it for want of that care which in Europe is taken to preserve Beauty, they are not in the least afraid "The Winds of the Heavens Should visit their faces too roughly"—were they brought up in the delicate manner European Women are, there would be a great many very fine women amongst these Islands— Colour, in my opinion, has very little to do with beauty provided it be a healthy one it is a handsome one whether fair, brown or black—I question if they have any Idea of Chastity being a virtue—you may see young Girls not more than 12 years old with bellies they can scarce carry—after Marriage they confine themselves to the Husband—if they are caught slipping the Husband commonly sends them home to their Relations, but the Gallant does not escape so well, his life often paying the forfeit of his incontinence. the Independent men, or Aree's are allowed to have 2 wives—If a women after 6 or 7 months cohabitation with her Husband does not prove with Child, their Union, if they please, may be dissolved & each party at liberty to choose another mate. the women always mess by themselves & are seldom allowed to eat flesh— if a girl becomes pregnant the man cannot be forced to marry her. When a man courts any girl for a wife, after having got her relations consent, he sleeps 3 nights at their house—if the bride is a Virgin he is allowed to take no liberties till the 3ᵈ Night, though he lyes with her each Night—the 3ᵈ Day he makes the Relations a present & the 4ᵗʰ takes the Bride home— they give no portions with the girls unless the Bride's father has no Male children or other Male Relations to bestow his property on. a case which must be very rare in these Islands—…

***

Opune—has but one child (a Girl) living; he has 2 Wives & 3 Concubines—Tereroa's Sister was formerly one of his wives—She has been dead some time his Daughter if She survives him will inherit his Dominions—for he is not likely to have any more Children, being now a very old man but is Still greatly loved by his own Subjects & feared by the other Islands—Opune, in spite of old age & Blindness, (his Eyes being very bad) nevertheless retains all the Chearfullness & Merriment of a Young Man, nor are his people ever happier than when in his Company—he is a great encourager of their Games & Revels (their Heavah of which I shall Speak presently) & has invented many new ones himself—I have given this Character of him from what Omy says, who stiles him a fighting man & a man of Laughter.—I never saw him—

Of these people's Character, I have as yet shewn you only the fair Side—My partiality towards them shall not induce me to Stop here—As I set down nought in Malice, so will I nothing extenuate.

In their dealings with us they are great thieves, our Goods being of such Value to them, that very few can withstand the temptation of a fair opportunity—nevertheless I have slept all Night in their houses 8 miles up the Country, without any attempt being made on me—theft amongst themselves is punished with Death—

They have some very barbarous customs, the worst of which is, when a man has as many children as he is able to maintain, all that come after are smothered: women will sometimes bargain with her husband on her first marrying him, for the Number of Children that shall be kept. They never keep any Children that are any ways deformed—every fifth Child if suffered to live is Seldom allowed to rank higher than a Towtow—yet notwithstanding all this, these Islands are exceeding populous—even the Smallest being full of inhabitants & perhaps were it not for the Custom just mentioned, these would be more than the Islands could well maintain—

Every Island has a high priest, some two, with inferior priests—of this latter Class was Omy—the Being whom they worship they call Mo-wee & sometime offer human sacrifices to him—this is not done at any particular sett times but when Mo-wee requires it—he appears to none but the high priests, who frequently pretend to see him flying—this gives the high priest great power & if he is a man of a vindictive temper, whoever offends him must feel it—Mo-wee always names the person & as soon as his desires are known to the high priest he sends his attendants to dispatch the destined victim who knows nothing of his fate till the minute of his death—having killed him, he is carried to the high Priest, who takes out his Eyes, which Mo-wee eats, & the body is buried—

Before they venture on any extraordinary Expedition, Mo-wee is consulted: if the priest brings bad News it is either laid aside or deferred till better success is promised. Temperance or Chastity is not in the least essential to the high priest's Character, he being at liberty to take any woman he chooses to honour so far, married or unmarried, for as long as he pleases. The great power of the high priest would be very inconvenient for the Chief Aree were it not that they most commonly exercise this office themselves.—The Kingsfisher is one of their inferior deities—& the high priest understands what they say—…

Questions:
1. *In what ways does Bumey betray disappointment or bias in his descriptions of the natives? In what ways does he demonstrate a deeper appreciation or tolerance?*
2. *For what causes might a Maori marriage be terminated?*
3. *What seems to be the Maori attitude towards old age? Towards infanticide?*
4. *What are the attributes of the deity, Mo-wee?*

14.9   The Prospects of Christian Conversion: Saint Francis Xavier

The following selection is an excerpt from the journals of Gaspar Correa, who sailed with Vasco da Gama in 1502. This incident occurred after a group of Portuguese had been killed in the trading station of Calcutta. Vasco da Gama sought to control the situation by exacting a bloody vengeance.

Source: "The Prospects of Christian Conversion" is from Henry James Coleridge, ed., *The Life and Letters of St. Francis Xavier,* 2nd edition (London: Burns and Oates, 1890), p. 86.

SAINT FRANCIS XAVIER

My own and only Father in the Heart of Christ, I think that the many letters from this place which have lately been sent to Rome will inform you how prosperously the affairs of religion go on in these parts, through your prayers and the good bounty of God. But there seem to be certain things which I ought myself to speak about to you; so I will just touch on a few points relating to these parts of the world which are so distant from Rome. In the first place, the whole race of the Indians, as far as I have been able to see, is very barbarous; and it does not like to listen to anything that is not agreeable to its own manners and customs, which, as I say, are barbarous. It troubles itself very little to learn anything about divine things and things which concern salvation. Most of the Indians are of vicious disposition, and are adverse to virtue. Their instability, levity, and inconstancy of mind are incredible; they have hardly any honesty, so inveterate are their habits of sin and cheating. We have hard work here, both in keeping the Christians up the mark and in this account you should take great care of us and help us continually by your prayers to God. You know very well what a hard business it is to teach people who neither have any knowledge of God nor follow reason, but think it a strange and intolerable thing to be told to give up their habits of sin, which have now gained all the force of nature by long possession. . . .

The experience which I have of these countries makes me think that I can affirm with truth, that there is no prospect of perpetuating our Society out here by means of the natives themselves, and that the Christian religion will hardly survive us who are now in the country; so that it is quite necessary that continual supplies of ours should be sent out from Europe. . . .

The Portuguese in these countries are masters only of the sea and of the coast. On the mainland they have only the towns in which they live. The natives themselves are so enormously addicted to vice as to be little adapted to receive the Christian religion. They so dislike it that it is most difficult to get them to hear us if we begin to preach about it, and they think it like death to be asked to become Christians. So for the present, we devote ourselves to keeping the Christians whom we have. Certainly, if the Portuguese were more remarkable for their kindness to the new converts, a great number would become Christians; as it is, the heathen see that the converts, are despised and looked down upon by the Portuguese, and so, as is natural, they are unwilling to become converts themselves. For all these reasons there is no need for me to labor in these countries, and as I have learned from good authorities that there is a country near China called Japan, the inhabitants of which are all heathen, quite untouched by Muslims or Jews, and very eager to learn what they do not know both in things divine and things natural, I have determined to go thither as soon as I can. . . .

Questions:
1. How does Xavier describe the Indians? By what criteria does he judge them?
2. According to Xavier, how are the Portuguese hindering the missionaries?

PART 15
Trade and Exploitation Across the Atlantic

15.1 The "Black Legend" of Spain: Bartolomé de las Casas

More than any other single individual, the Dominican friar Bartolomé de Las Casas was responsible for the birth of the "Black Legend," the vicious Spanish reputation that developed during the sixteenth and seventeenth centuries. Although the Black Legend became primarily an instrument of Anglo-Dutch propaganda against the Spanish, which Las Casas probably would never have accepted, his influence in its creation is undeniable. After witnessing the ravages and atrocities of Spanish colonists, Las Casas dedicated himself to the protection and defense of the Indians. He wrote the Short Account of the Destruction of the Indies in 1542 and dedicated it to the Spanish king Philip II in an effort to inform the crown of atrocities in the New World that, if not curtailed, would result in God's destruction of Spain. This book, a fierce and deeply atmospheric anatomy of genocide, established the image of the Spanish conquest of America for the next three centuries. It is testimony to the persuasive and enduring influence of the Black Legend that the Spanish government hoped to amend this pejorative image by hosting the 1992 Olympics in Barcelona.

Source: *A Short Account of the Destruction of the Indies* by Bartholome dé Las Casas, translated by Nigel Griffin (Penguin Classics, 1992) copyright © Nigel Griffin, 1992, pp. 14–15. Reproduced with permission of Penguin Books Ltd.

As we have said, the island of Hispaniola was the first to witness the arrival of Europeans and the first to suffer the wholesale slaughter of its people and the devastation and depopulation of the land. It all began with the Europeans taking native women and children both as servants and to satisfy their own base appetites; then not content with what the local people offered them of their own free will (and all offered as much as they could spare), they started taking for themselves the food that natives contrived to produce by the sweat of their brows, (which was in all honesty little enough). . . . Some of them started to conceal what food they had, others decided to send their women and children into hiding, and yet others took to the hills to get away from the brutal and ruthless cruelty that was being inflicted on them. The Christians punched them, boxed their ears and flogged them in order to track down the local leaders, and the whole shameful process came to a head when one of the European commanders raped the wife of the paramount chief of the entire island. It was then that the locals began to think up ways of driving the Europeans out of their lands and to take up arms against them. Their weapons, however, were flimsy and ineffective both in attack and in defense (and, indeed, war in the Americas is no more deadly than our jousting, or than many European children's games) and, with their horses and swords and lances, the Spaniards easily fended them off, killing them and committing all kind of atrocities against them.

They forced their way into native settlements, slaughtering everyone they found there, including small children, old men, pregnant women, and even women who had just given birth. They hacked them to pieces, slicing open their bellies with their swords as though they were so many sheep herded into a pen. They even laid wagers on whether they could manage to slice a man in two at a stroke, or cut an individual's head from his body, or disembowel him with a single blow of their axes. They grabbed suckling infants by the feet and, ripping them from their mothers' breasts, dashed them headlong against the rocks. . . . They slaughtered anyone and everyone in their path, on occasion running through a mother and her baby with a single thrust of their swords. They spared no one, erecting especially wide gibbets on which they could string their victims up with their feet just off the ground and then burn them alive thirteen at a time, in honor of our Savior and the twelve Apostles, or tie dry straw to their bodies and set fire to it. Some they chose to keep alive and simply cut their wrists, leaving their hands dangling, saying to them: "Take this letter"—meaning that their sorry condition would act as a warning to those hiding in the hills. The way they normally dealt with the native leaders and nobles was to tie them to a kind of griddle consisting of sticks resting on pitchforks driven into the ground and then grill them over a slow fire, with the result that they howled in agony and despair as they died a lingering death.

Questions:
1. What was the "Black Legend" of Spain?
2. What type of atrocities were committed by the Spanish conquistadors?

15.2 "Our Kingdom Is Being Lost": Nzinga Mbemba (Afonso I)

The next selection is a letter from the African King of Kongo, Nzinga Mbemba, who had converted to Christianity and adopted the name Afonso I (reigned ca. 1506–1543). Afonso had hoped to develop a prosperous state by cooperating with the Europeans. But by the time of his death, his kingdom had almost disintegrated. His concerns are expressed in a letter to the Portuguese king, Joao III, in 1526. It was evident that Portuguese exploitation and aggressive pursuit of slaves resulted in dissension and instability throughout the region.

Source: Copyright © 1964 by Basil Davidson, Reprinted by permission of Curtis Brown, Ltd.

Sir, Your Highness should know how our Kingdom is being lost in so many ways that it is convenient to provide for the necessary remedy, since this is caused by the excessive freedom given by your agents and officials to the men and merchants who are allowed to come to this Kingdom to set up shops with goods and many things which have been prohibited by us, and which they spread throughout our Kingdoms and Domains in such an abundance that many of our vassals, whom we had in obedience, do not comply because they have the things in greater abundance than we ourselves; and it was with these things that we had them content and subjected under our vassalage and jurisdiction, so it is doing a great harm not only to the service of God, but the security and peace of our Kingdoms and State as well.

And we cannot reckon how great the damage is, since the mentioned merchants are taking every day our natives, sons of the land and the sons of our noblemen and vassals and our relatives, because the thieves and men of bad conscience grab them wishing to have the things and wares of this Kingdom which they are ambitious of; they grab them and get them to be sold; and so great, Sir, is the corruption and licentiousness that our country is being completely depopulated, and Your Highness should not agree with this nor accept it as in your service. And to avoid it we need from your Kingdoms no more than some priests and a few people to teach in schools, and no other goods except wine and flour for the holy sacrament. That is why we beg of Your Highness to help and assist us in this matter, commanding your factors [agents] that they should not send here either merchants or wares, because it *our will that in these Kingdoms there should not be any trade of slaves nor outlet for them.* Concerning what is referred [to] above, again we beg of Your Highness to agree with it, since otherwise we cannot remedy such an obvious damage. Pray Our Lord in his mercy to have Your Highness under His guard and let you do forever the things of His service. . . .

Moreover, Sir, in our Kingdoms there is another great inconvenience which is of little service to God, and this is that many of our people, keenly desirous as they are of the wares and things of your Kingdoms, which are brought here by your people, and in order to satisfy their voracious appetite, seize many of our people, freed and exempt men, and very often it happens that they kidnap even noblemen and the sons of noblemen, and our relatives, and take them to be sold to the white men who are in our Kingdoms; and for this purpose they have concealed them; and others are brought during the night so that they might not be recognized.

And as soon as they are taken by the white men they are immediately ironed and branded with fire, and when they are carried to be embarked, if they are caught by our guards' men the whites allege that they have bought them but they cannot say from whom, so that it is our duty to do justice and to restore to the freemen their freedom, but it cannot be done if your subjects feel offended, as they claim to be.

And to avoid such a great evil we passed a law so that any white man living in our Kingdoms and wanting to purchase goods in any way should first inform three of our noblemen and officials of our court whom we rely upon in this matter, and these are Dom Pedro Manipanza and Dom Manuel Manissaba, our chief usher, and Gocalo Pires our chief freighter, who should investigate if the mentioned goods are captives or free men, and if cleared by them there will be no further doubt nor embargo for them to be taken and embarked. But if the white men do not comply with it they will lose the aforementioned goods. And if we do them this favor and concession it is for the part Your Highness has in it, since we know that it is in your service too that these goods are taken from our Kingdom, otherwise we should not consent to this. . . .

Question:
1. Why was his kingdom "out of balance" and what reforms did he suggest?

15.3   Olaudah Equiano, The Life of Olaudah Equiano, or Gustavus Vassa, The African

One African who survived the journey was Olaudah Equiano (ca. 1745–1797), an Ibo born in eastern Nigeria near Benin. When Equiano was ten years old, he and his sister were captured from their home by local robbers who quickly sold the children to slavers. Equiano served a series of masters, first in Barbados and later in Virginia; he was finally bought by a British naval officer who took him to Canada, England, and then back to the West Indies. This owner gave Equiano the new name of Gustavus Vassa. In 1766, by luck and frugal trading, Equiano had saved the hefty sum of forty pounds sterling, which was enough money to buy his freedom. As a free man, he returned to England, where he worked as a barber, a domestic servant, and a sailor.

In 1789, he published a two-volume set of memoirs in English, describing his life in Africa and his experiences as a slave. His account, excerpted in the following reading, became a best-seller in England and soon enabled Equiano; to become active in the English antislavery movement.

> **Source:** From Olaudah Equiano, *The Life of Olaudah Equiano, or Gustavus Vassa, The African,* Written by Himself (Boston: I. Knapp, 1837), 31–32, 43–44, 47–48, 50–52.

One day, when all our people were gone out to their works as usual and only I and my dear sister were left to mind the house, two men and a woman got over our walls, and in a moment seized us both, and without giving us time to cry out or make resistance they stopped our mouths and ran off with us into the nearest wood. Here they tied our hands and continued to carry us as far as they could till night came on, when we reached a small house where the robbers halted for refreshment and spent the night. . . .

The first object which saluted my eyes when I arrived on the coast was the sea, and a slave ship which was then riding at anchor and waiting for its cargo. These filled me with astonishment, which was soon converted into terror when I was carried on board. I was immediately handled and tossed up to see if I were sound by some of the crew, and I was now persuaded that I had gotten into a world of bad spirits and that they were going to kill me. Their complexions too differing so much from ours, their long hair and the language they spoke (which was very different from any I had ever heard) united to confirm me in this belief. Indeed such were the horrors of my views and fears at the moment that, if ten thousand worlds had been my own, I would have freely parted with them all to have exchanged my condition with that of the meanest slave in my own country. When I looked round the ship too and saw a large furnace or copper boiling and a multitude of black people of every description chained together, every one of their countenances expressing dejection and sorrow, I no longer doubted of my fate; and quite overpowered with horror and anguish, I fell motionless on the deck and fainted. When I recovered a little I found some black people about me, who I believed were some of those who had brought me on board and had been receiving their pay; they talked to me in order to cheer me, but all in vain. I asked them if we were not to be eaten by those white men with horrible looks, red faces, and loose hair. They told me I was not, and one of the crew brought me a small portion of spirituous liquor in a wine glass, but being afraid of him I would not take it out of his hand. One of the blacks there took it from him and gave it to me, and I took a little down my palate, which instead of reviving me, as they thought it would, threw me into the greatest consternation at the strange feeling it produced, having never tasted any such liquor before. Soon after this the blacks who brought me on board went off, and left me abandoned to despair. . . .

The stench of the hold while we were on the coast was so intolerably loathsome that it was dangerous to remain there for any time, and some of us had been permitted to stay on the deck for the fresh air; but now that the whole ship's cargo were confined together it became absolutely pestilential. The closeness of the place and the heat of the climate, added to the number in the ship, which was so crowded that each had scarcely room to run himself, almost suffocated us. This produced copious perspirations, so that the air soon became unfit for respiration from a variety of loathsome smells, and brought on a sickness among the slaves, of which many died, thus falling victims to the improvident avarice, as I may call it, of their purchasers. This wretched situation was again aggravated by the galling of the chains, now become insupportable, and the filth of the necessary tubs, into which the children often fell and were almost suffocated. The shrieks of the women and the groans of the dying rendered the whole a scene of horror almost inconceivable. Happily perhaps for myself I was soon reduced so low here that it was thought necessary to keep me almost always on deck, and from my extreme youth I was not put in fetters. . . .

At last we came in sight of the island of Barbados, at which the whites on board gave a great shout and made many signs of joy to us. We did not know what to think of this, but as the vessel drew nearer we plainly saw the harbour and other ships of different kinds and sizes, and we soon anchored amongst them off Bridgetown. Many merchants and planters now came on board, though it was in the evening. They put us in separate parcels and examined us attentively. They also made us jump, and pointed to the land, signifying we were to go there. We thought by this we should be eaten by these ugly men, as they appeared to us; and when soon after we were all put down under the deck again, there was much dread and trembling among us, and nothing but bitter cries to be heard all the night from these apprehensions, insomuch that at last the white people got some old slaves from the land to pacify us. They told us we were not to be eaten but to work, and were soon to go on land where we should see many of our country people. This report eased us much; and sure enough soon after we were landed there came to us Africans of all languages. We were conducted immediately to the merchant's yard, where we were all pent up together like so many sheep in a fold without regard to sex or age. As every object was new to me everything I saw filled me with surprise. What struck me first was that the houses were built with storeys, and in every other respect different from those in Africa: but I was still more astonished on seeing people on horseback. I did not know what this could mean, and indeed I thought these people were full of nothing but magical arts. While I was in this astonishment one of my fellow prisoners spoke to a countryman of his about the horses, who said they were the same kind they had in their country. I understood them though they were from a distant part of Africa, and I thought it odd I had not seen any horses there; but afterwards when I came to converse with different Africans I found they had many horses amongst them, and much larger than those I then saw. We were not many days in the merchant's custody before we were sold after their usual manner, which is this: On a signal given, (as the beat of a drum) the buyers rush at once into the yard where the slaves are confined, and make choice of that parcel they like best. The noise and clamour with which this is attended and the eagerness visible in the countenances of the buyers serve not a little to increase the apprehensions of the terrified Africans, who may well be supposed to consider them as the ministers of that destruction to which they think themselves devoted. In this matter, without scruple, are relations and friends separated, most of them never to see each other again. I remember in the vessel in which I was brought over, in the men's apartment there were several brothers who, in the sale, were sold in different lots; and it was very moving on this occasion to see and hear their cries at parting. O, ye nominal Christians! might not an African ask you, Do unto all men as you would men should do to you? Is it not enough that we are torn from our country and friends to toil for your luxury and lust of gain? Must every tender feeling be likewise sacrificed to your avarice? Are the dearest friends and relations, now rendered more dear by their separation from their kindred, still to be parted from each other and thus prevented from cheering the gloom of slavery with the small comfort of being together and mingling their sufferings and sorrows? Why are parents to lose their children, brothers their sisters, or husbands their wives? Surely this is a new refinement in cruelty which, while it has no advantage to atone for it, thus aggravates distress and adds fresh horrors even to the wretchedness of slavery.

Questions:
1. *What does this memoir tell us about the organization and extent of slavery in the eighteenth-century Atlantic world?*
2. *What does this selection indicate about Equiano's African home and African culture?*
3. *What does the memoir, particularly its title, The Life of Olaudah Equiano, or Gustavus Vassa, The African, tell us about the cultural effects of slavery upon Africans in the eighteenth century?*

15.4   Commerce, Slavery, and Religion in North Africa

The purchase of slaves by North African merchants through the agency of rulers on the southern Saharan fringes began as early as the ninth century a.d. and was brought to an end only at the beginning of the twentieth century. West African Muslim rulers played an important controlling role in all external trade, and North African merchants could operate only with their consent. From the nineteenth-century evidence we have from the northern regions of what is now Nigeria, it is clear that rulers had first choice of merchandise from the large caravans and paid for it in slaves—a commodity that could be obtained at will by raiding the large non-Muslim populations surrounding these Muslim states. The enslavement of non-Muslims was permitted by Islamic law as a by-product of jihād—"war for the expansion of the domain of Islam," but the random rounding up of non-Muslim populations to pay off a debt, such as is illustrated in the following piece, hardly comes under this rubric. Nevertheless, the narrator seeks some religious justification for carrying off black Africans into slavery inasmuch as their routinized mass "conversion" to Islam en route ensures their salvation. As he acknowledges, piety and commerce may be mutually reinforcing.

The following account was given to General E. Daumas, a French officer serving in Algeria in the 1830s, by a member of a caravan headed by a Tuareg guide (khabīr) called Cheggueun, which set out from Metlily in the Algerian Sahara to do business in Katsina in the far north of present-day Nigeria. Katsina was one of the emirates that formed part of a large Islamic empire founded in the early years of the nineteenth century with its capital at Sokoto.

Source: Abridged and trans. John O. Hunwick from Gen. E. Daumas, Le Grand Désert. *Itinéraire d'une caravane du Sahara au pays des nègres, royaume de Haoussa,* 4th ed., (Paris, 1860), pp. 199–247.

THE SLAVE TRADE

We had been at Katsina for ten days and when the story had got around in the surrounding villages that a rich caravan had arrived, all the petty merchants hastened to the town. Moreover, since those of Katsina were pressing us it was decided to put our merchandise on sale and Cheggueun went to tell Omar[1] what we intended to do. The response of the serki (ruler) was that we could do as we liked, but that he would reserve the sale of all our broadcloths, in the name of the sultan. His oukil (agent) made a list the same day and took us to the palace to discuss the price with the serki himself.

"Khabir (caravan leader)," said Omar to our chief, "according to what my agent has told me, the broadcloths of your merchants are of inferior quality and are worth no more than a single slave, negro or negress, per cubit." "Sir, it shall be done according to your justice. We are your servants," replied Cheggueun, and we all put our fist on our chest as a sign of consent, for in fact we were getting a good deal. "Go in peace, then," replied the serki, "I do not have enough slaves to pay you today. But, by the grace of God, Mohammed Omar shall not fail in his word."

As we went out of the palace a regular low pitched sound caught our attention. It came from the center of the town and we made for it. It led us to the Makhzen (army) square where, from every street, a crowd came running like us. At the center of the square was placed a huge drum which a strapping Negro beat with a knobbed stick with all his might. This is the sultan's drum. It is never beaten for anything but assembling the army.

We had discovered the secret of the strange noise that had moved us and this proclamation of the chief of the Mekhazenia informed us for what purpose they were gathered: "This is the will of the serki. In the name of sultan Bello the Victorious,[2] may God bless him, all of you, are summoned to present yourselves here at daybreak, armed and mounted, with sufficient provisions to go, some to Zenfra [Zamfara] and others to Zendeur [Zinder] to hunt the idolatrous Koholanes[3]— enemies of the glorious sultan our master—may God curse them." "All that the sultan orders is good," responded the soldiers. "Let it be done according to the will of our lord and master."

The following day, in fact, the Mekhazenia (soldiery), prompt to the appointed meeting, divided themselves into two goums (companies), one taking the east and the other the south-west with orders to attack places without defences and to carry off the inhabitants as well as seizing all peasants busy cultivating their fields. At the same time orders were given to track down the idolatrous Koholanes in the interior.

Whilst waiting for the return of the goums that Omar had despatched to hunt Negroes, we went every day to the slave market where we bought at the following prices:

A Negro with beard	10 or 15,000 cowries

They are not considered as merchandise since one has little chance of preventing them from escaping.

An adult Negress, same price for	10 or 15,000 cowries the same reasons
An adolescent Negro	30,000 cowries
A young Negress	50–60,000 cowries
(The price varies according to whether she is more or less beautiful.)	
A male Negro child	45,000 cowries
A female Negro child	35–40,000 cowries

The seller gives the buyer the greatest possible chance to examine the slaves and one has three days to give notice of concealed faults.

THE RETURN OF OMAR'S GOUM

The goum of serki Omar had been on campaign for about a month when we learnt from a messenger that the double raid launched against Zinder and Zamfara had been completely successful and that the makhzen, bringing back two thousand slaves would return to Katsina the next day. In a few hours this good news had spread throughout the town and at daybreak the next day the entire population crowded the gardens on the east side where the two armies that had the previous day joined up ought to arrive.

A cloud of dust soon announced it and as they crossed the outer wall where the route was better marked and the terrain more solid, their confused mass began to make itself out from the veil of sand that they had raised on the plain. The prisoners walked at the head, men, women, children, the elderly, almost all naked or half covered in rags of blue cloth. The women and the elderly were unbound but tightly packed together; the children were piled onto camels with some sitting on their mothers' backs in a piece of cloth doing duty as a bag. The men had been chained, five or six to the same chain, their necks fixed in a strong iron ring closed by a padlock and their hands bound with palm ropes. The strongest and most resistant were tied down to the tails of horses. Women moaned and children cried. Men, in general, seemed more resigned, but the bloody cuts that the whip had made on their shoulders bore witness to their tough struggle with the horsemen of the serki.

The convoy steered itself towards the palace and its arrival was announced to Mohammed Omar by musicians. At the first sound of the music the serki came out of his palace followed by his agent and some dignitaries. On seeing him all the slaves threw themselves on their knees and the musicians attacked their instruments with a passion that bordered on fury. The serki, approaching the goum, complimented its leaders, examined the slaves and gave the order for them to be taken to the market. There they were placed in two rows in sheds, women on one side and men on the other, and on the next day we were invited to go and choose those which suited us. Cheggueun and the palace agent went with us and after very careful examination each of us obtained as many Negroes and Negresses as he had handed over cubits of broadcloth to the serki. Nevertheless, we only accepted those whose sound constitutions were a surety against the hazards of the long journey we had to make. The elderly, small children and pregnant women were sold to the people of Katsina or given by Omar as gifts to the leaders of his mekhazenias.

DEPARTURE OF THE CARAVAN

We were now in the month of April and the season was favorable for leaving. We hastened to gather provisions of maize, millet, dried meat, butter and honey sufficient for each person for three months and we bought baggage camels in sufficient number to insure against accidents en route and some oxhide tents. Finally, our caravan which had set out from Metlily (in Algeria) with sixty-four camels and only sixteen persons, was now augmented by four hundred slaves, of whom three hundred were women, and had a total of almost six hundred camels.

The people of Touat [Tuwāt][4] who joined with us, had increased in number similarly. They had purchased fifteen hundred slaves and their camels had risen in number to two thousand. Altogether we formed a company of about two thousand one hundred men and two thousand six hundred camels. Katsina had no square big enough to contain us and so, under the name of the Touat caravan, we went to establish ourselves in one of the great empty spaces set up in the middle of the gardens.

Finally we saw successively arriving the three caravans of Ghadames, Ghat and the Fezzan.[5] The first had penetrated as far as Nupe on the banks of the Bahar-el-Nil [river Niger] to the south of Sokoto. It brought back three thousand slaves and three thousand five hundred camels. The second had pushed down to Kano to the south-east of Katsina. It only numbered seven or eight hundred camels and four or five hundred slaves. The third came back from Sokoto and was no larger than the preceding one.

At daybreak our camels were loaded, the Negro children perched atop the baggage, the male Negroes secured by their chains in the center of the convoy and the Negro females grouped in eights or tens under the watch of men carrying whips. The departure signal was given and the first caravan moved. It was at this point that suddenly a confused noise of cries and sobs passed from one group of slaves to another and reached our own. All, together, wept and moaned, called out and uttered farewells. They were terrified of being eaten during the journey. Some rolled on the ground, clung to bushes and absolutely refused to walk. Nothing had any effect on them, neither kind words nor threats. They could only be got up with mighty lashes of the whip and by rendering them completely bloody. Despite their obstinacy, no one of them resisted this extreme measure. Moreover, joined together as they were, the less fearful or more courageous, struggling with the weaker ones, forced them to walk.

The first day we halted at only three leagues[6] from Katsina on a huge plain where we found pools and plenty of grass and wood. Each caravan established its camp separately. As soon as our camels had crouched down and after having, first and foremost, chained up our Negresses by the foot in groups of eight or ten, we forced our Negroes to help us, using their left hand which we had left free, in unloading our animals, marking out a circle with our loads and putting up the oxhide tents we had brought from Katsina within this perimeter. Two or three of the older Negresses whom we had not chained together, but who nevertheless had their feet shackled, were set to preparing something for us to dine on.

The next day we loaded up early and this time the Ghat caravan took the lead. Although calmer than they were the evening before, our slaves were still very irritable. To tire them out and weaken them we made the slaves carry their irons, their dishes and the mortars for pounding maize and millet. And so that our entire attention could be concentrated on them, each of us tied his camels together in a single file. Watching over them thus became easier and if one of them fell down or a load fell off, we could in this way halt them all at once and we avoided the whole group bolting as we got one on its feet or reloaded another.

ESCAPE, RECAPTURE, PUNISHMENT

[The narrator's personal slave, Mebrouk, could not reconcile himself to his condition, despite his owner's blandishments, and led a party of six slaves—all chained together for the night—in an escape. Two were recaptured; two others chained together were attacked by a lion and one was mauled to death while the other eventually died of fright. Mebrouk and one other slave were never found.]

When news of this event was noised abroad our khebirs, each followed by fifteen horsemen, set off at a gallop and explored the countryside far and wide. But it is full of scrub and so dotted with hillocks that they could only find two of the fugitives. As a lesson for the future, it remained for us to learn from the two recaptured fugitives by what clever means they and their companions had slipped their chains. But neither kindness nor patience on the part of Cheggueun who was interrogating them, could make their tongues wag and, seized by anger, he ordered that they should be flogged in front of the other slaves. In no time all these pagans were lined up on the side of a hillock. Two powerful men seized one of the two Negroes, threw him to the ground and sat astride his heels and neck. At the same time two chaouchs (assistants) had taken up their stations, canes in hand, one on the right and the other on the left of the guilty one.

"Go to it," said Cheggueun. At the first blow the canes were white. At the fiftieth they were red and blood ran on the thighs and sides of the victim. But the obstinate fellow had still said nothing. Only his fitful breathing and some movement of his loins bore witness to the fact that they were not beating a corpse. Finally he cried out, "Abi (father)! Serki (chief)! I will tell all. Stop the beating." A gesture from Cheggueun brought the chaouchs to a halt.

"Speak," he said to the Negro. "What did you do to break your chains and what happened to them?"

"O Serki! I touched them with my kerikeri (amulet) and made them melt."

"Chaouchs!" responded Cheggueun, "Beat him harder. He lies."

The canes descended on the liar so hard that they removed a strip of his skin.

"Abi! Serki! I will talk. I will talk," he cried.

"Dog of a pagan," said Cheggueun, "I will have you killed if you lie to me again."

"By my father's neck," replied the slave, "here is the truth. During the night, by slithering on the sand, Mebrouk came over to us. He had some hot water in a calabash and he poured some of this in the lock of our chains. Thus wetted, when we tapped it on its side we made the bolt slide and we opened it. Out of the five, however, two had to escape attached to one another, carrying the chain with them."

"O my children," Cheggueun said to us, "you hear him. Above all, those of you whose Negroes are chained up with old chains, never go to sleep without seeing with your eye and touching with your hand the padlocks which protect your fortune. Let this be a good lesson to you all!"

The slave was seated and the chaouchs helped him to stand up. Limping and groaning he dragged himself to the feet of his master, prostrated with his face on the ground and poured sand over himself as a sign of his repentance and submission. It had taken no less than one hundred and twenty strokes of the cane to drag out his secret from him and good justice would have required that his accomplice receive the same. But his owner objected that two such wounded men would be an embarrassment for everyone, that they might die of exhaustion and that his loss was already great. Cheggueun, who had a heart of gold, was easily convinced by these good reasons and he gave orders that on departure the next morning the sick man should be put on a camel.

WITH THE MARABOUTS

[The caravan halted at a place called Aghezeur, probably near Agades in present-day Niger, to take on provisions and to reclaim some items they had deposited there on the southbound journey in the keeping of a community of "marabouts" (Muslim holymen).]

With our preparations for departure complete we were of a mind to set out on the third day after our arrival, but the marabouts of the zaouïa (lodge) of Sidi Ahmed who had come to our camp and called us together for prayer held us back with these words: "O Muslims! These negroes you are bringing are idolators. We must make them know the One God; we must teach them to pray and how to perform ablutions; we must circumcise them today. God will reward you for it. Make your slaves assemble. By God's grace we know their language; we will put ourselves in the middle of them and teach them what it is good for them to know."

We understood well, for the Lord loves him who causes the number of His servants to be increased; moreover, there is, from the point of view of sales, a great advantage in turning an idolator into a Muslim. Almost all of our slaves already knew the *shahāda* (declaration of faith) and the name of the Prophet and God. Frequently, during leisure time at camp we would teach them the basic tenets of the religion, speaking broken gnāwiyya[7] to them while they spoke broken Arabic to us. To the best behaved we offered some concessions; to the obdurate some harsh discipline; thus self-interest, if not conviction, had readied them for the solemn ceremony which would today make them into Muslims.

In front of the *zāwiya* of Sidi Ahmed is a huge open space. Each one of us led his Negroes there and made them sit on the ground and soon their number sketched out a gigantic thick semi-circle facing the zaouïa. Like a muezzin calling to prayer, the imam climbed up on the mosque and uttered these words:

"God is One; He has no associates. He is unique of His kind and none is comparable to Him. He is the Sovereign and Incomparable Lord. He is from all time and shall endure for all time. Eternity shall not destroy Hım and time and the centuries do not change Him. He is the First, the Last, the Manifest and the Hidden. He knows what is in the inside of bodies. Nothing is similar to Him; He is superior to all things. His superiority and His exhaltation, instead of distancing Him from His worshippers, brings Him closer to His creatures. He is All-Seeing, All-Knowing, He is Omnipresent. He is Holy and no place can encompass Him. Only the saints can look upon Him in the places where His dwelling is sempiternal, as has been established by the verses of the Qur'ān and the accounts of the ancients. He is Living, He is Powerful, He is Almighty, He is Superb, He is Severe; idleness and weakness are remote from Him."

"He forgets not, He sleeps not. His is the command and to Him belongs the vastness of the universe. To Him belong honor and omnipotence. He created creatures and their acts. When He wishes a thing, it is. When He does not wish it, it is not. He is the Beginning and the End, the Doer of His will. Everything that is in the world—movement, rest, good, evil, profit, loss, faith, infidelity, obedience and disobedience—all come from God. There is no bird that flies with its wings, no beast that walks on its feet, no serpent that glides on its stomach, no leaf that grows or falls and no light or darkness without the almighty will of God. Everything that exists is created; God exists from eternity and all that has been created demonstrates His unity. Man's petition to God is prayer and prayer itself only exists by the will of God. If you put your confidence in God, He will care for you as He cares for the birds of the heavens who set out hungry and return full. He does not bring food to their nests, but he puts in them the instinct to search for it."

I would not dare to say that this speech made a lively impression on the Negroes, but the solemnity of the new spectacle for them, the receptivity with which we, their masters and the holy marabout, listened certainly made them ready for the carrying out of the religious act that would make them Muslims. When time for the operation came, though all or almost all showed themselves surprised, not one refused to undergo it, for they take pride in having no fear of pain. As soon as they had been marked with the symbol of the Muslims, they had their wounds staunched by us with an astringent powder made of dried ground leaves of arrar [juniper] and el-aazir, blended with butter.[8]

The marabouts then prayed over them in gnāwiyya, saying: "O you Negroes, give thanks to God! Yesterday you were idolators and today you are Muslims. Depart with your masters who will clothe you, feed you and love you like their brothers and children. Serve them well and they will give you your liberty in a while. If you are comfortable with them you shall stay there. If not you shall return to your land."

That day and the next we took particular care of our slaves. We fed them good meat and let them sleep in tents to keep them from the cold and dew of the nights. Thanks to such attentions our caravan did not lose a single one. In the other caravans, however, some of the older ones died.

Questions:
1. *How did the Muslim Holy men (Marabouts) influence the commerce in African slavery?*
2. *How does the organization of the slave trade in North Africa in the nineteenth century compare with the organization of the slave trade in West Africa in the eighteenth century (see Reading 7)?*

15.5 Thomas Nelson, Slavery and the Slave Trade of Brazil

Under pressure from Britain, Brazil agreed to abolish its slave trade in 1826, but contraband traffic in slaves continued unabated in subsequent decades. Meanwhile, Britain claimed the right to search and arrest suspected slave ships. During the 1840s, Thomas Nelson served as a surgeon aboard a British frigate, the H.M.S. Crescent, and his duties included the inspection and treatment of contraband slaves intercepted en route to Brazil. The following reading is an excerpt from his book describing the conditions of the Africans he encountered.

> **Source:** From Thomas Nelson, *Remarks on the Slavery and Slave Trade of the Brazils* (London: J. Halchard and Son, 1846), pp. 43–56 passim.

A few minutes after the vessel dropped her anchor, I went on board of her, and although somewhat prepared by the previous inspection of two full slavers to encounter a scene of disease and wretchedness, still my experience, aided by my imagination, fell short of the loathsome spectacle which met my eyes on stepping over the side. Huddled closely together on deck, and blocking up the gangways on either side, cowered, or rather squatted, three hundred and sixty-two negroes, with disease, want, and misery stamped upon them with such painful intensity as utterly beggars all powers of description. In one corner, apart from the rest, a group of wretched beings lay stretched, many in the last stage of exhaustion, and all covered with the pustules of smallpox. Several of these I noticed had crawled to the spot where the water had been served out, in the hope of procuring a mouthful more of the precious liquid; but unable to return to their proper places, lay prostrate around the empty tub. Here and there, amid the throng, were isolated cases of the same loathsome disease in its confluent or worst form, and cases of extreme emaciation and exhaustion, some in a state of perfect stupor, others looking piteously around, and pointing with their fingers to their parched mouths whenever they caught an eye who they thought would relieve them. On every side, squalid and sunken visages were rendered still more hideous by the swollen eyelids and the puriform discharge of a virulent ophthalmia, with which the majority appeared to be afflicted; added to this were figures shriveled to absolute skin and bone, and doubled up in a posture which originally want of space had compelled them to adopt, and which debility and stiffness of the joints compelled them to retain.

On looking more leisurely around, after the first paroxysm of horror and disgust had subsided, I remarked on the poop another wretched group, composed entirely of females. Some were mothers with infants who were vainly endeavoring to suck a few drops of moisture from the lank, withered, and skinny breasts of their wretched mothers; others were of every intermediate age. The most of them destitute even of the decency of a rag, and all presenting as woeful a spectacle of misery as it is possible to conceive.

While employed in examining the negroes individually, and separating and classifying the sick, who constituted by far the majority, I obtained a closer insight into their actual condition. Many I found afflicted with a confluent smallpox, still more with purulent ophthalmia, and the majority of what remained, with dysentery, ulcers, emaciation, and exhaustion. In several, two or three of these were met. Not the least distressing sight on that pest-laden deck was the negroes whom the ophthalmia had struck blind, and who cowered in seeming apathy to all that was going on around. This was indeed the ultimatum of wretchedness, the last drops of the cup of bitterness. Deprived of liberty, and torn from their native country, there was nothing more of human misery but to make them the victims of a physical darkness as deep as they had already been made of a moral one.

The stench on board was nearly overwhelming. The odor of the negroes themselves, rendered still stronger by their filthy and crowded condition, the sickening smell of the suppurative stage of smallpox, and the far more disgusting effluvium of dysenteric discharge, combined with bilge water, putrid jerked beef, and numerous other matters to form a stench, it required no little exertion of fortitude to withstand. To all this, hunger and thirst lent their aid to finish the scene; and so poignant were they, that the struggles to obtain the means of satisfying them were occasionally so great as to require the interference of the prize crew. The moment it could be done, water in abundance and a meal was provided them; and none but an eyewitness could form an idea of the eagerness with which the former luxury was coveted and enjoyed. For many days, it seems, the water had not only been reduced in quantity, but so filled with impurities, and so putrid, that nothing but the most stringent necessity could have induced the use of it. . . .

Early yesterday morning (11th of September, 1843) the decks of the *Crescent* were again thronged by a miserable crowd of liberated Africans. The vessel in which they had been conveyed from the "coast" was captured a few days ago by one of the boats belonging to H.M.S. *Frolic,* a little to the northward of Rio.

Previously to the removal of the negroes, Dr. Gunn (the surgeon of the *Crescent*) and myself went on board the slaver, and stepping over the side, were astonished at the smallness of the vessel, and the number of wretched negroes who had been thrust on board of her. Below, the hold was crowded to excess; and above, the deck was so closely packed with the poor creatures, that we had to walk along the top of the low bulwarks in order to get aft. Of the appearance of the negroes, no pen can give an adequate idea. In numbers, the different protuberances and anatomical peculiarities of the bones can be distinctly traced by the eye, and appear, on every motion, ready to break through the skin, which is, in fact, all that covers them. Nor has this been confined to appearance; in many, at the bend of the elbows and knee-joints, over the hip-joints and lower part of the spine, the integuments have given way, and caused the most distressing and ill-conditioned sores. A great number of the Africans, especially the younger, cannot stand upright even when assisted, and the moment they are left to themselves, they double up their knees under their chins, and draw their legs so closely to their bodies, that they scarcely retain the form of humanity. So weak and so cramped are the most of them that they had to be carried in the arms of the seamen, one by one, up the *Crescent's* ladder. All those not affected with contagious diseases are now on board the *Crescent,* and the most of them look like animated skeletons. From one of the Portuguese crew, who is at present under treatment for smallpox, I learn that the name of the vessel is the Vencedora, and that she left Benguela on the coast of Africa with four hundred and sixty slaves on board. But of this *number* only three hundred and thirty-eight have been counted over the side, a circumstance which will appear the less surprising when the space in which they were stowed comes to be considered. . . .

Just as the negroes who remained of the *Vencedora* had entirely recovered their wonted health and vigor, and were fit to be sent to one of our colonies, H.M.S. *Dolphin,* on the 15th of November, 1843, brought into harbor a full slaver, which she had captured a day or two before, a little to the northward of Rio. The crew of the slaver had actually run her ashore, and had begun to throw the negroes overboard into the sea, in order that they might be induced to swim for the land, when the boats of the *Dolphin* came up and obliged them to stop and effect their own escape.

This vessel is the largest I have yet seen employed in this traffic, and is better fitted and found than the common run of slavers; she is American built, and several of her fittings bear the name of American tradesmen. But, as usual, the Africans benefit nothing from the greater size of the vessel. The additional room has not been devoted to give increased accommodation, but to carry a greater number from the coast. The hold, instead of being fitted with one slave deck, has two; so that, in fact, the negroes have been as badly off, if not worse, than they would have been in a smaller vessel.

On attempting to go down into the hold, and satisfy myself with an examination before the Africans were removed, I was forced, after one or two unsuccessful attempts, to give it up;—the effluvium was perfectly overwhelming, and the heat so great, that the moment I left the square of the hatchway, the sensation approached suffocation. The decks furnished a melancholy spectacle of disease and wretchedness; but the most prominent and widely spread scourge is purulent ophthalmia. Numbers of the poor creatures are squatting down in corners or groping about the deck deprived of all sight. Their immensely swollen eyelids, contrasting with their haggard and wasted features, and the discharge which keeps constantly trickling down their cheeks, and which they have not even a rag to wipe away, gives them an appearance of ghastly, murky misery which it is impossible for me to describe.

Many eyes, I am afraid, are irretrievably lost, and several poor wretches must remain forever totally blind. Dysentery, too, that fellest of all diseases in the negro race, is at work amongst them, and will undoubtedly commit fearful ravages. Five hundred and seventy-two Africans were found on board. What the number was at starting there is no means of ascertaining. One of the crew, a slave, who acted on board in the capacity of a cook, and who preferred being captured by Englishmen to escaping with his master, told me that many had died and were thrown overboard during the passage. The exact number taken on board, however, he could not tell. In all probability, it was not under seven hundred; but of course this is only mere conjecture.

Questions:
1. *What diseases did Nelson describe as being most prevalent among the Africans who survived the Atlantic crossing? Roughly what proportion of slaves arrived in Brazil compared to those who left American ports?*
2. *Compare Nelson's account of conditions aboard slave ships with Equiano's personal memoir.*